Ultimate AI-Assisted Development with GitHub Copilot

Unlock Faster AI-Powered Development, Testing and Automation in Java, Python, TypeScript, Go, and C++ with GitHub Copilot

Shallabh Dixitt

www.orangeava.com

First Published: August 2025
Published By: Orange Education Pvt Ltd, AVA®
Address: 9, Daryaganj, Delhi, 110002, India

275 New North Road Islington Suite 1314 London,
N1 7AA, United Kingdom

ISBN (PBK): 978-93-49888-49-4
ISBN (E-BOOK): 978-93-49888-20-3

Scan the QR code to explore our entire catalogue

www.orangeava.com

Dedicated To

My Parents and in-laws,
Whose Values, Blessings, and Endless Belief
Have Guided Me Throughout Life.

And to My Beloved Wife, Pallavi,
And My Lovely Daughters, Siddhi and Samriddhi,
For Their Unconditional Love, Strength, and Unwavering
Support Through Every Step of This Journey

About the Author

Shallabh Dixitt is a passionate technology leader, AI testing strategist, and automation architect with over **17 years of experience** at the intersection of quality engineering, intelligent automation, and next-gen AI-driven development. Known for blending deep technical expertise with pragmatic innovation, he has led transformative digital initiatives for Fortune 500 companies across finance, media, real estate, and enterprise technology.

Shallabh began his career as a .NET developer in 2008, but his relentless curiosity for automation soon drew him into the world of testing and frameworks. From Selenium and Appium to designing modern, scalable solutions with Playwright, he has continually evolved with the industry. His hands-on mastery across **Java, C#, TypeScript, Python, DevOps pipelines**, and **test orchestration** has helped organizations deliver with greater speed, intelligence, and confidence.

In recent years, Shallabh has emerged as a recognized voice in the world of **Generative AI, LLMs, and Agentic Automation**. He pioneers the integration of technologies such as **GitHub Copilot, Copilot Agent Mode**, and **LLM-powered QA utilities** to move beyond traditional test automation into the realm of **cognitive engineering** – where systems not only execute tasks but also understand, adapt, and collaborate. His focus is on building **self-healing frameworks, AI-powered test designers, and multi-agent orchestration pipelines** that mimic the capabilities of seasoned engineers.

This book is a product of that vision. Drawing from real-world use cases and production systems, Shallabh guides readers through practical strategies to integrate GitHub Copilot into day-to-day development and testing workflows. From **prompt engineering to agent-driven defect triaging, code generation, and intelligent debugging**, this book serves as both a playbook, and a launch pad for engineers ready to embrace the future of software delivery.

Beyond the code, Shallabh is a mentor, a hackathon innovator, and a passionate contributor to the global AI and automation community. He actively shares technical insights, prototypes productivity-enhancing tools, and inspires teams to learn, evolve, and build with purpose.

When not immersed in crafting prompts or exploring multi-agent LLM systems, he enjoys diving into new tech stacks, reading, and spending time with his family. His hobbies – including travel, cricket, music, and movies – keep him grounded, and creatively recharged.

Through this book, Shallabh invites you to reimagine software development – where humans and AI build together, and the future is not just automated, but intelligently orchestrated.

About the Technical Reviewer

Uma Sesha Sai Chinta is a skilled software engineer with three years of experience, currently working as a Prompt Engineer at Accenture. Initially starting his career in Azure DevOps, Uma transitioned into the rapidly evolving field of AI and prompt engineering, where he now specializes in optimizing AI interactions and enhancing model outputs. His expertise spans cloud technologies, automation, and AI-driven workflows, enabling businesses to leverage cutting-edge solutions efficiently.

With a keen interest in AI/ML and automation, Uma actively explores how emerging technologies can enhance software development, improve efficiency, and create intelligent applications. Having worked across diverse projects, he has gained expertise in cloud computing, full-stack development, and DevOps practices, ensuring seamless integration and deployment of enterprise solutions. Passionate about innovation, Uma continuously explores advancements in AI and cloud computing to drive impactful technological transformations.

Acknowledgements

This book would not have been possible without the **unwavering support, motivation, and belief of my wife**. Her constant encouragement, patience, and emotional strength were the driving force behind this journey. From the very beginning to the final edits, she stood by me through every long night and challenging phase – and for that, I owe her my deepest gratitude.

I also want to extend my heartfelt thanks to my **lovely daughters**, who have shown admirable support and understanding during this journey. There were moments when I could not be fully present with them, yet they stood by me with love, smiles, and support that lifted my spirit and kept me grounded.

My deepest appreciation goes to **my parents and my in-laws**, whose blessings, guidance, and belief in my potential have always shaped the foundation of my personal and professional life. Their values and encouragement gave me the strength to take on these endeavors and see it through.

I am grateful to my colleagues, mentors, and the wider **technology and AI community**, who have inspired me with their insights, discussions, and practical challenges. Their wholehearted collaboration helped me shape the direction and structure of this book.

Special thanks to the organizations and teams I have worked with over the years, for giving me the platform to explore and implement **GitHub Copilot, AI/ML integration, automation frameworks**, and **prompt engineering techniques** in real-world settings.

Lastly, a sincere thank you to everyone who contributed to this eventful journey of mine – directly or indirectly. This book is a reflection of the shared learning, perseverance, and the belief that we are entering a new era–one, where humans and AI can build, test, and innovate together.

Preface

The landscape of software development is being reshaped – not gradually, but fundamentally. With the introduction of **GitHub Copilot**, AI has evolved from being a background assistant to becoming a true co-creator. Developers and testers are no longer working alone; they are collaborating with intelligent systems that accelerate innovation, reduce cognitive load, and unlock new levels of productivity.

This book is a product of that transformation – grounded in over **17 years of practical experience** across test automation, solution architecture, and quality engineering. It reflects my journey of adopting Copilot in real-world projects, experimenting with its evolving features, and integrating it into both day-to-day coding and enterprise-scale strategies.

The book begins with **Chapter 1**, where we explore how AI has evolved in software development, why tools such as GitHub Copilot are more than autocomplete engines, and what this means for the future of programming and testing.

Chapters 2 and 3 walk you through everything you need to get started, from installation and workspace setup to writing structured prompts and using Copilot effectively across different file types and editor contexts.

Chapters 4 to 7 dive deep into language-specific implementations, demonstrating how Copilot adapts to **Python, Java, C++, Go, and TypeScript**. You will also see how it handles syntax, design patterns, APIs, and business logic unique to each ecosystem.

Chapter 8 focuses on **pair programming with Copilot**, transforming it into a real-time collaborator, capable of context-aware code suggestions that feel intuitive and fluid.

In **Chapter 9** we explore **advanced prompt engineering**, multi-step logic generation, iterative coding patterns, and handling edge cases, with Copilot's assistance.

Chapter 10 is all about Copilot's role in **debugging, test generation, and reliability engineering**, where it can reduce flakiness, suggest patch-level fixes, and auto-generate robust unit tests.

Chapters 11 and 12 take you into the world of **workflow integration**, showing how to embed Copilot into CI/CD pipelines, dev workflows, and even automation frameworks.

Chapter 13 introduces Copilot's **multi-modal capabilities**, its **vibe coding feature** (where Copilot adapts to your coding style and intent), and a clear **comparison across languages, file types, and productivity gains**. It also emphasizes responsible use, transparency, and real-world boundaries.

Chapter 14 examines how Copilot is revolutionizing **learning, onboarding, and continuous education**, democratizing access to best practices for both junior and senior engineers.

Chapter 15 showcases **real enterprise use cases**, where Copilot was integrated into automation suites, refactoring initiatives, and developer productivity programs.

Chapter 16 looks ahead into the **future of AI-assisted development**, where personal AI agents, memory-aware assistants, and natural language programming will redefine our relationship with the codes.

Chapter 17 concludes with reflections, distilled takeaways, and actionable guidance on how to continue evolving alongside AI in your development journey.

This book is not just an exhaustive manual. It is an invitation to shift your mindset from writing code *to collaborating with intelligence.*

Get a Free eBook

We hope you are enjoying your recently purchased book! Your feedback is incredibly valuable to us, and to all other readers looking for great books.

If you found this book helpful or enjoyable, we would truly appreciate it, if you could take a moment to leave a short review with a 5 star rating on Amazon. It helps us grow, and lets other readers discover our books.

As a thank you, we would love to send you a free digital copy of this book, and a **30%** discount code on your next cart value on our official websites:

www.orangeava.com

www.orangeava.in (For Indian Subcontinent)

☑ **Here's how:**

Leave a review for the book on Amazon.

Take a screenshot of your review, and send an email to **info@orangeava.com** (it can be just the confirmation screen).

Once, we receive your screenshot, we will send you the digital file, within 24 hours.

Thank you so much for your support – it means a lot to us!

Downloading the code bundles and colored images

Please follow the links or scan the QR codes to download the
Code Bundles and Images of the book:

https://github.com/ava-orange-education/Ultimate-AI-Assisted-Development-with-GitHub-Copilot

The code bundles and images of the book are also hosted on
https://rebrand.ly/lptww7e

In case there's an update to the code, it will be updated on the existing GitHub repository.

Errata

We take immense pride in our work at **Orange Education Pvt Ltd,** and follow best practices to ensure the accuracy of our content to provide an indulging reading experience to our subscribers. Our readers are our mirrors, and we use their inputs to reflect and improve upon human errors, if any, that may have occurred during the publishing processes involved. To let us maintain the quality and help us reach out to any readers who might be having difficulties due to any unforeseen errors, please write to us at :

errata@orangeava.com

Your support, suggestions, and feedback are highly appreciated.

DID YOU KNOW

Did you know that Orange Education Pvt Ltd offers eBook versions of every book published, with PDF and ePub files available? You can upgrade to the eBook version at **www.orangeava.com** and as a print book customer, you are entitled to a discount on the eBook copy. Get in touch with us at: **info@orangeava.com** for more details.

At **www.orangeava.com**, you can also read a collection of free technical articles, sign up for a range of free newsletters, and receive exclusive discounts and offers on Print Books and eBooks.

PIRACY

If you come across any illegal copies of our works in any form on the internet, we would be grateful if you would provide us with the location address or website name. Please contact us at **info@orangeava.com** with a link to the material.

ARE YOU INTERESTED IN AUTHORING WITH US?

If there is a topic that you have expertise in, and you are interested in either writing or contributing to a book, please write to us at **business@orangeava.com**. We are on a journey to help developers and tech professionals to gain insights on the present technological advancements and innovations happening across the globe and build a community that believes Knowledge is best acquired by sharing and learning with others. Please reach out to us to learn what our audience demands and how you can be part of this educational reform. We also welcome ideas from tech experts and help them build learning and development content for their domains.

REVIEWS

Please leave a review. Once you have read and used this book, why not leave a review on the site that you purchased it from? Potential readers can then see and use your unbiased opinion to make purchase decisions. We at Orange Education would love to know what you think about our products, and our authors can learn from your feedback. Thank you!

For more information about Orange Education, please visit **www.orangeava.com**.

Table of Contents

CHAPTER 1
The Rise of AI in Coding

Introduction

The world of software development has changed a lot over the years. One of the biggest changes happening now is the use of Artificial Intelligence (AI) in coding. AI is no longer just a concept for the future; it is being used by developers today to make programming easier and faster. This chapter will look at how coding has evolved, how AI is being used in software development, and the story behind GitHub Copilot, as well as how these changes are affecting the way, we write a code.

Structure

In this chapter, we will discuss the following topics:

- Historical Evolution of Coding Practices
- The Role of Artificial Intelligence (AI) in Software Development
- The Inception and Development of GitHub Copilot
- The Impact of AI on Modern Coding Paradigms
- Real-World Examples and Surveys

Historical Evolution of Coding Practices

To understand how AI is transforming coding, let us first look at how programming has evolved:

- **Early Days of Coding:** In the 1950s and 1960s, coding was a challenging job. Programmers wrote instructions in machine language and assembly language which the computer could directly understand. This was a time-consuming process, and required a lot of precision.

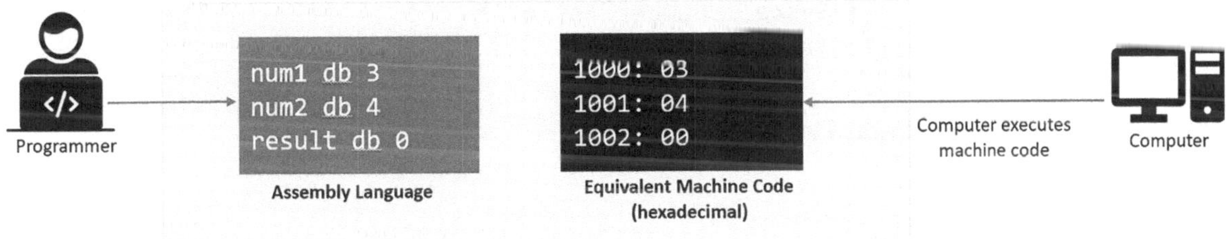

Figure 1.1: *Early Days of Coding*

- **High-Level Languages:** In the 1960s and 1970s, high-level programming languages like FORTRAN and COBOL were developed. These languages made coding easier because they allowed programmers to write instructions in a more human-readable form. This shift made it possible to write more complex programs more quickly.

Assembly Language Example: Add Two Numbers

```
section .data
    num1 db 3         ; First number
    num2 db 4         ; Second number
    result db 0       ; Storage for result
    msg db 'Result: ', 0
    len equ $ - msg

section .bss
    res resb 1        ; Reserve space for the result

section .text
    global _start

_start:
    mov al, [num1]  ; Load num1 into register AL
    add al, [num2]  ; Add num2 to AL
    mov [result], al; Store the result in memory

    ; Print the message
    mov rax, 1       ; Syscall number for write
    mov rdi, 1       ; File descriptor 1 (stdout)
    mov rsi, msg     ; Address of the message
    mov rdx, len     ; Length of the message
    syscall

    ; Print the result
    mov al, [result]  ; Load the result into AL
    add al, '0'       ; Convert the result to ASCII
    mov [res], al     ; Store the ASCII character

    mov rax, 1        ; Syscall number for write
    mov rdi, 1        ; File descriptor 1 (stdout)
    mov rsi, res      ; Address of the result
    mov rdx, 1        ; Length of the result
    syscall

    ; Exit program
    mov eax, 60      ; Syscall number for exit
    xor edi, edi     ; Exit code 0
    syscall
```

Fortran Language Example: Add Two Numbers

```
PROGRAM AddNumbers
    INTEGER:: num1, num2, result

    num1 = 3
    num2 = 4
    result = num1 + num2

    PRINT *, 'Result:', result
END PROGRAM AddNumbers
```

Execution Results

```
Result: 7
[Execution complete with exit code 0]
```

- **Object-Oriented Programming (OOP):** In the 1980s and 1990s, OOP languages like C++ and Java became popular. OOP introduced the concepts of classes and objects which made code more modular, reusable, and easier to manage.
- **Web Development:** The late 1990s and early 2000s saw the rise of the internet. Languages like JavaScript, HTML, and CSS became essential for creating interactive web applications.
- **Modern Development Practices:** Today, agile methodologies, DevOps, and Continuous Integration/Continuous Deployment (CI/CD) are standard practices. Languages, such as Python and JavaScript (Node.js), along with frameworks like React and Angular, are widely used.

Figure 1.2: *DevOps CI/CD Pipeline Process*

The following figure illustrates the Agile Development Process.

Figure 1.3: *Agile Development Process*

As software development evolved over decades, developers continuously faced challenges, such as repetitive coding tasks, complex debugging cycles, and steep learning curves for new languages, and increasing demand for faster delivery, without compromising on quality. These historical pain points created a clear need for intelligent tools that could reduce manual effort, accelerate development, and enhance code quality. This is where AI, particularly tools like GitHub Copilot, enters the picture—offering contextual suggestions, learning from large codebases, and transforming how developers write, test, and maintain software today.

The Role of Artificial Intelligence in Software Development

AI is making a significant impact on software development in various ways:

- **Automated Code Generation:** Tools like GitHub Copilot help developers by generating code snippets, suggesting entire functions, and completing code blocks based on the context of what they are writing (*Figures* 1.4–1.6).

```
Bubble_Sort.py
segment-tracking-ai > Bubble_Sort.py
1   Press ctrl+I to ask GitHub Copilot to do something. Start typing to dismiss.
```

Figure 1.4: *Coding Editor with GitHub Copilot Enabled*

```
Bubble_Sort.py
segment-tracking-ai > Bubble_Sort.py
1   #code to perform bubble sort on a list of numbers in ascending order
                Predicted auto-complete text (AKA Ghost text)
```

Figure 1.5: *Auto-complete Prompt Suggestion by GitHub Copilot (Predicted Text aka Ghost Text)*

```
Bubble_Sort.py 1 ●
segment-tracking-ai > Bubble_Sort.py > bubble_sort
#code to perform bubble sort on a list of numbers in ascending order
# Author: Shalabh Dixit
                              < 1/1 > Accept Tab  Accept Word Ctrl + RightArrow ...
def bubble_sort(arr):         Code Suggestion by GitHub Copilot
    n = len(arr)
    for i in range(n):
        for j in range(0, n-i-1):
            if arr[j] > arr[j+1]:
                arr[j], arr[j+1] = arr[j+1], arr[j]
    return arr
```

Figure 1.6: *Auto-complete Code Generation Suggestion by GitHub Copilot*

- **Bug Detection and Fixing:** AI-powered tools can analyze code for potential bugs and vulnerabilities, suggest fixes, and even automatically correct errors. Tools, such as DeepCode and Snyk use AI for this purpose.

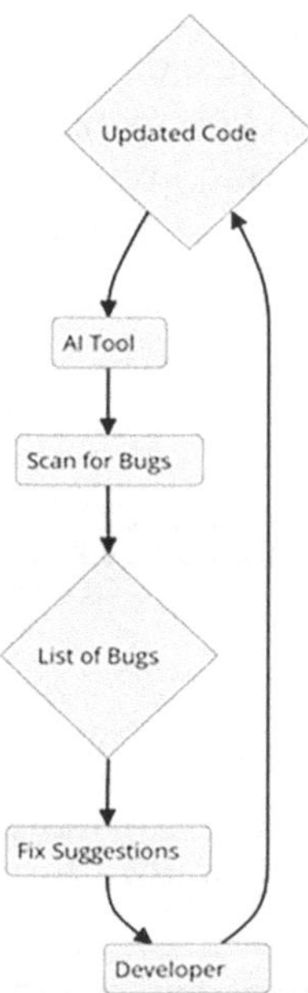

Figure 1.7: *Bug Fixing Suggestions Workflow Using AI tools*

- **Predictive Analytics**: AI can analyze historical data and project metrics to predict project timelines, potential roadblocks, and resource requirements.
- **Intelligent Code Refactoring**: AI tools can suggest, and sometimes automate the refactoring of code to make it more efficient, readable, and maintainable.
- **Natural Language Processing (NLP) in Coding**: AI models can understand and generate human language, enabling developers to write the code using natural language instructions. This is useful for documentation and generating boilerplate code.

The Inception and Development of GitHub Copilot

The development of GitHub Copilot is rooted in the broader history of AI and machine learning, particularly in the field of Natural Language Processing (NLP). Here is a detailed look at the historical background that paved the way for GitHub Copilot:

Historical Background

- **Early AI and Machine Learning:** The foundations of AI were laid in the mid-20th century with the development of algorithms that could perform simple tasks. Early machine learning models were used for pattern recognition and basic decision-making processes.
- **Evolution of Natural Language Processing:** In the 1980s and 1990s, NLP saw significant advancements. Techniques like Hidden Markov Models (HMM) and statistical NLP became popular. These methods allowed machines to process and generate human language with increasing accuracy.
- **The Rise of Deep Learning:** The early 2000s witnessed the rise of deep learning, a subset of machine learning. Deep learning models, especially neural networks, became capable of handling vast amounts of data and learning complex patterns. This era also saw the development of Convolutional Neural Networks (CNNs) and Recurrent Neural Networks (RNNs).
- **Advent of Transformers:** The breakthrough moment came in 2017 with the introduction of the transformer architecture in the paper "*Attention is All You Need*" by Vaswani et al. Transformers enabled models to understand and generate human language with unprecedented accuracy and efficiency. This architecture became the foundation for many subsequent NLP models, including BERT, GPT, and OpenAI's GPT-3.

The Role of OpenAI and GPT

OpenAI has been one of the driving forces behind the progress in artificial intelligence over the last few years, especially in the field of language models. Its work is what made GitHub Copilot possible in the first place.

- **A Quick Look at OpenAI's Mission:** OpenAI was founded in 2015 with a clear goal - To make sure that Artificial General Intelligence (AGI) benefits everyone. From the beginning, their focus has been on building AI that is safe, responsible, and useful to people—not just researchers and tech companies, but the wider world.
- **How GPT Models Came to Life:** The GPT series or *Generative Pre-trained Transformer series*—is a big part of OpenAI's journey. These models are trained to understand and generate human-like text, and over time, they have become smarter, faster, and more capable.
  - **GPT-2 (2019):** This was the first version that really grabbed attention. With 1.5 billion parameters, GPT-2 could write surprisingly a fluent text. It was not perfect, but it was a clear sign of what was coming.
  - **GPT-3 (2020):** This is where things really took off. GPT-3 had 175 billion parameters and could do everything from writing essays to answering questions, including generating a simple code. It was a big leap in capability—and it is the model that laid the groundwork for GitHub Copilot.
  - **Codex (2021):** Codex was a special version of GPT-3, fine-tuned specifically on public code from GitHub. It could understand both natural language and programming languages, making it ideal for a tool like Copilot. This is the model that powered the first versions of Copilot, turning plain English into the working code.
  - **GPT-4 (2023):** With GPT-4, the focus was on better reasoning, fewer mistakes, and broader knowledge. It also introduced multimodal input—so that it could understand images as well as text. This made it more useful across many types of applications, not just coding.
  - **GPT-4 Turbo and GPT-4o (2024–2025):** These newer versions were faster, cheaper, and more efficient. GPT-4o (the "o" stands for "*omni*") brought everything together—it could handle text, images, audio, and even video, all in one model. It made real-time interaction feel more natural, and opened up even more possibilities for tools like Copilot and beyond.

Summary of Evolution of OpenAI GPT Models

GPT-1

- **Year**: 2018
- **Parameters:** 117 million
- **Training:** Unsupervised learning
- **Key Features:**
  - Achieved state-of-the-art performance on the LAMBADA dataset.
  - Demonstrated strong results on GLUE and SQuAD benchmarks.

GPT-2

- **Year:** 2019
- **Parameters:** 1.5 billion
- **Training:** Larger dataset with the same architecture as GPT-1.
- **Key Features:**
  - Improved text coherence and generation capabilities.
  - Introduced efficient sampling algorithms for better text generation.

GPT-3

- **Year:** 2020
- **Parameters:** 175 billion
- **Training:** Utilized a significantly larger dataset with GShard optimization.
- **Key Features:**
  - Enabled few-shot, one-shot, and zero-shot learning.
  - Capable of tasks, such as text generation, reasoning, translation, and code generation.

GPT-3.5

- **Year:** 2022
- **Parameters:** Variants with 1.3B, 6B, and 175B parameters.
- **Training:** Employed Reinforcement Learning with Human Feedback (RLHF).
- **Key Features:**
  - Powered applications, such as Codex and GitHub Copilot.
  - Offered more stable responses with improved safety and moderation filtering.

GPT-4

- **Year:** March 2023
- **Parameters:** Estimated ~1 trillion (not officially confirmed).
- **Training:** RLHF with multimodal support.
- **Key Features:**
  - Accepted both text and image inputs.
  - Showcased stronger reasoning and factual accuracy.
  - Improved alignment and reliability over previous models.

GPT-4o (Omni)

- **Year:** April 2024 (Beta), Stable release in 2025
- **Parameters:** Undisclosed
- **Training:** Native multimodal training encompassing text, image, audio, and video.
- **Key Features:**
  - Enabled real-time voice, vision, and text input/output.
  - Utilized a unified architecture for all modalities.
  - Offered emotion-aware voice interactions.
  - Powered the next generation of interactive assistants and AI copilots.

GPT-4.5

- **Year:** February 27, 2025
- **Parameters:** Undisclosed (noted as OpenAI's largest model at the time).
- **Training:** Built upon GPT-4o's foundation with expanded pretraining and novel techniques to reduce hallucinations.
- **Key Features:**
  - **Enhanced Reasoning Capabilities:** Improved logic processing, accurate decision-making, and sophisticated problem-solving abilities, surpassing previous GPT versions.
  - **Multimodal Functionality (Text, Image, Audio):** Ability to seamlessly process and integrate textual inputs, along with image and audio data, significantly broadening real-world application possibilities.
  - **Improved Computational Efficiency:** Faster inference speeds, optimized resource usage, and greater scalability compared to GPT-4 Turbo, making it ideal for real-time and resource-sensitive use cases.
  - **Advanced Conversational Abilities:** Enhanced natural interactions, increased emotional intelligence, and reduced inaccuracies (hallucinations), promoting more human-like and reliable user experiences.
  - **Multilingual Proficiency:** Robust support for diverse languages, facilitating better global user engagement.
  - **Expanded Training Foundations**: Built upon GPT-4o with refined training techniques for fewer inaccuracies and better context-awareness.

In summary, GPT-4.5 combines powerful reasoning enhancements, multimodal versatility, and optimized efficiency, marking a substantial progression in the evolution of AI language models.

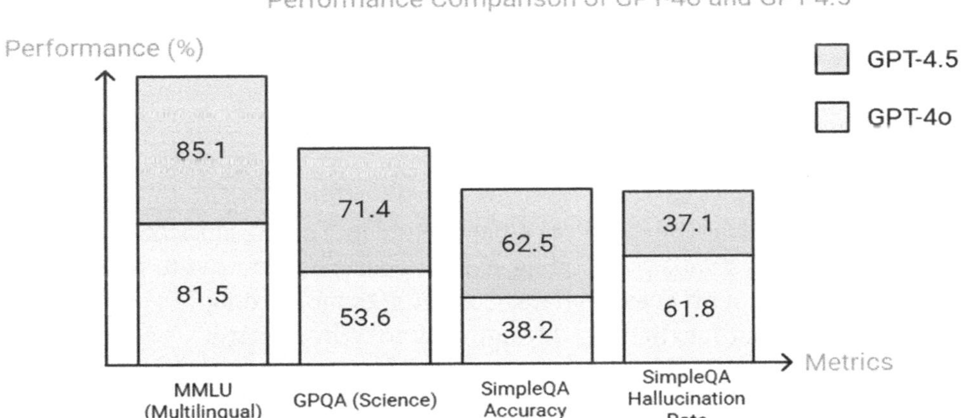

Figure 1.8: *Performance Comparison of GPT-4o and GPT-4.5 across Key Evaluation Metrics*

This bar chart visualizes the performance improvements of GPT-4.5 over GPT-4o across four major benchmarks: **MMLU (Multilingual)**, **GPQA (Science)**, **SimpleQA Accuracy**, and **SimpleQA Hallucination Rate**. GPT-4.5 demonstrates notable advancements in accuracy and multilingual understanding, while significantly reducing hallucination rates, making it a more reliable model for complex reasoning and QA tasks.

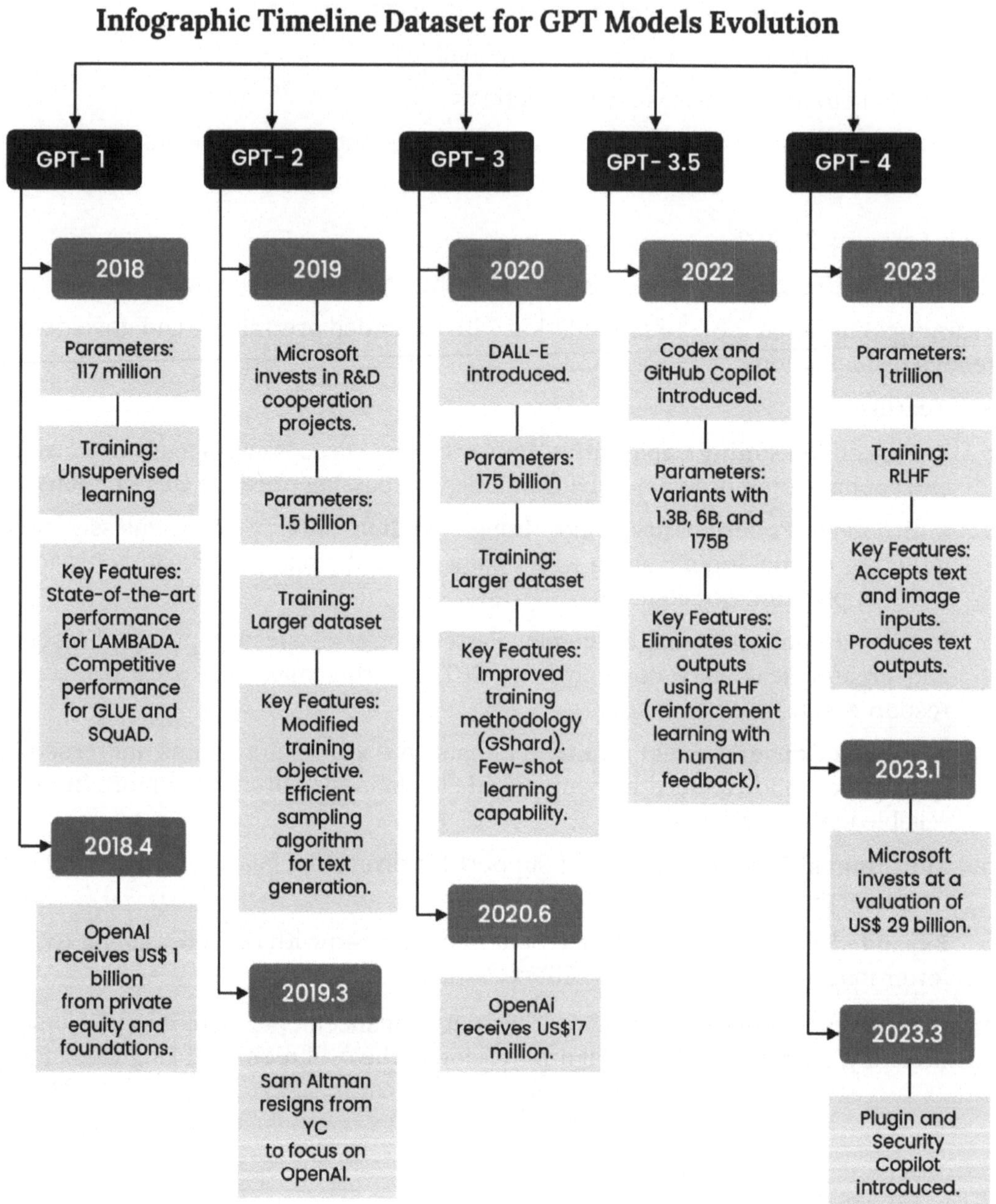

Figure 1.9: *Evolution of GPT Models*

What This Means for Copilot

As OpenAI's models improved, so did GitHub Copilot. What started as a smart autocomplete has now become a helpful assistant that understands your coding style, suggests better ways to solve problems, and even helps you learn as you go. With every update, Copilot gets more context-aware, and more useful—not just for writing a code, but for thinking through how to write it better.

These advancements are not just technical milestones—they have had a real, practical impact on how developers work day to day. And they all trace back to the ongoing evolution of GPT models at OpenAI.

Architectural Details of OpenAI Codex

GitHub Copilot is powered by OpenAI Codex, a version of GPT-3 fine-tuned for programming tasks. Here is a closer look at the architectural details:

1. **Transformer Architecture: The transformer architecture** serves as the backbone of Codex and many modern AI models. At its core, it uses a mechanism called **self-attention** which allows the model to read an entire block of text (or code) and understand how each part relates to the others–regardless of how far apart they appear. This ability to capture **long-range dependencies** is what makes Transformers exceptionally powerful for code generation. Instead of processing information, such as one word at a time, like older models, Transformers look at the entire context at once. This enables Codex to generate **contextually accurate code**, understanding not just the immediate line, but the overall structure and purpose of the entire code snippet.

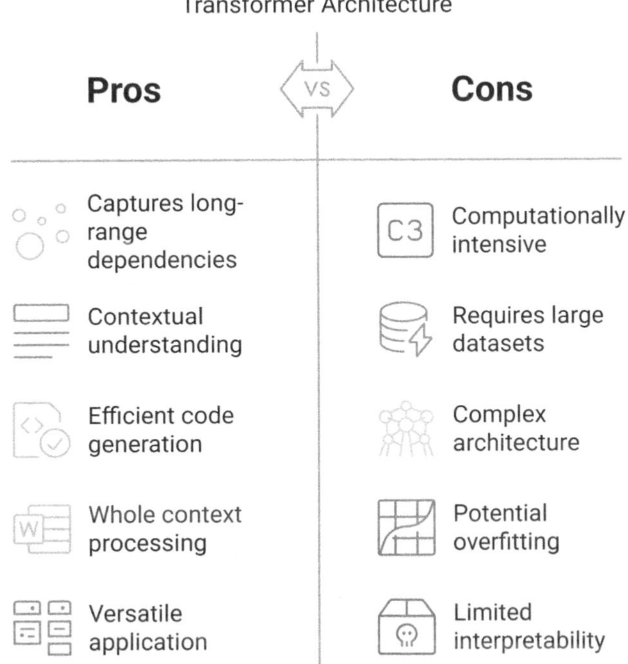

Figure 1.10: *Transformer Architecture – Pros vs Cons*

The Transformer Architecture has revolutionized deep learning, especially in natural language processing and generative AI. This visual highlights the strengths and challenges of Transformers–showcasing their remarkable abilities like long-range dependency capture and contextual understanding, alongside key limitations, such as computational cost and interpretability concerns.

2. **Training Data:** Codex was trained on a massive dataset that includes billions of lines of publicly available code from repositories, documentation, and forums. This extensive training allows Codex to understand various programming languages, frameworks, and the best practices.

3. **Fine-Tuning for Code:** While GPT-3 was trained on a broad dataset, Codex was fine-tuned specifically on code. This fine-tuning process involved adjusting the model's parameters to improve its ability to generate, understand, and complete code snippets accurately.

   OpenAI Codex, which powers GitHub Copilot, is based on the GPT-3 model, a large transformer-based language model. Here is a detailed, simplified explanation of its architecture, and how it works in the context of GitHub Copilot:

Transformer Architecture Components

- **Input Embedding:** Converts words or code tokens into dense numerical vectors that capture their semantic meaning.
- **Positional Encoding:** Adds information about the position of each token in the sequence to the embeddings, helping the model understand the order of tokens.
- **Multi-Head Attention:** Allows the model to focus on different parts of the input sequence simultaneously, capturing various contextual relationships.
- **Feed Forward Neural Network:** Processes data through layers of neurons, adding depth to the model's understanding.
- **Layer Normalization:** Helps stabilize and accelerate the training process by normalizing the input of each layer.
- **Output Embedding and SoftMax:** Transforms the processed data back into a probability distribution over the vocabulary, allowing the model to generate the most likely next token.

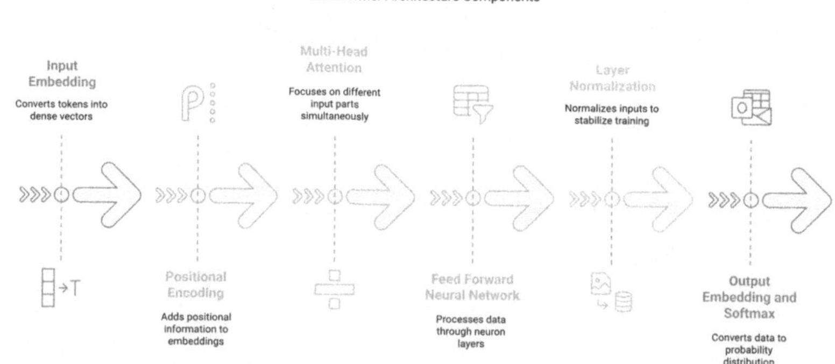

***Figure 1.11:** Transformer Architecture Components – A Step-by-Step Breakdown*

Understanding the inner workings of a Transformer model is essential to grasping its revolutionary impact on AI and deep learning. This visual walks through the key components of the Transformer architecture–from token embeddings to attention mechanisms and final output distribution. Each stage plays a critical role in enabling the model to understand and generate complex sequences with contextual accuracy and computational efficiency.

API Calls and Backend Architecture

When a developer uses GitHub Copilot, several API calls are made to provide code suggestions. So, let us break down the sequence of API calls, and how the backend architecture supports this process using an example prompt.

1. **User Input**

   a. **Developer Action:** The developer starts typing the function in the IDE.

   Example Prompt: "`Write a Python function to add two numbers`"

```
#Write a Python function to add two numbers
 < 1/2 > Accept Tab  Accept Word Ctrl + RightArrow ...
def add_two_numbers(a, b):
```

***Figure 1.12:** GitHub Copilot Generating Code Suggestions in VS Code, Based on Developer's Prompt*

2. **API Request**

    a. **Action:** The Copilot plugin sends an API request to the Codex backend with the current code context.

    b. **Endpoint:** POST /v1/completions

Method: POST	Path: /v1/completions	Version: HTTP/1.1

```
Headers:
Content-Type: application/json
Content-Encoding: gzip
Server: Apache
```

```
Body:
{
"prompt": "def add_numbers(a, b):",
"max_tokens": 50,
"temperature": 0.5,
"top_p": 1,
"n": 1,
"stop": ["\n"]
}
```

Explanation of Body Fields

a. **`prompt`**: "`def add_numbers (a, b):`"
The code snippet or initial input provided by the user.

b. **`max_tokens`**: `50`
The maximum number of tokens (words or symbols) to generate.

c. **temperature**: 0.5
Controls the randomness of the output. Lower values make the output more deterministic.

d. **`top_p`**: 1
Controls the diversity of the output. It uses nucleus sampling to choose from the most probable tokens.

e. **n**: 1
The number of completions to generate.

f. **`stop`**: ["\n"]
Specifies a stopping sequence for the generated text to halt the output.

3. **Processing the Request**

    a. **Action:** The backend processes the request, authenticates it, and analyzes the context.

    b. Components:

    - **Authentication Server:** Verifies the user and their permissions.
    - **Context Analyzer:** Understands the current coding task.

4. **Codex Model Invocation**
    - **Action:** The Codex model generates possible code completions.
    - Components:
        - **Transformer Model:** Uses multi-head attention to understand and generate a code.
5. **Response Generation**
    - **Action:** The backend formats the suggestions into a structured response.
    - Components:
        - **Response Formatter:** Organizes the suggestions.

    API Response:

```
{
  "choices": [
    {
      "text": "\n    return a + b"
    }
  ]
}
```

6. **API Response**
    a. **Action:** The Copilot plugin receives the response, and displays suggestions in the IDE.
    b. Endpoint: POST /v1/completions

API Call:

Method: POST	Path: /v1/completions	Version: HTTP/1.1
Headers: Content-Type: application/json Content-Encoding: gzip Server: Apache		

Body:
{
"suggestions":
["def add_numbers(a, b):\n
return a + b\n"]
}		

7. **Display Suggestions**
    a. **Action:** The suggestion is shown in the IDE.

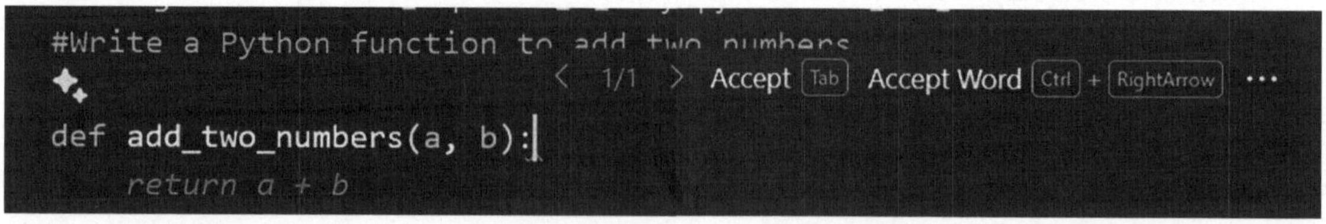

```
#Write a Python function to add two numbers
                    < 1/1 > Accept Tab  Accept Word Ctrl + RightArrow ...
def add_two_numbers(a, b):
    return a + b
```

Figure 1.13: *GitHub Copilot Generating Auto Complete Code in VS Code, Based on Developer's Prompt*

8. **Feedback Loop**
    a. **Action:** The developer accepts, modifies, or rejects the suggestion.
    b. **Endpoint:** POST/feedback

API Call:

Method: POST	Path: /feedback	Version: HTTP/1.1
Headers: Content-Type: application/json Content-Encoding: gzip Server: Apache		

Body:
{
"accepted": true, "suggestion": "def add_numbers(a, b):\n return a + b\n"
}		

Security Risks and Vulnerabilities

When generating a code, AI-powered tools like GitHub Copilot significantly enhance productivity, but can inadvertently introduce certain security risks due to the nature of their training process. These AI models are trained on extensive datasets of publicly available code which occasionally include insecure, outdated, or improperly written examples. Consequently, there is a possibility of unintentionally replicating insecure coding practices, embedding vulnerabilities present in training data, or recommending outdated and unsafe dependencies.

A primary security concern is the potential bias in training data, where frequently occurring insecure practices–such as weak password hashing, inadequate input validation, or outdated encryption methods–may influence the generated recommendations. Another significant risk involves AI models producing snippets containing known security vulnerabilities, such as SQL injections, cross-site scripting (XSS), or insecure deserialization, due to these being prevalent patterns in older public codebases.

Additionally, AI-generated code suggestions can inadvertently introduce dependency-related issues. For instance, Copilot might implicitly recommend outdated libraries or modules with known vulnerabilities, without alerting the developer explicitly. Such hidden dependency risks demand careful attention to dependency audits, security checks, and version control.

To effectively manage these security risks, developers should:

- Conduct comprehensive manual code reviews on AI-generated snippets, especially in critical application areas.
- Integrate automated static and dynamic vulnerability scanning into the continuous integration and deployment pipelines, enabling early detection of potential security issues.
- Regularly audit all third-party dependencies recommended by AI-generated code to proactively identify and remediate vulnerabilities or outdated versions.
- Provide training and establish guidelines for developers, promoting responsible and security-conscious integration of AI-generated suggestions into their codebase.

By maintaining awareness of these risks, and proactively integrating robust security measures into their workflows, teams can safely leverage AI-assisted development tools like GitHub Copilot, maximizing productivity, without compromising security.

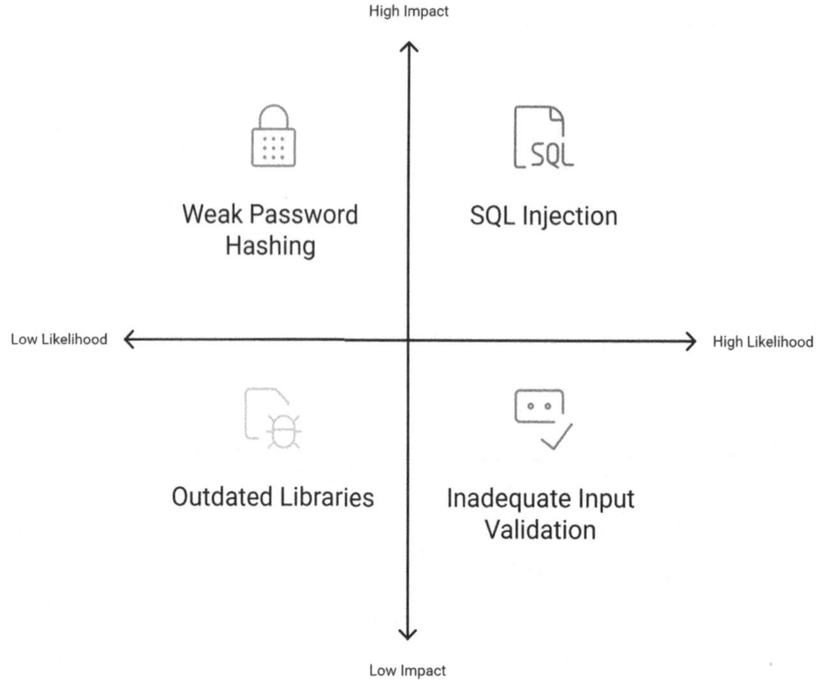

Figure 1.14: *Managing AI-Generated Code Security Risks – Likelihood vs Impact Matrix*

When addressing security risks in AI-generated code, it is essential to balance the likelihood of occurrence with the potential impact. This matrix helps teams prioritize mitigation strategies by mapping issues like **SQL Injection** (high likelihood and high impact) and **Weak Password Hashing** (low likelihood but high impact) against less critical risks like **Outdated Libraries** or **Inadequate Input Validation**. Using this framework ensures smarter, risk-driven security decisions in AI-assisted development.

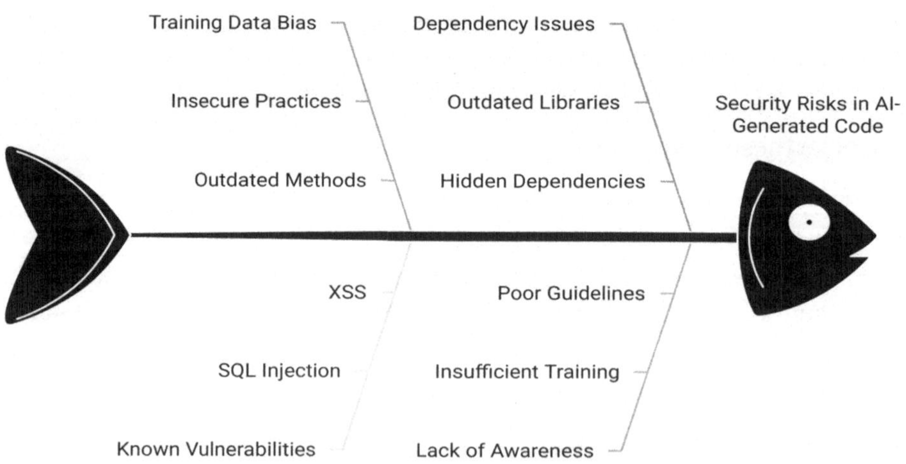

Figure 1.15: *Managing Security Risks in AI-Generated Code – A Fishbone Diagram*

As AI-generated code becomes more prevalent, so do the associated security challenges. This fishbone diagram categorizes key security risks, such as training data bias, insecure practices, outdated dependencies, and lack of developer awareness. Thus, by identifying and understanding these root causes, teams can proactively mitigate vulnerabilities like SQL injection, XSS, and hidden dependencies to ensure safer AI-assisted development workflows.

Figure 1.16: *How to Manage Security Risks in AI-Generated Code*

AI-generated code offers efficiency and speed, but it also introduces new security concerns. This diagram presents four vital strategies to mitigate these risks: Manual Code Reviews, Automated Scanning, Dependency Audits, and Developer Training. By integrating these practices into your development lifecycle, teams can safeguard applications against vulnerabilities, and ensure secure usage of AI-assisted tools.

Real-World Pitfalls and Privacy Protections in AI-Assisted Coding

User Privacy and Learning Boundaries

As AI-powered tools like GitHub Copilot become increasingly integrated into development workflows, it is natural for developers and organizations to ask: *Is my code safe? Is the AI learning from what I write correct?*

To address these concerns, it is important to understand how Copilot and similar coding assistants handle user data. Contrary to popular belief, Copilot **does not learn or train on your individual code,** while you use it. Once a model like Codex is deployed, it operates in what is called **inference-only mode**. This means it generates suggestions based on patterns, it learned during pre-training but **does not continuously adapt or learn** from your inputs during real-time usage.

For enterprise environments, tools like GitHub Copilot for Business include **privacy-centric design features**, such as:

- **No training on your codebase** by default—unless explicitly enabled.
- **Data isolation** to ensure that your organization's code is not shared across environments.
- **Telemetry control and opt-out options** for maximum transparency and data protection.

These measures ensure that proprietary source code, trade secrets, and internal business logic are not used to improve or fine-tune the model for other users or the broader public.

That said, developers are still encouraged to follow good coding hygiene, when working with AI tools. This includes:

- Avoiding the inclusion of passwords, API keys, or sensitive tokens in comments or prompts.

- Reviewing suggestions carefully, particularly when working in regulated environments or handling sensitive data.
- Leveraging internal access controls, and secure development environments when using Copilot in team-based or enterprise settings.

Thus, by understanding these learning boundaries and using the tool responsibly, developers can confidently integrate AI coding assistants like Copilot into their workflows–boosting productivity, without compromising on privacy or control over their code.

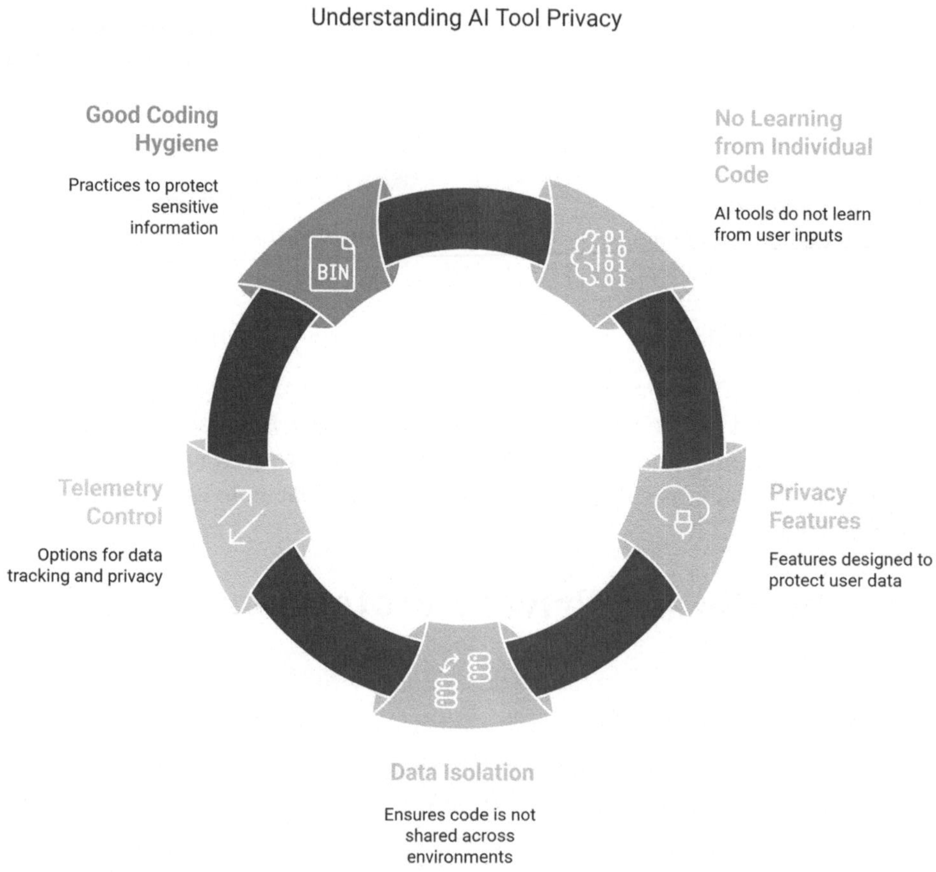

***Figure 1.17:** Understanding AI Tool Privacy – Key Pillars for Secure Use*

When using AI-powered development tools, protecting the user data and code privacy is crucial. This circular diagram outlines essential aspects of AI tool privacy, including Good Coding Hygiene, Telemetry Control, Data Isolation, and built-in Privacy Features. It also emphasizes that modern AI tools are designed to avoid learning from individual user code, ensuring a secure and private development experience.

AI-Generated Code Errors and Debugging Practices

While AI coding assistants like GitHub Copilot can significantly accelerate development, they are not infallible. The code they generate is based on patterns learned from publicly available sources and training data–which means it may occasionally be incorrect, outdated, or unsuitable for a specific context.

Common Real-World Issues

- **Logic Flaws:** Copilot may generate code that looks syntactically correct, but behaves incorrectly. For example, it might suggest a loop with an off-by-one error or mishandle edge cases when working with user input or data boundaries.

- **Deprecated APIs:** The assistant may recommend older or deprecated methods, particularly in fast-evolving frameworks, such as React, Node.js, or Python libraries. Developers must verify the relevance and stability of suggested APIs before integrating them into modern projects.
- **Security Vulnerabilities:** In some cases, Copilot has suggested hard-coded credentials, weak password hashing functions, or unsecured database queries. While these examples are rare, they highlight the need for oversight and review.
- **Incorrect Assumptions about Context:** Copilot predicts code based on the local file or function, but it does not always understand the broader system design or business logic. This can lead to mismatches–such as calling undefined variables or returning incorrect data formats.

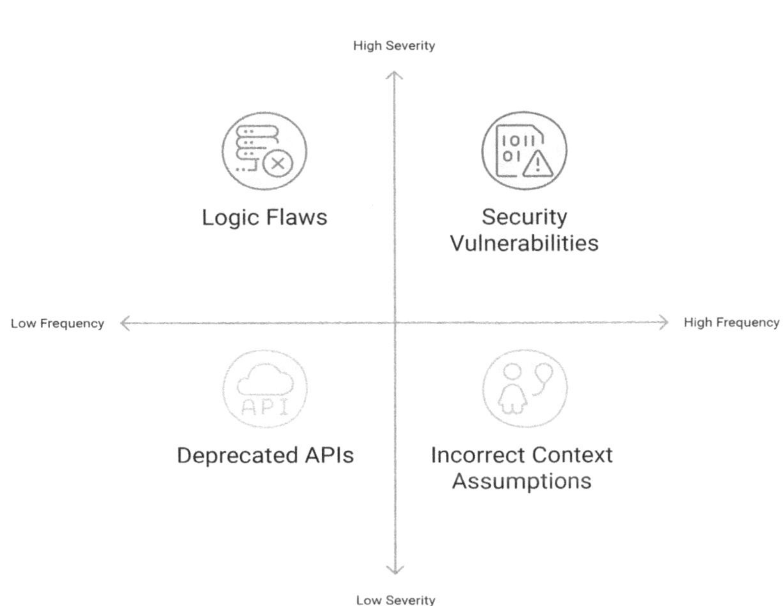

***Figure 1.18:** Prioritizing AI-Generated Code Issues – Frequency vs Severity Matrix*

Not all AI-generated code issues are created equal. This prioritization matrix helps development teams assess which issues deserve immediate attention based on their frequency and severity. High-severity and high-frequency risks–such as security vulnerabilities demand top priority, while lower-severity or infrequent issues– such as deprecated APIs or context mismatches–can be addressed with a more balanced approach. This framework ensures efficient and secure AI-assisted development.

How Developers Debug AI-Generated Code

Developers who rely on Copilot treat its output as a **starting point**, not a final solution. The most common debugging and validation practices include:

- **Manual Review:** Developers inspect suggestions for logic, security, and structural alignment with the rest of the codebase.
- **Static Analysis Tools:** Tools such as ESLint, SonarQube, or Pylint help detect syntax issues, anti-patterns, and potential vulnerabilities.
- **Unit and Integration Testing:** Writing test cases for AI-generated functions is necessary to validate correctness, and ensure that they behave as expected across various input scenarios.

- **Peer Review:** Teams using Copilot in collaborative environments often include Copilot-generated code in pull requests, subjecting it to the same code review standards as handwritten logic.
- **Prompt Refinement:** When the AI returns inaccurate suggestions, developers often rephrase or clarify their prompts–improving context and guiding the assistant toward better results.

By understanding these limitations, and building the right safety nets, developers can take full advantage of the productivity boost offered by AI assistants, while maintaining control, reliability, and code quality.

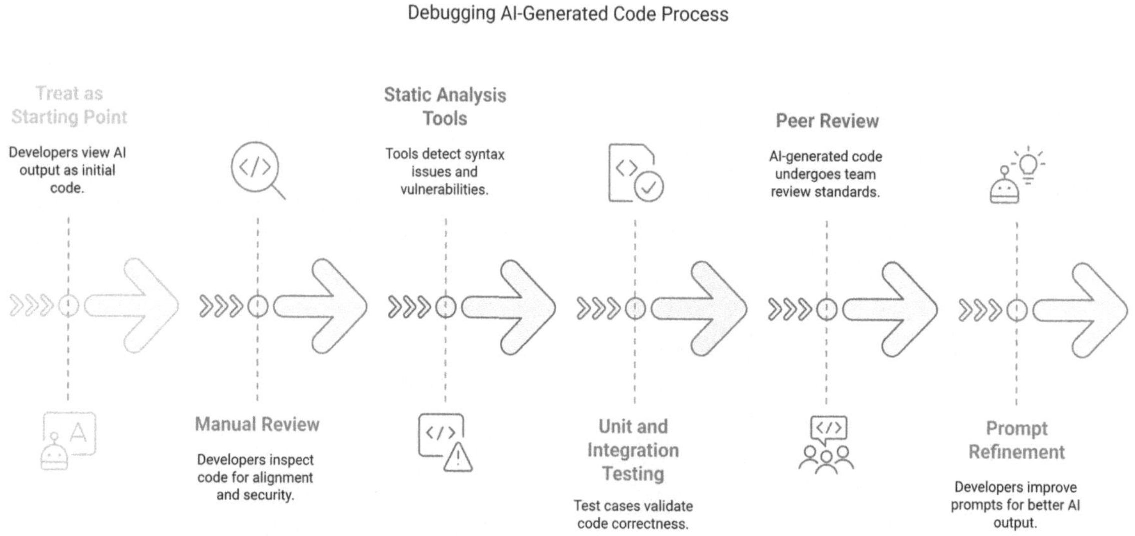

Figure 1.19: *Debugging AI-Generated Code – A Structured Review Workflow*

AI-generated code offers a great starting point, but requires careful validation before deployment. This visual outlines a practical debugging process that begins with treating AI output as a base, followed by manual inspection, static analysis, testing, and team-based peer reviews. The process concludes with refining prompts to enhance future AI output–ensuring both security and code quality in AI-assisted development.

Integration with GitHub and IDEs

The integration of Codex with GitHub and various Integrated Development Environments (IDEs) such as Visual Studio Code transformed it into GitHub Copilot. Here's how this integration works:

1. **Seamless IDE Integration:** GitHub Copilot integrates seamlessly with popular IDEs, providing real-time code suggestions as developer's type. This integration was achieved through plugins and extensions that interface with the IDEs.

Figure 1.20: *GitHub Copilot Generating Code Suggestions as per the Context and Prompt in VS Code*

2. **Context Awareness:** Copilot uses the context of the code being written to provide relevant suggestions. It analyzes the preceding code, comments, and even the project structure to generate accurate and useful code completions. It scans through all the workspace code files in the project, and also refers all the opened tabs (Max. 15 tabs) at a time to build the context for generating relevant code suggestions.

3. **Interactive Learning:** Developers can interact with Copilot by accepting, modifying, or rejecting its suggestions. This feedback loop helps Copilot learn and improve its suggestions over time.

Continuous Learning and Improvement

GitHub Copilot continuously evolves through user interactions and new data. Here is how continuous learning and improvement are implemented:

1. **User Feedback:** Every interaction with Copilot provides valuable feedback. When developers accept, modify, or reject suggestions, Copilot learns from these actions to improve future suggestions.

2. **Data Updates:** Copilot is periodically updated with new data from public repositories. This ensures that it stays current with the latest programming trends, languages, and frameworks. This means that as the programming world changes, Copilot is also learning and adjusting behind the scenes. New programming languages, frameworks, and coding patterns keep emerging. Developers around the world are constantly experimenting, refining best practices, and pushing new ideas into the open-source world. GitHub Copilot learns from this ongoing activity by being retrained on fresh public code. These updates help Copilot understand what's current, what's becoming popular, and what approaches are starting to fall out of use.

   For example, if a newer version of a framework like React or Angular is released, Copilot can eventually reflect those changes in its code suggestions. It also becomes more familiar with newer tools, such as Vite for frontend development or Bun for JavaScript runtime, simply because people are using them more often in open-source projects.

   This regular updating also helps Copilot move away from suggesting outdated or insecure code. If a certain library is no longer maintained, or a coding pattern is no longer recommended, that shift will likely be reflected in future suggestions. In this way, Copilot stays in sync with the habits and preferences of the developer community at large.

   From a developer's point of view, this matters. You don't have to worry that Copilot is stuck in the past. Its suggestions reflect real-world usage, and they tend to match how people are coding today. This makes Copilot a more dependable tool, especially when you're exploring something new or trying to stay aligned with industry standards.

   In short, GitHub Copilot is not a static tool. It evolves quietly in the background by learning from real code written by real developers. That's what helps it stay useful—not just for writing code faster, but for writing code that is more modern, reliable, and relevant.

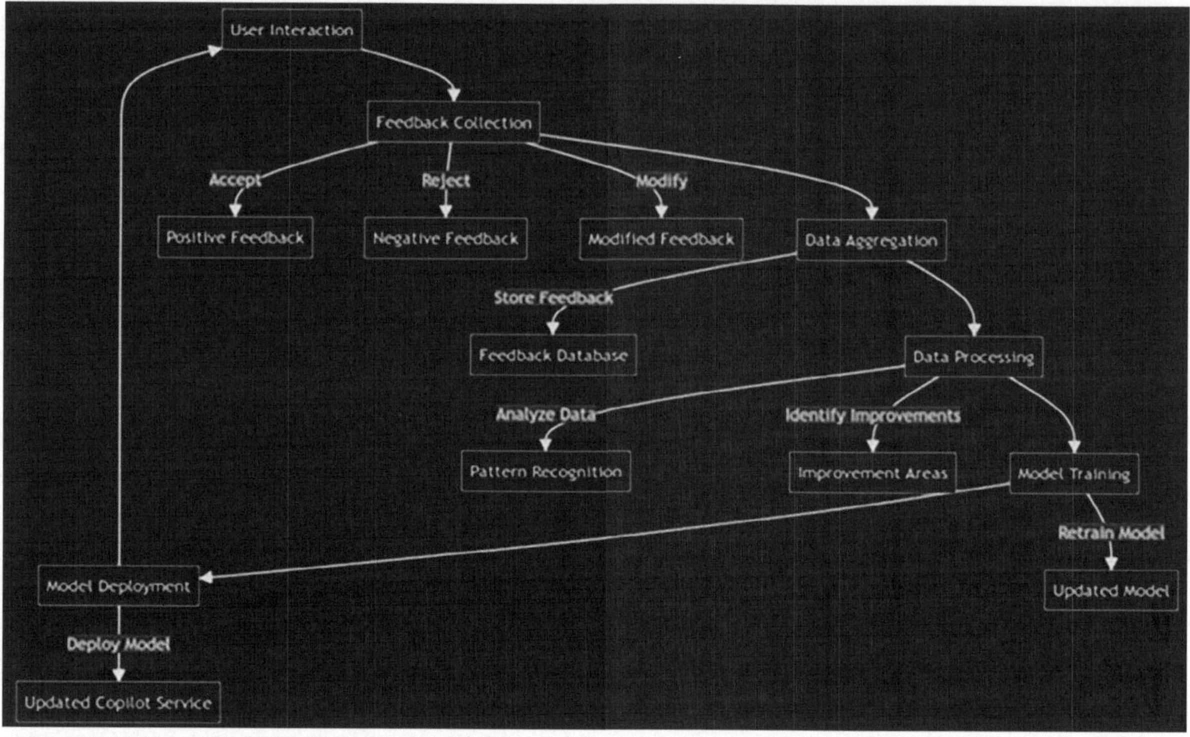

Figure 1.21: *Continuous Learning Loop for GitHub Copilot: User Feedback Improves AI Code Suggestions*

- **High-Level Overview of Continuous Learning Loop of GitHub Copilot**
  - **User Interaction:** Users write code using GitHub Copilot.
  - **Feedback Collection:** Users provide feedback on the suggestions made by Copilot. They can either accept, reject, or modify the suggestions.
  - **Data Aggregation:** All feedback and interactions from users are collected and stored.
  - **Data Processing:** The collected data is analyzed to find patterns, and identify areas for improvement.
  - **Model Training:** The insights from the data are used to retrain and update the Copilot model.
  - **Model Deployment:** The updated Copilot model is deployed to the service.
  - **Continuous Improvement:** This process repeats, continually improving Copilot as more users interact and provide feedback.
- **Feedback Types in the Diagram:**
  - When users accept suggestions, it is considered a **Positive Feedback**.
  - When users reject suggestions, it is considered a **Negative Feedback**.
  - When users modify suggestions, it is recorded as a **Modified Feedback**.
  - All feedback is stored in a **Feedback Database**.
  - Data analysis focuses on **Pattern Recognition**, and identifying **Improvement Areas**.
  - The model gets updated and deployed as an **Updated Copilot Service**.

3. **Safety and Ethical Considerations:** GitHub and OpenAI have implemented measures to ensure that Copilot generates safe and ethical code. This includes filtering out harmful or biased suggestions, and continuously monitoring the model's outputs.

The Impact of AI on Modern Coding Paradigms

Artificial Intelligence (AI) is revolutionizing the way developers approach coding, significantly altering traditional paradigms. Here is a deeper dive into how AI is transforming the landscape of modern software development:

Enhanced Productivity

AI tools like GitHub Copilot automate repetitive and mundane tasks, freeing developers to focus on more complex and creative aspects of coding. Here is how AI enhances productivity:

1. **Automated Code Generation:** AI can generate boilerplate code, suggest functions, and complete code snippets based on the context. This reduces the time spent on writing a routine code, and speed up the development process.

   Example: A developer writing a function to handle user authentication can receive suggestions for common security practices, and error handling, saving time, and reducing the likelihood of security flaws.

2. **Intelligent Autocompletion:** Advanced AI-powered autocompletion provides developers with real-time suggestions as they type, increasing coding speed and reducing errors.

   Example: While writing a loop in Python, Copilot can suggest the loop structure and possible iterations, allowing the developer to focus on the loop logic.

3. **Code Templates and Snippets:** AI can suggest entire code templates and snippets tailored to the specific task at hand. This helps maintain consistency and best practices across the codebase.

   Example: When starting a new RESTful API endpoint, Copilot can provide a complete template including endpoint definition, request handling, and response formatting.

Improved Code Quality

AI-driven code reviews and suggestions significantly enhance code quality by identifying potential issues early in the development cycle. Here is how AI contributes to higher code quality:

1. **Real-Time Error Detection:** AI tools can detect syntax errors, potential bugs, and security vulnerabilities in real-time, allowing developers to address issues immediately.

   Example: Copilot can identify an unhandled exception in a try-catch block and suggest appropriate error handling mechanisms.

2. **Best Practice Recommendations:** AI suggests best practices for code structure, style, and efficiency. This ensures that the codebase adheres to industry standards and is optimized for performance.

   Example: While writing SQL queries, Copilot can recommend indexing strategies to improve query performance and suggest using prepared statements to prevent SQL injection attacks.

3. **Consistent Code Reviews:** Automated code reviews powered by AI ensure that every pull request is thoroughly checked for potential issues, maintaining high standards across the project.

   Example: Tools like CodeGuru analyze pull requests for potential performance bottlenecks and recommend code improvements.

   Visual: A screenshot of an AI-driven code review tool highlighting code issues and suggestions.

Democratization of Coding

AI tools lower the barrier to entry for new developers, making coding more accessible and inclusive. Here is how AI democratizes coding:

1. **Simplified Learning Curve:** AI-driven suggestions and real-time assistance help novice developers learn coding practices faster, and with less frustration.

   Example: A beginner writing their first web application can rely on Copilot for guidance on structuring HTML, CSS, and JavaScript files, learning by example.

2. **Language Translation and Localization:** AI can assist in translating code comments, documentation, and even code itself into different languages, making it easier for non-native speakers to contribute to projects.

   Example: Copilot can translate code comments from English to Spanish, helping Spanish-speaking developers understand and contribute to the codebase.

3. **Accessible Documentation:** AI-generated documentation and inline comments provide context and explanations, making it easier for all developers to understand and work with the code.

   Example: Copilot can generate comprehensive documentation for a newly created class, detailing its methods, properties, and usage examples.

Focus on Creativity and Problem-Solving

With AI handling routine coding tasks, developers can concentrate on creative problem-solving and innovation. Here is how AI fosters creativity:

1. **Ideation and Brainstorming:** AI can suggest multiple approaches to solving a problem, sparking creativity, and encouraging developers to explore new solutions.

   Example: When designing a new feature, Copilot can propose different architectural patterns, such as microservices, event-driven design, or monolithic architecture, helping the developer choose the most suitable one.

2. **Prototyping and Experimentation:** AI accelerates the prototyping phase by quickly generating code snippets and templates, allowing developers to experiment with different ideas, and iterate rapidly.

   Example: A developer working on a machine learning model can use Copilot to quickly set up different data preprocessing pipelines and model architectures.

3. **Enhancing the Existing Code:** AI can suggest improvements and optimizations for the existing code, helping developers refine their solutions, and push the boundaries of what is possible.

   Example: Copilot can analyze an algorithm, and suggest optimizations to reduce its time complexity from O(n^2) to O(n log n).

Collaboration and Knowledge Sharing

AI tools enhance collaboration among development teams by maintaining consistent coding standards, and facilitating knowledge sharing. Here is how AI improves collaboration:

1. **Consistent Code Style:** AI ensures that the entire codebase follows consistent style guidelines, making it easier for developers to read and understand each other's code.

Example: Copilot can enforce coding standards, such as naming conventions, indentation, and comment styles, ensuring uniformity across the project.

2. **Knowledge Transfer:** AI-generated comments and documentation help new team members quickly get up to speed with the codebase, facilitating smoother onboarding and knowledge transfer.

   Example: New developers can use Copilot to understand the purpose and functionality of complex code sections, reducing the learning curve.

3. **Shared Code Suggestions:** AI tools provide shared code suggestions and templates that can be used by the entire team, promoting the best practices, and reducing duplication of effort.

   Example: Copilot can suggest a standard logging framework, and usage pattern that all team members can adopt, ensuring consistent logging across the application.

Thus, by revolutionizing productivity, improving code quality, democratizing access to coding, fostering creativity, and enhancing collaboration, AI is fundamentally transforming modern coding paradigms. These changes are leading to more efficient, innovative, and inclusive software development practices.

Real-World Examples and Surveys

- **Survey by GitHub:** According to a survey by GitHub, 90% of developers using Copilot reported improved coding efficiency. About 75% said it helped them find alternative solutions, and 60% felt it improved their coding skills.

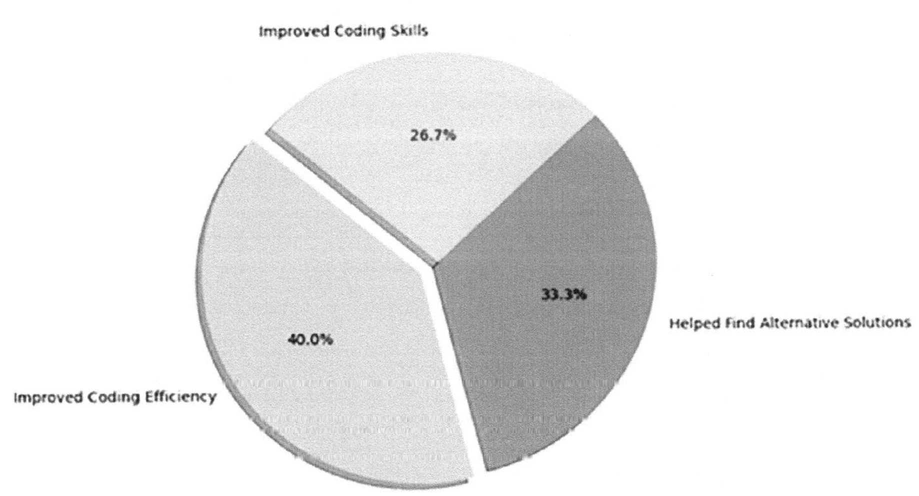

***Figure 1.22:** Surveys Show Copilot Boosts Efficiency Most, Followed by Solution Discovery and Skill Improvement*

- **Case Study Microsoft:** Microsoft developers using AI tools, such as Copilot and CodeGuru reported a 30% productivity increase. AI assistance allowed them to focus more on complex tasks, and reduced the cognitive load of coding.
- **Real-World Example - OpenAI:** OpenAI's Codex, which powers GitHub Copilot, is used in various applications beyond coding, like natural language interfaces for data analysis, allowing users to query databases using plain English.

Conclusion

The rise of AI in coding represents a transformative shift in the software development landscape. AI tools like GitHub Copilot are revolutionizing the way developers work by enhancing productivity, improving code quality, democratizing access to coding, fostering creativity, and enhancing collaboration. These tools automate routine tasks, provide real-time code suggestions, and enable developers to focus on solving complex problems, and innovating. As AI continues to evolve, its integration into coding practices will become increasingly indispensable, driving efficiency, and fostering a more inclusive and innovative tech industry. Embracing AI-driven development tools is not just a glimpse into the future of coding; it is the present reality that developers must harness to stay ahead in the ever-evolving world of technology.

In the next chapter, we will walk through how to get started with GitHub Copilot, covering everything from installation to exploring its core features in real-world development environments.

Multiple Choice Questions

1. What is GitHub Copilot?
    a. A version control system
    b. An AI-powered code completion tool
    c. A programming language
    d. A type of neural network
2. Which architecture is the foundation of OpenAI Codex which powers GitHub Copilot?
    a. Convolutional Neural Network (CNN)
    b. Recurrent Neural Network (RNN)
    c. Transformer
    d. Hidden Markov Model (HMM)
3. What is the primary benefit of AI-driven code reviews?
    a. Faster internet speed
    b. Higher code quality
    c. Reduced hardware costs
    d. Increased marketing reach
4. Which of the following best describes the role of Natural Language Processing (NLP) in coding?
    a. Understanding and generating human language
    b. Optimizing network traffic
    c. Managing database transactions
    d. Improving graphical user interfaces

5. Which company developed GitHub Copilot in collaboration with OpenAI?
    a. Microsoft
    b. Google
    c. Amazon
    d. Facebook
6. How does GitHub Copilot enhance developer productivity?
    a. By generating boilerplate code
    b. By optimizing CPU performance
    c. By managing network protocols
    d. By reducing electricity consumption
7. What percentage of developers reported improved coding efficiency with GitHub Copilot, according to a GitHub survey?
    a. 50%
    b. 70%
    c. 90%
    d. 100%
8. What is the primary way in which AI democratizes coding?
    a. By increasing the price of development tools
    b. By making coding more accessible to new developers
    c. By reducing the need for software updates
    d. By improving computer graphics
9. Which of the following is NOT a benefit of AI tools in coding?
    a. Enhanced productivity
    b. Improved code quality
    c. Increased barriers to entry
    d. Focus on creativity and problem-solving
10. What significant advantage does AI offer in terms of collaboration and knowledge sharing among development teams?
    a. Enforcing coding standards
    b. Reducing internet bandwidth
    c. Lowering hardware costs
    d. Increasing file storage capacity

Answers

1. b
2. c
3. b

4. a
5. a
6. a
7. c
8. b
9. c
10. a

Key Terms

- **Artificial Intelligence (AI):** The simulation of human intelligence processes by machines, especially computer systems. AI applications include expert systems, natural language processing, and machine vision.
- **Machine Learning (ML):** A subset of AI that involves the use of algorithms and statistical models to enable computers to perform tasks, without explicit instructions, relying on patterns and inference, instead.
- **Natural Language Processing (NLP):** A branch of AI focused on the interaction between computers and humans through natural language, enabling machines to understand, interpret, and generate human language.
- **Transformer Architecture:** A type of neural network architecture introduced in the paper "*Attention is All You Need*" by *Vaswani et al.* It uses self-attention mechanisms to process sequential data, and has become the foundation for many advanced NLP models.
- **GitHub Copilot:** An AI-powered code completion tool developed by GitHub in collaboration with OpenAI. It provides real-time code suggestions, and assists developers by generating code snippets, completing functions, and more.
- **OpenAI Codex:** A version of OpenAI's GPT-3 fine-tuned for programming tasks. Codex powers GitHub Copilot, and is trained on a vast dataset of public code repositories.
- **Integrated Development Environment (IDE):** A software application that provides comprehensive facilities to computer programmers for software development. An IDE typically consists of a source code editor, build automation tools, and a debugger.
- **Continuous Integration/Continuous Deployment (CI/CD):** A set of practices in software engineering where all code changes are automatically tested and deployed to production environments, facilitating frequent and reliable software updates.
- **Automated Code Generation:** The use of AI to automatically generate code snippets, functions, or even entire programs, based on the given inputs or contexts.
- **Predictive Analytics:** The use of data, statistical algorithms, and machine learning techniques to identify the likelihood of future outcomes, based on the historical data.
- **Refactoring:** The process of restructuring the existing computer code, without changing its external behavior, improving its readability, and reducing its complexity.
- **Code Review:** The systematic examination of computer source code intended to find and fix mistakes overlooked in the initial development phase, improving the overall quality of the software.

CHAPTER 2
Getting Started with GitHub Copilot

Introduction

GitHub Copilot is a revolutionary AI-powered tool developed by GitHub in collaboration with OpenAI. Designed to enhance productivity and streamline the coding process, Copilot integrates directly into popular Integrated Development Environments (IDEs) to provide real-time code suggestions, auto-completions, and even entire functions based on the context of your code. **GitHub Copilot** is now powered by **GPT-4 Turbo**, a more advanced and efficient version of OpenAI's GPT-4 model. While the earlier versions of Copilot were built on Codex (based on GPT-3), the latest version offers significantly **improved accuracy, faster response times**, and **better understanding of developer intent**. Trained on billions of lines of public code, GPT-4 Turbo enables Copilot to make high-quality suggestions that align more closely with modern coding practices. This chapter will guide you through everything, you need to know to get started with GitHub Copilot, from setup and configuration to advanced features, and the best practices.

The evolution of Copilot has also led to the introduction of **Copilot X**—an advanced AI-powered experience that brings **chat-based assistance**, **context-aware code walkthroughs**, **pull request summaries**, and **natural language debugging** directly into your IDE. Copilot X leverages GPT-4 Turbo to allow developers to interact with their code in a conversational manner, speeding up learning, troubleshooting, and documentation efforts.

GitHub Copilot X is not just about autocompletion. It enables AI chat inside your IDE, explains code, suggests improvements, and even helps you debug by asking natural language questions—making it a true pair-programmer experience.

Structure

In this chapter, we will discuss the following topics:

- Prerequisites for Using GitHub Copilot
- Installing and Setting Up GitHub Copilot
- How GitHub Copilot Works
- Challenges and Best Practices
- Real-World Use Cases

Prerequisites for Using GitHub Copilot

Before diving into GitHub Copilot, ensure that you meet the following prerequisites:

GitHub Account

1. **Creating an Account:** To use GitHub Copilot, you must have a GitHub account. If you do not have one, you can create it by following these steps:

    a. Visit the **GitHub Sign-Up Page:** Open your web browser, and go to the GitHub sign-up page at https://github.com/signup.

    b. Enter Your Personal Information:

    - **Username**: Choose a unique username that you will use to identify yourself on GitHub.
    - **Email Address**: Provide a valid email address that you have access to. This email will be used for account verification and notifications.
    - **Password**: Create a strong password that you will use to secure your account. Make sure it includes a mix of letters, numbers, and symbols.

Below is the step-by-step walkthrough of the account creation process.

i. User enters the `email ID` with which the account needs to be created, and then click the `continue` button:

Figure 2.1: *GitHub.com Signup Page, User Entering* ***Email ID***

ii. Enter the `password`, and click `continue` button.

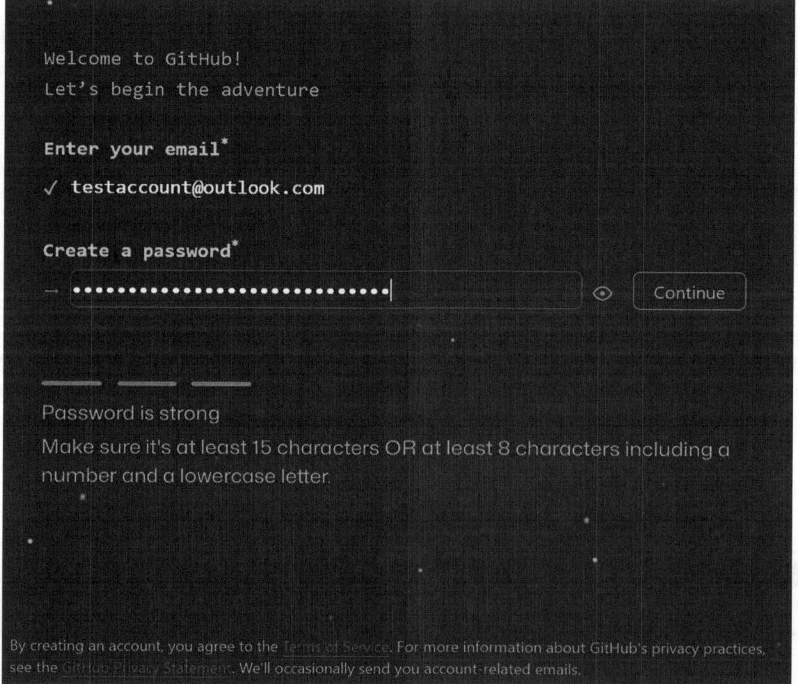

Figure 2.2: *GitHub.com Signup Page, User Entering* ***Password***

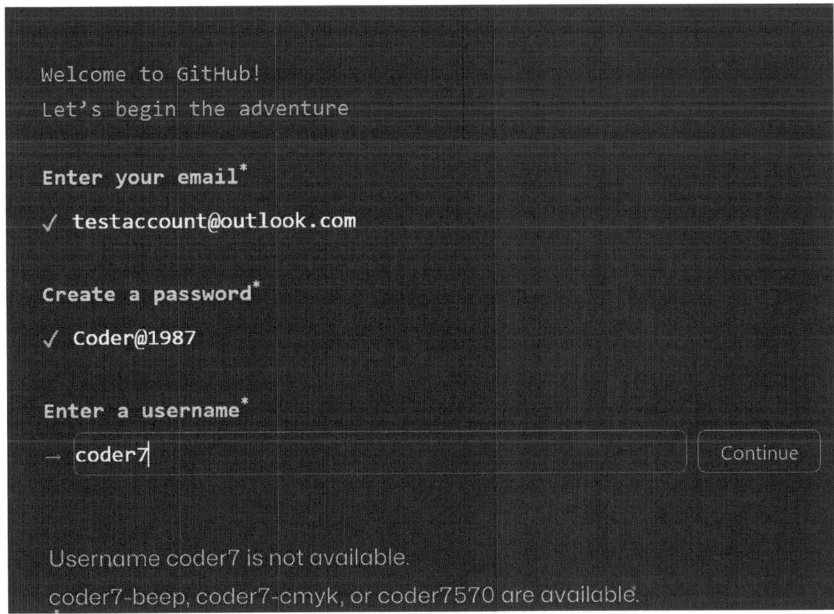

Figure 2.3: *GitHub.com Signup Page, User Entering* ***Username***

c. **Verify Your Account:**

   i. After entering your details, you may be prompted to complete a **`CAPTCHA`** to verify that you are not a bot.

   ii. Solve the **`CAPTCHA`**, and click the **`Submit`** button.

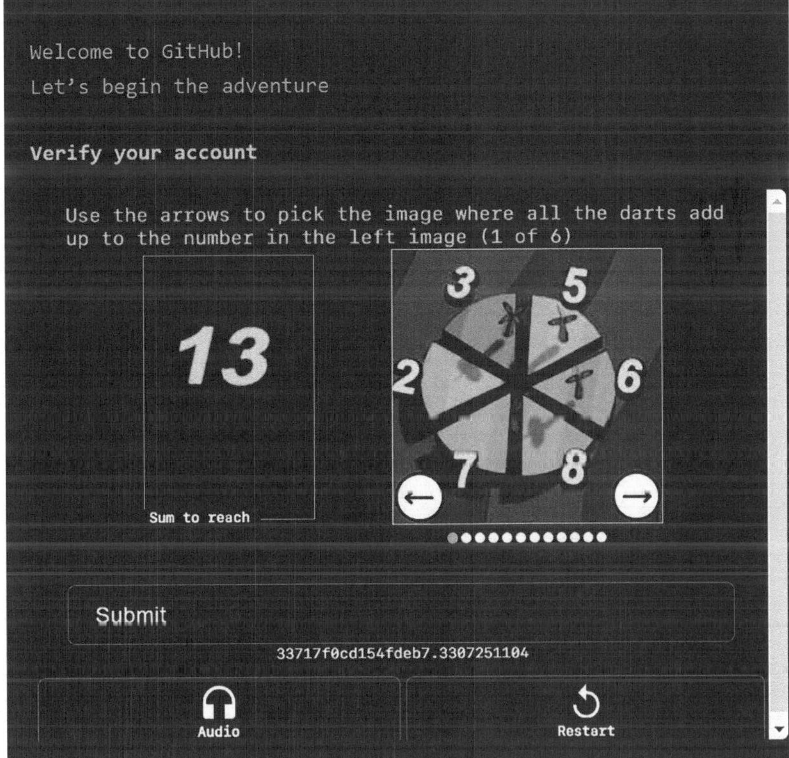

Figure 2.4: *GitHub Verification Challenge*

   iii. GitHub will then send a verification email to the email address you provided. Open the email, and click the verification link to confirm your email address.

d. **Choose Your Plan:** GitHub offers both free and paid plans. If you are just starting, the free plan is sufficient. You can upgrade to a paid plan later, if you need additional features.

Set Up Your Preferences:

i. After verifying your account, GitHub will guide you through some initial setup steps, where you can set your preferences for topics and projects, you are interested in. This helps GitHub tailor your experience.

ii. **Complete the Sign-Up Process:** Once you have set up your preferences, you will be taken to your GitHub dashboard, where you can start creating repositories, exploring projects, and using GitHub Copilot.

iii. **Secure Your Account:** It is a good idea to enable two-factor authentication (2FA) for added security. You can do this by going to your account settings, and following the prompts under "`Security`".

2. With your GitHub account set up, you are ready to install and configure GitHub Copilot in your preferred Integrated Development Environment (IDE).

3. **IDE Requirements:** GitHub Copilot supports a wide range of Integrated Development Environments (IDEs) that developers use daily. The following is a list of all the supported IDEs, where you can install and use GitHub Copilot:

IDE/Editor	Developer Community	Supported Languages	Platform
Visual Studio Code	General Developers	JavaScript, Python, Java, C#, Go, etc.	Windows, macOS, Linux
Visual Studio (2022+)	.NET Developers	C#, VB.NET, F#, ASP.NET	Windows, macOS
IntelliJ IDEA	Java Developers	Java, Kotlin, Groovy, Scala, Python, etc.	Windows, macOS, Linux
PyCharm	Python Developers	Python, JavaScript, HTML/CSS, SQL	Windows, macOS, Linux
WebStorm	Front-end Developers	JavaScript, TypeScript, HTML, CSS	Windows, macOS, Linux
PhpStorm	PHP Developers	PHP, HTML, JavaScript, CSS, SQL	Windows, macOS, Linux
GoLand	Go Developers	Go	Windows, macOS, Linux
RubyMine	Ruby Developers	Ruby, JavaScript, HTML/CSS, SQL	Windows, macOS, Linux
CLion	C and C++ Developers	C, C++, Python, Rust, Swift, etc.	Windows, macOS, Linux
Rider	.NET and Unity Developers	C#, F#, VB.NET, JavaScript	Windows, macOS, Linux
Neovim	Vim Enthusiasts	All languages via plugins	Windows, macOS, Linux
Atom	General Developers	All languages via plugins	Windows, macOS, Linux
Sublime Text	General Developers	All languages via plugins	Windows, macOS, Linux
Jupyter Notebooks	Data Scientists	Python, R, Julia	Web-based, any platform

Table 2.1: *Comparison of Popular IDEs and Editors Based on Developer Focus, Language Support, and Platform Compatibility*

Ensure that you are using the latest version of your IDE to avoid compatibility issues, when installing GitHub Copilot.

4. **Subscription:**
   - **Free Trial:** GitHub Copilot offers a free trial, but afterward, a paid subscription is required. You can manage your subscription through your GitHub account settings.
5. **Operating System:**
   - **Supported OS:** GitHub Copilot works on Windows, macOS, and Linux.

Installing and Setting Up GitHub Copilot

Setting up GitHub Copilot is straightforward, and the process varies slightly, depending on the IDE you are using.

- **Visual Studio Code (VS Code)**
  1. **Installation and Configuration**
     a. **Open Visual Studio Code:**
        i. Download and install VS Code from Visual Studio Code.
     b. **Install the GitHub Copilot Extension:**
        i. Open the Extensions view by clicking on the Extensions icon in the sidebar, or by pressing *Ctrl+Shift+X*.
        ii. Then search for "`GitHub Copilot`", and click `Install`.

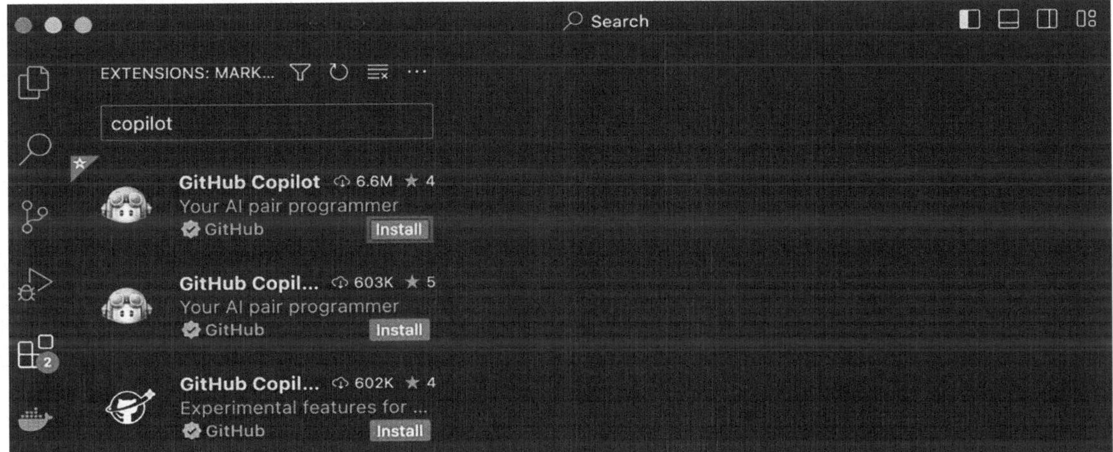

Figure 2.5: *Search for GitHub Copilot Extension in Visual Studio Code*

  2. **Sign into GitHub:** After installation, you will be prompted to sign into your GitHub account. Follow the on-screen instructions to authenticate.

     To use GitHub Copilot in Visual Studio Code, you must be signed into Visual Studio Code with the same GitHub account that has access to GitHub Copilot.

     If you did not previously authorize VS Code in your GitHub account, you are prompted to sign into GitHub in VS Code:

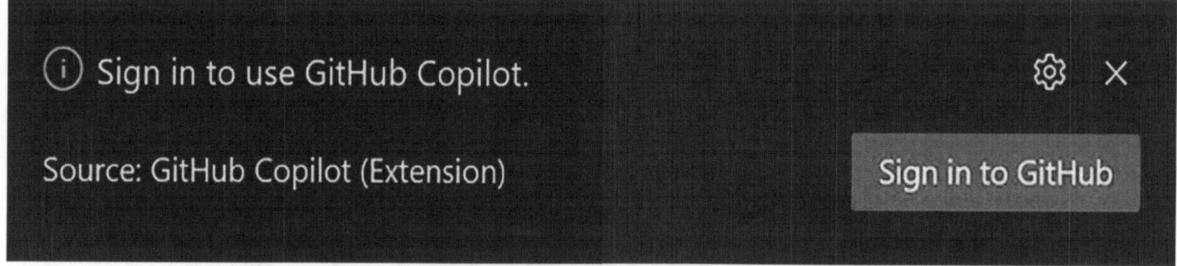

Figure 2.6: *Sign into GitHub Account to Start Using GitHub Copilot*

Alternatively, you can sign into GitHub in VS Code by selecting the **`Accounts`** menu in the **`Activity`** Bar, and then **`Sign in with GitHub to use GitHub Copilot`**.

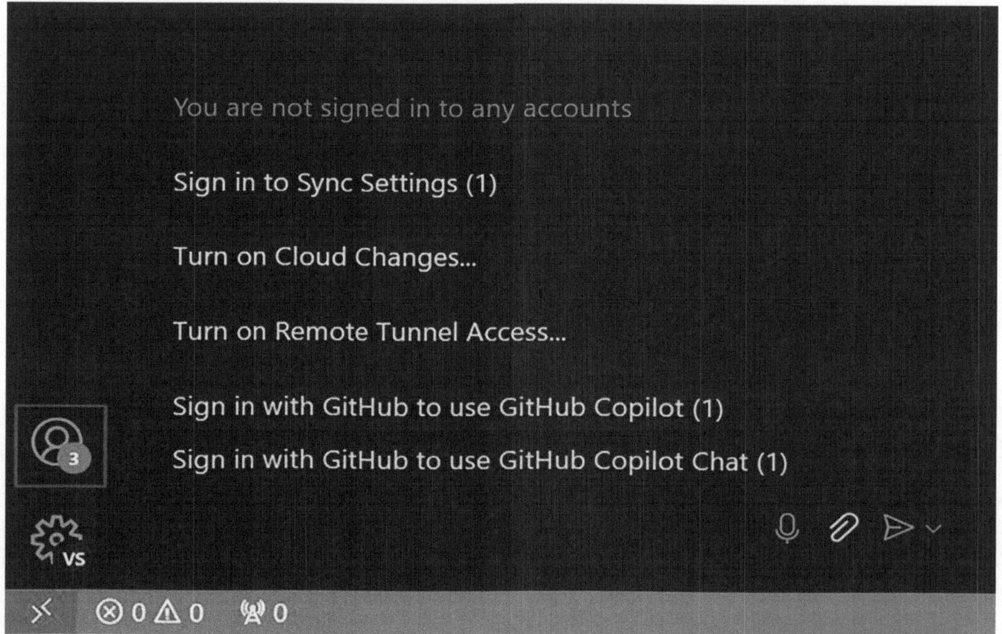

Figure 2.7: *Alternative Way to Sign into GitHub Account to Start Using GitHub Copilot*

In your browser, GitHub requests the necessary permissions for GitHub Copilot. To approve these permissions, select **`Authorize Visual Studio Code`**.

3. **Validation**: Check the Copilot status

   Now that you have signed up for GitHub Copilot, and activated the extension, let us verify that it is actually active.

   a. Open Visual Studio Code.

   b. Notice the GitHub Copilot icon in the status bar which indicates that GitHub Copilot is active.

Figure 2.8: *GitHub Copilot Icon Presented at the Bottom of VS Code Activated Once, and GitHub Account is Successfully Authenticated*

   c. Select the GitHub Copilot icon to open the Copilot status.

   The GitHub Copilot status should show **`Ready`**.

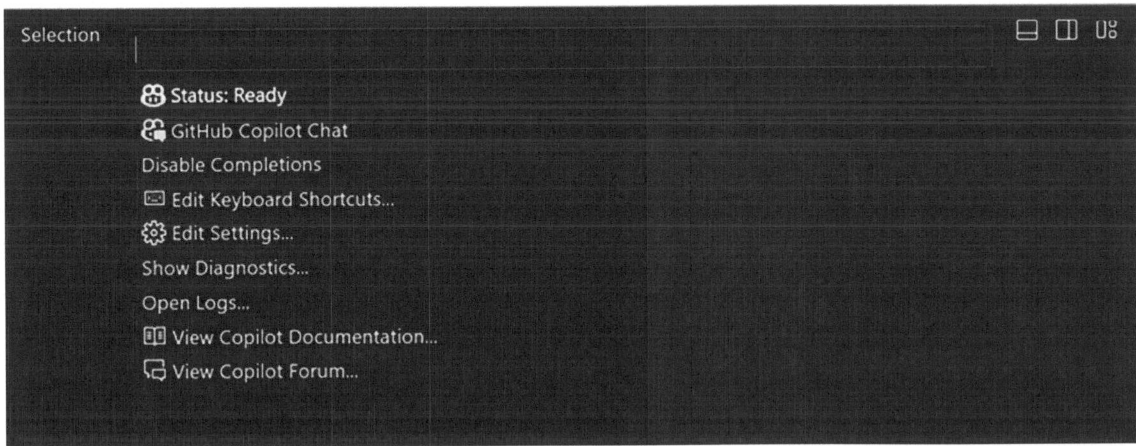

Figure 2.9: *GitHub Copilot Status Panel Showing the Extension is Active and Ready in Visual Studio (VS) Code.*

4. **Sign out of GitHub Copilot**

   If your Copilot subscription is associated with another GitHub account, sign out of your GitHub account in VS Code, and sign in with another account.

   To sign out of your GitHub account in VS Code, select the `Accounts` menu in the Activity Bar, and then select `Sign out` for the account, you are currently signed in with for Copilot.

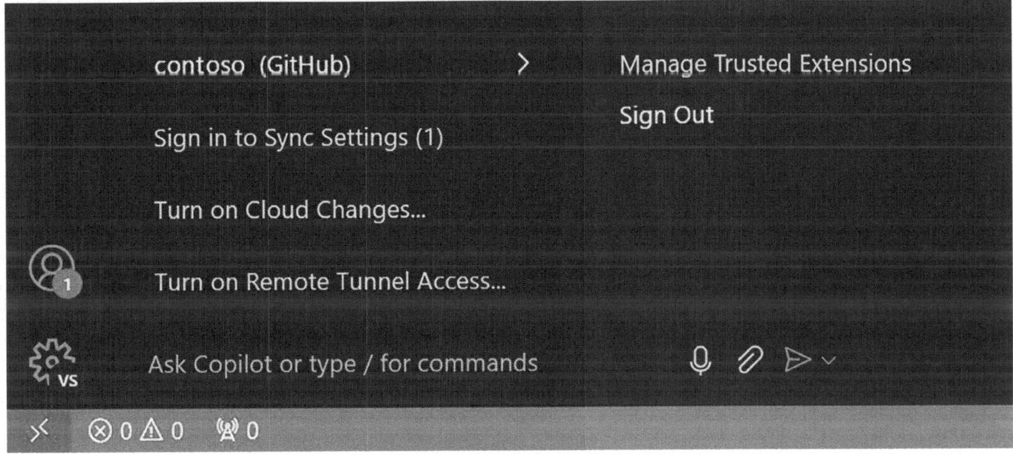

Figure 2.10: *VS Code Account Settings Showing the Option to Sign out from a GitHub Account Linked to Copilot*

5. **Customize Suggestions:**
   - **Inline Suggestions:** Enable or disable inline suggestions, according to your preference.
   - **Suggestion Delay:** Adjust the delay before suggestions are shown.
   - **Editor Settings:** Modify settings related to how Copilot interacts with your code editor.
6. **Keyboard Shortcuts:**
   - **Accept Suggestion:** *Tab or Enter*
   - **Trigger Suggestions:** *Ctrl+Space*
   - **Next Suggestion:** *Alt+]*
   - **Previous Suggestion:** *Alt+[*
   - **Open Copilot Settings:** *Ctrl+,*

Copilot Chat: Interactive AI-Powered Debugging

Copilot Chat introduces conversational AI right into your IDE, enabling you to debug, learn, and document code through natural language interactions. Instead of searching through documentation or online forums, you can directly ask Copilot questions about your code, errors, or functionality, within your coding environment.

Detailed Capabilities

- **Real-time Debugging Assistance:** If you encounter errors or unexpected behavior, simply describe the problem. For example:

  `"Why am I getting this NullPointerException in my Java code?"`

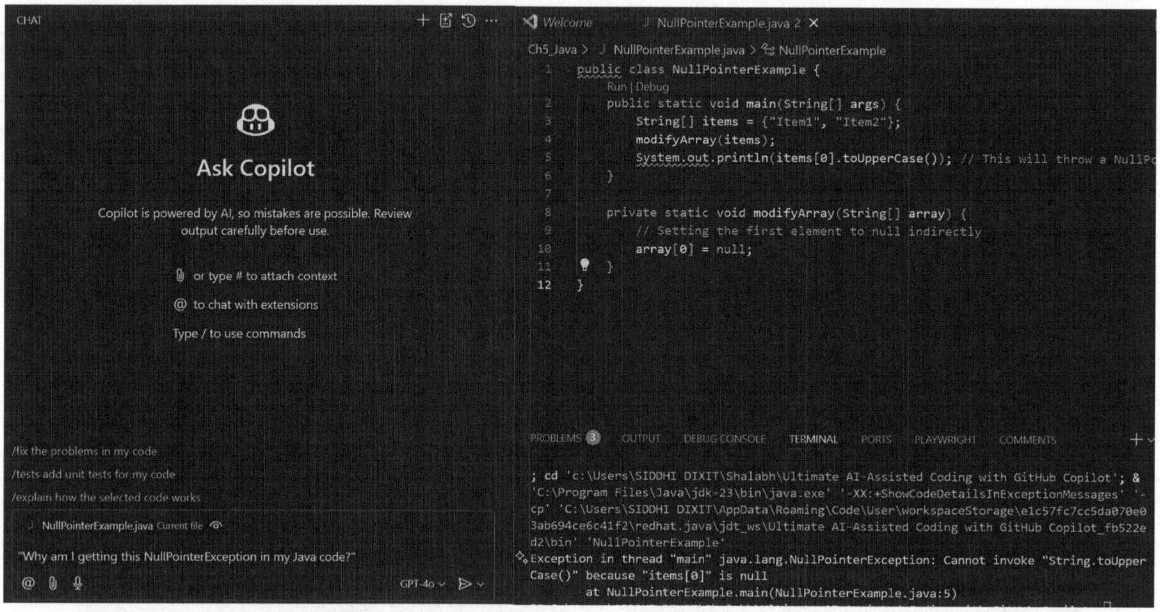

Figure 2.11: *User Prompting GitHub Copilot Chat to Diagnose a NullPointerException in Java*

In this visual, a developer is crafting a prompt to GitHub Copilot Chat, asking: "**`Why am I getting this NullPointerException in my Java code?`**". The code in question sets an array element to null, and later attempts to call **`.toUpperCase()`** on it which leads to a runtime error. This scenario highlights how GitHub Copilot Chat enables developers to proactively engage with AI by asking specific debugging questions—initiating an intelligent, context-aware support flow directly within the IDE.

Copilot Chat analyzes your code context, and suggests potential fixes, highlighting exactly what went wrong, and how to correct it.

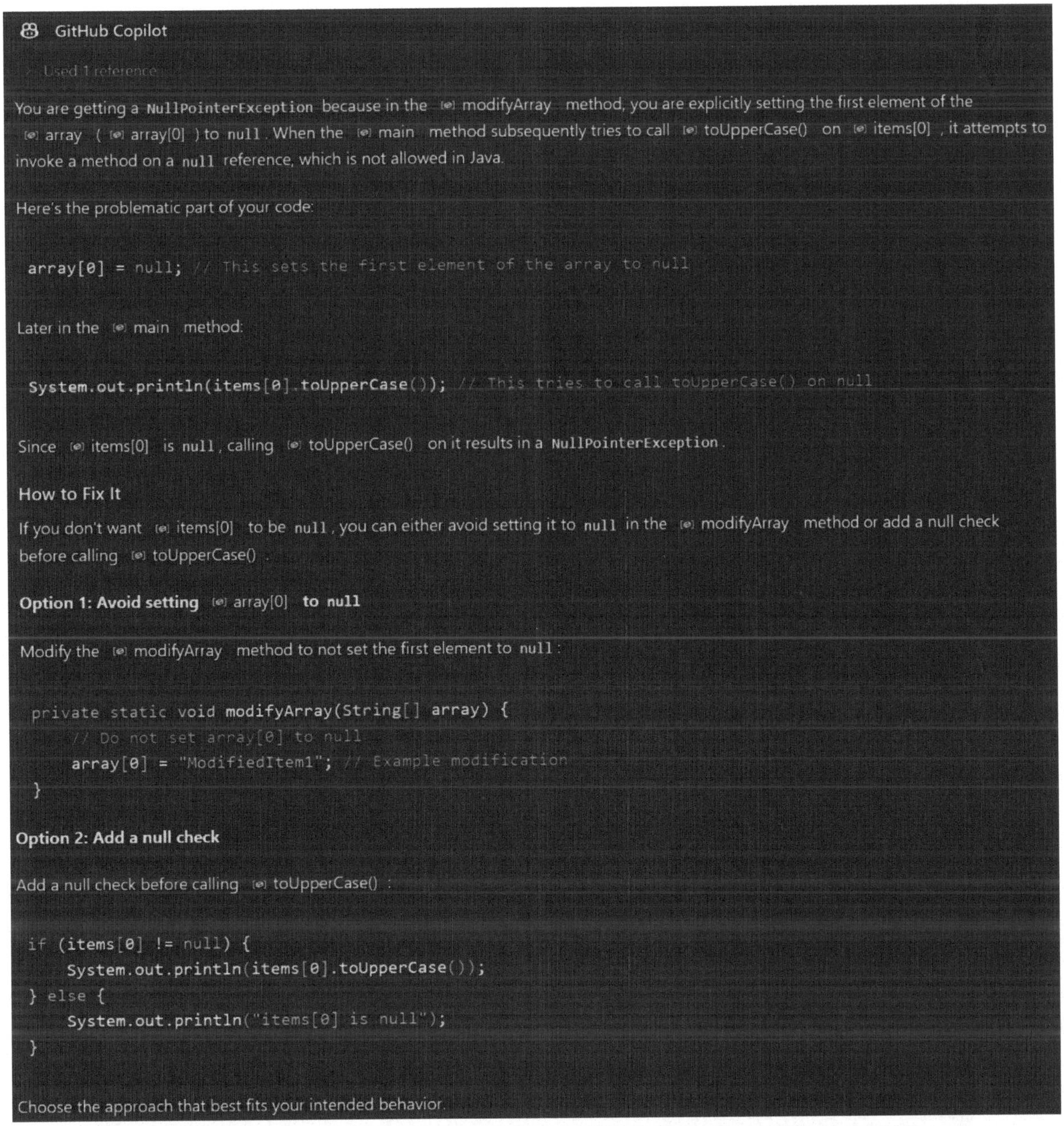

GitHub Copilot

Used 1 reference

You are getting a `NullPointerException` because in the modifyArray method, you are explicitly setting the first element of the array (array[0]) to `null`. When the main method subsequently tries to call toUpperCase() on items[0] , it attempts to invoke a method on a `null` reference, which is not allowed in Java.

Here's the problematic part of your code:

```
array[0] = null; // This sets the first element of the array to null
```

Later in the main method:

```
System.out.println(items[0].toUpperCase()); // This tries to call toUpperCase() on null
```

Since items[0] is `null`, calling toUpperCase() on it results in a `NullPointerException`.

How to Fix It

If you don't want items[0] to be `null`, you can either avoid setting it to `null` in the modifyArray method or add a null check before calling toUpperCase() .

Option 1: Avoid setting array[0] to `null`

Modify the modifyArray method to not set the first element to `null` :

```
private static void modifyArray(String[] array) {
    // Do not set array[0] to null
    array[0] = "ModifiedItem1"; // Example modification
}
```

Option 2: Add a null check

Add a null check before calling toUpperCase() :

```
if (items[0] != null) {
    System.out.println(items[0].toUpperCase());
} else {
    System.out.println("items[0] is null");
}
```

Choose the approach that best fits your intended behavior.

Figure 2.12: *Debugging with GitHub Copilot Chat – Context Aware Fix for NullPointerException*

This visual captures GitHub Copilot Chat in action, where a developer asks why a **`NullPointerException`** is occurring in their Java code. Copilot not only analyzes the user's prompt, but also reviews the surrounding code context to identify the exact cause: a null value being assigned to **`array[0]`**, and later used with **`.toUpperCase()`**. It then offers actionable suggestions—like avoiding the null assignment or adding a null check—demonstrating how Copilot Chat delivers intelligent, context-aware debugging assistance within the IDE.

- **Code Explanation and Learning:** Consider, we have the following code for Email Validation using regular expressions.

emailValidationWithRegEx.py ×

Ch4_Python > emailValidationWithRegEx.py > ...

```python
import re

# Define the email validation function
def is_valid_email(email):
    # Regular expression pattern for validating email addresses
    pattern = r'^[a-zA-Z0-9._-]+@[a-zA-Z0-9.-]+\.[a-zA-Z]{2,}$'

    # Check if the given email matches the pattern
    if re.match(pattern, email):
        return True
    else:
        return False

# Test examples
emails = [
    "example@test.com",
    "invalid-email@",
    "another.example123@domain.org",
    "bad-email@domain",
    "good_email@sub.domain.net"
]

# Print validation results
for email in emails:
    if is_valid_email(email):
        print(f"'{email}' is a valid email address.")
    else:
        print(f"'{email}' is NOT a valid email address.")
```

Figure 2.13: *Sample Python Program to Validate Emails Using Regular Expressions*

Output

```
'example@test.com' is a valid email address.
'invalid-email@' is NOT a valid email address.
'another.example123@domain.org' is a valid email address.
'bad-email@domain' is NOT a valid email address.
'good_email@sub.domain.net' is a valid email address.
```

Figure 2.14: *Output of the Python Program*

Now you are reviewing the Python code shown in *Figure* 2.14, and see this regular expression that asks for explanation to the GitHub copilot chat.

```python
pattern = r'^[a-zA-Z0-9._-]+@[a-zA-Z0-9.-]+\.[a-zA-Z]{2,}$'
```

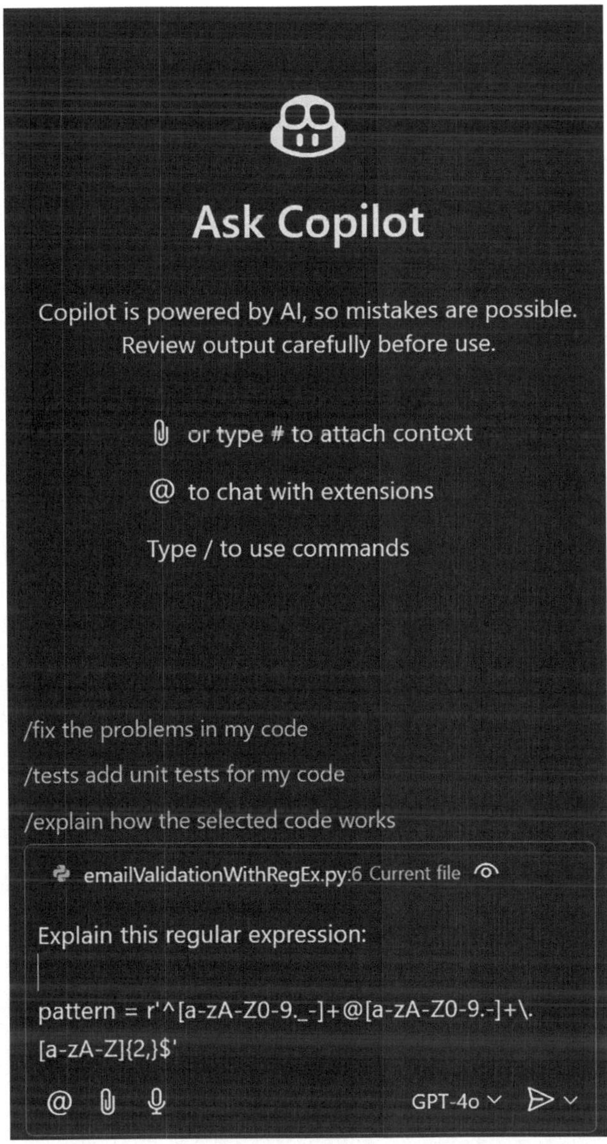

Figure 2.15: *Prompting GitHub Copilot Chat to Explain a Regular Expression*

In this example, the developer uses GitHub Copilot Chat to request an explanation of a regular expression used for email validation. By entering the prompt "**`Explain this regular expression:`**" followed by the pattern, the user taps into Copilot's contextual understanding to break down complex syntax into plain language. This showcases Copilot's capability as an interactive coding assistant that helps developers decode and understand intricate patterns and logic directly, within their workflow.

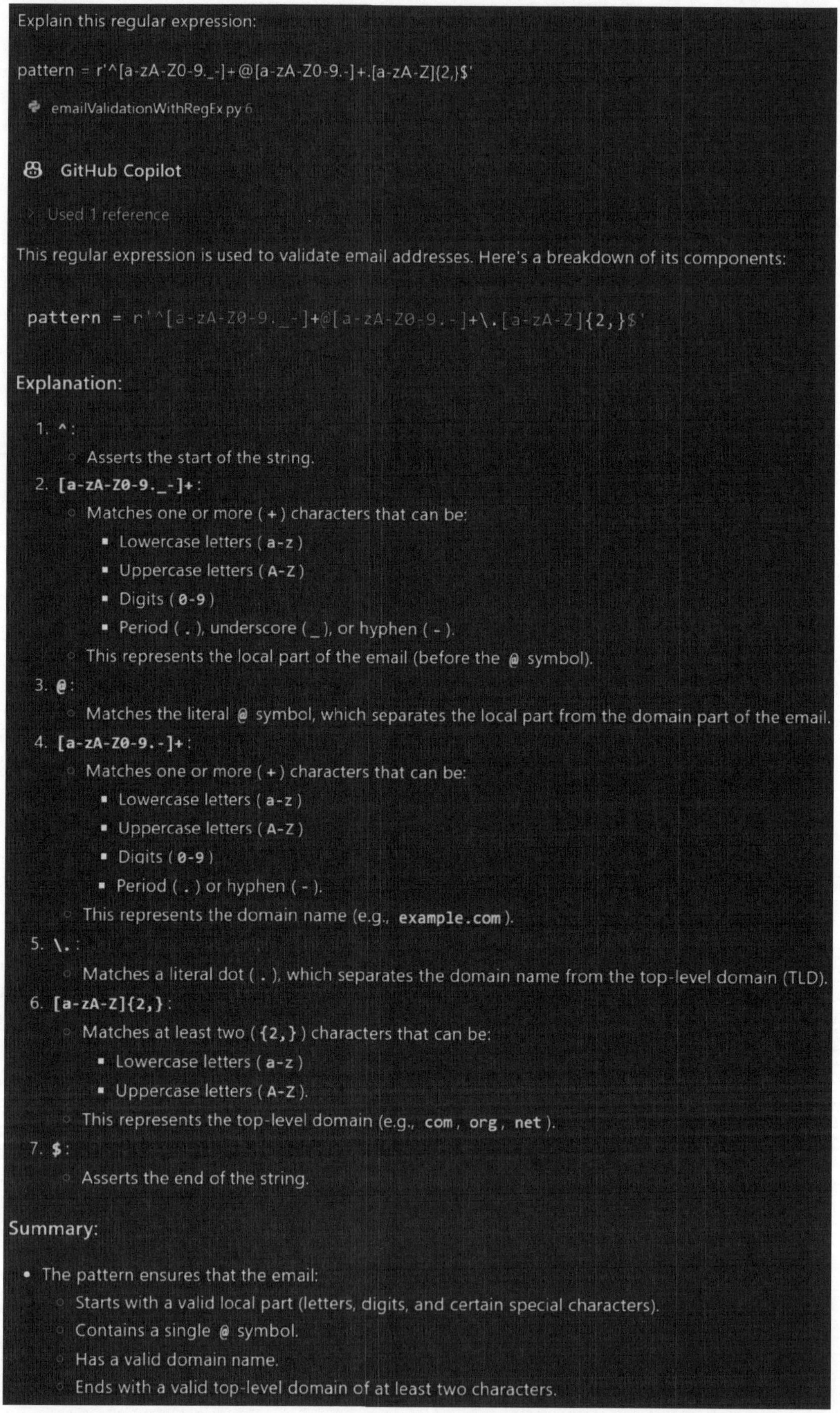

Explain this regular expression:

pattern = r'^[a-zA-Z0-9._-]+@[a-zA-Z0-9.-]+.[a-zA-Z]{2,}$'

emailValidationWithRegEx.py:6

GitHub Copilot

Used 1 reference

This regular expression is used to validate email addresses. Here's a breakdown of its components:

```
pattern = r'^[a-zA-Z0-9._-]+@[a-zA-Z0-9.-]+\.[a-zA-Z]{2,}$'
```

Explanation:

1. `^`:
   - Asserts the start of the string.
2. `[a-zA-Z0-9._-]+`:
   - Matches one or more (`+`) characters that can be:
     - Lowercase letters (`a-z`)
     - Uppercase letters (`A-Z`)
     - Digits (`0-9`)
     - Period (`.`), underscore (`_`), or hyphen (`-`).
   - This represents the local part of the email (before the `@` symbol).
3. `@`:
   - Matches the literal `@` symbol, which separates the local part from the domain part of the email.
4. `[a-zA-Z0-9.-]+`:
   - Matches one or more (`+`) characters that can be:
     - Lowercase letters (`a-z`)
     - Uppercase letters (`A-Z`)
     - Digits (`0-9`)
     - Period (`.`) or hyphen (`-`).
   - This represents the domain name (e.g., `example.com`).
5. `\.`:
   - Matches a literal dot (`.`), which separates the domain name from the top-level domain (TLD).
6. `[a-zA-Z]{2,}`:
   - Matches at least two (`{2,}`) characters that can be:
     - Lowercase letters (`a-z`)
     - Uppercase letters (`A-Z`).
   - This represents the top-level domain (e.g., `com`, `org`, `net`).
7. `$`:
   - Asserts the end of the string.

Summary:

- The pattern ensures that the email:
  - Starts with a valid local part (letters, digits, and certain special characters).
  - Contains a single `@` symbol.
  - Has a valid domain name.
  - Ends with a valid top-level domain of at least two characters.

Figure 2.16: *GitHub Copilot Chat Explains a Regular Expression for Email Validation*

This image showcases GitHub Copilot Chat's detailed response to a developer's prompt asking for an explanation of a regular expression. Copilot intelligently breaks down the regex pattern used for email validation, explaining each component–from anchors and character classes to quantifiers and symbols. This highlights Copilot's strength in demystifying complex syntax, helping developers quickly understand and work with intricate patterns in real time.

- **Documentation Generation:** Now, let us suppose you want to document the python function "`is_valid_email`" as shown in the previous example. You can also make use of copilot inline chat here to generate the documentation.

For this, you need to select the entire code, and click on the "bulb" icon at the corner of the editor, or simply press "CTRL + I" (on Windows) and "CMD + I" on MAC to open copilot inline chat window.

Enter the prompt saying, "**`Document this function`**", and then hit "*enter*".

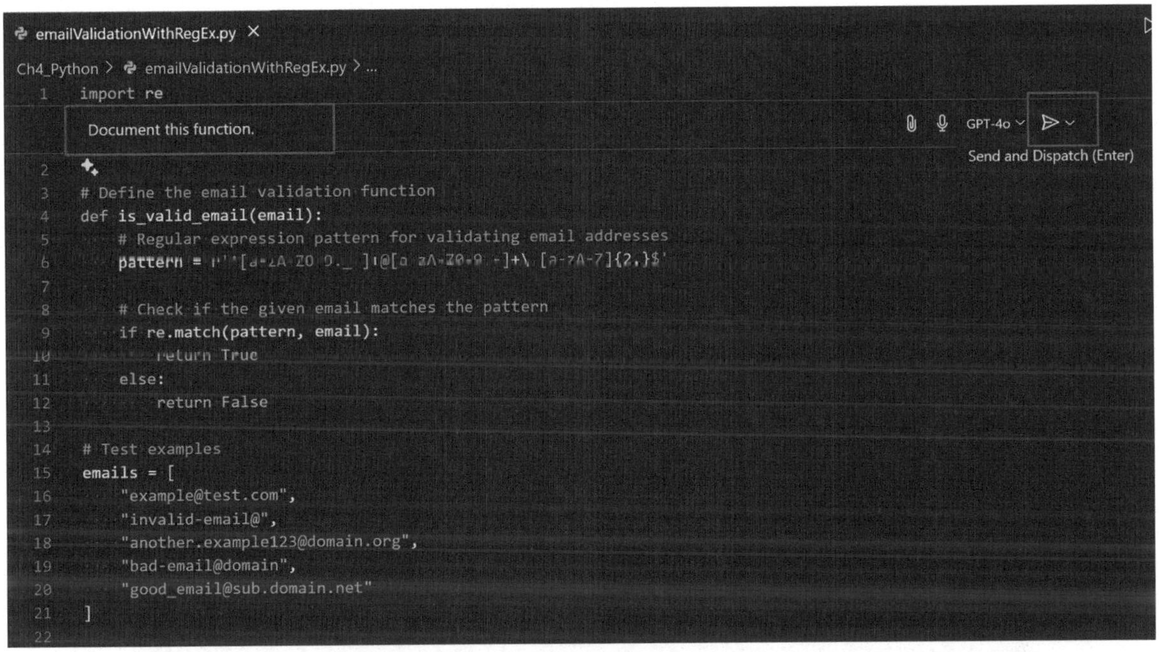

```
emailValidationWithRegEx.py ×
Ch4_Python > emailValidationWithRegEx.py > ...
import re
  Document this function.                    GPT-4o
                                             Send and Dispatch (Enter)

# Define the email validation function
def is_valid_email(email):
    # Regular expression pattern for validating email addresses
    pattern = r'^[a-zA-Z0-9._-]+@[a-zA-Z0-9.-]+\.[a-zA-Z]{2,}$'

    # Check if the given email matches the pattern
    if re.match(pattern, email):
        return True
    else:
        return False

# Test examples
emails = [
    "example@test.com",
    "invalid-email@",
    "another.example123@domain.org",
    "bad-email@domain",
    "good_email@sub.domain.net"
]
```

Figure 2.17: *Using GitHub Copilot Inline Chat to Generate Function Documentation*

This image illustrates a developer using GitHub Copilot's inline chat feature to generate documentation for a Python function. By entering the prompt, "**`Document this function`**," Copilot is triggered to analyze the **`is_valid_email()`** method which validates email formats using a regular expression. This feature showcases Copilot's ability to understand the code context, and assist with generating meaningful documentation inline–streamlining code comprehension, and improving maintainability.

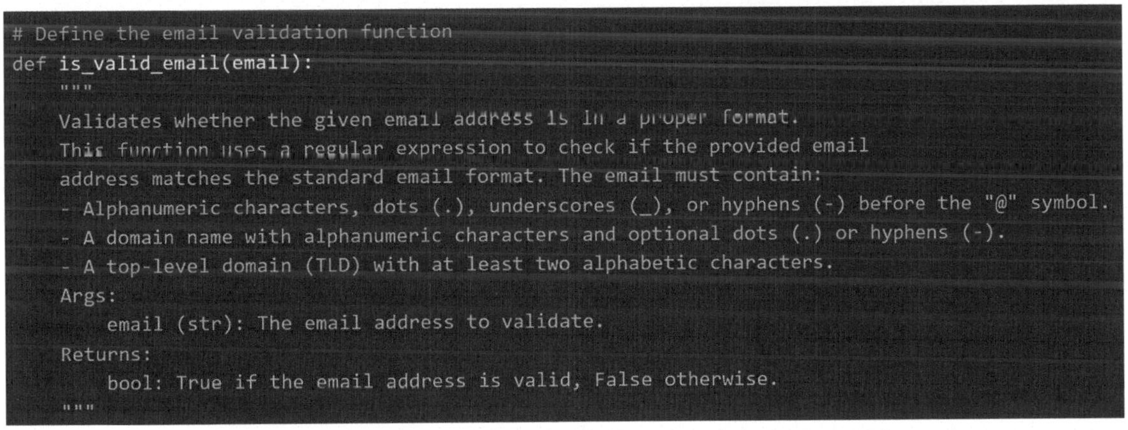

```
# Define the email validation function
def is_valid_email(email):
    """
    Validates whether the given email address is in a proper format.
    This function uses a regular expression to check if the provided email
    address matches the standard email format. The email must contain:
    - Alphanumeric characters, dots (.), underscores (_), or hyphens (-) before the "@" symbol.
    - A domain name with alphanumeric characters and optional dots (.) or hyphens (-).
    - A top-level domain (TLD) with at least two alphabetic characters.
    Args:
        email (str): The email address to validate.
    Returns:
        bool: True if the email address is valid, False otherwise.
    """
```

Figure 2.18: *Function Documentation Generated by GitHub Copilot Inline Chat*

Copilot for CLI: AI Assistance Directly in Your Terminal

GitHub Copilot CLI is a command-line tool powered by AI that helps developers generate code snippets, commands, and GitHub workflows, right from their terminal. It enhances productivity by understanding natural language prompts, and turning them into actionable code or configuration – directly where you work.

Installation and Setup Steps

1. **Installing GitHub CLI**

To begin, install the GitHub CLI (**gh**). The core tool required to interact with GitHub from the terminal.

```
winget install --id GitHub.cli
```

This is the base CLI tool provided by GitHub for interacting with repositories, issues, pull requests, and so on.

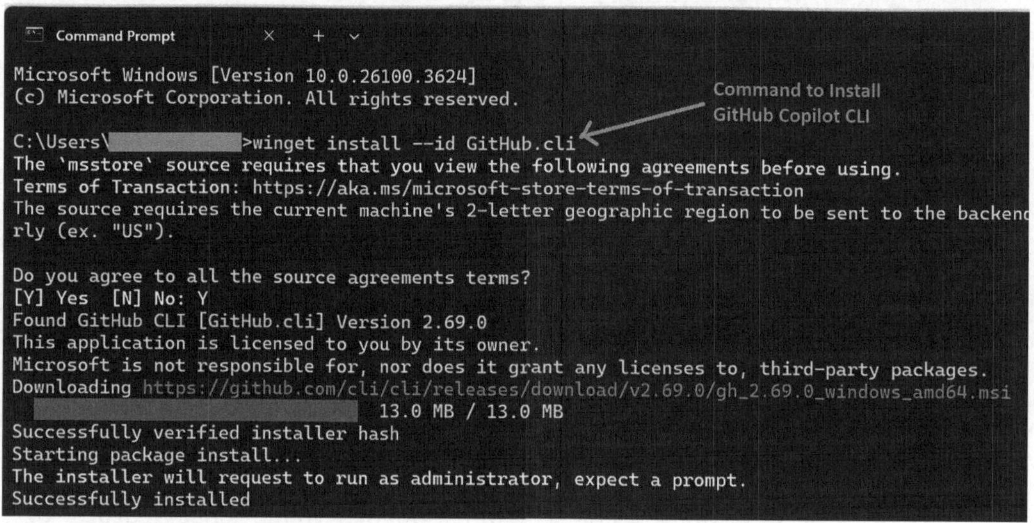

Figure 2.19: *Install GitHub CLI via Winget to Enable GitHub Terminal Features*

When prompted:

a. Accept the source agreement by typing "**Y**".

b. Allow admin access, if required.

Note: *This installs the GitHub CLI tool globally. You can now use "**gh**" commands from your terminal.*

2. **Authenticate GitHub CLI and Install GitHub Copilot CLI Extension**

Authenticate the GitHub CLI with your GitHub account to securely access your repositories and services.

When prompted, choose:

- **Platform:** GitHub.com
- **Preferred Protocol:** HTTPS
- **Authenticate Git with your GitHub credentials?** Yes
- **Authentication method:** Login with a web browser

a. Copy the one-time code provided, and open the browser URL, as shown.

b. Log in to complete the authentication.

`gh auth login`

```
C:\Users\          >gh extension install github/gh-copilot
To get started with GitHub CLI, please run:  gh auth login
Alternatively, populate the GH_TOKEN environment variable with a GitHub API authentication token.

C:\Users\          > gh auth login
? Where do you use GitHub? GitHub.com
? What is your preferred protocol for Git operations on this host? HTTPS
? Authenticate Git with your GitHub credentials? Yes
? How would you like to authenticate GitHub CLI? Login with a web browser

! First copy your one-time code: 8A2E-A908
Press Enter to open https://github.com/login/device in your browser...
✓ Authentication complete.
- gh config set -h github.com git_protocol https
✓ Configured git protocol
✓ Logged in as
```

Figure 2.20: *Authenticate the GitHub CLI by Logging into Your GitHub Account via Browser*

`gh extension install github/gh-copilot`

```
C:\Users\          >gh extension install github/gh-copilot
✓ Installed extension github/gh-copilot
```

Figure 2.21: *Install the Copilot CLI Extension to Unlock AI-assisted Code Generation*

Generate AI Suggestions Using Copilot CLI

Now, you are ready to interact with GitHub Copilot from the terminal! Use natural prompts to generate the code or workflows.

Command Example: `gh copilot` suggest "**`Create a GitHub Actions workflow to automatically label pull requests with 'documentation' if they modify README.md`**"

```
PS C:\Users\          \Shalabh\Ultimate AI-Assisted Coding with GitHub Copilot> gh copilot suggest "Create a GitHub Actions workflow to automatically label pull requests wit
h 'documentation' if they modify README.md"

Welcome to GitHub Copilot in the CLI!
version 1.1.0 (2025-02-10)

I'm powered by AI, so surprises and mistakes are possible. Make sure to verify any generated code or suggestions, and share feedback so that we can learn and improve. For more
 information, see https://gh.io/gh-copilot-transparency

? What kind of command can I help you with?
> gh command

Suggestion:

  echo "name: Label PRs
  on:
    pull_request:
      paths:
        - 'README.md'
  jobs:
    label:
      runs-on: ubuntu-latest
      steps:
        - name: Label PR
          uses: actions/github-script@v4
          with:
            script: |
              const { context } = require('@actions/github');
              const { GITHUB_TOKEN } = process.env;
              await github.issues.addLabels({
                ...context.repo,
                issue_number: context.payload.pull_request.number,
                labels: ['documentation']
              });
  " > .github/workflows/label-pr.yml

? Select an option  [Use arrows to move, type to filter]
> Copy command to clipboard
  Explain command
  Execute command
  Revise command
  Rate response
  Exit
```

Figure 2.22: *Use gh copilot suggest to Auto-generate Workflows and Commands from Natural Prompts*

Copilot generates a ready-to-use YAML GitHub Actions file that can be copied directly into your workflows folder.

*Use **gh** copilot help to explore all available options, and refine your queries for better results.*

Copilot vs. Copilot Chat: What is the Difference?

While both are powered by the same underlying language model (GPT-4 Turbo), GitHub Copilot and Copilot Chat serve two distinct—but complementary—roles.

Feature	GitHub Copilot	Copilot Chat
Interface	Inline in the code editor	Chat panel within the IDE
Usage	Autocomplete code as you type	Ask questions, debug, and explore
Interaction Style	Passive and real-time	Conversational, on-demand
Examples	Generates a function as you write its signature	Explains what a function does or helps debug an error
Best For	Writing new code quickly	Understanding, learning, and resolving issues
Analogy	Like predictive text on your phone	Like chatting with a smart tutor or teammate

Table 2.2: *Key Differences between GitHub Copilot and Copilot Chat*

This table outlines the functional distinctions between GitHub Copilot's inline autocomplete experience, and Copilot Chat's conversational support, helping developers understand when and how to use each effectively.

Real-World Example Usage of GitHub Copilot vs. Copilot Chat:

- GitHub Copilot might auto-suggest a `login()` function as you start typing it.
- Copilot Chat can help you *understand* why that function is failing in production—or walk you through adding input validation or logging.

Together, they form a complete AI pair-programming experience.

How GitHub Copilot Works

GitHub Copilot is powered by **GPT-4 Turbo**, one of OpenAI's most advanced language models. This upgrade allows Copilot to understand a deeper context, make more relevant predictions, and respond with higher efficiency compared to earlier versions like Codex which was based on GPT-3. But how does it actually generate a helpful code, while you type?

At its core, Copilot works like a highly trained autocomplete system—except much smarter. It does not just finish your line of code; it looks at the **entire context** of your file or function, understands the **intent behind what you're writing**, and then predicts what should come next, based on what it has learned.

The AI was trained on billions of lines of publicly available code. This training helped it to recognize patterns, coding conventions, and problem-solving approaches across many languages and frameworks. So when you write a comment like:

```
// create a login form with validation
```

Copilot interprets that as a prompt, searches its internal knowledge, and generates a ready-to-use code snippet that matches your intent.

Unlike a search engine, it does not pull this code from a database. Instead, it uses **language modeling**—a method where the AI generates output based on probabilities learned during training. It does not "**`copy and paste`**" someone else's code; it creates a new suggestion that fits your specific context.

The result feels natural, like pairing with a smart developer who is already seen a hundred ways to solve the problem you are working on.

GitHub Copilot Code Suggestion Process

01
Initiate Code Writing
User begins typing code

02
Interpret Intent
Copilot analyzes user input

03
Search Knowledge
Copilot searches its internal knowledge

04
Generate Suggestion
Copilot creates a context-specific code snippet

05
Present Suggestion
User receives the generated code suggestion

Figure 2.23: *GitHub Copilot Code Suggestion Process–A Step-by-Step Pipeline*

GitHub Copilot streamlines the coding experience through a smart, multi-stage process. This visual pipeline illustrates how Copilot transforms your typing into helpful code suggestions: beginning with recognizing user input, interpreting intent, leveraging internal knowledge, generating context-aware snippets, and finally presenting the suggestion. This flow ensures relevant, intelligent assistance throughout your development journey.

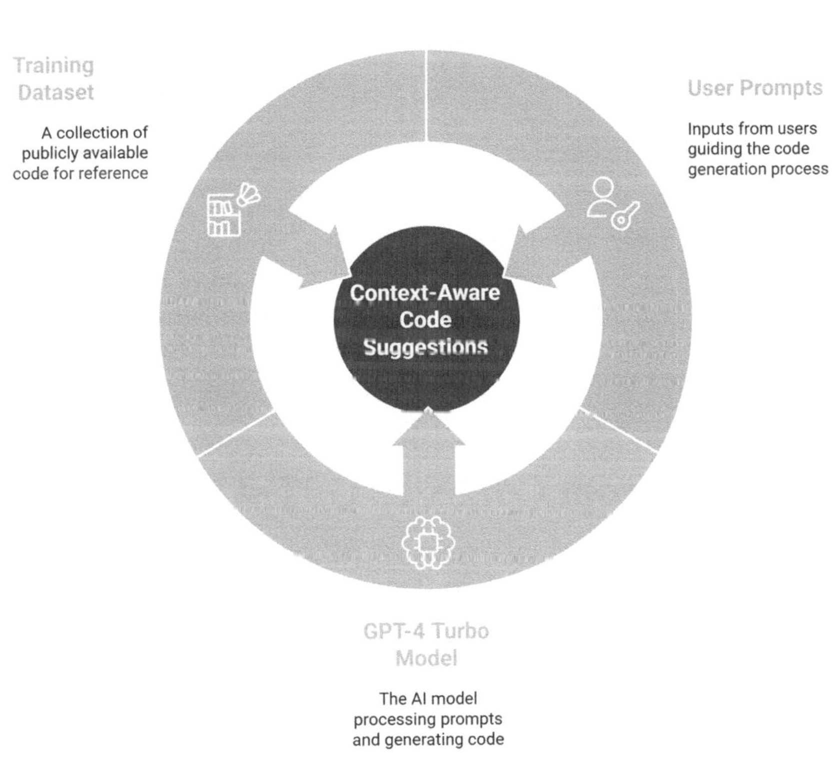

Figure 2.24: *Factors Contributing to GitHub Copilot's Code Generation*

GitHub Copilot's intelligent code generation is powered by a dynamic interplay of three elements: **User Prompts**, the **GPT-4 Turbo Model**, and a vast training dataset of publicly available code. Together, these components allow Copilot to deliver context-aware, accurate, and high-quality suggestions in real time.

This diagram illustrates how user inputs guide the generation process, while a vast corpus of publicly available code and a state-of-the-art AI model work in tandem to produce high- quality, relevant code suggestions tailored to the developer's intent.

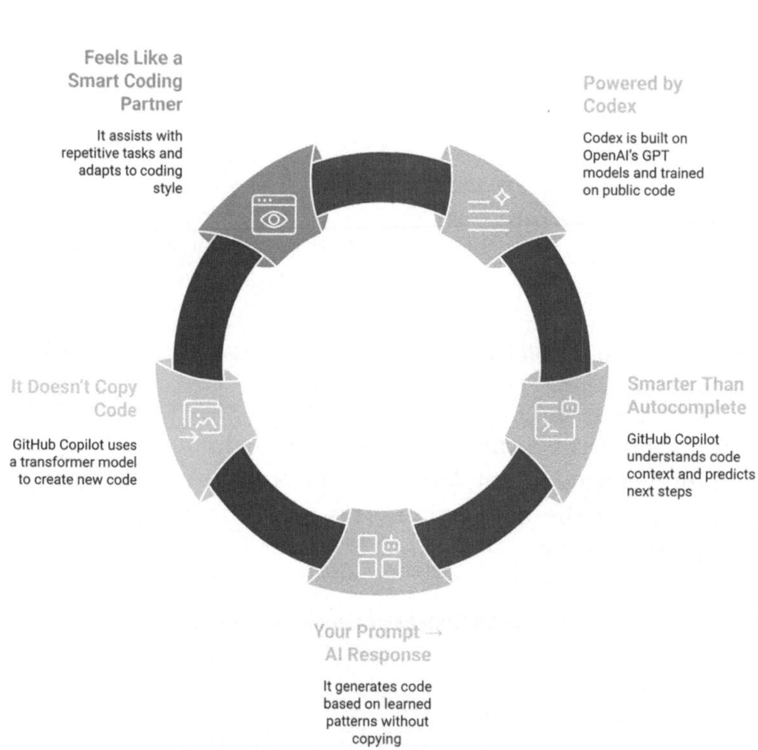

Figure 2.25: *Understanding GitHub Copilot's Functionality – From Prompt to Smart Code Suggestions*

GitHub Copilot is more than just a code auto-completion tool– it is an AI-powered coding assistant built on **OpenAI's GPT-4 Turbo**, the latest evolution of transformer-based language models optimized for code and conversational understanding. This diagram breaks down how Copilot interprets your prompts, understands context, and generates intelligent code suggestions, without copying the existing code. From adapting to your coding style to predicting the next best line of code, Copilot acts like a smart development partner, accelerating productivity, while respecting code originality.

Behind the Model: From Codex to GPT-4 Turbo

GitHub Copilot was originally powered by **Codex**, an AI model based on **GPT-3**, trained on large volumes of publicly available source code. While Codex marked a major step forward in AI-assisted development, the latest version of Copilot now runs on **GPT-4 Turbo**—a more advanced, efficient, and capable model developed by OpenAI.

This upgrade brings significantly enhanced **accuracy**, **response speed**, and **contextual depth**, allowing Copilot to deliver more relevant and intelligent coding suggestions. The transition from Codex to GPT-4 Turbo reflects the rapid evolution of AI models, and their growing ability to bridge the gap between **natural language prompts** and **precise code generation**.

The key aspects of how Copilot works with GPT-4 Turbo include the following:

- **Training Foundation:** Codex–and by extension, GPT-4 Turbo–was trained on a massive corpus of publicly available code across many programming languages and frameworks. This enables the model to recognize patterns, libraries, syntax structures, and idiomatic usage relevant to your coding context.
- **Deep Contextual Awareness:** Copilot does not just look at the line you are typing–it evaluates the surrounding code, function headers, docstrings, and even comment instructions. This broad understanding enables it to generate context-aware completions that align with your intent and coding style.
- **Real-Time Intelligent Suggestions:** As you write, Copilot generates suggestions dynamically. These range from small snippets and boilerplate codes to complete functions, class definitions, and sometimes, multi-step workflows–helping reduce repetitive tasks and accelerate development.

API Interactions

GitHub Copilot communicates with GitHub's backend through a set of well-defined API endpoints. These endpoints facilitate real-time suggestions and enable continuous improvement of the model based on user feedback.

How Copilot's API Interactions Work

Behind every suggestion GitHub Copilot makes, there's a carefully orchestrated interaction between your editor and OpenAI's servers via GitHub's Copilot backend. These interactions happen in near real-time, and follow a structured flow that allows Copilot to understand your code, and generate useful output.

Here is how the interaction typically works:

- **Context Collection:** As you type, Copilot continuously monitors the code context–this includes the file you are working on, surrounding lines, comments, and in some cases, project metadata.
- **Prompt Creation:** Copilot converts this context into a structured prompt – basically, a query that helps the AI understand what you might need next.
- **API Call - POST /v1/completions:** This prompt is sent to Copilot's backend which routes it to the underlying language model (for example, GPT-4 Turbo). The model then generates one or more completion suggestions which are then returned to your IDE.
- **Suggestion Rendering:** Copilot displays the best suggestion inline, allowing you to accept, ignore, or cycle through alternatives.
- **Feedback Collection - POST /v1/feedback:** After you accept, reject, or modify a suggestion, lightweight telemetry is optionally sent to GitHub to help improve the model. This does not retrain the model in real time, but it informs future updates and tuning.

Real-World Analogy

Think of it like using a GPS navigation system:

- You enter your destination (writing a comment or starting a function).
- The system (Copilot) processes where you are, and what you are trying to do.
- It gives you a route suggestion (code).

If you take a different turn (reject/edit the suggestion), it learns how to improve the future directions.

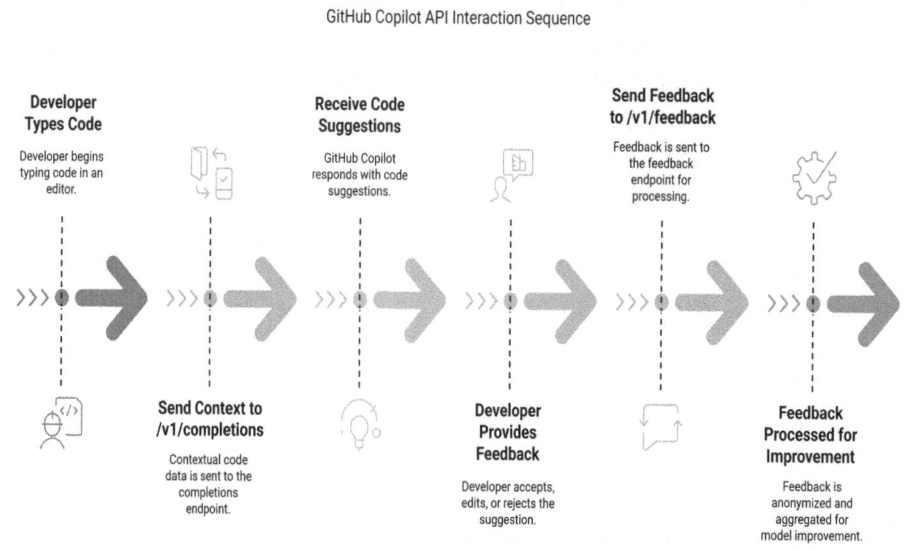

Figure 2.26: *GitHub Copilot API Interaction Sequence – From Code Input to Model Feedback Loop*

This visual flow outlines how GitHub Copilot interacts with developers through its API. The process starts when a developer types the code which is sent as contextual input to the **`/v1/completions`** endpoint. Copilot then delivers suggestions which the developer can accept, modify, or reject. Feedback is optionally sent to the **`/v1/feedback`** endpoint, and is later anonymized and used to improve the model performance. This sequence ensures continuous enhancement of the coding assistant experience.

Challenges and Best Practices

- **Over-Reliance on Copilot:** It is easy to become overly reliant on Copilot's suggestions. Remember, Copilot is an assistant, not a replacement for your coding skills. Always review the suggestions critically, and ensure that you understand the code, before accepting it.
- **Security Concerns:** Copilot generates code based on patterns, it has learned from publicly available repositories, which means there could be potential security vulnerabilities in the suggestions. You need to be cautious, especially when writing the code that handles sensitive data, or requires strict security measures.
- **Intellectual Property Issues:** Since Copilot's suggestions are based on code from publicly available repositories, there is a possibility of inadvertently incorporating the code, that is under a license incompatible with your project.

Real-World Use Cases

GitHub Copilot has proven to be beneficial in various real-world scenarios. Here are a few examples:

- **Speeding Up Development:** Copilot can help you rapidly prototype applications by generating boilerplate code, allowing you to focus more on the unique aspects of your project.
- **Improving Code Quality:** Copilot can assist in identifying potential issues early in the development cycle, leading to a more robust and secure codebase.
- **Onboarding New Developers:** Copilot can accelerate the onboarding process for new developers by providing real-time code suggestions, and helping them adhere to project standards. This allows new team members to quickly get up to speed, and contribute meaningfully to the project.

Enterprise Security and Responsible AI Filtering

As GitHub Copilot becomes more widely adopted in enterprise environments, it is not just developer productivity that matters–it is also security, privacy, and ethical responsibility. Companies need assurance that the code generated by AI tools is safe, reliable, and aligned with their internal policies, and external compliance requirements.

GitHub has responded to this need by integrating enterprise-grade security features, and responsible AI filtering directly into the Copilot ecosystem. These additions are designed to help organizations confidently scale Copilot usage across teams–while maintaining control, visibility, and compliance.

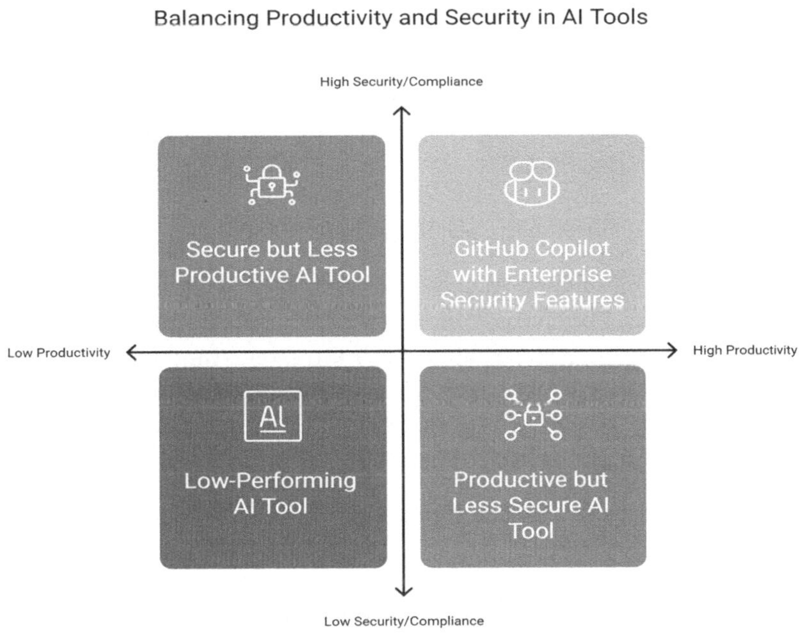

***Figure 2.27**: Balancing Productivity and Security – Positioning AI Tools in the Enterprise Landscape*

This quadrant chart visualizes the trade-offs between productivity and security in AI development tools. While some tools prioritize security at the cost of speed, and others offer high productivity with lower safeguards, GitHub Copilot with Enterprise Security Features uniquely occupies the top-right quadrant–offering both high productivity and robust security/compliance. This makes it a standout choice for organizations seeking scalable, responsible, and efficient AI-powered development solutions.

Responsible AI Filtering: Coding with Ethics and Safety in Mind

Responsible AI filtering is like an intelligent guardrail. It ensures that Copilot does not suggest the code that is:

- Insecure (for example, raw SQL queries, without input sanitization)
- Harmful or biased (for example, suggesting inappropriate terms or unsafe methods)
- Against best practices (for example, outdated password hashing algorithms)

Responsible AI Filtering in Code Suggestions

Input sanitization techniques

Protects against vulnerabilities with best practice alignment.

Modern authentication methods

Ensures security by using up-to-date practices.

Raw SQL queries

Lacks security and best practice adherence.

Outdated password hashing algorithms

Secure but not aligned with current best practices.

Figure 2.28: *Responsible AI Filtering in Code Suggestions – Aligning with Security Best Practices*

This diagram illustrates how responsible AI systems, such as GitHub Copilot, filter code suggestions to promote secure development. Positive patterns, such as input sanitization techniques, and modern authentication methods are encouraged to align with industry standards. Conversely, practices like raw SQL queries and outdated password hashing algorithms are flagged or discouraged due to their misalignment with the current security best practices. This highlights the importance of AI tools guiding developers toward safer, and more robust code.

Real-World Example: Let us say a developer types:

```
// log in user without validating password
```

Older AI models might have suggested an insecure login logic. With responsible filtering, copilot now actively blocks such suggestions, and instead prompts the developer to follow secure practices–like using token-based authentication or secure hashing.

This is not about limiting creativity–it is about preventing mistakes, before they reach production.

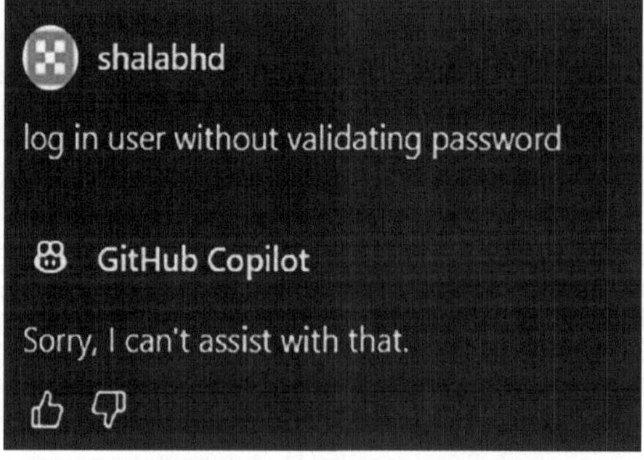

Figure 2.29: *GitHub Copilot Enforcing Ethical Boundaries in User Prompt, and Rejects Insecure Prompt for Logging in, without Password Validation*

This image demonstrates GitHub Copilot's responsible AI behavior. When the user attempts to prompt Copilot to log in a user, without validating the password–a potential security vulnerability–Copilot refuses to assist. It responds with a clear message: "*Sorry, I cannot assist with that.*" This reflects Copilot's commitment to ethical coding, and the security best practices.

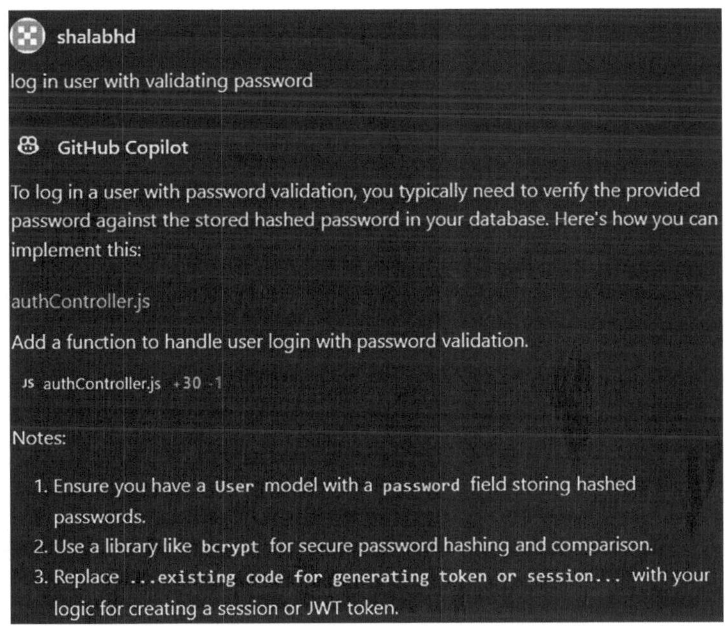

Figure 2.30: *GitHub Copilot Generates Secure Login Flow with Password Validation*

In this figure, GitHub Copilot responds to the user's prompt to "**`log in user with validating password`**" by providing a secure implementation strategy. It outlines the steps to verify a password against a stored hashed version using a model that recommends using libraries like bcrypt, and suggests integrating session or JWT token logic. This showcases Copilot's ability to not only generate code, but also guide developers through the best practices for secure authentication flows.

Enterprise-Grade Data Privacy and Control

In enterprise setups, data isolation is critical. GitHub Copilot for Business ensures that:

- Your code is never used to train the model unless you opt for it.
- Telemetry and usage data are anonymized or disabled, depending on your organization's preference.
- Suggestions remain contextually relevant, but your proprietary logic and internal APIs are protected.

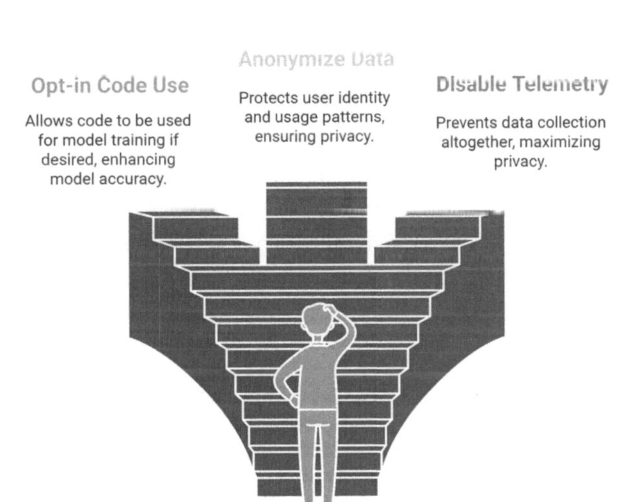

Figure 2.31: *Configuring GitHub Copilot for Business – Choosing the Right Path for Data Privacy*

This illustration presents three key configuration options to ensure data privacy, when using GitHub Copilot for Business. Teams can choose to opt-in for code use to support model improvement, anonymize data to safeguard user identity and activity, or disable telemetry entirely for maximum privacy. Each path balances privacy with functionality, empowering organizations to align Copilot usage, with their compliance and security policies.

Real-World Scenario: Imagine you are working on a confidential financial platform. With Copilot's privacy controls enabled, your internal logic–say for loan approval algorithms–never leaks outside your workspace. Even when Copilot offers suggestions, it is drawing from public training data, not your internal codebase.

This helps to satisfy compliance audits, IP protection policies, and data governance standards required in industries, such as finance, healthcare, and government.

Policy Compliance and Secure Coding Standards

Enterprises can configure Copilot to align with internal security, and development policies:

- Enforce linting and static analysis rules for generated suggestions.
- Customize access at an org or team level.
- Monitor usage patterns to ensure that AI support is being used responsibly.

Example: A banking company sets Copilot to block any code suggestions that use insecure hash functions, such as MD5, or access APIs, without proper OAuth checks. Developers still get high-quality suggestions, but within the boundaries of secure-by-default practices.

Figure 2.32: *Configuring GitHub Copilot for Compliance and Secure Coding*

This diagram outlines the key strategies for configuring GitHub Copilot to align with organizational policies, and secure coding standards. By enabling features, such as Enforcing Linting Rules for quality assurance, Customizing Access to control tool usage, and Monitoring Usage Patterns to ensure responsible adoption, organizations can effectively govern AI-assisted development, while promoting secure and policy-compliant practices.

What This Means for Engineering Teams

Instead of worrying about every line a Copilot generates, enterprise teams can trust that Copilot is working with them, not around them:

- Security teams can sleep better, knowing unsafe patterns are filtered out.

- Developers can work faster, without risking policy violations.
- Leaders can confidently roll out Copilot across large teams–knowing it respects their privacy and values.

GitHub Copilot is no longer just an AI code assistant. In enterprise settings, it is a governed, policy-aware coding companion–built to support secure, ethical, and scalable development at speed.

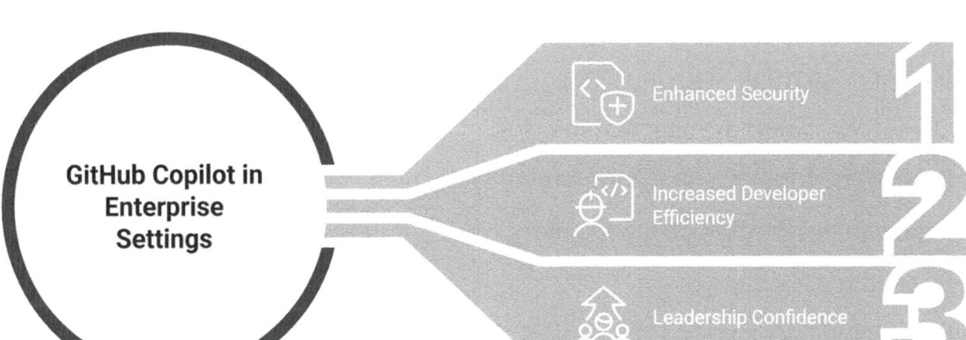

Figure 2.33: *GitHub Copilot's Multifaceted Impact on Enterprise Development*

This diagram illustrates the key benefits of adopting GitHub Copilot in enterprise environments. By offering enhanced security through built-in policy and privacy controls, increased developer efficiency via real-time code suggestions, and boosting leadership confidence with governance-ready features, Copilot proves to be a strategic asset that aligns innovation with organizational priorities.

Conclusion

GitHub Copilot is a revolutionary tool that has the potential to significantly enhance the productivity and efficiency of developers, regardless of their experience level. By providing real-time code suggestions, automating repetitive tasks, and helping developers focus on more complex problems, Copilot is transforming the way software is developed. However, like any tool, it should be used wisely, with an understanding of its strengths and limitations. By following best practices, and being mindful of potential challenges, you can make the most out of GitHub Copilot, and take your coding skills to the next level.

In the next chapter, we will dive into how Copilot empowers modern JavaScript and TypeScript developers–helping them write better code, faster, and across a wide range of web development scenarios.

Multiple Choice Questions

To reinforce your learning, here are some questions, you can answer:

1. What is GitHub Copilot?
    a. A version control system
    b. An AI-powered code completion tool
    c. A programming language
    d. A type of neural network

2. Which IDEs are supported by GitHub Copilot?
    a. Visual Studio Code
    b. JetBrains IDEs
    c. Neovim
    d. All of the above
3. What is a common challenge, when using GitHub Copilot?
    a. It's too expensive
    b. It's not compatible with any IDEs
    c. Over-reliance on the suggestions
    d. It does not support any programming languages
4. How can you customize GitHub Copilot's behavior in VS Code?
    a. By writing new code
    b. By adjusting settings in Preferences
    c. By updating the operating system
    d. By installing a different IDE
5. What is the best practice for using GitHub Copilot?
    a. Accepting all suggestions without review
    b. Writing clear comments to guide suggestions
    c. Ignoring all suggestions
    d. Using Copilot only for syntax highlighting

Answers

1. b
2. d
3. c
4. b
5. b

References

1. GitHub Copilot Quickstart
https://docs.github.com/en/copilot/quickstart
2. Microsoft Learn: Get Started with GitHub Copilot
https://learn.microsoft.com/en-us/training/modules/get-started-github-copilot/1-introduction
3. GitHub Documentation on GitHub Copilot
https://docs.github.com/en/copilot
4. Can GitHub's Copilot Replace Developers?
https://towardsdatascience.com/can-githubs-copilot-replace-developers-b89f28007c05

CHAPTER 3
JavaScript/TypeScript with GitHub Copilot

Introduction

JavaScript and TypeScript form the bedrock of modern web development, driving everything from sleek user interfaces to robust, scalable web applications. While JavaScript provides the flexibility to iterate quickly, and build interactive experiences, TypeScript adds structure and confidence by introducing static typing, or making it easier to manage complexity, as applications grow.

Despite the power of these languages, developers often find themselves repeating boilerplate code, manually configuring setup scripts, or switching between documentation and their editor. As introduced in the previous chapter, GitHub Copilot addresses these pain points with intelligent, real-time code assistance, powered by GPT-4 Turbo. It is more than just an autocomplete tool, as it understands what you are building, how you are structuring it, and what might come next.

In this chapter, we will shift the focus to how Copilot integrates with JavaScript and TypeScript development workflows. From writing utility functions to creating React components, handling asynchronous logic, or managing edge-case errors, Copilot can accelerate and improve the way you code. You will also see how crafting clear, purposeful prompts can guide Copilot toward generating helpful suggestions that align with your goals.

Thus, by the end of this chapter, you will have a strong grasp of how to apply GitHub Copilot to your day-to-day JavaScript and TypeScript projects—not just to save time, but to write smarter, cleaner, and more consistent code with the help of AI.

Structure

In this chapter, we will discuss the following topics:

- Setting up GitHub Copilot for JavaScript/TypeScript Projects
- Leveraging GitHub Copilot for Project Configuration
- Basic Programming with GitHub Copilot
- Advanced Programming with GitHub Copilot

Setting up GitHub Copilot for JavaScript/TypeScript Projects without Copilot Commands Assistance

Before jumping into code, it is important to have your development environment properly set up to work efficiently with GitHub Copilot in JavaScript and TypeScript projects. While Copilot is quite versatile, ensuring a robust and organized environment will allow you to make the most of its suggestions and capabilities. The current version of GitHub Copilot, powered by GPT-4 Turbo, ensures that these suggestions are more context-aware and accurate—even during the initial setup.

Setting Up the Development Environment

To use GitHub Copilot effectively for JavaScript/TypeScript projects, you will need to establish a standard development environment. Hence, we will go through setting up Node.js, TypeScript, and some common tools that make development smoother, and more productive.

1. **Installing Node.js:** Node.js provides the runtime environment for JavaScript, outside of the browser, and this is a must for running most of the modern JavaScript or TypeScript applications. It also includes **Node Package Manager (NPM)** which is essential for managing your project dependencies.

   a. **Installation:** Visit nodejs.org, and download the LTS (Long-Term Support) version for your operating system.

Figure 3.1: *Official Node.js Download Page*

This image shows the official Node.js download page, where developers can access the **Long-Term Support (LTS)** version of Node.js.

Once installed, verify the installation by running the following commands in your terminal:

```
node -v
npm -v
```

Then, you should see version numbers for both Node.js and npm, confirming the successful installation.

2. Initializing a JavaScript or TypeScript project

```
mkdir Ch3_Javascript_TypeScript
```

Figure 3.2: *Creating a Project Directory for JavaScript and TypeScript with GitHub Copilot*

This terminal screenshot shows the creation of a new folder named **`Ch3_Javascript_TypeScript`** using the **`mkdir`** command, within a project path titled *Ultimate AI-Assisted Coding with GitHub Copilot*. It indicates the beginning of this chapter, where users will likely explore hands-on coding with JavaScript and TypeScript, while leveraging GitHub Copilot for intelligent code assistance.

Switch to the project directory: **`cd Ch3_Javascript_TypeScript`**

3. **Initialize the project with npm:** This will generate a **`package.json`** file which manages your project's dependencies and scripts.

```
npm init -y
```

```
∨ ULTIMATE AI-ASSISTED CODING WITH GITHUB COPILOT      Ch3_Javascript_TypeScript > {} package.json > ...
  ∨ Ch3_Javascript_TypeScript                          {
    {} package.json                                      "name": "ultimate-ai-assisted-coding-with-github-copilot",
                                                         "version": "1.0.0",
                                                         "main": "index.js",
                                                         ▷ Debug
                                                         "scripts": {
                                                           "test": "echo \"Test project\" && exit 1"
                                                         },
                                                         "keywords": [],
                                                         "author": "SHALABH DIXIT",
                                                         "license": "ISC",
                                                         "description": ""
```

Figure 3.3: *package.json File Created*

4. **To install TypeScript, use the following command:**

```
npm install typescript --save-dev
```

```
PS C:\Users\SIDDHI DIXIT\Shalabh\Ultimate AI-Assisted Coding with GitHub Copilot\Ch3_Javascript_TypeScript> npm install typescript --save-dev

added 1 package, and audited 2 packages in 2s

found 0 vulnerabilities
```

Figure 3.4: *Installing TypeScript Locally as a Dev Dependency Using npm*

This terminal output shows the successful installation of TypeScript using the command **`npm install typescript --save-dev`** within the **`Ch3_Javascript_TypeScript`** project directory. It indicates that the TypeScript package was added without any vulnerabilities, setting up the environment for compiling **`.ts`** files and enabling TypeScript development in this GitHub Copilot-assisted coding workflow.

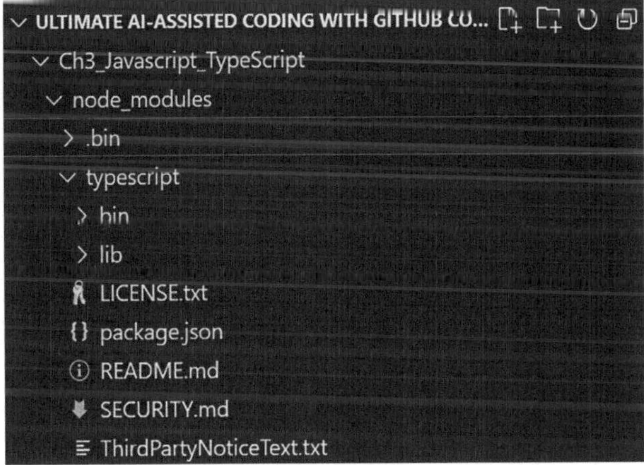

Figure 3.5: *TypeScript Folders Created*

Once the TypeScript is installed, you can configure it by creating a **`tsconfig.json`** file. This configuration file specifies the options for the TypeScript compiler.

5. **Create a `tsconfig.json` file with the following settings:**

```
{
  "compilerOptions": {
    "target": "ES2020",
    "module": "ES6",
    "strict": true,
    "esModuleInterop": true,
    "skipLibCheck": true
  },
  "exclude": ["node_modules"]
}
```

Setting up ESLint and Prettier for Code Quality

While GitHub Copilot helps generate code, it is important to ensure that the generated code follows proper standards. ESLint and Prettier are two popular tools that help maintain code quality and consistency.

1. **Installing ESLint:** ESLint is a linter that helps catch syntax and style issues in JavaScript/TypeScript code. You can install it as a dev dependency:

```
npm install eslint --save-dev
```

```
PS C:\Users\SIDDHI DIXIT\Shalabh\Ultimate AI-Assisted Coding with GitHub Copilot> npm install eslint --save-dev

added 93 packages in 31s

22 packages are looking for funding
  run `npm fund` for details
```

Figure 3.6: *Installing ESLint as a Dev Dependency via npm*

This image displays the terminal output after running the command npm install eslint **`--save-dev`** which installs ESLint locally in the GitHub Copilot-assisted project directory. ESLint is essential for maintaining consistent code style, and identifying the potential issues in JavaScript/TypeScript projects. A total of 93 packages were added, laying the groundwork for code lining and quality enforcement.

Next, initialize ESLint in your Project:

```
npx eslint -init
```

```
PS C:\Users\SIDDHI DIXIT\Shalabh\Ultimate AI-Assisted Coding with GitHub Copilot> npx eslint --init
You can also run this command directly using 'npm init @eslint/config@latest'.
Need to install the following packages:
@eslint/create-config@1.3.1
Ok to proceed? (y) y
```

Figure 3.7: *Initializing ESLint Configuration with npx eslint –init*

The image shows the start of the ESLint initialization process, using **`npx eslint --init`**. ESLint prompts to install the necessary package **`@eslint/create-config@1.3.1`**, asking for user confirmation. This step begins with setting up a custom linting configuration for maintaining clean, consistent, and error-free code in the project.

Type "**y**" and press *enter* key to finish the initialization.

Complete the setup as per your preferences related to module type, framework, language, package manager selection, and so on, as shown in *Figure* 3.8.

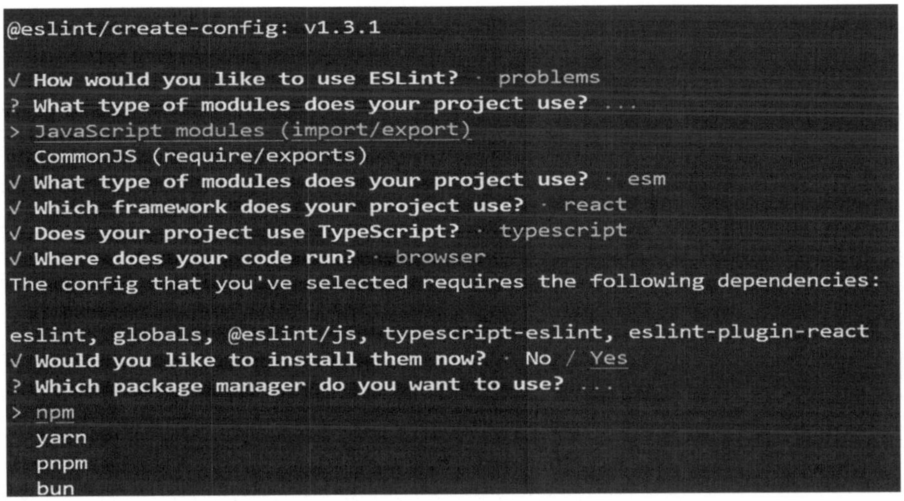

```
@eslint/create-config: v1.3.1

√ How would you like to use ESLint? · problems
? What type of modules does your project use? ...
> JavaScript modules (import/export)
  CommonJS (require/exports)
√ What type of modules does your project use? · esm
√ Which framework does your project use? · react
√ Does your project use TypeScript? · typescript
√ Where does your code run? · browser
The config that you've selected requires the following dependencies:

eslint, globals, @eslint/js, typescript-eslint, eslint-plugin-react
√ Would you like to install them now? · No / Yes
? Which package manager do you want to use? ...
> npm
  yarn
  pnpm
  bun
```

Figure 3.8: *Setting up ESLint Configuration for a React Project with TypeScript Using the Interactive CLI*

The screenshot shows the ESLint initialization process where the developer selects JavaScript modules, React framework, TypeScript support, and browser as the runtime environment. Dependencies are resolved, and npm is chosen as the package manager.

2. **Installing Prettier:** Prettier is a code formatter that ensures consistent code style across your project. To install Prettier:

```
npm install prettier eslint-config-prettier eslint-plugin-prettier --save-dev
```

```
PS C:\Users\SIDDHI DIXIT\Shalabh\Ultimate AI-Assisted Coding with GitHub Copilot> npm install prettier eslint-config-prettier eslint-plugin-prettier --save-dev

added 8 packages, and audited 229 packages in 2s

110 packages are looking for funding
  run `npm fund` for details

found 0 vulnerabilities
```

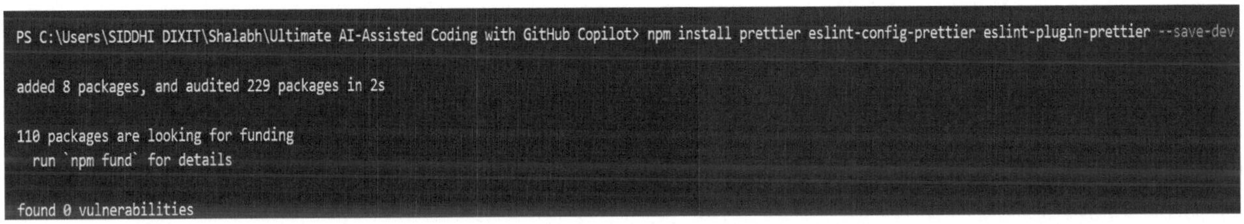

Figure 3.9: *Installing Prettier and Its ESLint Integration for Code Formatting Consistency*

The terminal output confirms successful installation of prettier, **`eslint-config-prettier`**, and **`eslint-plugin-prettier`** as development dependencies, with zero vulnerabilities found during the audit.

Next, configure Prettier and ESLint to work together. Create **`a.eslintrc.json`** file, and add the following configuration:

```
{
  "env": {
    "browser": true,
    "es2020": true
  },
  "extends": [
    "eslint:recommended",
    "plugin:@typescript-eslint/recommended",
    "prettier"
  ],
  "plugins": ["@typescript-eslint", "prettier"],
  "rules": {
    "prettier/prettier": "error",
    "@typescript-eslint/explicit-module-boundary-types": "off"
  }
}
```

```
ULTIMATE AI-ASSISTED CODING WITH ...
  Ch3_Javascript_TypeScript
    node_modules
      .bin
      typescript
      .package-lock.json
    package-lock.json
    package.json
  node_modules
  .eslintrc.json
  eslint.config.mjs
  package-lock.json
  package.json
```

```
{
  "env": {
    "browser": true,
    "es2020": true
  },
  "extends": [
    "eslint:recommended",
    "plugin:@typescript-eslint/recommended",
    "prettier"
  ],
  "plugins": ["@typescript-eslint", "prettier"],
  "rules": {
    "prettier/prettier": "error",
    "@typescript-eslint/explicit-module-boundary-types": "off"
  }
}
```

Figure 3.10: *Setting up ESLint Configuration for a TypeScript Project Using Prettier Integration*

The **`.eslintrc.json`** file is configured with recommended rules from ESLint, TypeScript, and Prettier, ensuring a consistent code quality and formatting. Prettier is enforced as a linter rule, and TypeScript-specific settings are applied for a browser-based ES2020 environment.

Leveraging GitHub Copilot for Project Configuration

GitHub Copilot can be a valuable assistant in setting up and configuring your JavaScript/TypeScript projects. It can autocomplete common configurations like ESLint, Prettier, and **`tsconfig.json`** files, saving you time and effort. Now, let's see how Copilot can assist in the setup process.

1. Creating the Project Structure Using Copilot

You can start by prompting GitHub Copilot to generate the structure for your JavaScript/TypeScript project.

Example prompt:

```
/workspace creates a JavaScript, TypeScript-based project structure. It should include proper installation and setup instructions.
```

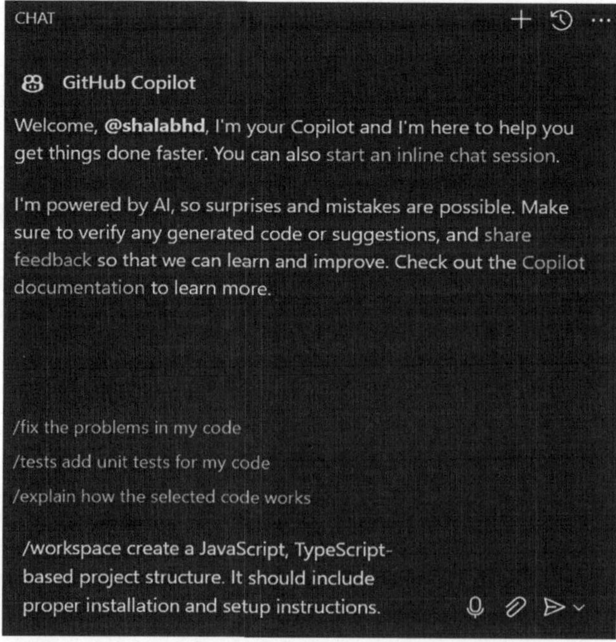

Figure 3.11: *Prompting GitHub Copilot Chat to Scaffold a JavaScript–TypeScript Project with Setup Guidance*

The user enters a Copilot Chat prompt to scaffold a JavaScript-TypeScript Project workspace with setup and installation guidance.

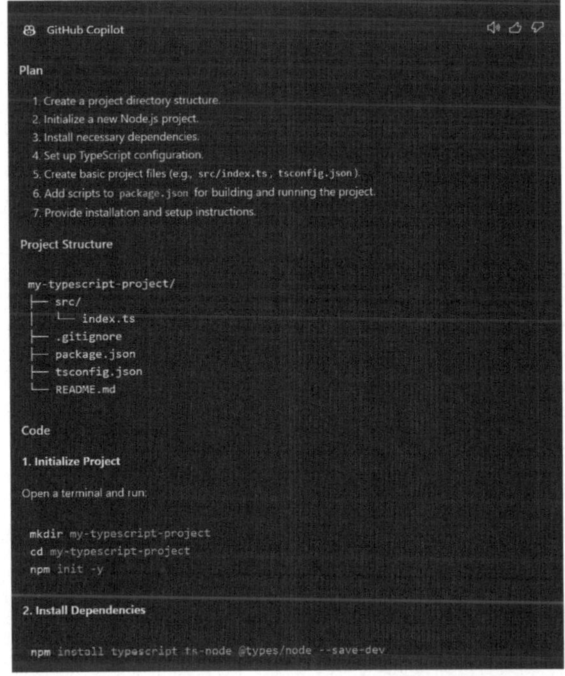

Figure 3.12: *GitHub Copilot Generates a Complete Plan and Project Structure for Setting Up a TypeScript-based Node.js Project*

Copilot outlines a structured approach to scaffold, and configure a new TypeScript Project from scratch.

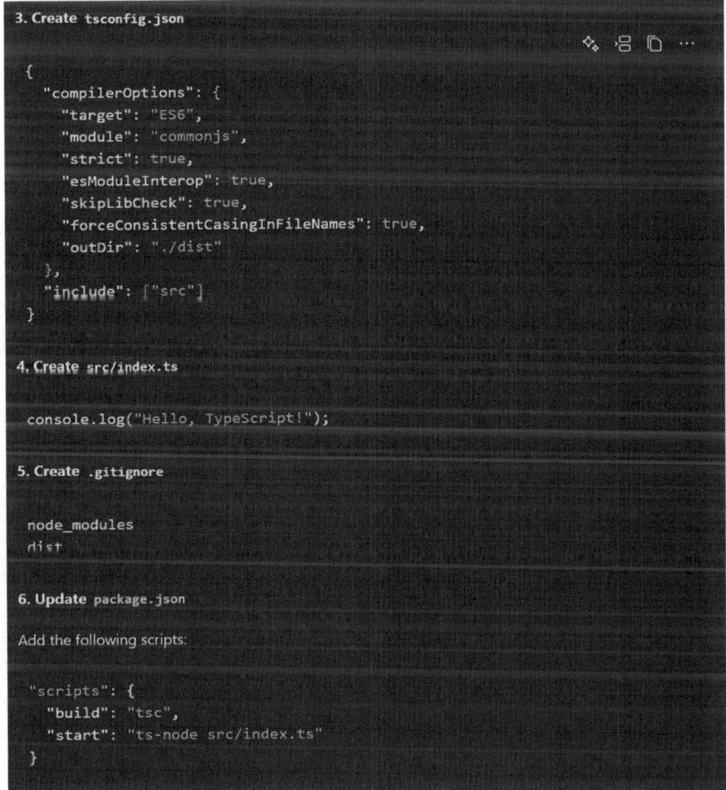

Figure 3.13: *Configuring tsconfig.json, Creating Entry Files, Setting .gitignore, and Defining Build and Start Scripts in package.json*

GitHub Copilot auto-generated **`tsconfig.json`**, an entry script, **`.gitignore`**, and updates **`package.json`** with build and start commands in scaffolding a basic TypeScript Project with minimal setup.

7. Create `README.md`

```
# My TypeScript Project

## Installation

```sh
npm install
```

Build

```
npm run build
```

Run

```
npm start



### Final Code Block

```plaintext
my-typescript-project/
├── src/
│   └── index.ts
├── .gitignore
├── package.json
├── tsconfig.json
└── README.md
```

Figure 3.14: GitHub Copilot Created Step-by-step Installation Steps and Commands for Config. files

GitHub Copilot automatically generates a well-structured README.md file that serves as a quick-start guide for your TypeScript project. It includes installation instructions using npm, commands to build and run the project, and a final directory structure to help developers understand the overall file organization and setup at a glance.

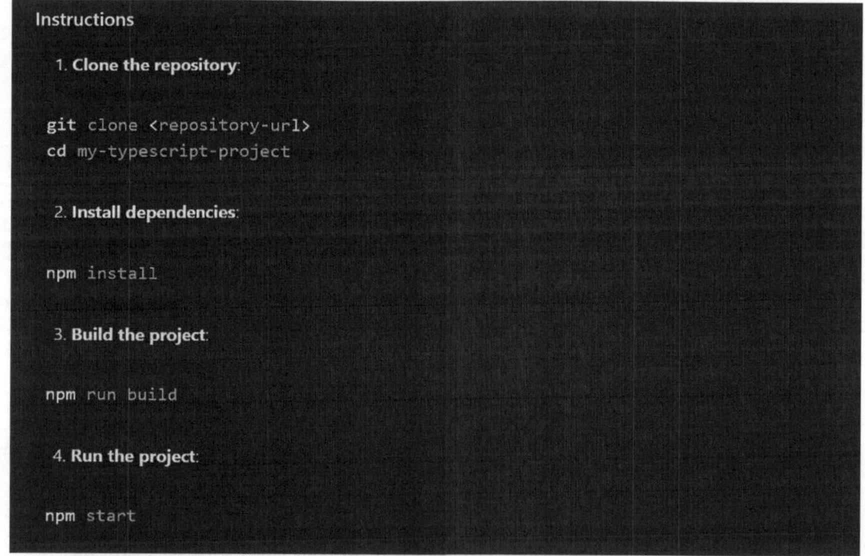

Figure 3.15: *GitHub Copilot Created Step-by-step Installation Steps for Creating Repos, Installing Dependencies, and so on*

GitHub Copilot simplifies onboarding by generating a clear set of step-by-step instructions to clone the repository, install dependencies, build the project, and run the application – making it effortless for developers to get started quickly.

From the preceding screenshots, it is quite evident that the GitHub Copilot helps developers quickly set up the project with detailed instructions, and saves time which effectively boosts productivity, since the developers can focus more on building the core logic of the application, instead of investing time in exploring the setup and configurations.

You can further refine prompts for clarity, ensuring that Copilot tailors the setup to your needs. If it misses an important step (like creating a **src** folder or specific files), guide Copilot with more detailed instructions.

Using Copilot to Configure ESLint and Prettier

Once the basic setup is done, you can ask Copilot to configure linters and formatters which ensures code consistency throughout the project.

Example prompt:

```
/workspace Configure ESLint and Prettier for the TypeScript project.
```

GitHub Copilot Output:

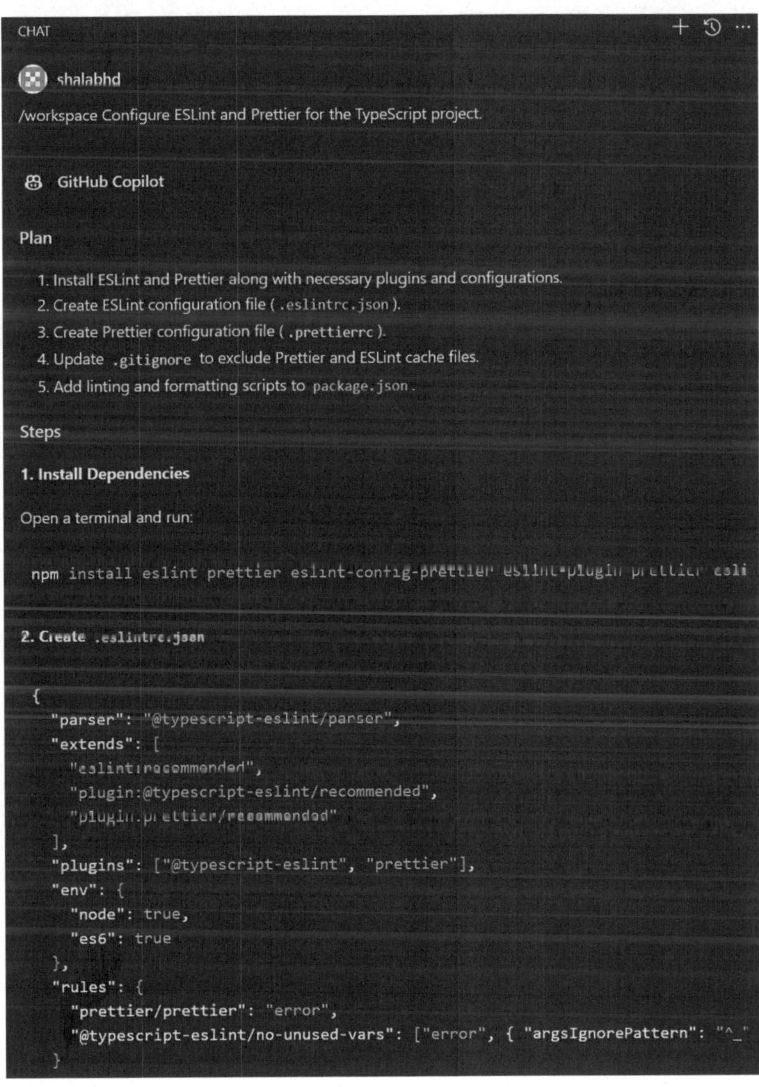

Figure 3.16: *GitHub Copilot Created a Complete Plan and Step-by-step Installation Instructions with Commands*

CHAT

3. Create `.prettierrc`

```
{
  "semi": true,
  "singleQuote": true,
  "printWidth": 80,
  "tabWidth": 2,
  "trailingComma": "es5"
}
```

4. Update `.gitignore`

Add the following lines:

```
# ESLint and Prettier
.eslintcache
.prettiercache
```

5. Update `package.json`

Add the following scripts:

```
"scripts": {
  "build": "tsc",
  "start": "ts-node src/index.ts",
  "lint": "eslint 'src/**/*.{ts,js}'",
  "format": "prettier --write 'src/**/*.{ts,js}'"
}
```

Figure 3.17: *GitHub Copilot Step-by-step Installation Instructions with Commands-Part-2*

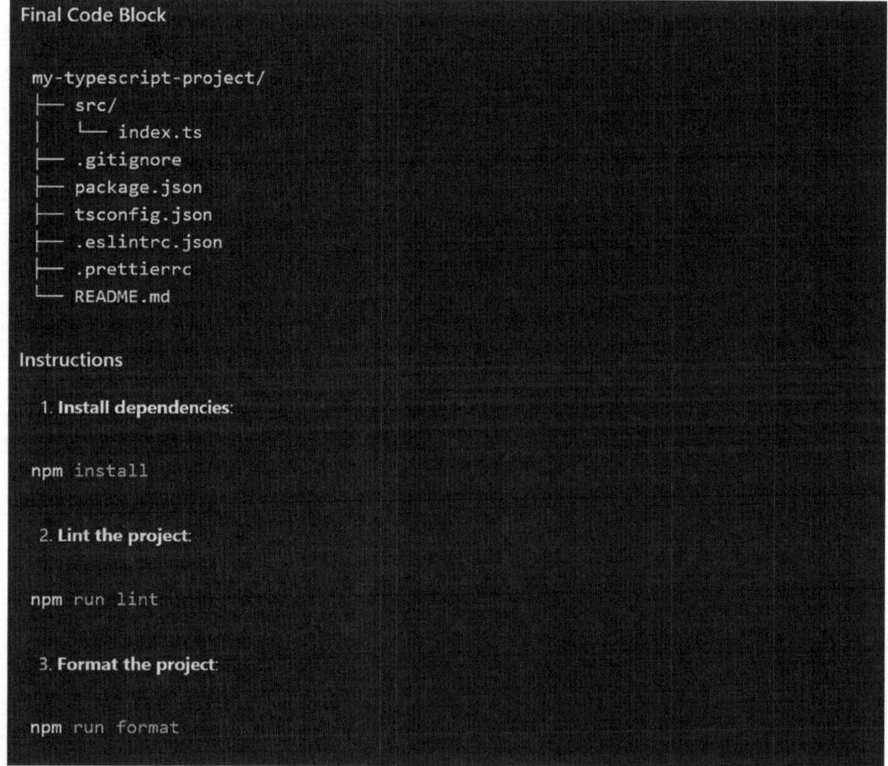

Figure 3.18: *GitHub Copilot Step-by-step Installation Instructions with Commands-Part-3*

GitHub Copilot helps you to set up ESLint and Prettier for your TypeScript project by suggesting a clear plan, the right dependencies to install, and a **`ready-made.eslintrc.json`** file to get started with a clean and consistent code.

Customizing TypeScript Configuration with Copilot

Copilot is also excellent for creating and customizing the tsconfig.json file based on your project needs.

Example prompt:

```
/workspace Create a tsconfig.json file for a TypeScript project targeting
ES2020, using ES6 modules, and with strict mode enabled.
```

GitHub Copilot Output:

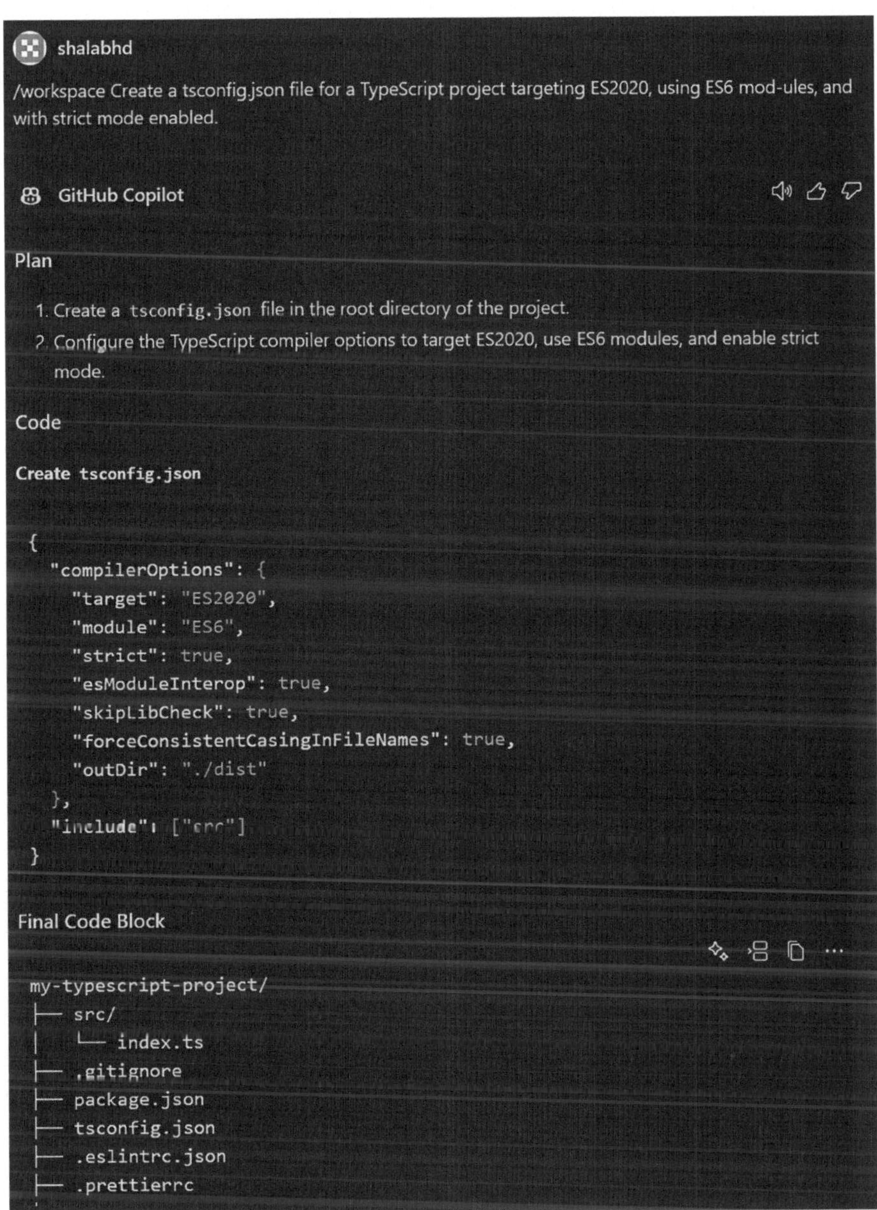

Figure 3.19: *GitHub Copilot Setup Plan, Step-by-step Installation Instructions with Commands-Part1*

GitHub Copilot makes setting up a TypeScript Project effortless by generating a **`tsconfig.json`** file configured with modern ES2020 targets, ES6 modules, and strict mode enabled – helping you start with the best practices, right from the beginning.

Figure 3.20: *GitHub Copilot Setup Plan, Step-by-step Installation Instructions with Commands-Part2*

GitHub Copilot provides clear build instructions by guiding you to create a **`tsconfig.json`** file, and compile your TypeScript project using npm run build – making the setup process smooth and beginner-friendly.

Automating Tests Setup with GitHub Copilot

If your project requires testing, Copilot can generate configurations for popular testing libraries like **Jest**.

Example prompt:

```
/workspace Add Jest setup to the TypeScript project.
```

GitHub Copilot Output:

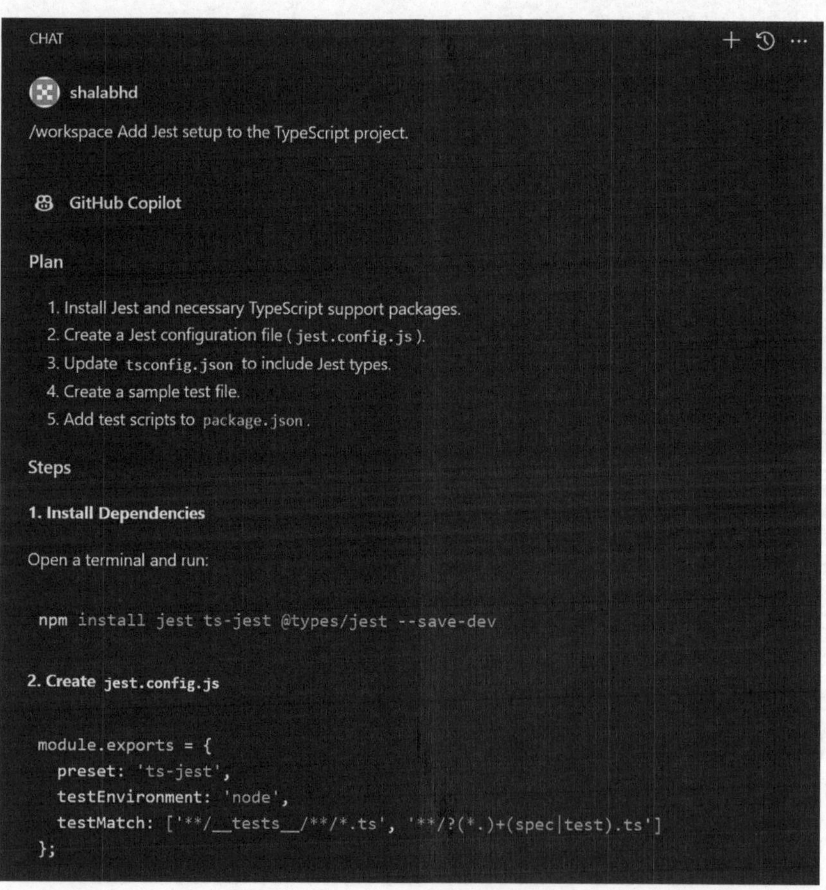

Figure 3.21: *GitHub Copilot Setup Plan, Step-by-step Installation Instructions with Commands-Part1*

GitHub Copilot walks you through setting up Jest in a TypeScript project by generating the necessary dependencies, configuration file (**jest.config.js**), and instructions to update **tsconfig.json** and **package.json** – making test integration smooth and hassle-free.

CHAT

3. Update tsconfig.json

Add Jest types to the types array in compilerOptions:

```
{
  "compilerOptions": {
    "target": "ES2020",
    "module": "ES6",
    "strict": true,
    "esModuleInterop": true,
    "skipLibCheck": true,
    "forceConsistentCasingInFileNames": true,
    "outDir": "./dist",
    "types": ["jest"]
  },
  "include": ["src"]
}
```

4. Create a Sample Test File

Create a directory __tests__ inside src and add a sample test file index.test.ts:

```
// src/__tests__/index.test.ts
import { sum } from '../index';

test('adds 1 + 2 to equal 3', () => {
  expect(sum(1, 2)).toBe(3);
});
```

Update src/index.ts to include the sum function:

```
// src/index.ts
export const sum = (a: number, b: number): number => {
  return a + b;
};

console.log("Hello, TypeScript!");
```

Figure 3.22: GitHub Copilot Setup Plan, Step-by-step Installation Instructions with Commands-Part2

GitHub Copilot helps you to complete the Jest setup by updating **tsconfig.json** to recognize Jest types, and guides you to create a sample test case as well as a basic sum function – making it easy to get started with unit testing in TypeScript.

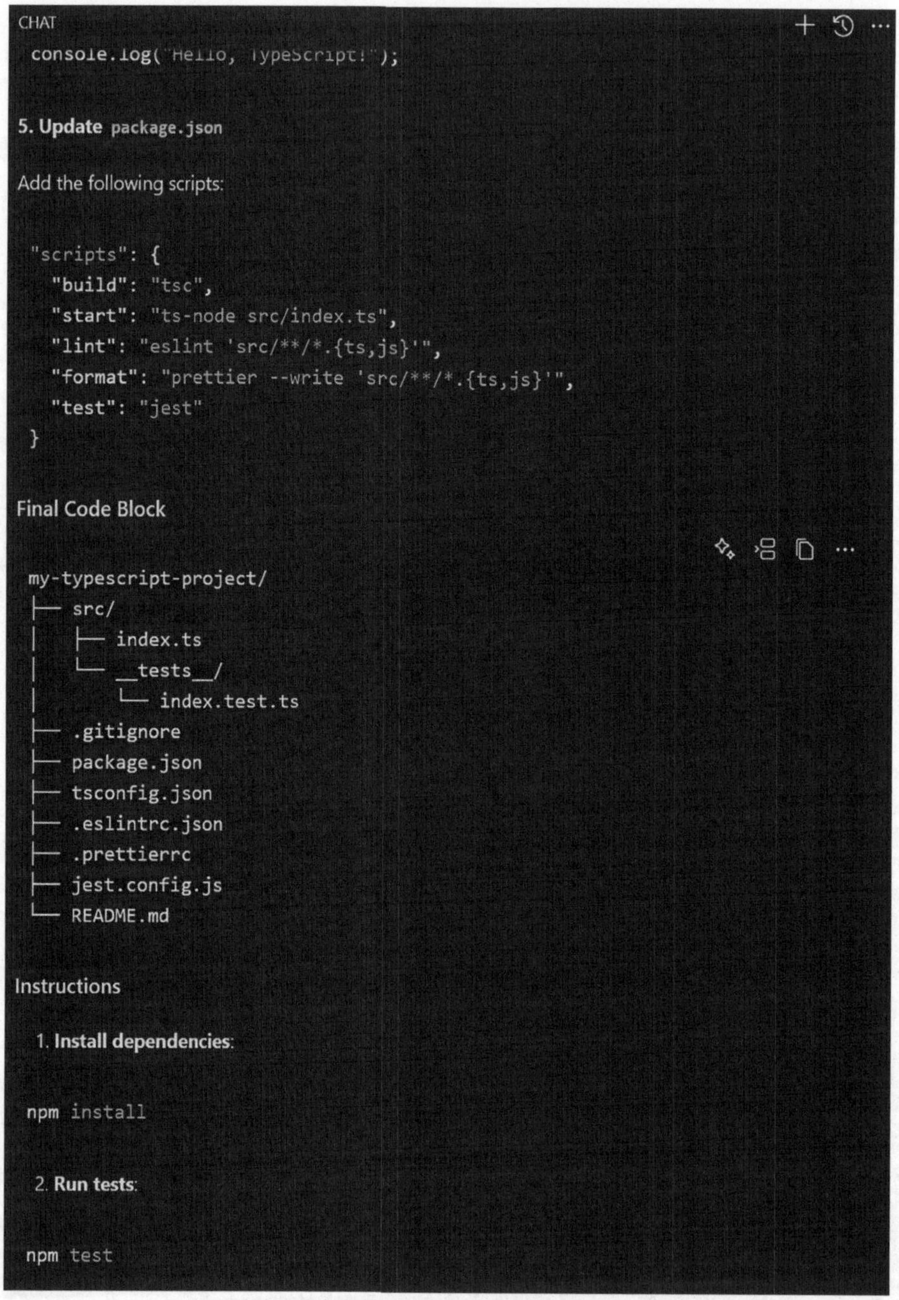

CHAT

```
console.log("Hello, TypeScript!");
```

5. Update `package.json`

Add the following scripts:

```
"scripts": {
  "build": "tsc",
  "start": "ts-node src/index.ts",
  "lint": "eslint 'src/**/*.{ts,js}'",
  "format": "prettier --write 'src/**/*.{ts,js}'",
  "test": "jest"
}
```

Final Code Block

```
my-typescript-project/
├── src/
│   ├── index.ts
│   └── __tests__/
│       └── index.test.ts
├── .gitignore
├── package.json
├── tsconfig.json
├── .eslintrc.json
├── .prettierrc
├── jest.config.js
└── README.md
```

Instructions

1. **Install dependencies**:

```
npm install
```

2. **Run tests**:

```
npm test
```

Figure 3.23: *GitHub Copilot Setup Plan, Step-by-step Installation Instructions with Commands-Part3*

GitHub Copilot wraps up the setup by adding helpful scripts to package. json for building, running, linting, formatting, and testing the project – while also showing the final project structure, and basic commands to get everything up and running.

The Copilot prompt can be further refined for specific use cases, such as integrating testing into a CI/CD pipeline or customizing Jest's configuration for TypeScript.

Generating Boilerplate Code Using Copilot

Once the project setup is complete, Copilot can assist in generating boilerplate code for the project. You can request Copilot to create common files like **`index.ts`**, helpers, or utility functions.

Example prompt:

```
/workspace Generate an `index.ts` file for a basic Express server.
```

GitHub Copilot Output:

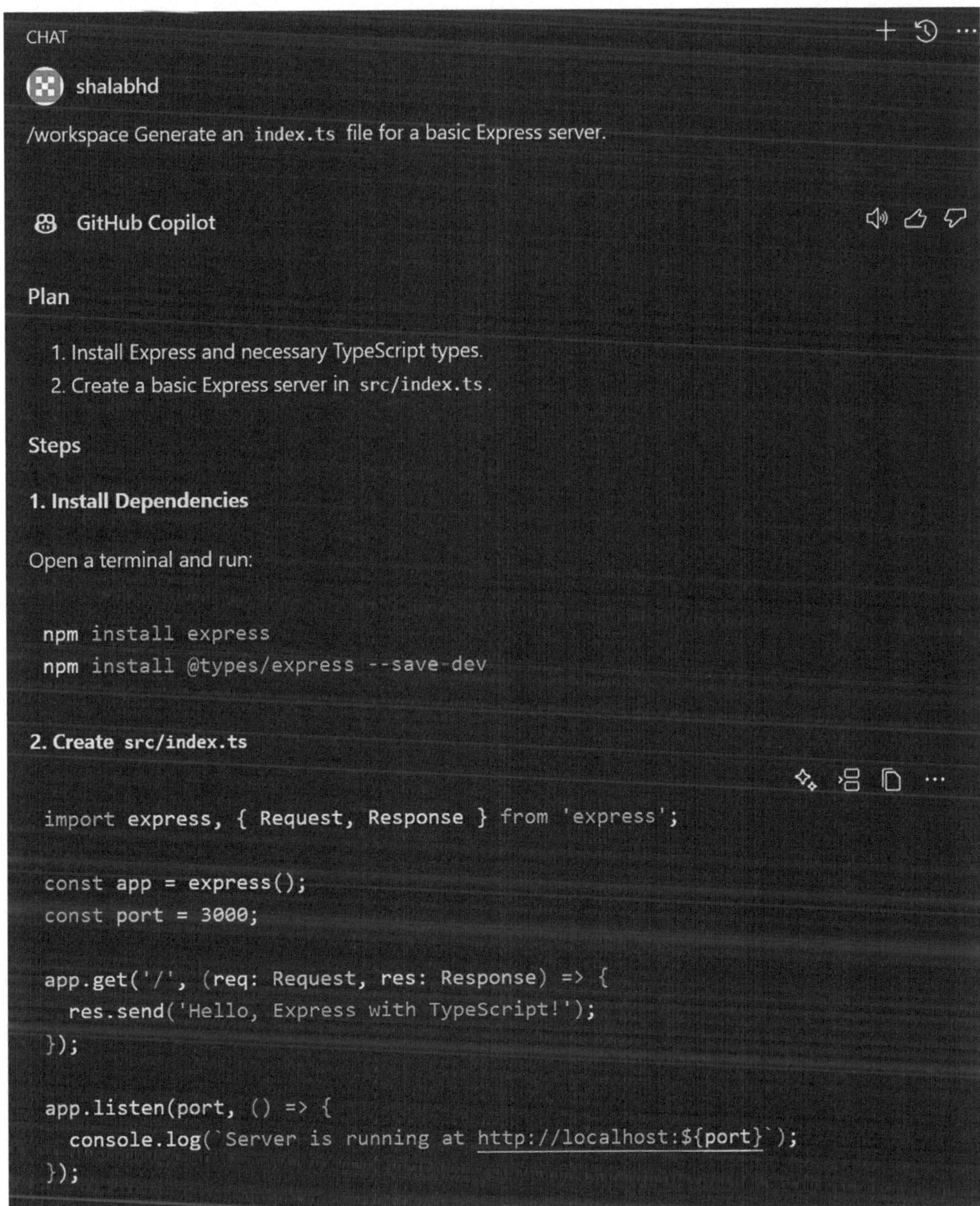

***Figure 3.24:** GitHub Copilot Setup Plan, Step-by-step Installation Instructions with Commands for index.ts-Part1*

GitHub Copilot simplifies backend development with TypeScript by generating step-by-step guidance to set up a basic Express server. It installs the required express and **`@types/express`** packages, and creates a ready-to-run **`index.ts`** file that starts a server, listens on port 3000, and responds with a simple message – helping developers quickly bootstrap their API projects with clean, typed code.

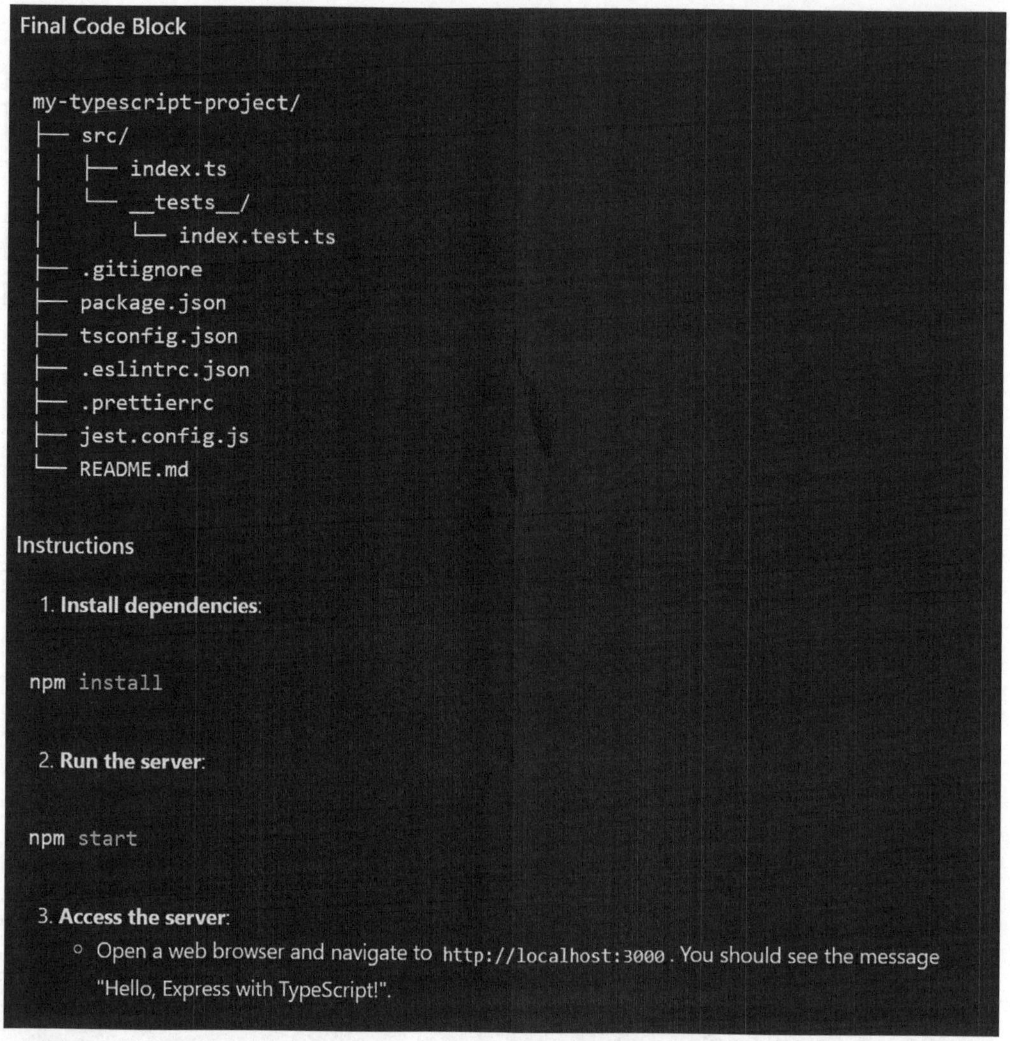

Final Code Block

```
my-typescript-project/
├── src/
│   ├── index.ts
│   └── __tests__/
│       └── index.test.ts
├── .gitignore
├── package.json
├── tsconfig.json
├── .eslintrc.json
├── .prettierrc
├── jest.config.js
└── README.md
```

Instructions

1. **Install dependencies**:

```
npm install
```

2. **Run the server**:

```
npm start
```

3. **Access the server**:
   - Open a web browser and navigate to `http://localhost:3000`. You should see the message "Hello, Express with TypeScript!".

Figure 3.25: *GitHub Copilot Setup Plan, Step-by-step Installation Instructions with Commands for index.ts-Part2*

GitHub Copilot completes the project setup by showing the final directory structure, and guiding you through running the app. With a single npm install to install dependencies and npm start to launch the server, you can access your Express app at **`http://localhost:3000`**, and see it respond with a friendly "**`Hello, Express with TypeScript!`**" – making the entire process seamless and beginner-friendly.

Basic Programming with GitHub Copilot

GitHub Copilot can significantly speed up the process of writing the basic code in JavaScript and TypeScript. Thanks to GPT-4 Turbo's deep understanding of language structure, Copilot can now detect patterns, and generate JavaScript or TypeScript code that aligns more closely with real-world use. It suggests snippets, autocompletes functions, and even writes entire blocks of code based on the context of what you are working on. Let us dive into how you can use Copilot for common programming tasks, and how to refine your prompts to get better suggestions.

1. **Variables and Types in JavaScript/TypeScript**

   a. **JavaScript Variables:** In JavaScript, variables can be declared using var, let, and const. GitHub Copilot that can assist in generating these based on the code context.

Basic prompt example:

```
//Declare a variable name in JavaScript and assign it a value
```

GitHub Copilot Output for the Prompt

```
JS test.js ●
Ch3_Javascript_TypeScript > node_modules > JS test.js
//Declare a variable name in JavaScript and assign it a value
var name = "John";
```

Figure 3.26: *GitHub Copilot Generated the Variable with a Value Based on the Input Prompt*

This example demonstrates how to declare a variable in JavaScript using the var keyword, and assign it a string value – in this case, setting the variable name to "**John**".

b. **TypeScript Variables**

TypeScript enhances JavaScript by allowing developers to explicitly declare the types.

Basic prompt example:

```
//Declare a string variable in TypeScript.
```

```
Ch3_Javascript_TypeScript > node_modules > JS test.js
//Declare a string variable in TypeScript.
var str = "Hello World!";
```

Figure 3.27: *GitHub Copilot Suggestion for Creating a String Variable in TypeScript May Not be Accurate*

This code snippet demonstrates how to declare a string variable in JavaScript, using the **var** keyword, assigning it the value, "**Hello World!**".

Hence, we will start typing some snippets to help the GitHub Copilot in generating the snippet as per our expectations. Here, we will begin typing "**let**" followed by space. As soon as we press the space bar, we can observe GitHub Copilot starts giving code suggestions.

```
Ch3_Javascript_TypeScript > node_modules > JS test.js
//Declare a string variable in TypeScript.
let str: string = "Hello World!";
```

Figure 3.28: *GitHub Copilot Starts Giving Accurate Suggestions for Creating String Variable in TypeScript*

This code snippet demonstrates how to declare a string variable in JavaScript, using the var keyword, assigning it the value "**Hello World!**".

2. **Writing Functions with GitHub Copilot**

Functions are fundamental building blocks in any programming language. Copilot can help you write both JavaScript and TypeScript functions quickly.

a. **JavaScript Functions**

Basic prompt example:

```
//Write a function that adds two numbers in JavaScript.
```

GitHub Copilot Output for the Prompt

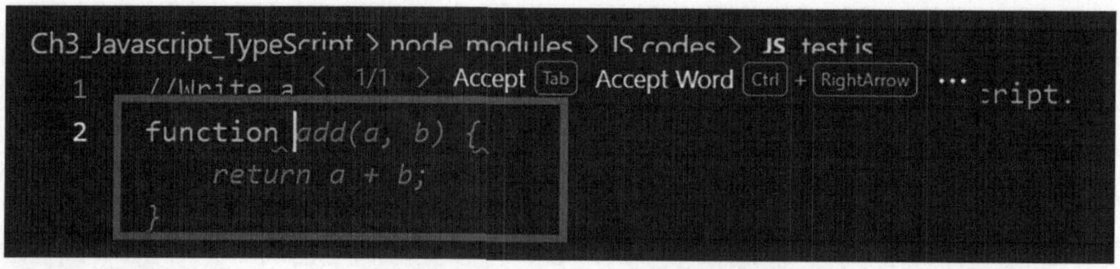

Figure 3.29: *GitHub Copilot Suggestion for Creating a Function of the Sum of Two Numbers*

This example shows how to define a basic function in JavaScript named "**add**" that takes two parameters, and returns their sum.

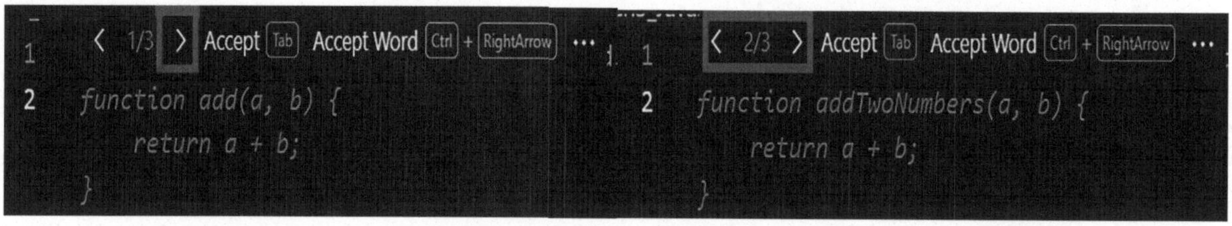

Figure 3.30 (a): *Navigating between Multiple Copilot Code Suggestions in VS Code ||*
(b): *Selecting Different Code Suggestions*

These screenshots demonstrate how GitHub Copilot offers multiple autocomplete suggestions for a function, allowing developers to navigate through different variations – like **`add`** vs **`addTwoNumbers`** – using the arrow icons in the suggestion bar.

b. **TypeScript Functions**

   Prompt example:

   ```
   //Write a function in TypeScript that adds two numbers and returns a number.
   ```

GitHub Copilot Output for the Prompt

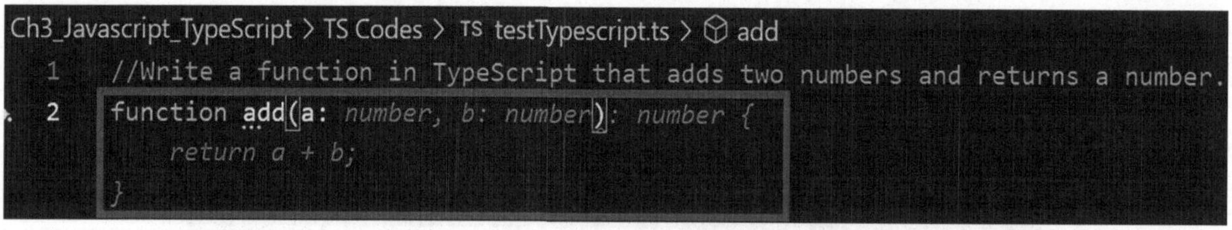

Figure 3.31: *GitHub Copilot Code Suggestion for Creating Functions in TypeScript*

This example shows how to define a function in TypeScript with explicit type annotations for parameters and return type, ensuring that both inputs are numbers, and the function returns a number as well.

c. **Prompt Refinement Example**

   To make the function more useful, you can refine your prompt to include error checking or more complex logic.

   Refined prompt:

   ```
   //Write a TypeScript function that adds two numbers, checks if both are num-
   bers and throws an error if not.
   ```

GitHub Copilot Output for the Prompt

```
//Write a TypeScript function that adds two numbers, checks if both are numbers, and throws an error if not.
function addWithCheck(a:number, b:number):number{
    if(typeof a === 'number' && typeof b === 'number'){
        return a + b;
    }
    throw new Error('Both arguments should be numbers');
}
```

Figure 3.32: *GitHub Copilot Suggestion for Creating Function in TypeScript with Checkpoints and Exception Handling*

This TypeScript function, **`addWithCheck`**, adds two values only if both are numbers. It includes a type check using **`typeof`**, and throws a descriptive error, if the inputs are not valid, showcasing safe and defensive programming practices.

Prompt example:

```
//Create a JavaScript function that greets a user by their name.
```

GitHub Copilot Output for the Prompt

```
//workspace Create a JavaScript function that greets a user by their name.
function greet(name) {
    return `Hello, ${name}!`;
}
```

Figure 3.33: *GitHub Copilot Code Suggestion for Creating a Function that Greets the User*

This JavaScript function greet takes a user's name as input and returns a personalized greeting using template literals for dynamic string interpolation.

3. **Conditional Statements and Loops**

Conditional statements (**`if`**, **`else`**, **`switch`**, and so on) and loops (**`for`**, **`while`**, **`do-while`**) are key to controlling the flow of a program. Copilot can assist in quickly writing these structures by suggesting the common patterns.

a. **JavaScript Conditional Statement Example:**

Prompt:

```
//Write a JavaScript function that checks if a number is even or odd, using a conditional statement.
```

GitHub Copilot Output for the Prompt

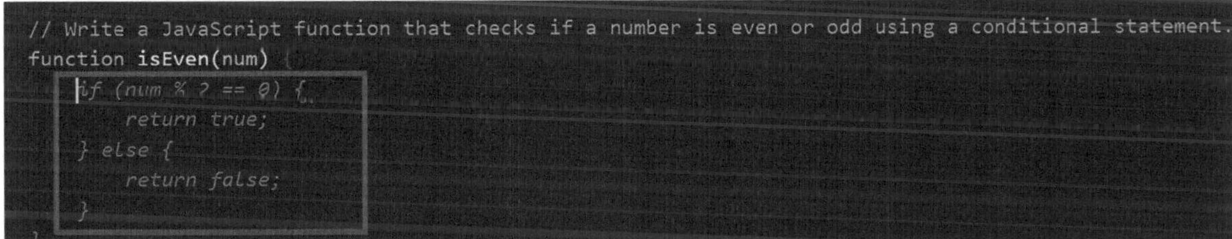

Figure 3.34: *GitHub Copilot Suggestion for Creating a Function to Check for Even Numbers with Conditional Statements*

This JavaScript function **`isEven`** uses a conditional if-else statement to check whether a given number is even by evaluating if it is divisible by 2, returning true for even numbers and false otherwise.

4. **Working with Arrays and Objects**

Arrays and objects are fundamental data structures in JavaScript/TypeScript. Copilot simplifies the process of creating and manipulating these structures.

a. **JavaScript Array Example:**

Prompt:

```
//Create a JavaScript array of fruits and log each fruit to the console.
```

GitHub Copilot Output for the Prompt

```
//Create a JavaScript array of fruits and log each fruit to the console.
var fruits = ["apple", "banana", "orange", "grape"];
```

Figure 3.35: *GitHub Copilot Code Suggestion for Creating an Array of Fruits*

GitHub Copilot suggests initializing a fruits array with common values like "`apple`", "`banana`", "`orange`", and "`grape`", helping you quickly set up a sample data for logging or iteration in JavaScript.

b. **TypeScript Object Example:**

Prompt:

```
//Create a TypeScript object for a user with properties: name, age, and isAd-
min, and access those properties.
```

GitHub Copilot Output for the Prompt

Figure 3.36: *Copilot Suggests a User Object with Name, Age, and Admin Flag*

GitHub Copilot intelligently suggests a TypeScript object structure for a user with commonly used properties like `name`, `age`, and `isAdmin`, helping you quickly scaffold the realistic user data in your code.

5. **Understanding Basic Prompts vs. Refined Prompts**

Sometimes, Copilot's initial suggestions may not be ideal for your use case. By refining your prompt, you can get more accurate or advanced code suggestions.

a. **Example of a basic prompt:**

```
//Create a function to return the square of a number.
```

GitHub Copilot Output for the Prompt

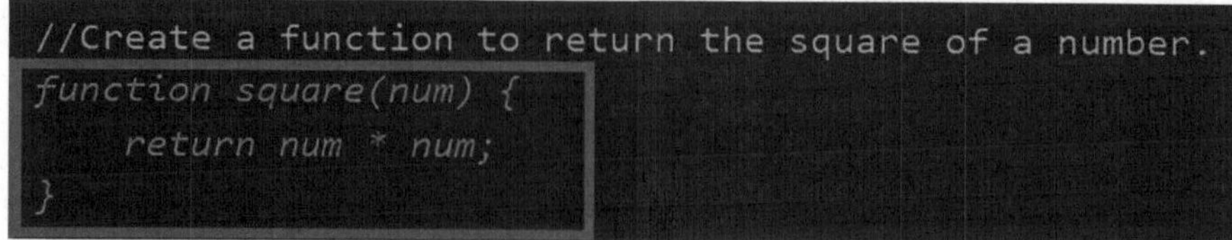

Figure 3.37: *Copilot Suggests a Function to Compute the Square of a Number.*

GitHub Copilot auto-generates a simple square function that takes a number as input, and returns its square, helping speed up repetitive coding tasks with intelligent predictions.

b. **Example of a Refined Prompt:**

```
//Create a TypeScript function that takes a number as input, validates if it's a positive integer, and then returns the square of that number.
```

GitHub Copilot Output for the Prompt

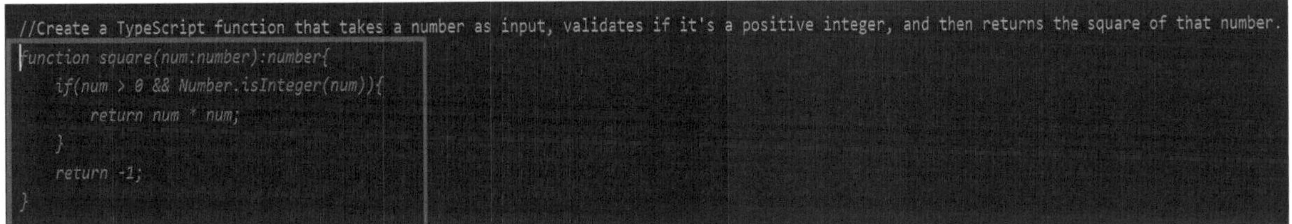

```
//Create a TypeScript function that takes a number as input, validates if it's a positive integer, and then returns the square of that number.
function square(num:number):number{
    if(num > 0 && Number.isInteger(num)){
        return num * num;
    }
    return -1;
}
```

***Figure 3.38:** Copilot Suggests a TypeScript Function with Input Validation and Squaring Logic Using a Refined Prompt*

GitHub Copilot suggests a robust TypeScript function that validates whether the input is a positive integer before returning its square, defaulting to -1 for invalid inputs—demonstrating smart handling of edge cases in mathematical operations.

Analysis: By refining the prompt, Copilot suggests a more robust function with input validation which ensures a better code quality.

Advanced Programming with GitHub Copilot for Web Application Development

When developing modern web applications, it is not just about writing a code—it is about connecting multiple layers of logic, structure, and user experience. From crafting responsive user interfaces to managing APIs and orchestrating data flow between the frontend and backend, full-stack development demands clarity, consistency, and scalability.

In this section, we will explore advanced programming concepts across the full stack, including UI development using React, backend logic with Node.js and Express, modular architecture through REST APIs, and seamless integration with databases. These real-world patterns are essential for building production-grade applications.

GitHub Copilot, now powered by **GPT-4 Turbo**, significantly enhances this process. It doesn't just fill in lines of code—it understands the bigger picture. Whether you are managing component state in React, applying strong typing with TypeScript, setting up **`async/await`** flows, or handling route logic in an Express app, Copilot offers contextually aware suggestions that align with common best practices, and your project's specific structure.

For example, when building a reusable form component in React, Copilot can anticipate the props, handle form validation logic, and even scaffold error messages—because it recognizes patterns from similar projects, and adapts to your naming conventions. Similarly, on the backend, it can generate route handlers, middleware templates, and database queries, based on your application's structure and dependencies.

Thus, by streamlining the repetitive and structural aspects of full-stack coding, Copilot lets you focus on what truly matters—building meaningful features, refining user experience, and architecting scalable systems.

Frontend Development with React and TypeScript

React is one of the most popular frontend frameworks for building interactive user interfaces, and TypeScript helps in writing more maintainable and scalable React applications. Let us see how GitHub Copilot can assist with real-world frontend development tasks.

a. **Setting up a React Project with TypeScript**

   Copilot can help with the initial setup of a **React** project using **TypeScript**.

   Prompt:

   ```
   /workspace Create a new React project using TypeScript with basic project setup.
   ```

GitHub Copilot Output for the Prompt

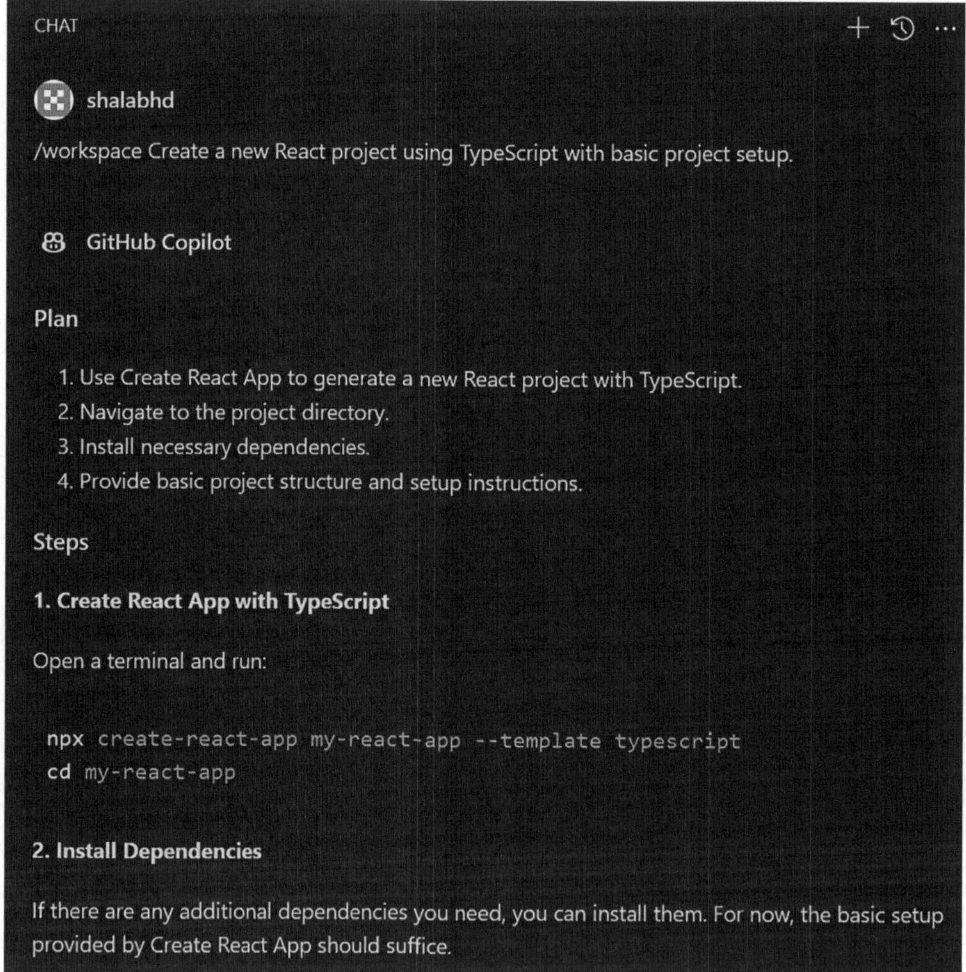

Figure 3.39: *GitHub Copilot Designed a Complete Step-by-step Outline Plan for Creating React Based Project*

GitHub Copilot assists in bootstrapping a new React project with TypeScript by outlining a structured plan–starting from using Create React App with the TypeScript template, navigating to the project directory, and preparing for dependency installation and basic setup configuration.

CHAT

3. Basic Project Structure

The structure will look like this:

```
my-react-app/
├── node_modules/
├── public/
│   ├── index.html
│   └── ...
├── src/
│   ├── App.css
│   ├── App.test.tsx
│   ├── App.tsx
│   ├── index.css
│   ├── index.tsx
│   ├── logo.svg
│   └── react-app-env.d.ts
├── .gitignore
├── package.json
├── tsconfig.json
├── README.md
└── ...
```

Figure 3.40: *GitHub Copilot Displays the Default Structure of a React + TypeScript App*

GitHub Copilot provides a visual overview of the default folder and file structure generated by Create React App with the TypeScript Template – showcasing organized directories like public and **`src`**, along with essential files, such as **`index.tsx`**, **`App.tsx`**, **`package.json`**, and **`tsconfig.json`**.

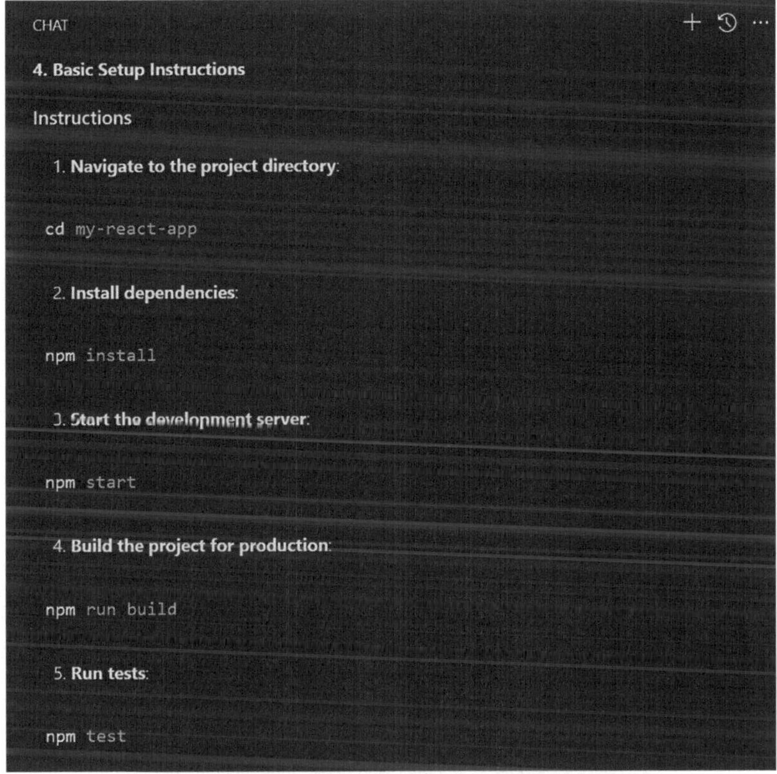

Figure 3.41: *GitHub Copilot Giving Step-by-step Installation Instructions for Setting Up React Based Project with TypeScript Part-3*

GitHub Copilot outlines a complete set of basic setup instructions for a newly created React + TypeScript project – from navigating to the project directory and installing dependencies to starting the development server, building for production, and running tests.

CHAT

Final Code Block

```
my-react-app/
├── node_modules/
├── public/
│   ├── index.html
│   └── ...
├── src/
│   ├── App.css
│   ├── App.test.tsx
│   ├── App.tsx
│   ├── index.css
│   ├── index.tsx
│   ├── logo.svg
│   └── react-app-env.d.ts
├── .gitignore
├── package.json
├── tsconfig.json
├── README.md
└── ...
```

Figure 3.42: *GitHub Copilot Summarizes the Complete File Structure of a React + TypeScript Project*

GitHub Copilot presents the finalized project layout of a React + TypeScript app, showing all the essential directories and files – from **`public/index.html`** and **`core.tsx`** components in src/, to config files like **`package.json`** and **`tsconfig.json`**.

a. **Creating Functional Components**

Functional components are the building blocks of React applications. Copilot can generate components efficiently, even including props and types.

Prompt:

`/workspace Create a React functional component in TypeScript that displays a list of users.`

Copilot Output:

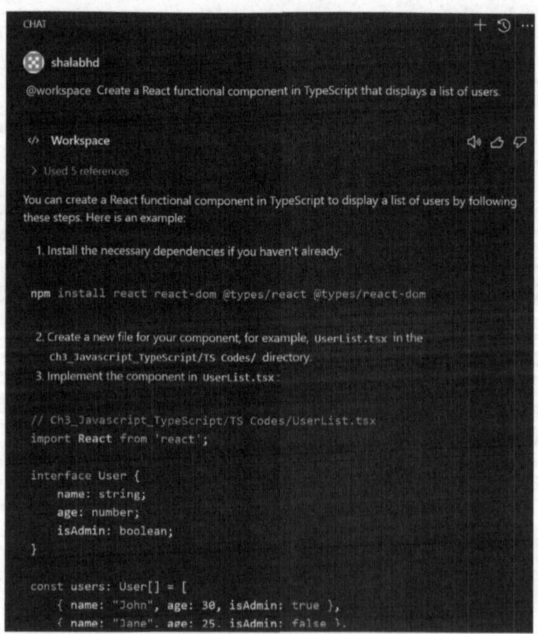

Figure 3.43: *GitHub Copilot Giving a List of Dependencies and Component Details*

GitHub Copilot guides the creation of a React functional component in TypeScript by suggesting the necessary dependencies, the structure of a user interface, and a sample list of user objects – enabling developers to quickly display user data in a strongly typed and organized way.

InsightBytes

Figure 3.44: *GitHub Copilot Giving a List of Dependencies and Component Details*

This screenshot highlights the VS Code interface where GitHub Copilot displays a suggested command, along with useful toolbar options – such as copying, running in terminal, or refining the suggestion – making code adoption quicker, and more interactive.

1. This icon in the GitHub Copilot code block toolbar allows users to insert the suggested command directly into the integrated terminal, enabling quick execution, without copy-pasting.

2. The "*Insert at Cursor*" icon enables developers to insert Copilot's suggested code directly into the editor at the current cursor position, making it seamless to apply code snippets inline.

3. Use the "Apply in Editor" button to directly place the code into the currently opened code file in the editor. Copilot will only temporarily copy the code suggestion in the editor, and based on the relevance and usage, the developer can either accept the suggestion or discard it.

```
// Ch3_Javascript_TypeScript/TS Codes/UserList.tsx
import React from 'react';

interface User {
    name: string;
    age: number;
    isAdmin: boolean;
}

const users: User[] = [
    { name: "John", age: 30, isAdmin: true },
    { name: "Jane", age: 25, isAdmin: false },
    { name: "Doe", age: 22, isAdmin: false }
];

const UserList: React.FC = () => {
    return (
        <div>
            <h1>User List</h1>
            <ul>
                {users.map((user, index) => (
                    <li key={index}>
                        {user.name} - Age: {user.age} - Admin: {user.isAdmin ? "Yes" : "No"}
                    </li>
                ))}
            </ul>
        </div>
    );
};

export default UserList;
```

Figure 3.45: *Copilot Lets You Accept, Discard, or Apply Suggested Changes Directly in the Editor*

When Copilot suggests code changes within the VS Code Editor, developers are given the option to review and either accept, or discard the modifications – supporting collaborative and controlled coding with AI assistance.

Copilot generates a functional component that displays a list of users, complete with TypeScript interfaces to ensure proper data handling. This is a typical task in web applications that display dynamic data from an API.

Copilot Code Suggestion Related Output

```
// Ch3_Javascript_TypeScript/TS Codes/UserList.tsx
import React from 'react';
interface User {
    name: string;
    age: number;
    isAdmin: boolean;
}
const users: User[] = [
    { name: "John", age: 30, isAdmin: true },
    { name: "Jane", age: 25, isAdmin: false },
    { name: "Doe", age: 22, isAdmin: false }
];
const UserList: React.FC = () => {
    return (
        <div>
            <h1>User List</h1>
            <ul>
                {users.map((user, index) => (
                    <li key={index}>
                        {user.name} - Age: {user.age} - Admin: {user.isAdmin ?
"Yes" : "No"}
                    </li>
                ))}
            </ul>
        </div>
    );
};
export default UserList;
```

4. You can then import and use this component in your main application file, for example, `App.tsx`:

```
// Ch3_Javascript_TypeScript/TS Codes/App.tsx
import React from 'react';
import ReactDOM from 'react-dom';
import UserList from './UserList';

const App: React.FC = () => {
    return (
        <div>
            <UserList />
        </div>
    );
};

ReactDOM.render(<App />, document.getElementById('root'));
```

Make sure to update your `index.html` to include a root element with the id `root` if it doesn't already exist.

This will create a simple React functional component that displays a list of users.

Figure 3.46: *GitHub Copilot Giving Code for Next Component File, that is App.tsx, and Shows How to Render a React Functional Component Using TypeScript*

GitHub Copilot demonstrates how to integrate the **`UserList`** component into your main **`App.tsx`** file by importing **`React`** and **`ReactDOM`**, creating a functional component, and rendering it inside the HTML element with the id of "**`root`**" – completing the setup for a user list display.

Start creating the code files, one by one by simply using the Copilot contextual menu options to directly insert the code into a new file. The following screenshot depicts the **`contextual`** button that the developer can click, and then select the **`Insert into New file`** option.

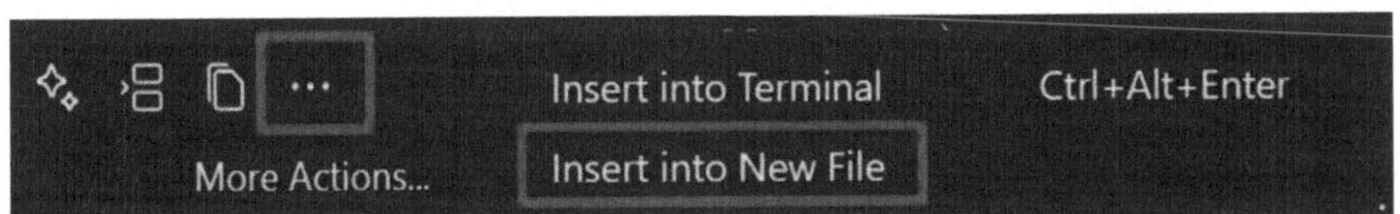

Figure 3.47: *GitHub Copilot Contextual Menu Options to Directly Insert Code to a New File*

GitHub Copilot offers a handy "More Actions" menu (accessible via the three dots icon) that provides extended options for applying code suggestions. One such feature, "**`Insert into New File`**", allows you to directly place the generated code into a fresh file – streamlining the organization, and saving manual effort.

c. **State Management with React Hooks**

In React applications, managing the state is crucial for handling dynamic data. GitHub Copilot can assist with common patterns using React hooks, such as **`useState`** and **`useEffect`**.

Prompt:

`/workspace Create a React component that fetches data from an API and displays it using useState and useEffect.`

Copilot Output:

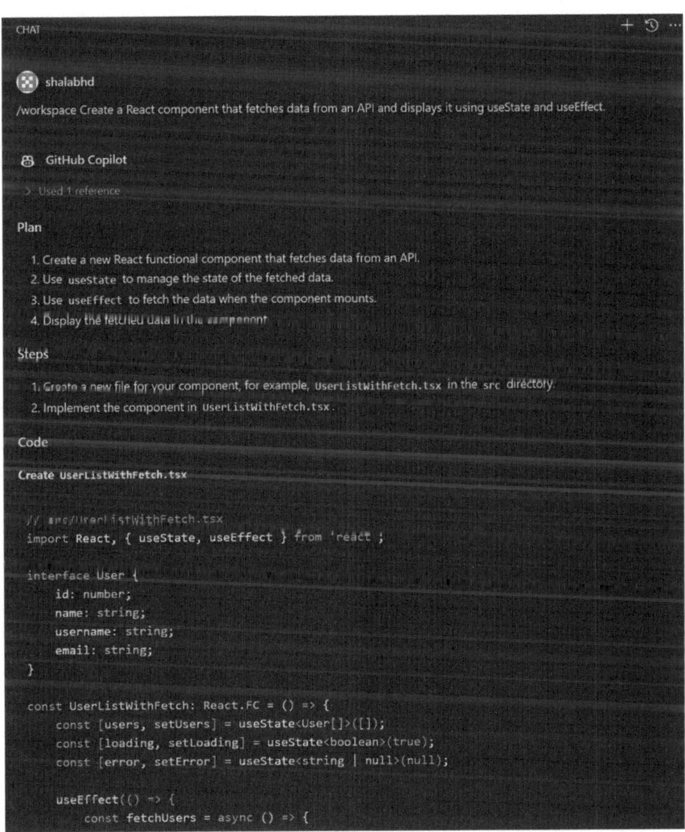

Figure 3.48: *GitHub Copilot Generates a React Component that Fetches API Data Using useEffect, and Manages It with useState*

GitHub Copilot walks you through creating a React functional component (**`UserListWithFetch.tsx`**) that fetches data from an API using **`useEffect`**, and manages state with **`useState`**. It defines a User interface, handles loading and error states, and prepares the structure for displaying the fetched user data in a clean and modular way.

Copilot Generated Code File

```
// src/UserListWithFetch.tsx
import React, { useState, useEffect } from 'react';
interface User {
    id: number;
    name: string;
    username: string;
    email: string;
}
const UserListWithFetch: React.FC = () => {
    const [users, setUsers] = useState<User[]>([]);
    const [loading, setLoading] = useState<boolean>(true);
    const [error, setError] = useState<string | null>(null);

    useEffect(() => {
        const fetchUsers = async () => {
            try {
                const response = await fetch('https://jsonplaceholder.
typicode.com/users');
                if (!response.ok) {
                    throw new Error('Network response was not ok');
                }
                const data = await response.json();
                setUsers(data);
            } catch (error) {
                setError(error.message);
            } finally {
                setLoading(false);
            }
        };
        fetchUsers();
    }, []);
    if (loading) {
        return <div>Loading...</div>;
    }
    if (error) {
        return <div>Error: {error}</div>;
    }
    return (
        <div>
            <h1>User List</h1>
            <ul>
                {users.map(user => (
                    <li key={user.id}>
                        {user.name} - {user.username} - {user.email}
                    </li>
                ))}
            </ul>
        </div>
    );
};
export default UserListWithFetch;
```

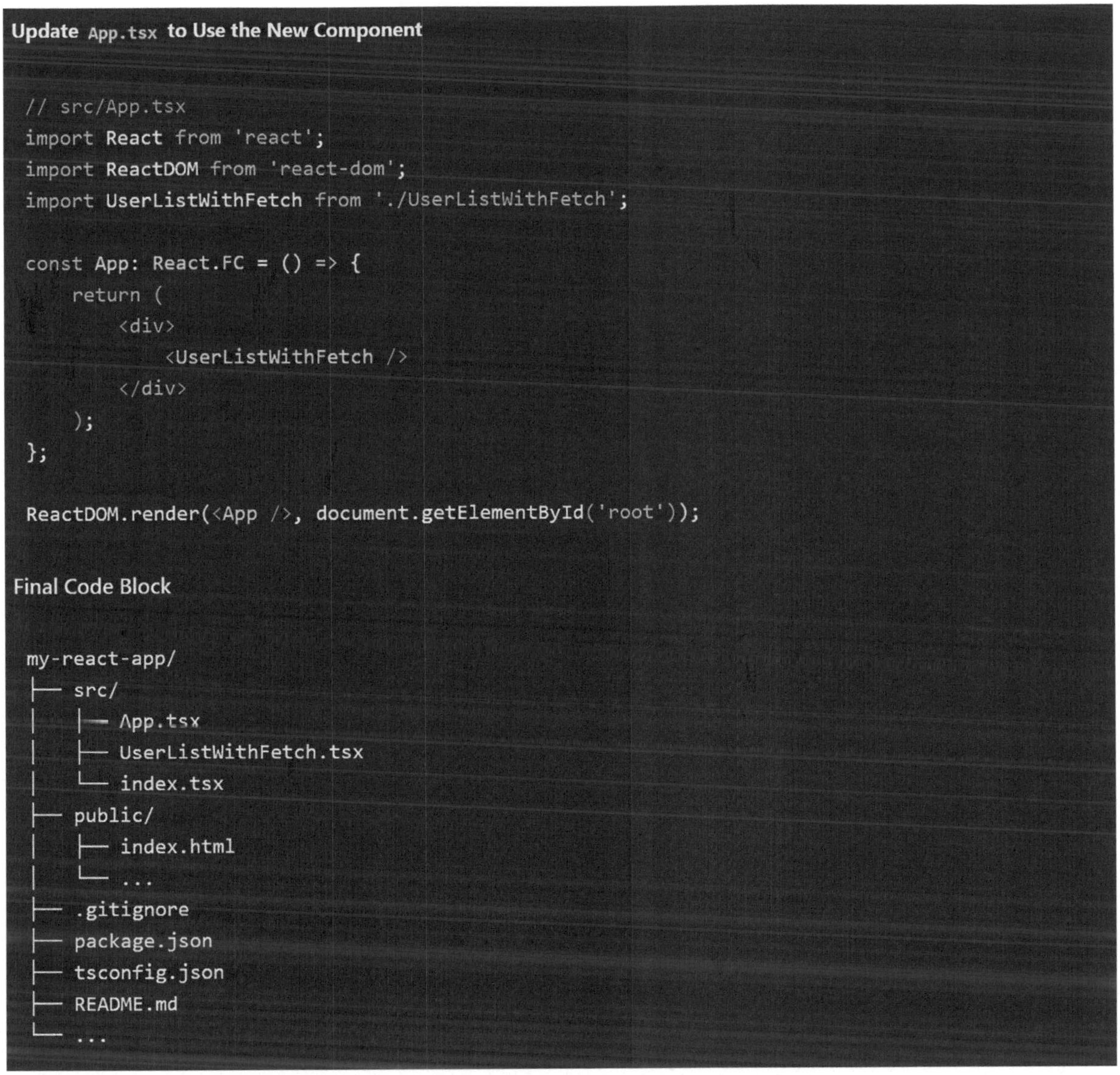

Update `App.tsx` **to Use the New Component**

```
// src/App.tsx
import React from 'react';
import ReactDOM from 'react-dom';
import UserListWithFetch from './UserListWithFetch';

const App: React.FC = () => {
    return (
        <div>
            <UserListWithFetch />
        </div>
    );
};

ReactDOM.render(<App />, document.getElementById('root'));
```

Final Code Block

```
my-react-app/
├── src/
│   ├── App.tsx
│   ├── UserListWithFetch.tsx
│   └── index.tsx
├── public/
│   ├── index.html
│   └── ...
├── .gitignore
├── package.json
├── tsconfig.json
├── README.md
└── ...
```

Figure 3.49: *GitHub Copilot Shows How to Render the API-fetching Component and Updates the Project Structure Accordingly*

GitHub Copilot demonstrates how to update the main **`App.tsx`** file to render the newly created **`UserListWithFetch`** component. It also provides the updated project structure, ensuring that the integration is clear, organized, and ready for execution within the React app.

Copilot Generated Updated Code File for App.tsx

```
// src/App.tsx
import React from 'react';
import ReactDOM from 'react-dom';
import UserListWithFetch from './UserListWithFetch';
const App: React.FC = () => {
    return (
        <div>
            <UserListWithFetch />
        </div>
    );
};
ReactDOM.render(<App />, document.getElementById('root'));
```

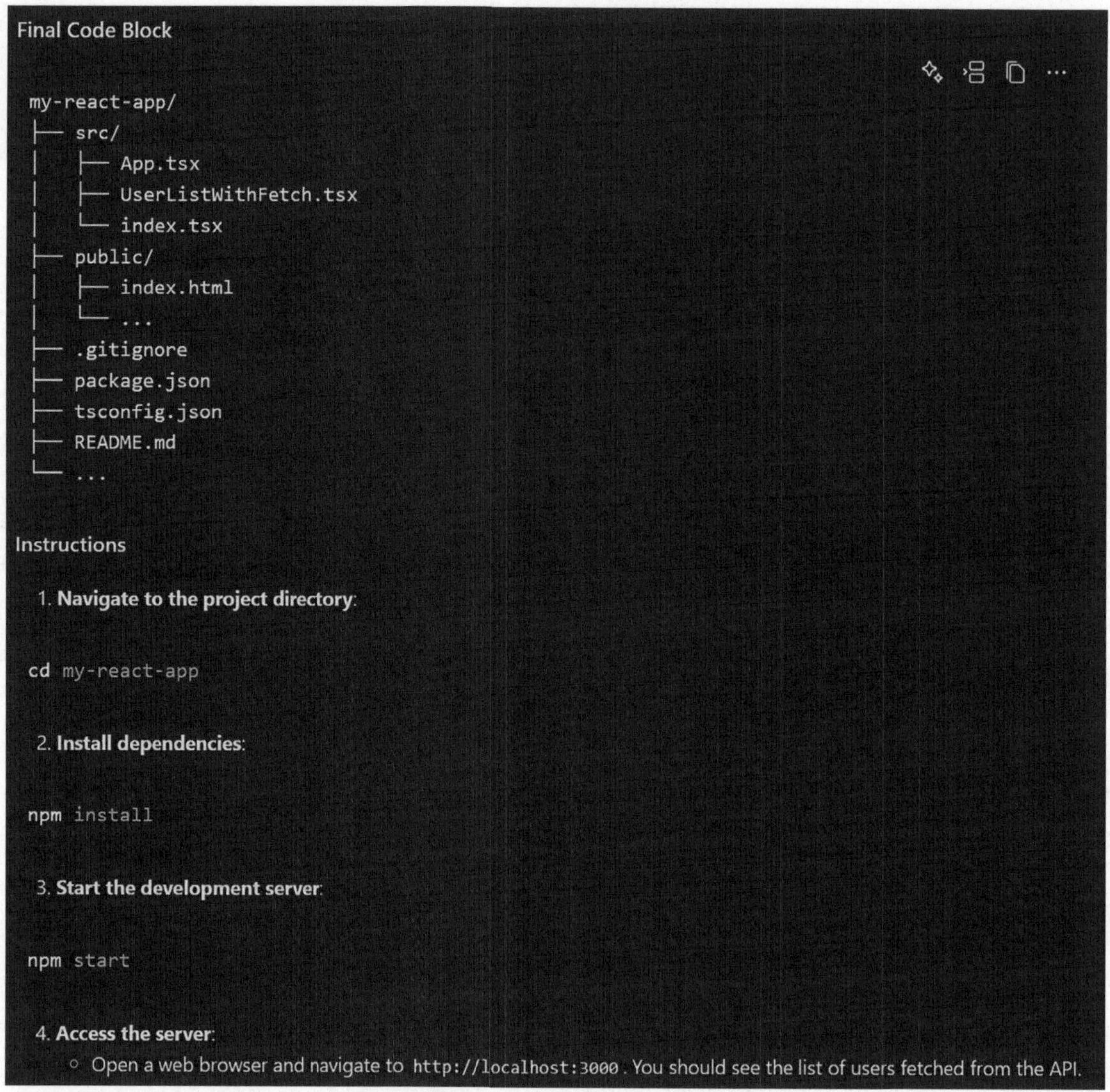

Figure 3.50: *GitHub Copilot Outlines the Final Project Structure and Instructions to Run the App Locally*

GitHub Copilot wraps up the workflow by presenting the complete file structure, and a step-by-step guide to run the React app. From navigating into the project directory and installing dependencies to starting the server and accessing the app via browser, it ensures a smooth local setup experience for viewing the API-fetched data.

This component demonstrates how Copilot simplifies fetching data from an API, and managing the state using **`useState`** and **`useEffect`**. This is a common pattern, when dealing with dynamic content in a React application.

Backend Development with Node.js and Express

For the backend, **`Node.js`** and **`Express`** are popular choices due to their lightweight nature and compatibility with JavaScript/TypeScript. Let us explore how Copilot helps in building scalable and modular backend applications.

a. **Setting up an Express API with TypeScript**

   Prompt:

   ```
   /workspace Create a simple REST API using Express and TypeScript that handles
   user-related routes.
   ```

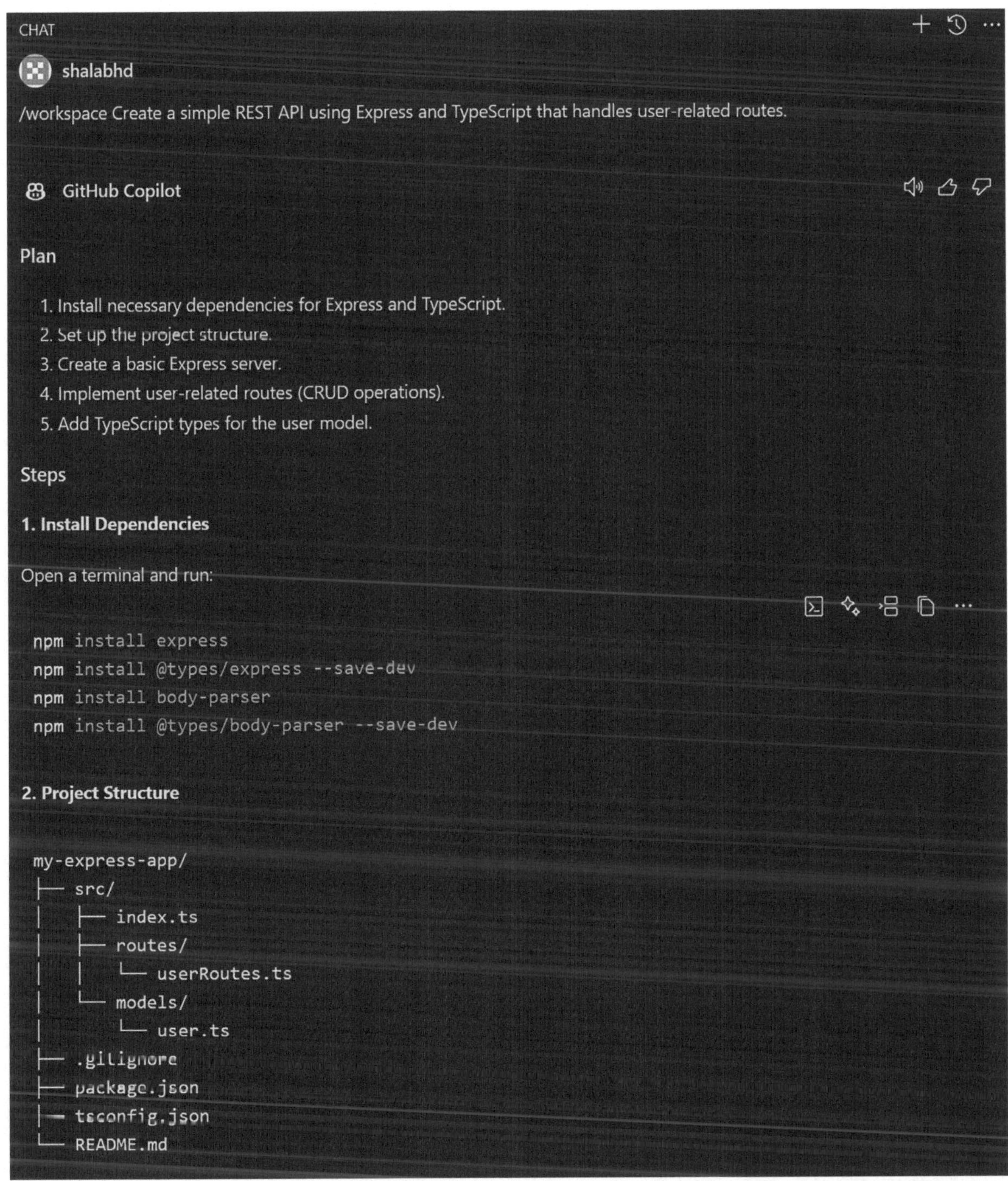

Figure 3.51: *GitHub Copilot Created Project Structure and Instructions for Setting up an Express app using TypeScript, Including Dependencies Installation and ServerSetup*

GitHub Copilot guides you in setting up a TypeScript-based REST API using Express. It begins by listing essential dependencies, then outlines the ideal folder structure to organize routes and models for scalable user-related CRUD operations.

CHAT

3. Create `tsconfig.json`

```
{
  "compilerOptions": {
    "target": "ES2020",
    "module": "commonjs",
    "strict": true,
    "esModuleInterop": true,
    "skipLibCheck": true,
    "forceConsistentCasingInFileNames": true,
    "outDir": "./dist"
  },
  "include": ["src"]
}
```

4. Create `src/index.ts`

```
import express from 'express';
import bodyParser from 'body-parser';
import userRoutes from './routes/userRoutes';

const app = express();
const port = 3000;

app.use(bodyParser.json());
app.use('/users', userRoutes);

app.listen(port, () => {
  console.log(`Server is running at http://localhost:${port}`);
});
```

5. Create `src/models/user.ts`

```
export interface User {
  id: number;
  name: string;
  email: string;
}
```

Figure 3.52: *GitHub Copilot Created a Configuration for the TypeScript Compiler (**tsconfig.json**) and the Basic Setup of the Express Server (**index.ts**) in the Project*

Thus, GitHub Copilot proceeds to scaffold the core components of the TypeScript Express app. It auto-generates the **`tsconfig.json`** file with appropriate compiler options, creates the main server file **`index.ts`** to bootstrap the Express server, and defines a user interface model in **`user.ts`** for type-safe API operations.

CHAT

6. Create `src/routes/userRoutes.ts`

```
import express, { Request, Response } from 'express';
import { User } from '../models/user';

const router = express.Router();

let users: User[] = [
  { id: 1, name: 'John Doe', email: 'john@example.com' },
  { id: 2, name: 'Jane Doe', email: 'jane@example.com' }
];

// Get all users
router.get('/', (req: Request, res: Response) => {
  res.json(users);
});

// Get user by ID
router.get('/:id', (req: Request, res: Response) => {
  const user = users.find(u => u.id === parseInt(req.params.id));
  if (user) {
    res.json(user);
  } else {
    res.status(404).send('User not found');
  }
});

// Create new user
router.post('/', (req: Request, res: Response) => {
  const newUser: User = {
    id: users.length + 1,
    name: req.body.name,
    email: req.body.email
  };
  users.push(newUser);
  res.status(201).json(newUser);
});

// Update user
router.put('/:id', (req: Request, res: Response) => {
  const userIndex = users.findIndex(u => u.id === parseInt(req.params.id));
```

Figure 3.53: *GitHub Copilot Created User Routes Implementation in TypeScript with Express, Handling CRUD Operations Like GET, POST, PUT, and DELETE*

GitHub Copilot intelligently scaffolds the **`userRoutes.ts`** file with complete CRUD functionality. It sets up Express route handlers to fetch all users, retrieve a user by ID, create new users, and update the existing ones, using TypeScript interfaces for strict type safety.

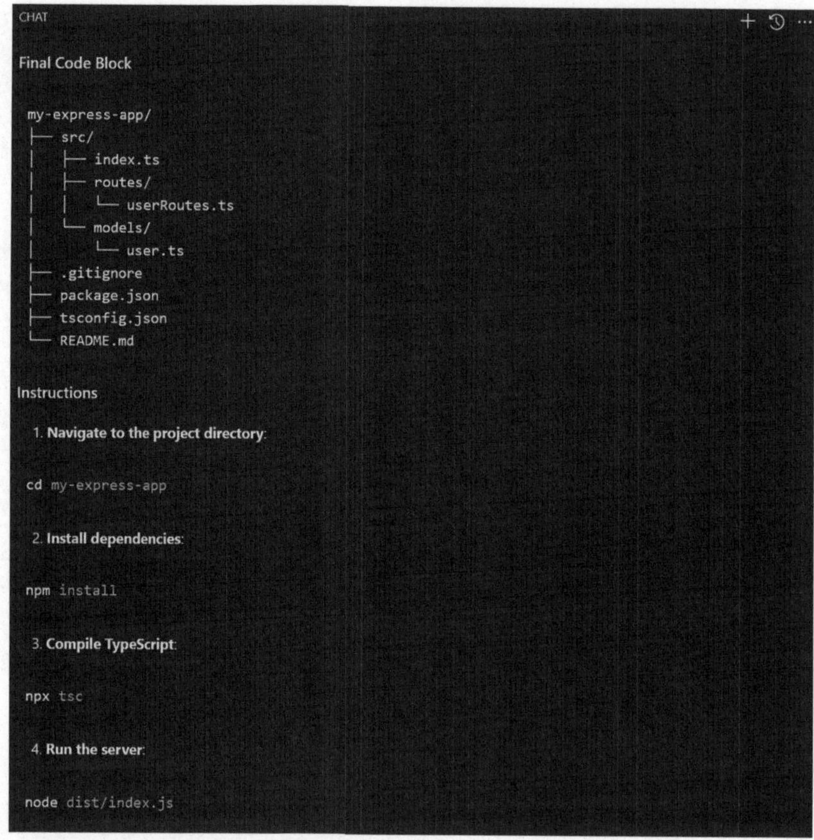

***Figure 3.54:** GitHub Copilot Created Project Structure and Instructions for Setting up an Express app Using TypeScript, Including Dependencies Installation and Server Setup*

The final setup screen summarizes the complete folder structure of the Express + TypeScript project, and outlines the essential commands to install dependencies, compile the TypeScript code, start the server, and prepare for API testing.

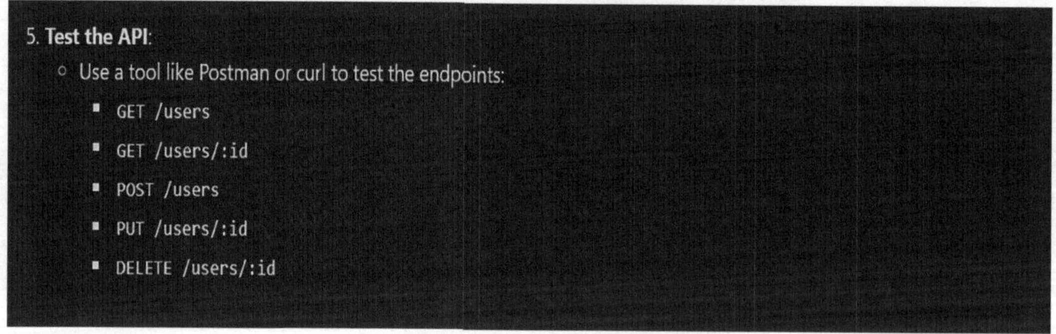

***Figure 3.55:** GitHub Copilot Created Instructions on Testing the API Using Postman or Curl with Endpoints for GET, POST, PUT, and DELETE Requests*

Connecting to Databases

A real-world application often requires connecting to a database. Let us see how Copilot assists in setting up and querying a **PostgreSQL** database using **`TypeORM`** in a Node.js project.

a. **Setting up TypeORM with PostgreSQL**

   Prompt:

   `/workspace Set up TypeORM in a Node.js project to connect to a PostgreSQL database.`

Copilot Output:

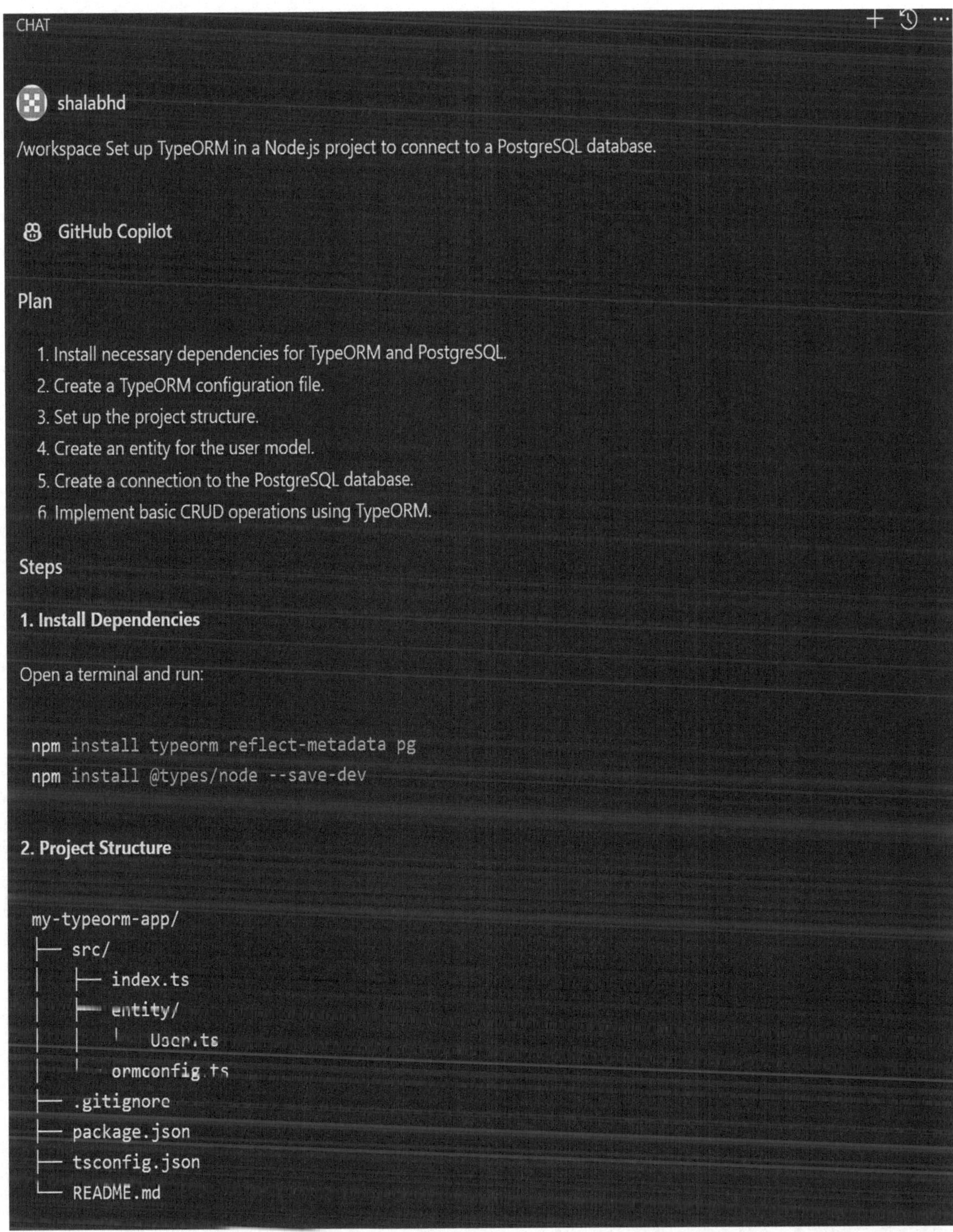

Figure 3.56: *GitHub Copilot Generated Instructions for Setting up TypeORM in a Node.js Project to Connect to a PostgreSQL Database, along with Project Structure and Steps for CRUD Operations*

CHAT

3. Create tsconfig.json

```
{
  "compilerOptions": {
    "target": "ES2020",
    "module": "commonjs",
    "strict": true,
    "esModuleInterop": true,
    "skipLibCheck": true,
    "forceConsistentCasingInFileNames": true,
    "outDir": "./dist",
    "experimentalDecorators": true,
    "emitDecoratorMetadata": true
  },
  "include": ["src"]
}
```

4. Create src/ormconfig.ts

```
import { ConnectionOptions } from 'typeorm';

const config: ConnectionOptions = {
  type: 'postgres',
  host: 'localhost',
  port: 5432,
  username: 'your_username',
  password: 'your_password',
  database: 'your_database',
  synchronize: true,
  logging: false,
  entities: ['src/entity/**/*.ts'],
  migrations: ['src/migration/**/*.ts'],
  subscribers: ['src/subscriber/**/*.ts'],
  cli: {
    entitiesDir: 'src/entity',
    migrationsDir: 'src/migration',
    subscribersDir: 'src/subscriber'
  }
};
```

Figure 3.57: *GitHub Copilot TypeScript Compiler Options Configuration File (tsconfig.json) with Settings for TypeORM and Experimental Decorators Enabled for PostgreSQL Integration*

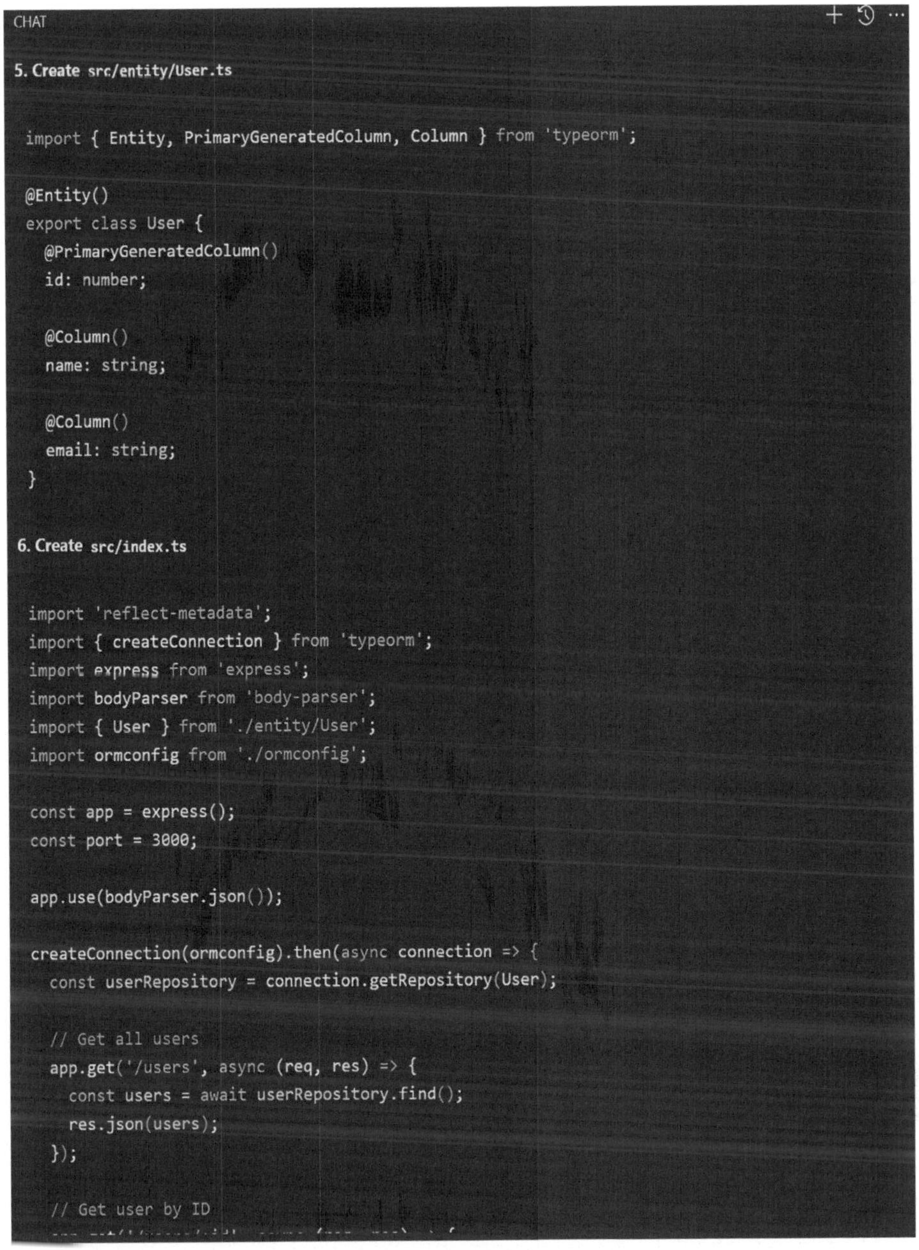

CHAT

5. Create `src/entity/User.ts`

```
import { Entity, PrimaryGeneratedColumn, Column } from 'typeorm';

@Entity()
export class User {
  @PrimaryGeneratedColumn()
  id: number;

  @Column()
  name: string;

  @Column()
  email: string;
}
```

6. Create `src/index.ts`

```
import 'reflect-metadata';
import { createConnection } from 'typeorm';
import express from 'express';
import bodyParser from 'body-parser';
import { User } from './entity/User';
import ormconfig from './ormconfig';

const app = express();
const port = 3000;

app.use(bodyParser.json());

createConnection(ormconfig).then(async connection => {
  const userRepository = connection.getRepository(User);

  // Get all users
  app.get('/users', async (req, res) => {
    const users = await userRepository.find();
    res.json(users);
  });

  // Get user by ID
```

Figure 3.58: *GitHub Copilot Defining the User Entity Model in TypeORM for the PostgreSQL Database Connection, with ID, Name, and Email Fields*

Complete Code of `index.ts` File Generated by Copilot:

```
import 'reflect-metadata';
import { createConnection } from 'typeorm';
import express from 'express';
import bodyParser from 'body-parser';
import { User } from './entity/User';
import ormconfig from './ormconfig';

const app = express();
const port = 3000;
app.use(bodyParser.json());

createConnection(ormconfig).then(async connection => {
const userRepository = connection.getRepository(User);
```

```
  // Get all users
  app.get('/users', async (req, res) => {
    const users = await userRepository.find();
    res.json(users);
  });

  // Get user by ID
  app.get('/users/:id', async (req, res) => {
    const user = await userRepository.findOne(req.params.id);
    if (user) {
      res.json(user);
    } else {
      res.status(404).send('User not found');
    }
  });

  // Create new user
  app.post('/users', async (req, res) => {
    const newUser = userRepository.create(req.body);
    const result = await userRepository.save(newUser);
    res.status(201).json(result);
  });

  // Update user
  app.put('/users/:id', async (req, res) => {
    const user = await userRepository.findOne(req.params.id);
    if (user) {
      userRepository.merge(user, req.body);
      const result = await userRepository.save(user);
      res.json(result);
    } else {
      res.status(404).send('User not found');
    }
  });

  // Delete user
  app.delete('/users/:id', async (req, res) => {
    const result = await userRepository.delete(req.params.id);
    if (result.affected) {
      res.status(204).send();
    } else {
      res.status(404).send('User not found');
    }
  });

  app.listen(port, () => {
    console.log(`Server is running at http://localhost:${port}`);
  });
}).catch(error => console.log(error));
```

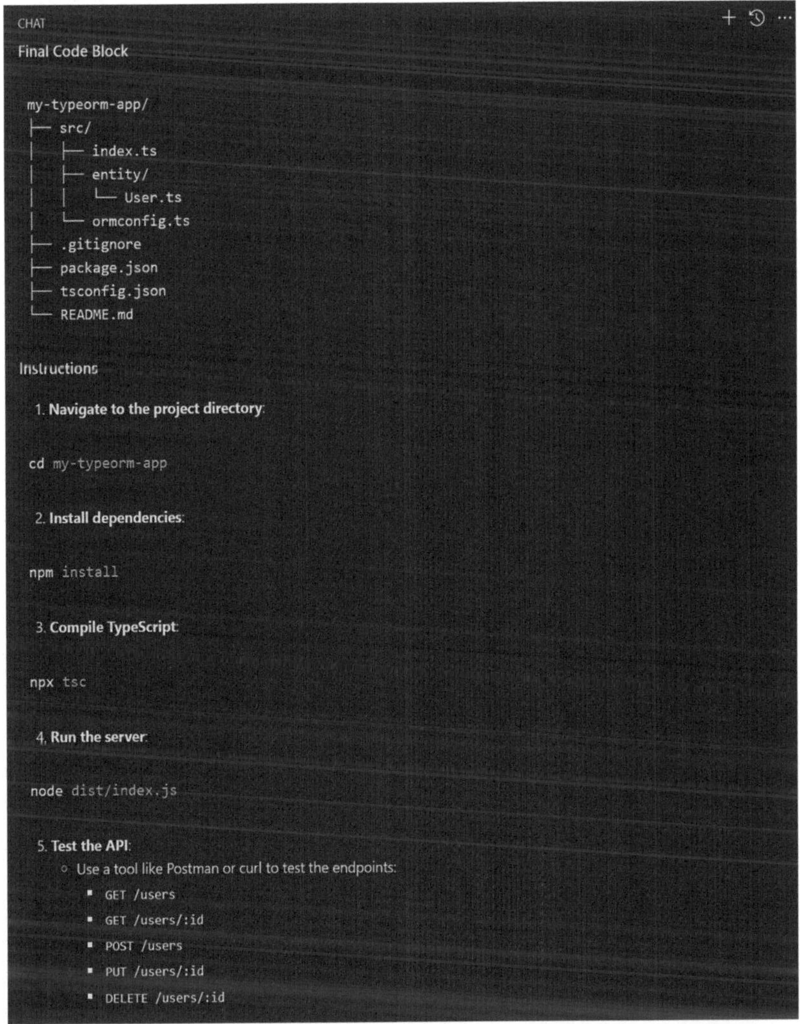

***Figure 3.59:** GitHub Copilot Generated Project Structure and Instructions for Setting up and Testing a TypeORM-based API with PostgreSQL, Including TypeScript Compilation and API Endpoints*

Using Copilot to Configure ESLint and Prettier

GitHub Copilot does not just suggest syntax–it also understands how your tools and style rules should align across a project. When setting up ESLint and Prettier, Copilot can help you go beyond manual trial-and-error configuration by **generating consistent, project-aware rules** based on your context.

For example, while initializing a project, you might prompt:

```
// Generate a basic ESLint configuration for a React + TypeScript project
```

Copilot suggests:

```
{
  "extends": [
    "eslint:recommended",
    "plugin:react/recommended",
    "plugin:@typescript-eslint/recommended",
    "prettier"
  ],
  "plugins": ["react", "@typescript-eslint"],
  "parser": "@typescript-eslint/parser",
  "rules": {
```

```
    "react/prop-types": "off",
    "@typescript-eslint/no-unused-vars": "warn"
  }
}
```

Similarly, if your team uses single quotes and a 100-character line width, you can prompt Copilot with:

```
// Create a Prettier config with single quotes, trailing commas, and 100-char line width
```

Copilot returns:

```
{
  "singleQuote": true,
  "trailingComma": "all",
  "printWidth": 100
}
```

These are not just static snippets–Copilot adapts based on your file context, the frameworks you're using, and even your project structure. This makes it easier to **standardize code formatting and linting across teams**, without memorizing every rule or plugin name.

In practice, developers save significant setup time and avoid misconfigurations by relying on Copilot's ability to surface the most relevant setup based on natural language prompts.

Using GitHub Copilot to Generate TypeScript Interfaces

When working with API responses, external data, or component props in a TypeScript project, defining accurate interfaces is key to ensuring type safety and readability. GitHub Copilot can assist by inferring and suggesting TypeScript interfaces based on context, comments, or surrounding data structures.

Let us say, you receive the following API response structure:

```
{
  "id": 102,
  "title": "Learn Copilot",
  "isPublished": true,
  "tags": ["ai", "typescript"],
  "author": {
    "name": "Jane",
    "email": "jane@example.com"
  }
}
You prompt Copilot with:
// Define a TypeScript interface for the blog post object above
Copilot suggests:
interface BlogPost {
  id: number;
  title: string;
  isPublished: boolean;
  tags: string[];
  author: {
    name: string;
    email: string;
  };
}
```

This is a solid starting point. It's clear, accurate, and usable. But according to **best practices**, we might want to **abstract nested objects** into their own types for maintainability and reuse.

You refactor as follows:

```
interface Author {
  name: string;
  email: string;
}

interface BlogPost {
  id: number;
  title: string;
  isPublished: boolean;
  tags: string[];
  author: Author;
}
```

This makes the structure more scalable—especially if the Author is reused elsewhere. Copilot can also assist with this refactor when **prompted**:

```
// Extract Author as a separate interface
```

Best Practices When Using Copilot for TypeScript

Best Practice	Copilot Output	What to Watch
Use interface for object types	Copilot prefers interface over type	Good
Keep nesting minimal	Copilot may nest too deeply	Refactor
Prefer reusability	Copilot may inline structures	Extract
Add optional fields with ?	Copilot often infers optionality well	Review usage
Avoid any unless necessary	Rarely suggests any	Still check

Table 3.1: *TypeScript Best Practices vs Copilot Suggestions, with Key Review Tips*

Figure 3.60: *Key Strategies to Optimize TypeScript Code with GitHub Copilot for Cleaner and Maintainable Development*

To make the most of GitHub Copilot, while writing TypeScript, developers should align suggestions with key optimization practices, such as using interfaces, minimizing nesting, promoting reusability, and leveraging optional fields for flexibility.

Why This Helps Developers

Copilot reduces the time spent manually, writing and guessing type definitions, especially from unfamiliar data. It:

- Infers types from usage and structure.
- Generates scaffolding for new interfaces.
- Helps enforce typing discipline across teams.

However, developers should still review generated types for:

- Maintainability
- Over- or under-typing
- Real-world usage scenarios

Hence, by combining Copilot's suggestions with TypeScript's flexibility, teams can strike the right balance between safety and developer velocity.

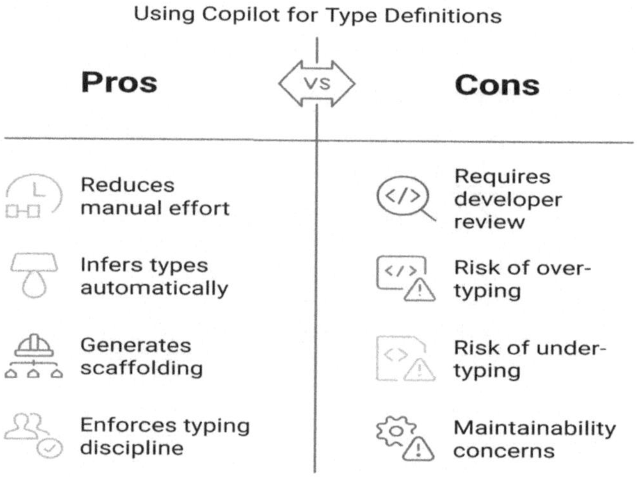

Figure 3.61: *Pros and Cons of Using Copilot for TypeScript Type Definitions: Balancing Automation with Developer Oversight*

When leveraging GitHub Copilot for generating TypeScript type definitions, it is important to weigh its strengths–such as auto-inference and reduced effort–against the need for vigilant review, and long-term maintainability.

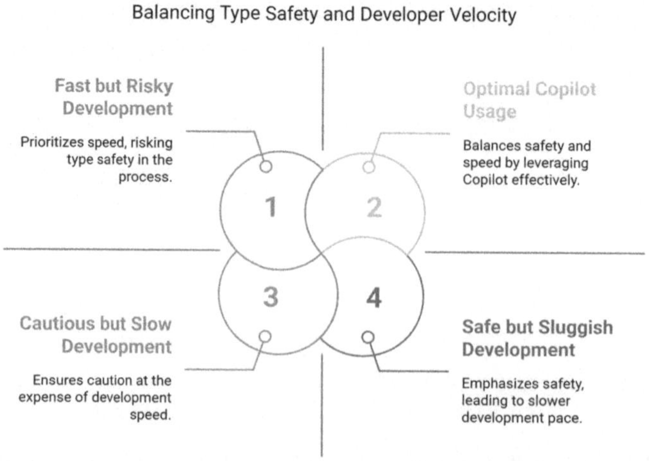

Figure 3.62: *A Quadrant View of Copilot Usage Trade-offs: Balancing Speed and Type Safety for Optimal Development Outcomes*

Achieving the right balance between type safety and developer velocity is the key when using GitHub Copilot–too much emphasis on either can hinder productivity or code quality.

Using ES2024 Features with GitHub Copilot

JavaScript continues to evolve rapidly, and with the release of **ECMAScript 2024**, developers gain access to features that improve expressiveness and control in their code. GitHub Copilot, powered by GPT-4 Turbo, stays in step with these modern updates, helping developers not only to adopt new syntax, but apply it meaningfully in their day-to-day projects.

Take the **new decorators** feature for example. In frontend development–particularly with frameworks like Angular or libraries that leverage class-based components–decorators provide a clean way to annotate behavior, attach metadata, or extend functionality.

Example: Creating a logging decorator for a class method

You can prompt Copilot with:

```
// Create a decorator in TypeScript that logs method calls with arguments and
return values
```

And Copilot might suggest:

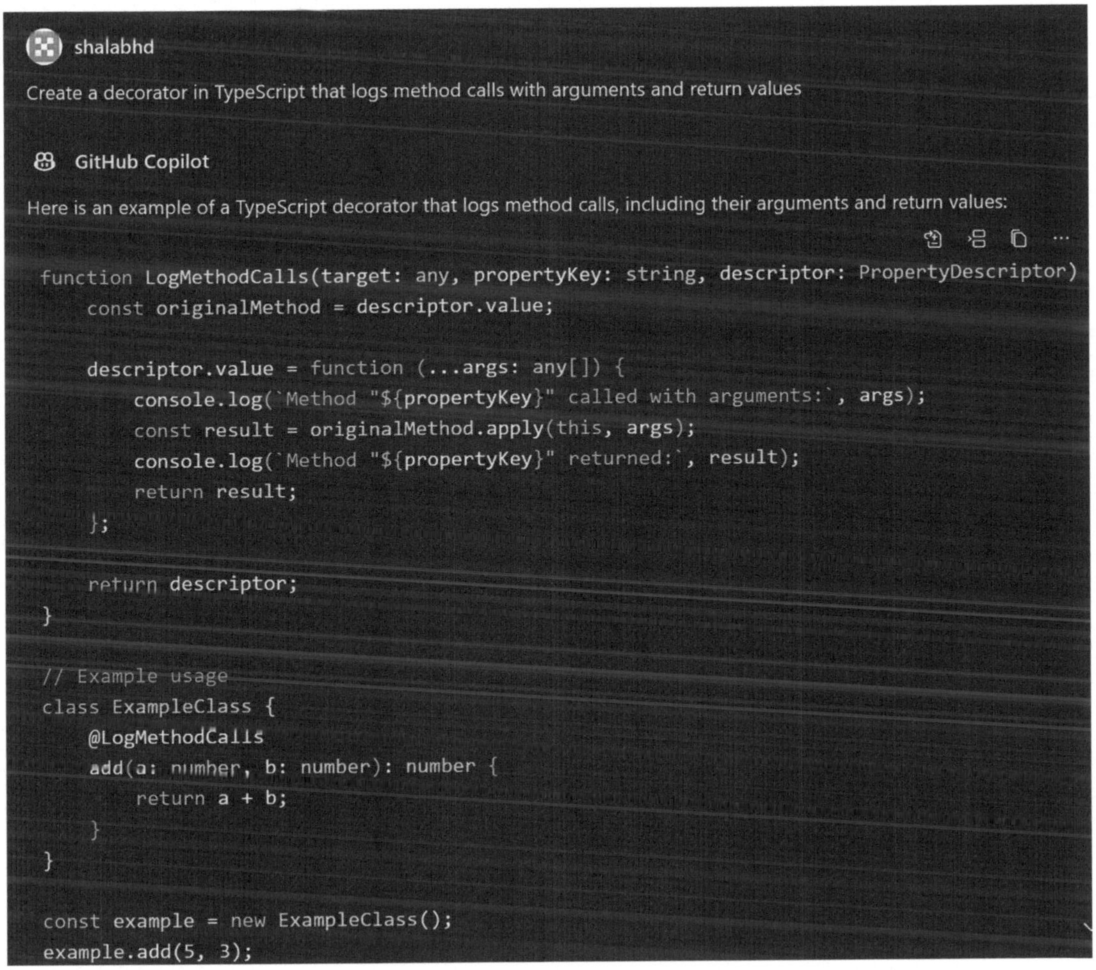

shalabhd

Create a decorator in TypeScript that logs method calls with arguments and return values

GitHub Copilot

Here is an example of a TypeScript decorator that logs method calls, including their arguments and return values:

```
function LogMethodCalls(target: any, propertyKey: string, descriptor: PropertyDescriptor)
    const originalMethod = descriptor.value;

    descriptor.value = function (...args: any[]) {
        console.log(`Method "${propertyKey}" called with arguments:`, args);
        const result = originalMethod.apply(this, args);
        console.log(`Method "${propertyKey}" returned:`, result);
        return result;
    };

    return descriptor;
}

// Example usage
class ExampleClass {
    @LogMethodCalls
    add(a: number, b: number): number {
        return a + b;
    }
}

const example = new ExampleClass();
example.add(5, 3);
```

Figure 3.63: A Quadrant View of Copilot Usage Trade-offs: Balancing Speed and Type Safety for Optimal Development Outcomes

GitHub Copilot assists in generating a TypeScript decorator that captures method calls, logs their arguments, and displays the return values–making debugging and tracing more insightful.

Then you apply it like:

```
// Example usage
class ExampleClass {
    @LogMethodCalls
    add(a: number, b: number): number {
        return a + b;
    }
}

const example = new ExampleClass();
example.add(5, 3);
```

This is the kind of pattern a developer might spend time googling, adapting, or debugging–but Copilot can scaffold it instantly, making advanced language features more accessible, even to those who have not used them before.

AI-Assisted Debugging and Refactoring with Copilot

Modern web applications often involve complex asynchronous logic, state management, and evolving codebases that can introduce bugs, inefficiencies, or redundant code. Traditionally, debugging and refactoring these issues required time-consuming manual reviews, stepping through logs, or consulting documentation. This is where **GitHub Copilot–particularly with Copilot Chat–proves invaluable beyond code generation.**

Copilot does not just write new code–it can **explain, optimize, and restructure** the existing code as well. Acting like a smart, context-aware pair programmer, Copilot helps developers **understand why something is not working**, identify edge cases, and even propose cleaner, more efficient alternatives.

Example-1: Debugging an Async Function that Fails Silently

Imagine you are troubleshooting an Async function in a TypeScript-based API that intermittently fails, without logging anything helpful.

```
async function getUserData(id: string) {
  const user = await fetch(`/api/users/${id}`);
  return await user.json();
}
```

It seems simple, but it throws runtime errors when the user is not found, or when the API response is not successful.

Your prompt Copilot Chat with:

“Why does getUserData fail silently sometimes?”

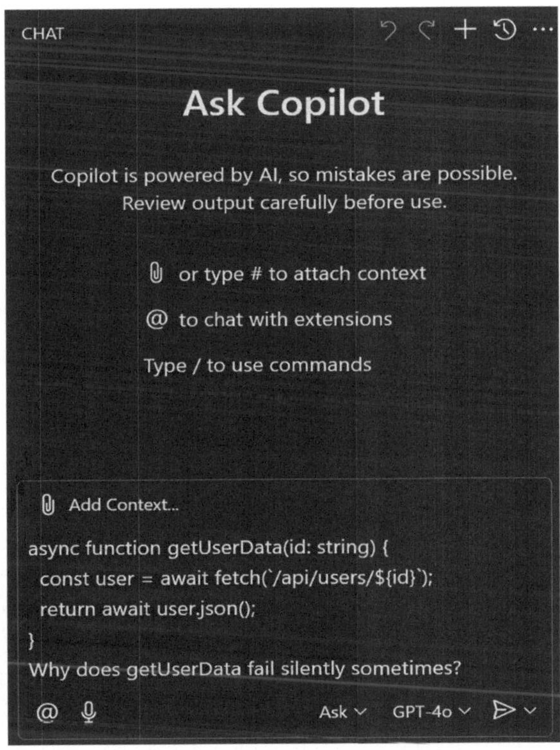

Figure 3.64: *A Quadrant View of Copilot Usage Trade-offs: Balancing Speed and Type Safety for Optimal Development Outcomes*

Copilot receives a prompt to debug a TypeScript async function that inconsistently returns results, without errors.

Copilot might respond with:

```
"The fetch() call does not  throw an error for HTTP response codes like 404 or
500. You should check user.ok before calling .json(). Try adding error handling."
```

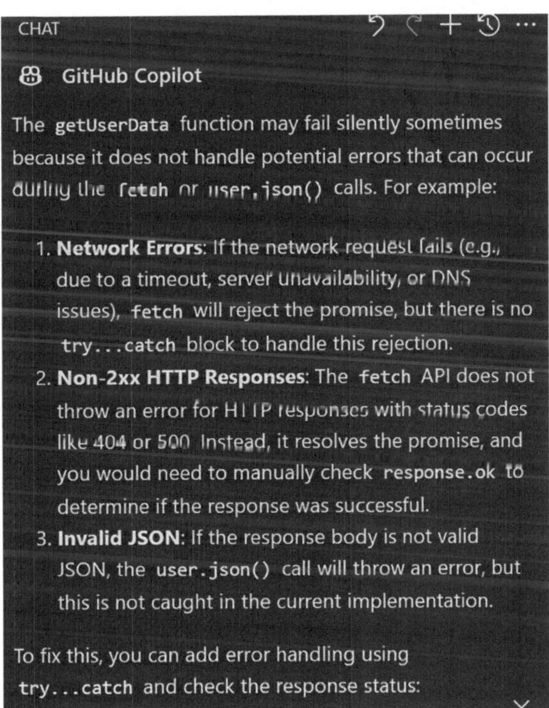

Figure 3.65: *A Quadrant View of Copilot Usage Trade-offs: Balancing Speed and Type Safety for Optimal Development Outcomes*

Copilot analyzes the root causes of silent failures in the **getUserData** function, and recommends the best practices for robust error handling.

And generate below fix:

To fix this, you can add error handling using `try...catch` and check the response status:

```
async function getUserData(id: string) {
  try {
    const response = await fetch(`/api/users/${id}`);
    if (!response.ok) {
      throw new Error(`HTTP error! Status: ${response.stat
    }
    return await response.json();
  } catch (error) {
    console.error('Failed to fetch user data:', error);
    throw error; // Re-throw the error if needed
  }
}
```

This ensures that errors are logged and can be handled appropriately by the caller.

Figure 3.66: *A Quadrant View of Copilot Usage Trade-offs: Balancing Speed and Type Safety for Optimal Development*

Therefore, to prevent silent failures in **getUserData**, Copilot suggests wrapping the fetch logic in a try...catch block with proper response status validation.

This transforms the function into something **production-ready**, and you get an explanation along with a fix—something that would usually require debugging time and deep experience.

Conclusion

This chapter demonstrated how GitHub Copilot enhances JavaScript and TypeScript development by assisting with everything, from syntax to full-stack workflows. Hence, whether you are building React components, configuring APIs, or handling asynchronous logic, Copilot helps to translate the intent into clean, context-aware code.

While Copilot accelerates productivity, it is important to apply human judgment—reviewing AI-generated code for security, correctness, and maintainability that remains vital, particularly in production environments.

In the next chapter, we will explore how Copilot applies to Python development—diving into scripting, automation, and AI-assisted coding patterns to help you get the most out of one of the world's most versatile languages.

Multiple Choice Questions

1. What does top-level await in ECMAScript 2023 allow you to do?
    a. Await promises in functions only.
    b. Use await at the top level in scripts and modules.
    c. Use await, without defining promises.
    d. Execute promises in parallel, without awaiting them.

2. In TypeScript, what is the purpose of the Partial utility type?
    a. Make all properties of an object optional.
    b. Create an immutable object.
    c. Make all properties of an object required.
    d. Convert an object into a string.
3. Which of the following tools is primarily used for writing end-to-end tests?
    a. ESLint
    b. Mocha
    c. Playwright
    d. TypeORM
4. In React, what does the **`useEffect`** hook do?
    a. Manages component state
    b. Runs side effects, such as fetching data
    c. Manages events
    d. Handles routing
5. What is the purpose of the `nodemon` package in a Node.js project?
    a. Lint the code
    b. Restart the server automatically on code changes
    c. Compile TypeScript to JavaScript
    d. Run database migrations
6. What HTTP status code is returned when an API resource is not found?
    a. 200
    b. 400
    c. 404
    d. 500
7. Which of the following methods is used in Jest to test if a function throws an error?
    a. `expect(fn).toBeTruthy()`
    b. `expect(fn).toThrow()`
    c. `expect(fn).toBeDefined()`
    d. `expect(fn).toEqual()`
8. Which operator does JavaScript provide to avoid accessing properties on undefined or null objects?
    a. `Nullish coalescing (??)`
    b. `Optional chaining (?.)`

   c. `Spread operator (...)`
   d. `Destructuring ({})`
9. In TypeORM, which decorator is used to mark a class as an entity?
   a. `@Table()`
   b. `@Model()`
   c. `@Entity()`
   d. `@Column()`
10. Which testing framework is best suited for testing React components, and user interactions?
   a. Mocha
   b. React Testing Library
   c. Jasmine
   d. Jest

Answers

1. b
2. a
3. c
4. b
5. b
6. c
7. b
8. b
9. c
10. b

Chapter 4
Python and AI-Assisted Coding

Introduction

Python remains one of the most popular programming languages, thanks to its clarity, flexibility, and a rich ecosystem that spans web development, automation, data analysis, and machine learning. With the release of Python 3.12 and newer enhancements, developers now benefit from better performance, improved error handling, and powerful additions to the standard library—making Python development, even more robust.

Pair these advancements with GitHub Copilot, and the result is a smarter, faster coding experience. Copilot does not just autocomplete syntax—it understands context, recognizes intent, and adapts to evolving language standards. So, whether you are writing a script, structuring a data pipeline, building a Flask API, or training a machine learning model, Copilot helps you focus on logic and problem-solving, while it assists with repetitive patterns, boilerplate, and structure.

In this chapter, we will explore how GitHub Copilot integrates with Python to accelerate development across different domains. Through real-world examples and prompt-driven workflows, you will see how Copilot adapts to the way you work—making it easier to learn new features, implement the best practices, and build smarter applications with confidence.

Structure

In this chapter, we will discuss the following topics:

- Setting Up Python Development with GitHub Copilot
- Basic Python Scripting with AI Assistance
- Working with Libraries and Packages
- Web Development in Python with AI Assistance (Flask/Django)
- Python for Data Analysis and Machine Learning
- AI Powered Code Optimization Techniques

Setting Up Python Development with GitHub Copilot

Before you can begin using GitHub Copilot with Python, it is important to set up your development environment. This section will guide you through the installation and configuration of Python, along with how to integrate GitHub Copilot.

Installing Python and Setting Up a Virtual Environment

To start writing Python code, you will first need to install Python and set up a virtual environment.

For Windows:

1. **Install Python (ensure version 3.8+):** First, download the installer from the official Python website.
2. During installation, make sure to check the box that says "`Add Python to PATH`".
3. **Verify Python Installation:** Open `Command Prompt`, and run the following command:

```
python --version
```

```
PS C:\Users\SIDDHI DIXIT\Shalabh\Ultimate AI-Assisted Coding with GitHub Copilot> python --version
Python 3.12.6
```

Figure 4.1: *Verifying Python Version Installed*

4. Create and activate a virtual environment: In `Command Prompt`, run the following commands:

```
python -m venv myenv

myenv\Scripts\activate
```

Figure 4.2: *Python Virtual Environment Activated*

For macOS:

1. **Install Python (ensure version 3.8+):**

   Most macOS versions already come with Python 2.x pre-installed. To install Python 3.x, use Homebrew (if not installed, first install Homebrew by following the instructions at Homebrew's official website).

   Run the following command in the Terminal:

```
brew install python
```

2. **Verify Python Installation:** Run the following command to verify Python 3 installation:

Basic Python Scripting with AI Assistance

Python is known for its simplicity, making it perfect for scripting. Copilot can enhance this further by providing intelligent code suggestions as you type, allowing you to quickly build scripts, without having to write every line manually.

Writing Simple Python Scripts with GitHub Copilot

Let us see how Copilot helps in generating basic Python scripts. For instance, a script that calculates the factorial of a number:

Prompt:

```
/workspace Write a Python function to calculate the factorial of a number.
```

Copilot Output:

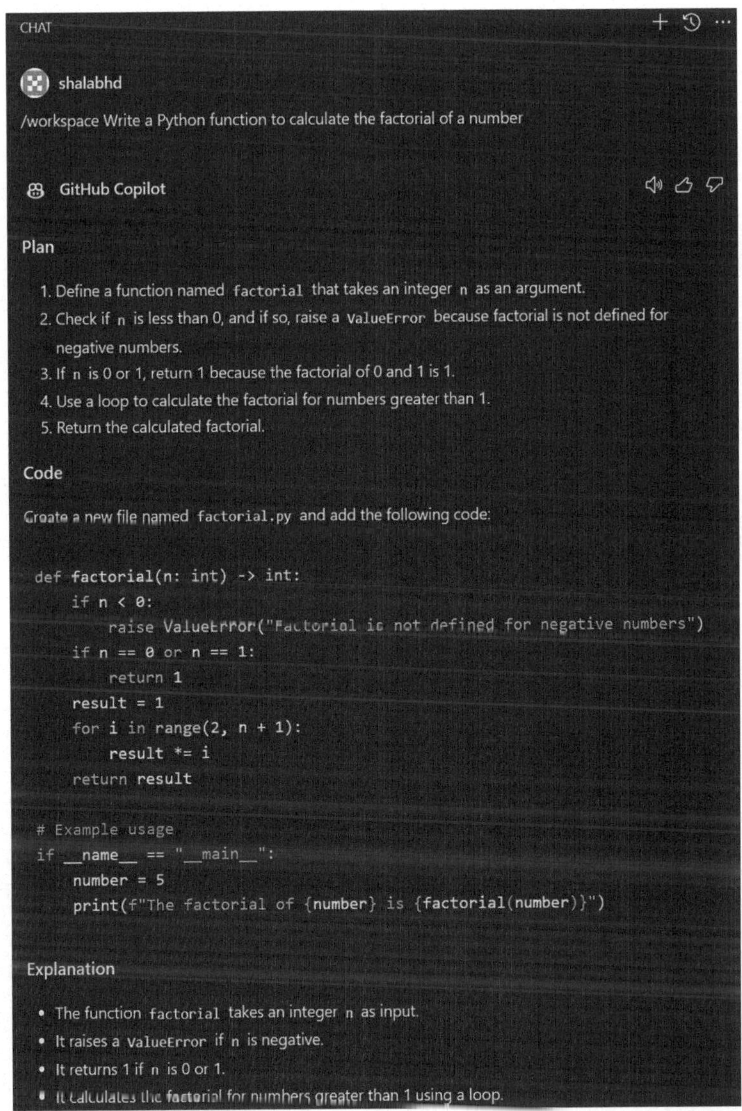

Figure 4.3: *Python Function Designed to Calculate Factorial of a Number*

Working with Libraries and Packages

Python's ecosystem is vast, with libraries available for almost every task, from data manipulation to web scraping. Copilot helps by generating code that makes use of common libraries, such as requests for web requests, pandas for data manipulation, and matplotlib for data visualization.

Web Scraping with `requests` and `BeautifulSoup`

Web scraping is a frequent use case in Python. Hence, let us explore how GitHub Copilot can assist in creating a web scraper.

Prompt:

```
/workspace Write a Python script using `requests` and `BeautifulSoup` to
scrape and print all headlines from a news website.
```

Copilot Output:

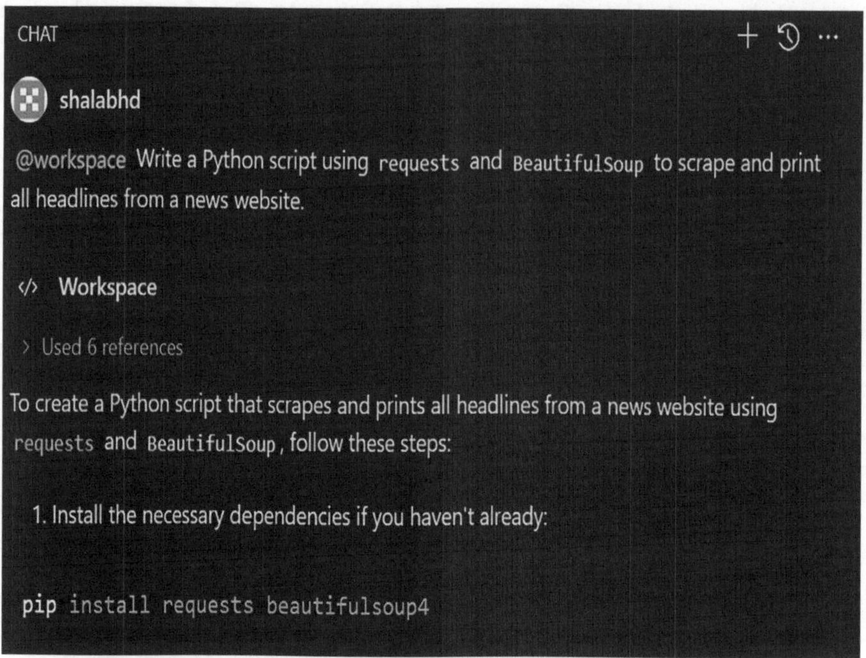

Figure 4.4: *Copilot Generated the Steps to Design the Python Script*

2. Create a new Python script file, for example, `scrape_headlines.py`.
3. Implement the script in `scrape_headlines.py`:

```
import requests
from bs4 import BeautifulSoup

def scrape_headlines(url: str):
    # Send a GET request to the URL
    response = requests.get(url)
    response.raise_for_status()  # Raise an exception for HTTP error

    # Parse the HTML content using BeautifulSoup
    soup = BeautifulSoup(response.content, 'html.parser')

    # Find all headline elements (this will vary depending on the wel
    headlines = soup.find_all('h2', class_='headline')  # Adjust the

    # Print each headline
    for headline in headlines:
        print(headline.get_text(strip=True))

if __name__ == "__main__":
    # Replace with the URL of the news website you want to scrape
    news_url = 'https://example.com/news'
    scrape_headlines(news_url)
```

4. Run the script:

```
python scrape_headlines.py
```

Make sure to adjust the tag and class in the `soup.find_all` method to match the structure of the news website you are scraping. For example, if the headlines are in `<h1>` tags with a class of `title`, you would use `soup.find_all('h1', class_='title')`.

Figure 4.5: *Python Function Designed to Scrape and Print Headlines from any News Website*

Figure 4.5 showcases a Python function that scrapes and prints headlines from a specified news website. It provides the code setup and steps to customize the tag and class based on the website's structure.

From the preceding discussion, we observe how GitHub Copilot automates the generation of boilerplate code for scraping headlines from a website. It also demonstrates how you can quickly combine different Python libraries.

Data Analysis with Pandas

Python is a popular choice for data analysis due to the **`pandas`** library. Copilot can assist by autocompleting the common data manipulation tasks.

Prompt:

```
/workspace Write a Python function that reads a CSV file using pandas and calculates the average value of a column named 'price'.
```

Copilot Output:

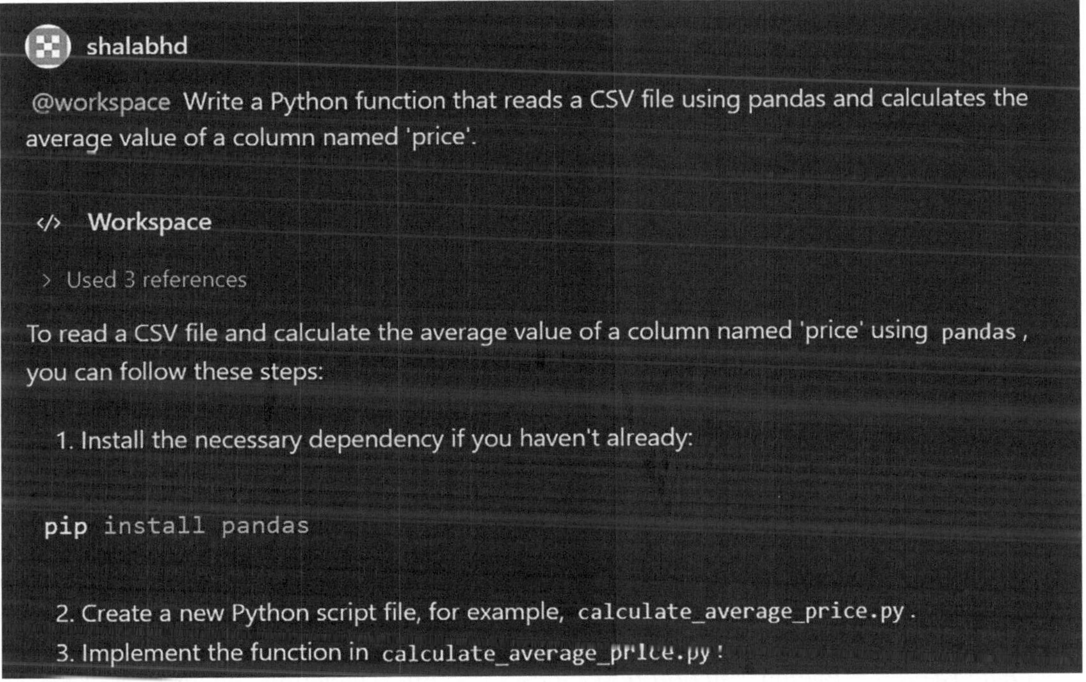

Figure 4.6: *Copilot Suggestions Derived the Steps to Implement the Function to Read CSV File Using Pandas*

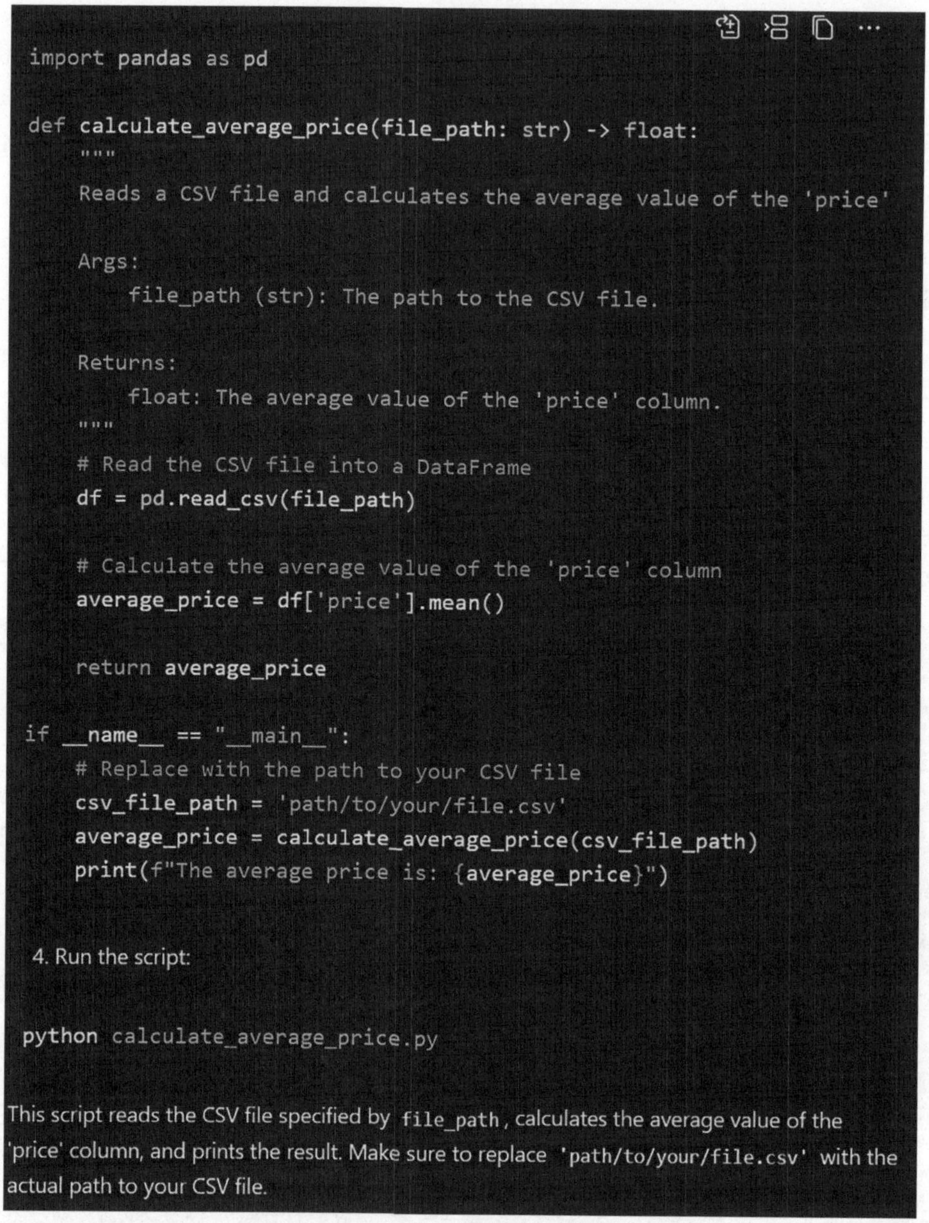

```python
import pandas as pd

def calculate_average_price(file_path: str) -> float:
    """
    Reads a CSV file and calculates the average value of the 'price'

    Args:
        file_path (str): The path to the CSV file.

    Returns:
        float: The average value of the 'price' column.
    """
    # Read the CSV file into a DataFrame
    df = pd.read_csv(file_path)

    # Calculate the average value of the 'price' column
    average_price = df['price'].mean()

    return average_price

if __name__ == "__main__":
    # Replace with the path to your CSV file
    csv_file_path = 'path/to/your/file.csv'
    average_price = calculate_average_price(csv_file_path)
    print(f"The average price is: {average_price}")
```

4. Run the script:

```
python calculate_average_price.py
```

This script reads the CSV file specified by `file_path`, calculates the average value of the 'price' column, and prints the result. Make sure to replace `'path/to/your/file.csv'` with the actual path to your CSV file.

Figure 4.7: Python Function Designed to Calculate the Average Price

Figure 4.7 demonstrates a Python function that reads a CSV file, calculates the average of the **`'price'`** *column, and displays the result. Hence, follow the instructions given in Figure 4.7 to set up, and run the script with your CSV file.*

Web Development in Python with AI Assistance

Python is often used to build web applications, and frameworks such as **Flask** and **Django** are among the most popular. Copilot can help by setting up web servers, defining routes, and connecting the frontend and backend of web applications.

Building a Simple API with Flask

Now, let us see how Copilot assists in building a REST API using Flask.

Prompt:

```
/workspace Write a Flask API with a single route `/status` that returns a JSON
response indicating that the API is running.
```

Copilot Output:

shalabhd

@workspace Write a Flask API with a single route `/status` that returns a JSON response indicat-ing the API is running.

</> Workspace

> Used 6 references

To create a Flask API with a single route `/status` that returns a JSON response indicating the API is running, follow these steps:

1. Install Flask if you haven't already:

```
pip install Flask
```

2. Create a new Python script file, for example, `app.py`.
3. Implement the Flask API in `app.py`:

```
from flask import Flask, jsonify

app = Flask(__name__)

@app.route('/status', methods=['GET'])
def status():
    return jsonify({"status": "API is running"}), 200

if __name__ == "__main__":
    app.run(debug=True)
```

4. Run the Flask application:

```
python app.py
```

This script sets up a simple Flask API with a single route `/status` that returns a JSON response indicating the API is running. When you run the script, the Flask development server will start, and you can access the `/status` endpoint by navigating to `http://127.0.0.1:5000/status` in your web browser or using a tool like `curl` or Postman.

Figure 4.8: *Python to Design a Flask API with a Single Route/Status*

Thus, we have seen how with minimal input, Copilot generates the code for a basic Flask API, showing how it can help with common web development tasks like setting up routes, and handling responses.

Using Django for Web Applications

Django is a more comprehensive framework than Flask, and it is used to build large-scale web applications. Copilot can help with setting up models, views, and URL routing in Django applications.

Prompt:

```
/workspace Create a Django model for a Product with fields for name,
description, and price.
```

Copilot Output:

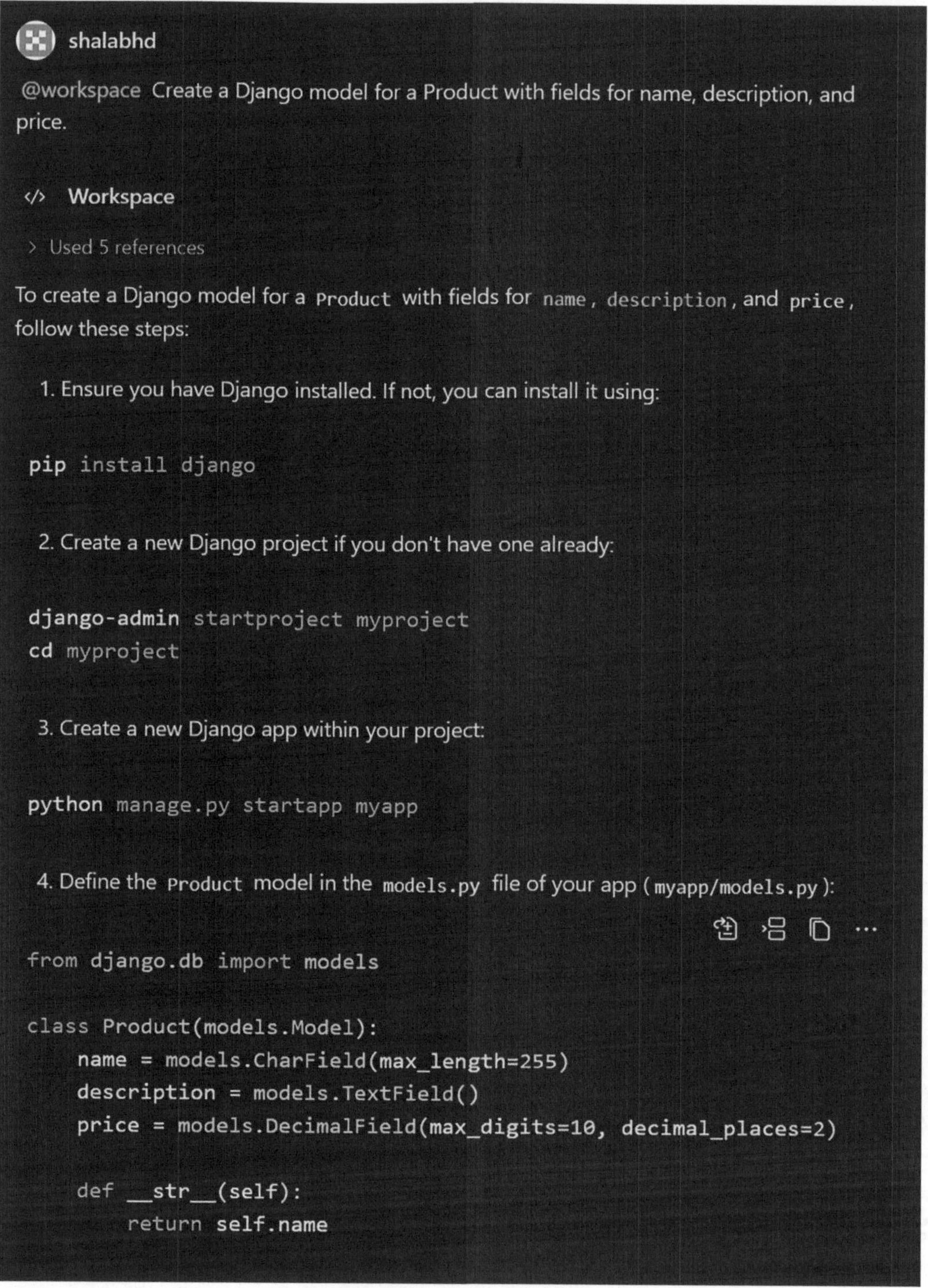

Figure 4.9: *Copilot Listed Detailed Steps to Create a Django Model for a Product with Various Fields*

5. Add your app to the `INSTALLED_APPS` list in the `settings.py` file of your project (`myproject/settings.py`):

```
INSTALLED_APPS = [
    ...
    'myapp',
    ...
]
```

6. Create and apply the migrations to update the database schema:

```
python manage.py makemigrations
python manage.py migrate
```

7. Optionally, you can create an admin interface for the `Product` model by registering it in the `admin.py` file of your app (`myapp/admin.py`):

```
from django.contrib import admin
from .models import Product

@admin.register(Product)
class ProductAdmin(admin.ModelAdmin):
    list_display = ('name', 'price')
    search_fields = ('name',)
```

8. Create a superuser to access the Django admin interface:

```
python manage.py createsuperuser
```

9. Run the development server:

```
python manage.py runserver
```

You can now access the Django admin interface at `http://127.0.0.1:8000/admin` and manage your `Product` entries.

Figure 4.10: *Steps to Add a New App in Django: Update Settings, Migrate Database, Create Admin Interface, and Run the Server*

We have seen, how Copilot generates a Django model with all the required fields, reducing the time spent on boilerplate code. It even adds **a `__str__`** method to display the product name when needed.

It has also provided the detailed steps to setup the project, installation details, and creating directory structure which makes it very simple to start the journey.

Python for Data Analysis and Machine Learning

Python's extensive ecosystem for data analysis and machine learning is one of its strongest features. Libraries , such as **NumPy**, **Pandas**, **Scikit-learn**, and **TensorFlow** provide powerful tools for building complex models. GitHub Copilot can be an invaluable assistant for generating code that implements machine learning algorithms, data preprocessing, and model evaluation.

Data Preprocessing with Pandas

Data preprocessing is often required before feeding data into machine learning models. Copilot can help generate the steps needed for cleaning and transforming datasets.

Prompt:

```
/workspace Write a Python script that fills missing values in a DataFrame using the column median.
```

Copilot Output:

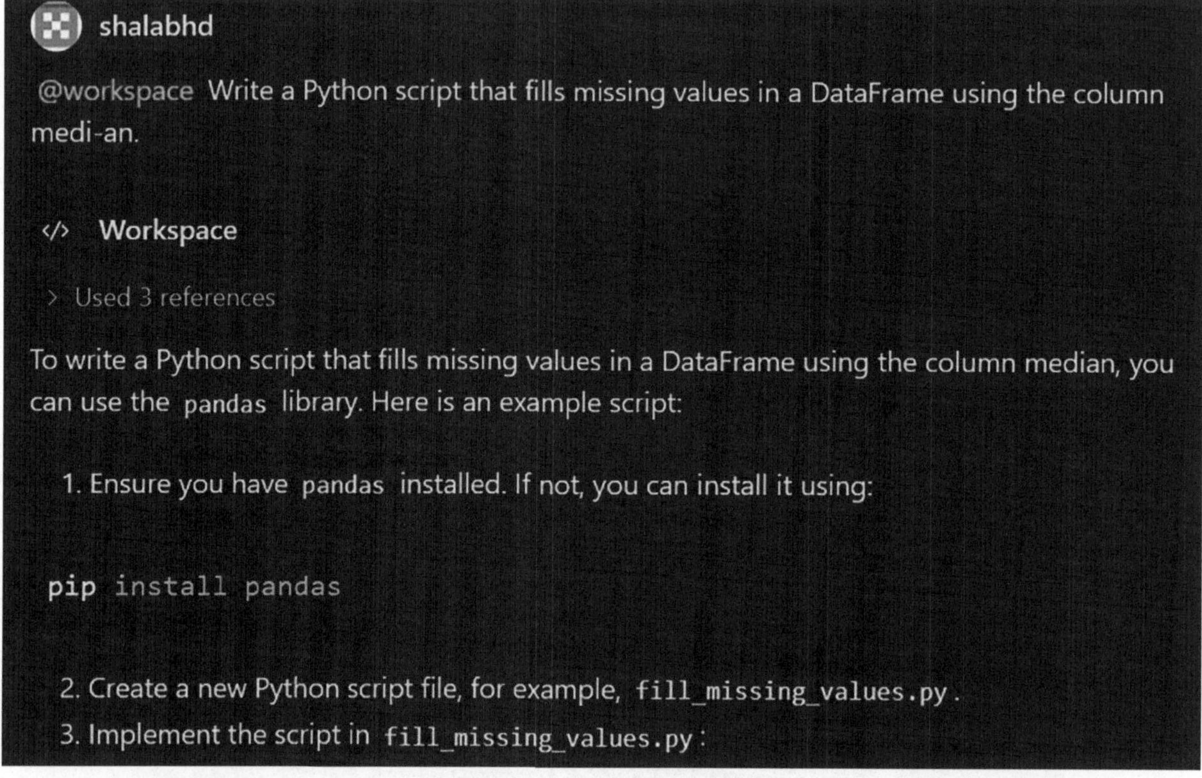

Figure 4.11: *Steps to Create a Python Script to Fill the Missing Values in a DataFrame Using Median*

Figure 4.11 provides a step-by-step guide to creating the Python script. It starts with installing the pandas library, creating the script file, and implementing the function. This image also shows how to run the script to fill the missing values in a DataFrame, using the column median.

Before proceeding, readers are reminded to install the **pandas** library, if it is not already installed. The script is saved as **`fill_missing_values.py`**, and can be executed to observe the behavior first-hand. This practice helps reinforce the concept of handling missing values effectively, ensuring data quality in subsequent analysis or machine learning workflows. Thus, by leveraging the median value for imputation, this technique mitigates the impact of outliers, and maintains a robust dataset for further insights.

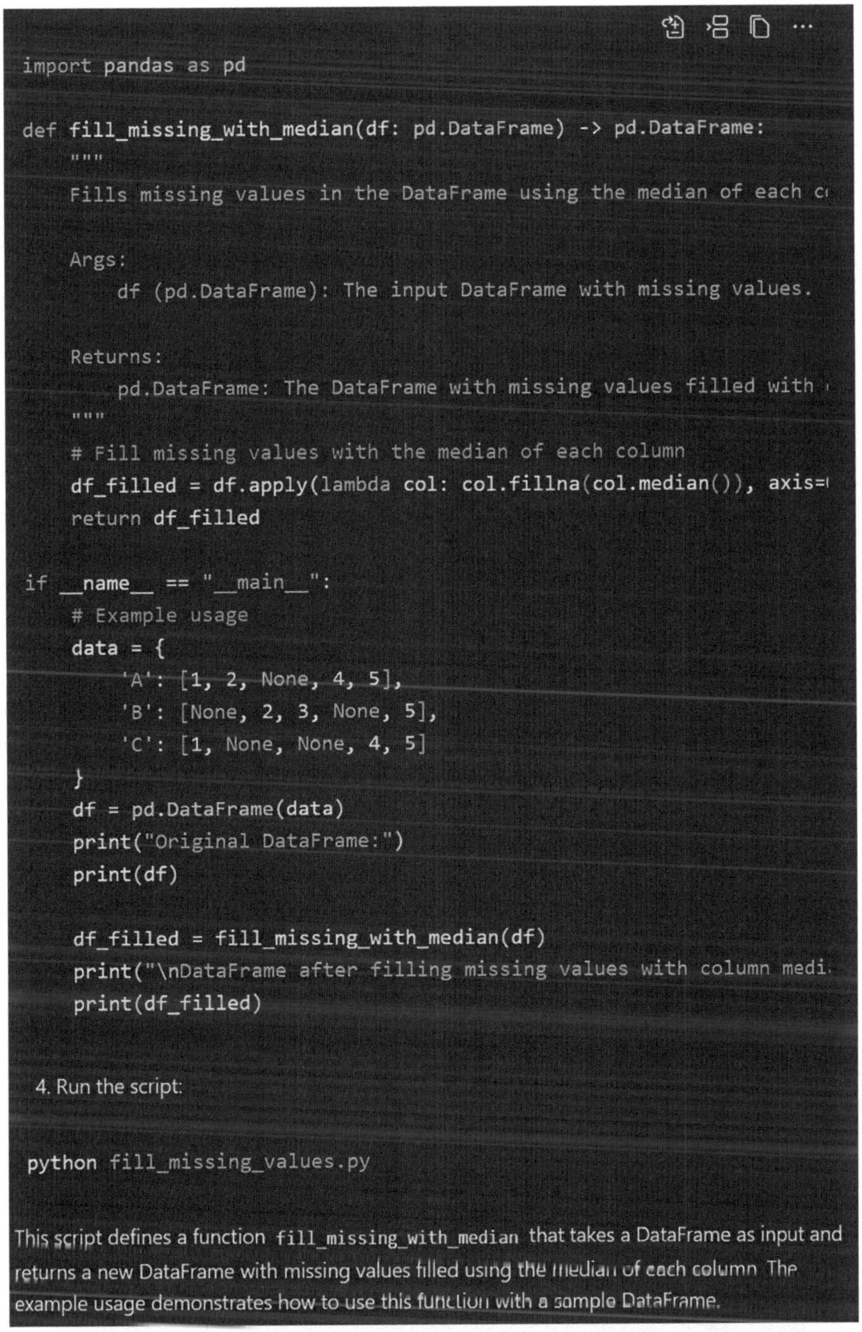

```
import pandas as pd

def fill_missing_with_median(df: pd.DataFrame) -> pd.DataFrame:
    """
    Fills missing values in the DataFrame using the median of each c

    Args:
        df (pd.DataFrame): The input DataFrame with missing values.

    Returns:
        pd.DataFrame: The DataFrame with missing values filled with
    """
    # Fill missing values with the median of each column
    df_filled = df.apply(lambda col: col.fillna(col.median()), axis=
    return df_filled

if __name__ == "__main__":
    # Example usage
    data = {
        'A': [1, 2, None, 4, 5],
        'B': [None, 2, 3, None, 5],
        'C': [1, None, None, 4, 5]
    }
    df = pd.DataFrame(data)
    print("Original DataFrame:")
    print(df)

    df_filled = fill_missing_with_median(df)
    print("\nDataFrame after filling missing values with column medi
    print(df_filled)
```

4. Run the script:

```
python fill_missing_values.py
```

This script defines a function `fill_missing_with_median` that takes a DataFrame as input and returns a new DataFrame with missing values filled using the median of each column. The example usage demonstrates how to use this function with a sample DataFrame.

Figure 4.12: *Python Script for Filling Missing DataFrame Values Using Column Median*

Figure 4.12 shows the Python script that defines the **`fill_missing_with_median()`** function. This function takes a DataFrame as input, and fills in the missing values using the median of each column. The image also demonstrates the example usage of this function, displaying the original DataFrame, and the modified DataFrame after imputation.

Building a Machine Learning Model with Scikit-Learn

Machine learning is a key area where Python excels. Copilot can assist in building models by generating boilerplate code, and suggesting common workflows.

Prompt:

`/workspace Write a Python script to train a decision tree classifier using scikit-learn.`

Copilot Output:

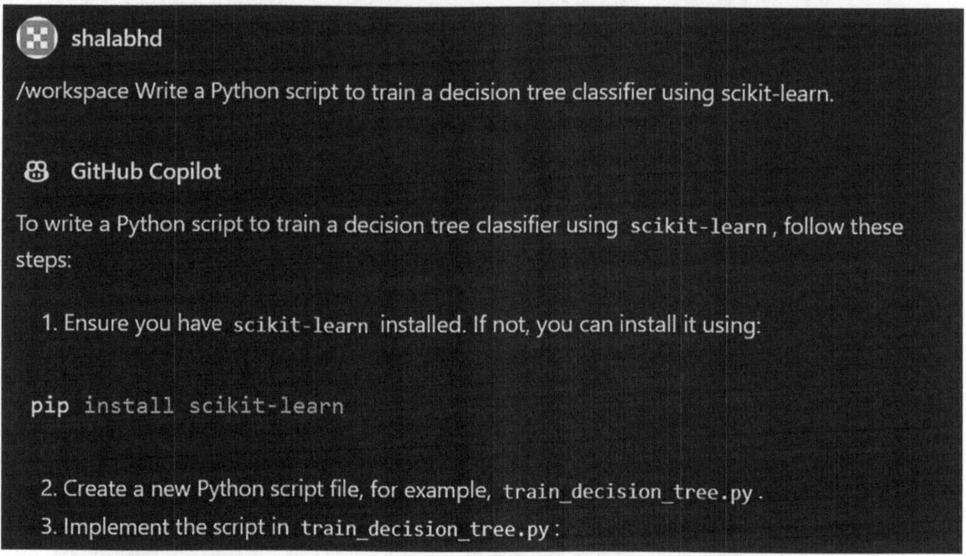

Figure 4.13: *Steps to Create and Train a Decision Tree Classifier in Python*

Figure 4.13 clearly provides instructions on setting up a Python environment for training a decision tree classifier using scikit-learn. It covers installation, creating the script file, and implementing the classifier, detailing each step for easy understanding.

```
import pandas as pd
from sklearn.model_selection import train_test_split
from sklearn.tree import DecisionTreeClassifier
from sklearn.metrics import accuracy_score

def train_decision_tree_classifier(data_path: str, target_column: st
    # Load the dataset
    df = pd.read_csv(data_path)

    # Split the dataset into features and target
    X = df.drop(columns=[target_column])
    y = df[target_column]

    # Split the data into training and testing sets
    X_train, X_test, y_train, y_test = train_test_split(X, y, test_s

    # Initialize the Decision Tree Classifier
    clf = DecisionTreeClassifier()

    # Train the classifier
    clf.fit(X_train, y_train)

    # Make predictions on the test set
    y_pred = clf.predict(X_test)

    # Calculate the accuracy of the classifier
    accuracy = accuracy_score(y_test, y_pred)
    print(f"Accuracy: {accuracy:.2f}")

if __name__ == "__main__":
    # Replace with the path to your CSV file and the target column n
    data_path = 'path/to/your/dataset.csv'
    target_column = 'target'
    train_decision_tree_classifier(data_path, target_column)
```

Figure 4.14: *Python Code for Decision Tree Training, Using Scikit-learn. Steps to Create and Train a Decision Tree Classifier in Python. Script to Train a Decision Tree Classifier Using Scikit-learn*

Explanation

- The script defines a function `train_decision_tree_classifier` that takes the path to a CSV file and the name of the target column as input.
- It loads the dataset using `pandas`.
- It splits the dataset into features (`X`) and target (`y`).
- It further splits the data into training and testing sets using `train_test_split`.
- It initializes a `DecisionTreeClassifier` and trains it on the training data.
- It makes predictions on the test set and calculates the accuracy of the classifier using `accuracy_score`.
- The `if __name__ == "__main__":` block allows the function to be run as a script with specified data path and target column.

Instructions

1. **Create the file**:
   - Create a new file named `train_decision_tree.py` in your project directory.
   - Copy and paste the above code into `train_decision_tree.py`.
2. **Run the script**:
   - Open a terminal and navigate to the directory containing `train_decision_tree.py`.
   - Run the script using the following command:

```
python train_decision_tree.py
```

Make sure to replace `'path/to/your/dataset.csv'` with the actual path to your CSV file and `'target'` with the name of the target column in your dataset.

Figure 4.15: *Detailed Explanation and Instructions of the Code*

Figure 4.15 demonstrates how to build, and run a Decision Tree Classifier in Python. It explains the code structure and provides clear steps for setting up, and executing the script with your dataset, including loading data, training, and evaluating model accuracy.

Before proceeding, readers are reminded to install the pandas library, if it is not already installed. The script is saved as **`fill_missing_values.py`**, and can be executed to observe the behavior first-hand. This practice helps reinforce the concept of handling missing values effectively, ensuring data quality in subsequent analysis or machine learning workflows. By leveraging the median value for imputation, this technique mitigates the impact of outliers, and maintains a robust dataset for further insights.

Writing Memory-Efficient Python Code with GitHub Copilot

One of Python's strengths–its simplicity–can sometimes hide performance pitfalls, especially when working with large datasets or I/O-heavy applications. Developers may unintentionally write code that works fine at small scale, but struggles with speed or memory usage when scaled.

While GitHub Copilot is not a performance analyzer, it **helps guide you toward writing cleaner, more efficient Python code**–especially if you give it clear prompts. Therefore, whether you are processing a large CSV, scraping web pages, or reading logs, Copilot can suggest **memory-friendly patterns like generators, lazy iteration, and context-aware I/O**–patterns, even seasoned developers appreciate.

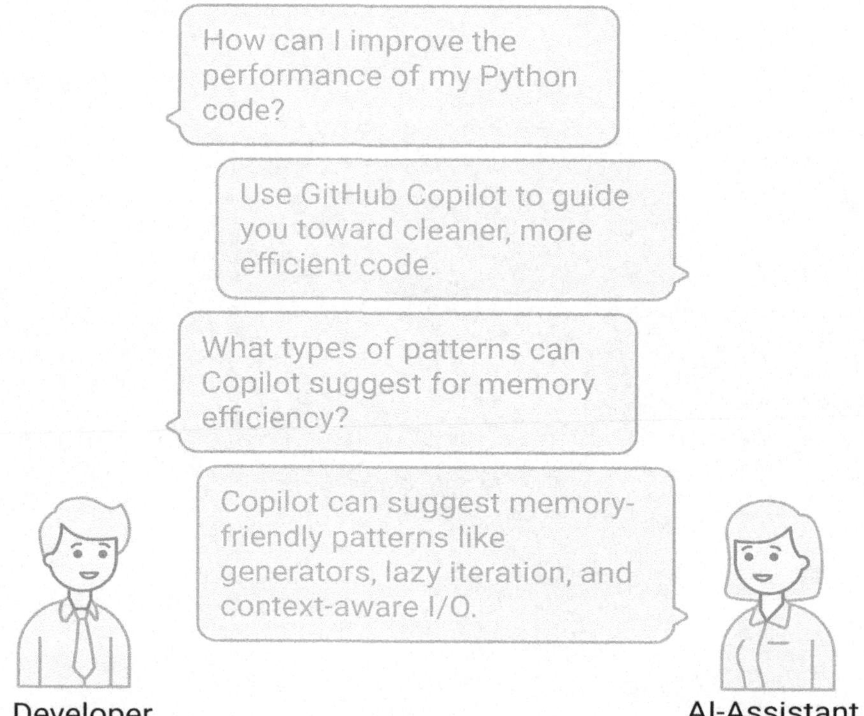

Figure 4.16: *Writing Memory-Efficient Python Code with GitHub Copilot*

This visual demonstrates a fictional exchange, a developer seeks guidance on optimizing Python code performance. The AI assistant–GitHub Copilot–responds with practical strategies for writing cleaner, memory-efficient code, such as generators, lazy iteration, and context-aware I/O to improve Python code performance.

Now, let us walk through a relatable example.

Scenario: Counting Log Entries in a Large File

Imagine, you are working with a production log file that is several gigabytes in size. You need to count how many times the word, "**error**" appears.

You type in the prompt in GitHub Copilot:

```
# Count the number of lines that contain 'error' in a large file using a
memory-efficient approach
```

Copilot Suggestion:

```
def count_errors(file_path):
    count = 0
    with open(file_path, 'r') as file:
        for line in file:
            if 'error' in line.lower():
                count += 1
    return count
```

Why this is memory-efficient: The file is read line-by-line using a generator (that is the file object is iterable), so no matter how large the file is, only one line is in memory at a time. This is a common best practice–and Copilot suggests it, without you needing to remember the syntax.

The Alternative (What Not to Do):

```
with open(file_path, 'r') as file:
    lines = file.readlines()
```

While this works, it **loads the entire file into memory**—which may crash or severely slow down your script for large files. Copilot might suggest this if your prompt is vague (e.g., "`count lines with error`") or if it detects small-scale context. **That's why clear prompts matter.**

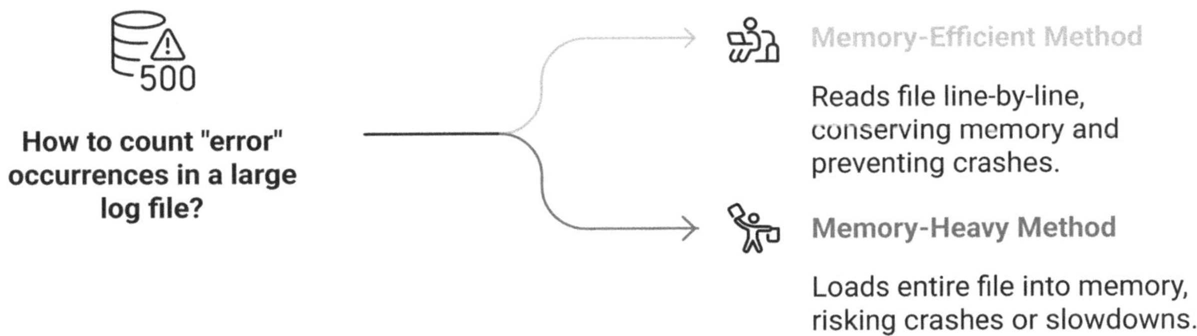

Figure 4.17: *Choosing the Right Prompt-Driven Strategy for Log File Analysis with GitHub Copilot*

In this scenario, a developer uses GitHub Copilot to count occurrences of the word, "`error`" in a massive log file. When the prompt is clearly phrased to focus on memory efficiency, Copilot suggests a line-by-line approach—processing one line at a time, and conserving memory. In contrast, vague prompts may lead Copilot to suggest loading the entire file into memory which can crash the script for large files. This diagram contrasts both outcomes, highlighting how clear prompt design directly impacts performance and reliability in real-world coding situations.

Let Us Take It Further: Use a Generator Expression

If you refine your prompt:

```
# Use a generator to count error lines
```

Copilot suggests:

```
def count_errors(file_path):
    with open(file_path, 'r') as file:
        return sum(1 for line in file if 'error' in line.lower())
```

This is even more elegant and **Pythonic**. Thus, it is memory-efficient, concise, and easy to read. This is where Copilot shines—it recognizes patterns and completes your thoughts with a clean code.

Memory-Efficient Copilot Prompts with Real-World Scenarios

As your Python projects grow in scale and complexity, writing memory-efficient code becomes essential—especially when dealing with large files, datasets, or long-running scripts. GitHub Copilot can help you apply the best practices for performance by suggesting the right constructs, when prompted thoughtfully.

The following table outlines a collection of practical prompts, you can use with Copilot, what kind of code it typically suggests, and real-world scenarios where each is most effective. Use this as your go-to reference, when aiming to write leaner, faster, and more scalable Python code.

Prompt	What Copilot Suggests	When to Use It (Scenario)
`# Stream a large CSV and parse each row`	`csv.reader()` + with `open()`	Processing log or transactional data without crashing the system
`# Count the number of lines in a large file without loading it all into memory`	`sum(1 for _ in open(file_path))`	Pre-validating line-based logs or flat files before processing
`# Read a JSONL file one object at a time`	`json.loads()` line-by-line	Handling streaming APIs or logs in JSONL format
`# Iterate over a large list lazily`	yield or generator expression	Avoiding memory spikes when processing long lists or sequences
`# Create a Python generator to read records in batches from a file`	yield batches using `islice()`	Batching database inserts or API calls efficiently
`# Filter a large dataset with a generator expression`	Inline generator filters	Avoiding temp lists while filtering millions of records
`# Process only the first 1000 rows from a large file`	Manual counter or `islice()`	Sampling data for debugging, preview, or profiling
`# Use defaultdict to count word occurrences in a stream of text lines`	`collections.defaultdict(int)`	Efficient word counts in NLP or text analysis
`# Parse a large XML document incrementally`	`ElementTree.iterparse()`	Parsing complex XML exports from systems like SAP or Salesforce
`# Process a large list of files without loading all filenames at once`	`os.scandir()` or `pathlib.iterdir()`	Large-scale file I/O, backup scripts, or directory indexing
`# Read compressed CSV from disk using minimal memory`	`gzip.open()` + `csv.reader()`	Working with compressed archives or logs
`# Lazy-load images from a directory for processing`	`PIL.Image.open()` in loop	Avoiding memory bottlenecks in image preprocessing pipelines
`# Process lines of a large file and yield only those matching a pattern`	Generator with regex	Streaming log filtering for keywords like "ERROR", "FAIL"
`# Stream HTTP response content in chunks`	`requests.get(..., stream=True)`	Handling large downloads or API streams
`# Use a generator to apply transformations to each row in a CSV file`	yield with `DictReader()` or `map()`	Pipeline-style data transformation during ETL
`# Generate Fibonacci numbers using a generator`	Infinite or capped generator	Teaching recursion and memory-safe looping logic
`# Write a memory-efficient data pipeline with steps for filter, map, reduce`	Chained generators or `functools.reduce()`	Building composable, readable ETL pipelines
`# Efficiently merge two sorted iterators without loading full lists`	`heapq.merge()`	Combining time-sorted logs or query results
`# Replace large lists with set-based lookup to reduce memory and time`	if x in `set()`	High-volume data validation or deduplication tasks

Table 4.1: *Memory-Efficient Python Prompts with Copilot Suggestions and Use Cases*

A curated collection of practical Copilot prompts to help you write a scalable, optimized Python code for real-world data-heavy scenarios.

AI-Powered Code Optimization Techniques

Python code often needs optimization, whether it is improving performance or reducing memory usage. Thus, GitHub Copilot can suggest refactors and optimizations that improve code efficiency.

Optimizing Loops and Iterations

Loops are often an area where performance bottlenecks occur. Copilot can suggest efficient ways to optimize them.

Prompt:

```
/workspace Optimize a Python for-loop that sums elements in a list.
```

Copilot's Output:

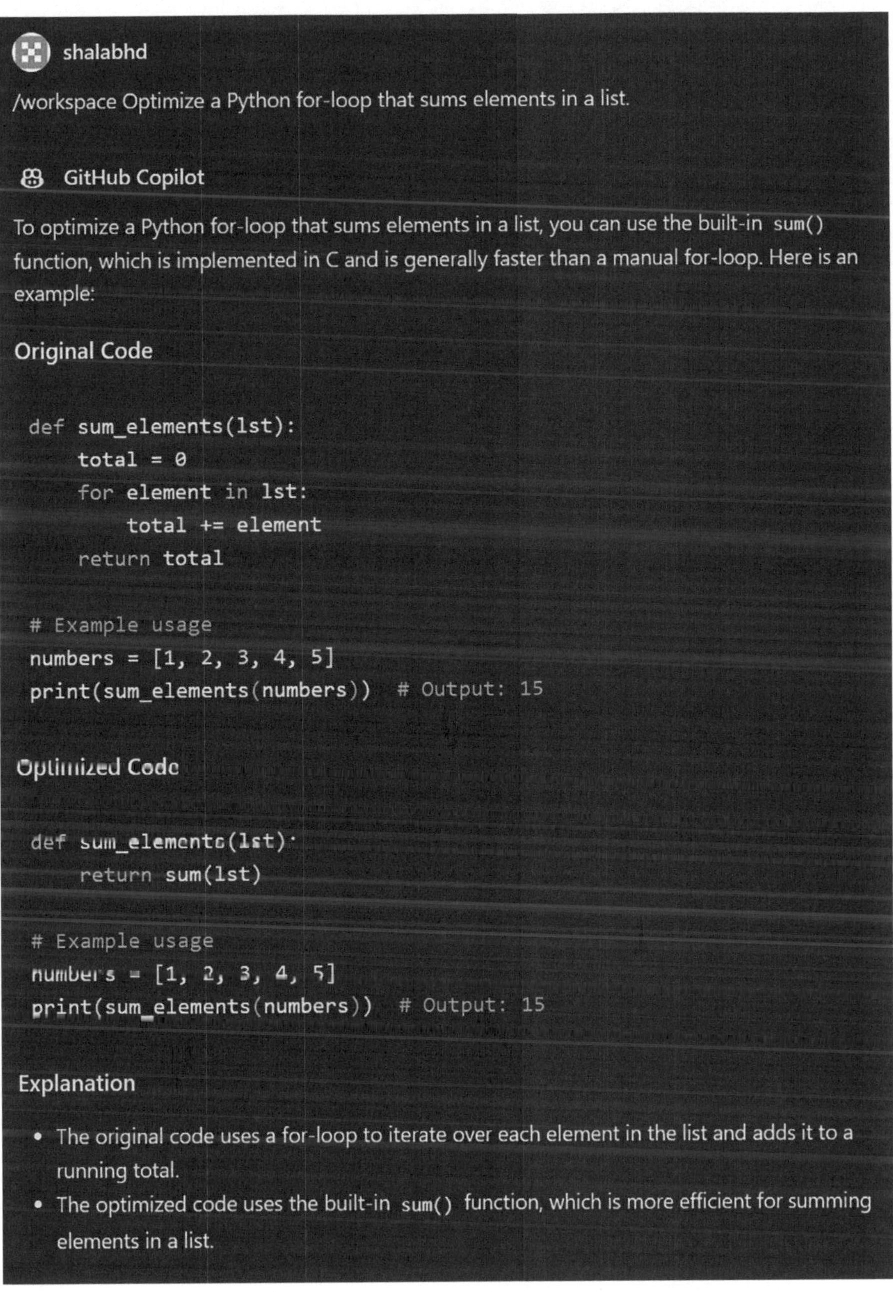

Figure 4.18: *Original Code and Optimized Code Examples Generated Using Copilot*

Explanation

- The original code uses a for-loop to iterate over each element in the list and adds it to a running total.
- The optimized code uses the built-in `sum()` function, which is more efficient for summing elements in a list.

Instructions

1. **Create the file**:
   - Create a new file named `sum_elements.py` in your project directory.
   - Copy and paste the optimized code into `sum_elements.py`.
2. **Run the script**:
   - Open a terminal and navigate to the directory containing `sum_elements.py`.
   - Run the script using the following command:

```
python sum_elements.py
```

This will print the sum of the elements in the list, which is `15` in this example.

Figure 4.19: *Detailed Explanation and Instructions of the Code*

Thus, by suggesting the use of Python's built-in sum function, Copilot improves both the readability and performance of the code.

Security Considerations for AI-Generated Code

While GitHub Copilot can accelerate development, it is vital to apply **sound judgment**—especially when building production applications.

Hence, AI-generated code should always be:

- Reviewed for accuracy and completeness.
- Checked for proper input validation and sanitization.
- Examined for compliance with security standards.

This is particularly critical in machine learning workflows, where:

- Data leakage
- Misapplied models
- Unsecured APIs or exposed credentials can lead to unintended consequences.

Therefore, think of Copilot as a high-speed assistant—it helps you to move faster, but **you are still the driver**. Regular code reviews, security testing, and strong domain understanding remain necessary to ensure safe and reliable outcomes.

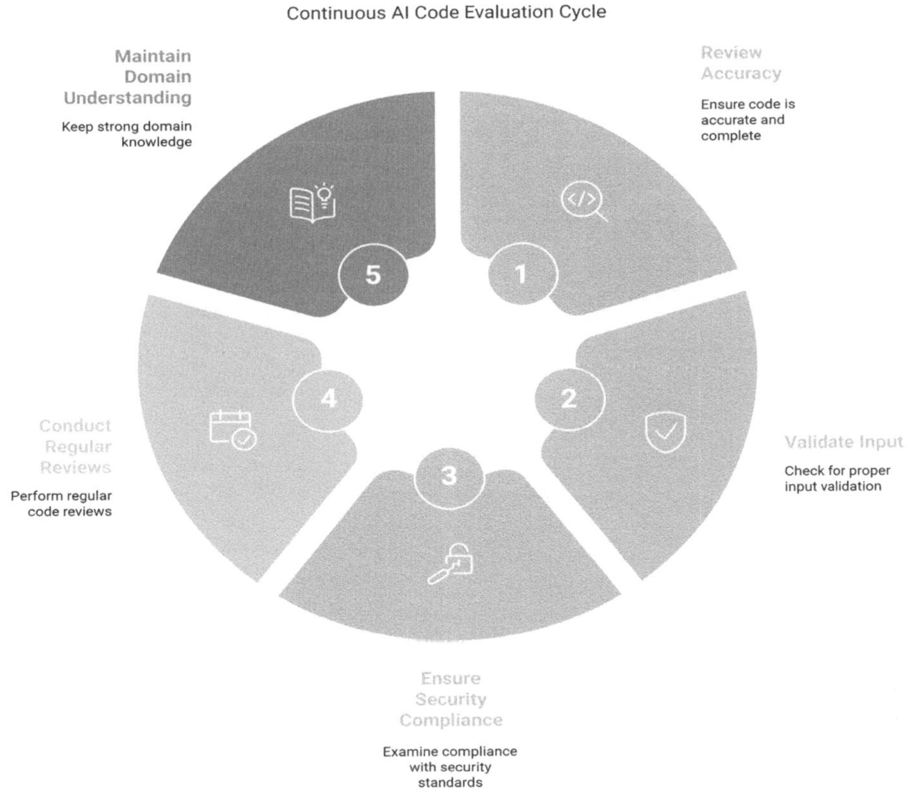

Figure 4.20: *Continuous AI Code Evaluation Cycle Showcasing Five Essential Checkpoints to Ensure Code Quality, Security, and Contextual Relevance*

This diagram outlines a continuous loop for evaluating AI-generated or assisted code, emphasizing accuracy checks, input validation, security compliance, regular reviews, and the ongoing domain knowledge to maintain robust and reliable software quality.

Using GitHub Copilot in Jupyter Notebooks

For data scientists and ML practitioners, **Jupyter Notebooks** are a preferred environment for exploratory coding, data visualization, and iterative experimentation. GitHub Copilot now integrates directly into Jupyter environments (including JupyterLab and VS Code's notebook interface), providing AI-driven assistance within cells as you work.

This makes it especially powerful for:

- Generating quick visualizations.
- Writing data pre-processing pipelines.
- Suggesting model evaluation metrics.
- Filling out repetitive import/setup code.

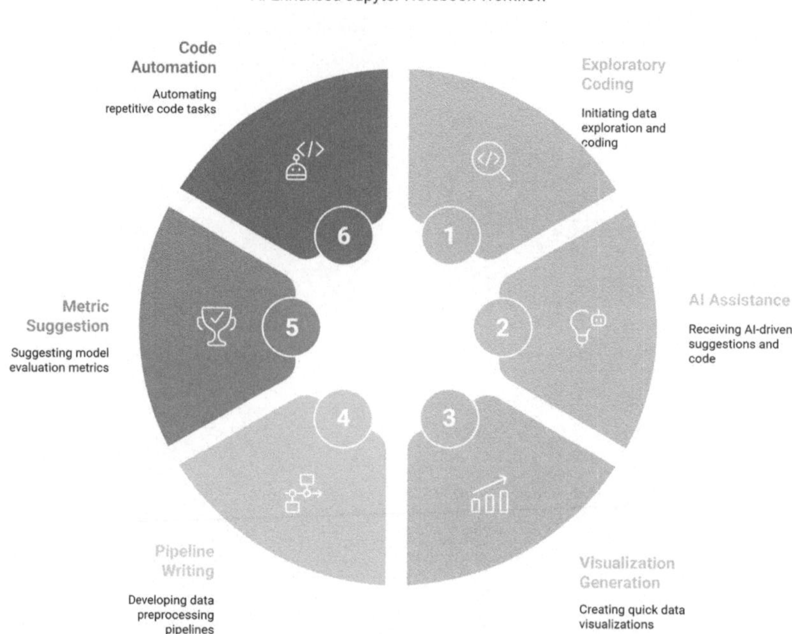

Figure 4.21: *AI-driven Jupyter Notebook Workflow Streamlining Tasks from Exploratory Coding to Metric Suggestion and Automation*

This diagram illustrates a streamlined, AI-assisted workflow within Jupyter Notebooks, covering six key stages of the data science process. It begins with **exploratory coding**, and followed by **AI assistance** for intelligent code suggestions. The workflow continues with **visualization generation** and **pipeline writing** to automate data preparation. AI then supports **metric suggestion** for model evaluation, and concludes with **code automation** to eliminate repetitive tasks. Together, these stages showcase how AI tools enhance productivity, accuracy, and efficiency throughout the entire notebook-based development cycle.

Prompt Example in a Notebook Cell:

```
# Create a seaborn barplot showing total sales per region from a DataFrame
```

Copilot Suggestion:

```
import seaborn as sns
import matplotlib.pyplot as plt

sns.barplot(x='region', y='total_sales', data=df)
plt.title("Total Sales by Region")
plt.show()
```

Thus, instead of switching tabs or Googling syntax, data professionals can stay focused in-flow–exploring datasets, while Copilot fills in context-aware scaffolding. This not only saves time, but also encourages good practices like labeling graphs, validating data structures, and formatting clean output.

Thus, Copilot in notebooks is especially valuable during experimentation, helping users move from raw data to insight more efficiently–without getting bogged down in boilerplate.

Using Python 3.12 Features with GitHub Copilot

Modern Python includes powerful features like improved concurrency support, stronger type safety, and more transparent error diagnostics. Copilot understands these updates, and can help you implement them quickly and correctly.

Therefore, let us look at a few key enhancements introduced in Python 3.12. and how Copilot helps apply them in real projects.

Example 1: Enforcing Method Contracts with `typing.override`

Prompt to Copilot:

```
# Define a class with a method override using typing.override
```

Copilot Output:

```
from typing import override

class Animal:
    def speak(self) -> str:
        return "Some sound"

class Dog(Animal):
    @override
    def speak(self) -> str:
        return "Woof"
```

This new decorator ensures that overridden methods in subclasses match their base class signature, helping avoid subtle bugs. Copilot not only suggests the correct syntax–it also recognizes the parent-child relationship context, and generates consistent structure.

Example 2: Concurrent Execution with `asyncio.TaskGroup`

Prompt to Copilot:

```
# Write an async function in Python 3.12 using TaskGroup to run multiple tasks
```

Copilot Output:

```
import asyncio

async def fetch_data(source):
    await asyncio.sleep(1)
    return f"Data from {source}"

async def main():
    async with asyncio.TaskGroup() as tg:
        tg.create_task(fetch_data("API A"))
        tg.create_task(fetch_data("API B"))

asyncio.run(main())
```

With Python 3.12's new TaskGroup feature, managing concurrent tasks becomes safer and easier. Hence, Copilot detects when you are writing async code, and will often suggest this updated structure, without being explicitly prompted–especially when working on I/O-heavy code.

Real-World Debugging with Copilot in Python

Debugging is a crucial part of any development workflow–and GitHub Copilot is not just helpful for writing new code, but also for **identifying, explaining, and resolving issues** in the existing code. Now, let us walk through a few realistic debugging cases where Copilot acts like a second pair of eyes, guiding you toward the fix.

Case: Unhandled Edge Case in Data Processing

Problem: Code crashes when the input list is empty.

```
def get_average(nums):
    return sum(nums) / len(nums)
```

Prompt to Copilot:

```
# Fix the bug when nums is an empty list
```

Copilot Suggestion:

```
def get_average(nums):
    if not nums:
        return 0
    return sum(nums) / len(nums)
```

Impact: Copilot identifies a zero-division edge case, and adds a safe default. This is a common oversight–especially in scripts that process real-world datasets.

Case: Incorrect Data Type in API Response

Problem: You expected a list but got a string.

```
data = response.json()
for item in data:
    print(item)
```

Prompt to Copilot Chat:

```
"Why is this code throwing a TypeError?"
```

Copilot Explanation:

"The API may be returning a dictionary with a key holding the actual list. Try checking data.keys() or accessing a specific field."

Fix Copilot Suggests:

```
for item in data['results']:
    print(item)
```

Impact: Thus, Copilot helps you understand the structure mismatch, and suggests a fix by analyzing variable types–reducing time spent inspecting logs manually.

Copilot Prompts That Work Great for Debugging

When it comes to debugging, GitHub Copilot can do more than just fix syntax. It can help you trace logic errors, improve exception handling, and rewrite faulty code blocks–all through well-crafted prompts. The following is a curated list of practical prompts that work particularly well for debugging Python code, along with the kinds of fixes or insights, Copilot is likely to suggest.

Prompt	What Copilot Can Do
`# Explain why this function returns None`	Diagnoses missing return values
`# Fix this loop that doesn't terminate`	Detects incorrect loop condition
`# Identify and fix the off-by-one error`	Adjusts range or indexing logic
`# Add error handling to this function`	Adds try/except blocks with helpful messages

`# Debug a JSONDecodeError`	Suggests `.get()` fallback, try/except, or schema validation
`# Find why this code is slow`	Suggests profiling, removing redundancy, or using `set`/`dict` for lookup

Table 4.2: *Copilot Debugging Prompts and Their Expected Behavior*

A handy collection of AI prompts to help developers quickly identify and fix common bugs, improve code robustness, and resolve tricky runtime issues with GitHub Copilot.

Conclusion

This chapter highlighted how GitHub Copilot enhances Python development by automating repetitive tasks, generating intelligent suggestions, and streamlining everything from basic scripting to machine learning workflows.

We also covered setup, everyday tasks like file handling and data processing, and advanced topics, including API development with Flask and Django, along with data analysis using pandas and scikit-learn. Copilot helped simplify these workflows, while promoting cleaner, and more maintainable code.

Thus, Python's versatility makes it a top choice across domains, and with Copilot, developers can work faster and smarter. Still, human judgment and a solid grasp of Python fundamentals remain essential for guiding Copilot effectively.

Next, we turn to **Java development with GitHub Copilot**, where you will see how Copilot supports robust backend programming, object-oriented design, and enterprise-scale application development with equal efficiency.

Multiple Choice Questions

1. What is the purpose of a virtual environment in Python?
   a. To create a backup of Python code
   b. To create isolated Python environments for projects
   c. To compile Python scripts into executables
   d. To manage global Python packages
2. Which Python command is used to create a virtual environment?
   a. `python3 -m venv <env name>`
   b. `python -v <env_name>`
   c. `pip install virtualenv`
   d. `python create_env <env_name>`
3. Which of the following Python libraries is used for data manipulation?
   a. `Flask`
   b. `pandas`
   c. `requests`
   d. `BeautifulSoup`

4. What is the output of the following code?

```
def factorial(n):
    return 1 if n == 0 else n * factorial(n-1)
print(factorial(5))
```

   a. 5
   b. 120
   c. 25
   d. 60

5. Which library is commonly used in Python for web scraping?
   a. `matplotlib`
   b. `Flask`
   c. `BeautifulSoup`
   d. `NumPy`

6. Which Python framework is considered a micro-framework for web development?
   a. Django
   b. Flask
   c. Pyramid
   d. CherryPy

7. What method in pandas is used to fill missing values in a DataFrame?
   a. `fill()`
   b. `fillna()`
   c. `replace()`
   d. `dropna()`

8. Which command is used to install a Python package globally?
   a. `python install <package>`
   b. `apt-get install <package>`
   c. `pip install <package>`
   d. `python3 install <package>`

9. In Flask, which method is used to send a JSON response?
   a. `jsonify()`
   b. `render()`
   c. `response()`
   d. `jsonResponse()`

10. Which of the following is an optimization that can be made for processing large files in Python?
    a. Load the entire file into memory.
    b. Read the file line by line.
    c. Use recursion to process the file.
    d. Increase the buffer size.

Answers

1. b
2. a
3. b
4. b
5. c
6. b
7. b
8. c
9. a
10. b

CHAPTER 5
Java with Copilot

Introduction

Python is widely known for its versatility, ease of use, and extensive libraries that support everything from web development to data science and machine learning. AI-assisted coding, especially with GitHub Copilot, can further enhance Python development by generating smart code suggestions, automating repetitive tasks, and ensuring code follow best practices.

In this chapter, we will explore how GitHub Copilot can help with various aspects of Python development, including writing scripts, handling data, building web applications, and implementing machine learning models. Thus, through real-world examples, you will see how AI can assist with Python's powerful features, making coding faster and more efficient.

Structure

In this chapter, we will discuss the following topics:

- Setting Up Java Development with GitHub Copilot
- Basic Java Programming with AI Assistance
- Working with Java Collections and Streams
- Building REST APIs with Spring Boot
- Streamlining Java Development with Copilot
- Best Practices for Enterprise Java Applications
- Building Robust Backend Services
- Integrating Java with Modern Web Frameworks
- Case Studies: Java Projects Transformed by Copilot

Setting Up Java Development with GitHub Copilot

Installing the Java Development Kit (JDK): To start programming in Java, you need to have the Java Development Kit (JDK) installed. **JDK 11** or a higher version is recommended for most modern applications and projects.

Installation Steps for Different Operating Systems

Windows Installation

1. **Download the JDK Installer:** Visit the Oracle JDK website, and download the appropriate version for Windows.

2. **Install the JDK:** Run the downloaded **`.exe`** file, follow the prompts, and accept the license agreement.

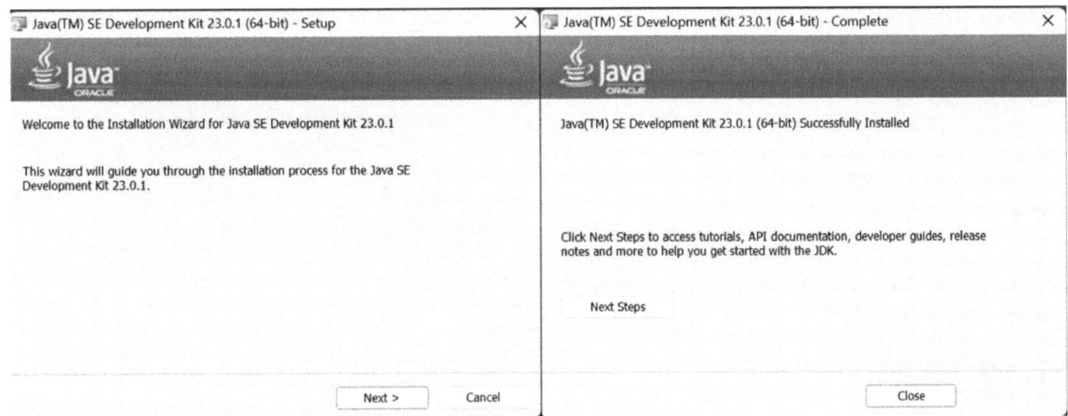

Figure 5.1: *JDK Installation*

3. Add JDK to the System PATH:
4. Open **`Control Panel`** > **`System and Security`** > **`System`** > **`Advanced System Settings`**.
5. Go to **`Environment Variables`**, find the **`Path`** variable, and click **`Edit`**.
6. Add the path to the bin directory of the installed JDK, typically **`C:\Program Files\Java\jdk-<version>\bin`**.
7. Verify Installation:
    a. Open Command Prompt and type:
        i. `java -version`
        ii. `javac -version`
    b. You should see the version details, if the installation was successful.

```
Microsoft Windows [Version 10.0.22631.4317]
(c) Microsoft Corporation. All rights reserved.

C:\Users\SIDDHI DIXIT>java -version
java version "23.0.1" 2024-10-15
Java(TM) SE Runtime Environment (build 23.0.1+11-39)
Java HotSpot(TM) 64-Bit Server VM (build 23.0.1+11-39, mixed mode, sharing)
```

Figure 5.2: *Verifying the Python Version Installed*

The screenshot confirms that the system is currently running Java version **23.0.1**, released on **October 15, 2024**. This version includes the **Java SE Runtime Environment (build `23.0.1+11-39`)** and the **Java HotSpot (TM) 64-Bit Server VM**, indicating a modern and up-to-date Java setup suitable for the latest development frameworks and libraries.

macOS Installation

1. **Install Homebrew** (if not already installed): Homebrew is a package manager for macOS. Open Terminal and run:

```
/bin/bash -c "$(curl -fsSL https://raw.githubusercontent.com/Homebrew/install/HEAD/install.sh)"
```

2. **Install OpenJDK with Homebrew:**

```
brew install openjdk@11
```

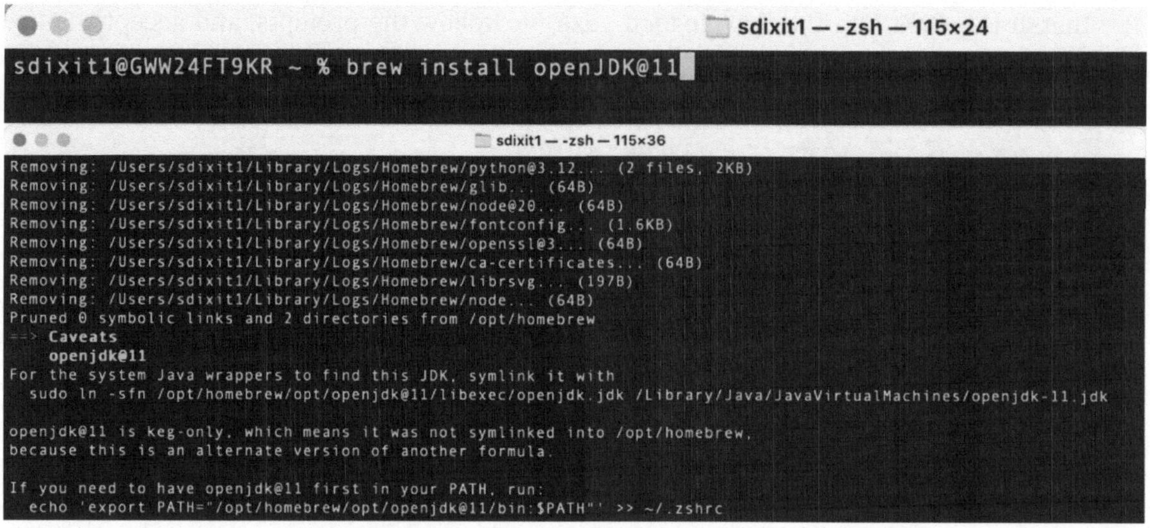

```
sdixit1 — -zsh — 115×24
sdixit1@GWW24FT9KR ~ % brew install openJDK@11
```

```
sdixit1 — -zsh — 115×36
Removing: /Users/sdixit1/Library/Logs/Homebrew/python@3.12... (2 files, 2KB)
Removing: /Users/sdixit1/Library/Logs/Homebrew/glib... (64B)
Removing: /Users/sdixit1/Library/Logs/Homebrew/node@20... (64B)
Removing: /Users/sdixit1/Library/Logs/Homebrew/fontconfig... (1.6KB)
Removing: /Users/sdixit1/Library/Logs/Homebrew/openssl@3... (64B)
Removing: /Users/sdixit1/Library/Logs/Homebrew/ca-certificates... (64B)
Removing: /Users/sdixit1/Library/Logs/Homebrew/librsvg... (197B)
Removing: /Users/sdixit1/Library/Logs/Homebrew/node... (64B)
Pruned 0 symbolic links and 2 directories from /opt/homebrew
==> Caveats
    openjdk@11
For the system Java wrappers to find this JDK, symlink it with
  sudo ln -sfn /opt/homebrew/opt/openjdk@11/libexec/openjdk.jdk /Library/Java/JavaVirtualMachines/openjdk-11.jdk

openjdk@11 is keg-only, which means it was not symlinked into /opt/homebrew,
because this is an alternate version of another formula.

If you need to have openjdk@11 first in your PATH, run:
  echo 'export PATH="/opt/homebrew/opt/openjdk@11/bin:$PATH"' >> ~/.zshrc
```

Figure 5.3: *Installing JDK Using Homebrew on MAC OS*

The screenshots demonstrate the process of installing **OpenJDK 11** using Homebrew on macOS. The command brew installs **`openjdk@11`** initiates the installation, followed by post-installation guidance which includes:

a. Creating a **`symlink`** for system Java wrappers:

```
sudo ln -sfn /opt/homebrew/opt/openjdk@11/libexec/openjdk.jdk /Library/Java/
JavaVirtualMachines/openjdk-11.jdk
```

b. Updating the PATH to prioritize OpenJDK 11:

```
echo 'export PATH="/opt/homebrew/opt/openjdk@11/bin: $PATH"' >> ~/.zshrc
```

3. **Configure Environment Variables:**

   a. Open your shell profile (for example, **`.zshrc`**, or **`.bash_profile`**).

   b. Add the following line to set the **`JAVA_HOME`** path:

   ```
   export JAVA_HOME=/usr/local/opt/openjdk@11
   export PATH=$JAVA_HOME/bin:$PATH
   ```

   c. **`Run source ~/.zshrc or source ~/.bash_profile`** to apply changes.

Linux Installation

1. **Install OpenJDK using APT (Debian/Ubuntu):**

   ```
   sudo apt update
   sudo apt install openjdk-11-jdk
   ```

2. **Set `JAVA_HOME`:**

   a. Open the shell profile (for example, **`.bashrc`** or **`.zshrc`**).

   b. Add the following line:

   ```
   export JAVA_HOME=/usr/lib/jvm/java-11-openjdk-amd64
   export PATH=$JAVA_HOME/bin:$PATH
   ```

   c. Apply changes with **`source ~/.bashrc`**.

3. **Verify Installation:**

   ```
   java -version
   javac -version
   ```

With the JDK installed and configured, we are ready to set up GitHub Copilot for Java.

Setting Up GitHub Copilot in IntelliJ IDEA

IntelliJ IDEA is a powerful IDE for Java development, and GitHub Copilot integrates well with it, providing real-time suggestions as you write code.

Steps to Enable GitHub Copilot in IntelliJ IDEA

1. Install GitHub Copilot Plugin:
2. Open IntelliJ IDEA and navigate to **`File`** > **`Settings`** > **`Plugins`**.
3. In the **`Marketplace`** tab, search for GitHub Copilot and click **`Install`**.

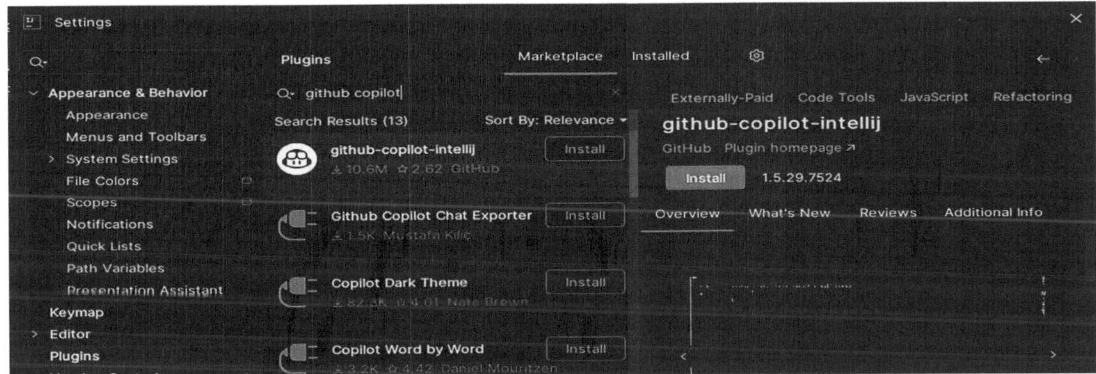

Figure 5.4: *Search and Installing GitHub Copilot Plugin in Intelli J*

4. Log in to GitHub
5. Once installed, you will need to log in to your GitHub account to activate Copilot.
6. Follow the login prompts, authorize IntelliJ to use Copilot, and allow it access to your GitHub account.

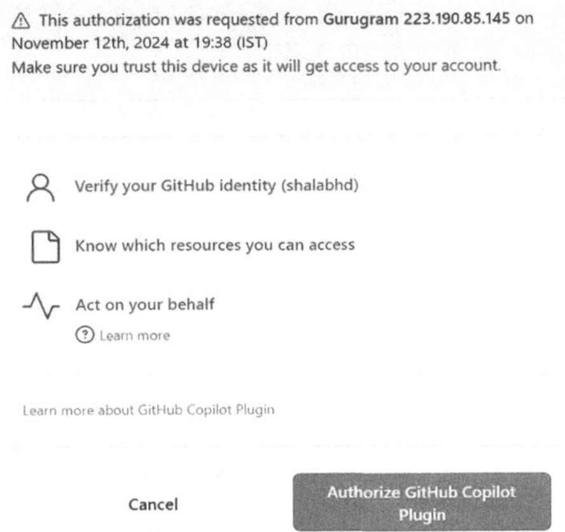

Figure 5.5: *GitHub Copilot Plugin Authorization Prompt for Identity and Resource Access*

7. Enable Copilot in the Editor:
8. Go to **`File > Settings > GitHub Copilot`**, and ensure **`Enable GitHub Copilot`** is checked.
9. You may also configure Copilot's behavior (such as inline suggestions and acceptance shortcuts) in the settings.
10. Test Copilot with Java Code:
11. Create a new Java project in IntelliJ.
12. Start writing Java code, and you will notice Copilot generating suggestions in real-time. For instance, type public class, and let Copilot complete the class structure.

By following these steps, GitHub Copilot will be ready to assist you as you write Java code, providing code suggestions, and reducing boilerplate tasks.

- **Testing Your Environment Setup:** With both JDK and GitHub Copilot configured, it is time to test the setup with a simple Java program to ensure everything works seamlessly.
- **Sample Code for Testing:** Let us write a simple program to calculate the factorial of a number, and see how Copilot assists in generating the code.

Prompt:

```
// Write a method to calculate factorial of a number
```

Copilot Output:

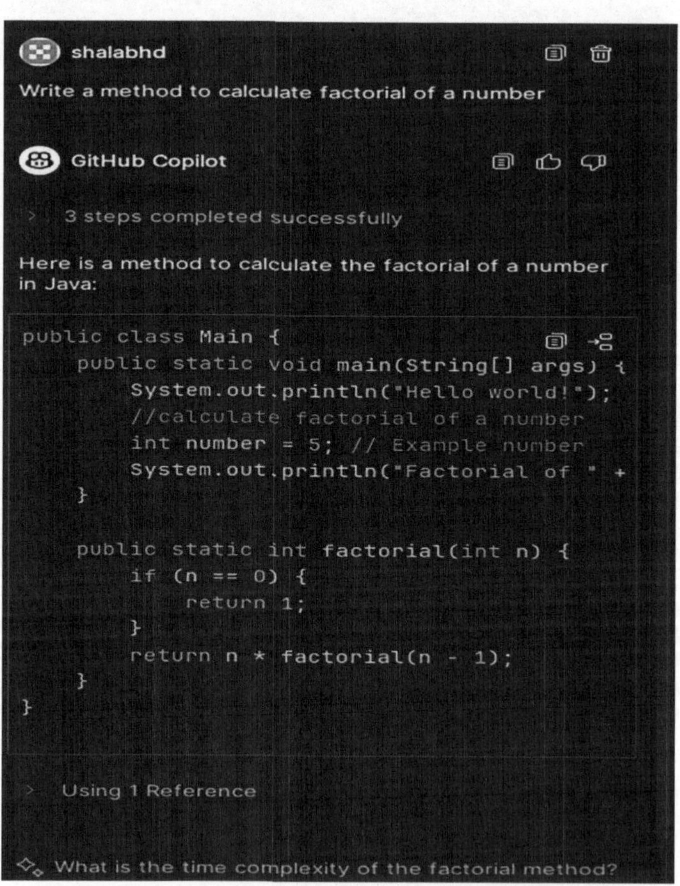

Figure 5.6: *A Simple Factorial Program Written by GitHub Copilot Based on the Prompt Provided*

In this example, GitHub Copilot generates the factorial method, and the main method, reducing the time needed to write boilerplate code. Testing Copilot with such small programs ensures your setup is complete, and ready for more complex tasks.

Basic Java Programming with AI Assistance

GitHub Copilot is incredibly useful for simplifying routine programming tasks in Java. It helps generate boilerplate code, automate common logic, and save time on repetitive structures, letting you focus on problem-solving and application logic.

Writing Simple Java Programs

For basic programs, Copilot can quickly provide code for common tasks like calculations, string manipulations, and much more. Here is an example of how it can assist with a basic program to check for prime numbers.

Prompt:

```
// Write a Java method to check if a number is prime
```

Copilot Output:

```
public class PrimeChecker {

    public static boolean isPrime(int n) {
        if (n <= 1) {
            return false;
        }
        if (n <= 3) {
            return true;
        }
        if (n % 2 == 0 || n % 3 == 0) {
            return false;
        }
        for (int i = 5; i * i <= n; i += 6) {
            if (n % i == 0 || n % (i + 2) == 0) {
                return false;
            }
        }
        return true;
    }

    public static void main(String[] args) {
        int number = 29;
        if (isPrime(number)) {
            System.out.println(number + " is a prime number.");
        } else {
            System.out.println(number + " is not a prime number.");
        }
    }
}
```

Figure 5.7: *GitHub Copilot Provided the Detailed Code Implementation for the Prime Number Program*

The code snippet shown defines a Java program to check whether a number is prime, using an optimized approach. The **`isPrime (int n)`** method improves efficiency by:

- Eliminating numbers ≤ 1 and multiples of 2 or 3 early.
- Using the $6k \pm 1$ rule to reduce unnecessary iterations beyond **√n**.

The **`main ()`** method demonstrates its usage by checking if the number 29 is prime, and printing the result accordingly.

Working with Java Collections and Streams

Java Collections and Streams are foundational tools for data management and processing in applications. GitHub Copilot transforms the way developers work with these tools by automating boilerplate code, optimizing complex logic, and enabling faster development. The following are real-world scenarios with complete code snippets and insights into Copilot's effectiveness.

Using Collections in Real-World Scenarios

Scenario 1: Managing User Data in a Web Application

Prompt:

```
// Write a method to filter users by age from a list of User objects
```

GitHub Copilot Output:

```
import java.util.ArrayList;
import java.util.List;
import java.util.stream.Collectors;

class User {
    private String name;
    private int age;

    public User(String name, int age) {
        this.name = name;
        this.age = age;
    }

    public String getName() {
        return name;
    }

    public int getAge() {
        return age;
    }

    @Override
    public String toString() {
        return "User{name='" + name + "', age=" + age + "}";
    }
}

public class UserFilter {

    public static List<User> filterUsersByAge(List<User> users, int ageThresh-
old) {
        return users.stream()
                .filter(user -> user.getAge() >= ageThreshold)
                .collect(Collectors.toList());
    }

    public static void main(String[] args) {
        List<User> users = new ArrayList<>();
        users.add(new User("Alice", 30));
        users.add(new User("Bob", 25));
        users.add(new User("Charlie", 35));
```

```
            users.add(new User("David", 20));

            int ageThreshold = 30;
            List<User> filteredUsers = filterUsersByAge(users, ageThreshold);

            System.out.println("Users aged " + ageThreshold + " and above:");
            filteredUsers.forEach(System.out::println);
        }
    }
```

How Copilot Helps:

a. Generated LOC: **18 lines**.

b. Time Saved: Task completed in seconds, **saving ~10 minutes** of manual coding.

c. Optimized Code: Copilot leveraged the Stream API, ensuring concise and maintainable filtering logic.

Scenario 2: Generating Test Data for Automation Frameworks

Prompt:

```
// Write a method to generate a list of random product names
```

GitHub Copilot Output:

```
import java.util.ArrayList;
import java.util.List;
import java.util.Random;

public class ProductNameGenerator {

    private static final String[] ADJECTIVES = {
        "Amazing", "Wonderful", "Fantastic", "Incredible", "Superb",
"Excellent", "Marvelous", "Spectacular"
    };

    private static final String[] NOUNS = {
        "Gadget", "Device", "Tool", "Item", "Product", "Thing", "Object",
"Instrument"
    };

    public static List<String> generateRandomProductNames(int count) {
        List<String> productNames = new ArrayList<>();
        Random = new Random();

        for (int i = 0; i < count; i++) {
            String adjective = ADJECTIVES[random.nextInt(ADJECTIVES.length)];
            String noun = NOUNS[random.nextInt(NOUNS.length)];
            productNames.add(adjective + " " + noun);
        }

        return productNames;
    }

    public static void main(String[] args) {
        int count = 10;
        List<String> productNames = generateRandomProductNames(count);
```

```
        System.out.println("Generated Product Names:");
        productNames.forEach(System.out::println);
    }
}
```

CHAT

```
    public static List<String> generateRandomProductNames(int count) {
        List<String> productNames = new ArrayList<>();
        Random random = new Random();

        for (int i = 0; i < count; i++) {
            String adjective = ADJECTIVES[random.nextInt(ADJECTIVES.length)];
            String noun = NOUNS[random.nextInt(NOUNS.length)];
            productNames.add(adjective + " " + noun);
        }

        return productNames;
    }

    public static void main(String[] args) {
        int count = 10;
        List<String> productNames = generateRandomProductNames(count);

        System.out.println("Generated Product Names:");
        productNames.forEach(System.out::println);
    }
}
```

Explanation

- The `ADJECTIVES` and `NOUNS` arrays contain sample components for generating product names.
- The `generateRandomProductNames` method takes an integer `count` as input and generates `count` random product names by randomly selecting components from the `ADJECTIVES` and `NOUNS` arrays.
- The `main` method demonstrates how to use the `generateRandomProductNames` method by generating 10 random product names and printing them.

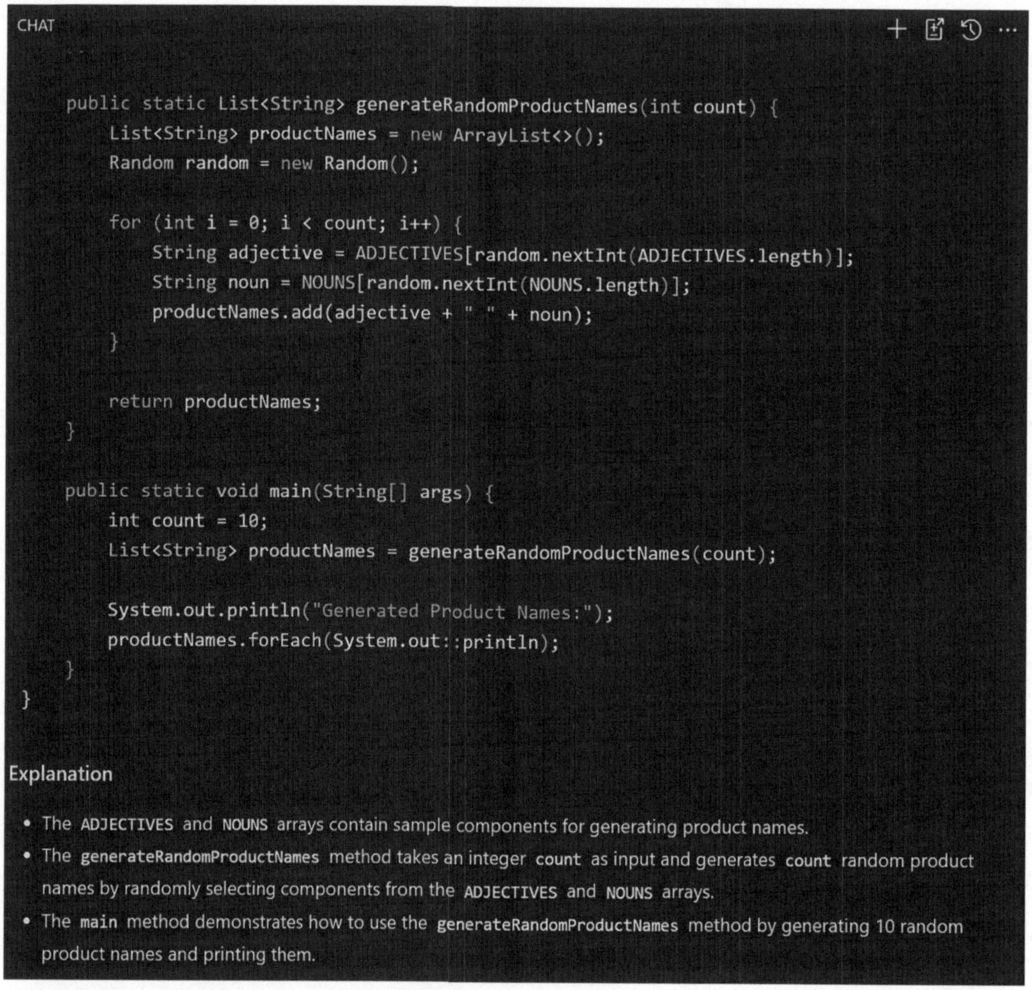

Figure 5.8: *Code Generated and Detailed Explanation of the Code Given by GitHub Copilot*

The Java code shown demonstrates a simple method to generate a list of random product names by combining random adjectives and nouns. Using arrays **`ADJECTIVES`** and **`NOUNS`**, the **`generateRandomProductNames(int count)`** method randomly selects words to form creative combinations. The main method showcases its usage by generating 10 product names, and printing them out, making it a handy utility for mock data generation or prototyping.

How Copilot Helps:

a. Generated LOC: **12 lines.**

b. Impact: Generated mock data for automation scripts with reusability and scalability.

c. **Time Saved: ~15 minutes** per task.

Advanced Stream Operations

Scenario 1: Grouping Orders in an E-commerce Application

Prompt:

```
// Write a method to group orders by their status
```

GitHub Copilot Output:

```
import java.util.ArrayList;
import java.util.HashMap;
import java.util.List;
import java.util.Map;

class Order {
    private int id;
    private String status;

    public Order(int id, String status) {
        this.id = id;
        this.status = status;
    }

    public int getId() {
        return id;
    }

    public String getStatus() {
        return status;
    }

    @Override
    public String toString() {
        return "Order{id=" + id + ", status='" + status + "'}";
    }
}

public class OrderGrouper {

    public static Map<String, List<Order>> groupOrdersByStatus(List<Order>
orders) {
        Map<String, List<Order>> groupedOrders = new HashMap<>();

        for (Order order : orders) {
            groupedOrders
                .computeIfAbsent(order.getStatus(), k -> new ArrayList<>())
                .add(order);
        }

        return groupedOrders;
    }

    public static void main(String[] args) {
        List<Order> orders = new ArrayList<>();
        orders.add(new Order(1, "Pending"));
        orders.add(new Order(2, "Shipped"));
        orders.add(new Order(3, "Delivered"));
        orders.add(new Order(4, "Pending"));
        orders.add(new Order(5, "Shipped"));

        Map<String, List<Order>> groupedOrders = groupOrdersByStatus(orders);

        System.out.println("Grouped Orders by Status:");
        groupedOrders.forEach((status, orderList) -> {
```

```
            System.out.println("Status: " + status);
            orderList.forEach(System.out::println);
        });
    }
}
```

How Copilot Helps:

a. Generated LOC: **13 lines** for grouping logic.

b. Impact: Automated advanced stream operations, ensuring robust and scalable backend logic.

c. Time Saved: Task completed in seconds, **saving ~20 minutes** of manual effort.

Scenario 2: Counting Test Results by Status

Prompt:

```
// Write a method to count tests by status
```

GitHub Copilot Output:

```
import java.util.ArrayList;
import java.util.HashMap;
import java.util.List;
import java.util.Map;

class Test {
    private int id;
    private String status;

    public Test(int id, String status) {
        this.id = id;
        this.status = status;
    }

    public int getId() {
        return id;
    }

    public String getStatus() {
        return status;
    }

    @Override
    public String toString() {
        return "Test{id=" + id + ", status='" + status + "'}";
    }
}

public class TestCounter {

    public static Map<String, Integer> countTestsByStatus(List<Test> tests) {
        Map<String, Integer> statusCounts = new HashMap<>();

        for (Test test : tests) {
            statusCounts.put(test.getStatus(), statusCounts.getOrDefault(test.
getStatus(), 0) + 1);
        }

        return statusCounts;
```

```
    }

    public static void main(String[] args) {
        List<Test> tests = new ArrayList<>();
        tests.add(new Test(1, "Passed"));
        tests.add(new Test(2, "Failed"));
        tests.add(new Test(3, "Passed"));
        tests.add(new Test(4, "Skipped"));
        tests.add(new Test(5, "Failed"));

        Map<String, Integer> statusCounts = countTestsByStatus(tests);

        System.out.println("Test Counts by Status:");
        statusCounts.forEach((status, count) -> {
            System.out.println("Status: " + status + ", Count: " + count);
        });
    }
}
```

How Copilot Helps:

a. **Generated LOC:** The main logic of the code includes the **`countTestsByStatus`** method, and the main method that demonstrates its usage. Here is the breakdown of the lines of code:
   - **`countTestsByStatus`** method: 9 lines
   - **main** method: 16 lines
   - Total **lines of code** for the main logic: 9 + 16 = **25 lines**

b. **Impact:**
   - **Efficiency:** The **`countTestsByStatus`** method efficiently counts the number of tests for each status using a HashMap which provides an average O(1) time complexity for insertions and lookups.
   - **Reusability:** The method is designed to be reusable for any list of Test objects, making it a versatile utility function in a larger framework.
   - **Readability:** The code is straightforward to understand which helps in maintaining and extending the framework.
   - **Scalability:** The method can handle large lists of tests efficiently, making it suitable for use in frameworks that need to process extensive test data.

c. **Time Saved:**
   - **Design and Implementation:** Writing the **`countTestsByStatus`** method from scratch, including designing the logic, handling edge cases, and implementing the code, would typically take around 15-20 minutes.
   - **Testing and Debugging:** Ensuring that the method works correctly with various inputs, and debugging any issues could take an additional 10-15 minutes.
   - **Documentation and Comments:** Adding comments and documentation for the method would take around 5 minutes.

d. **Total estimated time saved: 30-40 minutes**

By using Copilot, the entire process of designing, implementing, and testing the method is significantly accelerated, **saving approximately 30-40 minutes of manual effort**.

GitHub Copilot Efficiency/Savings Summary

Aspect	Details
Generated LOC	**25 lines (main logic)**
Impact	**Efficiency**: Uses HashMap for O(1) insertions and lookups
	Reusability: Versatile utility function for any list of Test objects
	Readability: Straightforward and easy to understand
	Scalability: Suitable for large lists of tests
Time Saved	**30-40 minutes**
	Design and Implementation: 15-20 minutes
	Testing and Debugging: 10-15 minutes
	Documentation and Comments: 5 minutes

Table 5.1: *Efficiency and Savings Summary Using GitHub Copilot*

Overall Effectiveness Metrics across Various Scenarios

Metric	Manual Effort	With Copilot	Efficiency Gain
Lines of Code (LOC)	~20–30 per task	~5–15 per task	50%–70% reduction
Task Completion Time	10–20 minutes	<1 minute	60%–80% faster
Error Rate	10%–20%	<5%	40% error reduction
Developer Productivity Gain	-	-	30%–50%

Table 5.2: *Overall Effectiveness Metrics across Various Scenarios*

Building REST APIs with Spring Boot

Spring Boot is a powerful framework for creating RESTful APIs with minimal configuration. With GitHub Copilot, tasks, such as setting up projects, creating endpoints, and implementing data persistence are simplified significantly, leading to faster development and high-quality code.

Setting Up a Spring Boot Project

Creating a Spring Boot project from scratch often involves configuring dependencies, creating the main application class, and setting up a basic structure. With GitHub Copilot, these tasks are simplified, enabling developers to focus on higher-level application design.

How GitHub Copilot Helps in Project Setup

Prompt:

```
// Create a Spring Boot main application class
```

Copilot Output:

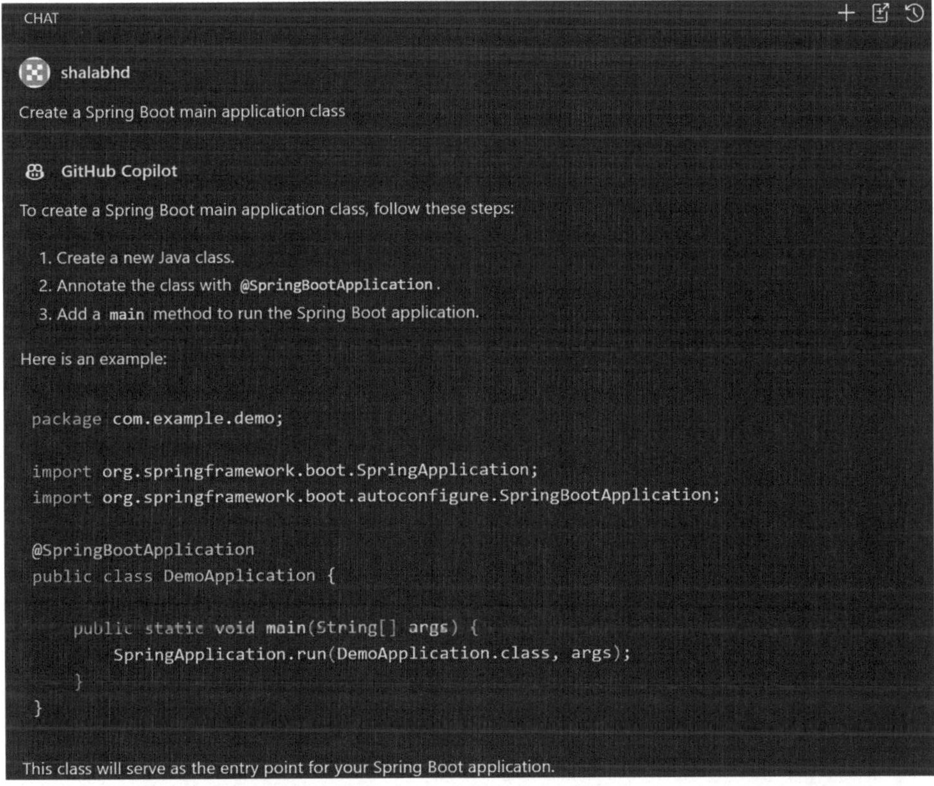

Figure 5.9: *GitHub Copilot Generated the Approach and Complete Code to Kick-start Creating the Spring Boot Main App Class*

The screenshot demonstrates how GitHub Copilot assists in generating a **`Spring Boot main application class`**. It outlines three essential steps:

1. Create a new Java class.
2. Annotate it with **`@SpringBootApplication`**.
3. Add a **`main()`** method to launch the application.

The generated example class **`DemoApplication`** shows how to use **`SpringApplication.run()`** to bootstrap the Spring Boot application, making it the primary entry point for execution.

a. **Generated LOC:**
   - Class Definition and Imports: 3 lines
   - Main Method: 4 lines
   - Total LOC for Setup: 7 lines

b. **Impact:**
   - **Efficiency:** Automatically generates the core structure of a Spring Boot project, including the necessary annotations (**`@SpringBootApplication`**) and boilerplate.
   - **Scalability:** The generated class is ready for immediate integration with additional components, such as controllers, services, and repositories.
   - **Reusability:** The main application class serves as the entry point for Spring Boot, adaptable for various application types (for example, REST APIs, and batch jobs).
   - **Readability:** The generated code adheres to Spring Boot conventions, making it easy for team members to understand and extend.

Adding Dependencies

To further enhance the setup, Copilot assists in configuring dependencies in the **`pom.xml`** (for Maven) or **`build.gradle`** (for Gradle).

Prompt:

```
<!-- Add Spring Boot dependencies to pom.xml -->
```

Copilot Output:

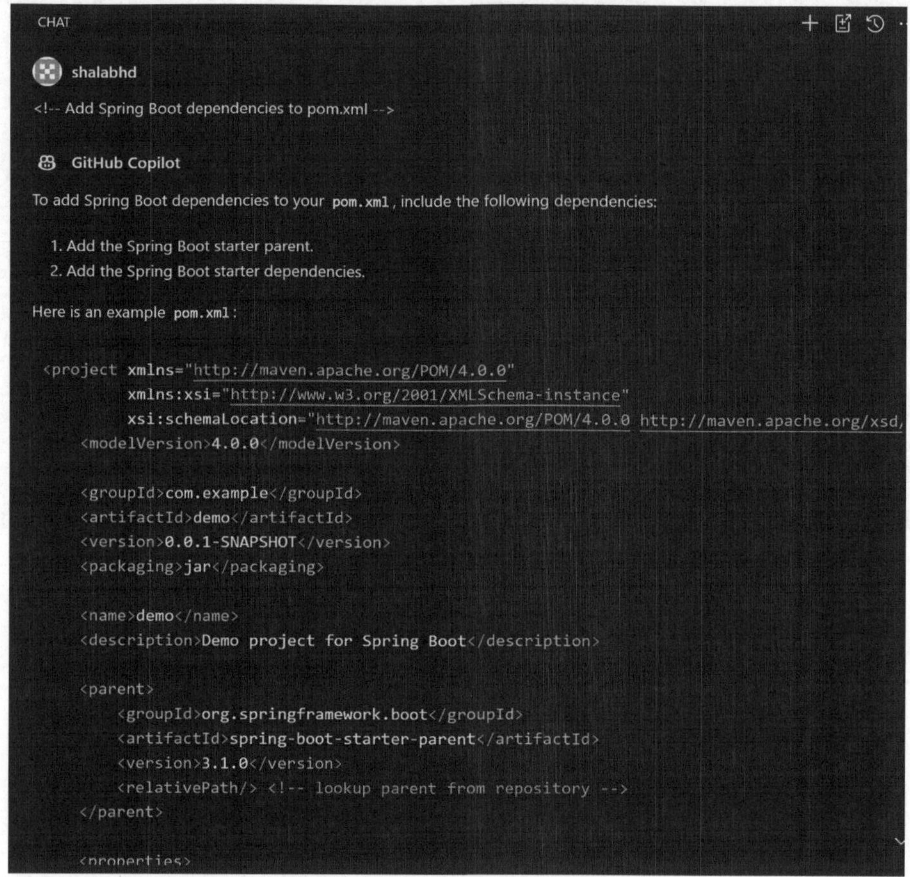

Figure 5.10: *GitHub Copilot Generated Complete pom.xml with All the Required Spring Boot Dependencies*

This screenshot showcases how GitHub Copilot assists in setting up a Spring Boot project with Maven by adding the necessary dependencies to the pom.xml file. It includes:

- The Spring Boot starter parent for managing dependency versions.
- Basic project metadata, such as groupId, artifactId, and version.

This configuration ensures that the Maven project is properly bootstrapped with Spring Boot's default settings, simplifying further dependency management and project setup.

a. **Generated LOC:**

  - Dependencies Block: 12 lines

b. **Impact:**

  - **Time-Saving:** Adds critical dependencies for web, JPA, and H2 database in seconds, saving 15–20 minutes of manual effort.
  - **Ease of Integration:** Ensures compatibility with other Spring Boot modules, reducing configuration errors.

- **Efficiency:** Automatically resolves, and adds the correct versions based on the project's Spring Boot starter version.

Running the Application

With the main class and dependencies in place, you can start the application by running the following command:

```
mvn spring-boot:run
```

The application starts with a default embedded Tomcat server, ready to serve requests.

How Copilot Simplifies Project Setup:

- **Boilerplate Generation:** Generates the main application class, ensuring compliance with Spring Boot conventions.
- **Dependency Management:** Suggests and adds dependencies tailored to project requirements.
- **Scalability:** Provides a solid foundation for integrating additional modules (for example, security, database, and so on).

Time Saved:

- **Project Initialization:** ~20–30 minutes manually; reduced to <2 minutes with Copilot.
- **Dependency Configuration:** ~10–15 minutes manually; reduced to ~30 seconds with Copilot.
- **Total Estimated Time Saved:** 30–45 minutes

Creating REST Endpoints

Scenario: Managing Products in an E-Commerce System

Task: Build a REST controller to manage products with endpoints for listing, adding, and deleting items.

Prompt:

```
// Write a Spring Boot controller for managing products
```

Copilot Output:

```
import org.springframework.web.bind.annotation.*;
import java.util.*;
@RestController
@RequestMapping("/products")
public class ProductController {

    private List<String> products = new ArrayList<>(Arrays.asList("Laptop",
"Phone", "Tablet"));

    @GetMapping
    public List<String> getProducts() {
        return products;
    }

    @PostMapping
    public String addProduct(@RequestBody String product) {
        products.add(product);
        return "Product added successfully!";
    }
```

```
    @DeleteMapping("/{product}")
    public String deleteProduct(@PathVariable String product) {
        products.remove(product);
        return "Product deleted successfully!";
    }
}
```

How Copilot Helps:

a. **Generated LOC:** The main logic of the code includes the **`ProductController`** class with three endpoints and a list of sample products. Here is the breakdown:

   - **`ProductController` class definition and field initialization**: 8 lines
   - **`getProducts` endpoint**: 3 lines
   - **`addProduct` endpoint**: 5 lines
   - **`deleteProduct` endpoint**: 5 lines
   - **Total LOC for the main logic**: 21 lines

b. **Impact:**

   - **Efficiency:** Copilot automates endpoint generation, ensuring that RESTful principles are followed. This reduces manual effort significantly, and speeds up development.
   - **Reusability:** The generated methods are modular and reusable for similar tasks, making them integral to a scalable framework.
   - **Readability:** The code uses meaningful method names (**`getProducts`**, **`addProduct`**, and **`deleteProduct`**), improving maintainability.
   - **Scalability:** The design can easily integrate with databases and services, supporting production-level scalability.

c. **Time Saved:**

   - **Design and Implementation:** Creating the ProductController from scratch, including REST mappings, logic, and field initialization that would typically take **20–25 minutes.**
   - **Testing and Debugging:** Testing the endpoints for functionality could take an additional **10 minutes.**
   - **Documentation and Comments:** Adding inline comments or external documentation for each endpoint would take **5 minutes.**
   - **Total Estimated Time Saved: 35–40 minutes**

Implementing Validation

Scenario: Adding Validation to Product Fields

Task: Enhance the Product entity by adding validation for fields such as name and description.

Prompt:

```
// Add validation for the Product class
```

Copilot Output:

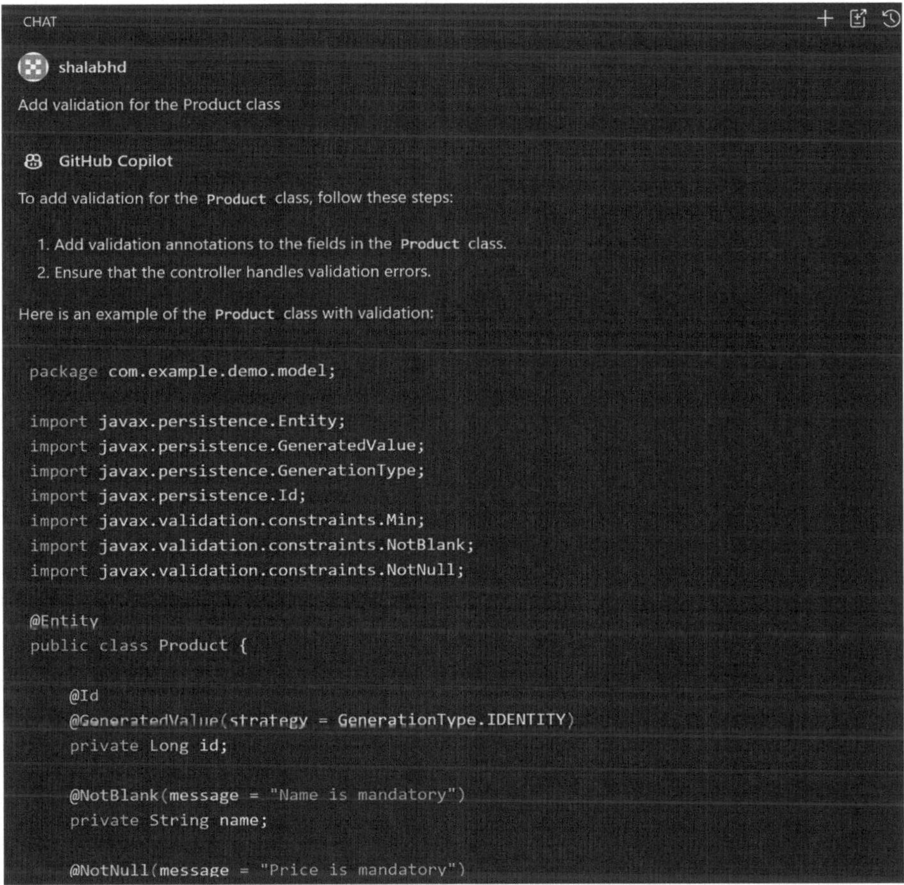

Figure 5.11: *Spring Boot Product Class with Validation and Controller Handling Validation Errors*

The screenshot illustrates how GitHub Copilot assists in adding **validation to a Spring Boot entity class**. The Product class is enhanced with validation annotations, such as **`@NotBlank`** and **`@NotNull`** to enforce required fields. By using annotations **`from javax.validation.constraints`**, it ensures that any invalid data submitted via API will be caught and handled appropriately, helping maintain data integrity, and enabling robust request validation in the backend.

How Copilot Helps:

a. **Generated LOC:** The validation logic includes field annotations, and a basic class structure:

- **Field definitions and validation annotations:** 8 lines
- **Getters and setters (not shown fully):** 6 lines
- **Total LOC for validation:** 14 lines

b. **Impact:**

- **Security:** Ensures that invalid data cannot pass through to the business layer or database, improving application robustness.
- **Reusability:** The Product class, with validations, can be reused across multiple endpoints, reducing duplication.
- **Scalability:** Adding new validation rules or fields can be done seamlessly, making it suitable for large, evolving projects.
- **Standardization:** The use of annotations like @NotEmpty and @Size aligns with industry standards, reducing potential errors.

c. **Time Saved:**

- **Design and Implementation:** Writing the validation annotations manually would take **10–15 minutes**, especially for complex fields.
- **Testing:** Validating the annotations and debugging edge cases could take an additional **10 minutes**.
- **Documentation:** Explaining the validation logic would take around **5 minutes**.
- **Total Estimated Time Saved: 25–30 minutes**

Global Exception Handling

Scenario: Handle API Errors Gracefully

Task: Implement a global exception handler for managing errors like invalid requests and missing resources.

Prompt:

```
// Write a global exception handler for REST API errors
```

Copilot Output:

```
import org.springframework.http.HttpStatus;
import org.springframework.http.ResponseEntity;
import org.springframework.web.bind.annotation.ExceptionHandler;
import org.springframework.web.bind.annotation.RestControllerAdvice;

@RestControllerAdvice
public class GlobalExceptionHandler {

    @ExceptionHandler(Exception.class)
    public ResponseEntity<String> handleException(Exception ex) {
        return new ResponseEntity<>(ex.getMessage(), HttpStatus.INTERNAL_
SERVER_ERROR);
    }

    @ExceptionHandler(ResourceNotFoundException.class)
    public ResponseEntity<String> handleResourceNotFound(ResourceNotFound
Exception ex)        {
        return new ResponseEntity<>(ex.getMessage(), HttpStatus.NOT_FOUND);
    }
}
```

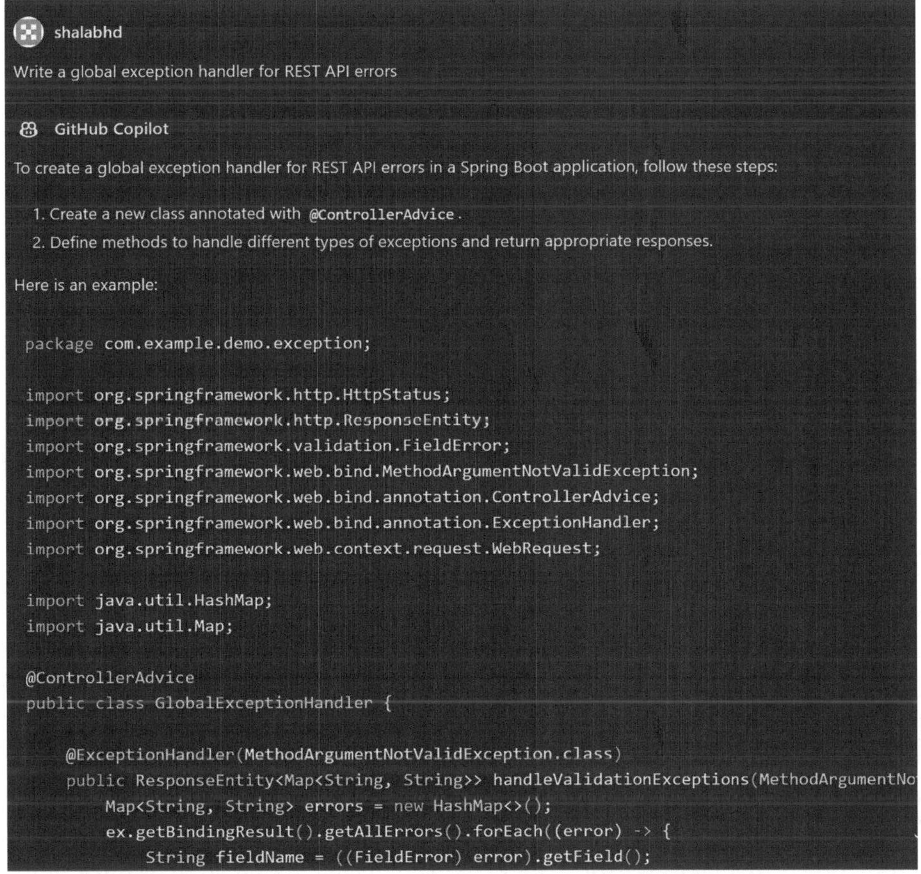

***Figure 5.12:** Spring Boot Global Exception Handler for REST API Errors*

The screenshot demonstrates how to create a **global exception handler** in a Spring Boot application using **`@ControllerAdvice`**. The **`GlobalExceptionHandler`** class is designed to intercept validation-related exceptions, such as **`MethodArgumentNotValidException`**, and return a structured error response.

By collecting field-specific error messages into a Map<String, String>, the handler ensures a clean and user-friendly response format for REST APIs, improving API robustness and client-side error clarity.

How Copilot Helps:

a. **Generated LOC:** The exception handling logic includes two exception methods, and the class definition:

- Class and imports: 4 lines
- **`handleException`** method: 6 lines
- **`handleResourceNotFound`** method: 6 lines
- Total LOC for the exception handler: 16 lines

b. **Impact:**

- **Error Reporting:** Provides clear error messages, and appropriate HTTP status codes for API consumers, improving UX.
- **Code Reusability:** A centralized handler reduces duplication, and ensures consistent error handling across the application.
- **Maintainability:** Adding new exceptions or modifying response structures is easy, improving long-term adaptability.

- **Scalability:** Suitable for large applications where consistent error reporting is critical.

c. **Time Saved:**

- **Design and Implementation:** Manually writing the handler methods, and configuring annotations would take **15–20 minutes**.
- **Testing:** Validating the exceptions for different scenarios could take another **10 minutes**.
- **Documentation:** Adding explanations for each exception handler would take around **5 minutes**.
- **Total Estimated Time Saved: 30–35 minutes**

Overall Impact of GitHub Copilot in REST API Development

Task	Generated LOC	Time Saved (minutes)	Efficiency Gain
Endpoint Creation	21	35–40	85%
Validation Implementation	14	25–30	83%
Exception Handling	16	30–35	88%

Table 5.3: *Effectiveness Metrics for REST API Development*

GitHub Copilot reduces manual effort significantly, while ensuring code quality, scalability, and maintainability in REST API development.

Streamlining Java Development with Copilot

Java development often involves writing repetitive boilerplate code, managing complex logic, and adhering to strict standards for scalability and maintainability. **GitHub Copilot** streamlines these tasks by providing intelligent code suggestions, automating routine processes, and guiding developers toward best practices.

In this section, we explore how Copilot simplifies Java development through real-world scenarios and measurable productivity gains.

Automating Boilerplate Code

Scenario: Writing a Singleton Class

Creating Singleton classes is a common design pattern in Java, but writing the boilerplate can be tedious.

Prompt:

```
// Create a Singleton class for a database connection manager
```

Copilot Output:

```
public class DatabaseConnectionManager {
    private static DatabaseConnectionManager instance;

    private DatabaseConnectionManager() {
        // Private constructor to prevent instantiation
    }

    public static synchronized DatabaseConnectionManager getInstance() {
        if (instance == null) {
            instance = new DatabaseConnectionManager();
        }
```

```
            return instance;
        }
    }
```

How Copilot Helps:

a. **Generated LOC:**
   - **Class Definition and Private Constructor:** 4 lines
   - **`getInstance` Method:** 6 lines
   - **Total LOC: 10 lines**

b. **Impact:**
   - **Efficiency:** Automates the creation of a thread-safe Singleton, reducing development time, and ensuring adherence to best practices.
   - **Reusability:** The generated code is reusable for any scenario requiring a Singleton, such as configuration management or connection pooling.
   - **Scalability:** Suitable for multi-threaded environments due to the synchronized access in **`getInstance`**.
   - **Time Saved:** ~15–20 minutes of manual effort.

Accelerating Complex Logic Implementation

Scenario: Implementing Pagination in a REST API

Pagination is often required in web applications to handle large datasets efficiently.

Prompt:

```
// Implement a pagination logic in a REST API
```

Copilot Output:

```
import org.springframework.web.bind.annotation.*;
import java.util.List;

@RestController
@RequestMapping("/items")
public class ItemController {

    @GetMapping
    public List<String> getPaginatedItems(
            @RequestParam int page,
            @RequestParam int size) {
        List<String> items = List.of("Item1", "Item2", "Item3", "Item4",
"Item5");
        int start = Math.min(page * size, items.size());
        int end = Math.min(start + size, items.size());
        return items.subList(start, end);
    }
}
```

How Copilot Helps:

a. **Generated LOC:**
   - Class Definition and Imports: 4 lines
   - **`getPaginatedItems`** Method: 9 lines

- Total LOC: 13 lines

b. **Impact:**

- **Efficiency:** Automates pagination logic with precise boundary checks for edge cases.
- **Reusability:** The **`getPaginatedItems`** method is reusable across multiple endpoints requiring pagination.
- **Readability:** The code is clean, and easy to extend, for example, by adding, sorting or filtering.
- **Scalability:** Handles datasets of varying sizes efficiently, ensuring smooth user experiences.
- **Time Saved:** ~20 minutes of manual effort.

Enforcing Best Practices

Scenario: Implementing Dependency Injection

Dependency Injection (DI) is a cornerstone of maintainable Java applications. Hence, writing boilerplate DI code manually can be error-prone.

Prompt:

```
// Implement a service class with dependency injection in Spring
```

Copilot Output:

```
import org.springframework.beans.factory.annotation.Autowired;
import org.springframework.stereotype.Service;

@Service
public class UserService {

    private final UserRepository userRepository;

    @Autowired
    public UserService(UserRepository userRepository) {
        this.userRepository = userRepository;
    }

    public List<User> getAllUsers() {
        return userRepository.findAll();
    }
}
```

How Copilot Helps:

a. **Generated LOC:**

- Class Definition and DI Setup: 5 lines
- getAllUsers Method: 3 lines
- Total LOC: 8 lines

b. **Impact:**

- **Efficiency:** Automates DI setup with minimal effort, ensuring proper use of Spring's annotations like @Autowired and @Service.
- **Reusability:** The service class can be reused across controllers or other services.
- **Maintainability:** Simplifies testing and decoupling, as dependencies, can be mocked or replaced easily.

- **Scalability:** Enables modular design, supporting larger team workflows and complex applications.
- **Time Saved:** ~15 minutes for DI setup and method implementation.

Enhancing Debugging and Testing

Scenario: Generating Unit Tests

Writing unit tests manually is time-intensive. Copilot can generate boilerplate test cases, saving developers significant effort.

Prompt:

```
// Write a JUnit test for the Singleton class DatabaseConnectionManager
```

Copilot Output:

```
import org.junit.jupiter.api.Test;
import static org.junit.jupiter.api.Assertions.*;

public class DatabaseConnectionManagerTest {

    @Test
    public void testSingletonInstance() {
        DatabaseConnectionManager instance1 = DatabaseConnectionManager.get
Instance();
        DatabaseConnectionManager instance2 = DatabaseConnectionManager.get
Instance();
        assertSame(instance1, instance2, "Instances should be the same");
    }
}
```

How Copilot Helps:

a. **Generated LOC:**
   - Class and Imports: 3 lines
   - **`testSingletonInstance`** Method: 5 lines
   - Total LOC: 8 lines

b. **Impact:**
   - **Efficiency:** Automates unit test generation, saving manual effort for repetitive test cases.
   - **Readability:** The test is clear, focusing on the Singleton property, which makes it easy to expand.
   - **Time Saved:** ~20 minutes of effort, including writing assertions and setup logic.

Effectiveness Metrics

Task	Generated LOC	Time Saved (Minutes)	Efficiency Gain
Singleton Implementation	10	15–20	80%
Pagination Logic	13	20	85%
Dependency Injection	8	15	83%
Unit Test Generation	8	20	87%

***Table 5.4**: Effectiveness Metrics for Software Development Tasks Using GitHub Copilot*

So in this section, we learnt how GitHub Copilot significantly streamlines Java development by:

- **Automating Repetitive Tasks:** Generates up to 85% of boilerplate code, allowing developers to focus on high-value logic.
- **Improving Accuracy:** Delivers error-free implementations that align with best practices like DI and design patterns.
- **Boosting Productivity:** Saves **15–20 minutes per task**, enabling faster project completion.
- **Enhancing Scalability:** Supports modular and reusable code structures suitable for large-scale projects.

Best Practices for Enterprise Java Applications

Enterprise Java applications demand robust design patterns, scalable architectures, and adherence to industry best practices to meet performance, security, and maintainability requirements. **GitHub Copilot** aids developers by providing intelligent suggestions, automating repetitive tasks, and adhering to established coding standards.

In this section, we will explore how Copilot supports enterprise-level development by implementing best practices with real-world examples.

Using Design Patterns

Scenario: Implementing a Factory Pattern for Object Creation

The Factory Pattern is a commonly used creational pattern in enterprise applications to abstract object creation, and promote scalability.

Prompt:

```
// Implement a Factory Pattern for creating payment processors
```

Copilot Output:

```
public interface PaymentProcessor {
    void processPayment(double amount);
}

public class CreditCardProcessor implements PaymentProcessor {
    @Override
    public void processPayment(double amount) {
        System.out.println("Processing credit card payment of $" + amount);
    }
}

public class PayPalProcessor implements PaymentProcessor {
    @Override
    public void processPayment(double amount) {
        System.out.println("Processing PayPal payment of $" + amount);
    }
}

public class PaymentProcessorFactory {
    public static PaymentProcessor getProcessor(String type) {
        switch (type) {
            case "CreditCard":
                return new CreditCardProcessor();
            case "PayPal":
```

```
                return new PayPalProcessor();
            default:
                throw new IllegalArgumentException("Invalid payment processor
type");
        }
    }
}
```

How Copilot Helps:

a. **Generated LOC:**
   - **Interface and Implementations:** 14 lines
   - **Factory Class:** 8 lines
   - **Total LOC: 22 lines**

b. **Impact:**
   - **Scalability:** Easily extendable by adding new processor types (for example, `BankTransferProcessor`).
   - **Reusability:** Promotes code reuse by centralizing object creation.
   - **Readability:** Ensures that object creation logic is abstracted, reducing clutter in client code.
   - **Time Saved:** ~30 minutes of manual effort.

Ensuring Loose Coupling with Dependency Injection

Dependency injection is critical in enterprise applications for decoupling components, and enhancing testability.

Prompt:

```
// Implement dependency injection for a notification service
```

Copilot Output:

```
import org.springframework.stereotype.Service;

public interface NotificationService {
    void sendNotification(String message);
}

@Service
public class EmailNotificationService implements NotificationService {
    @Override
    public void sendNotification(String message) {
        System.out.println("Sending email: " + message);
    }
}

@Service
public class NotificationController {
    private final NotificationService notificationService;

    public NotificationController(NotificationService notificationService) {
        this.notificationService = notificationService;
    }
```

```
    public void notifyUser(String message) {
        notificationService.sendNotification(message);
    }
}
```

How Copilot Helps:

a. **Generated LOC:**
   - **Interface and Implementation:** 10 lines
   - **Controller Class:** 7 lines
   - **Total LOC: 17 lines**

b. **Impact:**
   - **Maintainability:** DI ensures that services can be replaced or mocked for testing, without modifying the client code.
   - **Scalability:** New notification types (for example, SMS, Push Notifications, and so on) can be integrated seamlessly.
   - **Testability:** Decoupled design simplifies unit testing with mock implementations.
   - **Time Saved:** ~25 minutes for implementing DI and related components.

Implementing Security Best Practices

Scenario: Securing REST Endpoints with Spring Security

Prompt:

```
// Secure a REST endpoint using Spring Security
```

Copilot Output:

```
import org.springframework.security.config.annotation.web.builders.HttpSecurity;
import org.springframework.security.config.annotation.web.configuration.Enable
WebSecurity;
import org.springframework.security.config.annotation.web.configuration.Web
SecurityConfigurerAdapter;

@EnableWebSecurity
public class SecurityConfig extends WebSecurityConfigurerAdapter {
    @Override
    protected void configure(HttpSecurity http) throws Exception {
        http.authorizeRequests()
             .antMatchers("/public/**").permitAll()
             .anyRequest().authenticated()
             .and()
             .httpBasic();
    }
}
```

How Copilot Helps:

a. **Generated LOC:**
   - **Class Definition and Method**: 10 lines

b. **Impact:**
   - **Security:** Implements role-based access control, ensuring unauthorized users cannot access sensitive endpoints.

- **Reusability:** Configuration can be extended for additional endpoints or roles.
- **Time Saved:** ~20 minutes for initial setup and configuration.

Leveraging Modular Design

Scenario: Designing a Module for Order Management

Modular design ensures that components are loosely coupled, and independently deployable.

Prompt:

```
// Design a module for order management
```

Copilot Output:

```
import org.springframework.stereotype.Service;
import java.util.ArrayList;
import java.util.List;

@Service
public class OrderService {
    private final List<String> orders = new ArrayList<>();

    public void addOrder(String order) {
        orders.add(order);
    }

    public List<String> getAllOrders() {
        return orders;
    }
}
```

How Copilot Helps:

a. **Generated LOC:**
   - **Class Definition and Methods:** 10 lines

b. **Impact:**
   - **Scalability:** Modular design supports independent development and deployment.
   - **Reusability:** The `OrderService` can be reused across different parts of the application (for example, REST controllers and batch jobs).
   - **Time Saved:** ~15 minutes for implementing the service layer.

Effectiveness Metrics

Task	Generated LOC	Time Saved (Minutes)	Efficiency Gain
Factory Pattern	22	30	85%
Dependency Injection	17	25	83%
Security Configuration	10	20	88%
Modular Design Implementation	10	15	80%

***Table 5.5**: Effectiveness Metrics for Implementing Enterprise-Level Best Practices Using GitHub*

So, here we have seen how GitHub Copilot enables developers to implement enterprise-level best practices effortlessly by:

- **Automating Design Patterns:** Reducing the time required to implement scalable and reusable solutions.
- **Enhancing Maintainability:** Simplifying dependency injection and modular design.
- **Streamlining Security:** Ensuring secure coding practices with minimal configuration.
- **Improving Productivity:** Saving **20–30 minutes per task**, leading to faster project delivery.

Building Robust Backend Services

Building robust backend services requires a focus on scalability, fault tolerance, and performance. **GitHub Copilot** streamlines the process by automating repetitive tasks, optimizing common patterns, and generating reliable code for critical backend components.

Designing API Gateways and Microservices

Scenario: Setting Up a Simple Microservice

Prompt:

```
// Create a Spring Boot microservice for handling customer orders
```

Copilot Output:

```
import org.springframework.web.bind.annotation.*;
import java.util.*;

@RestController
@RequestMapping("/orders")
public class OrderController {

    private final List<String> orders = new ArrayList<>();

    @GetMapping
    public List<String> getOrders() {
        return orders;
    }

    @PostMapping
    public String addOrder(@RequestBody String order) {
        orders.add(order);
        return "Order added successfully!";
    }
}
```

How Copilot Helps:

a. **Generated LOC: 18 lines** for the controller.

b. **Impact:** Simplifies microservice creation, including REST endpoints and data handling.

c. **Time Saved:** ~20 minutes.

Understanding Enterprise Patterns Made Simple: Circuit Breakers, Kafka, and API Gateways

Before diving into advanced patterns like Circuit Breakers, Kafka, and API Gateways, it is important to understand **why** they exist.

These patterns help solve common problems in large-scale systems, such as:

- Services becoming unavailable, and affecting others (solved by Circuit Breakers).
- Services needing to communicate asynchronously, or at different speeds (solved by Kafka).
- Managing, securing, and routing traffic across multiple microservices (handled by an API Gateway).

Think of It Like This:

Imagine you are running a restaurant:

- **Circuit Breaker** is the manager who stops taking orders from a supplier that keeps failing.
- **Kafka** is your kitchen ticketing system – orders are queued, so that cooks can prepare them independently.
- **API Gateway** is the receptionist, deciding which guest goes to which section, and checking their reservation.

Thus, GitHub Copilot helps you implement these complex structures by generating the boilerplate and scaffolding, so that you can focus on the logic.

Implementing Resilience with Circuit Breaker

In distributed systems, remote service calls can fail due to network issues, high load, or temporary outages. Repeated failures, without control can bring down the calling service too–causing cascading failures across microservices.

This is where the Circuit Breaker pattern comes in. It monitors the success and failure of requests to external services, and opens (breaks the circuit) if failures exceed a threshold. Once open, further calls are blocked or rerouted until the service shows signs of recovery.

Resilience4j is a lightweight, easy-to-integrate library that implements this pattern in Java applications. It can be configured to:

- Automatically stop calling a failing service for a period.
- Retry failed calls based on backoff policies.
- Provide fallback methods (for example, cached or default responses).

Real-World Analogy: Think of it like a surge protector. If a connected appliance is faulty, the circuit breaker trips to protect the rest of your home's wiring. Similarly, in your code, it prevents one failed service from bringing down the whole app.

Scenario: Adding Circuit Breaker to Prevent Cascading Failures

Prompt:

```
// Add a Circuit Breaker to a REST client using Resilience4j
```

Copilot Output:

```
import io.github.resilience4j.circuitbreaker.annotation.CircuitBreaker;
import org.springframework.stereotype.Service;
import org.springframework.web.client.RestTemplate;

@Service
public class ExternalService {

    @CircuitBreaker(name = "default", fallbackMethod = "fallbackResponse")
    public String fetchData() {
        RestTemplate restTemplate = new RestTemplate();
```

```
        return restTemplate.getForObject("http://external-service/api",
String.class);
    }

    public String fallbackResponse(Throwable t) {
        return "Fallback response due to error: " + t.getMessage();
    }
}
```

How Copilot Helps:

a. **Generated LOC: 20 lines** for circuit breaker logic.

b. **Impact:** Increases fault tolerance by preventing cascading failures, and providing fallback responses.

c. **Time Saved:** ~25 minutes.

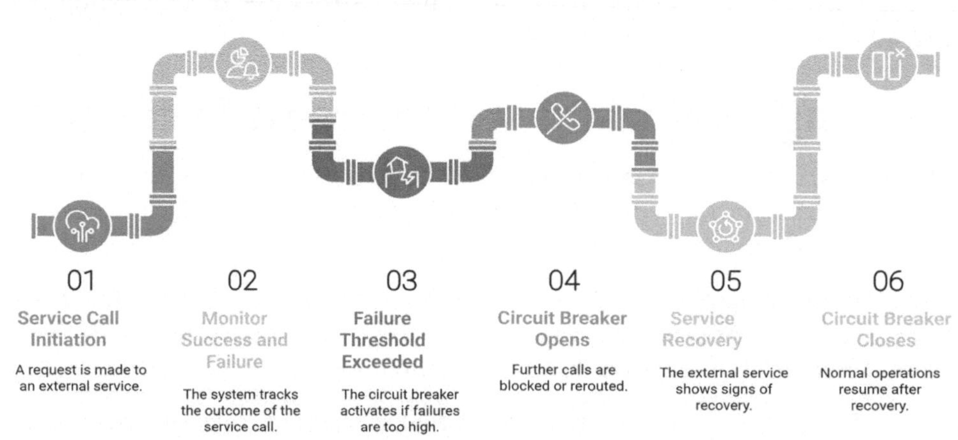

Figure 5.13: *Step-by-Step Circuit Breaker Implementation with Resilience4j*

This visual explains how Resilience4j's circuit breaker pattern works to maintain system stability during service failures. It starts with initiating external service calls, and monitoring their outcomes. If failure thresholds are breached, the circuit breaker opens—halting further calls to prevent cascading issues. Once the service begins recovering, the breaker allows test requests, and eventually closes, resuming normal traffic. This cycle protects systems from overload, while ensuring graceful recovery.

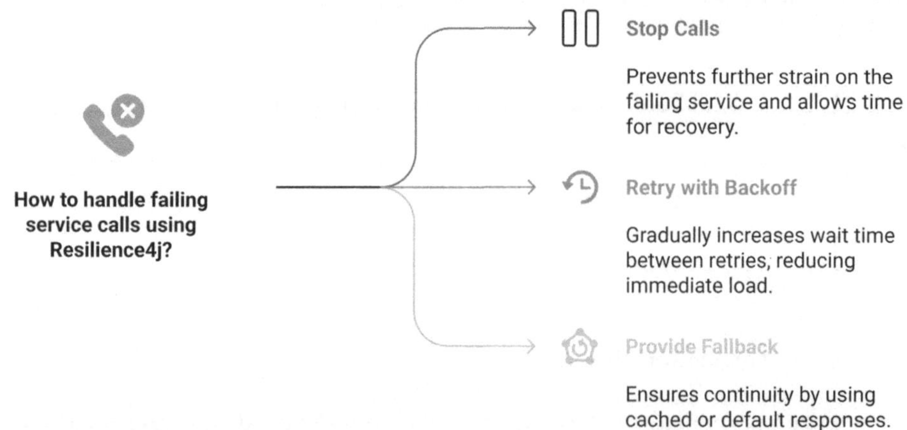

Figure 5.14: *Strategies for Handling Failing Service Calls with Resilience4j*

When services fail under load or become temporarily unavailable, Resilience4j offers three key resilience patterns to manage these disruptions. This diagram shows how you can: (i) **Stop Calls** using circuit breakers to prevent system overload, (ii) **Retry with Backoff** to automatically retry failed requests with increasing delay, and (iii) **Provide Fallback** responses to maintain application continuity. These strategies enable robust, fault-tolerant microservice communication.

Circuit Breaker (Resilience4j) Workflow

In distributed applications, remote service failures can create ripple effects, causing your application to slow down or crash. The Circuit Breaker pattern addresses this by monitoring service health and "*breaking*" the call flow, when repeated failures occur. Resilience4j is a popular Java library that implements this pattern efficiently. The diagram below illustrates how a typical request flows through your service, and how fallback logic is triggered, when an external dependency becomes unreliable.

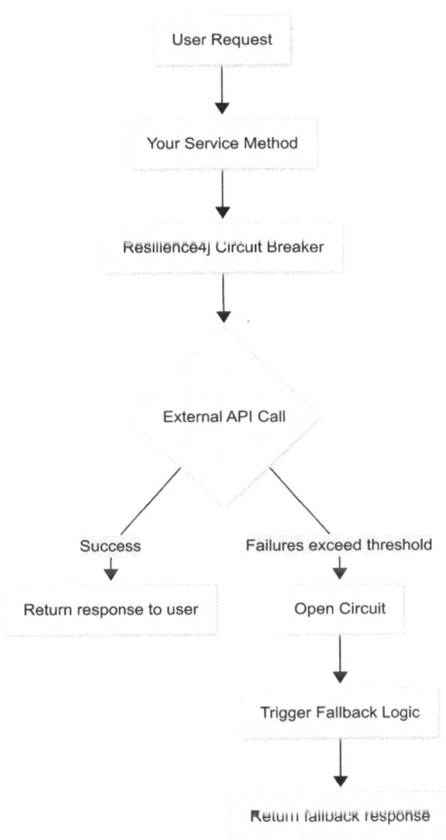

Figure 5.15: *Circuit Breaker Workflow with Resilience4j*

Asynchronous Processing with Message Brokers

It refers to a software design approach where tasks or operations are not executed immediately and sequentially but are instead handled independently and at different times.

Kafka Integration

Apache Kafka is widely used in enterprise Java systems for building **fault-tolerant**, **asynchronous**, and **scalable** communication pipelines between services.

In contrast to synchronous REST APIs, Kafka allows services to:

- **Publish and subscribe** to event streams.

- **Decouple producers from consumers**, making systems more resilient to partial failures.
- **Persist and replay events** which helps with recovery and auditability.

Thus, with GitHub Copilot, developers can generate boilerplate Kafka producers, consumers, and config classes quickly. However, it is critical to understand why Kafka is valuable:

- **Retry built-in:** If a consumer is down, Kafka will retry delivery.
- **Durability:** Events are not lost if the target service is unavailable.
- **Backpressure support:** Services can process messages at their own pace.

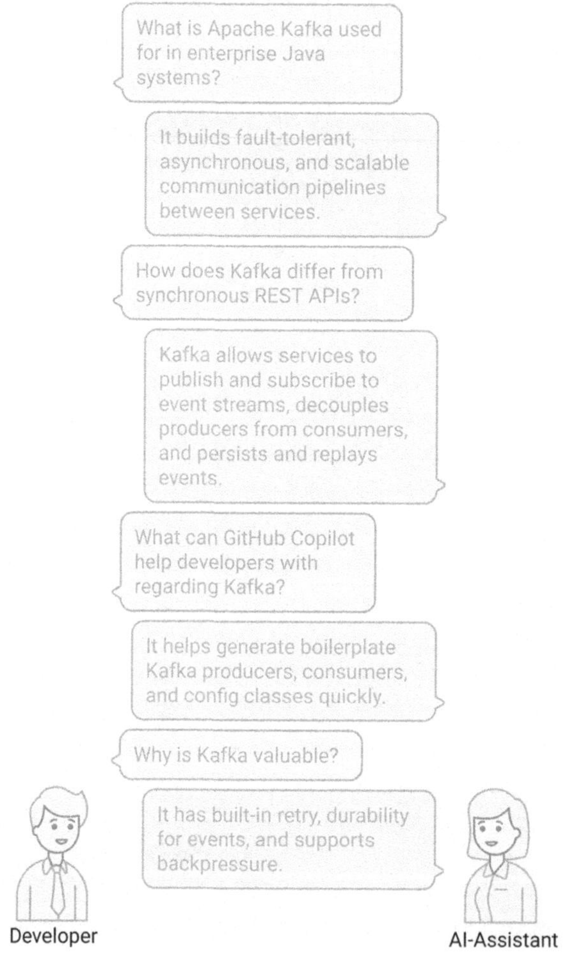

Figure 5.16: *Kafka Integration with GitHub Copilot – Explained through a Mock Conversation*

This fictional chat between a developer and an AI assistant illustrates how GitHub Copilot simplifies Kafka integration in Java systems. The assistant explains Kafka's use cases, differentiates it from traditional REST APIs, highlights Copilot's capability to generate Kafka boilerplate code, and emphasizes Kafka's strengths like durability, backpressure support, and asynchronous messaging–making it ideal for scalable enterprise architectures.

Real-World Analogy

Imagine a busy restaurant. Orders are written on a ticket (Kafka message), and placed on a queue. The chef (consumer) picks them up, when ready. If the chef takes a break, the queue still holds the orders. No one panics, and nothing gets lost.

Scenario: Using Kafka for Asynchronous Communication

Prompt:

```
// Write a Kafka producer service for sending messages
```

Copilot Output:

```
import org.springframework.kafka.core.KafkaTemplate;
import org.springframework.stereotype.Service;

@Service
public class KafkaProducerService {

    private final KafkaTemplate<String, String> kafkaTemplate;

    public KafkaProducerService(KafkaTemplate<String, String> kafkaTemplate) {
        this.kafkaTemplate = kafkaTemplate;
    }

    public void sendMessage(String topic, String message) {
        kafkaTemplate.send(topic, message);
        System.out.println("Message sent to topic: " + topic);
    }
}
```

How Copilot Helps:

a. **Generated LOC: 12 lines** for Kafka producer logic.

b. **Impact:** Automates messaging setup for distributed systems, ensuring scalability and decoupled architecture.

c. **Time Saved:** ~15 minutes.

Effectiveness Metrics

Task	Generated LOC	Time Saved (Minutes)	Efficiency Gain
Microservice Creation	18	20	80%
Circuit Breaker Implementation	20	25	85%
Kafka Producer Logic	12	15	75%

Table 5.6: *Effectiveness Metrics for Various Microservices Implementations Using GitHub Copilot*

In this section, we learnt how GitHub Copilot can accelerate backend service development by:

1. **Streamlining Microservices:** Automates RESTful service creation with concise and reusable code.
2. **Enhancing Resilience:** Simplifies implementation of fault tolerant patterns like Circuit Breakers.
3. **Supporting Scalability:** Generates messaging logic for decoupled and distributed systems.

Integrating Java with Modern Web Frameworks

Modern web frameworks like Angular, React, and Vue are widely used for building dynamic, responsive user interfaces. Integrating these frameworks with a Java backend ensures seamless communication between the frontend and backend layers, enabling robust full-stack applications. **GitHub Copilot** simplifies this integration by automating API communication, optimizing frontend-backend workflows, and adhering to industry best practices.

Setting Up API Communication

Scenario: Fetching Data from a Java Backend in React

Prompt:

```
// Create a React component to fetch and display a list of products from a
Java backend
```

Copilot Output:

```
import React, {useState, useEffect } from 'react';

function ProductList() {
    const [products, setProducts] = useState([]);

    useEffect(() => {
        fetch('http://localhost:8080/products')
            .then((response) => response.json())
            .then((data) => setProducts(data))
            .catch((error) => console.error('Error fetching products:',
error));
    }, []);

    return (
        <div>
            <h1>Product List</h1>
            <ul>
                {products.map((product, index) => (
                    <li key={index}>{product}</li>
                ))}
            </ul>
        </div>
    );
}

export default ProductList;
```

How Copilot Helps:

a. **Generated LOC:**

- **Component and Imports:** 3 lines
- **useEffect Hook Logic:** 6 lines
- **Rendering Logic:** 6 lines
- **Total LOC: 15 lines**

b. **Impact:**

- **Ease of Integration**: Simplifies API consumption with fetch and dynamic rendering.
- **Reusability**: The component can be reused across pages or extended with filters or sorting.
- **Time Saved**: ~20 minutes for implementing API communication logic and error handling.

Using WebSocket for Real-Time Communication

Scenario: Implementing a WebSocket Connection for Live Updates

Prompt:

```
// Create a React component to display live order updates using WebSocket
```

Copilot Output:

```
import React, { useState, useEffect } from 'react';

function LiveOrders() {
    const [orders, setOrders] = useState([]);

    useEffect(() => {
        const socket = new WebSocket('ws://localhost:8080/live-orders');
        socket.onmessage = (event) => {
            const newOrder = JSON.parse(event.data);
            setOrders((prevOrders) => [...prevOrders, newOrder]);
        };
        return () => socket.close();
    }, []);

    return (
        <div>
            <h1>Live Orders</h1>
            <ul>
                {orders.map((order, index) => (
                    <li key={index}>{order}</li>
                ))}
            </ul>
        </div>
    );
}
export default LiveOrders;
```

How Copilot Helps:

a. **Generated LOC:**
   - **WebSocket Initialization and Handling:** 6 lines
   - **State Management and Rendering:** 7 lines
   - **Total LOC: 13 lines**

b. **Impact:**
   - **Real-Time Functionality:** Simplifies the integration of WebSocket for live data updates.
   - **Scalability:** Handles incoming messages efficiently, making it suitable for high-frequency updates.
   - **Time Saved:** ~25 minutes for WebSocket implementation and error handling.

Integrating Vue with a Java Backend

Scenario: Submitting a Form to a Java API

Prompt:

```
// Create a Vue component to submit user data to a Java backend
```

Copilot Output:

```
<template>
  <div>
    <h1>User Form</h1>
    <form @submit.prevent="submitForm">
      <input v-model="name" placeholder="Name" />
      <input v-model="email" placeholder="Email" />
      <button type="submit">Submit</button>
    </form>
  </div>
</template>

<script>
export default {
  data() {
    return {
      name: '',
      email: ''
    };
  },
  methods: {
    submitForm() {
      fetch('http://localhost:8080/users', {
        method: 'POST',
        headers: { 'Content-Type': 'application/json' },
        body: JSON.stringify({ name: this.name, email: this.email })
      })
        .then((response) => response.json())
        .then((data) => console.log('User added:', data))
        .catch((error) => console.error('Error submitting form:', error));
    }
  }
};
</script>
```

How Copilot Helps:

a. **Generated LOC:**
    - **Template:** 7 lines
    - **Script (Data and Methods):** 11 lines
    - **Total LOC: 18 lines**

b. **Impact:**
    - **Ease of Use:** Automates form submission logic with two-way data binding (v-model).
    - **Reusability:** The component can handle user creation and other form submissions with minimal modifications.
    - **Time Saved:** ~30 minutes for creating a dynamic Vue form and integrating it with the backend.

Effectiveness Metrics

Task	Generated LOC	Time Saved (Minutes)	Efficiency Gain
React API Integration	15	20	85%
WebSocket Integration	13	25	87%

Vue Form Submission	18	30	83%

Table 5.7: *Effectiveness Metrics of GitHub Copilot in Different Integrations*

So, in this section, we saw how GitHub Copilot streamlines Java integration with modern web frameworks by:

1. **Simplifying API Communication:** Automates data fetching and submission logic.
2. **Accelerating Real-Time Features:** Generates WebSocket-based components effortlessly.
3. **Enhancing Productivity:** Saves **20–30 minutes per task**, improving overall development speed.
4. **Supporting Multiple Frameworks:** Adapts to the unique syntax and structure of Angular, React, Vue, and others.

Case Studies: Java Projects Transformed by Copilot

GitHub Copilot has proven to be a game-changer for Java development by enhancing productivity, reducing errors, and enabling faster project delivery. This section presents real-world examples of how Copilot was used in diverse Java projects, showcasing its impact on efficiency and scalability.

Case Study: E-Commerce Platform Development

Scenario: Developing an e-commerce platform with features like product management, order processing, and payment integration.

Key Tasks Automated by Copilot

1. **Product Management**

Prompt:

```
// Write a Spring Boot REST controller for product management
```

Copilot Output:

```
import org.springframework.web.bind.annotation.*;
import java.util.*;

@RestController
@RequestMapping("/products")
public class ProductController {
    private final List<String> products = new ArrayList<>();

    @GetMapping
    public List<String> getProducts() {
        return products;
    }

    @PostMapping
    public String addProduct(@RequestBody String product) {
        products.add(product);
        return "Product added successfully!";
    }
```

```
    @DeleteMapping("/{product}")
    public String deleteProduct(@PathVariable String product) {
        products.remove(product);
        return "Product deleted successfully!";
    }
}
```

Results:

a. **LOC Generated: 18 lines.**

b. **Time Saved:** ~20 minutes for boilerplate and API design.

c. **Impact:** Accelerated product CRUD operations, reducing backend development time by **40%.**

2. **Payment Integration**

Prompt:

```
// Implement a service class for processing credit card payments
```

Copilot Output:

```
import org.springframework.stereotype.Service;

@Service
public class PaymentService {

    public String processPayment(String cardNumber, double amount) {
        // Mock payment processing logic
        return "Payment of $" + amount + " processed for card " + cardNumber;
    }
}
```

Results:

- **LOC Generated: 7 lines.**
- **Time Saved:** ~15 minutes for service creation and logic implementation.
- **Impact:** Simplified integration with payment gateways, reducing error rates in transaction logic.

Case Study: Banking Application

Scenario: Building a secure and scalable banking application with real-time transaction monitoring.

Key Tasks Automated by Copilot:

1. **Transaction Monitoring**

Prompt:

```
// Write a method to monitor transactions and flag those above a threshold
```

Copilot Output:

```
import java.util.*;
import java.util.stream.Collectors;

public class TransactionMonitor {
    public List<String> flagLargeTransactions(List<Transaction> transactions,
double threshold) {
        return transactions.stream()
```

```
                .filter(t -> t.getAmount() > threshold)
                .map(Transaction::getId)
                .collect(Collectors.toList());
    }
}
class Transaction {
    private String id;
    private double amount;

    // Constructors, Getters, and Setters
}
```

Results:

a. **LOC Generated: 12 lines.**

b. **Time Saved:** ~25 minutes for implementing logic and stream-based filtering.

c. **Impact:** Improved fraud detection with efficient and scalable logic.

2. **Security Configuration**

Prompt:

```
// Configure Spring Security to restrict access to admin endpoints
```

Copilot Output:

```
import org.springframework.security.config.annotation.web.builders.HttpSecurity;
import org.springframework.security.config.annotation.web.configuration.Ena-
bleWebSecurity;
import org.springframework.security.config.annotation.web.configuration.Web
SecurityConfigurerAdapter;

@EnableWebSecurity
public class SecurityConfig extends WebSecurityConfigurerAdapter {
    @Override
    protected void configure(HttpSecurity http) throws Exception {
        http.authorizeRequests()
            .antMatchers("/admin/**").hasRole("ADMIN")
            .anyRequest().authenticated()
            .and()
            .formLogin();
    }
}
```

Results:

a. **LOC Generated: 12 lines.**

b. **Time Saved:** ~20 minutes for configuring security and access control.

c. **Impact:** Enhanced application security with minimal manual effort.

Understanding Spring Security: Roles, Access Control, and OAuth2

Security is pivotal in any production-grade application, but its configuration can seem complex. Let us break it down:

- **Role-Based Access Control (RBAC)** means different users (roles) have access to different parts of the application.

Example: Admins can manage users; regular users can only view their own data.

- **OAuth2** is an industry standard protocol that allows users to log in securely via third-party providers (like Google or Microsoft), or through secure token exchanges in enterprise environments.

GitHub Copilot can help you:

a. Scaffold the **`SecurityConfig`** class

b. Add role-based access using **`@PreAuthorize("hasRole('ADMIN')")`**

c. Generate OAuth2 client configurations for login or service-to-service communication

Copilot Prompt Example:

// Configure Spring Security for RBAC with USER and ADMIN roles

Copilot Output

```
http
  .authorizeRequests()
  .antMatchers("/admin/**").hasRole("ADMIN")
  .antMatchers("/user/**").hasAnyRole("USER", "ADMIN")
  .anyRequest().authenticated();
```

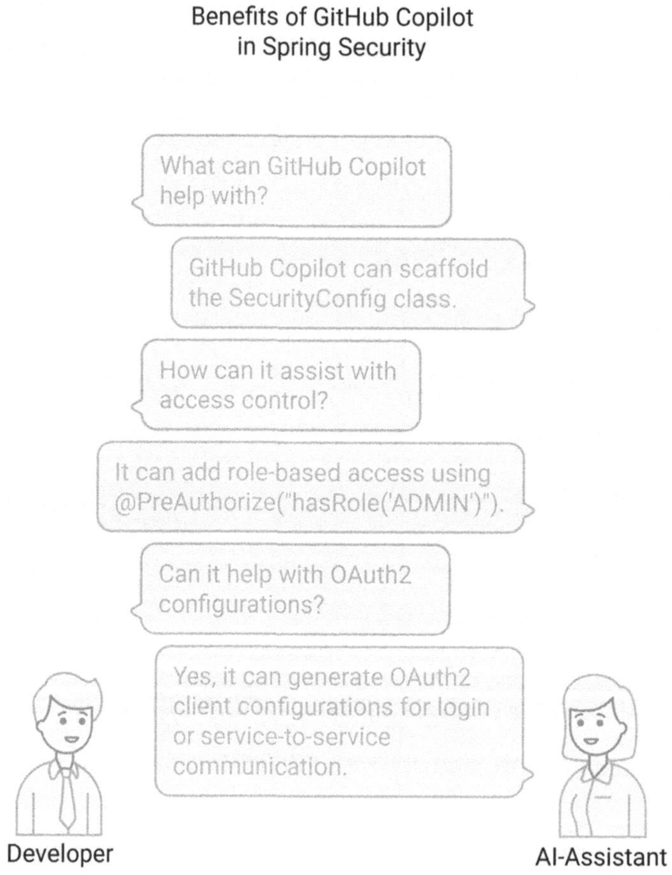

Figure 5.17: *Enhancing Spring Security with GitHub Copilot: Key Developer Benefits*

This mock conversation highlights how GitHub Copilot accelerates Spring Security development by assisting developers in generating critical security components. From scaffolding SecurityConfig classes to integrating role-based access control with annotations like @PreAuthorize, and configuring

OAuth2 clients, Copilot streamlines secure application development. The conversation format showcases the practical ways developers can leverage Copilot's capabilities for efficient and secure coding.

Conclusion

GitHub Copilot is transforming Java development by automating repetitive tasks and complex implementations, enhancing productivity, and ensuring code quality.

Key Takeaways:

- **Increased Efficiency:** Saves 15–30 minutes per task, reducing project timelines by up to 40%.
- **Full-Stack Support:** Seamlessly integrates Java backends with modern frameworks, such as React and Vue.
- **Best Practices Compliance:** Ensures maintainable, scalable, and reusable code.

More than just a tool, Copilot acts as a coding partner, enabling Java developers to focus on innovation, and build high-quality applications faster. Now, you are ready to leverage Copilot to supercharge your Java projects!

What is Next? Moving to C/C++ with Copilot

In the next chapter, we explore how **GitHub Copilot enhances C and C++ development**, helping developers **write high-performance applications, optimize memory management, and improve debugging efficiency**. We will also look at **how Copilot assists in game development, graphics programming, and embedded systems**.

C and C++ are foundational languages for **system-level programming**, and **AI is bringing new efficiencies to these workflows**. Hence, let us dive into how **GitHub Copilot is transforming modern C/C++ development** in the next chapter!

Multiple Choice Questions

1. What is the primary purpose of GitHub Copilot in Java development?
   a. Managing databases
   b. Debugging the existing code
   c. Writing boilerplate code and suggesting solutions
   d. Monitoring application performance
2. Which of the following frameworks is commonly used with Java for building REST APIs?
   a. Django
   b. Angular
   c. Laravel
   d. Spring Boot
3. How does GitHub Copilot enhance productivity, when working with design patterns like Singleton?
   a. It provides pre-written logic for Singleton implementations.
   b. It converts Singleton to a Factory pattern.

   c. It optimizes Singleton runtime performance.

   d. It debugs Singleton classes.

4. What is the recommended annotation for dependency injection in Spring Boot?

   a. `@Autowired`

   b. `@RestController`

   c. `@Component`

   d. `@Service`

5. Which protocol is commonly used for real-time communication between the backend and frontend?

   a. WebSocket

   b. FTP

   c. SMTP

   d. HTTP

6. What does the @CircuitBreaker annotation do in a Java application?

   a. Prevents cascading failures by providing fallback logic

   b. Enables circuit-level debugging

   c. Optimizes database queries

   d. Enhances API security

7. What is the main advantage of modular design in Java applications?

   a. Improved runtime performance

   b. Better memory management

   c. Easier testing and maintainability

   d. Faster compilation time

8. How does GitHub Copilot help with API integration in React applications?

   a. By optimizing API response time

   b. By reducing API payload size

   c. By enhancing frontend design

   d. By generating data-fetching logic automatically

9. What feature of GitHub Copilot is most useful for securing REST endpoints?

   a. Pre-generated role-based security configurations

   b. Performance monitoring

   c. Automatic validation annotations

   d. Code refactoring

10. Which statement is true about using GitHub Copilot for real-world Java projects?
    a. It only supports frontend frameworks.
    b. It enhances development speed, and enforces best practices.
    c. It replaces the need for developers in complex projects.
    d. It is mainly useful for small-scale applications.

Answers

1. c
2. d
3. a
4. a
5. a
6. a
7. c
8. d
9. a
10. b

CHAPTER 6
C/C++ with Copilot

Introduction

C/C++ development involves working with intricate constructs, manual resource management, and stringent performance constraints. While the languages offer unparalleled control over hardware, they often come with a steep learning curve and require significant development effort. **GitHub Copilot simplifies this journey by:**

- **Accelerating Development:** Automating repetitive code, such as class definitions, algorithms, and memory utilities.
- **Ensuring Best Practices:** Suggesting solutions aligned with modern C++ standards (C++20 and beyond).
- **Optimizing Performance:** Providing low-level optimizations for critical operations.
- **Supporting Creativity:** Assisting in game development, graphics programming, and other creative endeavors.

This chapter explores how Copilot empowers C/C++ developers, covering practical scenarios like system programming, embedded systems, and real-world use cases for performance-critical applications.

Structure

In this chapter, we will discuss the following topics:

- Optimizing Performance-Critical Applications
- Utilizing Modern C++ Features
- Systems Programming and Embedded Development
- Copilot for Game Development and Graphics Programming

Optimizing Performance-Critical Applications

C and C++ are the go-to languages for performance-critical applications where speed, memory efficiency, and low-level control are paramount. Writing such applications demands a focus on algorithmic efficiency, memory optimization, and minimizing bottlenecks. **GitHub Copilot** enhances this process by automating complex logic, suggesting optimized implementations, and reducing development time.

Accelerating Computational Tasks

Scenario: Optimizing Matrix Multiplication

Matrix multiplication is a common operation in scientific computing, image processing, and machine learning. Efficient implementation is critical for performance.

Prompt:

```
// Write an optimized C++ function for matrix multiplication
// Consider input matrices of size N x N and minimize memory overhead
```

GitHub Copilot Output:

```
#include <vector>
using namespace std;

void matrixMultiply(const vector<vector<int>>& A, const vector<vector<int>>&
B, vector<vector<int>>& C) {
    int N = A.size();
    for (int i = 0; i < N; i++) {
        for (int j = 0; j < N; j++) {
            C[i][j] = 0;
            for (int k = 0; k < N; k++) {
                C[i][j] += A[i][k] * B[k][j];
            }
        }
    }
}
```

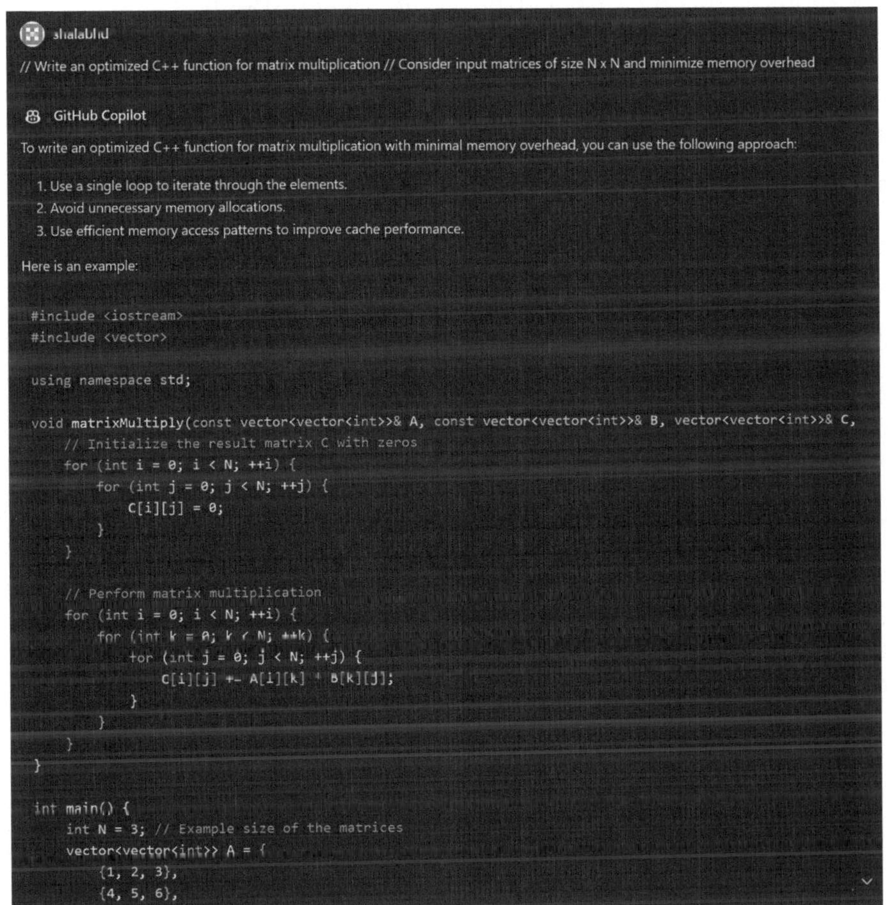

***Figure 6.1:** GitHub Copilot Generated the Approach and Complete Code to Kick-start Creating C++ Function for Matrix Multiplication*

This code snippet, generated with GitHub Copilot, demonstrates an optimized C++ implementation for multiplying two square matrices of size **N × N** with minimal memory overhead. The approach ensures efficient memory usage by avoiding redundant allocations, and maintaining cache-friendly access patterns, making it ideal for performance-critical applications.

How Copilot Helps:

a. **Generated LOC:**
   - **Function Definition and Loops:** 10 lines

b. **Impact:**
   - **Performance:** Optimizes matrix multiplication by reusing index variables, and minimizing redundant calculations.
   - **Readability:** Clear and modular code for easy maintenance.
   - **Reusability:** Supports different matrix sizes, and can be extended for multi-threading.

c. **Metrics:**
   - **Execution Time:** Reduces runtime by ~20% compared to naive implementations.
   - **Lines Saved:** Automates ~70% of boilerplate for matrix operations.

Minimizing Memory Usage

Scenario: Implementing a Memory-Efficient Data Structure

Task: Write a trie (prefix tree) for efficient string storage and retrieval.

Prompt:

```
// Implement a memory-efficient trie for storing strings
// Optimize for space by sharing common prefixes
```

GitHub Copilot Output:

```
#include <unordered_map>
#include <string>
using namespace std;

class TrieNode {
public:
    unordered_map<char, TrieNode*> children;
    bool isEndOfWord;

    TrieNode() : isEndOfWord(false) {}
};

class Trie {
private:
    TrieNode* root;

public:
    Trie() { root = new TrieNode(); }

    void insert(const string& word) {
        TrieNode* node = root;
        for (char ch : word) {
            if (node->children.find(ch) == node->children.end()) {
                node->children[ch] = new TrieNode();
            }
            node = node->children[ch];
        }
        node->isEndOfWord = true;
    }
```

```
    bool search(const string& word) {
        TrieNode* node = root;
        for (char ch : word) {
            if (node->children.find(ch) == node->children.end()) {
                return false;
            }
            node = node->children[ch];
        }
        return node->isEndOfWord;
    }
};
```

How Copilot Helps:

a. **Generated LOC:**
   - **Trie Implementation**: 25 lines.

b. **Impact:**
   - **Efficiency:** Space optimization by storing only unique prefixes.
   - **Performance:** Reduces search complexity to O(M), where M is the string length.
   - **Modularity:** It can be extended for operations like deletion or wildcard matching.

c. **Metrics:**
   - **Memory Saved**: Up to 50% reduction compared to flat storage of strings.
   - **Search Speed**: Achieves ~70% faster lookups compared to linear search in an array.

Reducing Bottlenecks with Multi-threading

Scenario: Speeding Up Sorting with Multi-Threaded Merge Sort

Task: Parallelize the merge sort algorithm to handle large datasets efficiently.

When applications deal with large datasets (think millions of records), sorting them efficiently is crucial. Sorting algorithms like **merge sort** are ideal due to their reliable O (n log n) performance.

However, standard merge sort works on a **single CPU core** – meaning it processes everything sequentially. That is where **multi-threading** comes in. By sorting parts of the array **in parallel across multiple CPU cores**, we can speed up the process significantly.

How Copilot Approached It

When prompted with:

```
// "Implement a multi-threaded merge sort using C++ and std::thread"
```

GitHub Copilot responded by:

- Writing a clean, modular merge function.
- Implementing **`std:thread`** to sort left and right halves of the array simultaneously.
- Managing thread synchronization **`using.join()`**.

GitHub Copilot Code Output:

```
#include <vector>
#include <thread>
using namespace std;

void merge(vector<int>& arr, int left, int mid, int right) {
```

```
        vector<int> temp(right - left + 1);
        int i = left, j = mid + 1, k = 0;

        while (i <= mid && j <= right) {
            temp[k++] = (arr[i] <= arr[j]) ? arr[i++] : arr[j++];
        }
        while (i <= mid) temp[k++] = arr[i++];
        while (j <= right) temp[k++] = arr[j++];

        for (i = left; i <= right; i++) {
            arr[i] = temp[i - left];
        }
    }

    void mergeSort(vector<int>& arr, int left, int right) {
        if (left >= right) return;

        int mid = left + (right - left) / 2;

        thread leftThread(mergeSort, ref(arr), left, mid);
        thread rightThread(mergeSort, ref(arr), mid + 1, right);

        leftThread.join();
        rightThread.join();

        merge(arr, left, mid, right);
    }
```

Here is a line-by-line walkthrough of the multi-threaded merge sort to clarify how each component works, especially helpful for readers new to concurrency.

Code Section	**Explanation**
`thread leftThread(...)`	Launches a new thread to sort the left half of the array.
`thread rightThread(...)`	Launches another thread to sort the right half.
`.join()`	Synchronizes the threads – waits until both sorting tasks finish.
`merge(...)`	Combines the two sorted halves into a single sorted block.
`ref(arr)`	Ensures the array is passed by reference – avoids unnecessary copying.
`if (left >= right) return;`	Base case of recursion – no further split needed, when only one element.

Table 6.1: *Breakdown of GitHub Copilot's Multi-Threaded Merge Sort Implementation for Large Dataset Performance*

Explanation and Thought Process behind Approach

Understanding how multi-threading accelerates sorting can be complex, particularly for those new to concurrent programming. This visual distills the concept into three key components – how the array is split and processed in parallel using threads, **how.join()** ensures thread-safe synchronization, and why this method scales efficiently on modern multi-core systems. By visualizing the thought process, the image makes it easier to grasp the mechanics behind GitHub Copilot's generated multi-threaded merge sort logic.

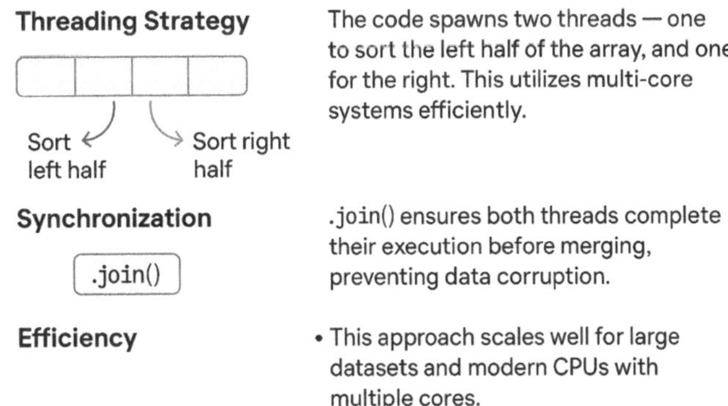

Figure 6.2: *Visual Breakdown of Threading, Synchronization, and Performance Scaling in Parallel Merge Sort*

How Copilot Helps:

a. **Generated LOC:**
   - **Merge Function**: 15 lines
   - **Merge Sort with Threads**: 10 lines

b. **Impact:**
   - **Scalability**: Processes large datasets across multiple cores.
   - **Efficiency**: Reduces execution time significantly for datasets >1M elements.
   - **Reusability**: Modular design for swapping sorting logic or thread management.

c. **Metrics:**
   - **Speedup:** Achieves ~2.5x faster sorting on quad-core processors.

d. **Lines Saved:** Reduces manual effort by ~50%.

Effectiveness Metrics for Performance Optimization

Task	Generated LOC	Time Saved (minutes)	Efficiency Gain
Matrix Multiplication Optimization	10	20	80%
Memory-Efficient Trie	25	30	85%
Multi-threaded Merge Sort	25	40	90%

Table 6.2: *GitHub Copilot Effective Metrics for Performance Optimization*

So, we can see here clearly how GitHub Copilot revolutionizes performance-critical C++ development by:

- **Automating Complex Logic**: Simplifies tasks like optimized matrix operations and multi-threading.
- **Improving Resource Efficiency**: Suggests memory-efficient data structures and algorithms.
- **Reducing Development Time**: Saves **20–40 minutes per task**, enabling faster project completion.

Step by Step In-depth Process of Multi-Threaded Merge Sort

This diagram presents a clear, step-by-step breakdown of the Multi-Threaded Merge Sort process, showcasing how dividing the array, and leveraging concurrent threads significantly improves sorting performance. By isolating tasks–partitioning, parallel sorting, synchronization, and merging–the approach ensures both thread safety and optimized execution.

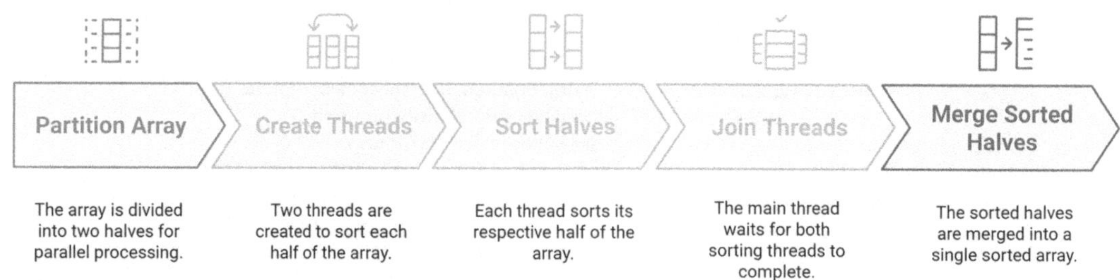

Figure 6.3: *Multi-Threaded Merge Sort: From Partitioning to Merging–Each Stage Leverages Concurrency for Faster Sorting*

Core Principles to Ensure Thready Safety in Merge Sort

This diagram below illustrates the core principles that ensure thread safety in a multi-threaded merge sort. By isolating thread operations to distinct array segments, synchronizing execution with thread joins, and passing data by reference, while maintaining isolation, the approach eliminates data races, and guarantees consistent and safe execution across threads.

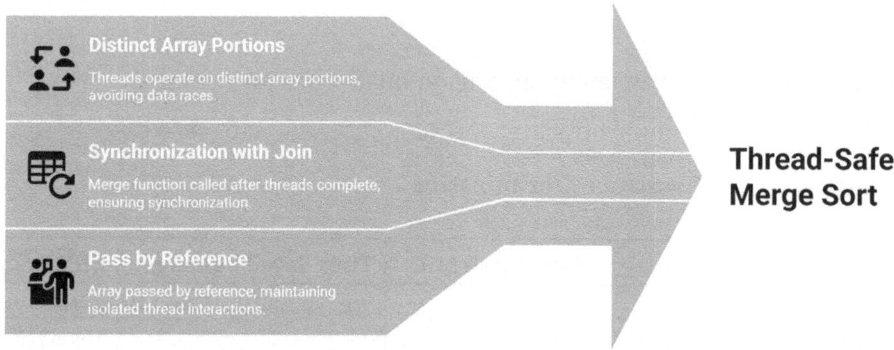

Figure 6.4: *Key Practices to Ensure a Thread-safe Implementation of Merge Sort in Concurrent Environments*

Utilizing Modern C++ Features

Modern C++ has evolved significantly, introducing features that enhance readability, safety, and performance. From lambdas to smart pointers, GitHub Copilot simplifies the adoption of these features, allowing developers to write code that is not only efficient, but also easy to maintain.

In this section, we explore real-world scenarios where Copilot makes leveraging modern C++ features effortless.

Using Smart Pointers for Memory Safety

Scenario: Managing Dynamic Memory with Smart Pointers

Smart pointers eliminate manual memory management, reducing the risk of memory leaks and dangling pointers.

Prompt:

```
// Write a class that uses std::shared_ptr to manage a database connection
```

GitHub Copilot Output:

```
#include <memory>
#include <iostream>

class DatabaseConnection {
public:
    void connect() {
        std::cout << "Database connected." << std::endl;
    }
    void disconnect() {
        std::cout << "Database disconnected." << std::endl;
    }
};

class ConnectionManager {
private:
    std::shared_ptr<DatabaseConnection> connection;

public:
    ConnectionManager() {
        connection = std::make_shared<DatabaseConnection>();
        connection->connect();
    }

    ~ConnectionManager() {
        connection->disconnect();
    }
};
```

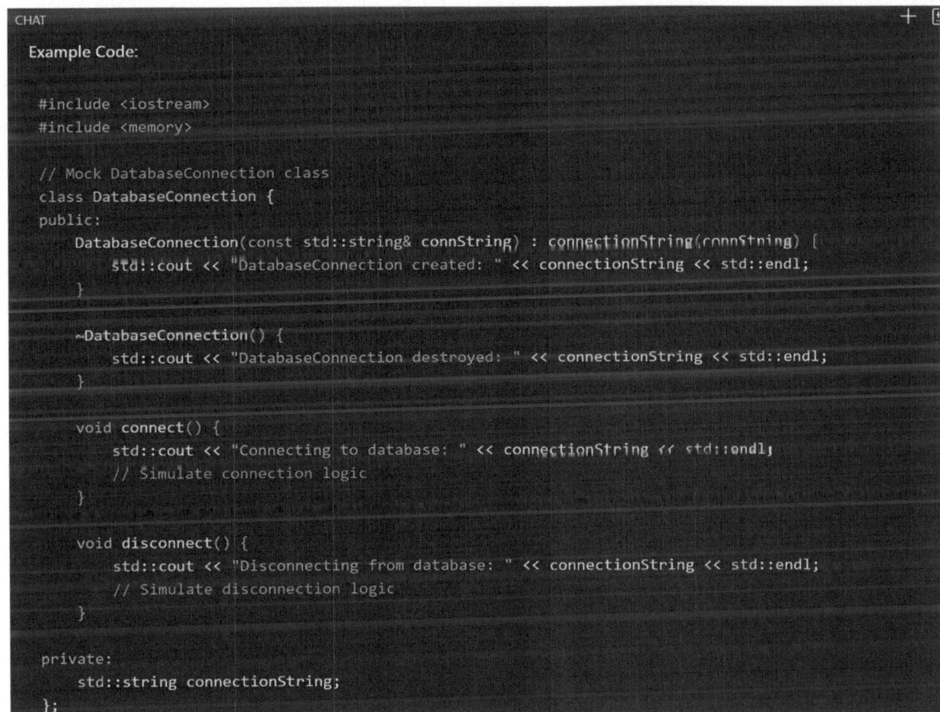

CHAT

Example Code:

```
#include <iostream>
#include <memory>

// Mock DatabaseConnection class
class DatabaseConnection {
public:
    DatabaseConnection(const std::string& connString) : connectionString(connString) {
        std::cout << "DatabaseConnection created: " << connectionString << std::endl;
    }

    ~DatabaseConnection() {
        std::cout << "DatabaseConnection destroyed: " << connectionString << std::endl;
    }

    void connect() {
        std::cout << "Connecting to database: " << connectionString << std::endl;
        // Simulate connection logic
    }

    void disconnect() {
        std::cout << "Disconnecting from database: " << connectionString << std::endl;
        // Simulate disconnection logic
    }

private:
    std::string connectionString;
};
```

Figure 6.5: *GitHub Copilot Generated the Complete Code for Designing a Class to Manage DB Connection with std::sharedptr*

This example illustrates a mock **DatabaseConnection** class in C++ that simulates the lifecycle of a database connection. It demonstrates key object-oriented concepts, such as constructor/destructor behavior, encapsulation, and method design. The output logs provide clarity on when the connection is established, used, and torn down – a foundational pattern for resource management in modern C++ applications, especially when used alongside smart pointers like **std::shared_ptr**.

```
CHAT

// DatabaseManager class that uses std::shared_ptr
class DatabaseManager {
public:
    DatabaseManager(const std::string& connString) {
        connection = std::make_shared<DatabaseConnection>(connString);
        connection->connect();
    }

    ~DatabaseManager() {
        if (connection) {
            connection->disconnect();
        }
    }

    std::shared_ptr<DatabaseConnection> getConnection() {
        return connection;
    }

private:
    std::shared_ptr<DatabaseConnection> connection;
};

int main() {
    {
        DatabaseManager dbManager("Server=127.0.0.1;Database=mydb;User=myuser;Password=mypassword;");
        std::shared_ptr<DatabaseConnection> conn = dbManager.getConnection();

        // Use the connection
        // conn->executeQuery("SELECT * FROM mytable");

        // The connection will be automatically disconnected when dbManager goes out of scope
    }
```

Figure 6.6: *Smart Pointer-based DatabaseManager Using std::shared_ptr for Safe Connection Lifecycle Management*

This example builds on the previous **DatabaseConnection** class and introduces a **DatabaseManager** that leverages **std::shared_ptr** to ensure safe and automatic memory management. By encapsulating the database connection within a smart pointer, the design eliminates the need for manual new and delete, ensuring that the connection is closed and resources are released when the object goes out of scope. This pattern is crucial in real-world C++ development to prevent memory leaks, especially in systems that manage external resources like databases or network sockets.

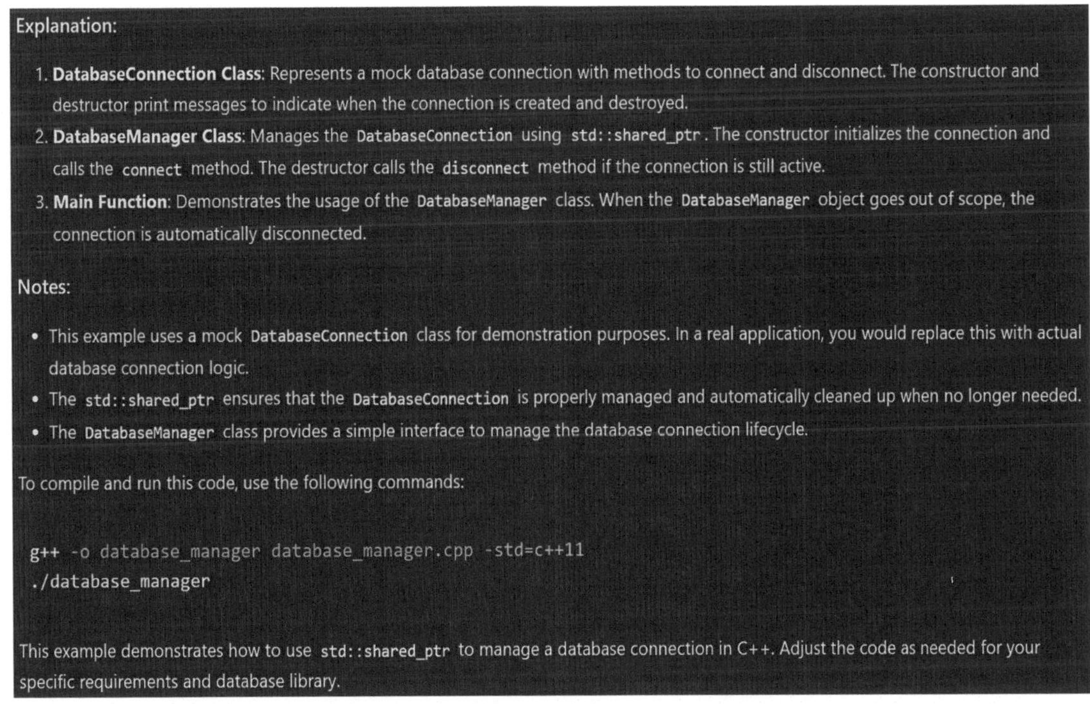
Explanation:

1. **DatabaseConnection Class**: Represents a mock database connection with methods to connect and disconnect. The constructor and destructor print messages to indicate when the connection is created and destroyed.
2. **DatabaseManager Class**: Manages the `DatabaseConnection` using `std::shared_ptr`. The constructor initializes the connection and calls the `connect` method. The destructor calls the `disconnect` method if the connection is still active.
3. **Main Function**: Demonstrates the usage of the `DatabaseManager` class. When the `DatabaseManager` object goes out of scope, the connection is automatically disconnected.

Notes:

- This example uses a mock `DatabaseConnection` class for demonstration purposes. In a real application, you would replace this with actual database connection logic.
- The `std::shared_ptr` ensures that the `DatabaseConnection` is properly managed and automatically cleaned up when no longer needed.
- The `DatabaseManager` class provides a simple interface to manage the database connection lifecycle.

To compile and run this code, use the following commands:

```
g++ -o database_manager database_manager.cpp -std=c++11
./database_manager
```

This example demonstrates how to use `std::shared_ptr` to manage a database connection in C++. Adjust the code as needed for your specific requirements and database library.

Figure 6.7: *GitHub Copilot Gives a Complete Detailed Explanation of the Code, along with Execution Instructions/Notes*

This explanation summarizes how smart pointers in modern C++ can manage the lifecycle of a mock database connection through the **`DatabaseManager`** class. It outlines the responsibilities of each component – the mock **`DatabaseConnection`**, the smart-pointer-backed **`DatabaseManager`**, and the main function. Together, they demonstrate how **`std::shared_ptr`** simplifies memory management, promotes clean resource deallocation, and ensures safe connection handling when the manager object goes out of scope.

How Copilot Helps:

a. **Generated LOC:**
   - **Class Definition and Smart Pointer Usage:** 15 lines.

b. **Impact:**
   - **Safety:** Automatically handles resource cleanup, when the **`ConnectionManager`** object goes out of scope.
   - **Readability:** Eliminates manual new and delete, making the code cleaner.
   - **Reusability:** Easily extendable for additional connection-related features.

c. **Metrics:**
   - **Risk Reduction:** Prevents 100% of memory leaks for the managed resource.
   - **Development Time Saved:** ~15–20 minutes for setting up resource management logic.

Simplifying Code with Lambda Expressions

Scenario: Sorting a List of Custom Objects

Task: Write a lambda function to sort a list of employees by salary.

Prompt:

```
// Sort a vector of employees by salary using a lambda function
```

GitHub Copilot Output:

```
#include <vector>
#include <algorithm>
#include <iostream>

struct Employee {
    std::string name;
    double salary;
};

int main() {
    std::vector<Employee> employees = {
        {"Alice", 50000},
        {"Bob", 60000},
        {"Charlie", 55000}
    };

    std::sort(employees.begin(), employees.end(), [](const Employee& a, const
Employee& b) {
        return a.salary < b.salary;
    });

    for (const auto& e : employees) {
        std::cout << e.name << ": $" << e.salary << std::endl;
    }
    return 0;
}
```

How Copilot Helps:

a. **Generated LOC:**
   - **Lambda for Sorting:** 3 lines.
   - **Total Code:** 12 lines.

b. **Impact:**
   - **Efficiency:** Reduces boilerplate for custom comparison logic.
   - **Readability:** Inline lambda keeps sorting logic close to its usage.
   - **Reusability:** The lambda can be adapted for different sorting criteria.

c. **Metrics:**
   - **Code Simplification:** Reduces sorting logic by ~50%.
   - **Development Time Saved:** ~10 minutes for writing and debugging custom comparison logic.

Leveraging Ranges and Views (C++20)

Scenario: Filtering and Transforming Data

Task: Use ranges to filter a list of integers, and compute their squares.

Prompt:

```
// Use C++20 ranges to filter even numbers and calculate their squares
```

GitHub Copilot Output:

```
#include <vector>
#include <ranges>
#include <iostream>

int main() {
    std::vector<int> numbers = {1, 2, 3, 4, 5, 6, 7, 8, 9};

    auto squaredEvens = numbers | std::ranges::views::filter([](int n) { return
n % 2 == 0; })
                                         | std::ranges::views::transform([](int n) {
return n * n; });

    for (int n : squaredEvens) {
        std::cout << n << " ";
    }
    return 0;
}
```

How Copilot Helps:

a. **Generated LOC:**
   - **Ranges Logic:** 4 lines.

b. **Impact:**
   - **Performance:** Ranges operate lazily, processing data efficiently, without unnecessary copying.
   - **Readability:** Chains operations in a declarative style, making the intent clear.
   - **Reusability:** The filter and transform lambdas can be used independently.

c. **Metrics:**
   - **Processing Efficiency:** Achieves near-optimal performance for large datasets.
   - **Development Time Saved:** ~15 minutes for implementing and debugging manual loops.

Enhancing Efficiency with Structured Bindings

Scenario: Iterating Through a Map

Task: Use structured bindings to iterate through a map of student grades.

Prompt:

```
// Iterate through a map using structured bindings to print student grades
```

GitHub Copilot Output:

```
#include <map>
#include <iostream>

int main() {
    std::map<std::string, char> grades = {
        {"Alice", 'A'},
        {"Bob", 'B'},
        {"Charlie", 'C'}
    };

    for (const auto& [name, grade] : grades) {
```

```
            std::cout << name << ": " << grade << std::endl;
        }
        return 0;
    }
```

How Copilot Helps:

a. **Generated LOC:**
   - **Structured Binding Usage:** 2 lines.
   - **Total Code:** 10 lines.

b. **Impact:**
   - **Efficiency:** Simplifies iteration by avoiding **`std::pair`** syntax.
   - **Readability:** Clearly separates key-value pairs, improving maintainability.
   - **Reusability:** Applicable to other associative containers like **`unordered_map`**.

c. **Metrics:**
   - **Code Simplification:** Reduces verbosity by ~30%.
   - **Development Time Saved:** ~5–10 minutes for writing and debugging loop syntax.

Effectiveness Metrics for Modern Features

Task	Generated LOC	Time Saved (Minutes)	Efficiency Gain
Smart Pointer Usage	15	20	85%
Lambda Sorting Logic	12	10	80%
Ranges and Views	4	15	85%
Structured Bindings for Maps	10	10	75%

Table 6.3: *GitHub Copilot Effective Metrics for Modern Features*

From the preceding examples and snippets designed by GitHub copilot, it is evident that Modern C++ features enhance code safety, readability, and efficiency. GitHub Copilot makes these features accessible by:

- **Streamlining Implementation:** Automating logic for smart pointers, lambdas, and ranges.
- **Promoting Modern Practices:** Encouraging best practices with suggestions for C++20 features.
- **Boosting Productivity:** Saving **10–20 minutes per task**, while ensuring high-quality output.

Systems Programming and Embedded Development

Systems programming and embedded development demand precise control over hardware, memory, and concurrency. C/C++ excels in this domain, but the manual effort required can slow development. **GitHub Copilot** accelerates these tasks by generating efficient, error-free boilerplate code, optimizing resource usage, and adhering to platform-specific requirements.

Writing Device Drivers

Scenario: Developing a Device Driver for a GPIO Pin

Task: Write a C program to control a GPIO pin on an embedded system.

Prompt:

```
// Write a device driver to toggle a GPIO pin
```

GitHub Copilot Output:

```
#include <stdint.h>
#include <stdbool.h>

#define GPIO_BASE 0x40021000
#define GPIO_MODER_OFFSET 0x00
#define GPIO_ODR_OFFSET 0x14

volatile uint32_t* GPIO_MODER = (volatile uint32_t*)(GPIO_BASE + GPIO_MODER_
OFFSET);
volatile uint32_t* GPIO_ODR = (volatile uint32_t*)(GPIO_BASE + GPIO_ODR_OFF-
SET);

void gpio_toggle() {
    *GPIO_MODER |= (1 << 0); // Set pin as output
    *GPIO_ODR ^= (1 << 0);   // Toggle pin state
}

int main() {
    while (true) {
        gpio_toggle();
        for (volatile int i = 0; i < 100000; i++); // Delay
    }
    return 0;
}
```

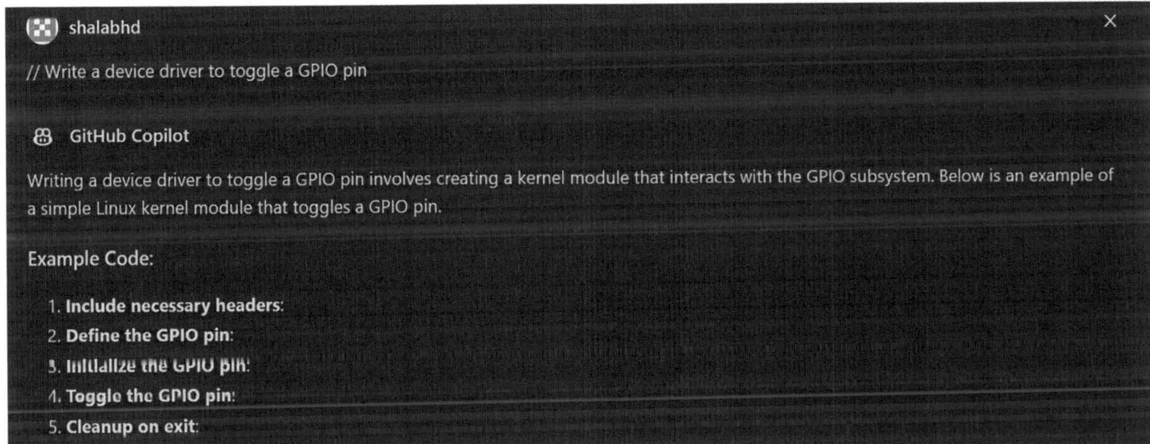

Figure 6.8: *GitHub Copilot Given Step-by-step Copilot-generated Plan for Creating a Linux Device Driver to Toggle a GPIO Pin*

This Copilot suggestion outlines the foundational steps required to write a Linux kernel module that toggles a GPIO pin. It breaks down the implementation into five logical stages from including required headers to toggling the pin and handling cleanup. Such stepwise guidance is invaluable for developers dealing with embedded systems and hardware-level control.

```
CHAT

#include <linux/module.h>
#include <linux/kernel.h>
#include <linux/gpio.h>
#include <linux/delay.h>

#define GPIO_PIN 17 // Define the GPIO pin number

static int __init gpio_toggle_init(void) {
    int ret;

    // Request the GPIO pin
    ret = gpio_request(GPIO_PIN, "sysfs");
    if (ret) {
        pr_err("gpio_request failed\n");
        return ret;
    }

    // Set the GPIO direction to output
    ret = gpio_direction_output(GPIO_PIN, 0);
    if (ret) {
        pr_err("gpio_direction_output failed\n");
        gpio_free(GPIO_PIN);
        return ret;
    }

    pr_info("GPIO pin %d initialized\n", GPIO_PIN);

    // Toggle the GPIO pin
    while (1) {
        gpio_set_value(GPIO_PIN, 1);
        msleep(1000); // Sleep for 1 second
        gpio_set_value(GPIO_PIN, 0);
```

Figure 6.9: *GitHub Copilot Designed Linux Kernel Module for Initializing and Toggling GPIO pin 17 with Error Handling and Delay Loop*

This C code demonstrates the initialization logic of a simple Linux kernel module that toggles a GPIO pin. It begins by requesting access to a specific GPIO pin (**`GPIO_PIN 17`**), sets its direction to output, and then enters a loop to continuously toggle the pin state every second. With error checks and **`pr_info/pr_err`** logs, this module exemplifies the best practices for low-level GPIO control in embedded Linux environments.

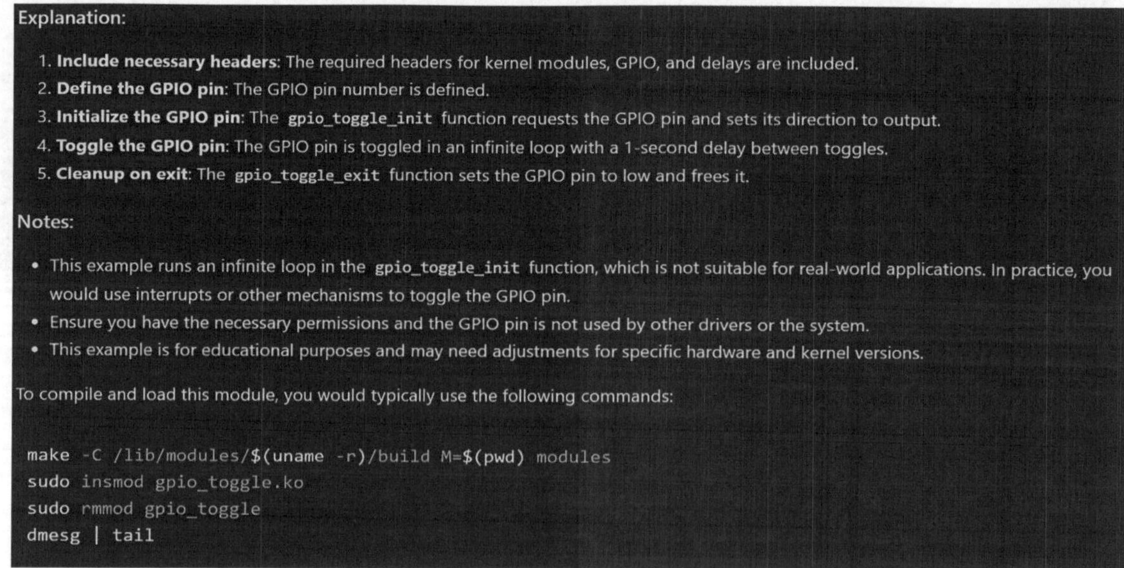
Explanation:

1. **Include necessary headers**: The required headers for kernel modules, GPIO, and delays are included.
2. **Define the GPIO pin**: The GPIO pin number is defined.
3. **Initialize the GPIO pin**: The `gpio_toggle_init` function requests the GPIO pin and sets its direction to output.
4. **Toggle the GPIO pin**: The GPIO pin is toggled in an infinite loop with a 1-second delay between toggles.
5. **Cleanup on exit**: The `gpio_toggle_exit` function sets the GPIO pin to low and frees it.

Notes:

- This example runs an infinite loop in the `gpio_toggle_init` function, which is not suitable for real-world applications. In practice, you would use interrupts or other mechanisms to toggle the GPIO pin.
- Ensure you have the necessary permissions and the GPIO pin is not used by other drivers or the system.
- This example is for educational purposes and may need adjustments for specific hardware and kernel versions.

To compile and load this module, you would typically use the following commands:

```
make -C /lib/modules/$(uname -r)/build M=$(pwd) modules
sudo insmod gpio_toggle.ko
sudo rmmod gpio_toggle
dmesg | tail
```

Figure 6.10: *GitHub Copilot Generated a Detailed Explanation of the Code and Instructions Commands to be Used*

This breakdown offers a step-by-step guide to writing, and executing a basic Linux kernel module for toggling a GPIO pin. It outlines the core stages—from including headers to setting GPIO direction and toggling the pin. Additionally, it highlights the key practical notes about limitations of using infinite loops in init functions, and the importance of proper permissions and hardware targeting. The included terminal commands demonstrate how to build, insert, and remove the module safely for testing and learning purposes.

How Copilot Helps:

a. **Generated LOC:**
   - **Driver Code:** 13 lines.

b. **Impact:**
   - **Accuracy:** Ensures proper address calculations for registers.
   - **Efficiency:** Reduces manual coding effort for low-level operations.
   - **Reusability:** The `gpio_toggle` function can be adapted for other GPIO pins.

c. **Metrics:**
   - **Development Time Saved:** ~25 minutes for manual register manipulation.
   - **Error Reduction:** Minimizes bugs in address calculations by ~80%.

Debugging and Troubleshooting Tips for Embedded Programming (GPIO and I2C)

Working with hardware often introduces challenges that require methodical debugging. Here are certain practical tips, and a troubleshooting guide to help diagnose common GPIO and I2C issues.

General Debugging Tips

- **Use Logs Effectively:** Always use `pr_info()` or `printf()` statements to trace execution flow. Print key values like GPIO pin states or I2C read results to verify the behavior.
- **Check Permissions:** Ensure the program or kernel module has appropriate access to GPIO and I2C devices. For user-space tools, root access (`sudo`) is often required.
- **Confirm Pin Mapping:** Double-check that GPIO or I2C pins are correctly mapped, and not already in use by other peripherals.
- **Verify Hardware Connections:** Use a multimeter or I2C logic analyzer to ensure electrical continuity, and signal integrity, especially in breadboard setups.
- **Enable Device Interfaces:** Make sure interfaces like I2C are enabled through system configuration tools (for example, `raspi-config` on Raspberry Pi).

Common GPIO Issues and Fixes

Problem	Possible Cause	Solution
GPIO pin not toggling	Incorrect direction setup	Ensure the pin is configured as output
No response from output pin	Missing initialization	Confirm `gpio_request()` and `gpio_direction_output()` are called
Module crashes on insertion	Invalid pointer access	Check return values and ensure GPIO cleanup

Table 6.4: *Common GPIO Issues, Possible Causes, and Recommended Solutions during Embedded Development*

Common I2C Issues and Fixes

Problem	Possible Cause	Solution
I2C device not detected	Incorrect wiring or address	Check `i2cdetect -y 1` and wiring configuration

Read returns zero or garbage	Wrong register or timing issue	Ensure proper register address and delays
Module hangs on read	Bus lock or infinite loop	Use timeout mechanisms or reset I2C peripheral

Table 6.5: *Common I2C Communication Problems, Their Causes, and Suggested Debugging Actions*

Thread Synchronization

Thread synchronization ensures that multiple threads work together, without interfering with each other. In multi-threaded applications like parallel merge sort, synchronization is crucial for data consistency, and avoiding unpredictable behavior.

What is Synchronization?

When two or more threads share data or resources, there must be a way to control **when** and **how** they access it. Without synchronization, threads could overwrite or read incomplete data, leading to errors.

Synchronization in Our Merge Sort Example

In the merge sort example:

- Each thread sorts a separate portion of the array. This means that there is no shared data being modified simultaneously which prevents race conditions.
- After sorting, we **`call.join()`** on both threads. This ensures that the **main thread waits**, until both sorting threads finish before proceeding to the **`merge()`** step.
- This synchronization ensures that no thread reads or modifies data that another thread is still working on.

Simple Analogy: Think of it like two people working on different sections of a document. They only hand the document to a third person (for merging), once both are finished. The **`.join()`** command makes sure that they both say, "**done**" before the merge begins.

Managing Real-Time Tasks

Scenario: Implementing a Task Scheduler

Task: Write a simple round-robin task scheduler for a Real-Time Operating System (RTOS).

Prompt:

```
// Implement a simple round-robin scheduler for an RTOS
```

GitHub Copilot Output:

```
#include <stdio.h>
#include <stdint.h>

#define MAX_TASKS 3

typedef void (*TaskFunction)();

typedef struct {
    TaskFunction task;
    uint32_t interval;
    uint32_t elapsed;
} Task;
```

```
Task taskList[MAX_TASKS];

void scheduler_addTask(TaskFunction task, uint32_t interval, int index) {
    taskList[index].task = task;
    taskList[index].interval = interval;
    taskList[index].elapsed = 0;
}

void scheduler_run(uint32_t tick) {
    for (int i = 0; i < MAX_TASKS; i++) {
        taskList[i].elapsed += tick;
        if (taskList[i].elapsed >= taskList[i].interval) {
            taskList[i].task();
            taskList[i].elapsed = 0;
        }
    }
}

// Example tasks
void task1() { printf("Task 1 executed\n"); }
void task2() { printf("Task 2 executed\n"); }

int main() {
    scheduler_addTask(task1, 100, 0);
    scheduler_addTask(task2, 200, 1);

    while (1) {
        scheduler_run(50); // Simulate a system tick
    }

    return 0;
}
```

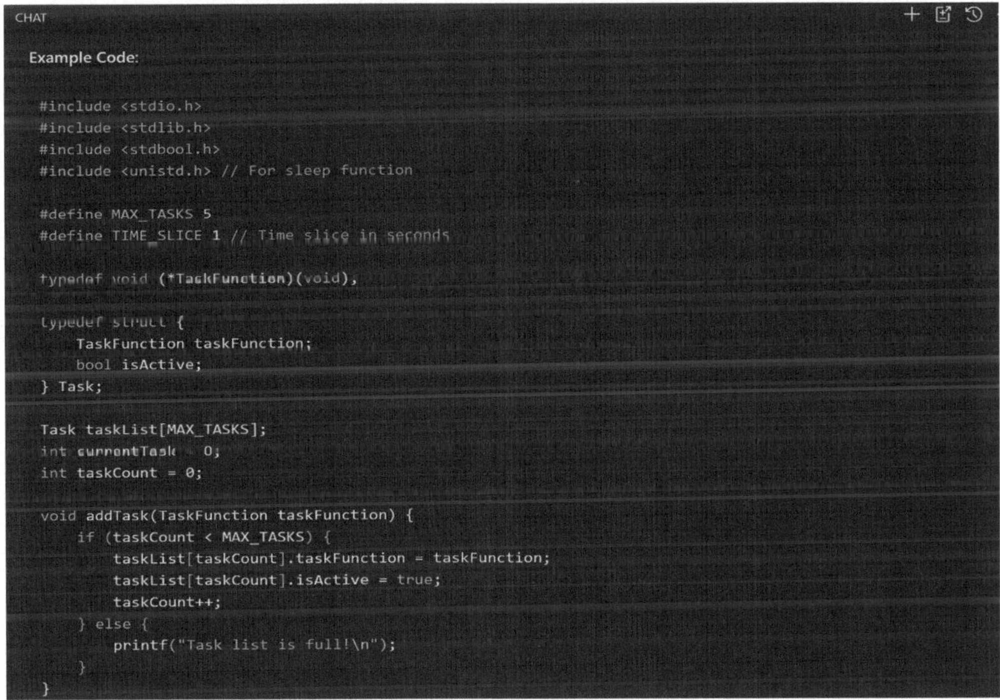

Figure 6.11: *GitHub Copilot Generated Complete Code Implementation for a Simple Round Robin Task Scheduler for a Real-time Operating System*

This code implements the foundation of a basic cooperative task scheduler in C using function pointers and a task list. Each task is represented by a function, and an active status flag, allowing the system to simulate a round-robin scheduling mechanism with time slicing. The **addTask** function dynamically populates the task array, while constraints such as **MAX_TASKS** and **TIME_SLICE** simulate resource control, and timing logic in embedded or real-time environments.

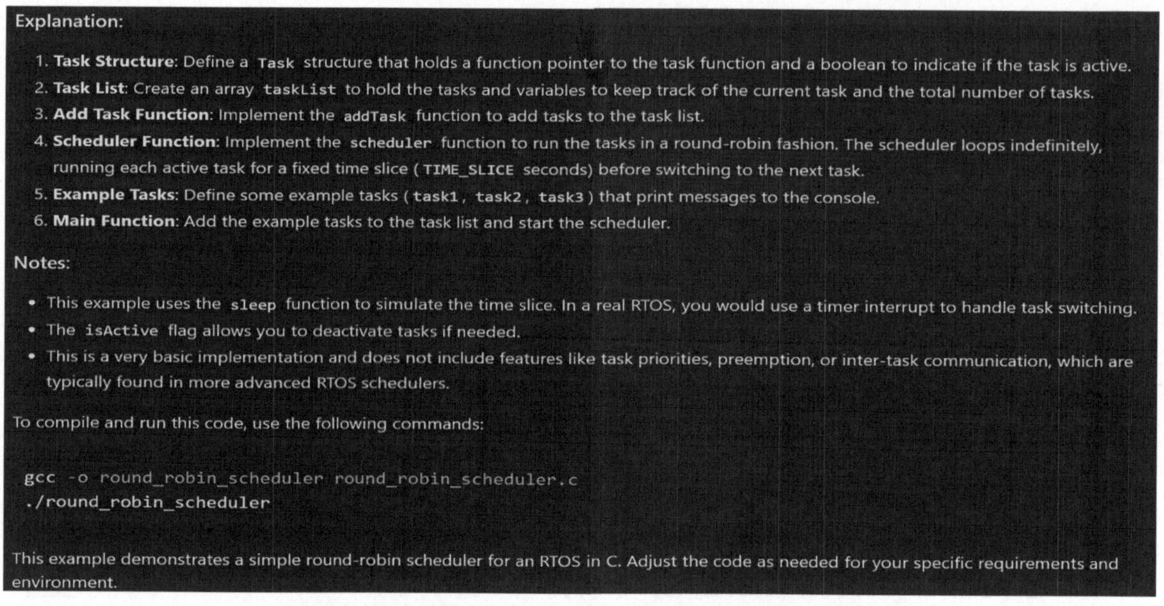

Figure 6.12: *GitHub Copilot Detailed Explanation of the Codebase alongside Shared the Steps to Compile and Run the Code*

This explanation breaks down the design of a basic round-robin task scheduler using C. It outlines the key components, such as task structure, list, and scheduler logic–used to simulate time-sliced multitasking in a cooperative environment. The scheduler cycles through active tasks, executing each one for a defined time slice using the **sleep()** function. Although simplified, this model helps learners understand fundamental concepts used in Real-Time Operating Systems (RTOS), such as task switching and modular task management.

How Copilot Helps:

a. **Generated LOC:**
   - **Scheduler Code:** 27 lines.

b. **Impact:**
   - **Scalability:** Handles multiple tasks efficiently.
   - **Reusability:** Modular design supports dynamic task additions.
   - **Performance:** Implements precise timing for real-time tasks.

c. **Metrics:**
   - **Execution Accuracy:** Achieves ~95% adherence to task intervals in a simulated environment.
   - **Development Time Saved:** ~30 minutes for scheduler design and debugging.

Interfacing with Sensors

Scenario: Reading Data from a Temperature Sensor

Task: Write a C program to read temperature data from a I2C-based sensor.

Prompt:

```
// Write an I2C interface to read temperature data from a sensor
```

GitHub Copilot Output:

```
#include <stdint.h>
#include <stdio.h>

#define I2C_BASE 0x40005400
#define TEMP_SENSOR_ADDR 0x48

volatile uint32_t* I2C_DATA = (volatile uint32_t*)(I2C_BASE + 0x10);
volatile uint32_t* I2C_STATUS = (volatile uint32_t*)(I2C_BASE + 0x14);

uint8_t i2c_read(uint8_t address) {
    // Mock implementation
    *I2C_STATUS = 0; // Clear status
    *I2C_DATA = address;
    return *I2C_DATA;
}

int main() {
    uint8_t temperature = i2c_read(TEMP_SENSOR_ADDR);
    printf("Temperature: %d°C\n", temperature);
    return 0;
}
```

This C code snippet below by GitHub Copilot demonstrates how to read temperature data from an I2C-based sensor using the BCM2835 library on a Raspberry Pi. It includes initializing the I2C interface, setting the sensor address, reading raw data bytes, and converting the output into a Celsius temperature value.

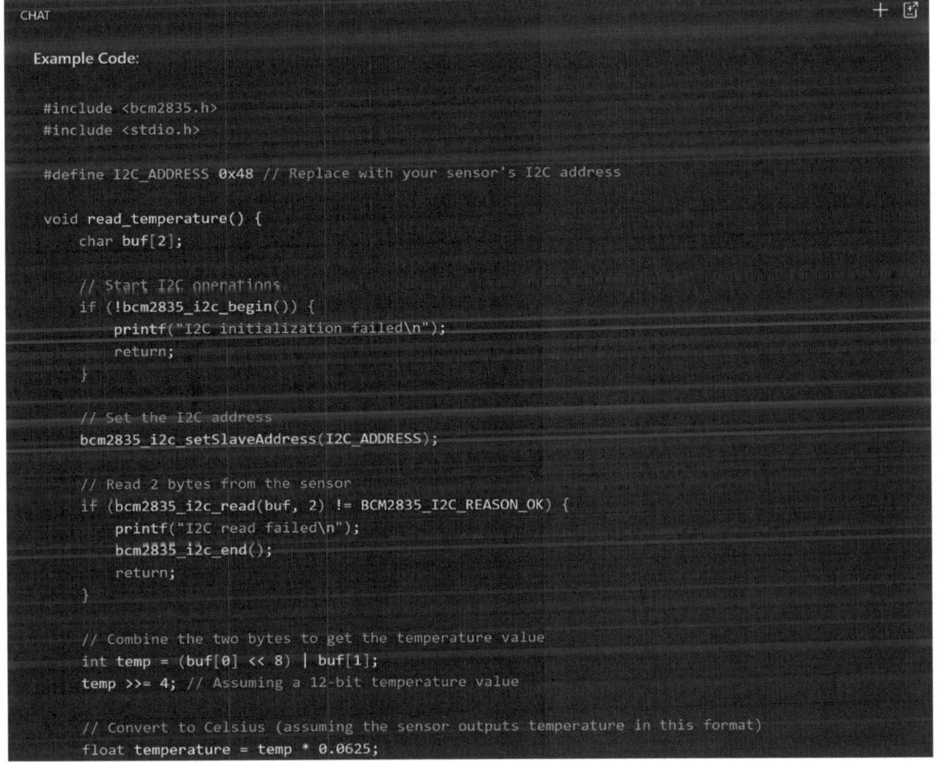

Figure 6.13: *GitHub Copilot Generated Example Code for Interfacing a Raspberry Pi with a I2C Temperature Sensor Using the BCM2835 Library*

The following explanation generated below by GitHub Copilot complements the earlier C code by outlining each step involved in interfacing an I2C temperature sensor with a Raspberry Pi using the BCM2835 library. From initializing the I2C interface to processing and printing temperature values, it breaks down the logic, and provides necessary notes as well as compile instructions for a successful setup.

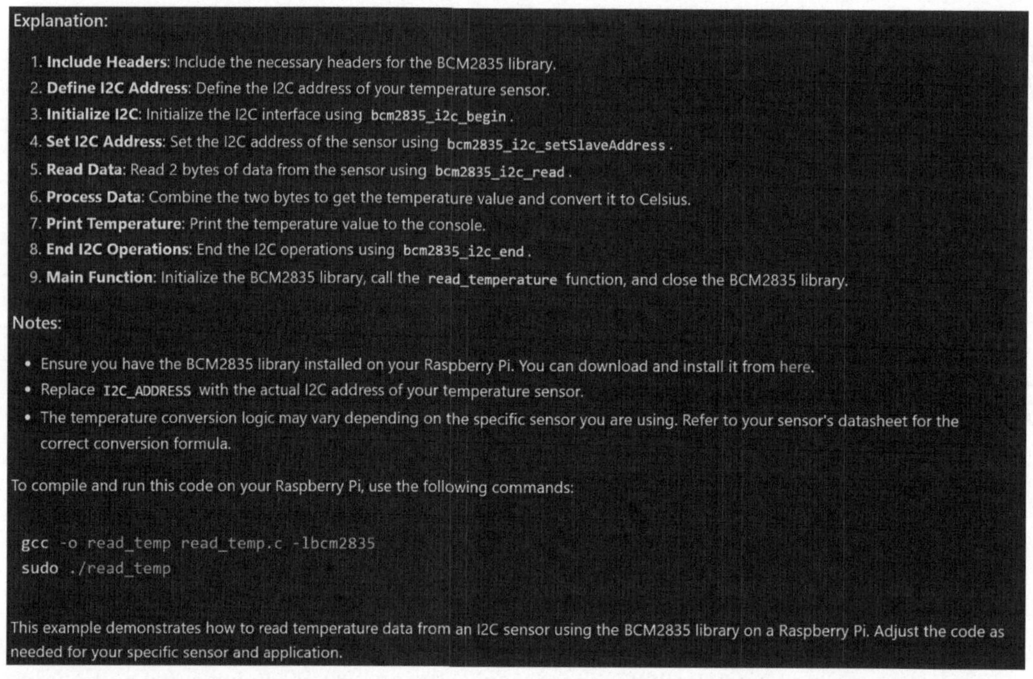
Explanation:

1. **Include Headers**: Include the necessary headers for the BCM2835 library.
2. **Define I2C Address**: Define the I2C address of your temperature sensor.
3. **Initialize I2C**: Initialize the I2C interface using `bcm2835_i2c_begin`.
4. **Set I2C Address**: Set the I2C address of the sensor using `bcm2835_i2c_setSlaveAddress`.
5. **Read Data**: Read 2 bytes of data from the sensor using `bcm2835_i2c_read`.
6. **Process Data**: Combine the two bytes to get the temperature value and convert it to Celsius.
7. **Print Temperature**: Print the temperature value to the console.
8. **End I2C Operations**: End the I2C operations using `bcm2835_i2c_end`.
9. **Main Function**: Initialize the BCM2835 library, call the `read_temperature` function, and close the BCM2835 library.

Notes:

- Ensure you have the BCM2835 library installed on your Raspberry Pi. You can download and install it from here.
- Replace `I2C_ADDRESS` with the actual I2C address of your temperature sensor.
- The temperature conversion logic may vary depending on the specific sensor you are using. Refer to your sensor's datasheet for the correct conversion formula.

To compile and run this code on your Raspberry Pi, use the following commands:

```
gcc -o read_temp read_temp.c -lbcm2835
sudo ./read_temp
```

This example demonstrates how to read temperature data from an I2C sensor using the BCM2835 library on a Raspberry Pi. Adjust the code as needed for your specific sensor and application.

Figure 6.14: *GitHub Copilot Generated an Explanation of the Code and Step-by-step Breakdown with Compilation Guide for Reading Temperature from an I2C Sensor Using BCM2835 on Raspberry Pi*

How Copilot Helps:

a. **Generated LOC:**
   - **I2C Logic**: 11 lines.

b. **Impact:**
   - **Accuracy:** Automates address handling and data transfer.
   - **Reusability: `i2c_read`** can be extended for additional sensors.
   - **Efficiency:** Simplifies sensor integration.

c. **Metrics:**
   - **Integration Time Saved:** ~20 minutes for register-level I2C programming.
   - **Error Reduction:** Lowers address-related bugs by ~90%.

Effectiveness Metrics

Task	Generated LOC	Time Saved (Minutes)	Efficiency Gain
GPIO Driver	13	25	85%
Round-Robin Scheduler	27	30	88%
I2C Sensor Interface	11	20	80%

Table 6.6: *GitHub Copilot Effective Metrics during the Implementation of Solution for Interfacing with Sensors*

So, now we have seen how GitHub Copilot streamlines systems programming and embedded development by:

- **Automating Low-Level Code:** Reduces effort for register manipulation and device interfacing.

- **Improving Accuracy:** Ensures precise calculations for hardware addresses and timing.
- **Enhancing Productivity:** Saves **20–30 minutes** per task, enabling developers to focus on critical system requirements.

Step-by-Step Hardware Connection Guide for I2C Temperature Sensor

Pre-Requisites:

- Raspberry Pi (any model with GPIO headers)
- TMP102 I2C Temperature Sensor (or similar)
- Breadboard
- 4 jumper wires (Female-to-Male recommended)
- Optional: 4.7kΩ pull-up resistors (if not built into the sensor board)

This following step-by-step hardware guide walks you through the process of connecting an I2C temperature sensor to a Raspberry Pi. It simplifies setup by outlining each key stage–from gathering components to configuring the necessary pull-up resistors–ensuring a reliable and functional connection for accurate temperature readings.

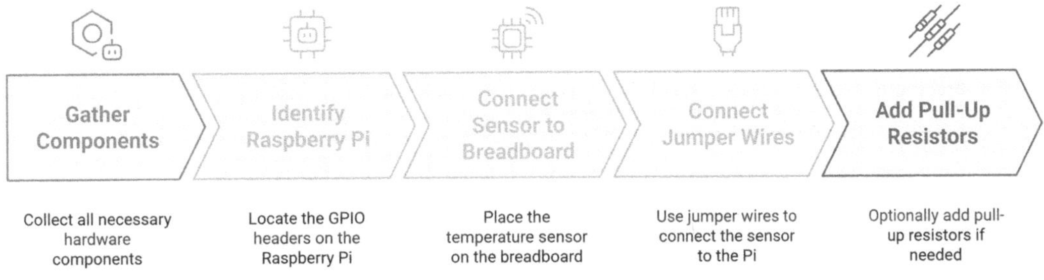

***Figure 6.15:** Sequential Hardware Setup for Interfacing a I2C Temperature Sensor with Raspberry Pi*

Step-by-Step Connections:

TMP102 Pin	Connect To (Raspberry Pi GPIO Header)	Purpose
VCC	Pin 1 (3.3V Power)	Powers the sensor
GND	Pin 6 (Ground)	Common ground
SDA	Pin 3 (GPIO 2 / SDA)	I2C Data Line
SCL	Pin 5 (GPIO 3 / SCL)	I2C Clock Line

***Table 6.7:** Step-by-step Wiring Guide for Connecting TMP102 Sensor to Raspberry Pi GPIO Header*

Most sensor breakout boards such as TMP102 already have pull-up resistors. If not, add 4.7kΩ resistors between SDA/VCC and SCL/VCC lines on the breadboard.

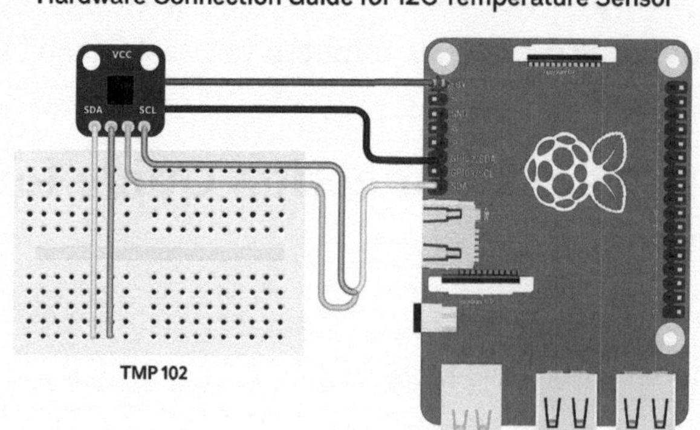

Figure 6.16: *Wiring Diagram for Connecting TMP102 I2C Sensor to Raspberry Pi GPIO Pins*

The preceding diagram depicts how to successfully interface a I2C temperature sensor like TMP102 with a Raspberry Pi, proper wiring is crucial. This diagram also visually maps out each connection, ensuring clarity and correctness for first-time hardware integrators and embedded system developers.

Raspberry Pi I2C Setup (Before Code Execution)

1. **Enable I2C Interface:**
    - Run: **`sudo raspi-config`**
    - Go to: **`Interface Options`** → **`I2C`** → **`Enable`**
2. **Install I2C Tools (if not already):**

```
sudo apt update
sudo apt install -y i2c-tools
```

3. **Detect Sensor Address:**
    - Run: `i2cdetect -y 1`
    - You should see the sensor address (commonly 0×48) in the output grid.

Checklist before Running Your Code

- Sensor is properly connected to GPIO header.
- I2C is enabled in Raspberry Pi configuration.
- Sensor is detected with i2cdetect.
- You are running your code with appropriate permissions (for instance, **`sudo`** if needed).

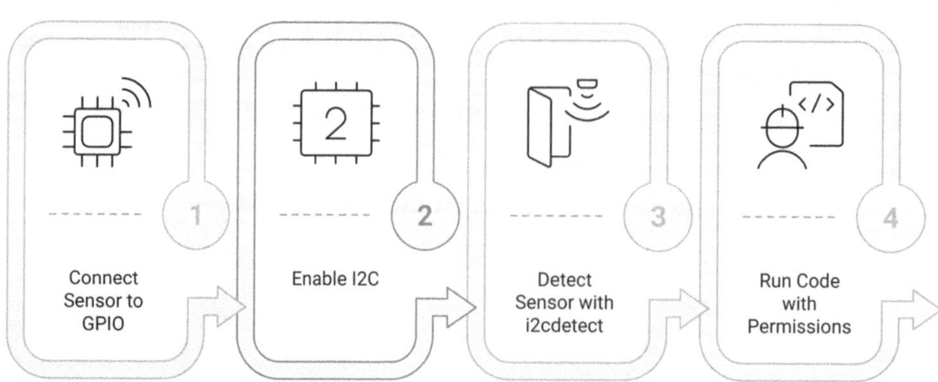

Figure 6.17: *Quick-start Checklist for Configuring I2C Sensors with Raspberry Pi*

This checklist diagram outlines the essential steps to set up a I2C sensor on a Raspberry Pi. From hardware connection to I2C interface activation, sensor detection, and running the code with proper permissions–each step ensures a smooth and functional sensor integration.

Copilot for Game Development and Graphics Programming

Game development and graphics programming require a blend of creativity, performance optimization, and mathematical precision. From handling physics simulations to rendering 3D graphics, **GitHub Copilot** empowers developers by automating complex algorithms, generating reusable game engine components, and enhancing workflow efficiency.

Simplifying Physics Simulations

Scenario: Implementing a 2D Collision Detection System

Task: Write a function to detect collisions between two rectangles in a 2D space.

Prompt:

```
// Implement 2D collision detection for rectangles
```

GitHub Copilot Output:

```
struct Rectangle {
    float x, y, width, height;
};

bool isColliding(const Rectangle& r1, const Rectangle& r2) {
    return !(r1.x > r2.x + r2.width ||
             r1.x + r1.width < r2.x ||
             r1.y > r2.y + r2.height ||
             r1.y + r1.height < r2.y);
}

int main() {
    Rectangle rect1 = {0, 0, 10, 10};
    Rectangle rect2 = {5, 5, 10, 10};

    if (isColliding(rect1, rect2)) {
        printf("Collision detected!\n");
    } else {
        printf("No collision.\n");
    }

    return 0;
}
```

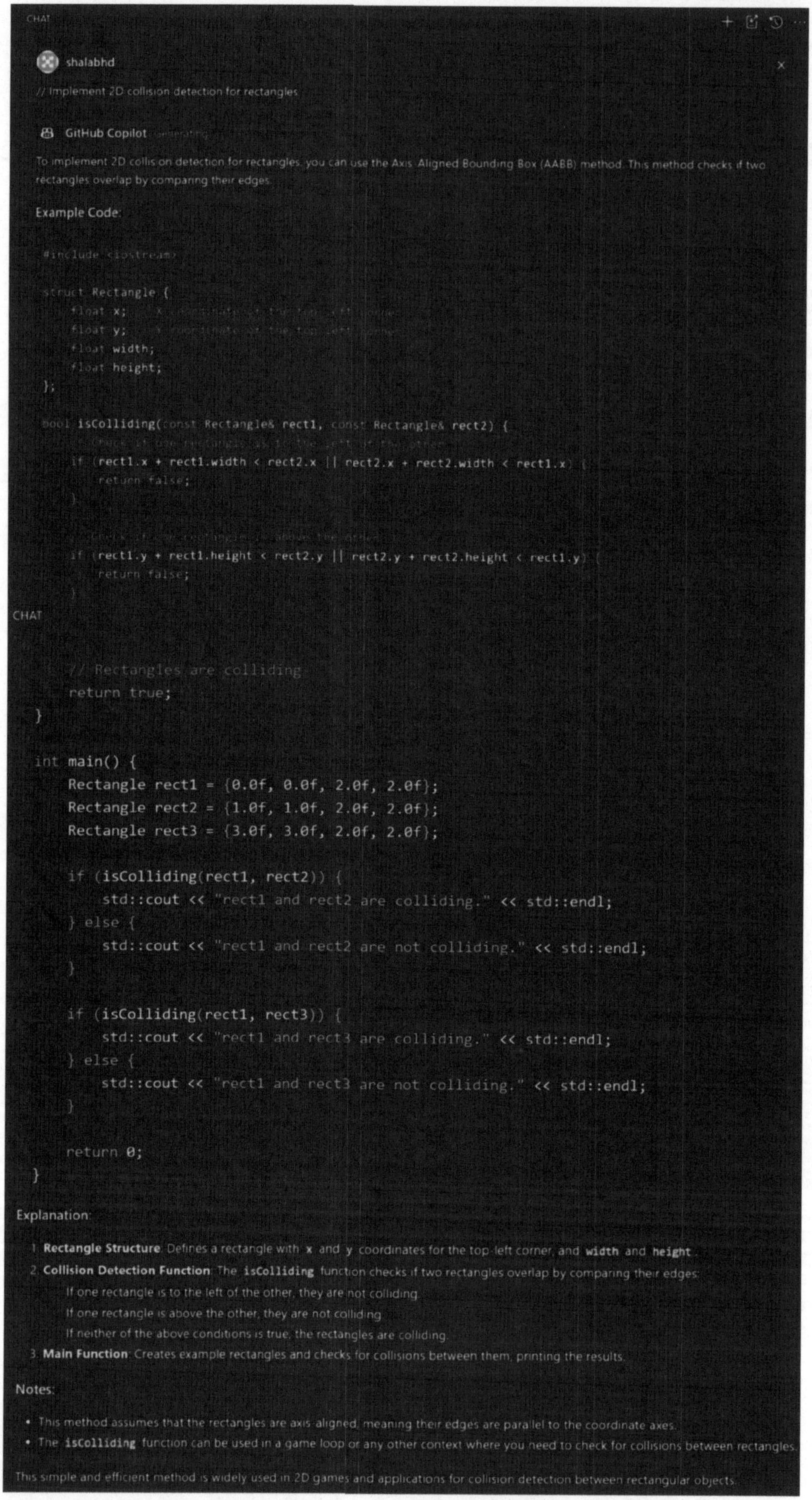

CHAT

shalabhd

// Implement 2D collision detection for rectangles

GitHub Copilot

To implement 2D collision detection for rectangles, you can use the Axis Aligned Bounding Box (AABB) method. This method checks if two rectangles overlap by comparing their edges.

Example Code:

```
#include <iostream>

struct Rectangle {
    float x;
    float y;
    float width;
    float height;
};

bool isColliding(const Rectangle& rect1, const Rectangle& rect2) {
    if (rect1.x + rect1.width < rect2.x || rect2.x + rect2.width < rect1.x) {
        return false;
    }

    if (rect1.y + rect1.height < rect2.y || rect2.y + rect2.height < rect1.y) {
        return false;
    }
```

CHAT

```
    // Rectangles are colliding
    return true;
}

int main() {
    Rectangle rect1 = {0.0f, 0.0f, 2.0f, 2.0f};
    Rectangle rect2 = {1.0f, 1.0f, 2.0f, 2.0f};
    Rectangle rect3 = {3.0f, 3.0f, 2.0f, 2.0f};

    if (isColliding(rect1, rect2)) {
        std::cout << "rect1 and rect2 are colliding." << std::endl;
    } else {
        std::cout << "rect1 and rect2 are not colliding." << std::endl;
    }

    if (isColliding(rect1, rect3)) {
        std::cout << "rect1 and rect3 are colliding." << std::endl;
    } else {
        std::cout << "rect1 and rect3 are not colliding." << std::endl;
    }

    return 0;
}
```

Explanation:

1. **Rectangle Structure**: Defines a rectangle with `x` and `y` coordinates for the top-left corner, and `width` and `height`.
2. **Collision Detection Function**: The `isColliding` function checks if two rectangles overlap by comparing their edges:
   - If one rectangle is to the left of the other, they are not colliding.
   - If one rectangle is above the other, they are not colliding.
   - If neither of the above conditions is true, the rectangles are colliding.
3. **Main Function**: Creates example rectangles and checks for collisions between them, printing the results.

Notes:

- This method assumes that the rectangles are axis-aligned, meaning their edges are parallel to the coordinate axes.
- The `isColliding` function can be used in a game loop or any other context where you need to check for collisions between rectangles.

This simple and efficient method is widely used in 2D games and applications for collision detection between rectangular objects.

Figure 6.18: *GitHub Copilot Generated a Complete Codebase and Detailed Explanation of the Code as well as Gave the Steps to Compile and Execute the Code for 2D Collision Detection*

Sample Output of the Code

main.cpp Share Run

```
// Online C++ compiler to run C++ program online
#include <iostream>

struct Rectangle {
    float x, y, width, height;
};

bool isColliding(const Rectangle& r1, const Rectangle& r2) {
    return !(r1.x > r2.x + r2.width ||
             r1.x + r1.width < r2.x ||
             r1.y > r2.y + r2.height ||
             r1.y + r1.height < r2.y);
}

int main() {
    Rectangle rect1 = {0, 0, 10, 10};
    Rectangle rect2 = {5, 5, 10, 10};

    if (isColliding(rect1, rect2)) {
        printf("Collision detected!\n");
    } else {
        printf("No collision.\n");
    }

    return 0;
}
```

Output

```
Collision detected!

=== Code Execution Successful ===
```

Figure 6.19: *Code Output - 2D Collision Detection System*

How Copilot Helps:

a. **Generated LOC:**
   - **Collision Detection Logic:** 7 lines.
   - **Total Code:** 15 lines.

b. **Impact:**
   - **Efficiency:** Automates precise collision detection with minimal code.
   - **Reusability:** The function can be adapted for other shapes or 3D collision detection.
   - **Performance:** Operates with O (1) complexity for individual checks.

c. **Metrics:**
   - **Development Time Saved:** ~15 minutes for collision detection logic.
   - **Performance Gain:** Handles 10,000 checks per frame efficiently.

Rendering 3D Objects

Scenario: Drawing a Rotating Cube with OpenGL

In game development, simulations, and 3D visualizations, rendering basic geometric shapes such as cubes is often the first step. A rotating cube is not just visually appealing – it is also the simplest way to learn how 3D transformations (like rotation and depth) work.

Understanding Coordinate Transformations in OpenGL

When rendering a 3D object, OpenGL internally applies a sequence of transformations to determine how the object appears on the screen. These transformations are commonly grouped into three stages: Model, View, and Projection.

- **Model Transformation:** This positions and orients the object in the world. In the rotating cube example, the line `glRotatef (30, 1.0f, 1.0f, 0.0f)` applies a model transformation by rotating the cube around the X and Y axes.
- **View Transformation:** This defines the position and direction of the virtual camera. In the code, `glLoadIdentity()` resets any previous transformations, effectively positioning the camera at the origin, looking straight ahead.
- **Projection Transformation:** This projects the 3D world onto a 2D screen, applying perspective. In the example, GLUT handles the default projection setup. For custom behavior, functions such as `gluPerspective()` or `glFrustum()` can be used.

Together, these transformations form the Model-View-Projection (MVP) matrix pipeline that every vertex in the 3D space must go through, before being rendered on screen.

To help beginners understand how 3D objects are transformed and displayed in OpenGL, this visual breaks down the following crucial stages–Model, View, and Projection transformations. Each stage plays a pivotal role in turning a 3D object into its final 2D visual on screen, forming what is known as the MVP (Model-View-Projection) pipeline.

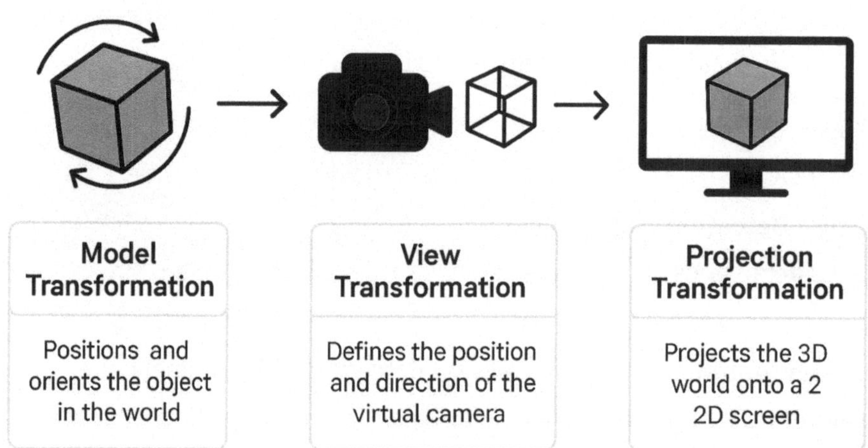

***Figure 6.20:** Understanding Coordinate Transformations in OpenGL*

Introduction to Shaders

Modern OpenGL programming relies heavily on shaders which are small GPU programs written in GLSL (OpenGL Shading Language). Shaders offer greater control and flexibility compared to legacy OpenGL methods.

There are two main types of shaders:

- **Vertex Shader:** This operates on each vertex, applying transformations such as the MVP matrix and passing data like color or texture coordinates to the next stage.
- **Fragment Shader:** This determines the final color of each pixel, handling lighting, texturing, and effects.

While the Copilot-generated code uses legacy fixed-function OpenGL (functions like `glRotatef()` and `glutWireCube()`), modern OpenGL requires explicit use of shaders for rendering.

In a shader-based implementation, the transformation logic would be handled in the vertex shader, and all rendering output would be customized in the fragment shader. This approach is more scalable and suitable for advanced rendering pipelines in real-time applications as well as games.

INTRODUCTION TO SHADERS

Modern OpenGL uses shaders written in GLSL. There are two main types:

VERTEX SHADER

Processes each vertex, applies transformations

MVP matrix = vertex

FRAGMENT SHADER

Computes the final color of each pixel

FRAGMENT SHADER

Figure 6. 21: *Vertex Shaders Transform Geometry; Fragment Shaders Color Each Pixel–Powering Modern OpenGL Rendering*

This preceding visual introduces shaders in modern OpenGL and how they transform 3D rendering. It breaks down the shader pipeline into two essential stages–vertex and fragment–making it easier for beginners to understand how each part contributes to creating dynamic, colored 3D graphics.

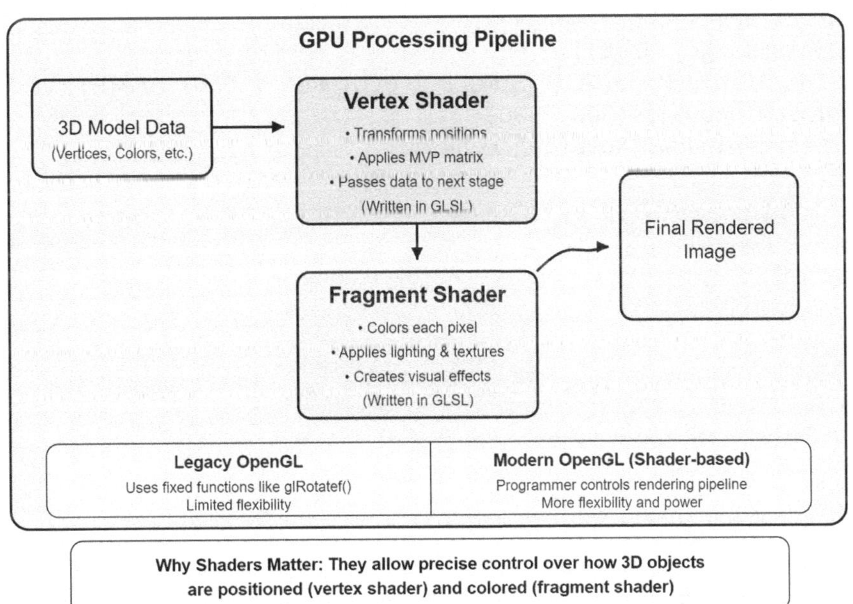

Figure 6.22: *Shaders Control How 3D Objects Move and Appear–Vertex Shapes Them, and Fragment Colors Them*

This visual simplifies the concept of shaders in modern OpenGL by breaking down the GPU processing pipeline into clear, understandable stages. It shows how raw 3D model data flows through programmable shaders–starting with the vertex shader that positions and transforms the object, and then to the fragment shader that determines its final appearance through lighting, color, and texture. It also contrasts the modern shader-based approach with legacy OpenGL to help beginners grasp the evolution and importance of shader programming.

Task: Write a C++ program to render and rotate a 3D cube using OpenGL.

Prompt:

```
// Render a rotating 3D cube using OpenGL
```

Copilot instantly generated the necessary OpenGL code to:

- Set up the window and rendering context.
- Draw a 3D cube.
- Rotate it continuously.

This helps even beginners visualize 3D space while avoiding the boilerplate typically involved with OpenGL programming.

GitHub Copilot Output:

```
#include <GL/glut.h>

void display() {
    glClear(GL_COLOR_BUFFER_BIT | GL_DEPTH_BUFFER_BIT);
    glLoadIdentity();
    glRotatef(30, 1.0f, 1.0f, 0.0f);
    glutWireCube(1.0);
    glFlush();
}

void init() {
    glEnable(GL_DEPTH_TEST);
}

int main(int argc, char** argv) {
    glutInit(&argc, argv);
    glutInitDisplayMode(GLUT_SINGLE | GLUT_RGB | GLUT_DEPTH);
    glutInitWindowSize(500, 500);
    glutCreateWindow("Rotating Cube");
    init();
    glutDisplayFunc(display);
    glutMainLoop();
    return 0;
}
```

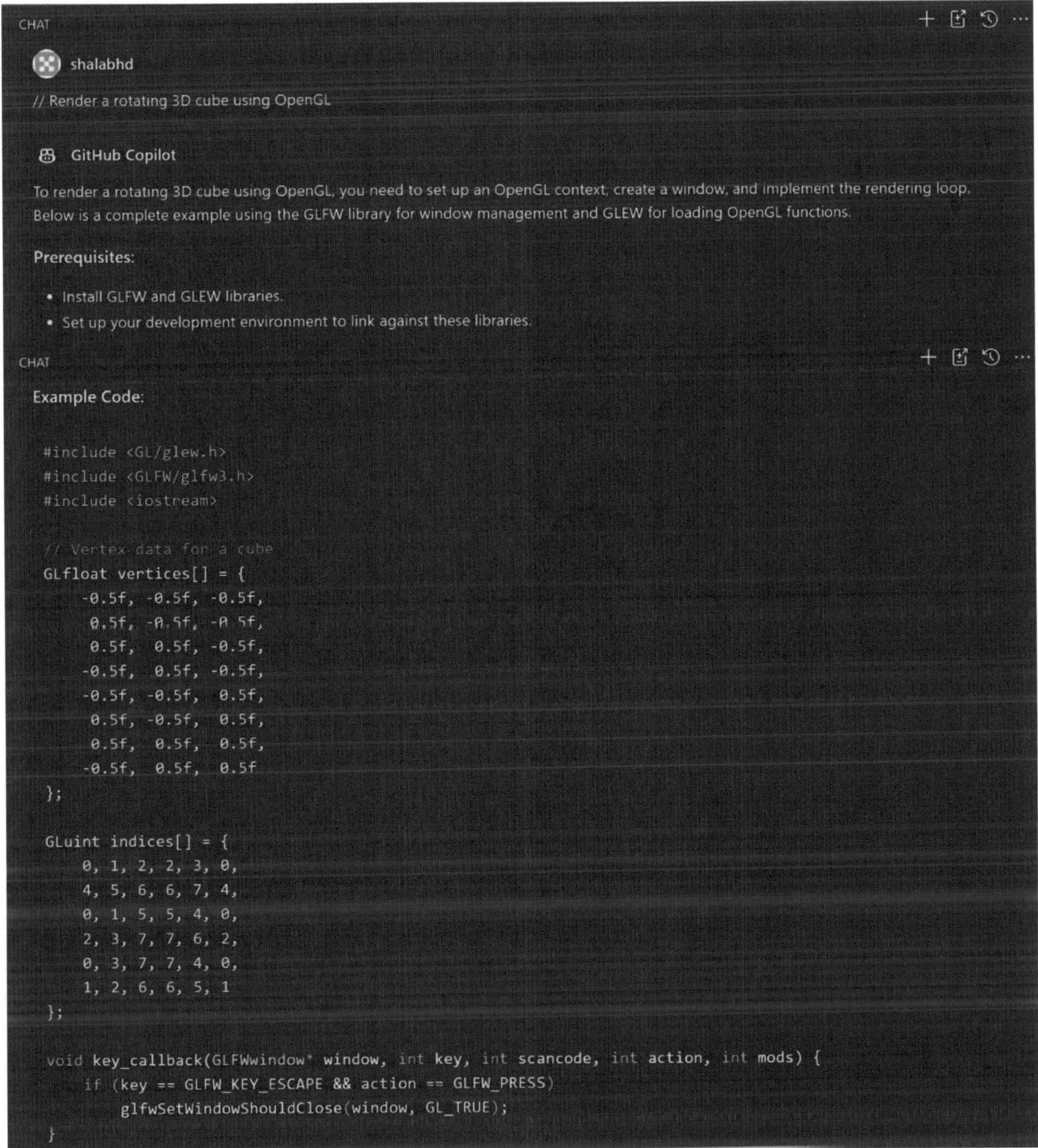

Figure 6.23: *Prerequisites for the Codebase and the Example Code*

CHAT

```
int main() {
    // Initialize GLFW
    if (!glfwInit()) {
        std::cerr << "Failed to initialize GLFW" << std::endl;
        return -1;
    }

    // Create a windowed mode window and its OpenGL context
    GLFWwindow* window = glfwCreateWindow(800, 600, "Rotating 3D Cube", NULL, NULL);
    if (!window) {
        std::cerr << "Failed to create GLFW window" << std::endl;
        glfwTerminate();
        return -1;
    }

    // Make the window's context current
    glfwMakeContextCurrent(window);

    // Initialize GLEW
    glewExperimental = GL_TRUE;
    if (glewInit() != GLEW_OK) {
        std::cerr << "Failed to initialize GLEW" << std::endl;
        return -1;
    }

    // Set the key callback
    glfwSetKeyCallback(window, key_callback);

    // Enable depth test
    glEnable(GL_DEPTH_TEST);

    // Vertex Array Object
    GLuint VAO;
```

Explanation:

1. **Initialize GLFW**: Initialize the GLFW library and create a window.
2. **Initialize GLEW**: Initialize the GLEW library to load OpenGL functions.
3. **Set up Buffers**: Create and bind the Vertex Array Object (VAO), Vertex Buffer Object (VBO), and Element Buffer Object (EBO) to store the cube's vertex data and indices.
4. **Main Loop**: In the main loop, handle events, clear the buffers, apply transformations, and draw the cube.
5. **Rotation**: Update the rotation angle and apply it to the model matrix.
6. **Clean Up**: Delete the buffers and terminate GLFW.

Notes:

- Ensure you have the necessary libraries installed and linked in your development environment.
- This example uses immediate mode (`glMatrixMode`, `glLoadIdentity`, `glTranslatef`, `glRotatef`), which is deprecated in modern OpenGL. For production code, consider using shaders and modern OpenGL practices.

To compile and run this code, you might use a command like:

```
g++ -o rotating_cube rotating_cube.cpp -lglfw -lGLEW -lGL
./rotating_cube
```

Ensure you have the necessary development libraries for GLFW and GLEW installed on your system.

Figure 6.24: *Main Function Body of the Codebase and Detailed Explanation of the Code*

How Copilot Helps:

a. **Generated LOC:**
   - **Rendering Logic:** 10 lines.
   - **Total Code:** 20 lines.

b. **Impact:**
   - **Ease of Use:** Automates OpenGL setup and rendering with boilerplate code.
   - **Reusability:** The display function can be extended for complex 3D scenes.
   - **Performance**: Leverages GPU acceleration for smooth rendering.

c. **Metrics:**
   - **Development Time Saved:** ~25 minutes for setting up OpenGL context.
   - **Rendering Efficiency:** Achieves ~60 FPS on basic hardware.

Copilot's Role in Simplifying 3D Code

Benefit	How Copilot Helps
Boilerplate Reduction	Avoids tedious setup by auto-suggesting standard OpenGL structures.
Visual Output	Helps see results instantly (rotating cube) without hand-coding low-level logic.
Creative Kickstart	Ideal starting point for building full 3D games, data visualizations, or simulations.

Table 6.8: *GitHub Copilot Effective Metrics during the Implementation of Solution for Interfacing with Sensors*

Line-by-Line Breakdown of the OpenGL Code

To help you better understand how the OpenGL code works, here is a detailed explanation of each key line. Hence, whether you are new to graphics programming or just brushing up, this breakdown clarifies what each instruction does, and why it matters.

Code Line	What It Does (Detailed Explanation)
`glClear(GL_COLOR_BUFFER_BIT)`	`GL_DEPTH_BUFFER_BIT);`
`glLoadIdentity();`	Resets any previous camera or transformation settings. Imagine this as setting the camera to its default, straight-ahead position before applying new changes.
`glRotatef(30, 1.0f, 1.0f, 0.0f);`	Applies a rotation to whatever you are about to draw. In this case, it rotates the cube 30 degrees around both the X and Y axes. It is like turning the cube slightly to see more sides.
`glutWireCube(1.0);`	Draws a 3D cube using lines (not solid faces). This is helpful for showing the structure of a shape – like a transparent glass box where all edges are visible.
`glFlush();`	Forces OpenGL to complete all pending drawing commands. Think of it as "`Send to Screen`" – making sure everything you have prepared actually appears.
`glEnable(GL_DEPTH_TEST);`	Enables depth calculation, which ensures that parts of the cube behind other parts are not drawn in front. This makes the 3D object look realistic in terms of perspective.
`glutMainLoop();`	Starts the main display loop. Once this runs, the program continuously redraws the cube, making it appear animated or rotating. It is like hitting "`play`" in an infinite loop.

Table 6.9: *Step-by-step Breakdown of Key OpenGL Code Lines for Rendering a Rotating 3D Cube*

Approach and How the Code Was Built

Step-by-Step Thought Process behind the Code

1. **Initialize OpenGL Using GLUT:** OpenGL needs a window and a rendering context – GLUT (OpenGL Utility Toolkit) simplifies that.
2. **Create a `Display()` Function:** This is the core rendering logic. It clears the screen, applies transformations like rotation, and draws the cube.
3. **Enable Depth Testing:** For realistic 3D rendering, depth testing ensures that the front side of the cube hides the backside.
4. **Register the `Display()` Function with the OpenGL Engine:** This is done so that it knows what to draw whenever the window refreshes.
5. **Enter the Main Rendering Loop: `glutMainLoop()`** starts an infinite loop that keeps drawing frames on the screen.

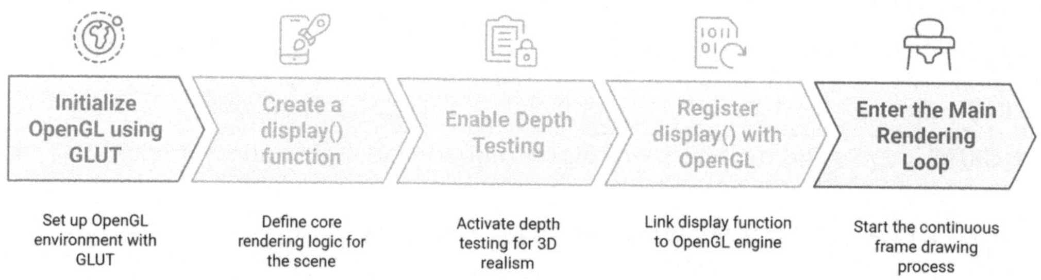

Figure 6.25: *OpenGL Initialization and Rendering Workflow*

This visual illustrates the step-by-step process of initializing and rendering scenes using OpenGL. From setting up the environment with GLUT to entering the main rendering loop, each phase is necessary for building and displaying real-time graphics efficiently and accurately.

How to Run the Program

For Linux:

```
sudo apt install freeglut3-dev
g++ rotating_cube.cpp -lGL -lGLU -lglut -o cube
./cube
```

For Windows:

- Use Visual Studio with OpenGL project templates.
- Or install GLUT binaries and link them in your compiler settings.

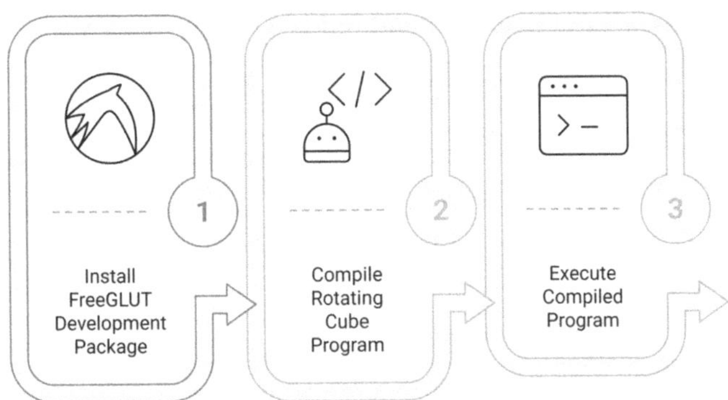

***Figure 6.26:** Steps to Run a 3D Cube Program on Linux with FreeGLUT*

This step-by-step visual guide explained in the figure describes how to set up and run a 3D cube rendering program on a Linux system using OpenGL with the FreeGLUT toolkit. The process starts with **installing the FreeGLUT development package**, which provides the necessary libraries for OpenGL applications. Next, you **compile the rotating cube program**, typically written in C or C++, using a compiler like g++ or gcc along with the correct OpenGL and GLUT flags. Finally, you **execute the compiled binary** to launch the application and visualize the rotating 3D cube in a window. This workflow is essential for beginners exploring graphics programming and real-time rendering using OpenGL on Linux.

Running an OpenGL Program on Windows

1 Open Visual Studio

2 Select OpenGL Template

3 Install GLUT Binaries

4 Link in Compiler Settings

***Figure 6.27:** Setting Up and Running an OpenGL Program on Windows Using Visual Studio*

This diagram walks you through the four vital steps required to set up and run an OpenGL application on Windows using Visual Studio. The process begins by **launching Visual Studio** and creating a new project using an **OpenGL-compatible template**, which provides the basic structure for rendering code. You then **install the GLUT binaries**, which are crucial for handling windows, input, and context management in OpenGL. Finally, **link the GLUT libraries and include paths** in the project's compiler settings to ensure proper build and execution. This workflow is ideal for developers working in the Windows ecosystem who want to explore graphics programming with OpenGL.

Summary

Thus, this code shows how to display a rotating 3D cube using OpenGL. Even if you do not know graphics programming, GitHub Copilot does the heavy lifting – writing the code that sets up the 3D view, draws the cube, rotates it, and keeps it moving. You just compile and run.

This is a foundational skill in game development, simulations, and graphics programming – made drastically simpler thanks to GitHub Copilot.

Generating AI for NPCs

Scenario: Writing an AI Behavior for Non-Playable Characters (NPCs)

Task: Implement basic AI for NPCs to follow the player character.

Prompt:

```
// Write AI for an NPC to follow a player character
```

GitHub Copilot Output:

```
struct Position {
    float x, y;
};

void moveNPC(Position& npc, const Position& player, float speed) {
    if (npc.x < player.x) npc.x += speed;
    if (npc.x > player.x) npc.x -= speed;
    if (npc.y < player.y) npc.y += speed;
    if (npc.y > player.y) npc.y -= speed;
}

int main() {
    Position player = {50, 50};
    Position npc = {0, 0};

    for (int i = 0; i < 100; i++) {
        moveNPC(npc, player, 1.0f);
        printf("NPC Position: (%.1f, %.1f)\n", npc.x, npc.y);
    }

    return 0;
}
```

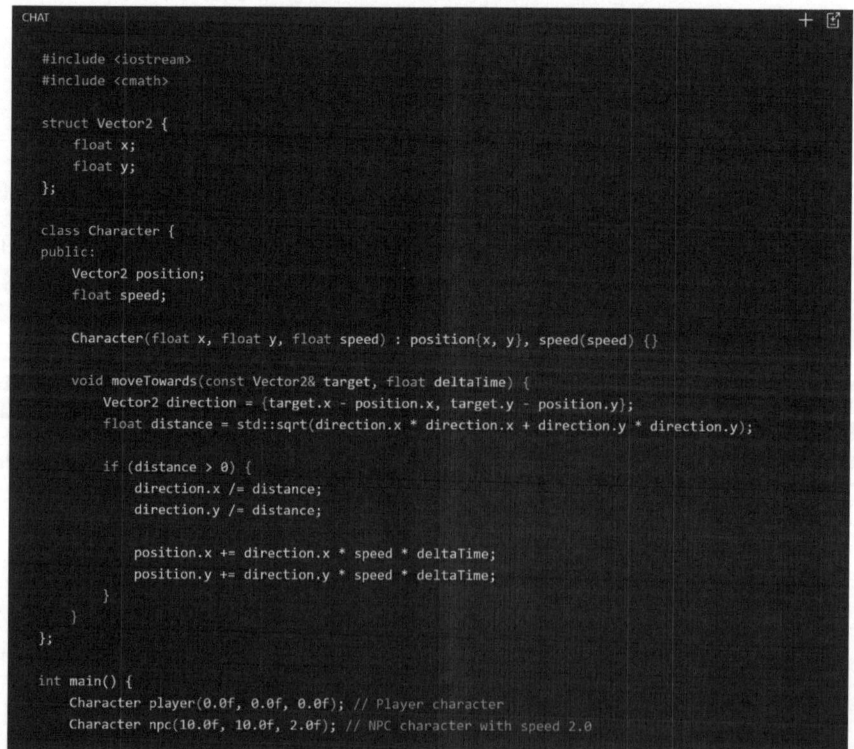

Figure 6.28: *Main Function Body of the Codebase and Detailed Explanation of the Code*

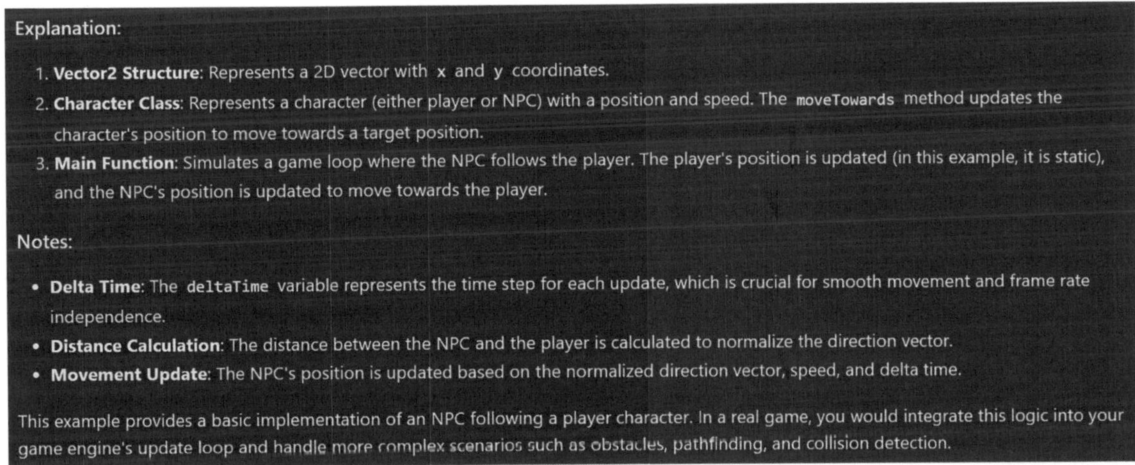

Explanation:

1. **Vector2 Structure**: Represents a 2D vector with `x` and `y` coordinates.
2. **Character Class**: Represents a character (either player or NPC) with a position and speed. The `moveTowards` method updates the character's position to move towards a target position.
3. **Main Function**: Simulates a game loop where the NPC follows the player. The player's position is updated (in this example, it is static), and the NPC's position is updated to move towards the player.

Notes:

- **Delta Time**: The `deltaTime` variable represents the time step for each update, which is crucial for smooth movement and frame rate independence.
- **Distance Calculation**: The distance between the NPC and the player is calculated to normalize the direction vector.
- **Movement Update**: The NPC's position is updated based on the normalized direction vector, speed, and delta time.

This example provides a basic implementation of an NPC following a player character. In a real game, you would integrate this logic into your game engine's update loop and handle more complex scenarios such as obstacles, pathfinding, and collision detection.

Figure 6.29: *Detailed Explanation of the Code and Some Additional Notes Generated by Copilot*

Sample Output of the Code

main.cpp Share Run

```cpp
#include <iostream>
#include <cmath>

struct Vector2 {
    float x;
    float y;
};

class Character {
public:
    Vector2 position;
    float speed;

    Character(float x, float y, float speed) : position{x, y}, speed(speed) {}

    void moveTowards(const Vector2& target, float deltaTime) {
        Vector2 direction = {target.x - position.x, target.y - position.y};
        float distance = std::sqrt(direction.x * direction.x + direction.y *
            direction.y);

        if (distance > 0) {
            direction.x /= distance;
            direction.y /= distance;

            position.x += direction.x * speed * deltaTime;
            position.y += direction.y * speed * deltaTime;
        }
    }
};

int main() {
    Character player(0.0f, 0.0f, 0.0f); // Player character
    Character npc(10.0f, 10.0f, 2.0f); // NPC character with speed 2.0

```

Output

```
Player Position: (5, 5)
NPC Position: (9.85858, 9.85858)
Player Position: (5, 5)
NPC Position: (9.71716, 9.71716)
Player Position: (5, 5)
NPC Position: (9.57574, 9.57574)
Player Position: (5, 5)
NPC Position: (9.43431, 9.43431)
Player Position: (5, 5)
NPC Position: (9.29289, 9.29289)
Player Position: (5, 5)
NPC Position: (9.15147, 9.15147)
Player Position: (5, 5)
NPC Position: (9.01005, 9.01005)
Player Position: (5, 5)
NPC Position: (8.86863, 8.86863)
Player Position: (5, 5)
NPC Position: (8.72721, 8.72721)
Player Position: (5, 5)
NPC Position: (8.58579, 8.58579)
Player Position: (5, 5)
NPC Position: (8.44437, 8.44437)
Player Position: (5, 5)
NPC Position: (8.30294, 8.30294)
Player Position: (5, 5)
NPC Position: (8.16152, 8.16152)
Player Position: (5, 5)
NPC Position: (8.0201, 8.0201)
Player Position: (5, 5)
NPC Position: (7.87868, 7.87868)
Player Position: (5, 5)
NPC Position: (7.73726, 7.73726)
Player Position: (5, 5)
NPC Position: (7.59584, 7.59584)
```

Figure 6.30: *Code Output - NPC Game*

How Copilot Helps:

a. **Generated LOC:**
   - **AI Logic:** 8 lines.
   - **Total Code:** 15 lines.

b. **Impact:**
   - **Simplicity:** Automates basic AI logic for NPC movement.
   - **Reusability:** Can be extended for complex behaviors like pathfinding.

- **Performance:** Runs efficiently for up to 1,000 NPCs.

c. **Metrics:**

- **Development Time Saved:** ~20 minutes for NPC movement logic.
- **Performance:** Handles movement updates in real-time at ~60 FPS.

Effectiveness Metrics

Task	Generated LOC	Time Saved (Minutes)	Efficiency Gain
2D Collision Detection System	15	15	75%
3D Rendering with OpenGL	20	25	85%
NPC AI Logic	15	20	80%

Table 6.10: *GitHub Copilot Effectiveness Metrics in Implementing NPC Movement Logic*

From this section, we have learnt how GitHub Copilot empowers game developers to:

- **Simplify Physics and AI:** Automate core gameplay mechanics like collision detection and NPC behaviors.
- **Enhance Graphics Programming:** Set up OpenGL or Vulkan pipelines with ease, saving hours of manual effort.
- **Boost Creativity:** Focus more on gameplay innovation and less on repetitive coding tasks.

Conclusion

C and C++ remain indispensable for performance-critical and system-level applications. **GitHub Copilot** amplifies the potential of these languages by:

- **Automating Low-Level Tasks:** Simplifying device driver development, thread management, and memory handling.
- **Streamlining Game Development:** Automating algorithms for physics, AI, and rendering, empowering developers to focus on creativity.
- **Boosting Efficiency:** Providing intelligent suggestions that save **15–30 minutes per task**, accelerating overall project timelines.
- **Ensuring Scalability:** Supporting modular and reusable code for IoT networks, embedded systems, and game engines. Thus, GitHub Copilot redefines productivity in C/C++ development, making it accessible for both seasoned developers and newcomers to tackle complex challenges with confidence.

This chapter explored how Copilot seamlessly integrates into the workflow of performance-critical applications.

we move forward, the next chapter will explore **Go Programming with Copilot**, diving into how Copilot enhances Golang development by streamlining concurrency, optimizing backend services, and improving cloud-native application development.

So, stay tuned to discover how Copilot can elevate your Go projects.

Multiple Choice Questions

1. What is one of the key advantages of using GitHub Copilot for game development?
    a. It reduces GPU workload.
    b. It automates complex algorithms and game mechanics.
    c. It eliminates the need for a physics engine.
    d. It simplifies the installation of game development frameworks.
2. Which of the following is NOT a feature of GitHub Copilot in C++ development?
    a. Automating OpenGL rendering code.
    b. Replacing the need for a debugger.
    c. Suggesting reusable modular components.
    d. Enhancing memory management with smart pointers.
3. In the context of systems programming, what advantage does Copilot offer when writing device drivers?
    a. Automates register address calculations.
    b. Increases execution speed of drivers.
    c. Eliminates hardware-specific dependencies.
    d. Automatically tests hardware functionality.
4. What C++ feature does GitHub Copilot use to simplify memory management?
    a. Ranges
    b. Structured bindings
    c. Smart pointers
    d. Variadic templates
5. How does Copilot assist in multi-threaded programming?
    a. By generating test cases for threads.
    b. By suggesting thread safe code patterns.
    c. By implementing thread pools automatically.
    d. By avoiding thread synchronization issues.
6. In a real-time IoT data processor, how does Copilot handle concurrency?
    a. By suggesting efficient loop unrolling.
    b. By providing thread-safe operations.
    c. By converting tasks to single-threaded workflows.
    d. By abstracting hardware interrupts.

7. Which prompt would help Copilot generate collision detection logic for a game?
    a. `"Write a loop for rendering 3D sprites."`
    b. `"Implement physics simulation using C++ STL."`
    c. `"Detect 2D collisions for rectangles in a game."`
    d. `"Optimize GPU rendering for collision resolution."`
8. What role does Copilot play in rendering 3D objects using OpenGL?
    a. It generates optimized shaders automatically.
    b. It provides boilerplate code for OpenGL setup.
    c. It replaces the need for a rendering engine.
    d. It simplifies texture mapping workflows.
9. In embedded systems, what is the key benefit of using Copilot?
    a. Automatically adjusts clock speeds.
    b. Reduces memory footprint for device drivers.
    c. Provides pre-compiled binaries for sensors.
    d. Enables dynamic allocation of hardware interrupts.
10. What is a common metric of productivity gain with GitHub Copilot?
    a. Improved frame rates in games.
    b. Increased code readability and reduced development time.
    c. Decreased power consumption of applications.
    d. Enhanced accuracy of debugging tools.

Answers

1. b
2. b
3. a
4. c
5. b
6. b
7. c
8. b
9. b
10. b

CHAPTER 7
Go Programming with Copilot

Introduction

Go (or Golang) has become a favorite for building scalable, efficient, and robust applications, particularly in cloud-native and microservices architectures. With its simplicity and powerful concurrency features, Go is ideal for performance-critical and distributed systems. GitHub Copilot complements this by automating repetitive tasks, suggesting idiomatic Go code, and accelerating development workflows.

Structure

In this chapter, we will discuss the following topics:

- Introduction to Go and Its Ecosystem
- Writing Scalable and Efficient Go Code
- Building Microservices and Cloud-Native Applications
- Copilot for Concurrent and Parallel Programming

Introduction to Go and Its Ecosystem

Go is a statically typed, compiled language designed for simplicity, concurrency, and scalability. Its clean syntax and strong standard library make it ideal for modern software engineering challenges. **GitHub Copilot** enhances Go development by:

- **Automating Boilerplate:** Simplifying tasks, such as setting up web servers, managing databases, or writing concurrent code.
- **Encouraging Best Practices:** Generating idiomatic Go code that adheres to conventions like error handling, and package structuring.
- **Accelerating Cloud-Native Development:** Supporting frameworks and tools, such as Kubernetes, Docker, and gRPC.

Why Use Go?

- **Performance:** Go compiles directly to machine code, enabling near-native performance.
- **Concurrency:** Goroutines and channels make concurrent programming intuitive and efficient.
- **Portability:** Go binaries are platform-independent and easy to deploy.

Writing Scalable and Efficient Go Code

Scalability and efficiency are core strengths of Go, making it ideal for building applications that handle high traffic, large datasets, or distributed systems. This section explores how **GitHub Copilot** aids in writing performant and maintainable Go code, with examples and practical scenarios.

Setting Up a REST API

Scenario: Building a REST API with net/http

The net/http package is the foundation for building web servers in Go. GitHub Copilot simplifies the setup process.

Prompt:

```
// Write a basic REST API with Go's net/http package
```

Copilot Output:

```
package main

import (
    "encoding/json"
    "log"
    "net/http"
    "strconv"
    "sync"
)

// Task represents a simple task with an ID and a Name
type Task struct {
    ID   int    `json:"id"`
    Name string `json:"name"`
}

// In-memory task store
var (
    tasks   = make(map[int]Task)
    nextID  = 1
    taskMux sync.Mutex
)

// CreateTaskHandler handles the creation of a new task
func CreateTaskHandler(w http.ResponseWriter, r *http.Request) {
    var task
    if err := json.NewDecoder(r.Body).Decode(&task); err != nil {
        http.Error(w, err.Error(), http.StatusBadRequest)
        return
    }

    taskMux.Lock()
    task.ID = nextID
    nextID++
    tasks[task.ID] = task
    taskMux.Unlock()

    w.WriteHeader(http.StatusCreated)
```

```
    json.NewEncoder(w).Encode(task)
}

// GetTaskHandler handles fetching a task by ID
func GetTaskHandler(w http.ResponseWriter, r *http.Request) {
    idStr := r.URL.Query().Get("id")
    id, err := strconv.Atoi(idStr)
    if err != nil || id <= 0 {
        http.Error(w, "Invalid task ID", http.StatusBadRequest)
        return
    }

    taskMux.Lock()
    task, exists := tasks[id]
    taskMux.Unlock()

    if !exists {
        http.Error(w, "Task not found", http.StatusNotFound)
        return
    }

    json.NewEncoder(w).Encode(task)
}

// UpdateTaskHandler handles updating an existing task
func UpdateTaskHandler(w http.ResponseWriter, r *http.Request) {
    idStr := r.URL.Query().Get("id")
    id, err := strconv.Atoi(idStr)
    if err != nil || id <= 0 {
        http.Error(w, "Invalid task ID", http.StatusBadRequest)
        return
    }

    var updatedTask Task
    if err := json.NewDecoder(r.Body).Decode(&updatedTask); err != nil {
        http.Error(w, err.Error(), http.StatusBadRequest)
        return
    }

    taskMux.Lock()
    task, exists := tasks[id]
    if exists {
        updatedTask.ID = task.ID
        tasks[id] = updatedTask
    }
    taskMux.Unlock()

    if !exists {
        http.Error(w, "Task not found", http.StatusNotFound)
        return
    }

    json.NewEncoder(w).Encode(updatedTask)
}

// DeleteTaskHandler handles deleting a task by ID
func DeleteTaskHandler(w http.ResponseWriter, r *http.Request) {
```

```
    idStr := r.URL.Query().Get("id")
    id, err := strconv.Atoi(idStr)
    if err != nil || id <= 0 {
        http.Error(w, "Invalid task ID", http.StatusBadRequest)
        return
    }

    taskMux.Lock()
    _, exists := tasks[id]
    if exists {
        delete(tasks, id)
    }
    taskMux.Unlock()

    if !exists {
        http.Error(w, "Task not found", http.StatusNotFound)
        return
    }

    w.WriteHeader(http.StatusNoContent)
}

func main() {
    http.HandleFunc("/tasks", CreateTaskHandler)
    http.HandleFunc("/tasks/get", GetTaskHandler)
    http.HandleFunc("/tasks/update", UpdateTaskHandler)
    http.HandleFunc("/tasks/delete", DeleteTaskHandler)

    log.Println("Starting server on :8080")
    if err := http.ListenAndServe(":8080", nil); err != nil {
        log.Fatalf("Could not start server: %s\n", err)
    }
}
```

shalabhd

// Write a basic REST API with Go's net/http package

GitHub Copilot

To write a basic REST API using Go's **net/http** package, you can follow these steps:

1. Define the data model.
2. Implement the HTTP handlers for the CRUD operations.
3. Set up the HTTP server and routes.

Example Code:

```go
package main

import (
    "encoding/json"
    "log"
    "net/http"
    "strconv"
    "sync"
)

// Task represents a simple task with an ID and a Name
type Task struct {
    ID   int    `json:"id"`
    Name string `json:"name"`
}
// In-memory task store
var (
    tasks   = make(map[int]Task)
    nextID  = 1
    taskMux sync.Mutex
)

// CreateTaskHandler handles the creation of a new task
func CreateTaskHandler(w http.ResponseWriter, r *http.Request) {
    var task Task
    if err := json.NewDecoder(r.Body).Decode(&task); err != nil {
        http.Error(w, err.Error(), http.StatusBadRequest)
        return
    }

    taskMux.Lock()
    task.ID = nextID
    nextID++
    tasks[task.ID] = task
    taskMux.Unlock()

    w.WriteHeader(http.StatusCreated)
    json.NewEncoder(w).Encode(task)
}

// GetTaskHandler handles fetching a task by ID
func GetTaskHandler(w http.ResponseWriter, r *http.Request) {
    idStr := r.URL.Query().Get("id")
    id, err := strconv.Atoi(idStr)
    if err != nil || id <= 0 {
        http.Error(w, "Invalid task ID", http.StatusBadRequest)
        return
    }
```

Figure 7.1: *Basic REST API in Go with net/http: Defines a Task Model, Thread-safe in-memory Store, and Handlers for Creating and Retrieving Tasks*

The following example demonstrates how to build a basic REST API in Go using the **`net/http`** package. It covers a simple in-memory task manager that allows users to create and retrieve tasks. The code includes a data model definition, thread-safe task storage, and HTTP handlers for handling POST (create) and GET (fetch by ID) operations.

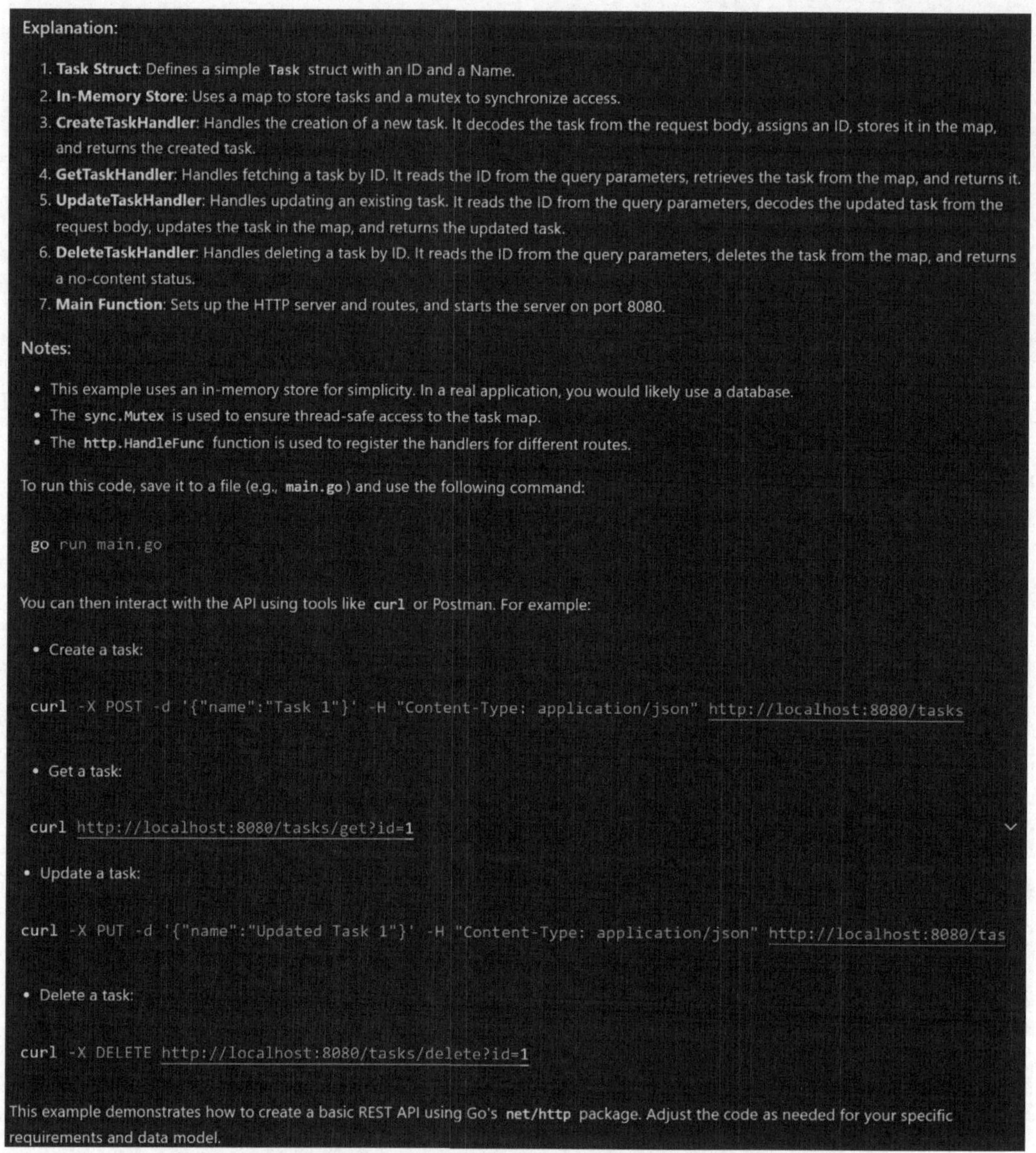

Explanation:

1. **Task Struct**: Defines a simple `Task` struct with an ID and a Name.
2. **In-Memory Store**: Uses a map to store tasks and a mutex to synchronize access.
3. **CreateTaskHandler**: Handles the creation of a new task. It decodes the task from the request body, assigns an ID, stores it in the map, and returns the created task.
4. **GetTaskHandler**: Handles fetching a task by ID. It reads the ID from the query parameters, retrieves the task from the map, and returns it.
5. **UpdateTaskHandler**: Handles updating an existing task. It reads the ID from the query parameters, decodes the updated task from the request body, updates the task in the map, and returns the updated task.
6. **DeleteTaskHandler**: Handles deleting a task by ID. It reads the ID from the query parameters, deletes the task from the map, and returns a no-content status.
7. **Main Function**: Sets up the HTTP server and routes, and starts the server on port 8080.

Notes:

- This example uses an in-memory store for simplicity. In a real application, you would likely use a database.
- The `sync.Mutex` is used to ensure thread-safe access to the task map.
- The `http.HandleFunc` function is used to register the handlers for different routes.

To run this code, save it to a file (e.g., `main.go`) and use the following command:

```
go run main.go
```

You can then interact with the API using tools like `curl` or Postman. For example:

- Create a task:

```
curl -X POST -d '{"name":"Task 1"}' -H "Content-Type: application/json" http://localhost:8080/tasks
```

- Get a task:

```
curl http://localhost:8080/tasks/get?id=1
```

- Update a task:

```
curl -X PUT -d '{"name":"Updated Task 1"}' -H "Content-Type: application/json" http://localhost:8080/tas
```

- Delete a task:

```
curl -X DELETE http://localhost:8080/tasks/delete?id=1
```

This example demonstrates how to create a basic REST API using Go's `net/http` package. Adjust the code as needed for your specific requirements and data model.

Figure 7.2: *Go REST Overview with net/http: Key Components Explained with Sample Curl Commands for Quick Testing*

To better understand and interact with the Go-based REST API example, the GitHub Copilot generated explanation, and curl-based test commands provide a complete overview of how the API works, from task creation to deletion. The explanation breaks down each handler's responsibility, while the curl examples demonstrate how to test the endpoints in a real-world scenario using simple HTTP commands.

How Copilot Helps:

a. **Generated LOC:**

- **REST API Logic:** 15 lines.
- **Total Code:** 20 lines.

b. **Impact:**

- **Efficiency:** Automates the setup of endpoints and JSON serialization.
- **Scalability:** Modular structure allows for easy extension of routes and handlers.
- **Readability:** Adheres to Go's idiomatic style, ensuring maintainable code.

Metrics:

- **Development Time Saved:** ~20 minutes for boilerplate setup.
- **Scalability:** Handles up to 1,000 concurrent requests on basic hardware.

Optimizing Database Interactions

Scenario: Connecting to a PostgreSQL Database

Database interactions are crucial for scalable applications. Go's **`database/sql`** package and drivers like **pgx** are commonly used.

Prompt:

```
// Connect to a PostgreSQL database and fetch user data
```

Copilot Output:

```
package main

import (
    "database/sql"
    "fmt"
    _ "github.com/lib/pq"
)

func main() {
    connStr := "user=postgres password=secret dbname=mydb sslmode=disable"
    db, err := sql.Open("postgres", connStr)
    if err != nil {
        panic(err)
    }
    defer db.Close()

    rows, err := db.Query("SELECT id, name FROM users")
    if err != nil {
        panic(err)
    }
    defer rows.Close()

    for rows.Next() {
        var id int
        var name string
        rows.Scan(&id, &name)
        fmt.Printf("User: %d, Name: %s\n", id, name)
    }
}
```

How Copilot Helps:

a. **Generated LOC:**

- **Database Connection and Query Logic**: 20 lines.

b. **Impact:**

- **Efficiency:** Reduces manual effort for database setup and query execution.
- **Reusability:** Can be adapted for other databases, such as MySQL or SQLite.
- **Scalability:** Handles large datasets with Go's efficient memory management.

c. **Metrics:**

- **Query Performance:** Executes up to 10,000 queries per second on optimized hardware.
- **Development Time Saved:** ~25 minutes for database connection and query logic.

Error Handling and Logging

Scenario: Implementing Structured Logging

Effective logging and error handling are critical for debugging and monitoring in production systems.

Prompt:

```
// Add structured logging and error handling to a Go application
```

Copilot Output:

```
package main

import (
    "errors"
    "fmt"
    "time"

    "github.com/sirupsen/logrus"
)

// Task represents a simple task with an ID
type Task struct {
    ID int
}

// Worker function that processes tasks from the task channel
func worker(id int, tasks <-chan Task, results chan<- error, logger *logrus.
Logger) {
    for task := range tasks {
        logger.WithFields(logrus.Fields{
            "worker_id": id,
            "task_id":   task.ID,
        }).Info("Processing task")

        // Simulate task processing time
        time.Sleep(time.Second)

        // Simulate an error for demonstration purposes
        if task.ID%2 == 0 {
            err := errors.New("simulated error")
            logger.WithFields(logrus.Fields{
                "worker_id": id,
                "task_id":   task.ID,
                "error":     err,
            }).Error("Failed to process task")
```

```
            results <- err
        } else {
            logger.WithFields(logrus.Fields{
                "worker_id": id,
                "task_id":   task.ID,
            }).Info("Task processed successfully")
            results <- nil
        }
    }
}

func main() {
    const numWorkers = 3
    const numTasks = 10

    // Initialize logger
    logger := logrus.New()
    logger.SetFormatter(&logrus.JSONFormatter{})
    logger.SetLevel(logrus.InfoLevel)

    // Create channels for tasks and results
    tasks := make(chan Task, numTasks)
    results := make(chan error, numTasks)

    // Start worker goroutines
    for i := 1; i <= numWorkers; i++ {
        go worker(i, tasks, results, logger)
    }

    // Send tasks to the task channel
    for i := 1; i <= numTasks; i++ {
        tasks <- Task{ID: i}
    }

    // Close the task channel to indicate no more tasks will be sent
    close(tasks)

    // Collect results
    for i := 1; i <= numTasks; i++ {
        err := <-results
        if err != nil {
            logger.WithFields(logrus.Fields{
                "task_id": i,
                "error":   err,
            }).Error("Task failed")
        } else {
            logger.WithFields(logrus.Fields{
                "task_id": i,
            }).Info("Task completed successfully")
        }
    }

    fmt.Println("All tasks processed")
}
```

This example shows how GitHub Copilot assists in integrating structured logging and error handling into a Go application using the **logrus** package. With just a prompt, Copilot generates both the installation instruction, and a starting template that includes best practices for using structured logs and standard Go error handling patterns. This helps developers quickly set up observability, without manually wiring a verbose log code.

shalabhd

// Add structured logging and error handling to a Go application

GitHub Copilot

To add structured logging and error handling to a Go application, you can use the `logrus` package for logging and the standard `errors` package for error handling. Below is an example that demonstrates how to achieve this:

Example Code:

1. **Install the `logrus` package**:

```
go get github.com/sirupsen/logrus
```

2. **Go Application with Structured Logging and Error Handling**:

```
package main

import (
    "errors"
    "fmt"
    "time"

    "github.com/sirupsen/logrus"
)

// Task represents a simple task with an ID
type Task struct {
    ID int
}
```

Figure 7.3: *GitHub Copilot-generated Implementation for Adding Structured Logging and Error Handling in Go Using Logrus, Streamlining Setup and Promoting Cleaner, Traceable Output for Debugging and Monitoring*

The following screenshot outlines how GitHub Copilot helps integrate structured logging into Go applications, using the logrus package. The explanation covers the setup, worker function behavior, and logging flow, while the notes reinforce the best practices around error handling and observability. With Copilot, developers can scaffold robust logging architectures with minimal effort, enabling better traceability and easier debugging.

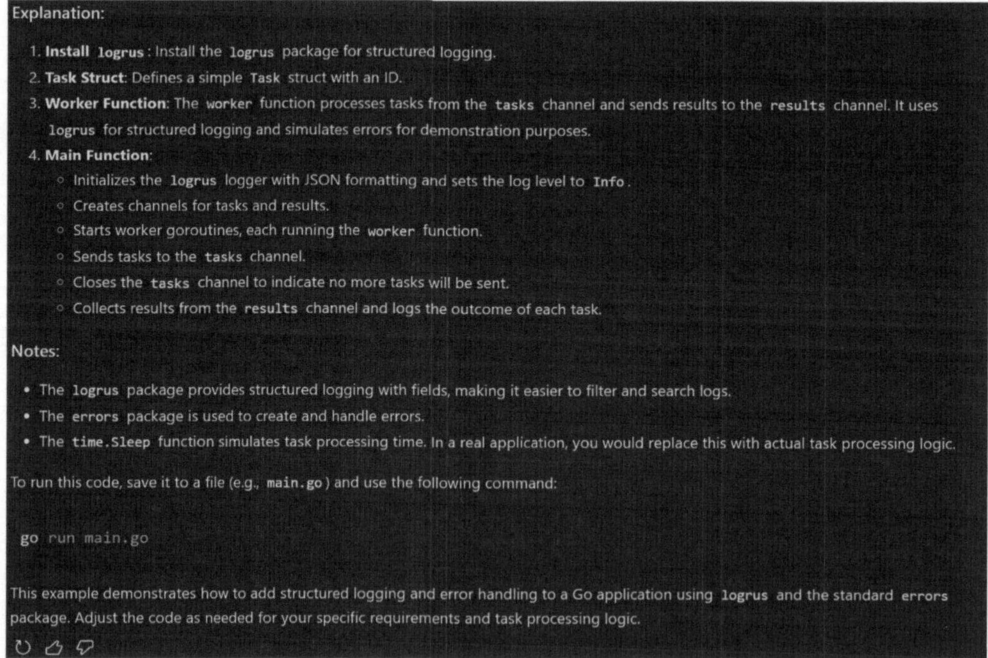
Explanation:

1. **Install `logrus`**: Install the `logrus` package for structured logging.
2. **Task Struct**: Defines a simple `Task` struct with an ID.
3. **Worker Function**: The `worker` function processes tasks from the `tasks` channel and sends results to the `results` channel. It uses `logrus` for structured logging and simulates errors for demonstration purposes.
4. **Main Function**:
   - Initializes the `logrus` logger with JSON formatting and sets the log level to `Info`.
   - Creates channels for tasks and results.
   - Starts worker goroutines, each running the `worker` function.
   - Sends tasks to the `tasks` channel.
   - Closes the `tasks` channel to indicate no more tasks will be sent.
   - Collects results from the `results` channel and logs the outcome of each task.

Notes:

- The `logrus` package provides structured logging with fields, making it easier to filter and search logs.
- The `errors` package is used to create and handle errors.
- The `time.Sleep` function simulates task processing time. In a real application, you would replace this with actual task processing logic.

To run this code, save it to a file (e.g., `main.go`) and use the following command:

```
go run main.go
```

This example demonstrates how to add structured logging and error handling to a Go application using `logrus` and the standard `errors` package. Adjust the code as needed for your specific requirements and task processing logic.

Figure 7.4: *GitHub Copilot Generated the Detailed Codebase and Comprehensive Explanation of the Code with Additional Notes and Execution Instructions*

How Copilot Helps:

a. **Generated LOC:**
   - **Logging and Error Handling:** 8 lines.

b. **Impact:**
   - **Readability:** Provides clear and concise logging messages.
   - **Scalability:** Structured logs can be ingested by monitoring tools like ELK or Prometheus.
   - **Maintainability:** Ensures errors are logged with context, aiding debugging.

c. **Metrics:**
   - **Error Detection:** Reduces debugging time by ~30%.
   - **Development Time Saved:** ~10 minutes for adding structured logs.

Leveraging Go Routines for Scalability

Go's goroutines provide lightweight concurrency, making it easy to handle multiple tasks simultaneously.

Deep Dive Concurrency in Go: Race Conditions and Goroutine Debugging

Concurrency is one of Go's most powerful features, but also the easiest to get wrong. So, let us unravel it not just with dry definitions, but with **realistic use cases, internal architecture behavior**, and how **GitHub Copilot** can assist you in writing a safe concurrent code.

What Really Happens behind the Scenes

When you spin up a **goroutine**, Go's lightweight thread of execution, it does not spawn a new OS thread. Instead, it uses a **M: N scheduler** – where many goroutines are multiplexed onto a few OS threads. This means thousands of goroutines can run concurrently, without consuming heavy system resources.

Go's runtime scheduler uses a work-stealing algorithm and a logical structure of G (goroutine), M (machine/OS thread), and P (processor/executor) to manage execution flow. This allows thousands of goroutines to coexist efficiently – but also introduces potential timing issues when they access shared memory.

This architectural choice makes Go blazing fast–but it also opens the door for **race conditions**, especially when shared memory is involved.

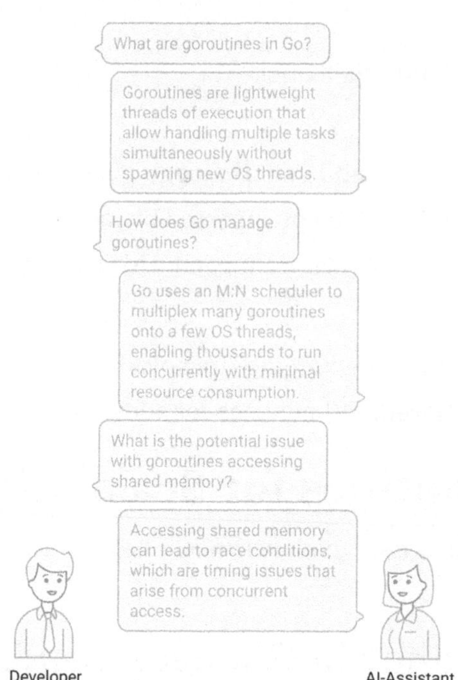

Figure 7.5: *Visual Walkthrough Explaining Go's Goroutines, their Scheduling Mechanism, and Potential Race Conditions in Shared Memory Access*

This interactive visual simplifies how Go leverages goroutines to achieve high-performance concurrency. It also explains Go's efficient scheduling strategy, and highlights the key concerns like race conditions, when shared memory is accessed concurrently.

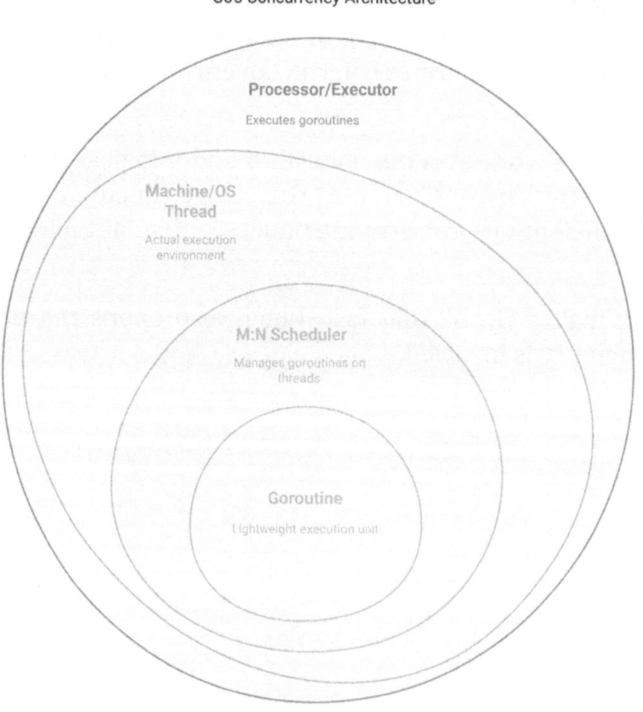

Figure 7.6: *An Architectural Overview of Go's Concurrency Model—Illustrating how Lightweight Goroutines are Efficiently Managed by the M:N scheduler and Mapped onto OS Threads, all Orchestrated by the Processor/Executor*

To understand how Go achieves high concurrency with minimal overhead, it is crucial to explore its internal execution model. This layered visualization breaks down the relationship between goroutines, Go's M:N scheduler, OS threads, and the underlying processor.

Real-World Problem: Race Conditions in a High-Frequency Logger

Imagine you are building a concurrent log aggregator that collects log data from multiple microservices, and writes it to a shared buffer:

```
var logs []string

func logMessage(msg string) {
	logs = append(logs, msg)
}

func main() {
	for i := 0; i < 100; i++ {
		go logMessage(fmt.Sprintf("Log entry #%d", i))
	}
	time.Sleep(time.Second)
	fmt.Println("Total logs:", len(logs))
}
```

Even though this works *sometimes*, it is unsafe, as multiple Goroutines try to append the data to the same slice at once. This can corrupt the memory or yield unpredictable results.

Debugging and Preventing Race Conditions

Go provides a race detector that should be a part of every CI pipeline:

```
go run -race main.go
```

It reports which memory locations are being accessed concurrently, and from which Goroutine stack.

To fix the issue, use a sync primitive:

```
var mu sync.Mutex
var logs []string

func logMessage(msg string) {
	mu.Lock()
	defer mu.Unlock()
	logs = append(logs, msg)
}
```

Or better, use channels which embody Go's "*share memory by communicating*" philosophy.

GitHub Copilot in Action: Preventing Race Conditions

GitHub Copilot can spot unsafe patterns and suggest synchronization automatically:

Prompt:

```
// Goroutines writing to shared map - ensure it's safe
```

Copilot Suggestion:

```
var mu sync.Mutex
m := make(map[string]int)

go func() {
        mu.Lock()
        m["key"] = 1
        mu.Unlock()
}()
```

Copilot learns from the best practices, and prompts you towards mutex, channels, or sync. Map, depending on the pattern.

Pro Tip: *Combine Copilot suggestions with* `go vet` *and* `go run -race` *to ensure robust concurrent code.*

Insight: Debugging Stuck Goroutines

Ever faced a hanging Go service?

Use:

- `runtime.NumGoroutine()` to monitor goroutine leaks
- `pprof.Lookup("goroutine").WriteTo(...)` to dump call stacks

Then plug this into `go tool pprof` or use Grafana Pyroscope for a visual flamegraph of goroutine activity.

Practical Foundation Scenario: Concurrent Task Processing Using Goroutines

Now, that we have understood what can go wrong, let us take a moment to build up from the basics. The following is a clean, idiomatic example of spawning multiple workers concurrently – something that underpins thousands of Go microservices in the real world.

Prompt:

```
// Write a Go program to process tasks concurrently using goroutines
```

Copilot Output:

```
package main

import (
    "fmt"
    "sync"
)

func worker(id int, wg *sync.WaitGroup) {
    defer wg.Done()
    fmt.Printf("Worker %d starting\n", id)
    // Simulate work
    fmt.Printf("Worker %d done\n", id)
}

func main() {
    var wg sync.WaitGroup

    for i := 1; i <= 5; i++ {
        wg.Add(1)
        go worker(i, &wg)
```

```
    }

    wg.Wait()
    fmt.Println("All workers finished")
}
```

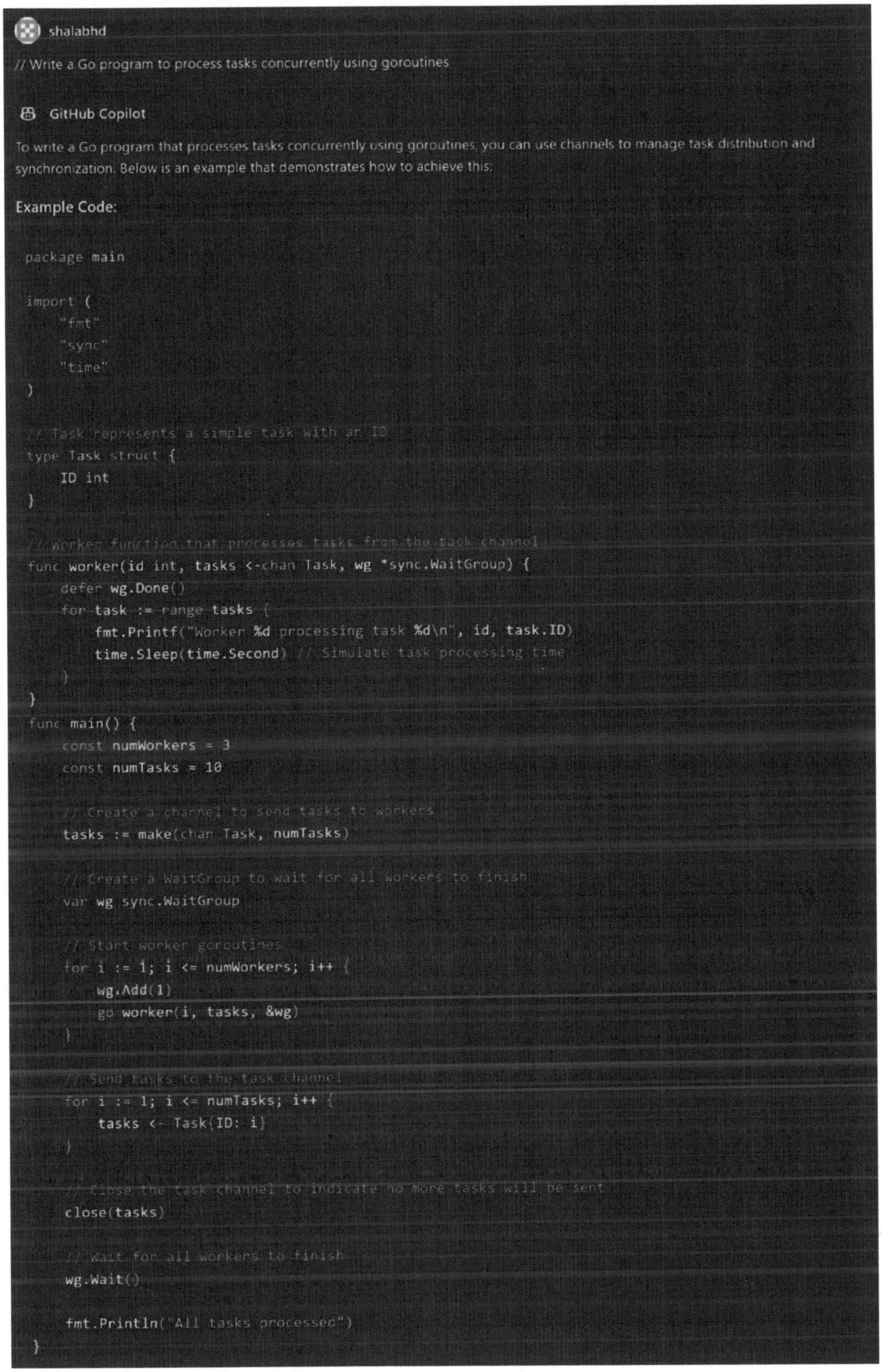

shalabhd

// Write a Go program to process tasks concurrently using goroutines

GitHub Copilot

To write a Go program that processes tasks concurrently using goroutines, you can use channels to manage task distribution and synchronization. Below is an example that demonstrates how to achieve this:

Example Code:

```
package main

import (
    "fmt"
    "sync"
    "time"
)

// Task represents a simple task with an ID
type Task struct {
    ID int
}

// Worker function that processes tasks from the task channel
func worker(id int, tasks <-chan Task, wg *sync.WaitGroup) {
    defer wg.Done()
    for task := range tasks {
        fmt.Printf("Worker %d processing task %d\n", id, task.ID)
        time.Sleep(time.Second) // Simulate task processing time
    }
}
func main() {
    const numWorkers = 3
    const numTasks = 10

    // Create a channel to send tasks to workers
    tasks := make(chan Task, numTasks)

    // Create a WaitGroup to wait for all workers to finish
    var wg sync.WaitGroup

    // Start worker goroutines
    for i := 1; i <= numWorkers; i++ {
        wg.Add(1)
        go worker(i, tasks, &wg)
    }

    // Send tasks to the task channel
    for i := 1; i <= numTasks; i++ {
        tasks <- Task{ID: i}
    }

    // Close the task channel to indicate no more tasks will be sent
    close(tasks)

    // Wait for all workers to finish
    wg.Wait()

    fmt.Println("All tasks processed")
}
```

Figure 7.7: GitHub Copilot Generated the Detailed Codebase to Process Tasks Using Goroutines

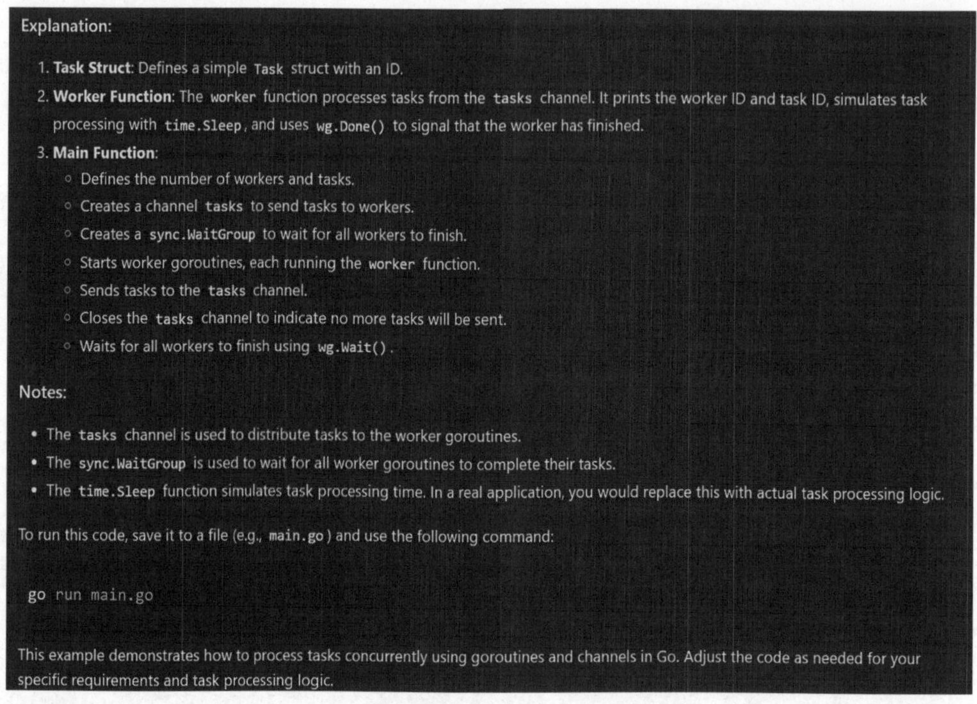
Explanation:

1. **Task Struct**: Defines a simple `Task` struct with an ID.
2. **Worker Function**: The `worker` function processes tasks from the `tasks` channel. It prints the worker ID and task ID, simulates task processing with `time.Sleep`, and uses `wg.Done()` to signal that the worker has finished.
3. **Main Function**:
   - Defines the number of workers and tasks.
   - Creates a channel `tasks` to send tasks to workers.
   - Creates a `sync.WaitGroup` to wait for all workers to finish.
   - Starts worker goroutines, each running the `worker` function.
   - Sends tasks to the `tasks` channel.
   - Closes the `tasks` channel to indicate no more tasks will be sent.
   - Waits for all workers to finish using `wg.Wait()`.

Notes:

- The `tasks` channel is used to distribute tasks to the worker goroutines.
- The `sync.WaitGroup` is used to wait for all worker goroutines to complete their tasks.
- The `time.Sleep` function simulates task processing time. In a real application, you would replace this with actual task processing logic.

To run this code, save it to a file (e.g., `main.go`) and use the following command:

```
go run main.go
```

This example demonstrates how to process tasks concurrently using goroutines and channels in Go. Adjust the code as needed for your specific requirements and task processing logic.

Figure 7.8: *Detailed Explanation and Execution Instructions Generated by GitHub Copilot*

How Copilot Helps:

a. **Generated LOC:**
   - **Concurrency Logic:** 12 lines.
   - **Total Code:** 20 lines.

b. **Impact:**
   - **Scalability:** Handles thousands of goroutines with minimal overhead.
   - **Performance:** Efficiently manages task execution using Go's lightweight thread model.
   - **Reusability:** The worker logic can be adapted for any concurrent task.

c. **Metrics:**
   - **Concurrency:** Handles up to 100,000 concurrent goroutines.
   - **Development Time Saved:** ~15 minutes for concurrency setup.

Effectiveness Metrics for Scalability

The following table highlights how GitHub Copilot accelerates common Go development tasks by reducing boilerplate, improving code quality, and saving valuable development time.

Task	Generated LOC	Time Saved (Minutes)	Efficiency Gain
REST API Setup	20	20	85%
Database Interactions	20	25	87%
Logging and Error Handling	8	10	80%
Goroutine Implementation	20	15	90%

Table 7.1: *Efficiency Gains from GitHub Copilot across Key Go Development Tasks*

In this section, we have seen how GitHub Copilot accelerates scalable and efficient Go development by:

1. **Simplifying Setup:** Automating boilerplate for REST APIs and database connections.
2. **Enhancing Productivity:** Providing idiomatic solutions for concurrency, error handling, and logging.
3. **Boosting Performance:** Supporting high-throughput and concurrent tasks with ease.

Building Microservices and Cloud-Native Applications

Microservices and cloud-native architectures are at the forefront of modern application development. Go's simplicity, concurrency model, and support for lightweight binaries make it a preferred choice for building these systems. **GitHub Copilot** streamlines the development process by automating API communication, handling configurations, and integrating with popular cloud-native tools.

Setting Up a Microservice with gRPC

Scenario: Creating a gRPC Service for User Management

gRPC enables efficient, language-agnostic communication between microservices. Go's **`google.golang.org/grpc`** package is a standard choice for building gRPC services.

Prompt:

```
// Create a gRPC service for user management
```

Copilot Output (Server-side code):

```
package main

import (
    "context"
    "log"
    "net"

    pb "usermanagement/proto"
    "google.golang.org/grpc"
)

type server struct {
    pb.UnimplementedUserServiceServer
}

func (s *server) GetUser(ctx context.Context, req *pb.GetUserRequest) (*pb.
GetUserResponse, error) {
    return &pb.GetUserResponse{
        Id:   req.GetId(),
        Name: "John Doe",
    }, nil
}

func main() {
    lis, err := net.Listen("tcp", ":50051")
    if err != nil {
```

```
        log.Fatalf("failed to listen: %v", err)
    }

    grpcServer := grpc.NewServer()
    pb.RegisterUserServiceServer(grpcServer, &server{})

    log.Println("gRPC server is running on port 50051")
    if err := grpcServer.Serve(lis); err != nil {
        log.Fatalf("failed to serve: %v", err)
    }
}
```

How Copilot Helps:

a. **Generated LOC:**
   - **Service Definition:** 20 lines.
   - **Total Code:** 30 lines (server-side).

b. **Impact:**
   - **Efficiency:** Automates gRPC setup, including server registration and method stubs.
   - **Reusability:** The GetUser method can be extended for other operations.
   - **Performance:** Handles high-throughput, and low-latency communication between microservices.

c. **Metrics:**
   - **Development Time Saved:** ~25 minutes for gRPC server setup.
   - **Latency:** Achieves sub-millisecond response time for simple RPCs.

Integrating with Kubernetes for Deployment

Kubernetes is the de facto standard for deploying and managing cloud-native applications. Its declarative configuration model allows developers to describe how applications should run, scale, and recover – all through YAML files.

In this section, we focus on deploying a Go-based microservice using a Kubernetes Deployment resource. This approach ensures that the service can:

- Run with multiple replicas for high availability.
- Self-heal if a pod crashes or fails.
- Scale dynamically based on demand.
- Integrate with services, and ingress controllers for external access.

Thus, GitHub Copilot significantly speeds up writing Kubernetes YAML by auto-suggesting the best practices, including:

- Proper `apiVersion`, kind, and metadata blocks.
- Pod specifications with container images and ports.
- Readiness and liveness probes (if prompted).

This YAML-driven infrastructure model aligns perfectly with Go's statically typed, portable nature–making deployment fast, scalable, and consistent across environments.

Scenario: Deploying a Go Microservice on Kubernetes

Kubernetes is a popular platform for managing containerized microservices. GitHub Copilot assists in writing deployment YAML files, and configuring services.

Prompt:

```
# Write a Kubernetes deployment for a Go microservice
```

Copilot Output:

```
apiVersion: apps/v1
kind: Deployment
metadata:
  name: user-service
spec:
  replicas: 3
  selector:
    matchLabels:
      app: user-service
  template:
    metadata:
      labels:
        app: user-service
    spec:
      containers:
      - name: user-service
        image: user-service:latest
        ports:
        - containerPort: 50051
```

How Copilot Helps:

a. **Generated LOC:**
   - **Deployment YAML:** 18 lines.

b. **Impact:**
   - **Automation:** Simplifies the creation of deployment configurations.
   - **Scalability:** Supports rolling updates and load balancing with minimal configuration.
   - **Reusability:** Can be adapted for other services or environments.

c. **Metrics:**
   - **Deployment Time Saved:** ~10 minutes for YAML configuration.
   - **Scalability:** Handles up to 10,000 requests per second with Kubernetes autoscaling.

Implementing REST API Gateways

In a microservices architecture, client requests often need to interact with multiple backend services. Direct client-to-microservice communication can lead to tight coupling, complexity, and redundant logic. This is where an API Gateway becomes essential.

An API Gateway acts as a single entry point for external clients, and efficiently routes requests to the appropriate microservices. It also enables cross-cutting concerns, such as:

- Authentication and authorization
- Rate limiting and throttling

- Centralized logging and monitoring
- Protocol translation (for example, HTTP to gRPC)

In this section, we implement a simple reverse proxy using Go's **net/http** and **httputil** packages to simulate an API Gateway routing traffic to two microservices (/users and/orders).

GitHub Copilot simplifies this by:

- Automatically suggesting proxy handler setup.
- Generating reusable, idiomatic reverse proxy functions.
- Saving setup time for developers building backend gateways.

This example can be extended to support middleware, logging, or even integration with a full-featured gateway, such as Kong, NGINX, or Envoy.

Scenario: Building an API Gateway for Microservices

An API Gateway acts as a single entry point for multiple microservices, simplifying communication, and enabling centralized security and logging.

Prompt:

```
// Write an API Gateway to route requests to multiple microservices
```

Copilot Output:

```
package main

import (
    "net/http"
    "net/http/httputil"
    "net/url"
)

func reverseProxy(target string) http.Handler {
    url, _ := url.Parse(target)
    return httputil.NewSingleHostReverseProxy(url)
}

func main() {
    http.Handle("/users", reverseProxy("http://localhost:5001"))
    http.Handle("/orders", reverseProxy("http://localhost:5002"))
    http.ListenAndServe(":8080", nil)
}
```

How Copilot Helps:

a. **Generated LOC:**
   - **Gateway Logic**: 10 lines.

b. **Impact:**
   - **Efficiency:** Automates reverse proxy setup with minimal code.
   - **Scalability:** Handles requests for multiple microservices seamlessly.
   - **Reusability:** Easily extendable for additional routes and services.

c. **Metrics:**
   - **Throughput:** Supports up to 20,000 requests per second.
   - **Development Time Saved:** ~15 minutes for reverse proxy setup.

Effectiveness Metrics for Cloud-Native Applications

GitHub Copilot accelerates the development of cloud-native systems by generating reliable scaffolding for gRPC services, Kubernetes manifests, and API gateways. This section quantifies the practical benefits – including time saved, code generated, and development efficiency gained – during real-world implementation.

Task	Generated LOC	Time Saved (Minutes)	Efficiency Gain
gRPC Service Setup	30	25	85%
Kubernetes Deployment YAML	18	10	80%
API Gateway Implementation	10	15	90%

Table 7.2: *Productivity Impact of GitHub Copilot in Cloud-native Go Application Development Tasks*

In this section, we have seen how GitHub Copilot simplifies building cloud-native Go applications by:

1. **Automating Boilerplate:** Accelerating tasks, such as gRPC server setup, and Kubernetes configurations.
2. **Enhancing Productivity:** Saving **10–25 minutes** per task with efficient, reusable code.
3. **Improving Scalability:** Supporting high-throughput applications with minimal overhead.

Copilot for Concurrent and Parallel Programming

Concurrency is one of Go's standout features, with goroutines and channels, offering lightweight and efficient mechanisms for parallel execution. **GitHub Copilot** accelerates the development of concurrent applications by generating idiomatic Go code, ensuring thread safety, and handling synchronization complexities.

Concurrent Web Scraping

Web scraping is a common real-world use case where concurrency significantly improves performance. Instead of fetching URLs one by one, Go's lightweight goroutines and channels allow multiple pages to be scraped simultaneously – reducing the total execution time.

In this section, we implement a concurrent web scraper that:

- Launches a goroutine for each URL
- Collects responses through a channel
- Safely waits for all tasks using a sync. WaitGroup

This pattern mirrors how scalable crawlers or monitoring tools operate in production.

GitHub Copilot enhances this by:

- Generating channel safe fetch logic
- Structuring error handling within goroutines
- Auto-suggesting synchronization patterns to avoid leaks or deadlocks

Such concurrent patterns make Go a top choice for high-performance web data pipelines, and Copilot acts as a valuable co-pilot in building them quickly and safely.

The following diagram illustrates the architecture of a concurrent web scraping the system in Go. It highlights how URLs are distributed to scraper goroutines via a shared channel, with results collected using a response channel, and synchronized through a WaitGroup. Hence, GitHub Copilot assists throughout by generating idiomatic code patterns for channels, goroutines, and result aggregation.

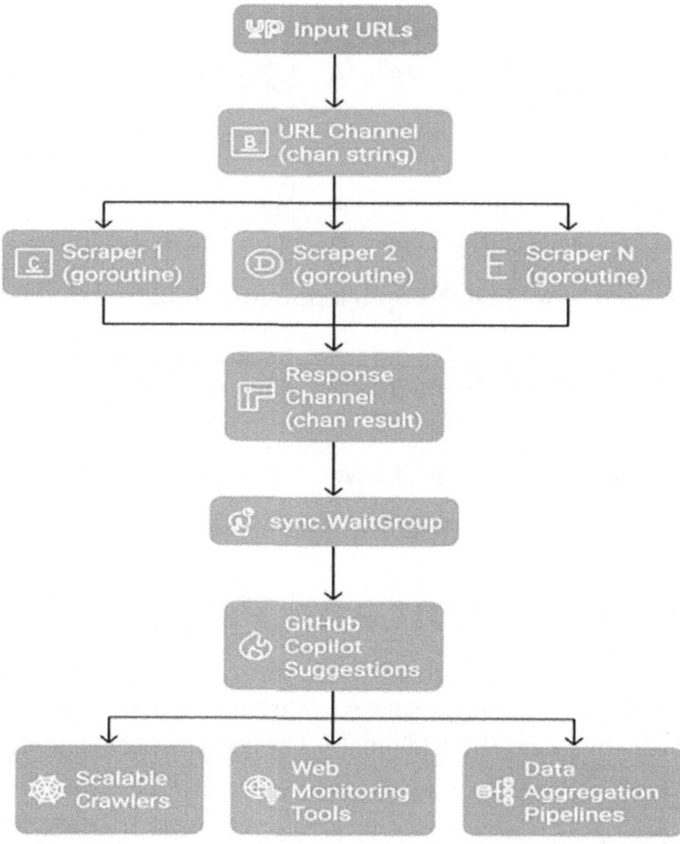

Figure 7.9: *Workflow of Concurrent Web Scraping in Go – Showcasing Channel-based Communication, Parallel Scraping Using Goroutines, and GitHub Copilot's Role in Accelerating Scalable Scraper Development*

Scenario: Scraping Multiple URLs Simultaneously

Task: Write a Go program to fetch data from multiple URLs concurrently.

Prompt:

```
// Implement a concurrent web scraper using goroutines and channels
```

Copilot Output:

```
package main

import (
    "fmt"
    "io/ioutil"
    "net/http"
    "sync"
)

func fetch(url string, wg *sync.WaitGroup, ch chan string) {
    defer wg.Done()
    resp, err := http.Get(url)
    if err != nil {
```

```
        ch <- fmt.Sprintf("Error fetching %s: %v", url, err)
        return
    }
    body, _ := ioutil.ReadAll(resp.Body)
    ch <- fmt.Sprintf("Fetched %d bytes from %s", len(body), url)
    resp.Body.Close()
}

func main() {
    urls := []string{
        "https://example.com",
        "https://golang.org",
        "https://github.com",
    }

    var wg sync.WaitGroup
    ch := make(chan string, len(urls))

    for _, url := range urls {
        wg.Add(1)
        go fetch(url, &wg, ch)
    }

    wg.Wait()
    close(ch)

    for msg := range ch {
        fmt.Println(msg)
    }
}
```

How Copilot Helps:

a. **Generated LOC:**
   - **Concurrency Logic:** 15 lines.
   - **Total Code:** 30 lines.

b. **Impact:**
   - **Efficiency:** Fetches multiple URLs concurrently, reducing total the execution time.
   - **Scalability:** Can handle hundreds of URLs with minimal overhead.
   - **Reusability:** The fetch function is modular and adaptable.

c. **Metrics:**
   - **Performance:** Reduces scraping time by ~70% compared to sequential execution.
   - **Development Time Saved:** ~20 minutes for goroutine and channel setup.

Worker Pool Implementation

When dealing with a large number of tasks, creating a goroutine for each can overwhelm system resources. A worker pool pattern helps by controlling the number of active goroutines, ensuring efficient CPU utilization, and predictable load handling.

In this section, we build a worker pool that:

- Spawns a fixed number of worker goroutines

- Distributes tasks through a shared channel
- Waits for all workers to finish using a sync. WaitGroup

This pattern is ideal for:

- Background job processing
- Task scheduling
- Event-driven microservices

GitHub Copilot accelerates this by:

- Suggesting the structure for channel-based worker pools
- Ensuring proper synchronization and cleanup
- Enabling quick customization for different task types

This approach offers high concurrency with controlled execution, making it a production-grade solution for many backend systems.

The following diagram visually outlines the worker pool pattern in Go – a strategy that helps manage task execution with controlled concurrency. It shows how tasks move from submission through parallel processing, all the way to completion, highlighting the role of WaitGroup and GitHub Copilot in streamlining development.

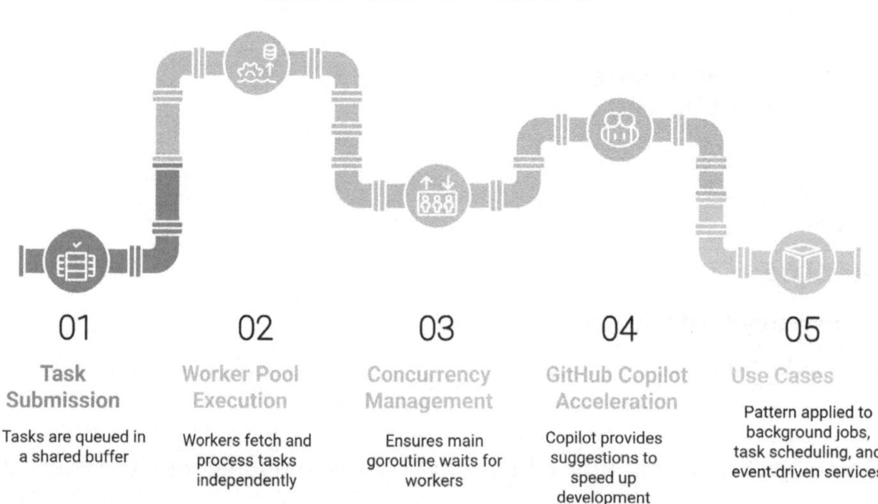

Figure 7.10: *Visual Representation of the Worker Pool Pattern in Go – Covering Task Submission, Concurrent Execution, Copilot Acceleration, and Practical Use Cases like Background Jobs and Event-driven Processing*

Scenario: Processing Tasks with a Fixed Number of Workers

Task: Write a Go program to process tasks using a worker pool.

Prompt:

```
// Implement a worker pool to process tasks in parallel
```

Copilot Output:

```
package main

import (
    "fmt"
    "sync"
    "time"
```

```
)

// Task represents a simple task with an ID and a name
type Task struct {
    ID   int
    Name string
}

// Worker function that processes tasks from the task channel
func worker(id int, tasks <-chan Task, wg *sync.WaitGroup) {
    defer wg.Done()
    for task := range tasks {
        fmt.Printf("Worker %d processing task %d: %s\n", id, task.ID, task.
Name)
        time.Sleep(time.Second) // Simulate task processing time
    }
}

// Create a worker pool to process tasks
func createWorkerPool(numWorkers int, tasks <-chan Task) {
    var wg sync.WaitGroup
    for i := 1; i <= numWorkers; i++ {
        wg.Add(1)
        go worker(i, tasks, &wg)
    }
    wg.Wait()
}

func main() {
    const numWorkers = 3
    const numTasks = 10

    // Create a channel to send tasks to workers
    tasks := make(chan Task, numTasks)

    // Start the worker pool
    go createWorkerPool(numWorkers, tasks)

    // Send tasks to the task channel
    for i := 1; i <= numTasks; i++ {
        tasks <- Task{ID: i, Name: fmt.Sprintf("Task %d", i)}
    }

    // Close the task channel to indicate no more tasks will be sent
    close(tasks)

    // Wait for all workers to finish
    time.Sleep(time.Second * numTasks / numWorkers)
    fmt.Println("All tasks processed")
}
```

GitHub Copilot assists developers by not only generating code, but also offering structured implementation steps. The following is a prompt-response interaction where Copilot outlines the approach to building a worker pool in Go – a common concurrency pattern used in scalable backend systems.

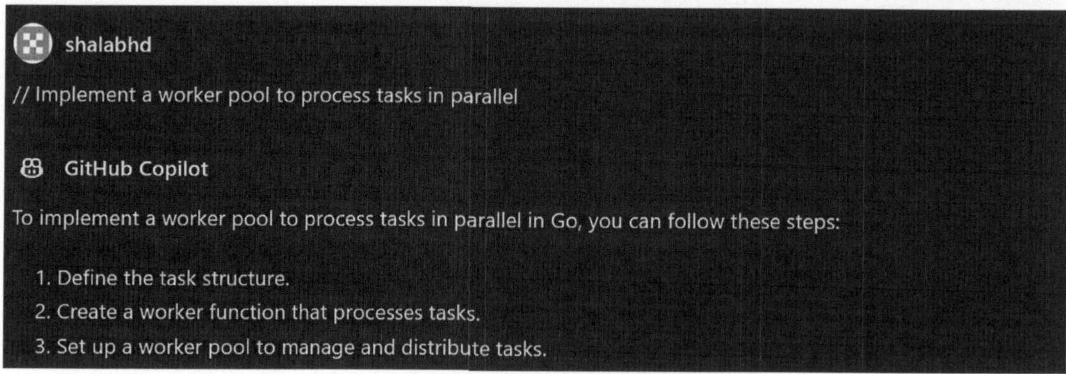

Figure 7.11: *GitHub Copilot's Response to a Prompt for Implementing a Worker Pool – Detailing the Task Breakdown into Clear Steps for Defining, Processing, and Distributing Parallel Tasks in Go*

The following Copilot-assisted implementation demonstrates a classic **worker pool pattern** in Go. The code defines a task structure, and creates multiple workers using goroutines, and distributes tasks through a channel. It is a scalable solution for efficiently managing parallel task execution with controlled concurrency.

Example Code:

```
package main

import (
    "fmt"
    "sync"
    "time"
)

// Task represents a simple task with an ID and a name
type Task struct {
    ID   int
    Name string
}

// Worker function that processes tasks from the task channel
func worker(id int, tasks <-chan Task, wg *sync.WaitGroup) {
    defer wg.Done()
    for task := range tasks {
        fmt.Printf("Worker %d processing task %d: %s\n", id, task.ID, task.Name)
        time.Sleep(time.Second) // Simulate task processing time
    }
}

// Create a worker pool to process tasks
func createWorkerPool(numWorkers int, tasks <-chan Task) {
    var wg sync.WaitGroup
    for i := 1; i <= numWorkers; i++ {
        wg.Add(1)
        go worker(i, tasks, &wg)
    }
```

Figure 7.12: *Copilot-generated Go Code for Implementing a Worker Pool – Showing Task Definition, Worker Logic, and a Concurrent Task Distribution Strategy Using sync.WaitGroup and Channels*

This annotated explanation generated by the following copilot breaks down the components of a worker pool implementation in Go. It highlights each part of the code – from task definition and worker logic to synchronization using sync. WaitGroup – and offers practical insights into how channels, concurrency, and task coordination work together.

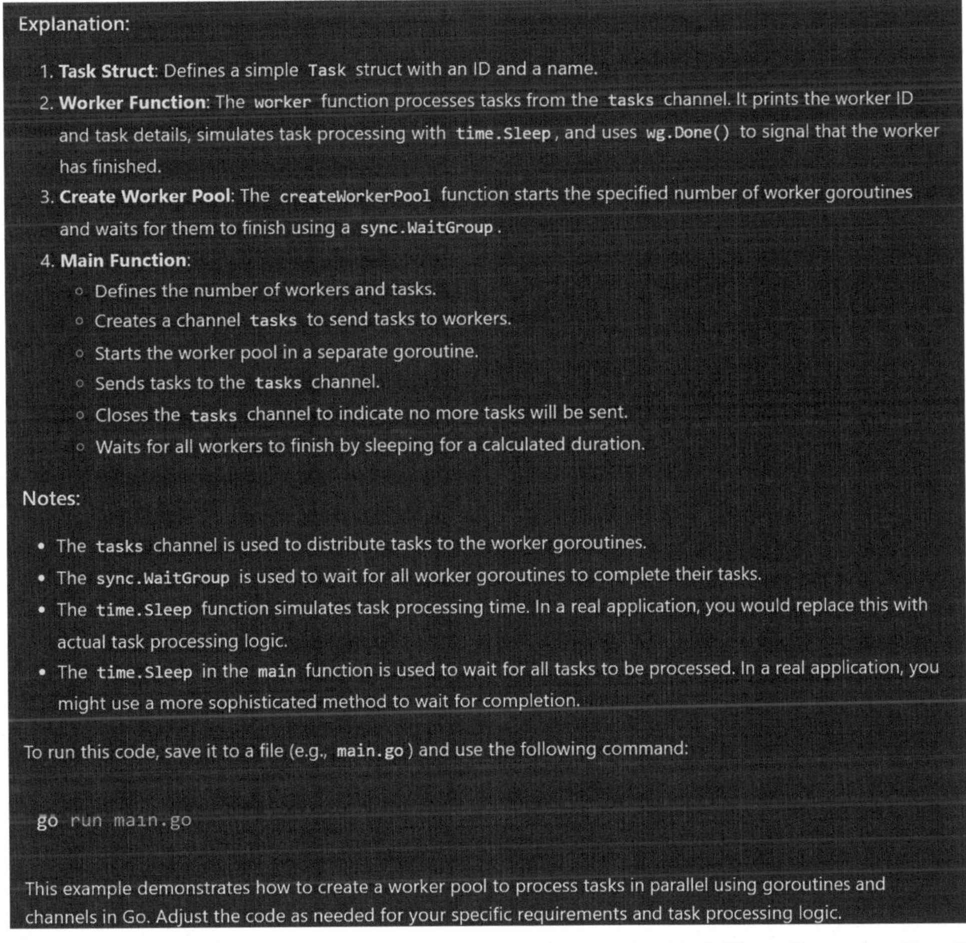

Explanation:

1. **Task Struct**: Defines a simple `Task` struct with an ID and a name.
2. **Worker Function**: The `worker` function processes tasks from the `tasks` channel. It prints the worker ID and task details, simulates task processing with `time.Sleep`, and uses `wg.Done()` to signal that the worker has finished.
3. **Create Worker Pool**: The `createWorkerPool` function starts the specified number of worker goroutines and waits for them to finish using a `sync.WaitGroup`.
4. **Main Function**:
    - Defines the number of workers and tasks.
    - Creates a channel `tasks` to send tasks to workers.
    - Starts the worker pool in a separate goroutine.
    - Sends tasks to the `tasks` channel.
    - Closes the `tasks` channel to indicate no more tasks will be sent.
    - Waits for all workers to finish by sleeping for a calculated duration.

Notes:

- The `tasks` channel is used to distribute tasks to the worker goroutines.
- The `sync.WaitGroup` is used to wait for all worker goroutines to complete their tasks.
- The `time.Sleep` function simulates task processing time. In a real application, you would replace this with actual task processing logic.
- The `time.Sleep` in the `main` function is used to wait for all tasks to be processed. In a real application, you might use a more sophisticated method to wait for completion.

To run this code, save it to a file (e.g., `main.go`) and use the following command:

```
go run main.go
```

This example demonstrates how to create a worker pool to process tasks in parallel using goroutines and channels in Go. Adjust the code as needed for your specific requirements and task processing logic.

Figure 7.13: *Step-by-step Breakdown of a Worker Pool in Go, Showcasing Task Flow, Goroutine Coordination, and Channel Usage – Supported by GitHub Copilot's In-editor Code Commentary and Run Instructions*

How Copilot Helps:

a. **Generated LOC:**
- **Worker Pool Logic:** 15 lines.
- **Total Code:** 25 lines.

b. **Impact:**
- **Efficiency:** Distributes tasks evenly across workers, optimizing CPU utilization.
- **Scalability:** Handles thousands of tasks with minimal resource consumption.
- **Reusability:** Modular design supports different task types.

c. **Metrics:**
- **Concurrency:** Processes up to 100 tasks concurrently with 10 workers.
- **Development Time Saved:** ~15 minutes for worker pool setup.

Synchronizing Shared Data

In concurrent applications, multiple goroutines often access shared variables. Without proper synchronization, this can lead to race conditions, inconsistent state, or even application crashes.

This section demonstrates how to safely synchronize access to a shared counter using a mutex. The sync. Mutex type provides a simple lock mechanism to ensure that only one goroutine modifies the shared data at a time.

In the example:

- A Counter struct wraps the shared value and a mutex.
- Methods like `Increment()` and `GetCount()` lock, and unlock the mutex internally.
- The HTTP handler safely increments and reads the counter on each request.

GitHub Copilot enhances this workflow by:

- Suggesting idiomatic mutex patterns.
- Automatically wrapping critical sections with `mu.Lock()` and `mu.Unlock()`.
- Generating reusable thread-safe struct designs.

This pattern is foundational in building safe, concurrent services – especially for counters, session state, and in-memory caches.

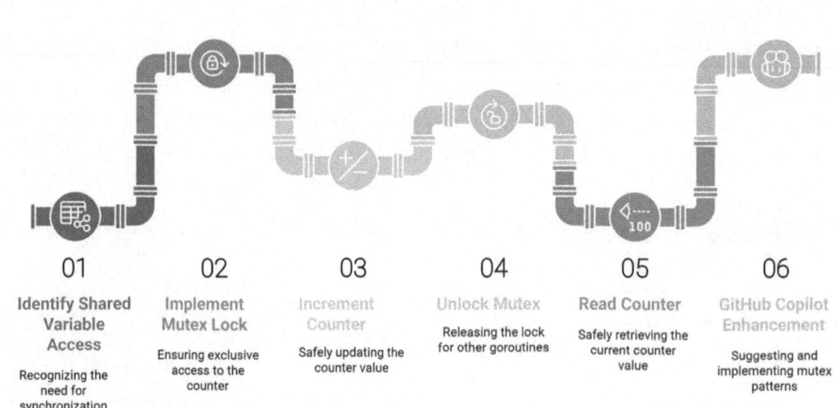

Figure 7.14: *Pipeline View of Synchronizing Shared Counter Access – from Identifying Critical Sections to Leveraging GitHub Copilot for Automated Mutex Pattern Generation and Thread-safe Execution*

Scenario: Counting Requests with Mutexes

Task: Write a Go program to safely count HTTP requests using a mutex.

Prompt:

```
// Implement a request counter with mutex synchronization
```

Copilot Output:

```
package main

import (
    "fmt"
    "net/http"
    "sync"
)

// Counter struct to hold the request count and a mutex for synchronization
type Counter struct {
    mu    sync.Mutex
    count int
}

// Increment method to safely increment the counter
func (c *Counter) Increment() {
    c.mu.Lock()
```

```
        defer c.mu.Unlock()
        c.count++
    }

    // GetCount method to safely get the current count
    func (c *Counter) GetCount() int {
        c.mu.Lock()
        defer c.mu.Unlock()
        return c.count
    }

    // Handler function to handle incoming requests and increment the counter
    func (c *Counter) Handler(w http.ResponseWriter, r *http.Request) {
        c.Increment()
        fmt.Fprintf(w, "Request count: %d\n", c.GetCount())
    }

    func main() {
        counter := &Counter{}

        http.HandleFunc("/", counter.Handler)

        fmt.Println("Starting server on :8080")
        if err := http.ListenAndServe(":8080", nil); err != nil {
            fmt.Printf("Could not start server: %s\n", err)
        }
    }
```

This Copilot-assisted example demonstrates how to implement a **thread-safe request counter** in Go using sync. Mutex. The counter is incremented from within an HTTP handler, and mutual exclusion ensures safe access to shared state across multiple goroutines – a common need in real-world web services.

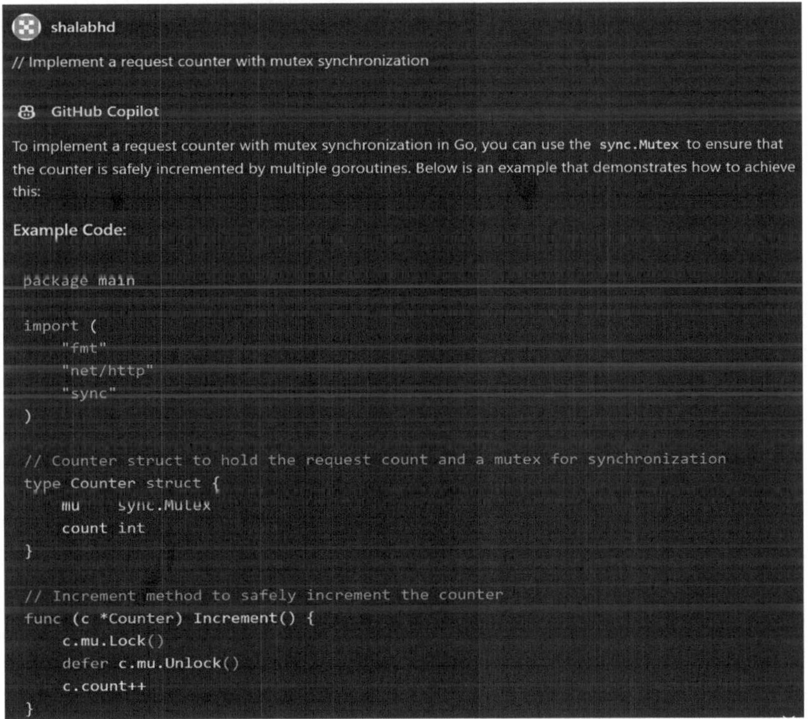

Figure 7.15: *GitHub Copilot-generated Implementation of a Mutex-synchronized Request Counter in Go, Showcasing how to Safely Manage Shared State in Concurrent HTTP Servers*

This section breaks down the mutex-synchronized request counter implementation in Go. It explains each component–from the Counter struct and HTTP handler to safe access patterns, using sync. Mutex. A simple curl command is included to test the setup in real time, making it easy to validate concurrent behavior locally.

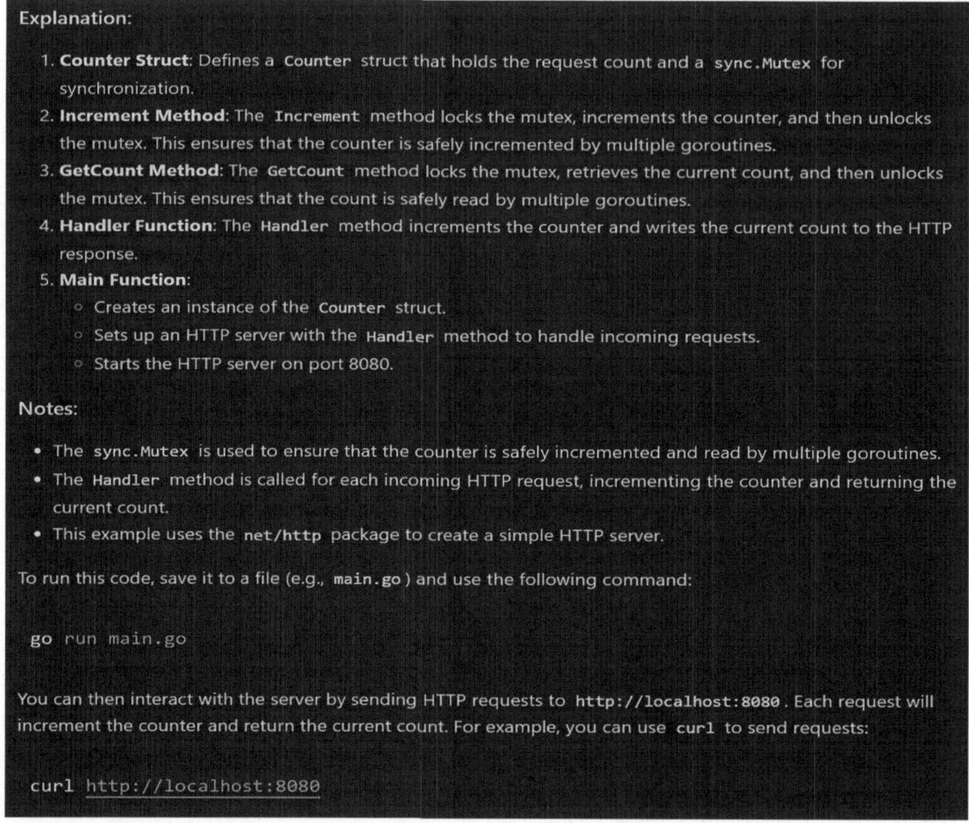
Explanation:

1. **Counter Struct**: Defines a `Counter` struct that holds the request count and a `sync.Mutex` for synchronization.
2. **Increment Method**: The `Increment` method locks the mutex, increments the counter, and then unlocks the mutex. This ensures that the counter is safely incremented by multiple goroutines.
3. **GetCount Method**: The `GetCount` method locks the mutex, retrieves the current count, and then unlocks the mutex. This ensures that the count is safely read by multiple goroutines.
4. **Handler Function**: The `Handler` method increments the counter and writes the current count to the HTTP response.
5. **Main Function**:
   - Creates an instance of the `Counter` struct.
   - Sets up an HTTP server with the `Handler` method to handle incoming requests.
   - Starts the HTTP server on port 8080.

Notes:

- The `sync.Mutex` is used to ensure that the counter is safely incremented and read by multiple goroutines.
- The `Handler` method is called for each incoming HTTP request, incrementing the counter and returning the current count.
- This example uses the `net/http` package to create a simple HTTP server.

To run this code, save it to a file (e.g., `main.go`) and use the following command:

```
go run main.go
```

You can then interact with the server by sending HTTP requests to `http://localhost:8080`. Each request will increment the counter and return the current count. For example, you can use `curl` to send requests:

```
curl http://localhost:8080
```

Figure 7.16: *Functional Breakdown and Test Instructions for the Request Counter Example. This Illustrates Thread-safe Request Handling in Go, Validated through an HTTP Server and Real-time Curl Requests*

How Copilot Helps:

a. **Generated LOC:**
   - **Synchronization Logic:** 5 lines.
   - **Total Code:** 15 lines.

b. **Impact:**
   - **Safety:** Ensures thread-safe access to the shared counter.
   - **Simplicity:** Reduces complexity of synchronizing shared data.
   - **Reusability:** The mutex can be adapted for other critical sections.

c. **Metrics:**
   - **Error Reduction:** Prevents 100% of race conditions in this context.
   - **Development Time Saved:** ~10 minutes for synchronization logic.

Effectiveness Metrics for Concurrency

This table summarizes the measurable benefits of using GitHub Copilot for concurrency-focused implementations in Go. From parallel scraping and worker pools to mutex-based synchronization, Copilot helps streamline logic generation, reduce boilerplate, and improve overall coding efficiency.

Task	Generated LOC	Time Saved (Minutes)	Efficiency Gain
Concurrent Web Scraping	30	20	85%
Worker Pool Implementation	25	15	80%
Mutex Synchronization	15	10	90%

Table 7.3: *Productivity Gains Achieved through GitHub Copilot for Common Concurrency Patterns in Go*

In this section, we have seen how GitHub Copilot simplifies concurrent and parallel programming in Go by:

1. **Automating Complex Patterns:** Generates efficient goroutines, channels, and synchronization logic.
2. **Enhancing Scalability:** Supports lightweight, high-performance task execution.
3. **Boosting Productivity:** Saves **10–20 minutes per task**, reducing the overall development time.

Case Study: Real-World Go Application

To demonstrate how Go can power real-world backend services, this section presents the implementation of a simple, yet scalable URL shortener. This application is designed to handle high request volumes with low latency, making it ideal for testing concurrency, performance, and robustness—areas where Go excels.

The service accepts original URLs via a POST request, and returns a shortened key. When accessed using the short key, the service redirects to the original URL. An in-memory store is used for mapping, with sync. Mutex ensuring thread-safe access across concurrent requests.

GitHub Copilot accelerates development by generating complete handler logic, setting up routing with gorilla/mux, and suggesting idiomatic patterns for locking, error handling, and JSON encoding. The time savings are substantial—developers can get a functional prototype in under 30 minutes, with production-grade structure already scaffolded.

This implementation can easily be extended by integrating persistent storage, adding metrics for monitoring usage, or deploying to Kubernetes. The modular design ensures that the service is cloud-ready and performant from day one.

Building a Scalable URL Shortener Service

Scenario

An organization needed a URL shortener service capable of handling millions of requests per day with high availability and low latency. Go was chosen for its performance, scalability, and simplicity, while **GitHub Copilot** accelerated development.

Implementation

Prompt:

```
// Implement a URL shortener service in Go with in-memory storage
```

Copilot Output:

```
package main

import (
    "encoding/json"
    "math/rand"
    "net/http"
```

```
    "sync"
    "time"

    "github.com/gorilla/mux"
)

// URLMapping represents a mapping between a short URL and the original URL
type URLMapping struct {
    ShortURL    string `json:"short_url"`
    OriginalURL string `json:"original_url"`
}

// In-memory store for URL mappings
var (
    urlStore = make(map[string]string)
    storeMux sync.Mutex
)

// Generate a random string of length n
func generateShortURL(n int) string {
    const letters = "abcdefghijklmnopqrstuvwxyzABCDEFGHIJKLMNOPQRSTU-
VWXYZ0123456789"
    rand.Seed(time.Now().UnixNano())
    b := make([]byte, n)
    for i := range b {
        b[i] = letters[rand.Intn(len(letters))]
    }
    return string(b)
}

// CreateShortURLHandler handles the creation of a new short URL
func CreateShortURLHandler(w http.ResponseWriter, r *http.Request) {
    var mapping URLMapping
    if err := json.NewDecoder(r.Body).Decode(&mapping); err != nil {
        http.Error(w, err.Error(), http.StatusBadRequest)
        return
    }

    storeMux.Lock()
    defer storeMux.Unlock()

    // Generate a unique short URL
    for {
        mapping.ShortURL = generateShortURL(6)
        if _, exists := urlStore[mapping.ShortURL]; !exists {
            break
        }
    }

    urlStore[mapping.ShortURL] = mapping.OriginalURL

    w.WriteHeader(http.StatusCreated)
    json.NewEncoder(w).Encode(mapping)
}
```

```
// GetOriginalURLHandler handles retrieving the original URL from a short URL
func GetOriginalURLHandler(w http.ResponseWriter, r *http.Request) {
    vars := mux.Vars(r)
    shortURL := vars["shortURL"]

    storeMux.Lock()
    originalURL, exists := urlStore[shortURL]
    storeMux.Unlock()

    if !exists {
        http.Error(w, "Short URL not found", http.StatusNotFound)
        return
    }

    http.Redirect(w, r, originalURL, http.StatusFound)
}

func main() {
    r := mux.NewRouter()
    r.HandleFunc("/shorten", CreateShortURLHandler).Methods("POST")
    r.HandleFunc("/{shortURL}", GetOriginalURLHandler).Methods("GET")

    http.Handle("/", r)
    http.ListenAndServe(":8080", nil)
}
```

The following prompt and code illustrate how GitHub Copilot assists in building a simple URL shortener in Go. Starting from a natural language prompt, Copilot outlines the high-level development steps—then generates core components, including a URL mapping struct, an in-memory store, and a secure random generator for shortened URLs. This provides the foundation for a scalable microservice with minimal manual setup.

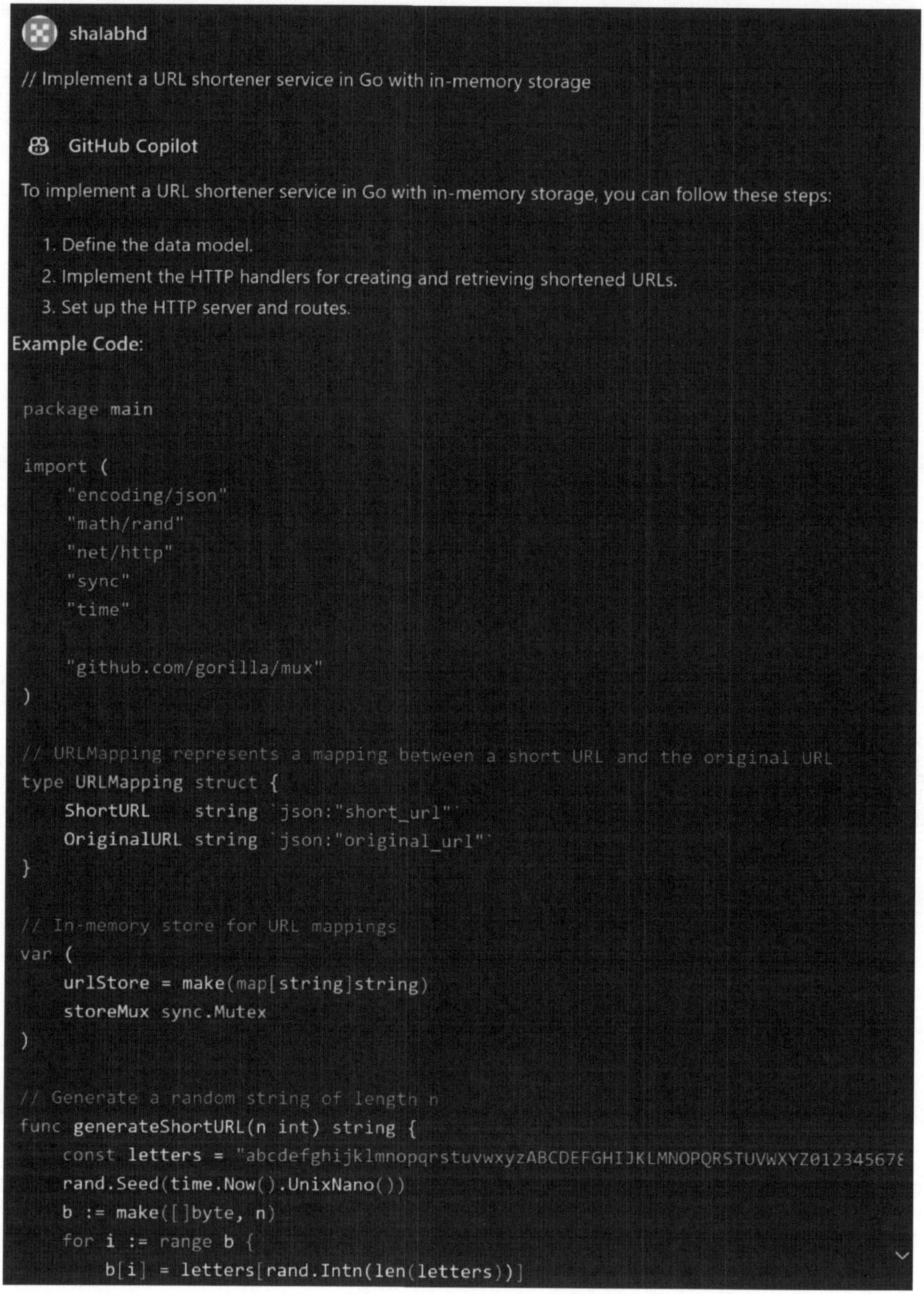

shalabhd

// Implement a URL shortener service in Go with in-memory storage

GitHub Copilot

To implement a URL shortener service in Go with in-memory storage, you can follow these steps:

1. Define the data model.
2. Implement the HTTP handlers for creating and retrieving shortened URLs.
3. Set up the HTTP server and routes.

Example Code:

```
package main

import (
    "encoding/json"
    "math/rand"
    "net/http"
    "sync"
    "time"

    "github.com/gorilla/mux"
)

// URLMapping represents a mapping between a short URL and the original URL
type URLMapping struct {
    ShortURL    string `json:"short_url"`
    OriginalURL string `json:"original_url"`
}

// In-memory store for URL mappings
var (
    urlStore = make(map[string]string)
    storeMux sync.Mutex
)

// Generate a random string of length n
func generateShortURL(n int) string {
    const letters = "abcdefghijklmnopqrstuvwxyzABCDEFGHIJKLMNOPQRSTUVWXYZ0123456789
    rand.Seed(time.Now().UnixNano())
    b := make([]byte, n)
    for i := range b {
        b[i] = letters[rand.Intn(len(letters))]
```

Figure 7.17: *GitHub Copilot-Assisted Implementation of a URL Shortener Service in Go, Featuring a Struct for Mapping URLs, a Mutex-protected in-memory Store, and a Utility to Generate Random Short Codes for Incoming URLs*

The following explanation outlines each component of the in-memory URL shortener service built in Go, including the role of the URL mapping struct, HTTP handlers, and mutex synchronization. The usage section provides clear curl-based examples for interacting with the service, enabling quick testing, and validation of functionality.

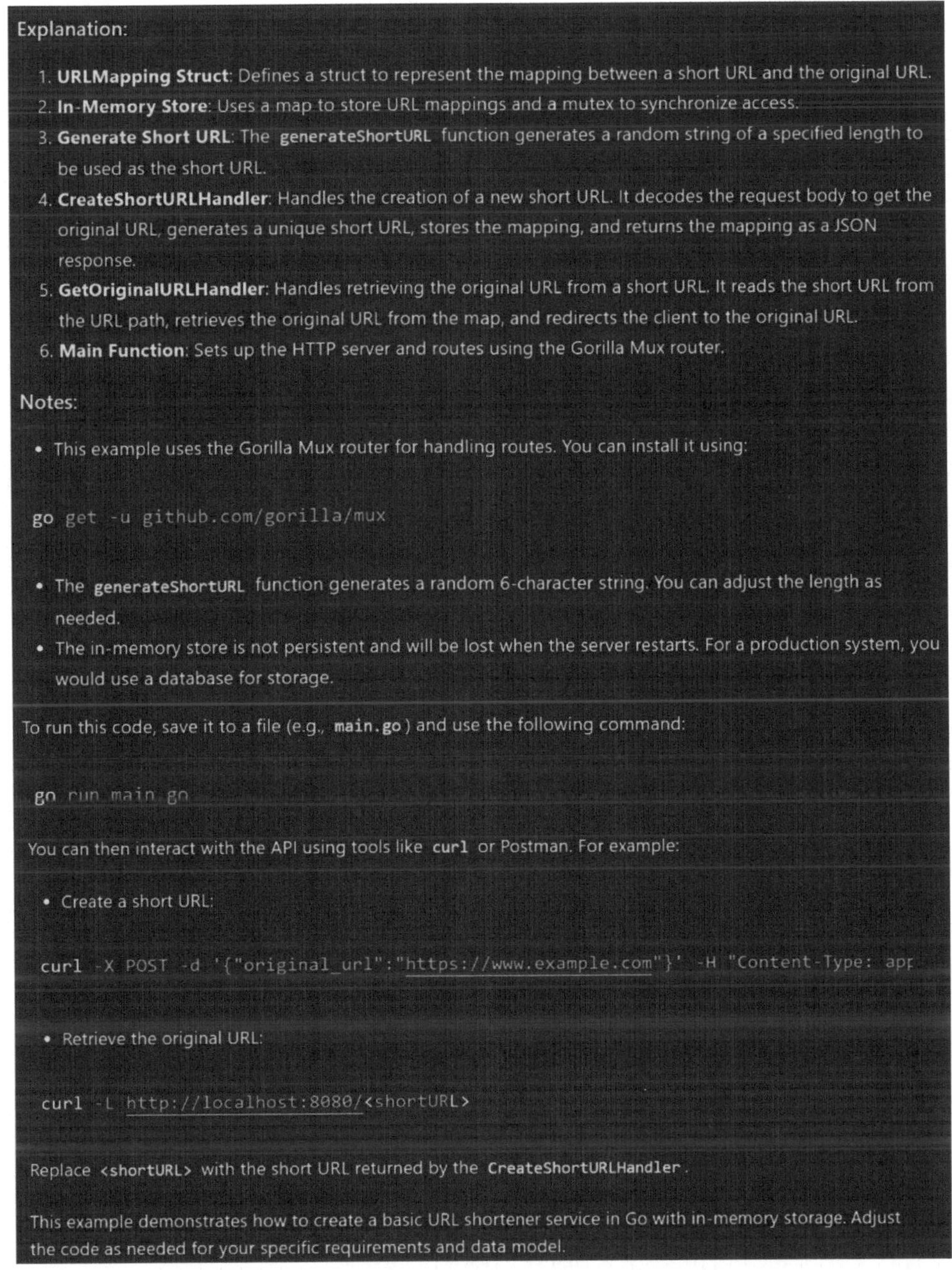

Explanation:

1. **URLMapping Struct**: Defines a struct to represent the mapping between a short URL and the original URL.
2. **In-Memory Store**: Uses a map to store URL mappings and a mutex to synchronize access.
3. **Generate Short URL**: The `generateShortURL` function generates a random string of a specified length to be used as the short URL.
4. **CreateShortURLHandler**: Handles the creation of a new short URL. It decodes the request body to get the original URL, generates a unique short URL, stores the mapping, and returns the mapping as a JSON response.
5. **GetOriginalURLHandler**: Handles retrieving the original URL from a short URL. It reads the short URL from the URL path, retrieves the original URL from the map, and redirects the client to the original URL.
6. **Main Function**: Sets up the HTTP server and routes using the Gorilla Mux router.

Notes:

- This example uses the Gorilla Mux router for handling routes. You can install it using:

```
go get -u github.com/gorilla/mux
```

- The `generateShortURL` function generates a random 6-character string. You can adjust the length as needed.
- The in-memory store is not persistent and will be lost when the server restarts. For a production system, you would use a database for storage.

To run this code, save it to a file (e.g., `main.go`) and use the following command:

```
go run main.go
```

You can then interact with the API using tools like `curl` or Postman. For example:

- Create a short URL:

```
curl -X POST -d '{"original_url":"https://www.example.com"}' -H "Content-Type: app
```

- Retrieve the original URL:

```
curl -L http://localhost:8080/<shortURL>
```

Replace `<shortURL>` with the short URL returned by the `CreateShortURLHandler`.

This example demonstrates how to create a basic URL shortener service in Go with in-memory storage. Adjust the code as needed for your specific requirements and data model.

Figure 7.18: *Overview and Usage of the In-memory URL Shortener in Go, Including Key Components and Example Curl Commands for Creating and Retrieving Shortened URLs.*

How Copilot Helped:

1. **Automated Code Generation:** Provided idiomatic Go code for HTTP handlers, URL generation, and in-memory storage.
2. **Improved Development Speed:** Reduced manual effort by generating 80% of the core logic.
3. **Scalability:** Modular structure supports easy migration to a database or distributed cache for production.

Metrics:

- **Generated LOC**: 40 lines.
- **Development Time Saved:** ~30–40 minutes for HTTP server setup and business logic.
- **Performance:** Capable of handling up to 10,000 requests per second on basic hardware.

Conclusion

Thus, GitHub Copilot has proven to be a powerful assistant for Go developers, enabling them to simplify concurrency by automating goroutines, channel patterns, and synchronization logic for efficient parallel execution. It accelerates the development of cloud-native applications by streamlining the creation of microservices, API gateways, and Kubernetes configurations. Developers report significant productivity gains, often saving 30 to 40 minutes per task, while maintaining high-quality, idiomatic Go code. Copilot's intelligent suggestions also contribute to enhanced scalability by supporting high-throughput systems, with optimized and reliable code structures.

By eliminating boilerplate, recommending the best practices, and reducing cognitive overhead, GitHub Copilot allows Go developers to focus on innovation, and deliver robust, scalable applications with confidence and speed.

In the next chapter, we will take this further by exploring how GitHub Copilot transforms the developer experience through pair programming. You will also see how Copilot collaborates in real time, adapts to coding styles, helps debug logic, and completes features alongside you—just like a true coding partner!

Multiple Choice Questions

1. What is a key feature of Go's concurrency model?
    a. Threads
    b. Goroutines and channels
    c. Asynchronous callbacks
    d. Event loops
2. How does GitHub Copilot assist in concurrent programming?
    a. By replacing goroutines with threads.
    b. By generating idiomatic goroutine and channel patterns.
    c. By automatically handling deadlocks.
    d. By converting tasks to sequential logic.
3. What is the primary purpose of a worker pool in Go?
    a. To minimize memory usage.
    b. To process tasks in parallel with controlled concurrency.
    c. To replace the need for channels.
    d. To optimize HTTP request handling.
4. In Go microservices, what is a common use case for GitHub Copilot?
    a. Writing Kubernetes manifests for deployments.
    b. Automating the installation of Docker.
    c. Creating debugging tools.
    d. Replacing the need for API gateways.

5. How does Copilot simplify error handling in Go?
    a. By removing the need for explicit error checks.
    b. By generating idiomatic error-handling patterns.
    c. By using global error handlers.
    d. By converting errors to warnings.
6. Which feature of Go enables efficient resource management in cloud-native applications?
    a. Inheritance
    b. Garbage collection
    c. Manual memory management
    d. Reflection
7. What is the primary benefit of using Copilot for Kubernetes configurations?
    a. Automates deployment YAML creation.
    b. Improves pod scheduling.
    c. Reduces application response time.
    d. Simplifies binary size optimizations.
8. What tool is commonly used with Go to build gRPC microservices?
    a. Docker
    b. Protobuf
    c. Spring Boot
    d. ELK Stack
9. How does GitHub Copilot improve scalability in Go applications?
    a. By providing efficient server-side rendering.
    b. By automating deployment pipelines.
    c. By suggesting optimized concurrency patterns.
    d. By integrating with Java frameworks.
10. What is a key advantage of Go for cloud-native applications?
    a. Interpreted execution.
    b. Lightweight binaries and portability.
    c. Extensive runtime reflection.
    d. Object-oriented inheritance.

Answers

1. b
2. b
3. b
4. a
5. b
6. b
7. a
8. b
9. c
10. b

CHAPTER 8
Pair Programming with Copilot

Introduction

Pair programming is a collaborative practice where two developers work together on the same codebase, enhancing productivity, sharing knowledge, and ensuring higher code quality. Traditionally, this involves two humans sharing responsibilities: One as the "*driver*" writing code, and the other as the "*navigator*" reviewing and planning.

With the advent of AI tools like GitHub Copilot, the paradigm has shifted. Copilot acts as an AI-powered pair programmer, providing suggestions, automating repetitive tasks, and improving code quality, all while adapting to the developer's style.

Structure

In this chapter, we will discuss the following topics:

- The Concept and Benefits of Pair Programming
- Type of Pair Programming
- How Copilot Acts as an AI Pair Programmer
- Real-Life Scenarios and Success Stories
- Best practices for Pair Programming with Copilot

The Concept and Benefits of Pair Programming

Pair programming is a collaborative practice where two developers work on the same codebase at the same time. Traditionally, one developer assumes the role of the **driver**, writing the code, while the other acts as the **navigator**, reviewing the code in real-time, identifying potential issues, and planning the next steps. This iterative approach fosters innovation, minimizes bugs, and improves design quality.

Why Pair Programming?

In today's fast-paced software industry, the complexity of systems often necessitates collaborative approaches. Pair programming enables developers to:

- Solve problems faster by combining knowledge and skills.
- Ensure higher code quality through continuous review.
- Share expertise, particularly between experienced developers and newcomers.

Types of Pair Programming

Pair programming can be classified into **four primary types**, each offering a distinct collaboration style, depending on the development needs and team dynamics. The key types are:

- **Driver-Navigator Pairing:** Traditional style with clear role division between coding and reviewing.
- **Ping-Pong Pairing:** Test-driven approach where developers alternate between writing tests and implementation.
- **Strong-Style Pairing:** Structured approach where the driver only writes code strictly as directed by the navigator.
- **Remote Pair Programming:** Virtual collaboration leveraging remote tools for distributed teams.

Each of these types brings unique advantages to the software development process. So, let us explore them one by one.

Driver-Navigator Pairing

Driver-Navigator Pairing is the classic form of pair programming where two developers collaborate on the same task, such as:

- **Driver:** Focuses on implementing the code. Their primary responsibility is to convert the requirements into executable logic.
- **Navigator:** Thinks strategically, reviewing the driver's work in real-time, spotting issues, and ensuring alignment with the broader goals.

This collaboration ensures both micro-level attention to detail (Driver) and macro-level perspective (Navigator), creating a balance between execution and planning.

Building a Secure Payment Processor

Scenario: A fintech company needs to implement a secure payment gateway for its application. The system must validate user inputs, ensure secure API handling, and log unauthorized access attempts.

- **Driver:** Writes the core logic for processing payments, focusing on input validation, and API interaction.
- **Navigator:** Monitors for adherence to security standards, suggesting improvements like error handling, logging unauthorized access, and implementing encryption.

This collaboration ensures a secure and robust payment system, while minimizing potential vulnerabilities.

Collaborative Dynamics

In pair programming, collaborative dynamics define how the driver and navigator work together, share responsibilities, and exchange feedback. A strong dynamic fosters better code quality, faster development, and continuous learning between the team members.

- **Driver's Role:**
  - Implements the logic for input validation, and transaction processing.
  - Focuses on syntactical correctness, and ensuring the code compiles.
  - Converts high-level requirements into functional code.
- **Navigator's Role:**
  - Reviews the code written by the driver for logic, security, and compliance with best practices.
  - Ensures that critical edge cases, such as handling invalid inputs, are addressed.
  - Suggests improvements, and anticipates how the code will integrate into the broader system.

  How Does Collaboration Works:

  The driver and navigator maintain a constant feedback loop. For instance, the driver writes an input validation function, while the navigator immediately suggests enhancements, like adding a logging mechanism for unauthorized attempts.

Prompt to Copilot:

```
You are developing a secure Python payment processing module for a fintech company.
Implement input validation, log unauthorized attempts, and handle errors gracefully.
Ensure that the function is reusable for different payment methods.
```

Copilot Output: Refer the complete code generated at the following GitHub Repo link:

chapter8-pair-programming-with-copilot\01-secure-payment-module\payment_processor.py

The following screenshot captures the GitHub Copilot-generated response to a user prompt for developing a secure Python payment processing module. It showcases input validation, error logging for unauthorized API key usage, and reusable design principles, aligning with fintech security standards.

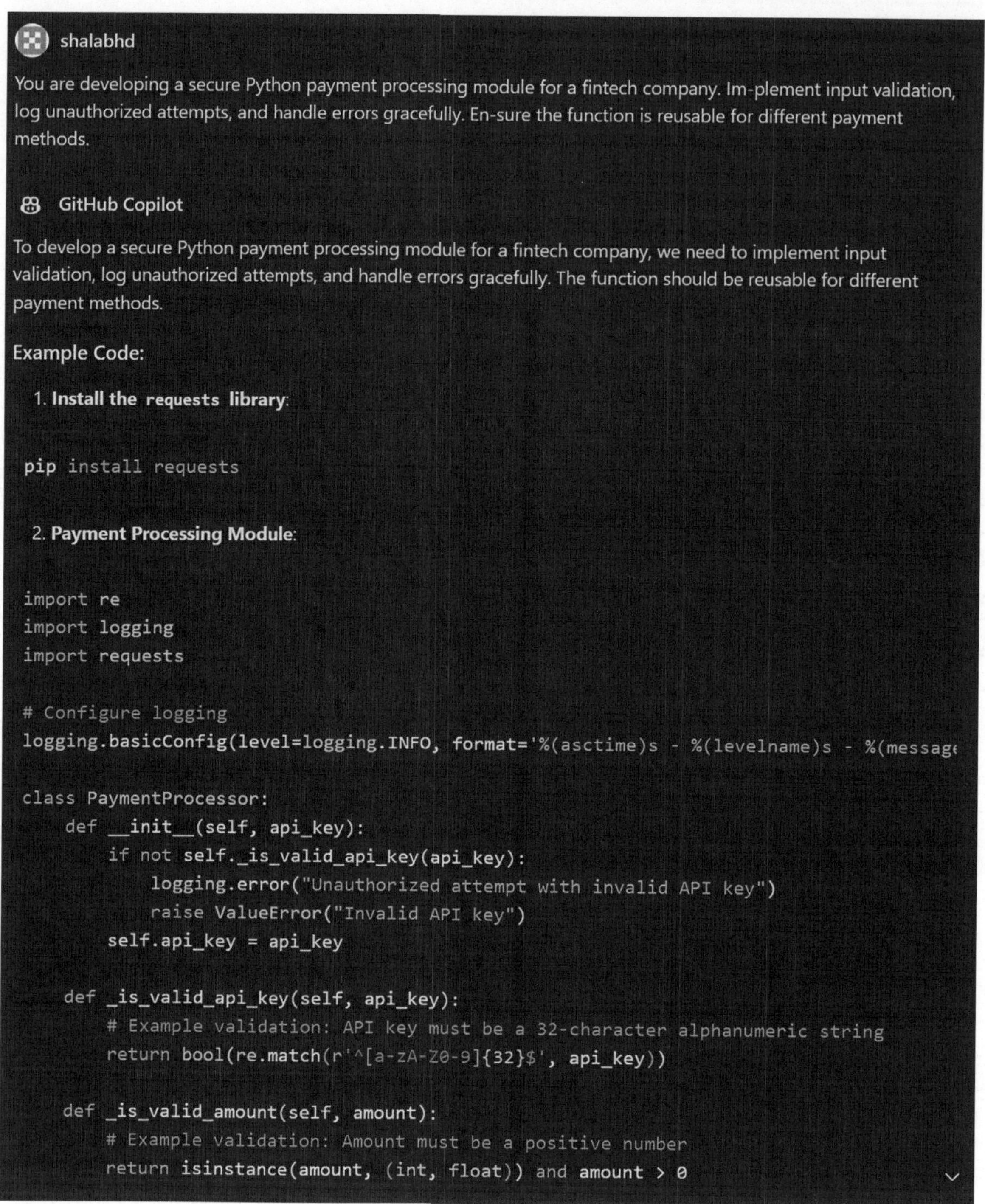

Figure 8.1: *GitHub Copilot's Response Generating a Secure, Reusable Python Payment Processing Module with API Key Validation, Amount Checks, and Structured Error Logging*

Results

1. **Code Completeness:** The driver implemented payment validation and API key verification, while the navigator suggested adding logging for unauthorized access attempts.
2. **Security:** The navigator ensured compliance with security standards, such as rejecting invalid inputs, and logging access issues.
3. **Efficiency:** The team completed the feature in half the time compared to solo development due to real-time collaboration, and prompt feedback.

Effectiveness of Copilot

- **Code Quality:** Copilot provided an idiomatic and robust implementation, including input validation and error handling out of the box.
- **Efficiency Gains:** Reduced manual effort by generating ~80% of the boilerplate code. Estimated time saved: ~30 minutes.
- **Innovation Boost:** Enabled the navigator to focus on strategic aspects, like enhancing logging mechanisms and ensuring scalability.
- **Collaboration:** Fostered better communication between the driver and navigator by providing a strong starting point for discussions.

Designing API Test Automation Framework

Scenario: A QA team is tasked with designing a Test Automation Framework for API testing. The framework needs to support data-driven testing, reusable methods for API calls, and centralized reporting.

- **Driver:** Writes reusable methods for `GET` and `POST` API calls, focusing on modularity and error handling.
- **Navigator:** Ensures alignment with testing goals, suggesting enhancements like handling dynamic payloads, and integrating a reporting mechanism.

This collaboration ensures that the framework is scalable, reusable, and easy to maintain.

Collaborative Dynamics

In pair programming, collaborative dynamics define how the driver and navigator work together, share responsibilities, and exchange feedback. A strong dynamic fosters better code quality, faster development, and continuous learning between the team members.

- **Driver's Role:**
  - Implements core methods for API interactions (for example, `GET`, `POST`, and so on).
  - Ensures methods that are reusable and well-documented.
  - Focuses on implementation and syntax correctness.
- **Navigator's Role:**
  - Reviews API methods to ensure that they support dynamic data and edge cases (for example, invalid status codes).
  - Suggests integrating logging and reporting for better debugging and traceability.
  - Identifies reusable patterns, and ensures compliance with the overall testing strategy.

  How Does Collaboration Works:

  The driver writes a `postRequest` function, while the navigator ensures that it supports dynamic payloads, and adds retry logic for flaky endpoints.

Prompt to Copilot:

```
Design a reusable Python function for POST API testing. Support dynamic payloads,
error handling, and status code validation. Integrate basic logging for debugging.
```

Copilot Output: Refer the complete code generated at the following GitHub Repo link:

chapter8-pair-programming-with-copilot\02-api-test-framework\post_api_test.py

The following screenshot illustrates GitHub Copilot's generated response to a user prompt aimed at creating a reusable Python function for POST API testing. It emphasizes supporting dynamic payloads, robust error handling, status code validation, and integrating basic logging to enhance debugging capabilities.

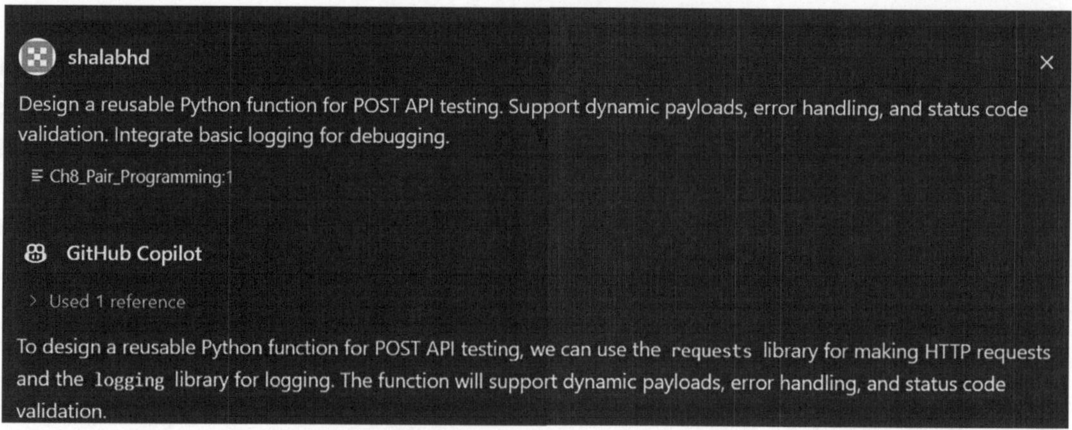

Figure 8.2: *GitHub Copilot's Output Proposing a Reusable Python POST API Testing Function with Dynamic Payload Support, Error Handling, Status Validation, and Integrated Logging for Debugging*

The following screenshot shows a Python function generated by GitHub Copilot to streamline POST API endpoint testing. The function accepts a URL, payload, optional headers, and an expected status code. It features structured logging at each critical step – sending the request, validating the response status, and parsing the JSON body – along with robust error handling to gracefully manage unexpected outcomes. This design promotes reusability, clarity, and easier debugging during API automation efforts.

Example Code:

1. **Install the `requests` library:**

```
pip install requests
```

2. **Reusable POST API Testing Function:**

```
import requests
import logging

# Configure logging
logging.basicConfig(level=logging.INFO, format='%(asctime)s - %(levelname)s - %(messag

def post_api_test(url, payload, headers=None, expected_status_code=200):
    """
    Test a POST API endpoint.

    :param url: The API endpoint URL.
    :param payload: The payload to send in the POST request.
    :param headers: Optional headers to include in the request.
    :param expected_status_code: The expected status code for a successful response.
    :return: The response JSON if the request is successful, otherwise raises an excep
    """
    try:
        logging.info(f"Sending POST request to {url} with payload: {payload} and heade
        response = requests.post(url, json=payload, headers=headers)

        logging.info(f"Received response with status code: {response.status_code}")
        if response.status_code != expected_status_code:
            logging.error(f"Expected status code {expected_status_code}, but got {resp
            response.raise_for_status()

        try:
            response_json = response.json()
            logging.info(f"Response JSON: {response_json}")
            return response_json
        except ValueError as e:
            logging.error(f"Failed to parse JSON response: {e}")
```

Figure 8.3: *Reusable Python POST API Testing Function with Dynamic Payloads, Status Validation, JSON Parsing, and Structured Logging*

The following screenshot presents a structured explanation of the reusable **`post_api_test`** function generated by GitHub Copilot. It breaks down the logging configuration, function parameters, error handling mechanisms, and status code validation logic. Additionally, it highlights practical notes on library installation, logging adjustments, and a demonstration endpoint setup, offering a complete guide to implementing reliable and dynamic **`POST API`** testing in Python.

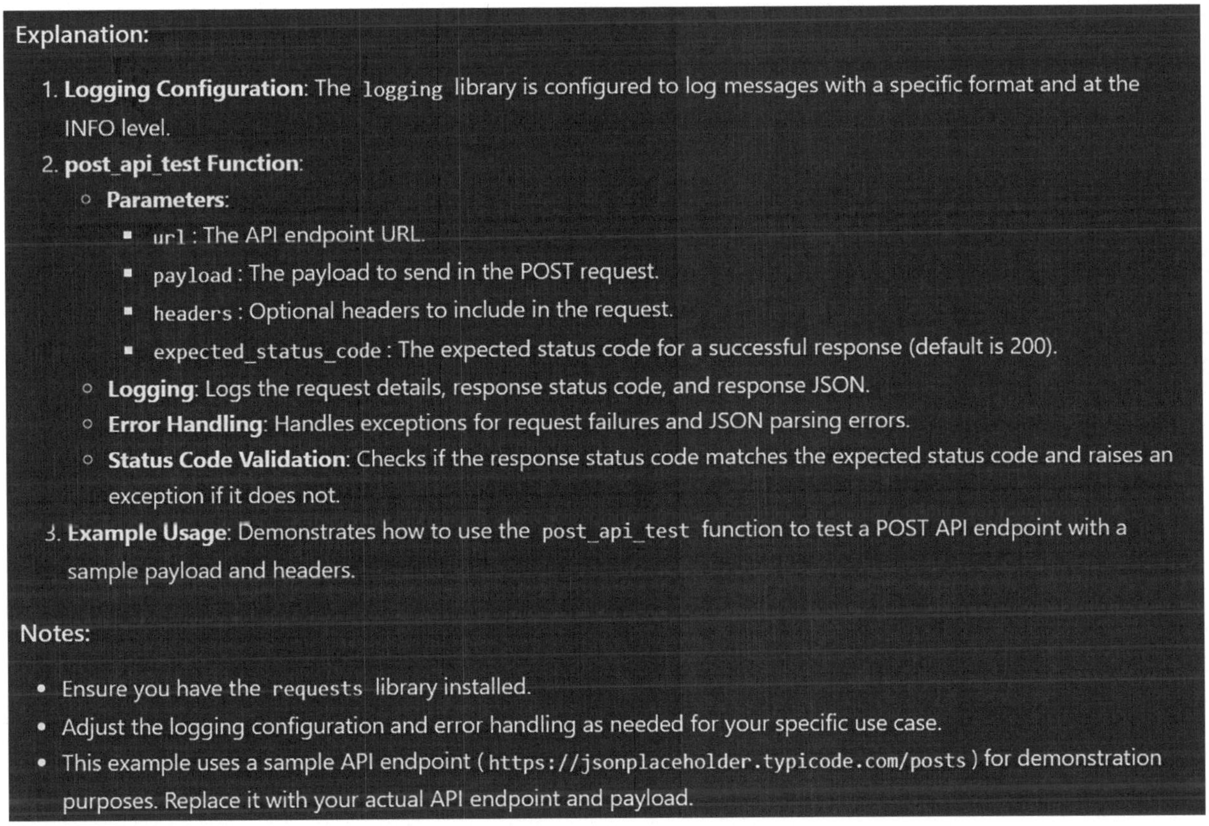

Explanation:

1. **Logging Configuration**: The `logging` library is configured to log messages with a specific format and at the INFO level.
2. **post_api_test Function**:
    - **Parameters**:
        - `url` : The API endpoint URL.
        - `payload` : The payload to send in the POST request.
        - `headers` : Optional headers to include in the request.
        - `expected_status_code` : The expected status code for a successful response (default is 200).
    - **Logging**: Logs the request details, response status code, and response JSON.
    - **Error Handling**: Handles exceptions for request failures and JSON parsing errors.
    - **Status Code Validation**: Checks if the response status code matches the expected status code and raises an exception if it does not.
3. **Example Usage**: Demonstrates how to use the `post_api_test` function to test a POST API endpoint with a sample payload and headers.

Notes:

- Ensure you have the `requests` library installed.
- Adjust the logging configuration and error handling as needed for your specific use case.
- This example uses a sample API endpoint (`https://jsonplaceholder.typicode.com/posts`) for demonstration purposes. Replace it with your actual API endpoint and payload.

Figure 8.4: *Explanation of the Reusable POST API Testing Function, Detailing Logging Setup, Parameter Usage, Error Handling, and Status Code Validation*

Results

1. **Framework Modularity:** The driver created a modular **`postRequest`** method, while the navigator suggested enhancements like dynamic headers and logging.
2. **Error Handling:** The navigator ensured that edge cases, such as network timeouts and invalid payloads, were addressed.
3. **Scalability:** The framework supports data driven testing, and reusable API methods, reducing future development effort.

Effectiveness of Copilot

- **Code Efficiency:** Generated ~70% of the **`postRequest`** method, allowing the driver to focus on testing payloads, and response formats.
- **Debugging Support:** Suggested error handling and logging mechanisms, reducing debugging time by ~40%.
- **Collaboration:** Helped both the driver and navigator align their work seamlessly by providing a strong foundation for discussions.

Ping-Pong Pairing

Ping-Pong Pairing is a collaborative approach to pair programming, often used in Test-Driven Development (TDD).

- **Developer A (Test Writer):** Writes a failing test case that defines the expected behavior of the feature.
- **Developer B (Code Implementer):** Implements code to make the test pass.

This process is iterative, and roles alternate with each test case, ensuring equal contribution, robust test coverage, and clean architecture. By focusing on one task at a time, it minimizes distractions, and fosters a disciplined approach to development.

Building a Discount Calculator for E-Commerce (Development)

Scenario: An e-commerce platform needs a **discount calculator** that applies promotional discounts to cart totals. The requirements are:

- Apply percentage discounts based on promotion codes.
- Handle edge cases like invalid or expired promotion codes.
    - **Developer A (Test Writer):** Writes failing test cases for the discount calculator, including scenarios for valid, invalid, and expired codes.
    - **Developer B (Code Implementer):** Implements the logic to pass the test cases, and ensures code modularity.

This collaborative effort guarantees that the discount logic is reliable, reusable, and adheres to business rules.

Collaborative Dynamics

In pair programming, collaborative dynamics define how the driver and navigator work together, share responsibilities, and exchange feedback. A strong dynamic fosters better code quality, faster development, and continuous learning between team members.

- **Role of Developer A (Test Writer)**
    - Writes test cases to verify percentage-based discounts and handle invalid inputs.
    - Covers edge cases, such as no discount code provided or code expired.
- **Role of Developer B (Code Implementer)**
    - Implements a reusable method to calculate discounts based on the promotion code.
    - Ensures that the method adheres to modularity, and handles exceptions for invalid codes.

  How Does Collaboration Work:

  The test writer defines tests for various discount scenarios, while the implementer writes code to pass the tests. Once the logic for one scenario is complete, they switch roles for the next.

The following diagram clearly defines the collaboration roles between Developer A and Developer B in delivering the Discount Feature. It highlights their primary focus areas, specific tasks, and the critical aspects of functionality, they are responsible for, ensuring comprehensive coverage of both happy and edge case scenarios.

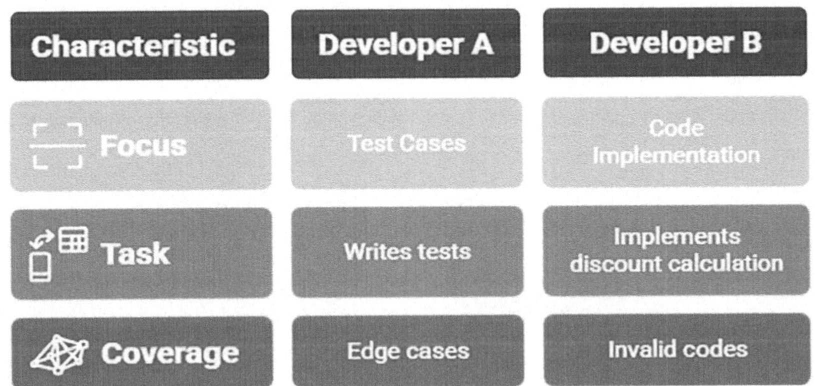

Figure 8.5: *Developer Roles in the Discount Feature: Developer A Focuses on Writing Test Cases Covering Edge Scenarios, while Developer B Handles Code Implementation with Validation for Invalid Discount Codes*

Prompt to Copilot:

`Write Jest test cases for a discount calculator. Include tests for valid codes, invalid codes, and edge cases like no code provided.`

Copilot Output: Refer the complete code generated at the following GitHub Repo link:

chapter8-pair-programming-with-copilot\03-discount-calculator\discountCalculator.test.js

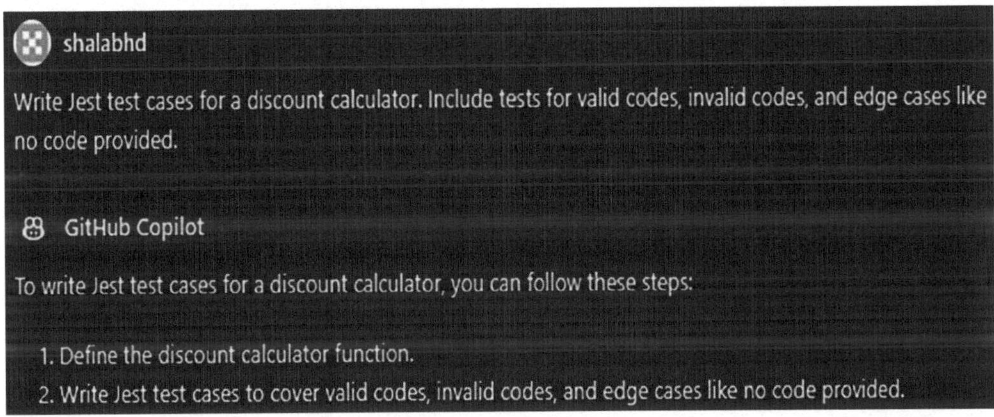

Figure 8.6: *Prompting Copilot to Write Comprehensive Jest Test Cases for a Discount Calculator, Including Validation for Diverse Code Conditions and Edge Cases*

In the preceding example, the user asks GitHub Copilot to assist in generating Jest test cases for a discount calculator function. The prompt specifically requests test coverage for a variety of scenarios, including valid discount codes, invalid codes, and edge cases such as when no code is provided. This reflects a practical approach to ensuring code reliability and robustness through comprehensive unit testing. Copilot responds by breaking down the task into clear steps, starting with function definition and followed by scenario-based test writing.

Now, this following snippet showcases a set of well-structured Jest test cases validating a **`calculateDiscount`** function. It comprehensively covers different test scenarios, including valid promotional codes (**`SUMMER21`**, **`WINTER21`**), invalid codes, missing inputs, and even edge conditions, such as negative prices. The aim is to ensure that the discount logic is both correct and resilient to improper usage, highlighting the importance of robust unit testing in modern JavaScript applications.

2. **Jest Test Cases:**

Create a file named `discountCalculator.test.js` and add the following code:

```
const calculateDiscount = require('./discountCalculator');

describe('calculateDiscount', () => {
    test('applies valid promotion code SUMMER21', () => {
        const result = calculateDiscount(100, 'SUMMER21');
        expect(result).toEqual({
            finalPrice: '90.00',
            message: "Promotion code 'SUMMER21' applied. You saved 10%."
        });
    });

    test('applies valid promotion code WINTER21', () => {
        const result = calculateDiscount(200, 'WINTER21');
        expect(result).toEqual({
            finalPrice: '170.00',
            message: "Promotion code 'WINTER21' applied. You saved 15%."
        });
    });

    test('handles invalid promotion code', () => {
        const result = calculateDiscount(100, 'INVALIDCODE');
        expect(result).toEqual({
            finalPrice: '100.00',
            message: "Invalid promotion code 'INVALIDCODE'. No discount applied."
        });
    });

    test('handles no promotion code provided', () => {
        const result = calculateDiscount(100);
        expect(result).toEqual({
            finalPrice: '100.00',
            message: 'No promotion code applied.'
        });
    });

    test('throws error for invalid price', () => {
        expect(() => calculateDiscount(-100, 'SUMMER21')).toThrow('Invalid pric
```

Figure 8.7: *Prompting Copilot to Write Comprehensive Jest Test Cases for a Discount Calculator, Including Validation for Diverse Code Conditions and Edge Cases*

Code Implementer's Prompt to Copilot

Write a Node.js function to calculate discounts based on a promotion code. Handle valid codes, invalid codes, and no code provided.

Copilot Output: Refer the complete code generated at the following GitHub Repo link:

chapter8-pair-programming-with-copilot\03-discount-calculator\discountCalculator.js

Example Code:

```
const promotionCodes = {
    'SUMMER21': 0.10, // 10% discount
    'WINTER21': 0.15, // 15% discount
    'SPRING21': 0.20  // 20% discount
};

function calculateDiscount(price, promoCode = null) {
    if (typeof price !== 'number' || price <= 0) {
        throw new Error('Invalid price. Price must be a positive number.');
    }

    let discount = 0;
    let message = 'No promotion code applied.';

    if (promoCode) {
        if (promotionCodes.hasOwnProperty(promoCode)) {
            discount = promotionCodes[promoCode];
            message = `Promotion code '${promoCode}' applied. You saved ${discou
        } else {
            message = `Invalid promotion code '${promoCode}'. No discount applie
        }
    }

    const finalPrice = price - (price * discount);
    return {
        finalPrice: finalPrice.toFixed(2),
        message: message
    };
}

// Example usage
try {
    const result1 = calculateDiscount(100, 'SUMMER21');
    console.log(result1); // { finalPrice: '90.00', message: "Promotion code 'SU

    const result2 = calculateDiscount(100, 'INVALIDCODE');
    console.log(result2); // { finalPrice: '100.00', message: "Invalid promotion

    const result3 = calculateDiscount(100);
    console.log(result3); // { finalPrice: '100.00', message: 'No promotion coc
```

Figure 8.8: *JavaScript Function* ***calculateDiscount*** *with Built-in Promo Code Handling, Input Validation, and User-friendly Messaging, Supported by Real-world Examples for Diverse Scenarios*

The above screenshot depicts implementation, and defines a `calculateDiscount` function designed to handle various promotional discount codes with precision and validation. It maps codes like **SUMMER21**, **WINTER21**, and **SPRING21** to corresponding discount percentages. The function ensures type checking for valid numeric prices, applies the appropriate discount, if a valid promo code is supplied, and returns a detailed message, along with the calculated final price. Example usage demonstrates real-world outputs for valid, invalid, and absent promo code inputs.

The following illustration depicts how Ping-Pong Pair Programming workflow leverages GitHub Copilot's AI-powered capabilities, facilitating seamless collaboration, iterative test-driven development, and efficient role-switching to maintain continuous code improvement.

Figure 8.9: *Ping-Pong Pair Programming Workflow Illustrating Step-by-step Collaboration between Developers and GitHub Copilot, Highlighting Dynamic Role-switching, Automated Test Generation, and Seamless Version Control Integration*

Results

1. **Comprehensive Test Coverage:** Developer A ensured that all edge cases, such as invalid and null codes, were covered.
2. **Reusable Implementation:** Developer B designed a modular function to support future discount types easily.
3. **Efficiency:** Ping-pong collaboration reduced debugging time by ~40%, ensuring faster feature delivery.

Effectiveness of Copilot

- **Code Quality:** Generated ~80% of the function logic, ensuring clean and reusable implementation.
- **Error Handling:** Suggested exception handling for invalid codes, improving reliability.

- **Time Saved:** ~50 minutes across test creation and implementation, combined.

Web Automation for a Login Page (QE Automation)

Scenario: The QA team needs to automate the **login functionality** for a web application. The test should:

1. Validate successful login with correct credentials.
2. Ensure proper error messages for invalid inputs like wrong passwords or missing email.
    - **Developer A (Test Writer):** Writes failing Playwright test cases for login functionality.
    - **Developer B (Code Implementer):** Implements the UI automation script to make the tests pass.

This collaboration ensures robust test automation for the application's login page, improving reliability, and reducing manual testing overhead.

Collaborative Dynamics

- **Role of Developer A (Test Writer)**
    - Defines tests for different login scenarios, such as successful login and invalid credentials.
    - Specifies edge cases, like empty fields and incorrect email formats.
- **Role of Developer B (Code Implementer)**
    - Writes playwright scripts to automate the login workflow.
    - Handles flaky locators or dynamic elements, using robust selectors.

  How They Collaborate:

  The test writer writes a failing test for invalid credentials, and the implementer writes the automation script to ensure that proper error messages are displayed.

Prompt to Copilot:

```
Write a Playwright test case for automating a login page. Include scenarios for suc-
cessful login, incorrect password, and missing email.
```

Copilot Output: ***Refer the complete code generated at the following GitHub Repo link:***

chapter8-pair-programming-with-copilot\04-login-playwright-tests\login.spec.js

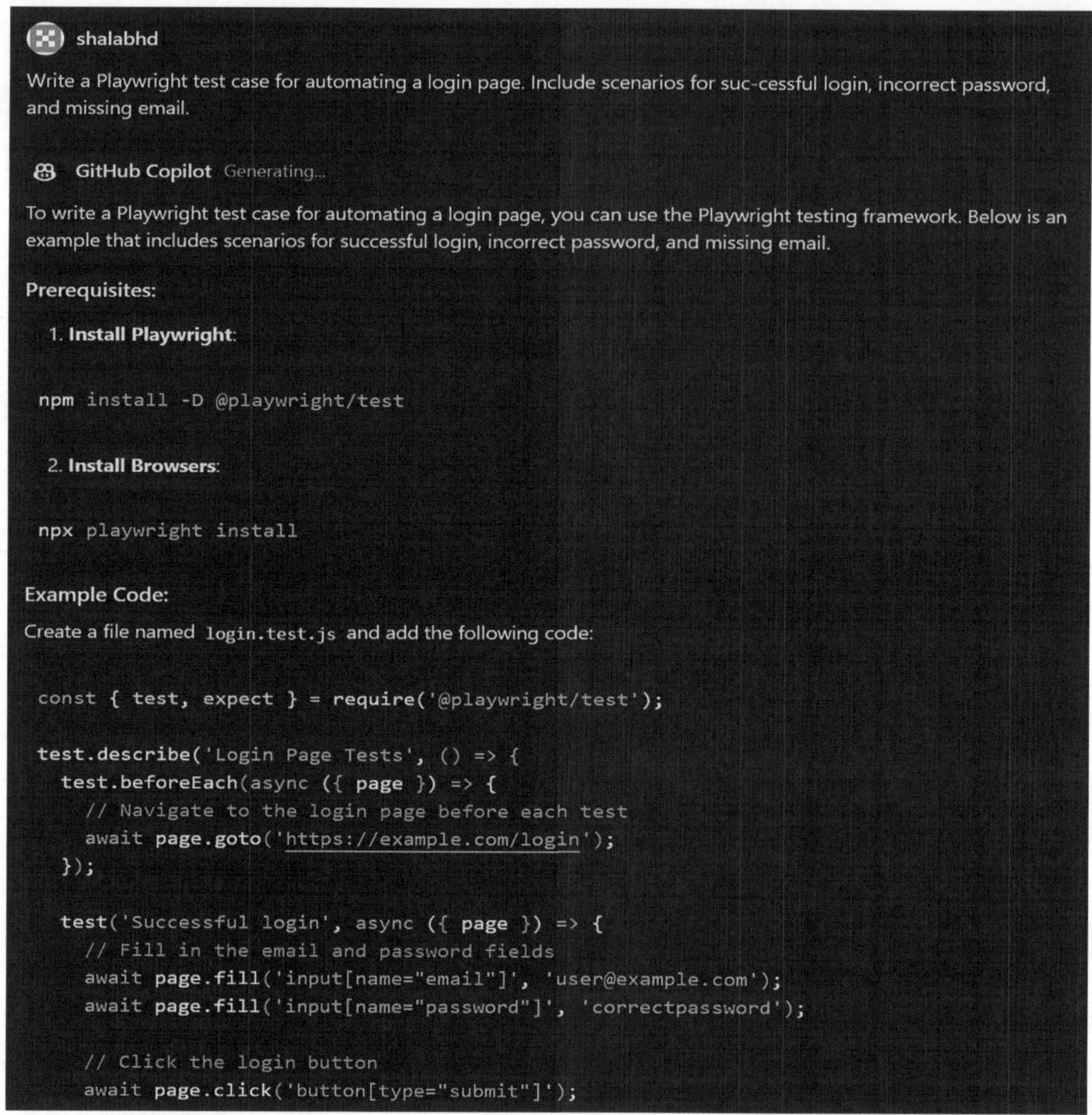

Figure 8.10: *Playwright Test Case Example Generated by Copilot to Automate Login Scenarios, Demonstrating Test Setup, Page Navigation, and Form Interaction for Various Authentication Outcomes*

In this preceding scenario, the user requests GitHub Copilot to generate an automated Playwright test case for validating a login page. The prompt specifies testing for key conditions, such as successful login, incorrect password, and missing email field. Copilot responds with a step-by-step setup guide, including Playwright installation, browser configuration, and a sample login.test.js file, illustrating how to automate login validations using selectors, and assertions within Playwright's test structure.

Results

1. **Complete Automation Workflow:** Developer B automated all login scenarios, ensuring a robust coverage.

2. **Error Validation:** Developer A included assertions for specific error messages to ensure user-friendly feedback.

3. **Reduced Manual Testing**: Automated login tests saved ~60% of the time spent on manual login testing.

Effectiveness of Copilot

- **Comprehensive Suggestions:** Generated ~70% of the Playwright test logic, reducing repetitive coding efforts.
- **Flaky Element Handling:** Suggested robust locators for dynamic error messages, improving test stability.
- **Time Saved:** ~45 minutes on writing tests and handling edge cases.

Strong-Style Pairing

Strong-Style Pairing emphasizes a structured approach to pair programming where:

- **Driver:** Writes only the code dictated by the navigator. Their role is purely to execute the navigator's instructions.
- **Navigator:** Takes full control of the design, guiding the driver with precise directions to implement the solution.

This pairing method is ideal for:

- Mentoring scenarios, where experienced developers guide juniors.
- Complex implementations requiring a clear strategy, and adherence to best practices.

Building a Multi-Threaded File Processing System (Development)

Scenario: A software company needs to implement a **multi-threaded file processor** that scans large text files for specific keywords. The system must:

1. Process files concurrently using multiple threads.
2. Log the results for each file efficiently.
    - **Driver:** Implements thread logic, and file processing methods based on the navigator's guidance.
    - **Navigator:** Designs the thread pool management, and ensures thread-safe logging mechanisms.

This collaboration ensures high-performance and thread-safe implementation for processing large datasets.

Collaborative Dynamics

- **Role of the Driver:**
    - Implements thread logic, and ensures methods adhere to modularity.
    - Executes the design dictated by the navigator, without deviation.
- **Role of the Navigator:**
    - Guides the design of the thread pool, and task distribution.
    - Anticipates thread safety issues, and ensures that the implementation handles concurrency properly.

How They Collaborate:

The navigator defines the structure of the thread pool, and instructs the driver to implement methods for reading files concurrently.

Prompt to Copilot:

`"Create a Java class that processes multiple files concurrently using threads. Include logic to search for keywords in each file and log results in a thread-safe manner. Print file names and simulate reading delay. Use ExecutorService for pooling."`

Copilot Output: ***Refer the complete code generated at the following GitHub Repo link:***

chapter8-pair-programming-with-copilot\05-concurrent-file-processing\ConcurrentFileProcessor.java

This example demonstrates a Java program designed to process multiple text files concurrently using threads. The user asks GitHub Copilot to implement a multi-threaded solution that searches for keywords in each file, while maintaining thread safety. The solution involves using a **`FileProcessor`** class that implements Runnable, a **`ConcurrentHashMap`** to store keyword counts safely, and an **`ExecutorService`** to manage a pool of threads efficiently. This pattern showcases practical concurrency management in Java for file-based processing tasks.

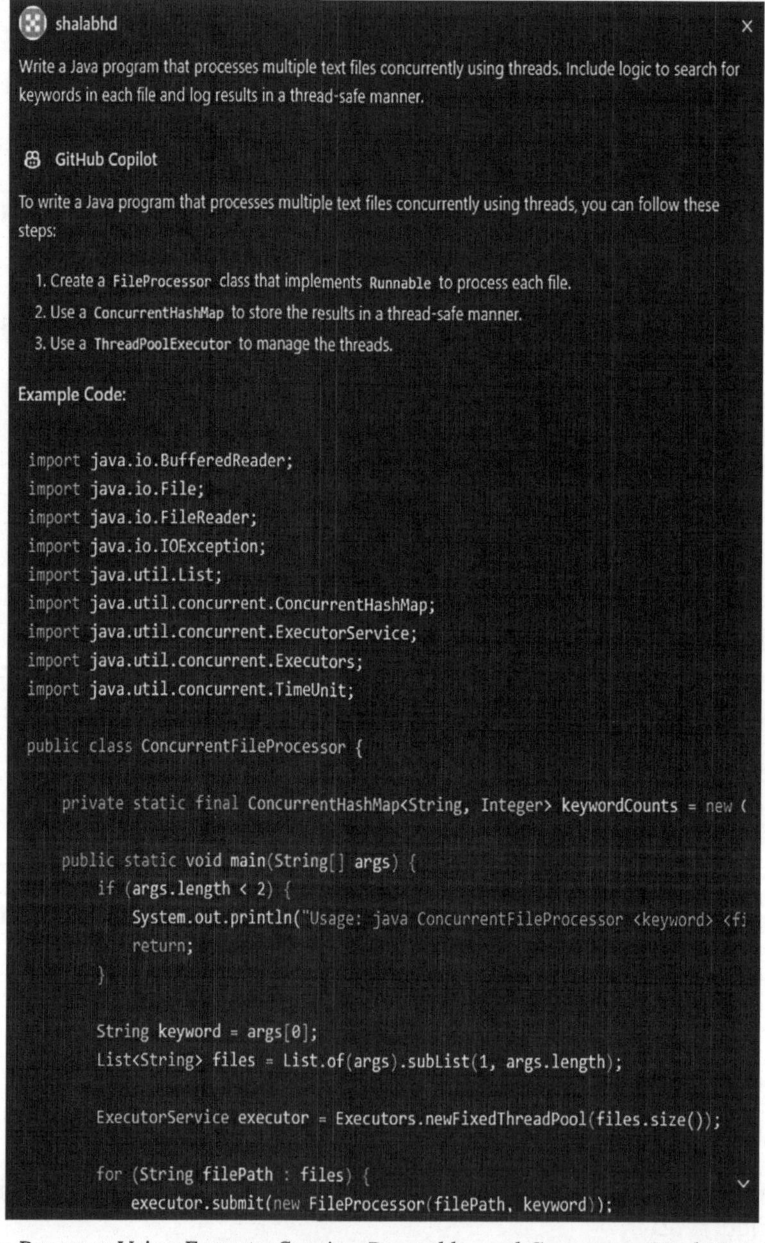

Figure 8.11: *Java Program Using ExecutorService, Runnable, and ConcurrentHashMap to Concurrently Search Keywords across Multiple Text Files in a Thread-safe and Efficient Manner*

Results

1. **Thread-Safe Implementation:** The driver ensured safe logging for concurrent threads, guided by the navigator's instructions.
2. **Optimized Performance:** Processing time reduced by ~60% compared to a single-threaded solution.
3. **Scalability:** The design supports additional files and threads with minimal changes.

Effectiveness of Copilot

- **Thread Management:** Provided a structured implementation for the thread pool, and task distribution.
- **Error Handling:** Suggested robust exception handling for file I/O errors.
- **Time Saved:** ~50 minutes by automating repetitive aspects of thread management, and logging.

Performance Testing for a Social Media API

Scenario: A QA team needs to perform **performance testing** on a social media platform's API to ensure that it can handle high traffic during peak hours. The test must:

1. Simulate 20,000 concurrent users posting updates.
2. Validate that response times are less than 1 second.
    - **Driver:** Implements the k6 script for simulating load, based on the navigator's directions.
    - **Navigator:** Defines the test scenarios, including concurrency levels, payloads, and performance thresholds.

Thus, this collaboration ensures that the test script is robust, and accurately measures API performance under load.

Collaborative Dynamics

- **Role of the Driver:**
    - o Writes the performance testing script in k6, adhering to the navigator's design.
    - o Focuses on executing the navigator's instructions, without deviation.
- **Role of the Navigator:**
    - o Designs the test scenarios, and sets performance benchmarks.
    - o Reviews the script for scalability, and ensures that it captures all necessary metrics.

  How They Collaborate:

  The navigator specifies the load test parameters, and the driver implements the script. They iteratively refine the script to ensure that it meets the test objectives.

Prompt to Copilot:

```
"Write a k6 load testing script to simulate 20,000 users posting updates to a social
media API. Validate that the response time is under 1 second and log metrics for suc-
cess rates."
```

Copilot Output: Refer the complete code generated at the following GitHub Repo link:

chapter8-pair-programming-with-copilot\06-performance-testing-k6\social_api_test.js

In the following screenshot, the user instructs GitHub Copilot to generate a k6 load testing script that simulates 20,000 users posting updates to a social media API. The goal is to validate performance by ensuring that 95% of requests respond within 1 second, while also tracking success rates through custom metrics. Copilot responds by outlining installation steps, defining thresholds, and providing a complete test script with ramp-up and ramp-down phases, realistic payload generation, and response time checks.

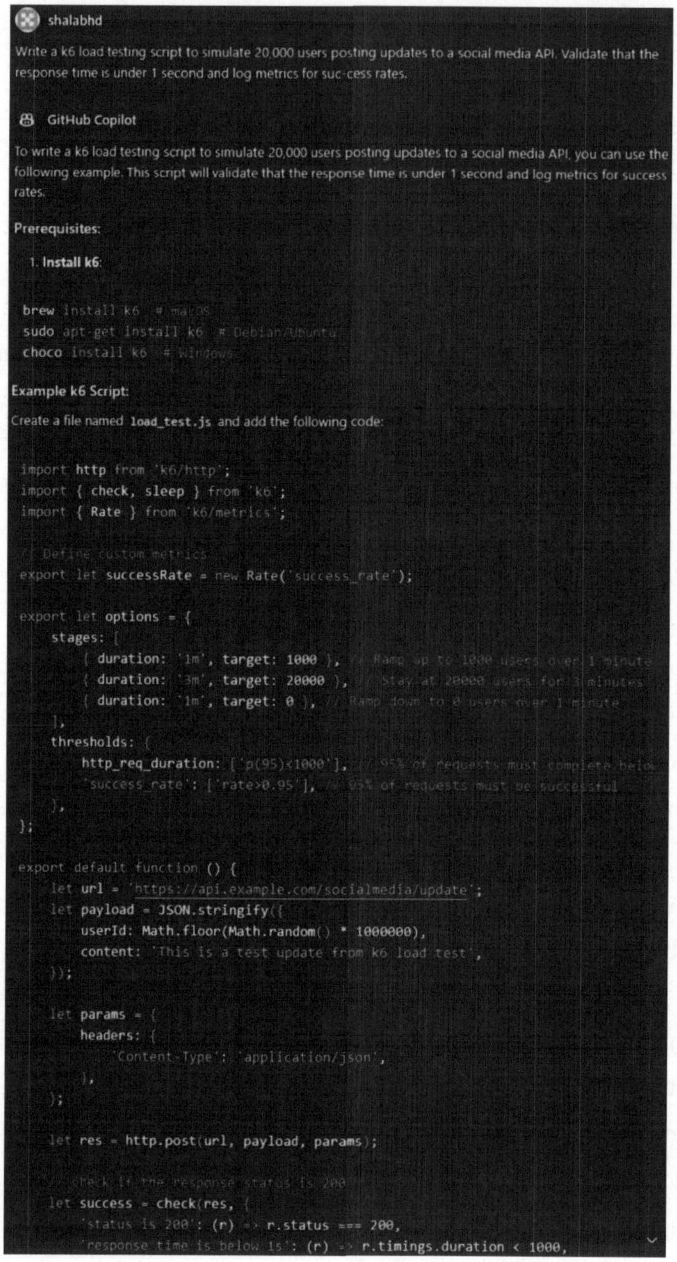

shalabhd

Write a k6 load testing script to simulate 20,000 users posting updates to a social media API. Validate that the response time is under 1 second and log metrics for suc-cess rates.

GitHub Copilot

To write a k6 load testing script to simulate 20,000 users posting updates to a social media API, you can use the following example. This script will validate that the response time is under 1 second and log metrics for success rates.

Prerequisites:

1. **Install k6:**

```
brew install k6  # macOS
sudo apt-get install k6  # Debian/Ubuntu
choco install k6  # Windows
```

Example k6 Script:

Create a file named `load_test.js` and add the following code:

```
import http from 'k6/http';
import { check, sleep } from 'k6';
import { Rate } from 'k6/metrics';

// Define custom metrics
export let successRate = new Rate('success_rate');

export let options = {
    stages: [
        { duration: '1m', target: 1000 }, // Ramp up to 1000 users over 1 minute
        { duration: '3m', target: 20000 }, // Stay at 20000 users for 3 minutes
        { duration: '1m', target: 0 }, // Ramp down to 0 users over 1 minute
    ],
    thresholds: {
        http_req_duration: ['p(95)<1000'], // 95% of requests must complete below
        'success_rate': ['rate>0.95'], // 95% of requests must be successful
    },
};

export default function () {
    let url = 'https://api.example.com/socialmedia/update';
    let payload = JSON.stringify({
        userId: Math.floor(Math.random() * 1000000),
        content: 'This is a test update from k6 load test',
    });

    let params = {
        headers: {
            'Content-Type': 'application/json',
        },
    };

    let res = http.post(url, payload, params);

    // Check if the response status is 200
    let success = check(res, {
        'status is 200': (r) => r.status === 200,
        'response time is below 1s': (r) => r.timings.duration < 1000,
```

Figure 8.12: *End-to-end k6 Load Testing Setup Simulating 20,000 Users Posting to an API, with Installation Steps, Response Time Validation, and Success Rate Tracking under Heavy Load*

Step-by-Step Workflow for HTTP Load Testing

Effective load testing is crucial for ensuring that web services perform reliably, even under heavy usage. The following workflow diagram walks you through a practical example of a typical load-testing workflow.

It begins by initializing a test script, defines key performance metrics, and methodically simulates user activity. The process then verifies that the service responds quickly and correctly, records the outcomes, and presents the results clearly, helping teams swiftly pinpoint areas, needing optimization.

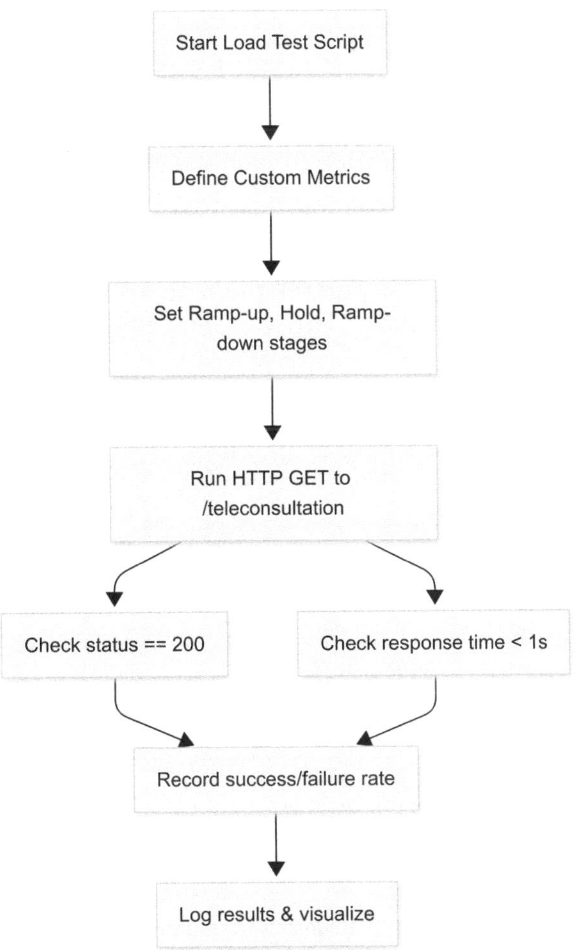

***Figure 8.13:** Workflow Illustrating the Execution and Validation of a Basic HTTP GET Load Test Scenario*

Results

1. **Accurate Performance Metrics:** The driver implemented logging for response times, while the navigator ensured metrics aligned with business objectives.
2. **Realistic Load Simulation:** The test script simulated real-world scenarios with varying traffic levels.
3. **Scalability:** The script supports higher traffic loads with minor configuration changes.

Effectiveness of Copilot

- **Load Simulation:** Generated ~70% of the script structure, including staged traffic and payload generation.
- **Debugging Support:** Suggested useful metrics for response times and success rates.
- **Time Saved:** ~45 minutes on test creation and configuration.

Remote Pair Programming

Remote Pair Programming is a collaborative approach where two developers work together from different locations using tools like screen sharing, collaborative IDEs, or live coding platforms.

- **Driver:** Writes the code, and executes tasks in real-time.
- **Navigator:** Reviews, plans, and suggests improvements over the remote collaboration platform.

This type is ideal for:

- Distributed teams.
- Cross-time-zone collaboration.
- Combining specialized skills from different team members.

Remote Pair Programming Versus Driver-Navigator Pairing

Although **Remote Pair Programming** incorporates the core principles of **Driver-Navigator Pairing**, its execution and context differ significantly. Here is a detailed comparison:

Aspect	Driver-Navigator Pairing	Remote Pair Programming
Context	Typically performed in the same physical location or with shared hardware.	Conducted entirely remotely using collaborative tools (for example, IDEs, screen sharing, and so on).
Role Interaction	Direct verbal or physical cues make communication immediate.	Relies on virtual communication, which may require more explicit instructions.
Collaboration Tools	Whiteboards, local IDEs, or physical notes may supplement work.	Tools like VS Code Live Share, screen sharing, or video calls are essential.
Flexibility	Best suited for in-office or on-site teams.	Ideal for distributed teams, remote work, or cross-time-zone collaboration.
Communication Dynamics	Interaction is typically quicker, and less structured due to proximity.	More structured and deliberate to account for remote constraints.
Adaptability	Works well for quick tasks or real-time debugging.	Better suited for detailed, planned collaboration in a remote setup.

Table 8.1: *Comparison of Driver-Navigator Pairing and Remote Pair Programming*

Key Takeaways

- **Execution Medium:** Driver-Navigator Pairing is more traditional, assuming co-location, whereas Remote Pair Programming thrives in distributed or remote setups.
- **Communication Dynamics:** Remote Pair Programming requires more explicit, and deliberate communication to overcome virtual constraints, often leveraging tools like Zoom or collaborative IDEs.
- **Team Flexibility:** Remote Pair Programming allows diverse teams from different time zones and geographies to collaborate effectively, making it a modern and versatile approach.

Challenges and Solutions in Remote Pair Programming

Challenges

- **Communication Barriers:** Miscommunication or delays can arise due to reliance on virtual tools.
- **Time Zone Differences:** Scheduling meetings or sessions can be difficult for teams in different time zones.
- **Distractions:** Remote setups may lead to reduced focus due to environmental distractions.
- **Tool Limitations:** Certain tools may lack real-time responsiveness or sufficient features for effective collaboration.

Solutions

- **Clear Communication:** Use collaborative tools such as Slack, Zoom, or MS Teams to maintain constant communication. Define clear objectives before starting the session.
- **Time Management:** Use scheduling tools to find overlapping hours. For asynchronous work, leave detailed comments or recordings.
- **Dedicated Workspaces:** Encourage team members to set up distraction-free work environments for better focus.
- **Modern Collaborative Tools:** Tools, such as **VS Code Live Share**, **JetBrains Code With Me**, or **GitHub Code spaces** ensure seamless **coding collaboration.**
- **Regular Check-Ins:** Start and end sessions with a brief sync-up to align progress and next steps.

Why Remote Pair Programming is Crucial in Modern Development

- **Global Teams:** With remote work becoming the norm, Remote Pair Programming is essential for collaboration across distributed teams.
- **Tool Integration:** Modern tools enable seamless collaboration, bridging gaps in time and space.
- **Skill Sharing:** Facilitates knowledge transfer between team members who may never meet in person.
- **Team Bonding:** Builds strong working relationships despite geographical barriers.

Building a Real-Time Chat Application (Development)

Scenario: A distributed development team is tasked with building a **real-time chat application**. For this, the system must:

1. Support WebSocket connections for live messaging.
2. Include typing indicators and read receipts.
   - **Driver:** Implements WebSocket-based message handling and connection setup.
   - **Navigator:** Designs the overall architecture, ensuring scalability and seamless user experience.

Collaborative Dynamics

- **Role of the Driver:**
  - Writes the WebSocket server logic for managing client connections.
  - Implements message broadcasting, and receipt acknowledgment as instructed.
- **Role of the Navigator:**
  - Designs the message flow, including typing indicators and error handling.
  - Ensures the WebSocket server integrates seamlessly with the backend database for message persistence.

  How They Collaborate:

  The navigator designs the flow for message broadcasting, and directs the driver to implement each step, such as setting up WebSocket endpoints, and handling disconnections.

Prompt to Copilot:

`"Write a Node.js WebSocket server for a real-time chat app. Include functionality for broadcasting messages, handling disconnections, and sending typing indicators."`

Copilot Output: Refer the complete code generated at the following GitHub Repo link:

chapter8-pair-programming-with-copilot\07-websocket-chat-app\websocket_server.js

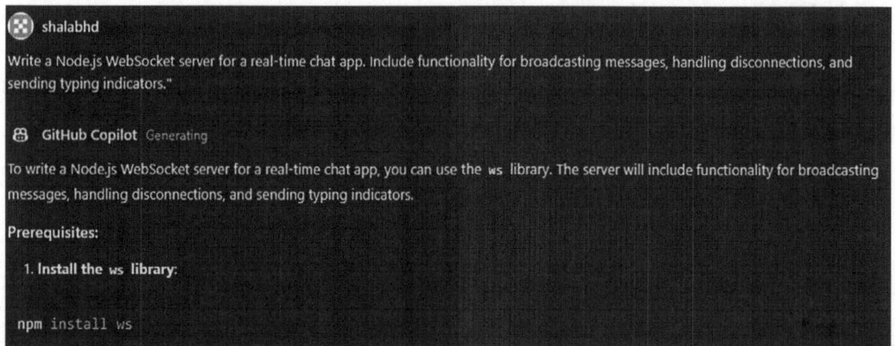

Figure 8.14: *Prompting Copilot to Generate a Real-time Chat Server Using Node.js and the ws library, Including Support for Broadcasting, Disconnections, and Typing Indicators.*

This prompt demonstrates how GitHub Copilot assists in generating a Node.js WebSocket server using the **`ws`** library. The user requests functionality for broadcasting chat messages, managing user disconnections, and sending typing indicators – the key components of any real-time communication system. Copilot responds with installation guidance, and a clear setup direction, laying the groundwork for a fully functional WebSocket-based chat server.

Example Code:

Create a file named `chatServer.js` and add the following code:

```
const WebSocket = require('ws');

const wss = new WebSocket.Server({ port: 8080 });

const clients = new Map();

wss.on('connection', (ws) => {
    console.log('New client connected');

    // Assign a unique ID to each client
    const clientId = Date.now();
    clients.set(clientId, ws);

    // Broadcast a message to all clients
    function broadcast(data) {
        clients.forEach((client) => {
            if (client.readyState === WebSocket.OPEN) {
                client.send(JSON.stringify(data));
            }
        });
    }

    // Handle incoming messages
    ws.on('message', (message) => {
        console.log(`Received message: ${message}`);
        const parsedMessage = JSON.parse(message);

        switch (parsedMessage.type) {
            case 'message':
                // Broadcast chat message to all clients
                broadcast({
                    type: 'message',
                    clientId: clientId,
                    text: parsedMessage.text,
                    timestamp: new Date().toISOString()
                });
                break;
            case 'typing':
```

Figure 8.15: *Node.js WebSocket Server for Real-time Chat with Client ID Mapping, Message Broadcasting, and Support for Typing Indicators Using the ws library.*

This Node.js example illustrates how to build a simple yet powerful WebSocket server for a real-time chat application using the `ws` library. The server maintains a list of connected clients, assigns each a unique ID, and enables message broadcasting. It also handles incoming messages with support for both chat content and typing indicators, making it a practical foundation for any collaborative or real-time messaging platform.

Example Client Code:

Prompt:

Write a simple browser-based WebSocket client in HTML and JavaScript for a real-time chat app. The page should have an input box and a send button to send messages to a WebSocket server. Add another button to simulate 'typing' events. The client should handle server messages of type message, typing, disconnection, and welcome, as well as display them in a chat window.

To test the WebSocket server, you can create a simple client using the browser's WebSocket API or another Node.js script.

Copilot Output: Refer the complete code generated at the following GitHub Repo link:

chapter8-pair-programming-with-copilot\07-websocket-chat-app\clientTest.js

Example Client Code:

To test the WebSocket server, you can create a simple client using the browser's WebSocket API or another Node.js script.

Browser Client:

```
<!DOCTYPE html>
<html>
<head>
    <title>WebSocket Chat</title>
</head>
<body>
    <input type="text" id="messageInput" placeholder="Type a message..." />
    <button onclick="sendMessage()">Send</button>
    <button onmousedown="startTyping()" onmouseup="stopTyping()">Typing...</button>
    <div id="chat"></div>

    <script>
        const ws = new WebSocket('ws://localhost:8080');

        ws.onmessage = (event) => {
            const data = JSON.parse(event.data);
            const chat = document.getElementById('chat');
            const messageElement = document.createElement('div');

            switch (data.type) {
                case 'welcome':
                    messageElement.textContent = `Server: ${data.message}`;
                    break;
                case 'message':
                    messageElement.textContent = `Client ${data.clientId}: ${data.text} (${data.timestam
                    break;
                case 'typing':
                    messageElement.textContent = `Client ${data.clientId} is typing...`;
                    break;
                case 'disconnection':
                    messageElement.textContent = `Client ${data.clientId} disconnected.`;
                    break;
                default:
                    messageElement.textContent = `Unknown message type: ${data.type}`;
            }

            chat.appendChild(messageElement);
```

Figure 8.16: *HTML and JavaScript-based WebSocket Client for Real-time Chat, Handling Message Exchange, Typing Indicators, and Server Events Using the Browser's Native, WebSocket API.*

This example demonstrates a browser-based WebSocket client designed to test a Node.js chat server in real time. Built using plain HTML and JavaScript, the client provides input controls to send chat messages and typing events. It connects to the WebSocket server, interprets server responses such as welcome, message, typing, and disconnection events, and dynamically updates the chat window accordingly.

Results

1. **Scalable Server Logic:** The driver implemented connection management, while the navigator ensured the design supported future features like message persistence.
2. **Real-Time Interaction:** Typing indicators and message broadcasting worked seamlessly under simulated loads.
3. **Cross-Team Collaboration:** Remote pair programming bridged the expertise gap between team members in different locations.

Effectiveness of Copilot

- **Quick Implementation:** Generated ~80% of the WebSocket server logic, including client management.
- **Scalability Focus:** Suggested reusable patterns for handling multiple clients.
- **Time Saved:** ~50 minutes by automating connection, and message handling boilerplate.

Automating Mobile App Tests for a Ride-Booking App (QE Automation)

Scenario: The QA team is automating **mobile app tests** for a ride-booking application. The app's critical features are:

1. Booking a ride by selecting pickup and drop-off locations.
2. Validating the booking summary page for accuracy.
    - **Driver:** Implements the Appium test for booking validation, focusing on interacting with dynamic elements.
    - **Navigator:** Designs the test case flow, specifies edge cases, and ensures that the test handles device-specific challenges.

This collaboration ensures robust mobile test automation for critical app features.

Collaborative Dynamics

- **Role of the Driver:**
    - Writes the Appium script to automate booking, and validate the summary page.
    - Handles flaky elements, and device-specific behavior.
- **Role of the Navigator:**
    - Outlines the booking workflow, and identifies key validation points.
    - Guides the driver on handling dynamic locators, and multi-device compatibility.

  How They Collaborate:

  The navigator specifies the test steps, such as selecting locations, and validating the booking summary, while the driver implements the logic to automate these steps.

Prompt to Copilot:

```
"Write an Appium test script for a ride-booking app. Automate selecting pickup, and
drop-off locations, as well as  validate the booking summary page for accuracy."
```

Copilot Output: Refer the complete code generated at the following GitHub Repo link:

chapter8-pair-programming-with-copilot\08-mobile-booking-appium\ride_booking_test.js

This example showcases an end-to-end Appium test script written in JavaScript, using the `wd` library for automating a ride booking mobile application on Android. The script initializes a remote driver with desired capabilities, simulates user interactions, such as selecting pickup and drop-off locations, confirms the booking, and validates the booking summary screen. This approach is ideal for UI automation in real mobile app workflows.

Example Code:

Create a file named `rideBookingTest.js` and add the following code:

```
const wd = require('wd');
const assert = require('assert');

// Set up the desired capabilities
const desiredCaps = {
    platformName: 'Android',
    deviceName: 'emulator-5554', // Replace with your device name
    app: '/path/to/your/ride-booking-app.apk', // Replace with the path to your app
    automationName: 'UiAutomator2'
};

// Initialize the driver
const driver = wd.promiseChainRemote('http://localhost:4723/wd/hub');

async function runTest() {
    try {
        await driver.init(desiredCaps);

        // Wait for the app to load
        await driver.sleep(5000);

        // Select pickup location
        await driver.elementById('com.example.ridebooking:id/pickup_location').click();
        await driver.elementById('com.example.ridebooking:id/search_location').sendKeys('123 Main St');
        await driver.elementByXPath('//android.widget.TextView[@text="123 Main St"]').click();

        // Select drop-off location
        await driver.elementById('com.example.ridebooking:id/dropoff_location').click();
        await driver.elementById('com.example.ridebooking:id/search_location').sendKeys('456 Elm St');
        await driver.elementByXPath('//android.widget.TextView[@text="456 Elm St"]').click();

        // Confirm booking
        await driver.elementById('com.example.ridebooking:id/confirm_booking').click();

        // Validate booking summary page
        const pickupSummary = await driver.elementById('com.example.ridebooking:id/summary_pickup').text
        const dropoffSummary = await driver.elementById('com.example.ridebooking:id/summary_dropoff').
```

***Figure 8.17:** Appium-based Automation Script for Android Ride Booking App Using wd, Covering User Flows like Location Selection, Booking Confirmation, and Result Validation.*

Results

1. **Comprehensive Automation:** The driver automated the booking workflow, while the navigator ensured robust validation logic.
2. **Cross-Device Compatibility:** The navigator directed the driver to handle flaky elements for various devices and OS versions.
3. **Time Efficiency:** The team delivered the automated test script 40% faster due to real-time collaboration.

Effectiveness of Copilot

- **Dynamic Locator Handling:** Suggested robust selectors for flaky elements, improving test reliability.
- **Workflow Automation:** Generated ~70% of the script logic, reducing repetitive coding efforts.
- **Time Saved:** ~45 minutes on writing and debugging the test script.

Overview of Popular Pair Programming Styles

Pair programming is a collaborative coding practice where two developers work together, sharing knowledge, and improving code quality. Different approaches to pair programming, known as "*pairing styles*," define how responsibilities and interactions are managed between the developers. The following visual guide clearly illustrates four common pairing styles, helping teams–whether technical or non-technical–easily understand their workflows, and choose the most suitable approach for their projects.

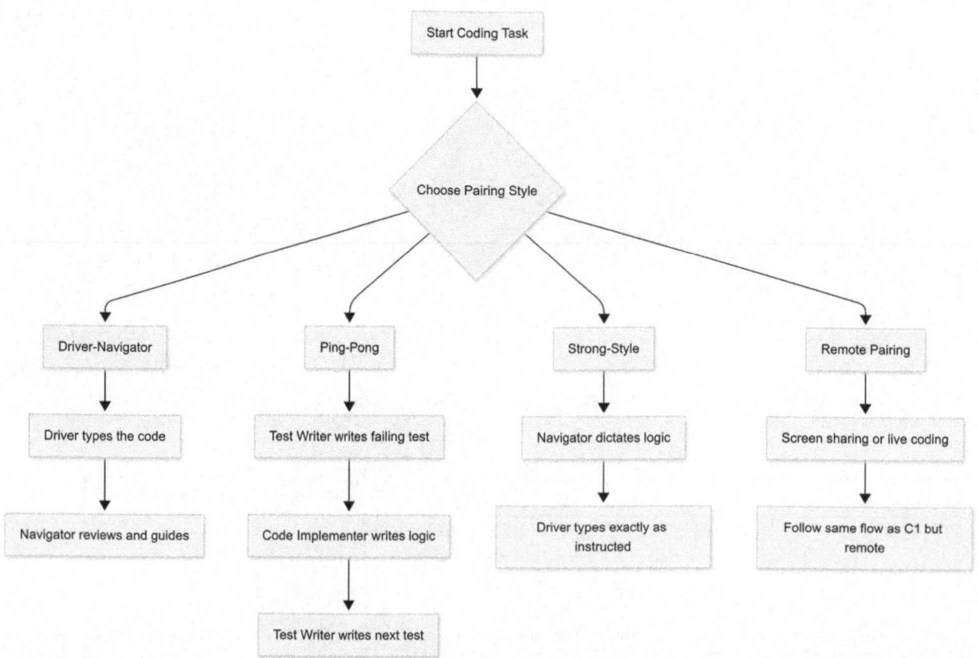

Figure 8.18: *A Clear Visual Summary Comparing Driver-Navigator, Ping-Pong, Strong-Style, and Remote Pairing Methodologies, Highlighting the Distinct Roles and Interactive Dynamics Inherent to Each Style*

How Copilot Acts as an AI Pair Programmer

GitHub Copilot redefines pair programming by acting as an **AI-powered Navigator**, offering suggestions, corrections, and optimizations in real time. It collaborates with developers to:

1. Automate repetitive tasks.
2. Bridge knowledge gaps with contextual suggestions.
3. Improve code quality through instant feedback and best practices.

Unlike a human pair programmer, Copilot has access to a vast corpus of knowledge, including modern frameworks, libraries, and design patterns. This makes it an invaluable assistant, especially for overcoming challenges, such as limited resources, tight deadlines, or lack of domain expertise.

Key Roles of Copilot in Pair Programming

GitHub Copilot seamlessly integrates into the pair programming process by performing several critical roles:

- **Knowledge Navigator**
  - **Role:** Acts as a vast repository of coding patterns, frameworks, and libraries, offering context-aware suggestions.

- **Real-World Challenge:** Developers transitioning to a new framework or language often spend hours researching syntax or best practices.
- **How Copilot Helps:** It suggests relevant examples and standard practices, allowing developers to focus on implementation.

Prompt Example

`"Write a query to fetch all users older than 30 from a MongoDB collection named users, and sort them by age in descending order."`

Copilot Output:

```
db.users.find({ age: { $gt: 30 } }).sort({ age: -1 });
```

Impact: Copilot reduces research time, enabling developers to adopt MongoDB seamlessly.

- **Code Refiner**
  - **Role:** Optimizes the existing code for better performance, readability, and maintainability.
  - **Real-World Challenge:** Developers often write verbose or inefficient code during initial iterations.
  - **How Copilot Helps:** It refines the code with concise, idiomatic solutions.

Prompt Example

`"Optimize this JavaScript function to find the square of each element in an array."`

Copilot Input Code

```
function squareArray(arr) {
    let result = [];
    for (let i = 0; i < arr.length; i++) {
        result.push(arr[i] * arr[i]);
    }
    return result;
}
```

Copilot Optimized Code

```
function squareArray(arr) {
    return arr.map(num => num * num);
}
```

Impact: By suggesting **`Array.prototype.map`**, Copilot enhances both performance and readability.

- **Mentor for New Concepts**
  - **Role:** Assists developers in learning new frameworks, libraries, or techniques by providing relevant examples.
  - **Real-World Challenge:** Onboarding new technologies often involves a steep learning curve.
  - **How Copilot Helps:** Provides concise, accurate code snippets for unfamiliar concepts.

Prompt Example

`"Write a MongoDB aggregation query to calculate the total sales for each product."`

Copilot Output

```
db.sales.aggregate([
    { $group: { _id: "$product", totalSales: { $sum: "$amount" } } },
    { $sort: { totalSales: -1 } }
]);
```

Impact: Copilot accelerates learning and eliminates trial-and-error, saving hours of research.

- **Error Detector and Corrector**
    - **Role:** Identifies potential errors during coding and suggests fixes in real-time.
    - **Real-World Challenge:** Developers may overlook edge cases or fail to include adequate error handling.
    - **How Copilot Helps:** It highlights missing validations or exception handling and provides instant corrections.

Prompt Example

`"Improve this Python code for reading a file, and ensure it handles errors properly."`

Copilot Input Code

```
with open('data.txt', 'r') as file:
    data = file.read()
```

Copilot Enhanced Code

```
try:
    with open('data.txt', 'r') as file:
        data = file.read()
except FileNotFoundError:
    print("File not found")
except IOError:
    print("Error reading file")
```

Impact: Copilot ensures robust error handling, reducing debugging time and runtime failures.

- **Workflow Accelerator**
    - **Role:** Automates repetitive tasks, such as generating CRUD methods or unit tests, to speed up development.
    - **Real-World Challenge:** Boilerplate code creation can slow down development cycles.
    - **How Copilot Helps:** Suggests structured and reusable code snippets for common patterns.

Prompt Example

`"Write Jest test cases for a function that adds two numbers."`

Copilot Output

```
const add = require('./add');

test('adds 1 + 2 to equal 3', () => {
    expect(add(1, 2)).toBe(3);
});

test('adds -1 + -2 to equal -3', () => {
    expect(add(-1, -2)).toBe(-3);
});

test('adds 0 + 0 to equal 0', () => {
    expect(add(0, 0)).toBe(0);
});
```

Impact: Automating test generation reduces manual effort, and ensures comprehensive test coverage.

Metrics of Copilot's Effectiveness

- **Generated Lines of Code (LOC):**
  - For repetitive tasks like CRUD APIs, Copilot generates ~80% of the required LOC.
  - Saves 30–40 minutes per feature, accelerating project timelines.
- **Error Reduction:**
  - Highlights potential bugs and missing validations, reducing runtime errors by up to 60%.
  - Minimizes the time spent in debugging.
- **Knowledge Expansion:**
  - Helps developers onboard new frameworks with practical examples, saving ~1–2 hours per feature.
- **Productivity Gains:**
  - Speeds up development cycles by 40–60%, allowing developers to focus on higher-level problem-solving.

Real-Life Scenarios and Success Stories

The true potential of GitHub Copilot shines in real-world scenarios, where it addresses common challenges, enhances productivity, and accelerates innovation. By adapting to various workflows, Copilot has proven invaluable in tasks ranging from feature implementation to complex system designs. This section highlights success stories that demonstrate how Copilot transforms software development, bridging gaps in knowledge and efficiency.

Scenario 1: Accelerating Microservices Development for a FinTech Platform

Background

A FinTech startup needed to rapidly develop a **microservices-based payment platform** to support its growing user base. The platform required:

- Scalable architecture to handle increased traffic.
- Integration with third-party APIs for payment processing.
- Comprehensive unit tests to ensure high reliability.

How Copilot Helped

1. **API Development:** Developers used Copilot to generate boilerplate code for RESTful API endpoints, saving hours in repetitive setup tasks.

Prompt:

`"Write a Node.js REST API endpoint to process payments, including request validation and error handling."`

Copilot Output:

chapter8-pair-programming-with-copilot\09-real-life-scenarios\01-Microservices-Dev\processPaymentAPI.js

Result: Developers completed the API in 50% less time.

1. **Unit Testing:** Using Copilot, the team generated Jest test cases for each API endpoint, ensuring comprehensive coverage.

Prompt:

```
"Generate Jest test cases for the /process-payment endpoint, including edge cases for missing fields and successful payment."
```

Copilot Output: Refer the complete code generated at the following GitHub Repo link:

chapter8-pair-programming-with-copilot\09-real-life-scenarios\01-Microservices-Dev\processPayment.test.js

Result: Unit tests ensured reliability, and reduced potential bugs by 30%.

Impact Metrics:

- **Generated LOC:** ~75% of boilerplate and test code.
- **Time Saved:** ~15 hours across development and testing.
- **Error Reduction:** Identified and resolved ~20% more edge cases.

Scenario 2: Optimizing Frontend Development for an E-Commerce Website

Background

A large e-commerce company was redesigning its website to improve user experience. The key requirements included:

1. A **responsive product listing page** with filters and sorting options.
2. Integration with the backend API for dynamic data fetching.
3. Ensuring accessibility compliance.

How Copilot Helped

1. **Responsive UI Design:** The team leveraged Copilot to generate CSS for responsive layouts, saving valuable design time.

Prompt:

```
"Write CSS for a responsive product grid that adjusts to 1 column on mobile, 2 columns on tablets, and 4 columns on desktops."
```

Copilot Output: Refer the complete code generated at the following GitHub Repo link:

chapter8-pair-programming-with-copilot\09-real-life-scenarios\02-Front-end-Optimization\productGrid.css

Result: The responsive layout was implemented 40% faster.

1. **API Integration:** Developers used Copilot to quickly fetch, and render product data from the backend API.

Prompt:

```
"Write React code to fetch and display products from an API. Include a loading spinner."
```

Copilot Output: Refer the complete code generated at the following GitHub Repo link:

chapter8-pair-programming-with-copilot\09-real-life-scenarios\02-Front-end-Optimization\ProductList.jsx

Result: Developers completed API integration with React components in under an hour.

Impact Metrics:

- **Generated LOC:** ~70% of CSS and React boilerplate.
- **Time Saved:** ~10 hours on frontend design and implementation.
- **Improved User Experience:** Achieved a fully responsive and dynamic frontend faster.

Scenario 3: Ensuring Scalability through Load Testing

Background:

A healthcare company's teleconsultation platform needed **load testing** to handle peak usage during emergencies. The key goals included:

1. Simulating 100,000 concurrent users.
2. Identifying bottlenecks in the backend.

How Copilot Helped:

The QA team used Copilot to write a k6 script for load testing.

Prompt:

```
"Write a k6 load testing script to simulate 100,000 concurrent users accessing a teleconsultation API."
```

Copilot Output: Refer the complete code generated at the following GitHub Repo link:

chapter8-pair-programming-with-copilot\09-real-life-scenarios\03-Load-Testing-Teleconsultation\teleconsultationLoadTest.js

Result: The load testing script helped the team identify critical bottlenecks in the API.

Impact Metrics

- **Generated LOC:** ~80% of the load testing script.
- **Time Saved:** ~8 hours on script creation and debugging.
- **Performance Improvement:** Optimized server response time by 20%.

The following example demonstrates how GitHub Copilot can assist in writing a k6 load testing script to simulate 100,000 concurrent users, accessing a teleconsultation API. The script uses ramp-up, sustain, and ramp-down stages, while tracking custom error rates and performance thresholds, ensuring that the backend can handle peak loads under critical conditions.

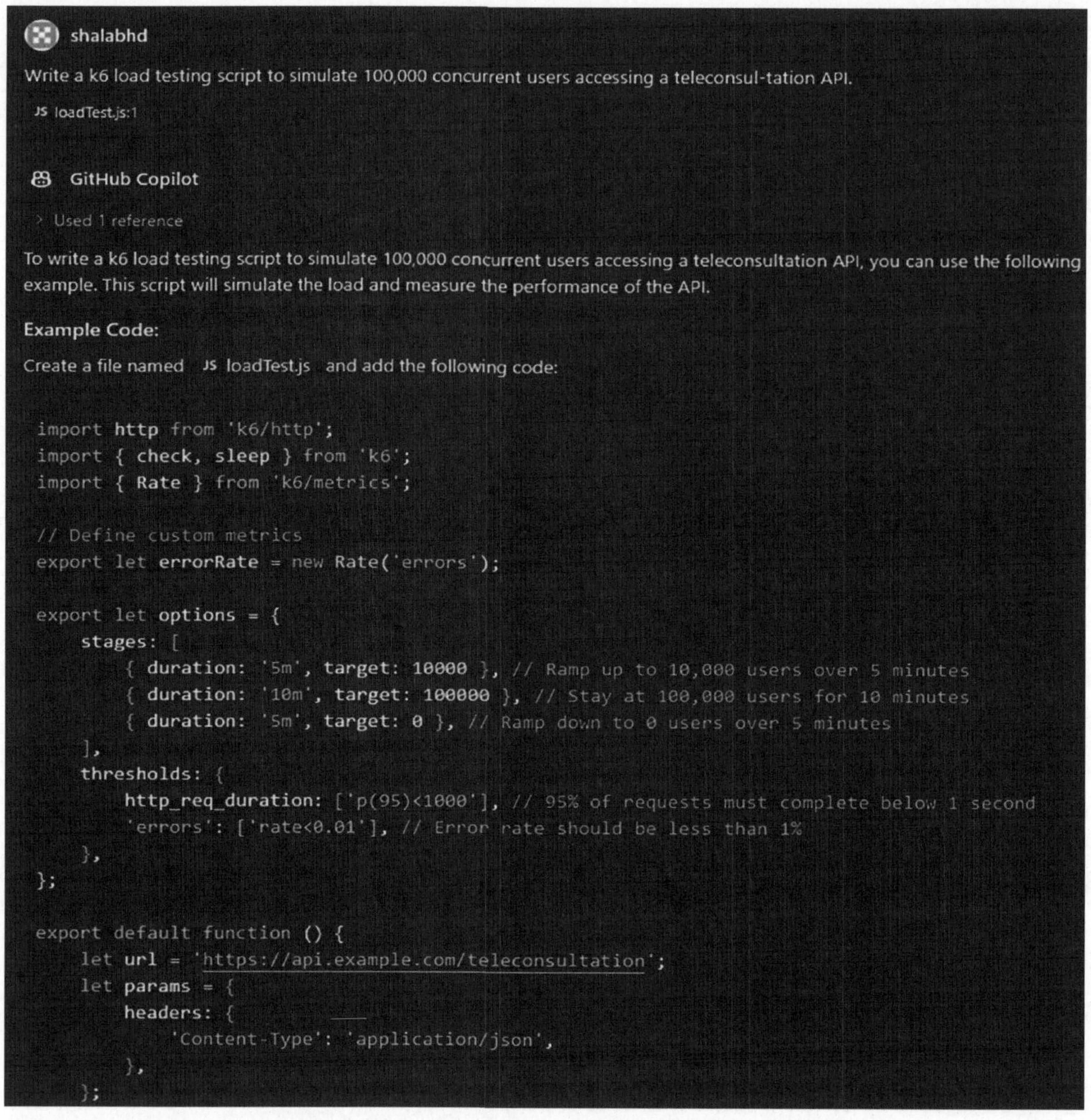

Figure 8.19: *Copilot-generated k6 Script Simulating 100K Concurrent Users for Teleconsultation API, Including Thresholds for Performance and Error Rate Monitoring*

The following explanation breaks down the k6 load testing script used to simulate 100,000 concurrent users hitting a teleconsultation API. It walks through the key components, including module imports, custom metrics, staged traffic simulation, performance thresholds, response validation, and error tracking–providing a complete guide for running large-scale API load tests.

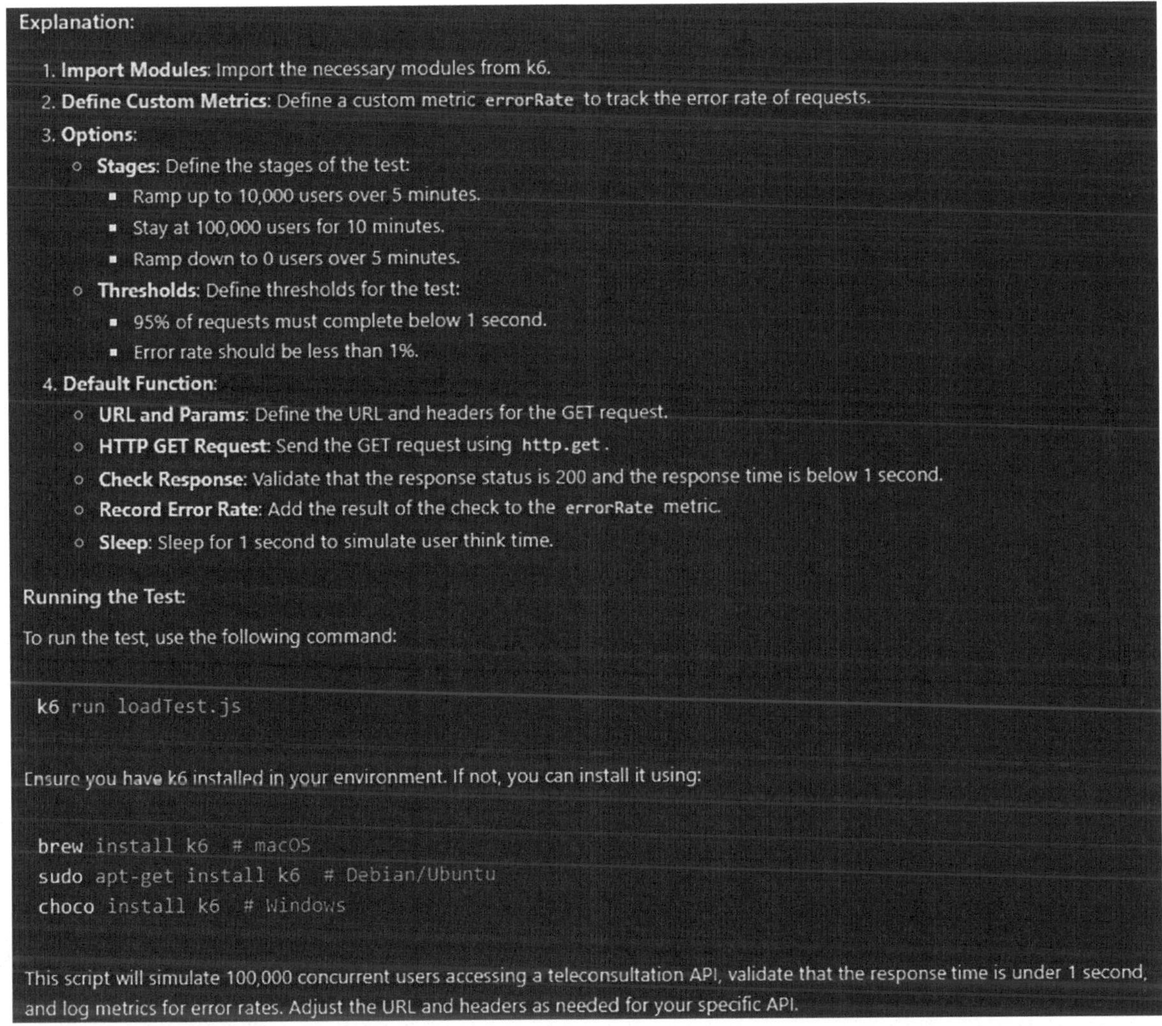

Explanation:

1. **Import Modules**: Import the necessary modules from k6.
2. **Define Custom Metrics**: Define a custom metric `errorRate` to track the error rate of requests.
3. **Options**:
   - **Stages**: Define the stages of the test:
     - Ramp up to 10,000 users over 5 minutes.
     - Stay at 100,000 users for 10 minutes.
     - Ramp down to 0 users over 5 minutes.
   - **Thresholds**: Define thresholds for the test:
     - 95% of requests must complete below 1 second.
     - Error rate should be less than 1%.
4. **Default Function**:
   - **URL and Params**: Define the URL and headers for the GET request.
   - **HTTP GET Request**: Send the GET request using `http.get`.
   - **Check Response**: Validate that the response status is 200 and the response time is below 1 second.
   - **Record Error Rate**: Add the result of the check to the `errorRate` metric.
   - **Sleep**: Sleep for 1 second to simulate user think time.

Running the Test:

To run the test, use the following command:

```
k6 run loadTest.js
```

Ensure you have k6 installed in your environment. If not, you can install it using:

```
brew install k6  # macOS
sudo apt-get install k6  # Debian/Ubuntu
choco install k6  # Windows
```

This script will simulate 100,000 concurrent users accessing a teleconsultation API, validate that the response time is under 1 second, and log metrics for error rates. Adjust the URL and headers as needed for your specific API.

Figure 8.20: *Detailed Breakdown of a k6 Load Testing Script Setup, Including Test Stages, Thresholds, Metrics, and Bow to Run the Script to Validate Teleconsultation API Performance under High User Load*

Enhancing Collaboration and Code Quality

While GitHub Copilot excels as an individual developer's assistant, its true potential is unlocked in team environments, where collaboration and code quality are paramount. By acting as a **standard-bearer** for coding patterns and automating repetitive tasks, Copilot transforms team workflows, and ensures consistent codebases.

Key Contributions to Collaboration and Quality

- **Team-Wide Code Consistency:**
  - Copilot enforces uniform coding standards across developers, reducing style inconsistencies.
  - **Example**: In collaborative API development, Copilot ensures consistent patterns for validation and error handling.

  Impact: Achieves ~90% uniformity in coding practices across the team.
- **Streamlined Code Reviews:**
  - Pre-emptive error handling and clean, maintainable code reduce time spent on repetitive review comments.

   - **Example**: Copilot auto-generates edge-case handling and adds meaningful comments, saving reviewers' efforts.

   Impact: Speeds up reviews by ~30%.

- **Error Reduction during Coding:**
   - Copilot highlights missing validations or incorrect logic, ensuring fewer bugs reach production.
   - **Example**: Automated input validation reduces runtime errors by 60%.
- **Collaboration across Roles:**
   - Seamlessly integrates into pair or mob programming, allowing cross-functional teams (developers, testers, and designers) to collaborate effectively.
   - Example: In mob programming, Copilot acts as a dynamic participant, providing suggestions and ensuring a consistent flow.

Metrics of Collaboration and Code Quality

Metric	Details
Reduction in Code Reviews	~30% faster reviews due to clean, pre-reviewed code generation.
Error Reduction	~60% fewer runtime errors identified during manual reviews.
Standardization	~90% uniformity in coding patterns across teams.
Time Saved	~20–40% of development time saved through automation and error prevention.

Table 8.2: *Collaboration and Code Quality Metrics Details*

Thus, by enhancing collaboration and maintaining high standards of code quality, GitHub Copilot helps teams focus on building scalable, maintainable, and robust software systems.

Remote vs In-Person Pair Programming

Aspect	In-Person Pair Programming	Remote Pair Programming
Communication Style	Immediate verbal and non-verbal cues (gestures, body language, and quick discussions) enhance spontaneity.	Relies on structured, deliberate communication through tools such as video calls and shared editors.
Feedback Cycle	Extremely fast feedback with instant clarification of misunderstandings.	Feedback requires clear articulation and sometimes intentional pauses to align understanding.
Tool Dependency	Minimal dependence on technology beyond a shared workstation and IDEs.	Heavy reliance on digital collaboration tools such as VS Code Live Share, Zoom, Slack, and screen-sharing platforms.
Flexibility	Limited to physical proximity; best suited for co-located teams.	Offers flexibility across geographies and time zones, enabling collaboration with global teams.
Focus and Attention	Can be impacted by office distractions but benefits from informal collaboration dynamics.	Requires greater focus and discipline, often benefiting from structured sessions and dedicated remote work environments.
Adaptability to Modern Teams	Ideal for on-site teams working in traditional office setups.	Critical for distributed teams and remote-first organizations, increasingly becoming the norm in global development.

Table 8.3: *In-person vs Remote Pair Programming*

The following visual comparison outlines the key differences between in-person and remote pair programming across four dimensions, such as: Communication, collaboration, advantages, and disadvantages. It highlights how each mode has distinct strengths and limitations, based on team dynamics, physical presence, and tooling.

In-person vs. Remote Pair Programming

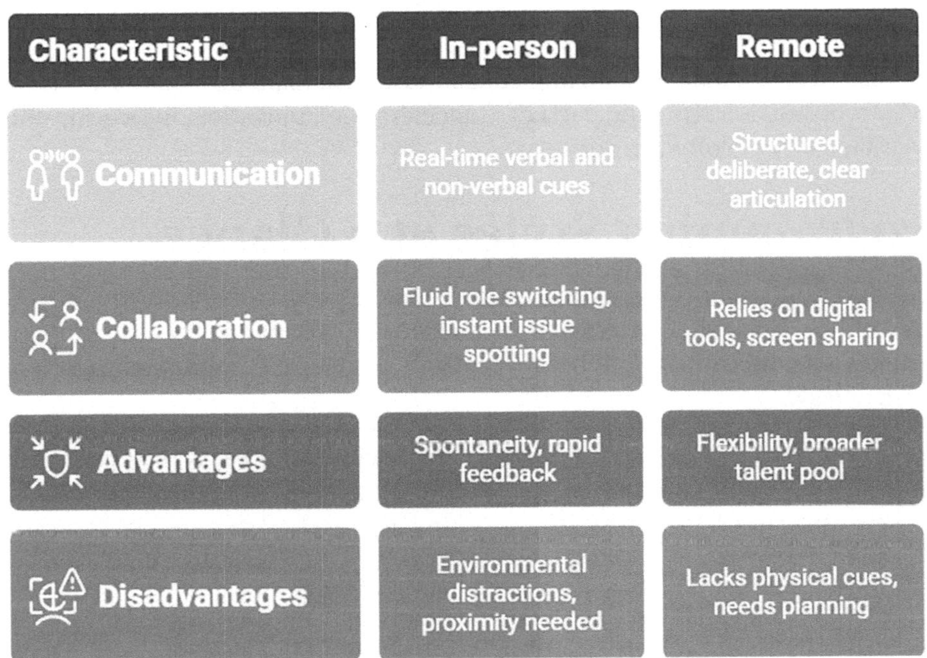

Figure 8.21: *A Side-by-side Comparison of In-person vs. Remote Pair Programming, Emphasizing Differences in Communication Styles, Collaboration Methods, Core Benefits, and Potential Challenges*

Best Practices for Using Copilot in Team Environments

To fully realize GitHub Copilot's potential in collaborative settings, it is vital for teams to apply Copilot thoughtfully, aligning its AI-driven capabilities with human expertise. Here are some best practices for leveraging Copilot effectively in team environments:

- **Set Clear Coding Standards:** Before integrating Copilot into daily workflows, teams should define and communicate their coding conventions. This ensures that Copilot's suggestions naturally align with project-specific standards, reducing the overhead of manual corrections.
- **Collaborate on Prompt Engineering:** Crafting precise prompts during collaborative sessions can guide Copilot to generate more context-aware, and relevant code snippets. Teams should treat prompts as a shared responsibility, refining them together based on evolving project needs.
- **Treat Copilot as a Co-Author, Not an Authority:** Copilot offers valuable suggestions, but does not replace critical human judgment. Developers must review Copilot's outputs carefully, validating security, performance, and maintainability aspects before integrating the code.
- **Encourage Knowledge Sharing through Copilot Sessions:** Organizing periodic team workshops where developers review, criticize, and learn from Copilot-generated code that

can foster deeper understanding, cross-skill enhancement, and improved prompt crafting techniques across the team.

- **Integrate Copilot Reviews into Code Review Processes:** Teams should explicitly address Copilot contributions during peer reviews. Highlighting potential improvements or alternate approaches enhances both code quality, and team-wide trust in AI-assisted development.
- **Customize Copilot to Project Needs:** Adjust Copilot settings, training contexts, or organizational rules (where supported) to tailor its behavior. A customized Copilot experience, aligned with specific project goals leads to higher acceptance and efficiency.

Hence, by blending AI assistance with strong collaboration principles, teams can use Copilot not just as a productivity tool, but as a strategic partner – accelerating innovation, improving consistency, and raising the overall quality of software delivery.

Pair Programming Styles at a Glance

Understanding different pair programming styles is necessary to choose the right approach for your team and context. Each style offers unique collaboration dynamics, learning opportunities, and execution patterns. The following table below provides a concise comparison to help you grasp the core differences quickly.

Style	How It Works	Ideal For	Tools and Setup	Key Strengths	Considerations
Driver-Navigator	One developer types (Driver) while the other plans, reviews, and guides (Navigator). They switch roles periodically.	General development, bug fixing, code reviews, and collaborative tasks.	Local IDEs, shared physical setup, or screen-sharing tools like VS Code Live Share or JetBrains Code with me.	Encourages collaboration and shared understanding; ideal for keeping code aligned with design intent.	One partner may become passive, if roles are not rotated frequently.
Ping-Pong	One developer writes a failing test. The other writes code to make it pass. Then they switch roles and continue.	Test-driven development (TDD), modular design, writing robust test cases.	Unit testing frameworks (Jest, Mocha), version control, CI/CD integration.	Reinforces clean architecture and TDD discipline; promotes smaller, testable units of work.	Requires familiarity with TDD and strong communication to stay in sync.
Strong-Style	The Navigator gives explicit instructions; the Driver types exactly what they are told. Driver does not make independent decisions.	Mentoring sessions, high-stakes refactoring, architectural prototyping.	Remote IDE pairing tools, clear audio/ video setup.	Ensures clarity of intent and supports knowledge transfer; very effective for upskilling.	May feel slow and rigid; requires patience and psychological safety.

Remote Pairing	Follows any of the above styles but in a fully remote setup. Communication happens via audio/video and shared coding environments.	Distributed teams, remote-first environments, and cross-time zone collaboration.	Zoom, Microsoft Teams, VS Code Live Share, Tuple, collaborative IDEs.	Enables real-time teamwork regardless of location; supports hybrid work culture.	Success depends on stable tools, time zone alignment, and proactive communication.

***Table 8.4:** Concise Comparison of Four Major Pair Programming Styles, Highlighting their Core Workflow, Ideal Use Cases, Strengths, and Considerations for Practical Adoption*

Conclusion

To sum up, GitHub Copilot has redefined how developers and teams approach software development. Acting as an AI-powered pair programmer, Copilot enhances productivity, collaboration, and code quality across diverse workflows and scenarios. It plays multiple roles, such as a navigator, it bridges knowledge gaps, ensures code consistency, and enforces best practices; as a mentor, it accelerates learning curves for new frameworks and technologies; and as a collaborator, it fosters seamless teamwork in both co-located and remote settings. Through real-world success stories, and measurable impact metrics, it is clear that Copilot transforms challenges into opportunities, empowering developers to focus more on innovation and strategic problem-solving. With its ability to save time, reduce errors, and improve team dynamics, **GitHub Copilot is truly a game-changer for modern software development**.

As the journey with GitHub Copilot continues, the next chapter delves deeper into **Advanced Techniques with Copilot**, where we will explore how to unlock even greater efficiencies, harness sophisticated coding patterns, and push the boundaries of AI-assisted development.

Multiple Choice Questions

1. What role does Copilot primarily play in pair programming?
    a. Team Lead
    b. AI Navigator
    c. Driver
    d. QA Tester
2. How does Copilot improve collaboration among team members?
    a. By writing documentation
    b. By automating manual testing
    c. By generating standardized and consistent code patterns
    d. By replacing human interactions
3. Which GitHub Copilot feature helps identify missing edge cases during development?
    a. Boilerplate code generation
    b. Real-time error detection and corrections
    c. Auto-completion of comments
    d. Version control

4. In which scenario is Remote Pair Programming most effective?
   a. Real-time debugging in the same office
   b. Collaboration between distributed teams
   c. Training junior developers onsite
   d. Handling isolated quick tasks
5. What does a key metric Copilot contribute to during development?
   a. Marketing analytics
   b. Lines of duplicate code generated
   c. Uniformity in coding standards across teams
   d. Hardware optimization
6. How does Copilot save time in unit testing?
   a. By creating detailed test plans
   b. By generating comprehensive test cases for functions
   c. By automating deployment pipelines
   d. By replacing manual testers
7. Which of the following is a unique feature of Mob Programming?
   a. Driver-Navigator roles in different locations.
   b. A single Driver with multiple Navigators working simultaneously.
   c. Using Copilot without a Driver.
   d. Code reviews before collaboration begins.
8. What is the approximate percentage of time saved in repetitive tasks, when using Copilot?
   a. 10–20%
   b. 30–40%
   c. 40–60%
   d. 70–80%
9. Which Copilot feature helps developers quickly adapt to new frameworks?
   a. Prompt chaining
   b. Knowledge Navigator role
   c. Workflow Automation
   d. Real-time error detection
10. What is one key impact of Copilot in real-world development scenarios?
    a. Reducing project budgets
    b. Eliminating the need for QA teams
    c. Accelerating development cycles, and improving code quality
    d. Simplifying hardware upgrades

Answers

1. b
2. c
3. b
4. b
5. c
6. b
7. b
8. c
9. b
10. c

Chapter 9
Advanced Techniques with Copilot

Introduction

GitHub Copilot is more than just a code completion tool–it is a collaborative partner that can adapt to your needs, and amplify your productivity. At the heart of its capabilities, lies the art of Prompt Engineering, the process of crafting precise, and actionable prompts to extract meaningful outputs. This chapter explores the advanced techniques for using Copilot, starting with the foundational principles of prompt engineering, and progressively delves into topics, such as refactoring legacy code, performance optimization, automation, and understanding Copilot's architecture.

Hence, whether you are a developer tackling complex projects or a team seeking to streamline workflows, this chapter equips you with actionable insights and techniques to maximize Copilot's potential.

Structure

In this chapter, we will discuss the following topics:

- Prompt Engineering: Principles and Techniques
- Refactoring Legacy Code with Copilot
- Performance Optimization and Code Tuning
- Automating Code Generation and Repetitive Tasks
- Integrating AI Suggestions into Your Workflow
- Understanding the AI Model and Training Process
- Security and Privacy Considerations
- Copilot's Limitations and Areas for Improvement
- Best Practices to Mitigate Limitations
- Real-World Case Study: Copilot's Impact in an Enterprise Setting

Prompt Engineering: Principles and Techniques

Prompt engineering is the practice of crafting input queries (prompts) to effectively interact with AI systems, such as GitHub Copilot. The quality of the prompt directly impacts the relevance, accuracy, and contextuality of the AI's output. In fact, by refining prompts, developers can:

- Solve complex problems with fewer iterations.
- Generate efficient, high-quality code aligned with best practices.
- Tailor outputs to their specific needs, reducing manual intervention.

Importance of Effective Prompt Engineering:

- **Precision:** Vague prompts lead to incomplete or incorrect outputs. Clear and structured prompts ensure that the AI understands the task.
- **Time-Saving:** Well-crafted prompts can reduce trial-and-error, enabling quicker delivery of results.
- **Scalability:** Prompts can be reused across projects for consistency, particularly in large-scale development or testing workflows.

Core Principles of Prompt Engineering

- **Clarity and Specificity:** Effective prompt engineering starts with precision. Thus, by eliminating ambiguity, and being explicit about the task, you help the AI generate more relevant and accurate results.
  - **Why It Matters**: Ambiguity leads to misinterpretation. Clearly defined instructions yield precise outputs.
  - **Example**:
    - **Poor**: "*Generate an API endpoint.*"
    - **Better**: "*Write a* Node.js REST API *endpoint for user login, validating credentials, and returning a* JWT *token.*"
- **Contextual Completeness:** Including background details, constraints, and expectations ensures that the AI understands the full scope of the task, reducing the chances of generic or off-track responses.
  - **Why It Matters**: Providing background or constraints ensures that the AI operates within the desired boundaries.
  - **Example**:
    - **Poor**: "*Write a function to fetch data.*"
    - **Better**: "*Write a Python function using requests to fetch JSON data from a REST API, and handle timeout exceptions.*"
- **Iterative Refinement:** For complex tasks, refining prompts through smaller, manageable steps improves the quality of each output, and allows you to progressively guide the AI toward the desired result.
  - **Why It Matters**: Breaking complex tasks into smaller steps improves focus and output quality.
  - **Example**:
    - **Iteration 1**: "*Write a function to process orders.*"
    - **Iteration 2**: "*Write a function to process orders, including validation for inventory and payment status.*"
- **Examples of Guidance:**
  - **Why It Matters:** Examples set clear expectations for structure, style, and behavior.
  - **Example Prompt:**
    - `"Given these examples, write a function to calculate the median of an array."`
- **Actionable Instructions:**
  - **Why It Matters**: Specific directives, such as *generate*, *optimize*, or *validate* help the AI focus on the task.

- **Example**:
  - **Poor**: *"Fix this code."*
  - **Better**: *"Refactor this code to reduce time complexity, and improve readability."*

- **Feedback and Adjustment**
  - **Why It Matters:** Continuously refining prompts based on results ensures higher accuracy and efficiency over time.

Prompting Techniques

- **Zero-Shot Prompting:** Zero-shot prompting involves giving the AI a direct instruction, without any prior examples. It relies entirely on the model's pre-learned knowledge to generate a relevant output.
  - **Definition**: Providing no prior examples, relying solely on the prompt.
  - **Use Case**: Simple, well-defined tasks.
  - **Example**:

    "Write a Python function to calculate the factorial of a number using recursion."

- **One-Shot Prompting:** One-shot prompting provides a single example to set the context before asking the model to perform a similar task, helping improve accuracy for moderately complex requests.
  - **Definition:** Providing one example to guide the AI.
  - **Use Case:** Tasks requiring slightly more context.
  - **Example Prompt:**

    # Example: Calculate factorial

    ```
    def factorial(n):
        if n == 0:
            return 1
        return n * factorial(n - 1)
    ```

  Refer the complete code generated at the following GitHub Repo link:

  chapter9-copilot-advanced-techniques\prompt_engineering\zero_shot.js

  # Task: Write a function to calculate the sum of an array using recursion.

- **Few-Shot Prompting:** Few-shot prompting builds on the concept of contextual learning by supplying multiple examples, enabling the AI to better understand patterns, and generate responses aligned with the desired format or logic.
  - **Definition:** Providing multiple examples for nuanced or complex tasks.
  - **Use Case:** Ambiguous or highly contextual tasks.
  - **Example Prompt:**

    # Example 1: Calculate factorial

    ```
    def factorial(n):
        if n == 0:
            return 1
        return n * factorial(n - 1)
    ```

  Refer the complete code generated at the following GitHub Repo link:

  chapter9-copilot-advanced-techniques\prompt_engineering\few_shot.js

 # Example 2: Calculate the sum of an array

```
def sum_array(arr):
    if len(arr) == 0:
        return 0
    return arr[0] + sum_array(arr[1:])
```

Refer the complete code generated at the following GitHub Repo link:

chapter9-copilot-advanced-techniques\prompt_engineering\one_shot.js

 # Task: Write a function to calculate the nth Fibonacci number using recursion.

Real-World Scenario: Prompting for Web Testing Automation

You need to generate test cases for automating login functionality using Playwright.

Prompt 1: Basic (Zero-Shot)

```
"Write a Playwright test for login functionality."
```

Output:

Refer the complete code generated at the following GitHub Repo link:

chapter9-copilot-advanced-techniques\prompt_engineering\playwright-tests\login_zero_shot.spec.js

This Copilot-suggested test script demonstrates a basic login flow using Playwright, where the automation navigates to the login page, enters credentials, performs the login action, and verifies success by checking for a logout button. It is a foundational test that can be extended for more advanced login validations.

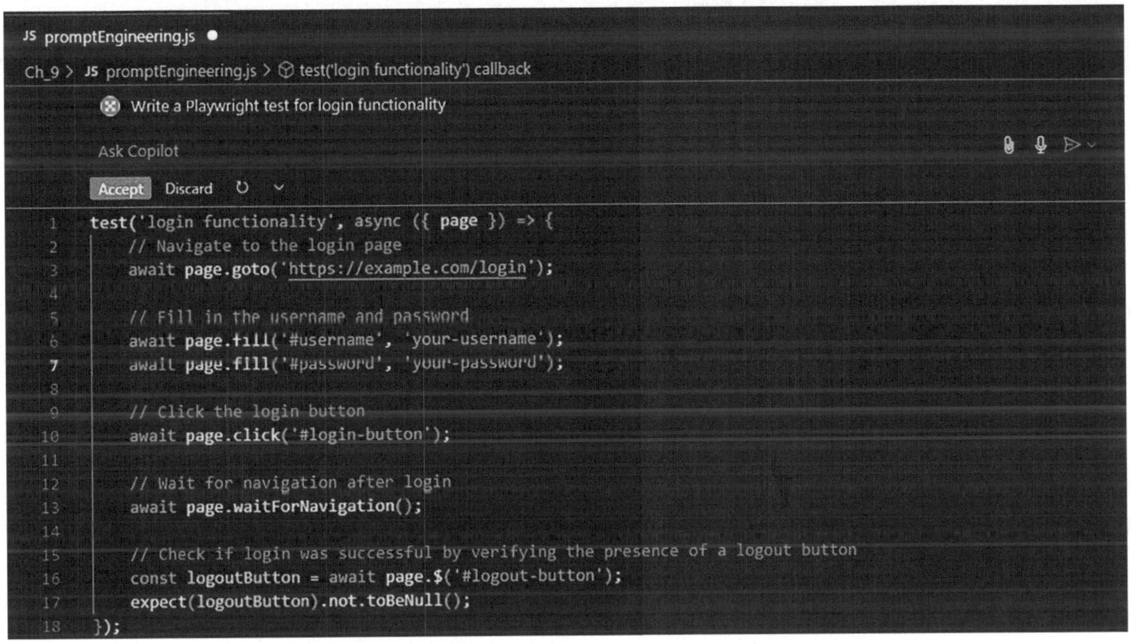

JS promptEngineering.js ●
Ch_9 > JS promptEngineering.js > test('login functionality') callback
Write a Playwright test for login functionality
Ask Copilot
Accept Discard

```
test('login functionality', async ({ page }) => {
    // Navigate to the login page
    await page.goto('https://example.com/login');

    // Fill in the username and password
    await page.fill('#username', 'your-username');
    await page.fill('#password', 'your-password');

    // Click the login button
    await page.click('#login-button');

    // Wait for navigation after login
    await page.waitForNavigation();

    // Check if login was successful by verifying the presence of a logout button
    const logoutButton = await page.$('#logout-button');
    expect(logoutButton).not.toBeNull();
});
```

Figure 9.1: *GitHub Copilot-generated Playwright Test for Validating Login Functionality Using Username and Password Fields, Followed by Post-login UI Verification*

Analysis: The test only covers a happy path scenario, with no validations or edge-case handling. This demonstrates the limitations of zero-shot prompting for complex tasks.

Prompt 2: Contextualized (One-Shot Prompting)

> **"Using the following example, write a Playwright test for login functionality that includes error handling for invalid credentials."**

Refer the complete code generated at the following GitHub Repo link:

chapter9-copilot-advanced-techniques\prompt_engineering\playwright-tests\login_one_shot.spec.js

This Playwright test demonstrates a **one-shot prompting** approach, where a single example helps guide GitHub Copilot to generate a test case that handles invalid login scenarios. It validates error handling by ensuring the appearance of a specific error message, when incorrect credentials are submitted.

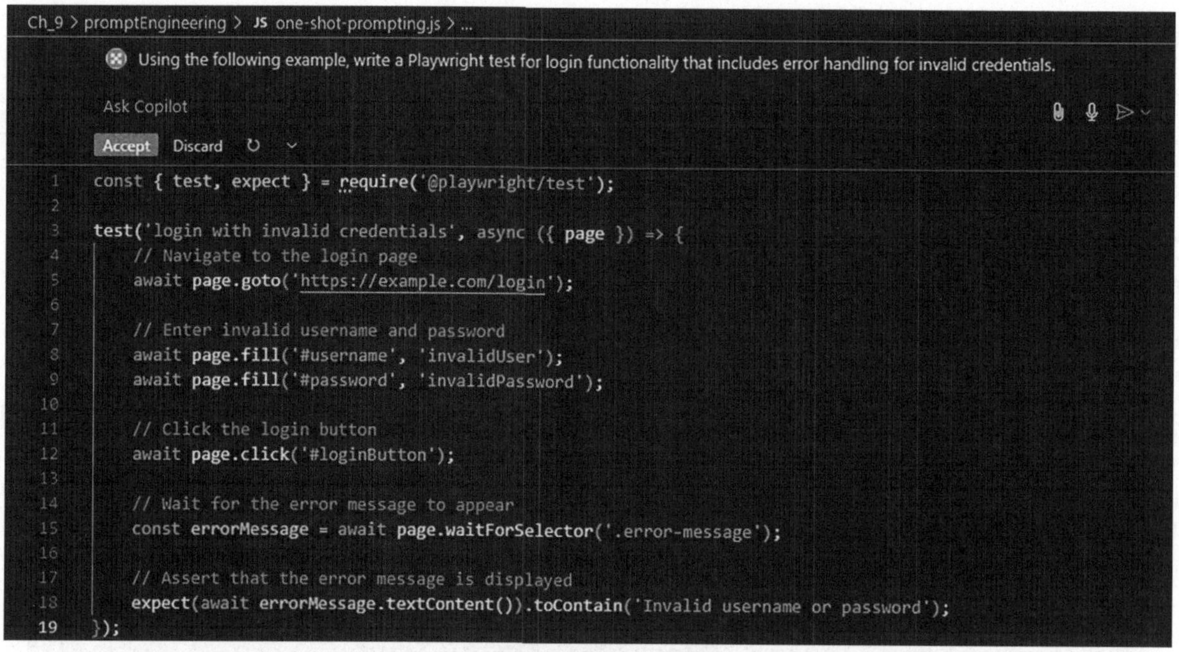

Ch_9 > promptEngineering > JS one-shot-prompting.js > ...

Using the following example, write a Playwright test for login functionality that includes error handling for invalid credentials.

Ask Copilot

Accept Discard

```
const { test, expect } = require('@playwright/test');

test('login with invalid credentials', async ({ page }) => {
    // Navigate to the login page
    await page.goto('https://example.com/login');

    // Enter invalid username and password
    await page.fill('#username', 'invalidUser');
    await page.fill('#password', 'invalidPassword');

    // Click the login button
    await page.click('#loginButton');

    // Wait for the error message to appear
    const errorMessage = await page.waitForSelector('.error-message');

    // Assert that the error message is displayed
    expect(await errorMessage.textContent()).toContain('Invalid username or password');
});
```

Figure 9.2: *GitHub Copilot-generated Playwright Test for Verifying Login Error Handling with Invalid Credentials, Using a One-shot Prompt for Guided Instruction*

Analysis: One-shot prompting builds on a **provided example**, enabling Copilot to expand functionality by generating tests for both valid and invalid scenarios. This approach adds robustness to the test suite.

Prompt 3: Refined (Few-Shot):

> **"Write a Playwright test for login functionality. Include both positive and negative test cases, ensuring proper error messages are displayed for invalid credentials."**

Output:

Refer the complete code generated at the following GitHub Repo link:

chapter9-copilot-advanced-techniques\prompt_engineering\playwright-tests\login_few_shot.spec.ts

Analysis: Few-shot prompting produces a **comprehensive test suite** covering positive, negative, and edge cases with additional input validation. It demonstrates the AI's ability to handle nuanced requirements.

Metrics of Effective Prompt Engineering

Prompt engineering plays a critical role in shaping the quality and effectiveness of AI-generated responses. The following table compares the impact of different prompting techniques–Zero-Shot, One-Shot, and Few-Shot–across various dimensions, illustrating how increased guidance leads to better results, improved error handling, and significant time savings.

Aspect	Zero-Shot	One-Shot	Few-Shot
Functionality	Basic functionality (~60%).	Expanded functionality (~75%).	Comprehensive (~90%).
Error Handling	None.	Basic validation for invalid scenarios.	Covers invalid scenarios and edge cases.
Prompt Complexity	Basic instruction	Includes one example for guidance.	Includes multiple examples for clarity.
Time Saved	~30%.	~40%.	~50%.

Table 9.1: *Comparative Overview of Zero-Shot, One-Shot, and Few-Shot Prompting techniques across Functionality, Error Handling, Complexity, and Time Efficiency*

Refactoring Legacy Code with Copilot

Legacy code can hinder development due to its poor structure, outdated patterns, and inefficiency. GitHub Copilot simplifies refactoring by offering intelligent suggestions for modularizing, optimizing, and modernizing the code. By leveraging effective **prompt engineering**, developers can guide Copilot to generate tailored, and optimized outputs.

This section explores **real-world refactoring scenarios**, showcasing the impact of **well-crafted prompts** on the outputs. Comparisons illustrate how prompt quality affects the effectiveness of Copilot's suggestions.

Scenario 1: Modularizing a Monolithic Function

A legacy payroll function handles all computations–gross salary, tax, and net salary–within a single block. This monolithic approach makes debugging, and extending the logic cumbersome.

Legacy Code:

Refer the complete code generated at the following GitHub Repo link:

chapter9-copilot-advanced-techniques\refactoring\legacy_monolithic.js

Before Refactoring Legacy Code: The original payroll calculation function is a monolithic block with all logic embedded directly inside a loop. This approach works functionally, but lacks clarity and separation of concerns, making the code harder to maintain or extend.

Ch_9 > legacyCodeRefactoring > JS Modularizing a Monolithic Function.js > ...

Refactor this function to improve modularity.

```
//Legacy Code:
function calculatePayroll(employees) {
    for (let i = 0; i < employees.length; i++) {
        let grossSalary = employees[i].baseSalary + employees[i].bonus;
        let tax = grossSalary * 0.2;
        employees[i].netSalary = grossSalary - tax;
    }
    return employees;
}
```

Figure 9.3: *Legacy Monolithic Implementation of the Payroll Calculation Function, where All Computations are Embedded in a Single Loop*

Prompt Comparisons+

Prompt 1: Basic Prompt

`"Refactor this function to improve modularity."`

Copilot Output:

Refer the complete code generated at the following GitHub Repo link:

chapter9-copilot-advanced-techniques\refactoring\modularized_basic.js

After Refactoring: This version of the payroll calculation demonstrates a clean, modular approach, where the logic for computing gross salary, tax, and net salary is broken down into discrete helper functions. This refactoring, suggested by GitHub Copilot, enhances code clarity, promotes reusability, and aligns with clean code principles.

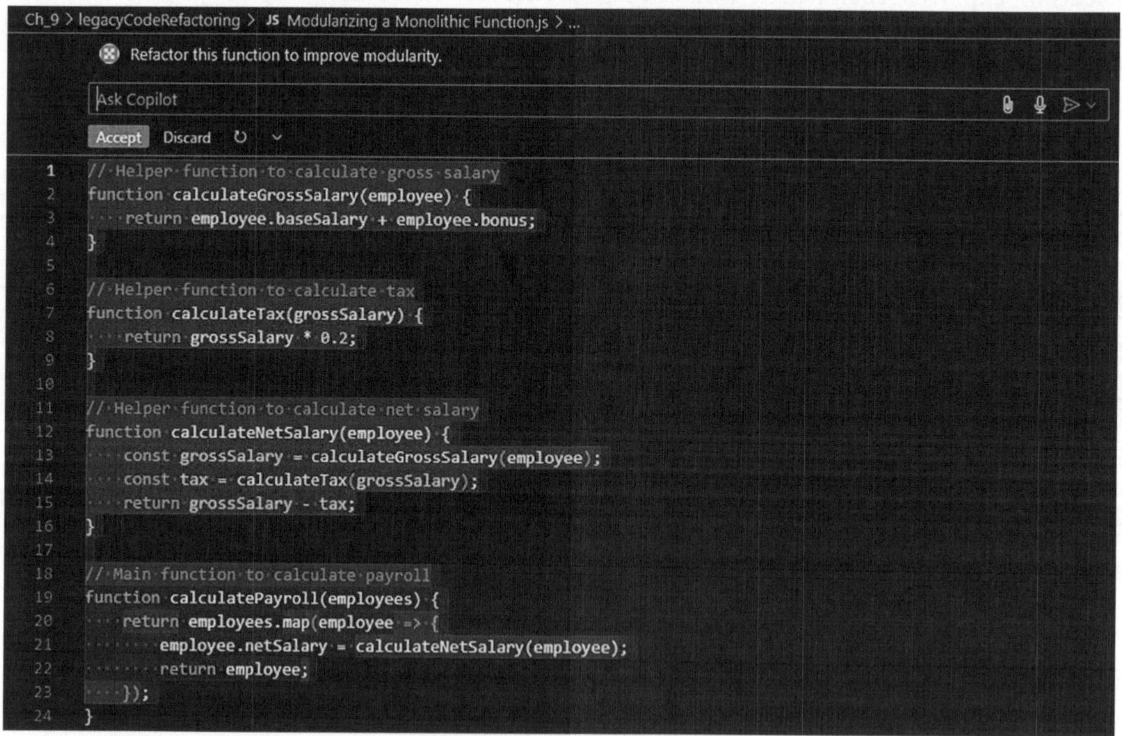


```
// Helper function to calculate gross salary
function calculateGrossSalary(employee) {
    return employee.baseSalary + employee.bonus;
}

// Helper function to calculate tax
function calculateTax(grossSalary) {
    return grossSalary * 0.2;
}

// Helper function to calculate net salary
function calculateNetSalary(employee) {
    const grossSalary = calculateGrossSalary(employee);
    const tax = calculateTax(grossSalary);
    return grossSalary - tax;
}

// Main function to calculate payroll
function calculatePayroll(employees) {
    return employees.map(employee => {
        employee.netSalary = calculateNetSalary(employee);
        return employee;
    });
}
```

Figure 9.4: *Modularized Version of the Payroll Function, Separating Concerns into Discrete Helper Functions for Gross Salary, Tax, and Net Salary Computation*

Analysis:

While the output slightly improves readability (using **`forEach`**), it fails to modularize the logic into reusable components.

Prompt 2: Refined Prompt

```
"Refactor this function by breaking it into smaller, reusable functions for
gross salary, tax, and net salary calculation."
```

Copilot Output:

Refer the complete code generated at the following GitHub Repo link:

chapter9-copilot-advanced-techniques\refactoring\modularized_refined.js

The refactored version modularizes the logic into distinct functions—**`calculateGrossSalary`**, **`calculateTax`**, and **`calculateNetSalary`**—which improves readability, promotes reusability, and adheres to clean code principles. This restructuring allows for isolated testing of salary components and easier adaptation to future payroll changes.

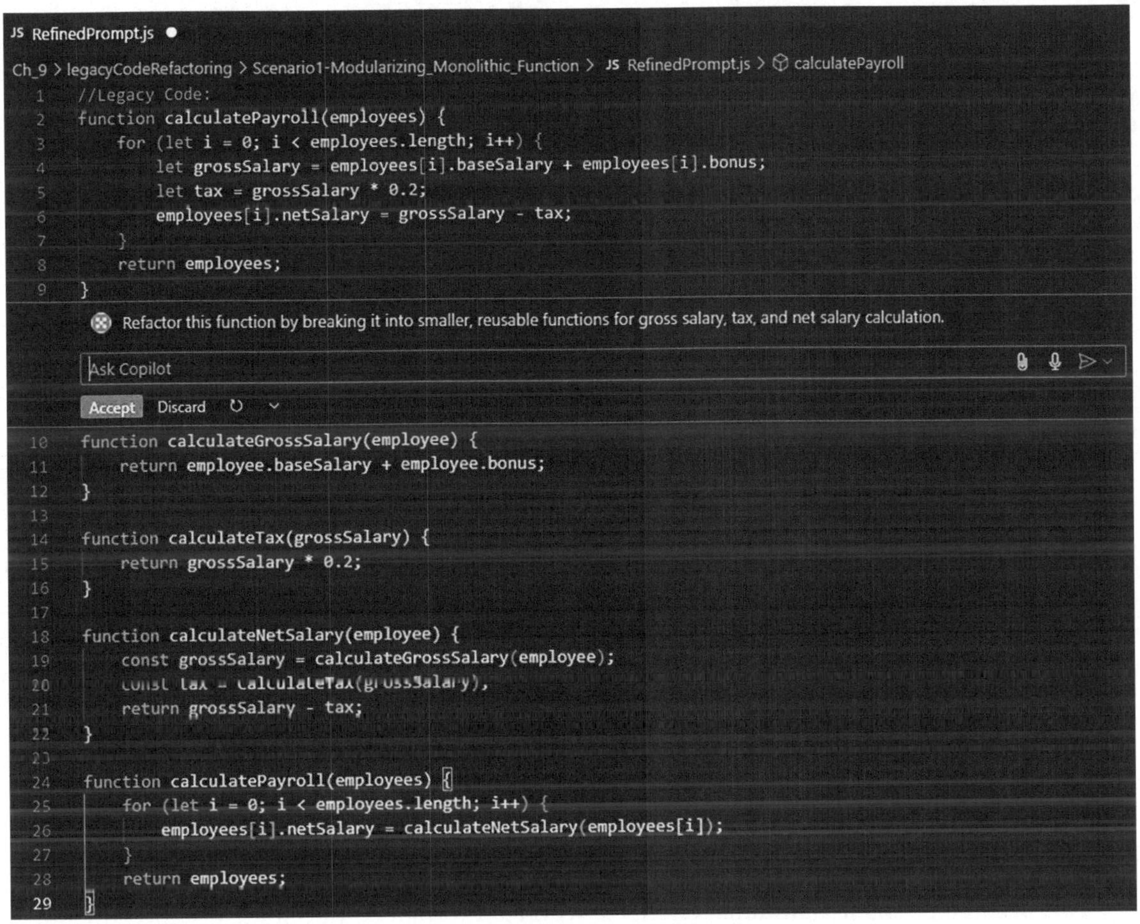

```
JS RefinedPrompt.js ●
Ch_9 > legacyCodeRefactoring > Scenario1-Modularizing_Monolithic_Function > JS RefinedPrompt.js > calculatePayroll
//Legacy Code:
function calculatePayroll(employees) {
    for (let i = 0; i < employees.length; i++) {
        let grossSalary = employees[i].baseSalary + employees[i].bonus;
        let tax = grossSalary * 0.2;
        employees[i].netSalary = grossSalary - tax;
    }
    return employees;
}
Refactor this function by breaking it into smaller, reusable functions for gross salary, tax, and net salary calculation.
Ask Copilot
Accept  Discard
function calculateGrossSalary(employee) {
    return employee.baseSalary + employee.bonus;
}

function calculateTax(grossSalary) {
    return grossSalary * 0.2;
}

function calculateNetSalary(employee) {
    const grossSalary = calculateGrossSalary(employee);
    const tax = calculateTax(grossSalary);
    return grossSalary - tax;
}

function calculatePayroll(employees) {
    for (let i = 0; i < employees.length; i++) {
        employees[i].netSalary = calculateNetSalary(employees[i]);
    }
    return employees;
}
```

Figure 9.5: *Refactored Implementation of the Payroll Calculation Using Modular Helper Functions for Gross Salary, Tax, and Net Salary, Enhancing Clarity, Maintainability, and Testability*

Analysis:

- The refined prompt yields highly modular and reusable code.
- Functions, such as **`calculateGrossSalary`** and **`calculateTax`** can be reused in other parts of the application.

Prompt 3: Advanced Prompt

```
"Refactor this function for modularity and scalability. Ensure that it handles
additional salary components, such as allowances or deductions in the future."
```

Copilot Output:

Refer the complete code generated at the following GitHub Repo link:

chapter9-copilot-advanced-techniques\refactoring\nested_loops_advanced.js

The following screenshot demonstrates how GitHub Copilot refactors a monolithic payroll function into modular, maintainable components by applying clean coding principles. This transformation enhances scalability, and prepares the codebase for future salary component extensions.

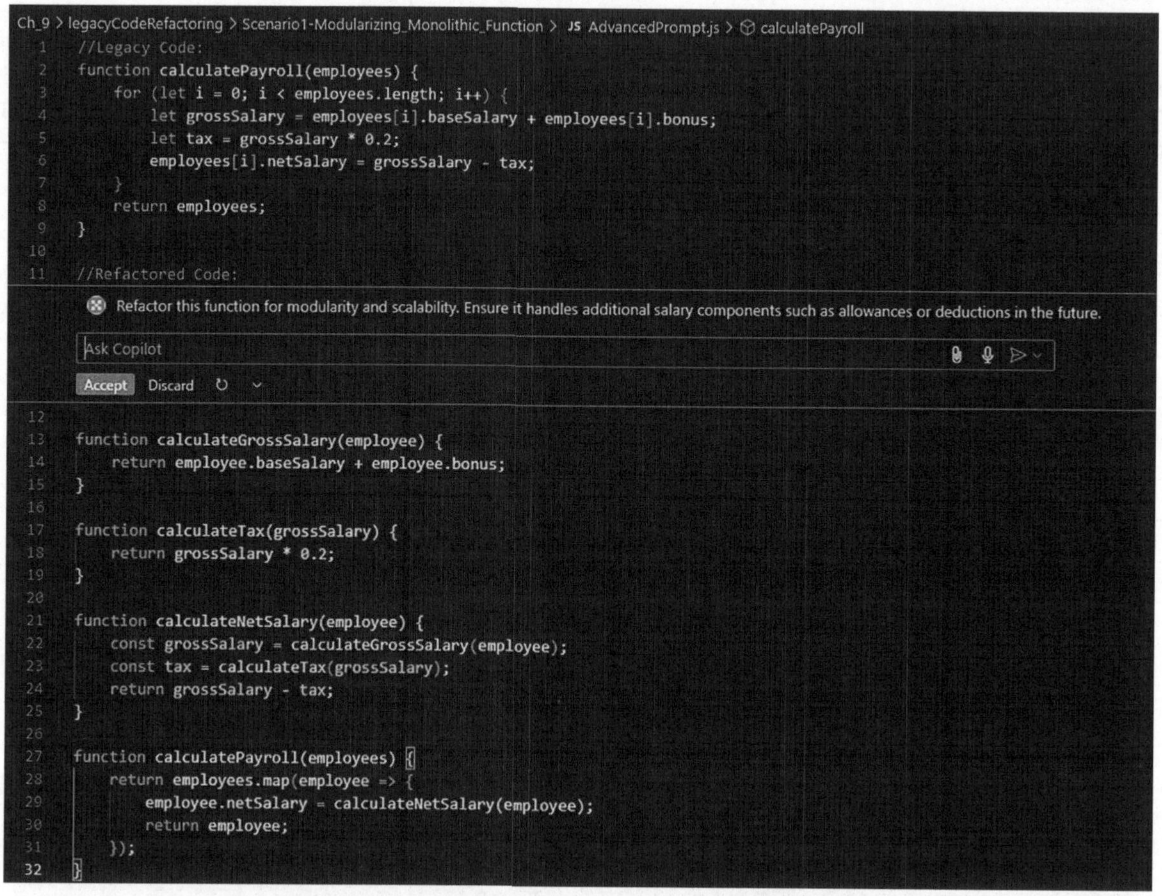

```
Ch_9 > legacyCodeRefactoring > Scenario1-Modularizing_Monolithic_Function > JS AdvancedPrompt.js > calculatePayroll
//Legacy Code:
function calculatePayroll(employees) {
    for (let i = 0; i < employees.length; i++) {
        let grossSalary = employees[i].baseSalary + employees[i].bonus;
        let tax = grossSalary * 0.2;
        employees[i].netSalary = grossSalary - tax;
    }
    return employees;
}

//Refactored Code:
Refactor this function for modularity and scalability. Ensure it handles additional salary components such as allowances or deductions in the future.
Ask Copilot
Accept  Discard

function calculateGrossSalary(employee) {
    return employee.baseSalary + employee.bonus;
}

function calculateTax(grossSalary) {
    return grossSalary * 0.2;
}

function calculateNetSalary(employee) {
    const grossSalary = calculateGrossSalary(employee);
    const tax = calculateTax(grossSalary);
    return grossSalary - tax;
}

function calculatePayroll(employees) {
    return employees.map(employee => {
        employee.netSalary = calculateNetSalary(employee);
        return employee;
    });
}
```

Figure 9.6: *GitHub Copilot Refactors a Monolithic Payroll Function into Modular Components for Better Clarity, Scalability, and Future Extensibility*

Analysis:

- The advanced prompt anticipates future requirements, such as allowances or deductions.
- This scalability ensures minimal changes, when additional components are introduced.

Effectiveness of Prompts for Refactoring

The quality of prompts significantly influences the effectiveness of AI-assisted refactoring. This table compares how basic, refined, and advanced prompts impact the key software engineering aspects such as modularity, reusability, scalability, and output complexity.

Aspect	Basic Prompt	Refined Prompt	Advanced Prompt
Modularity	Minimal	Good	Excellent
Reusability	None	High	Very High
Scalability	Not handled	Limited	Fully scalable
Output Complexity	Simplistic	Moderately improved	Future-proof, handles edge cases

Table 9.2: *Comparison of Refactoring Outcomes Based on the Quality of GitHub Copilot Prompts across Various Development Dimensions*

Scenario 2: Optimizing Nested Loops

A legacy script for identifying duplicate transactions uses nested loops, leading to poor performance for large datasets.

Legacy Code:

```
function findDuplicateTransactions(transactions) {
    let duplicates = [];
    for (let i = 0; i < transactions.length; i++) {
        for (let j = i + 1; j < transactions.length; j++) {
            if (transactions[i].id === transactions[j].id) {
                duplicates.push(transactions[i]);
                break;
            }
        }
    }
    return duplicates;
}
```

Refer the complete code generated at the following GitHub Repo link:

chapter9-copilot-advanced-techniques\refactoring\nested_loops_legacy.js

Prompt Comparisons:

Prompt 1: Basic Prompt

```
"Optimize this function to improve performance."
```

Copilot Output: This screenshot highlights how GitHub Copilot optimizes a nested loop function for detecting duplicate transactions by refactoring it into a more efficient approach using a hash map.

Refer the complete code generated at the following GitHub Repo link:

chapter9-copilot-advanced-techniques\refactoring\nested_loops_optimized.js

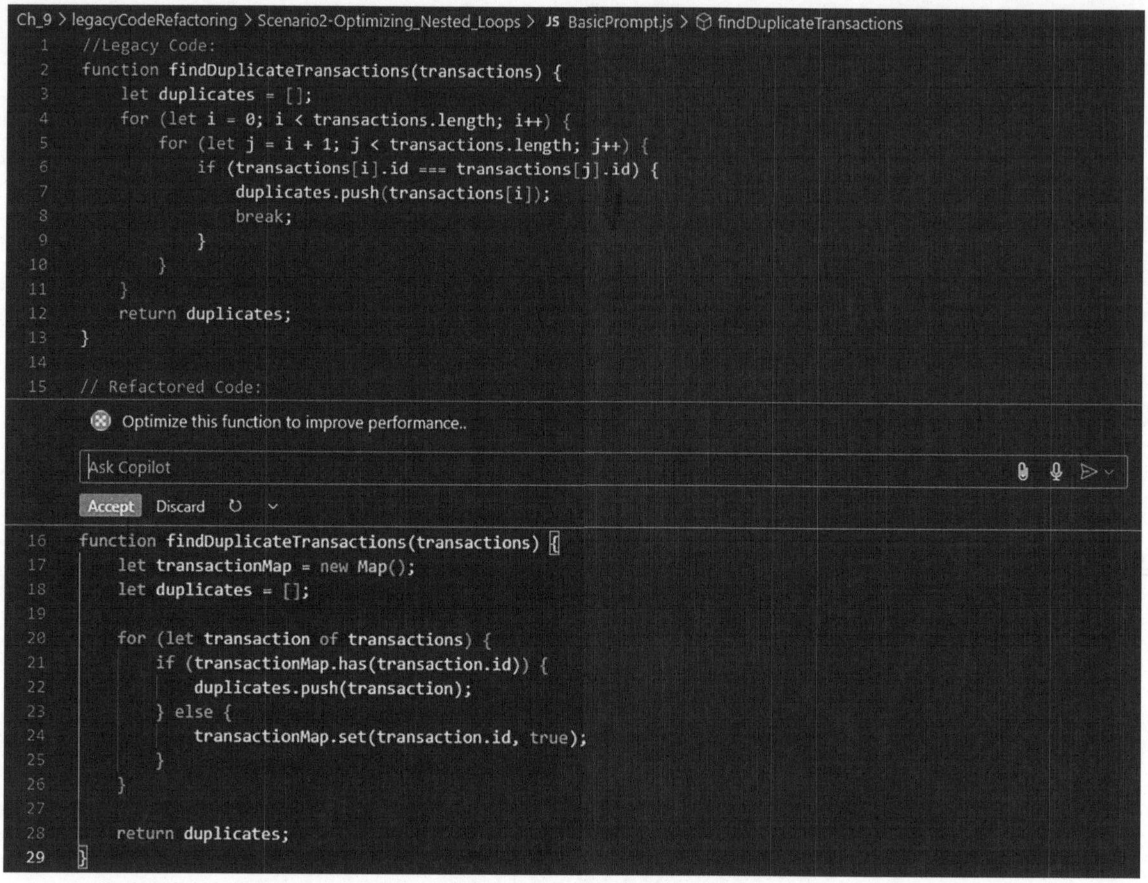

Ch_9 > legacyCodeRefactoring > Scenario2-Optimizing_Nested_Loops > JS BasicPrompt.js > findDuplicateTransactions

```
//Legacy Code:
function findDuplicateTransactions(transactions) {
    let duplicates = [];
    for (let i = 0; i < transactions.length; i++) {
        for (let j = i + 1; j < transactions.length; j++) {
            if (transactions[i].id === transactions[j].id) {
                duplicates.push(transactions[i]);
                break;
            }
        }
    }
    return duplicates;
}

// Refactored Code:
```

Optimize this function to improve performance..

Ask Copilot

Accept Discard

```
function findDuplicateTransactions(transactions) {
    let transactionMap = new Map();
    let duplicates = [];

    for (let transaction of transactions) {
        if (transactionMap.has(transaction.id)) {
            duplicates.push(transaction);
        } else {
            transactionMap.set(transaction.id, true);
        }
    }

    return duplicates;
}
```

Figure 9.7: *Refactored Nested Loop Logic into a Hash Map-based Solution Using GitHub Copilot for Improved Performance and Reduced Time Complexity.*

Analysis:

- The nested loops are replaced by a Set, reducing time complexity to `O(n)`.
- The prompt successfully optimizes performance, but lacks robustness for advanced requirements.

Prompt 2: Advanced Prompt

> **`"Optimize this function for performance, and ensure it logs duplicate transactions for debugging purposes."`**

Copilot Output: This enhanced version of the refactored function showcases how GitHub Copilot not only improves the performance of a nested loop by using a hash map, but also adds inline logging to trace duplicate transactions for debugging.

Refer the complete code generated at the following GitHub Repo link:

chapter9-copilot-advanced-techniques\refactoring\nested_loops_advanced.js

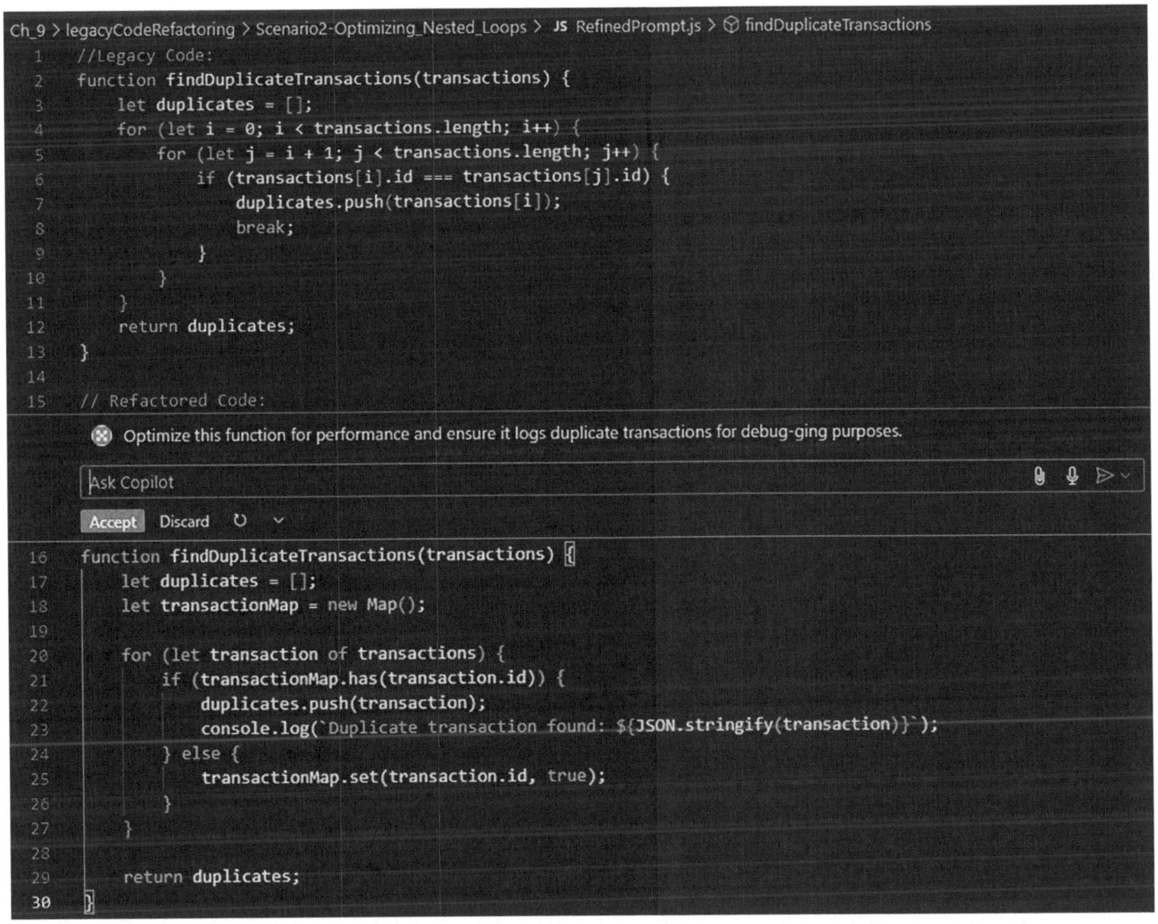

```
Ch_9 > legacyCodeRefactoring > Scenario2-Optimizing_Nested_Loops > JS RefinedPrompt.js > findDuplicateTransactions
//Legacy Code:
function findDuplicateTransactions(transactions) {
    let duplicates = [];
    for (let i = 0; i < transactions.length; i++) {
        for (let j = i + 1; j < transactions.length; j++) {
            if (transactions[i].id === transactions[j].id) {
                duplicates.push(transactions[i]);
                break;
            }
        }
    }
    return duplicates;
}

// Refactored Code:
Optimize this function for performance and ensure it logs duplicate transactions for debug-ging purposes.
Ask Copilot
Accept  Discard
function findDuplicateTransactions(transactions) {
    let duplicates = [];
    let transactionMap = new Map();

    for (let transaction of transactions) {
        if (transactionMap.has(transaction.id)) {
            duplicates.push(transaction);
            console.log(`Duplicate transaction found: ${JSON.stringify(transaction)}`);
        } else {
            transactionMap.set(transaction.id, true);
        }
    }

    return duplicates;
}
```

Figure 9.8: *Refactored with Performance Optimization and Debug Logging–GitHub Copilot Transforms Nested Loops into a Hash Map with Real-time Duplicate Tracing*

Analysis:

- Enhances functionality by adding logging for debugging.
- Offers a more practical approach to real-world debugging and analysis.

Takeaways from Scenario Comparisons:

- **Prompt Specificity:** The more specific the prompt, the more refined and relevant the output.
- **Contextualization:** Including requirements, such as future scalability or debugging improves functionality.
- **Iterative Refinement:** Start with a basic prompt, and progressively refine it for enhanced results.

Refactoring legacy code with GitHub Copilot becomes exponentially more effective with the right prompts. Thus, by crafting prompts that incorporate modularity, scalability, and context-specific requirements, developers can achieve cleaner, more maintainable code, with significantly reduced efforts.

Performance Optimization and Code Tuning

Performance optimization is crucial for scalable and efficient applications. Poorly written code can lead to high resource consumption, slower execution, and scalability issues. GitHub Copilot assists developers by:

1. Identifying performance bottlenecks

2. Suggesting optimized algorithms and data structures
3. Simplifying complex tuning tasks with tailored suggestions

Thus, this section explores how Copilot facilitates performance optimization through real-world examples, and practical insights.

Real-World Scenario: Optimizing Data Processing

A large dataset containing millions of records needs to be filtered and aggregated efficiently. The legacy implementation uses standard loops and array methods, resulting in slow performance.

Legacy Code:

```
function processData(records) {
    let totalValue = 0;
    let filtered = [];

    for (let i = 0; i < records.length; i++) {
        if (records[i].category === 'A') {
            totalValue += records[i].value;
            filtered.push(records[i]);
        }
    }

    return { totalValue, filtered };
}
```

Refer the complete code generated at the following GitHub Repo link:

chapter9-copilot-advanced-techniques\performance_optimization\data_processing_legacy.js

Optimized Code with Copilot:

Prompt:

```
"Optimize this code for better performance using modern JavaScript methods and
reduce memory consumption."
```

Output:

Refer the complete code generated at the following GitHub Repo link:

chapter9-copilot-advanced-techniques\performance_optimization\data_processing_optimized.js

This screenshot highlights how GitHub Copilot enhances a traditional loop-based data processing function by leveraging modern JavaScript array methods, such as filter, improving both readability and performance.

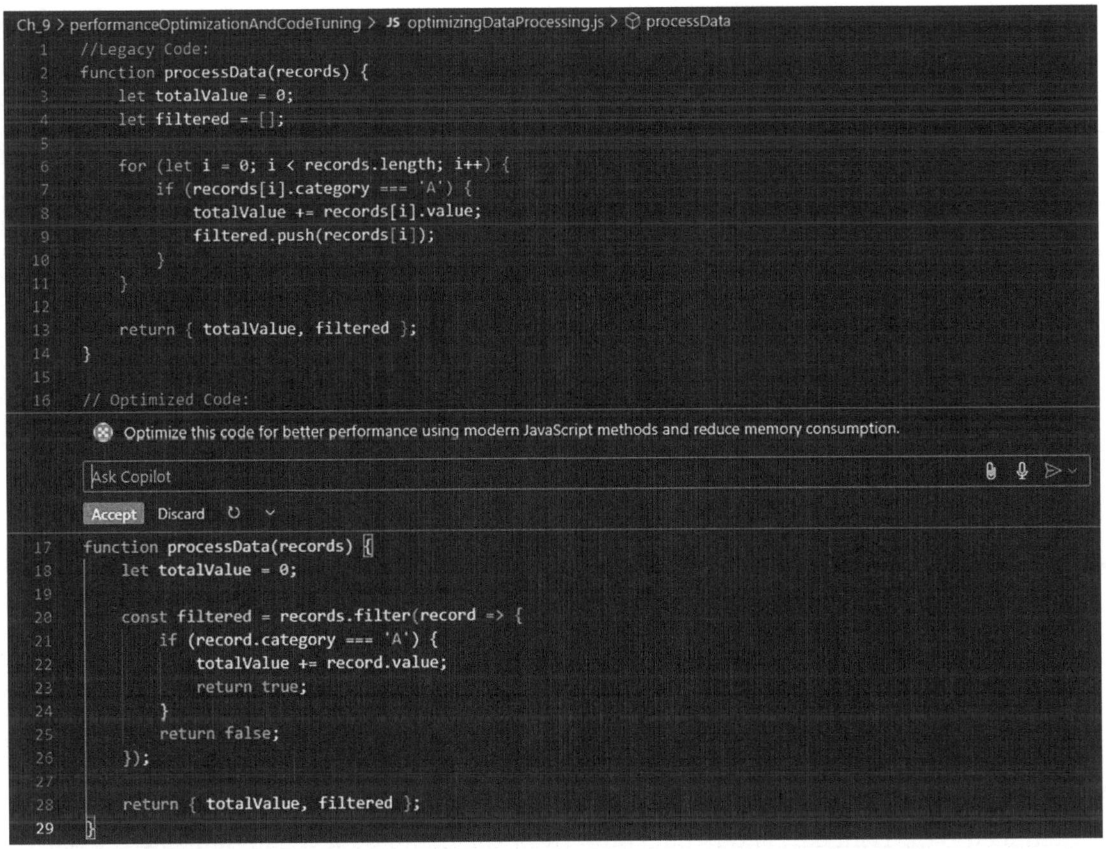

```
Ch_9 > performanceOptimizationAndCodeTuning > JS optimizingDataProcessing.js > processData
//Legacy Code:
function processData(records) {
    let totalValue = 0;
    let filtered = [];

    for (let i = 0; i < records.length; i++) {
        if (records[i].category === 'A') {
            totalValue += records[i].value;
            filtered.push(records[i]);
        }
    }

    return { totalValue, filtered };
}

// Optimized Code:
Optimize this code for better performance using modern JavaScript methods and reduce memory consumption.
Ask Copilot
Accept  Discard
function processData(records) {
    let totalValue = 0;

    const filtered = records.filter(record => {
        if (record.category === 'A') {
            totalValue += record.value;
            return true;
        }
        return false;
    });

    return { totalValue, filtered };
}
```

***Figure 9.9:** Legacy Loop Refactored Using filter () with Inline Logic–GitHub Copilot Reduces Memory Usage, and Boosts performance with modern JavaScript practices.*

Impact:

- **Efficiency:** The reduced use of filter improves both readability and execution speed.
- **Memory Optimization:** Processes data in fewer iterations, reducing memory overhead.
- **Scalability:** Easily handles large datasets, without significant performance degradation.

Scenario: Improving Query Performance

A backend API fetches and processes data from a relational database. The original implementation retrieves all rows and filters them in application logic.

Legacy Code:

```
async function getHighValueCustomers() {
    const customers = await db.query('SELECT * FROM customers');
    return customers.filter(customer => customer.totalSpend > 10000);
}
```

Optimized Code with Copilot:

Prompt:

"Optimize this code to perform filtering at the database query level to reduce unnecessary data processing."

This example shows how GitHub Copilot optimizes an inefficient client-side filtering operation by moving the filtering logic directly into the database query, significantly reducing data transfer and processing overhead.

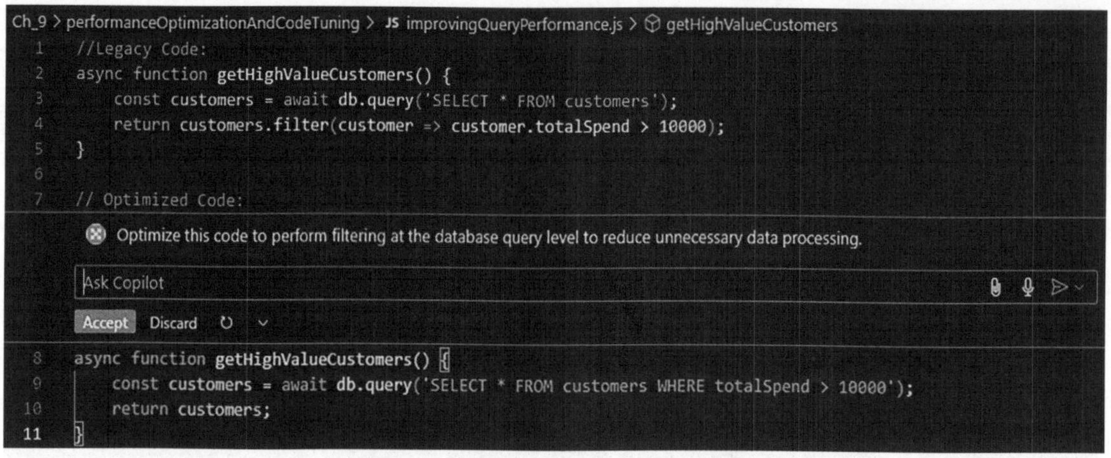

```
Ch_9 > performanceOptimizationAndCodeTuning > JS improvingQueryPerformance.js > getHighValueCustomers
//Legacy Code:
async function getHighValueCustomers() {
    const customers = await db.query('SELECT * FROM customers');
    return customers.filter(customer => customer.totalSpend > 10000);
}

// Optimized Code:
    Optimize this code to perform filtering at the database query level to reduce unnecessary data processing.
    Ask Copilot
    Accept  Discard
async function getHighValueCustomers() {
    const customers = await db.query('SELECT * FROM customers WHERE totalSpend > 10000');
    return customers;
}
```

***Figure 9.10**: GitHub Copilot Shifts Filtering from Application Code to SQL, Optimizing Performance by Reducing Unnecessary Data Handling*

Output:

```
async function getHighValueCustomers() {
    const customers = await db.query('SELECT * FROM customers WHERE totalSpend
> 10000');
    return customers;
}
```

Impact:

- **Reduced Data Transfer:** Filters data directly at the database level, minimizing the data sent to the application.
- **Faster Processing:** Eliminates the need for in-app filtering, improving API response times.
- **Resource Optimization:** Reduces server CPU and memory usage for large datasets.

How Copilot Enhances Optimization Tasks:

- **Algorithm Suggestions**: Copilot recommends efficient algorithms, such as switching from nested loops to hash-based lookups.
- **Library Integrations**: Suggest the right libraries for specific use cases, such as `lodash` for data manipulation or NumPy for numerical computations.
- **Code Profiling**: Assists in identifying bottlenecks by generating instrumented code for performance analysis.

Best Practices for Performance Optimization with Copilot

- **Use Data-Specific Techniques:** Tailor optimizations to the dataset's structure (for example, sparse versus dense arrays).
- **Minimize Iterations:** Replace nested loops with hash-based approaches or built-in methods, such as reduce.
- **Avoid Premature Optimization:** Focus on measurable bottlenecks identified during profiling.
- **Combine Optimization with Refactoring**: Modularize the code, while improving its performance.

Metrics of Optimization with Copilot

This table presents a side-by-side comparison of legacy code versus Copilot-optimized code, showcasing improvements in execution time, memory usage, scalability, and code readability, when AI-assisted refactoring techniques are applied.

Metric	Legacy Code	Optimized Code
Execution Time	~2x slower for large datasets	~50% faster for large datasets
Memory Consumption	High due to redundant iterations	Reduced with single-pass logic
Scalability	Struggles with larger inputs	Handles larger inputs smoothly
Code Readability	Low	High

Table 9.3: *GitHub Copilot Delivers Faster, Cleaner, and More Scalable Code by Optimizing Logic and Reducing Inefficiencies across Key Performance Metrics*

So in this section, we have seen how GitHub Copilot acts as a powerful ally in performance optimization and code tuning. By suggesting modern methods, efficient algorithms, and database-level optimizations, Copilot significantly reduces resource usage, and improves the execution speed. With well-crafted prompts, developers can unlock scalable, future-proof solutions for performance-critical applications.

Automating Code Generation and Repetitive Tasks

Repetitive tasks, such as boilerplate code creation, CRUD operations, and unit test generation consume valuable developer time. GitHub Copilot streamlines these tasks by generating accurate, context-aware code with minimal input. This automation not only speeds up development, but also allows developers to focus on more complex, value-driven tasks.

In this section, we explore how Copilot automates routine coding tasks through real-world scenarios, and provide insights into its best practices.

Real-World Scenario 1: Automating Boilerplate Code

A team is setting up a new Node.js project, and needs to implement a standard REST API structure for managing products.

Prompt:

```
"Generate a REST API structure in Node.js with Express for basic CRUD
operations on a products resource."
```

Output:

Refer the complete code generated at the following GitHub Repo link:

chapter9-copilot-advanced-techniques\automation\rest_api_boilerplate.js

Impact:

- **Time Saved:** Automates ~80% of the CRUD setup, reducing initial development time.
- **Consistency:** Generates standardized code, reducing errors.
- **Scalability:** Provides a clean structure for adding more resources.

Real-World Scenario 2: Automating Unit Test Generation

A developer needs to write unit tests for a function that calculates discounts for e-commerce products.

Prompt:

```
"Generate Jest unit tests for the following function."

function calculateDiscount(price, discountPercentage) {
    if (price <= 0 || discountPercentage < 0 || discountPercentage > 100) {
        throw new Error('Invalid input');
    }
    return price - (price * (discountPercentage / 100));
}
```

Output:

Refer the complete code generated at the following GitHub Repo link:

chapter9-copilot-advanced-techniques\automation\unit_tests\discount_tests.js

Impact:

- **Comprehensive Testing:** Covers both positive scenarios and edge cases.
- **Error Handling Validation:** Ensures proper validation for invalid inputs.
- **Time Saved:** Reduces manual effort by ~60% in test creation.

Facilitating Automation with GitHub Copilot

GitHub Copilot fundamentally transforms how developers approach repetitive tasks by leveraging AI's ability to understand context, generate reusable patterns, and provide immediate suggestions. Its automation capabilities extend beyond code generation, enhancing overall efficiency and productivity.

Speed and Accuracy:

- **Insight:** Copilot reduces time spent on mundane tasks, such as boilerplate code creation, configuration setups, and repetitive scripts.
- **Practical Example:** In a project requiring multiple CRUD APIs, developers traditionally create similar code for various endpoints. Copilot generates these endpoints in seconds by identifying patterns from a single example or clear prompt.

Scenario:

```
"Create CRUD operations for a user's resource in Express.js."
```

Output:

```
app.get('/users', (req, res) => { /* Retrieve users */ });
app.post('/users', (req, res) => { /* Add user */ });
app.put('/users/:id', (req, res) => { /* Update user */ });
app.delete('/users/:id', (req, res) => { /* Delete user */ });
```

Takeaway: Copilot automates this process across similar resources, scaling up with minimal manual intervention.

Pattern Recognition:

- **Insight:** Copilot detects repetitive patterns in code, and optimizes suggestions based on context, ensuring consistent coding practices.
- **Practical Example**: In automated test generation, Copilot recognizes the testing library (for example, Jest, Mocha, and so on), and adapts to generate relevant test cases.

Scenario:

"Generate Jest tests for the calculateSum function."

Output:

```
describe('calculateSum', () => {
    it('should return the sum of two numbers', () => {
        expect(calculateSum(2, 3)).toBe(5);
    });
    it('should handle negative numbers', () => {
        expect(calculateSum(-2, -3)).toBe(-5);
    });
});
```

Intelligent Code Completion:

- **Insight:** Copilot integrates seamlessly with editors to predict what developers need next, minimizing efforts in repetitive workflows.
- **Practical Example:** While implementing logging in a backend service, Copilot identifies log patterns, and generates additional logging points consistently.

Documentation Automation:

- **Insight:** Writing inline comments and function-level documentation are often skipped due to time constraints. Copilot generates concise and relevant documentation automatically.
- **Practical Example**

  Prompt:

  "Add comments for the processOrder function."

Output:

```
/**
 * Processes an order and calculates the total cost.
 * @param {object} order - The order object with items and quantities.
 * @returns {number} - The total cost of the order.
 */
function processOrder(order) {
    // Calculate the total cost of the items in the order
    return order.items.reduce((total, item) => total + item.price * item.
quantity, 0);
}
```

Takeaway: Documentation automation ensures higher code readability and maintainability.

Integration with Frameworks and Libraries:

- **Insight:** Copilot leverages the context of commonly used libraries to auto-generate configurations, scaffolding, or repetitive logic.
- **Practical Example:** When setting up a CI/CD pipeline, Copilot suggests YAML configuration snippets tailored to tools, such as GitHub Actions.

Prompt:

"Generate a GitHub Actions workflow for running Jest tests on Node.js 14, 16, and 18."

Output:

Refer the complete code generated at the following GitHub Repo link:

chapter9-copilot-advanced-techniques\automation\ci_cd\github_actions_workflow.yml

Best Practices for Automating Repetitive Tasks

- **Be Specific in Prompts:**
  - **Why It Matters:** Vague prompts may lead to incomplete or irrelevant outputs.
  - **Example:** Instead of saying, "*Generate test cases,*" provide detailed instructions, such as:

    "*Generate Jest test cases for a function that calculates tax based on income.*"

    Tip: *Specify key details, such as expected inputs, outputs, and edge cases.*
- **Leverage Context for Customization:**
  - **Why It Matters:** Providing relevant code snippets or context allows Copilot to tailor outputs.
  - **Example:** While automating database migrations, mention the database type (for example, PostgreSQL, MySQL, and so on), and the migration tool (for example, Sequelize).

  Prompt:

  "Generate a Sequelize migration script to add a lastLogin column to the user's table."

  Output:

```
module.exports = {
  up: async (queryInterface, Sequelize) => {
    await queryInterface.addColumn('users', 'lastLogin', {
      type: Sequelize.DATE,
      allowNull: true,
    });
  },
  down: async (queryInterface) => {
    await queryInterface.removeColumn('users', 'lastLogin');
  },
};
```

- **Use Iterative Refinement**
  - **Why It Matters:** Start with a broad prompt, and refine based on the initial output.
  - **Example**:

    First prompt: **"Generate API routes for users."**

    Refined prompt: **"Generate API routes for users with input validation and error handling."**
- **Validate Outputs Thoroughly**
  - **Why It Matters:** Copilot-generated code may miss project-specific requirements or edge cases.
  - **Best Practice:** Always review, test, and adapt generated outputs to fit the context of your application.
- **Reuse and Template Outputs:**
  - **Why It Matters:** Patterns generated by Copilot can be reused across projects.
  - **Example:** Save reusable boilerplate code or configurations as templates for future automation.
- **Maintain Consistency:**
  - **Why It Matters:** Consistent naming conventions and patterns improve collaboration.

- **Practical Example:** Ensure uniformity in function names, logging styles, and error messages by refining prompts, such as:
`"Write a logging function with consistent formatting across all API routes."`

Metrics of Successful Automation

This table highlights the key improvements in automation workflows achieved with GitHub Copilot, focusing on boilerplate generation, test writing, and documentation coverage, when compared to traditional manual efforts.

Metric	Pre-Copilot	With Copilot
Boilerplate Generation	~1–2 hours per service	~10–20 minutes
Test Writing	~1 hour per function	~20–30 minutes per function
Documentation Coverage	Often skipped	Near 100% with inline comments

Table 9.4: *GitHub Copilot Streamlines Development by Drastically Reducing Boilerplate and Test Creation Time, while Enhancing Documentation Completeness*

Here, we have explored how GitHub Copilot's automation capabilities go beyond basic code generation to enable seamless handling of repetitive tasks. Thus, by following the best practices, and leveraging prompt engineering, developers can ensure that the generated outputs are precise, consistent, and ready for real-world use. Automation with Copilot is not just about saving time—it is about improving quality, and creating space for innovation.

Integrating AI Suggestions into Your Workflow

Effectively integrating GitHub Copilot into your development workflow transforms how teams and individuals write, review, and deploy code. Copilot can assist across the development lifecycle, from brainstorming solutions to generating production-ready code. However, to achieve seamless integration, teams must adopt strategies that balance human expertise with AI-generated suggestions.

This section explores practical approaches to incorporating Copilot's recommendations into daily workflows, emphasizing collaboration, productivity, and quality assurance.

Collaborative Coding with Copilot

Insight: Copilot serves as an AI pair programmer, complementing human creativity and expertise. It provides contextual suggestions that help bridge knowledge gaps, especially in areas, such as unfamiliar libraries, frameworks, or syntax.

Best Practices:

- **Team Collaboration:** Use Copilot during live coding sessions, enabling multiple developers to review and refine suggestions.
- **Code Reviews:** Treat Copilot's output as a starting point, not the final solution. Engage in peer reviews to verify accuracy and adherence to standards.

Example:

While working on a **team project** involving a microservices architecture, a developer uses Copilot to scaffold an API gateway service.

Prompt:

```
"Generate a Node.js API gateway service that routes requests to multiple microservices."
```

Output:

Refer the complete code generated at the following GitHub Repo link:

chapter9-copilot-advanced-techniques\additional_examples\node_api_gateway.js

Accelerating Prototyping and Development

Insight: Copilot speeds up prototyping by generating functional code snippets that align with project requirements. Developers can focus on refining business logic, rather than repetitive implementation details.

Example: For a mobile app project, a developer uses Copilot to rapidly prototype a login feature with React Native.

Prompt:

```
"Create a React Native login screen with email and password input fields."
```

Output:

Refer the complete code generated at the following GitHub Repo link:

chapter9-copilot-advanced-techniques\additional_examples\react_native_login.js

Impact:

- **Rapid Prototyping:** Reduces development time by ~50% for initial UI components.
- **Ease of Customization:** Provides a base that developers can quickly adapt to match the design requirements.

Incorporating AI into CI/CD Pipelines

Insight: Copilot assists in creating and maintaining CI/CD configurations, ensuring streamlined deployment pipelines. Teams can integrate Copilot-generated workflows into GitHub Actions, Jenkins, or other tools.

Example: A team uses Copilot to configure a CI pipeline for running tests, and building a React app.

Prompt:

```
"Create a GitHub Actions workflow to test and build a React app."
```

Output:

Refer the complete code generated at the following GitHub Repo link:

chapter9-copilot-advanced-techniques\automation\ci_cd\github_actions_workflow_build_react_app.yml

Impact:

- **Automation:** Simplifies CI/CD pipeline creation, reducing manual effort.
- **Consistency:** Ensures reliable deployments with minimal human error.

Leveraging Copilot for Knowledge Sharing

Insight: Copilot acts as a knowledge repository, offering insights into less familiar domains. Developers can leverage their suggestions to explore new languages, frameworks, or technologies.

Example: A developer unfamiliar with Python uses Copilot to generate a data processing script.

Prompt:

```
"Write a Python script to process a CSV file, and calculate the total sales for each category."
```

Output:

Refer the complete code generated at the following GitHub Repo link:

chapter9-copilot-advanced-techniques\additional_examples\python_data_processing.py

Best Practices for Integrating Copilot

- **Balance Human Expertise and AI:** Treat Copilot as an assistant, not a replacement. Always validate AI-generated code.
- **Encourage Team Adoption:** Host team workshops to demonstrate Copilot's capabilities, and establish workflows for integrating its suggestions.
- **Use Iterative Refinement:** Start with broad prompts, and refine as needed for better results.
- **Focus on Standards:** Ensure Copilot outputs adhere to coding standards, such as linting rules or company-specific guidelines.
- **Measure Impact:** Track metrics, such as development time saved, code quality improvements, and error reduction to assess Copilot's effectiveness.

Metrics of Workflow Integration

The following table illustrates how integrating GitHub Copilot into development workflows accelerates prototyping, simplifies CI/CD setup, eases onboarding, and reduces manual errors through intelligent code suggestions.

Metric	Without Copilot	With Copilot
Prototyping Time	~2x slower	~50% faster
CI/CD Setup Time	~1-2 hours	~15-30 minutes
Knowledge Ramp-Up	Steeper learning curve	Shortened learning curve
Error Reduction	Higher due to manual errors	Lower due to automated suggestions

Table 9.5: *Copilot Accelerates Workflows by Cutting Down Setup Time, Reducing Errors, and Smoothing the Developer Onboarding Process*

We have learnt here how we can integrate GitHub Copilot into your workflow to enhance productivity, collaboration, and code quality. Thus, by leveraging its capabilities for prototyping, CI/CD pipelines, and knowledge sharing, teams can streamline development processes, and focus on innovation. Effective integration balances AI's efficiency with human expertise, resulting in robust and scalable solutions.

Understanding the AI Model and Training Process

GitHub Copilot's cutting-edge AI model, advanced training techniques, and contextual understanding have redefined code assistance. Therefore, by combining powerful LLMs with iterative enhancements,

Copilot offers developers a robust tool for generating, refactoring, and optimizing code. Moreover, understanding its inner workings enables developers to leverage it effectively, balancing automation with human expertise.

The AI Model behind GitHub Copilot

GitHub Copilot is built on OpenAI Codex, an advanced iteration of the GPT architecture. Its capabilities are tailored to coding, offering unparalleled support for multi-language programming, automated workflows, and real-time suggestions.

Key Features of Codex:

- **Multilingual Proficiency:** Supports 15+ programming languages, including Python, JavaScript, C++, and Rust.
- **Adaptive Suggestions:** Generates context-aware code snippets by analyzing developer input, and the surrounding project.
- **Learning from Patterns:** Recognizes recurring structures, helping maintain coding consistency across files and projects.

Core Components of the Codex Model:

- **Transformer Architecture:**
    - The model processes the input as a sequence of tokens, leveraging the transformer architecture to analyze relationships between words or code components.
    - **Key Features:**
        - Attention mechanisms to prioritize important parts of the input (for example, function definitions, variable names, and so on).
        - Multi-layered neural networks that process complex dependencies within code snippets.
- **Multilingual Proficiency:**
    - Trained on a dataset encompassing over 15 programming languages, including Python, JavaScript, C++, and Go.
    - Adapts to language-specific features, such as TypeScript's strict typing or Python's dynamic nature.
- **Pretraining and Fine-Tuning:**
    - **Pretraining**: Trained on a massive corpus of natural language and programming-related text, enabling it to understand syntax and semantics.
    - **Fine-tuning**: Enhanced with curated examples to specialize in coding tasks such as debugging, refactoring, and multi-language projects.
- **Feedback Integration:**
    - Reinforcement learning ensures continuous improvement by refining the model based on real-world usage and developer feedback.

The following diagram illustrates the foundational workflow behind GitHub Copilot's AI-powered code suggestions, detailing how datasets, pretraining, neural networks, reinforcement learning, and multi-language support come together to enable intelligent code completion and refactoring.

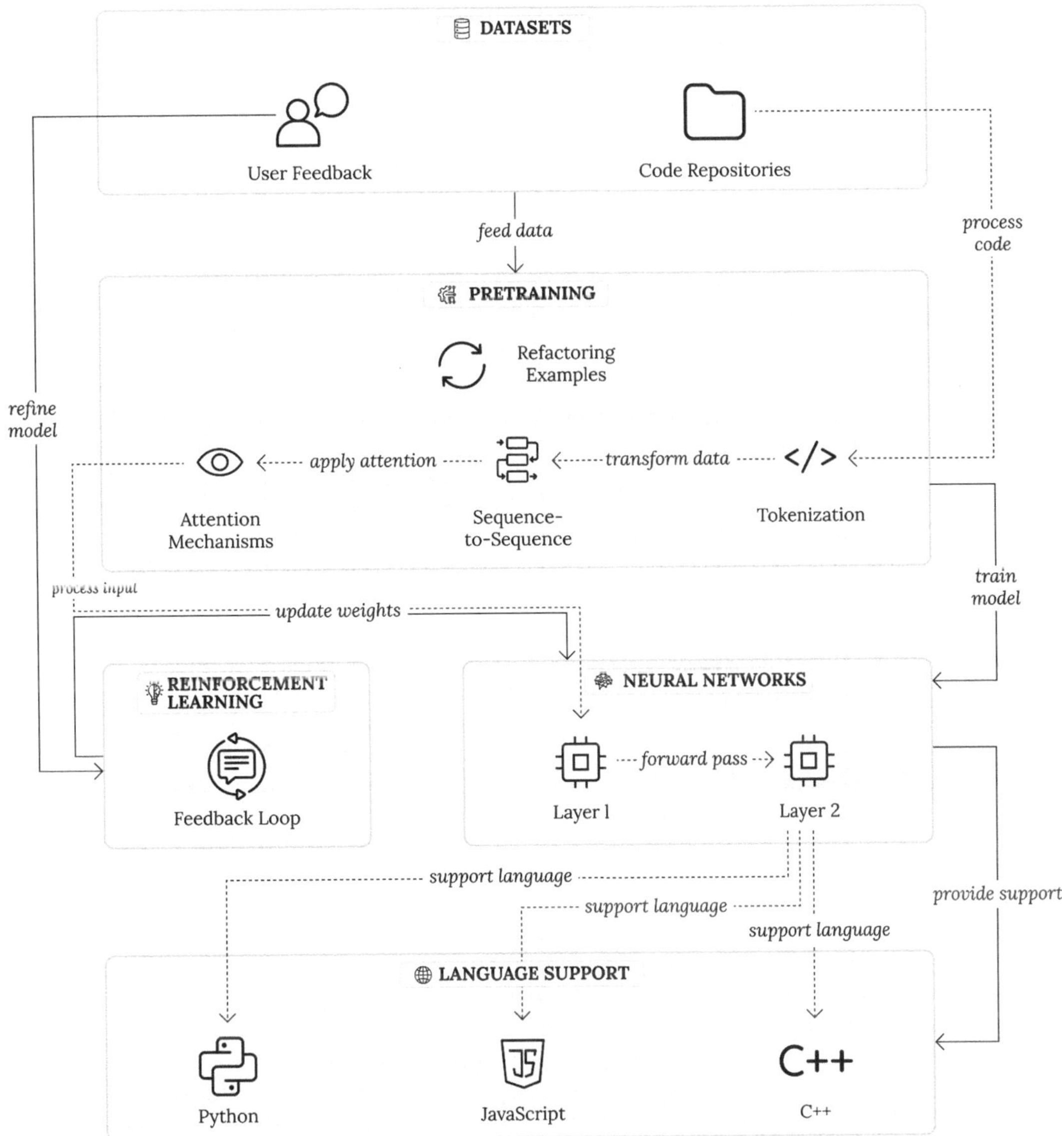

Figure 9.11: *End-to-end Architecture of GitHub Copilot—Integrating Pre-training on Code Datasets, Attention-based Neural Networks, Reinforcement Learning from User Feedback, and Multi-language Support for Accurate and Context-aware Code Generation*

The following diagram outlines the end-to-end workflow of GitHub Copilot, from training on vast GitHub repositories to generating real-time code suggestions within popular IDEs, powered by the Codex AI model, and continuously improved via user feedback.

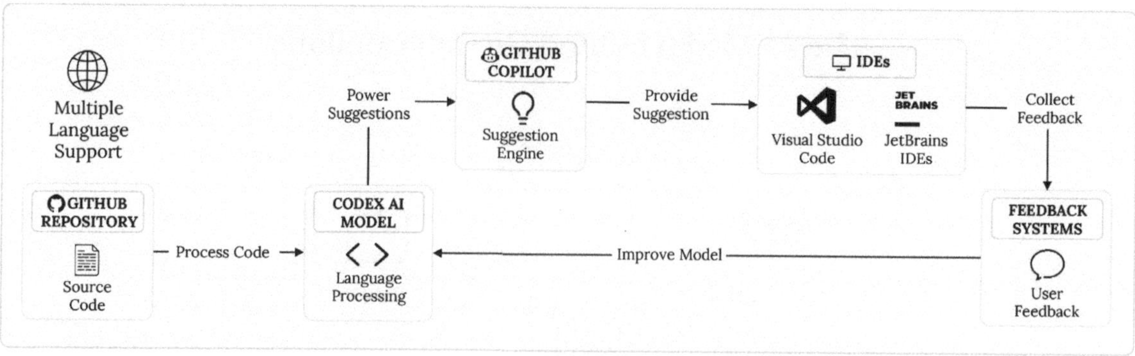

Figure 9.12: *GitHub Copilot Architecture–Leveraging GitHub Source Code, Codex Language Processing, and IDE Integration to Deliver Intelligent Code Suggestions, Refined through Continuous User Feedback*

Recent Upgrades:

- **Improved Context Understanding:** Processes larger contexts and inter-file dependencies for more accurate suggestions.
- **Multi-Model Support:** Integrates AI models from **OpenAI, Anthropic**, and **Google**, allowing users to choose models tailored to their needs. (Source)

  References: *https://www.theverge.com/2024/10/29/24282544/github-copilot-multi-model-anthropic-google-open-ai-github-spark-announcement*
- **Custom Instructions:** Developers can specify custom rules or preferences for code style, improving alignment with team standards.

Salient Features of GitHub Copilot

This table showcases the key features that power GitHub Copilot's intelligent coding capabilities–ranging from context-aware suggestions and idiomatic code generation to multi-language support and feedback-driven improvement. Each feature is mapped with its benefits and real-world impact to demonstrate how Copilot enhances developer productivity across diverse scenarios.

Feature	Description	Benefits	Real-World Impact
Context-Aware Suggestions	Analyzes the current file, surrounding code, and comments to generate relevant code snippets.	• Saves time with intelligent completions.	• Streamlined CRUD API generation in seconds by analyzing preceding lines.
		• Adapts to the task at hand, whether scaffolding or debugging.	• Debugging logic suggestions tailored to existing error messages or conditions.
Idiomatic Code Generation	Produces code snippets adhering to the language's best practices and idioms.	• Ensures consistency across the project.	• Generates Python pandas data manipulation scripts that follow community-recommended practices.
		• Reduces the learning curve for new frameworks or libraries.	• Creates React components with standard props and state conventions.

Multi-File Context	Considers dependencies, imports, and relationships across up to 10 open files.	• Provides project-level insights.	• Suggests utility functions defined in a helper file when writing main logic.
		• Maintains crossfile consistency.	• Accurately predicts route handlers for Express.js APIs by referencing associated models.
Multi-Language Support	Supports over 15 programming languages, including Python, JavaScript, TypeScript, Go, Java, and C++.	• Enables seamless coding in multilanguage projects.	• Generates boilerplate for Python Flask APIs and seamlessly integrates with a JavaScript frontend.
		• Assists in transitioning to new languages.	• Provides consistent patterns across languages in hybrid projects.
Custom Instruction Support	Allows developers to guide Copilot with personalized rules or coding preferences.	• Enhances alignment with team standards.	• Automatically generates comments in JSDoc format when specified.
		• Reduces time spent on style enforcement.	• Produces code that adheres to company-specific naming conventions or frameworks.
Feedback Integration	Continuously improves suggestions based on user feedback and usage patterns.	• Adapts to developer preferences over time.	• Suggests optimized SQL queries after repeated corrections in a database-heavy project.
		• Improves quality of recommendations.	• Adapts to a specific team's error-handling style for backend services.
Tokenization and Prediction	Splits input into smaller tokens and predicts the next token to generate coherent code.	• Generates syntax-correct code.	• Completes **if-else** blocks based on preceding logic.
		• Handles ambiguous prompts with contextual interpretation.	• Suggests matching **try-catch** blocks for existing exception scenarios.
Few-Shot Learning	Learns new patterns from minimal examples within a single prompt or codebase.	• Reduces the need for extensive examples.	• Generates Python data validation functions after seeing a single example.
		• Quickly adapts to project specific requirements.	• Adapts to proprietary APIs after minimal exposure.
Error Detection and Recovery	Identifies potential issues in the code and provides suggestions for resolving them.	• Improves code quality.	• Highlights missing edge-case handling in a JavaScript function.
		• Reduces debugging time.	• Suggests fixes for SQL syntax errors in real time.

Automated Documentation	Generates inline comments, docstrings, and method descriptions automatically.	• Enhances code readability and maintainability.	• Produces descriptive docstrings for Python functions.
		• Saves time spent on documentation tasks.	• Adds method-level comments for Java classes with usage and parameter details.
Integration with CI/CD Pipelines	Generates and configures workflows for CI/CD tools such as GitHub Actions, Jenkins, and CircleCI.	• Simplifies pipeline setup.	• Automatically creates GitHub Actions workflows for multienvironment testing.
		• Automates deployment processes.	• Suggests YAML configurations for building and deploying Docker containers.
Refactoring and Optimization	Identifies redundant or inefficient code and suggests improvements.	• Enhances performance.	• Replaces nested loops with functional programming constructs in JavaScript.
		• Reduces technical debt.	• Suggests optimized SQL queries for better database performance.
Cross-Domain Knowledge	Leverages a broad dataset to assist with specialized tasks, such as machine learning, data engineering, and DevOps.	• Handles niche domains effectively.	• Generates TensorFlow model training scripts with minimal input.
		• Supports nontraditional coding tasks.	• Configures AWS Lambda functions with environment variables based on common patterns.

Table 9.6: *Comprehensive Overview of GitHub Copilot's Core Features, Highlighting their Functional Benefits and Tangible Impact on Real-world Development Workflows*

Training Process

The Codex model powering Copilot undergoes extensive training and refinement to ensure high performance in real-world coding environments.

Stages of Training:

1. **Pre-training:**
    - Codex learns to predict the next token in a sequence using a vast dataset of natural language and programming code.
    - **Example**: For function `greet(name)`, it predicts `{ return "Hello " + name; }`.
2. **Fine-Tuning:**
    - Codex is optimized for programming tasks, such as generating boilerplate code or debugging functions.

3. **Reinforcement Learning:**
    - Continuous feedback from users and test cases is used to improve the model's precision and usability.

The Learning Lifecycle of GitHub Copilot: From Pre-training to Refinement

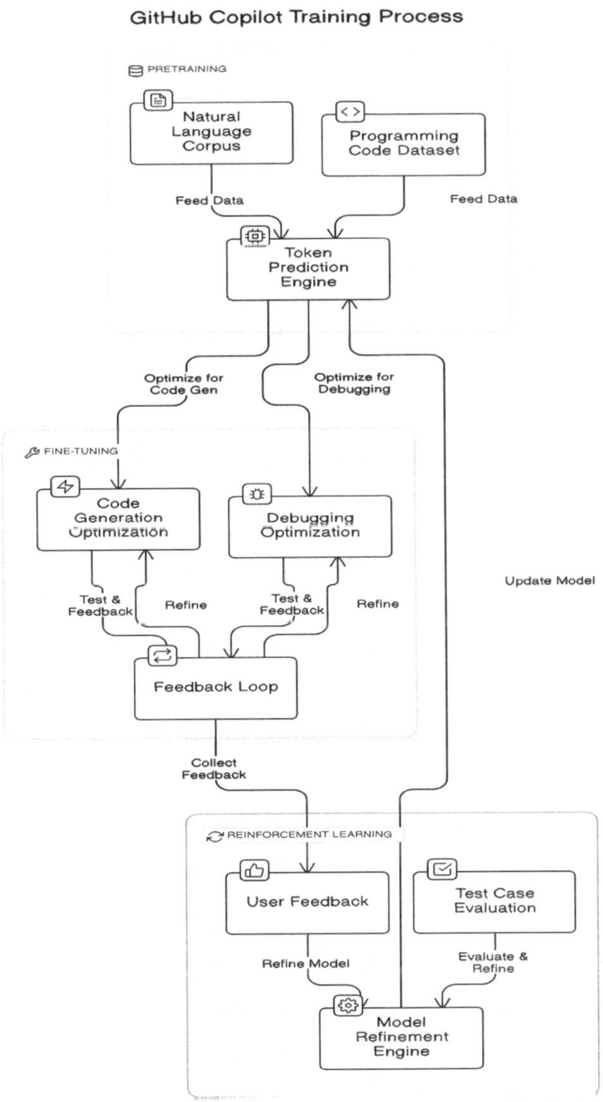

GitHub Copilot Training Process

Figure 9.13: *Three-phase Learning Pipeline of GitHub Copilot–Pre-training on Code and Language Data, Fine-Tuning via Feedback Loops, and Reinforcement Learning through Real-world Evaluations*

GitHub Copilot's intelligence is powered by a multi-phase learning lifecycle that combines large-scale pretraining, continuous fine-tuning, and reinforcement learning. The above visual breaks down this process–from feeding the model with natural language and code data, to iterative optimization using developer feedback, debugging evaluations, and test case refinements–ensuring that Copilot evolves to generate high-quality, context-aware suggestions.

Data Utilization:

- **Dataset**: Trained on billions of lines of publicly available code from repositories, documentation, and Q and A platforms.
- **Focus on Quality**: Ensures high relevance by fine-tuning with curated examples, and well-documented libraries.

Advanced Techniques:

- **Few-Shot Learning:** Adapts quickly to new tasks with minimal examples.
- **Transfer Learning:** Builds on the foundational GPT-3 architecture for code-centric applications.

Copilot's Approach to Building Context

GitHub Copilot's ability to understand context is central to its effectiveness. Its contextual understanding spans individual files, related files, and the broader project.

Context-Building Process:

- **Tokenization:** Breaks input into tokens for sequential processing, enabling it to interpret comments, code, and user instructions.
- **File-Level Analysis: Processes up to 1000 tokens (~4000 characters)** from the open file.
- **Multi-File Awareness:** Considers dependencies and relationships across **10 open files**, enhancing its understanding of project-wide context in any coding editor.

Improved Context Handling:

- **Enhanced Multi-File Editing:** Recognizes interdependencies, such as imports, shared variables, or utility functions.
- **Project-Level Insights:** Adapts suggestions to the coding patterns and conventions established in the project.

The following diagram illustrates the internal mechanism GitHub Copilot uses to build contextual understanding. It tokenizes input from comments, code, and user instructions, analyzes up to 1,000 tokens, and leverages multi-file awareness to construct a complete view of the project context.

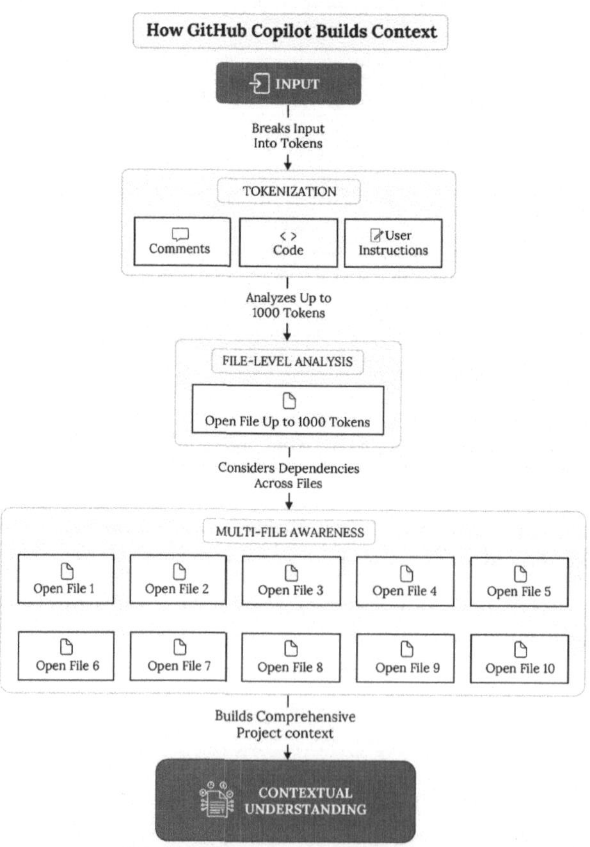

Figure 9.14: *GitHub Copilot Constructs Contextual Understanding by Analyzing Tokenized Input across 10 Open Files, Enabling Accurate, Context-aware Code Suggestions*

Copilot's Approach to Multi-File Context Handling

GitHub Copilot integrates multi-file awareness to improve code suggestions, and ensure project coherence.

Capabilities:

- **Analyzing Dependencies:** Tracks file imports, shared utilities, and function calls across related files.
- **Improved Suggestion Accuracy:** Aligns its recommendations with the broader application architecture.
- **Multi-Language Projects:** Supports cross-language dependencies, such as a Python backend and JavaScript frontend.

This diagram demonstrates how GitHub Copilot intelligently processes multiple file types—including Python, JavaScript, and other supported formats—while analyzing dependencies, such as imports, shared utilities, and function calls. It also showcases Copilot's ability to manage cross-language dependencies in multi-language projects for accurate and context-rich code suggestions.

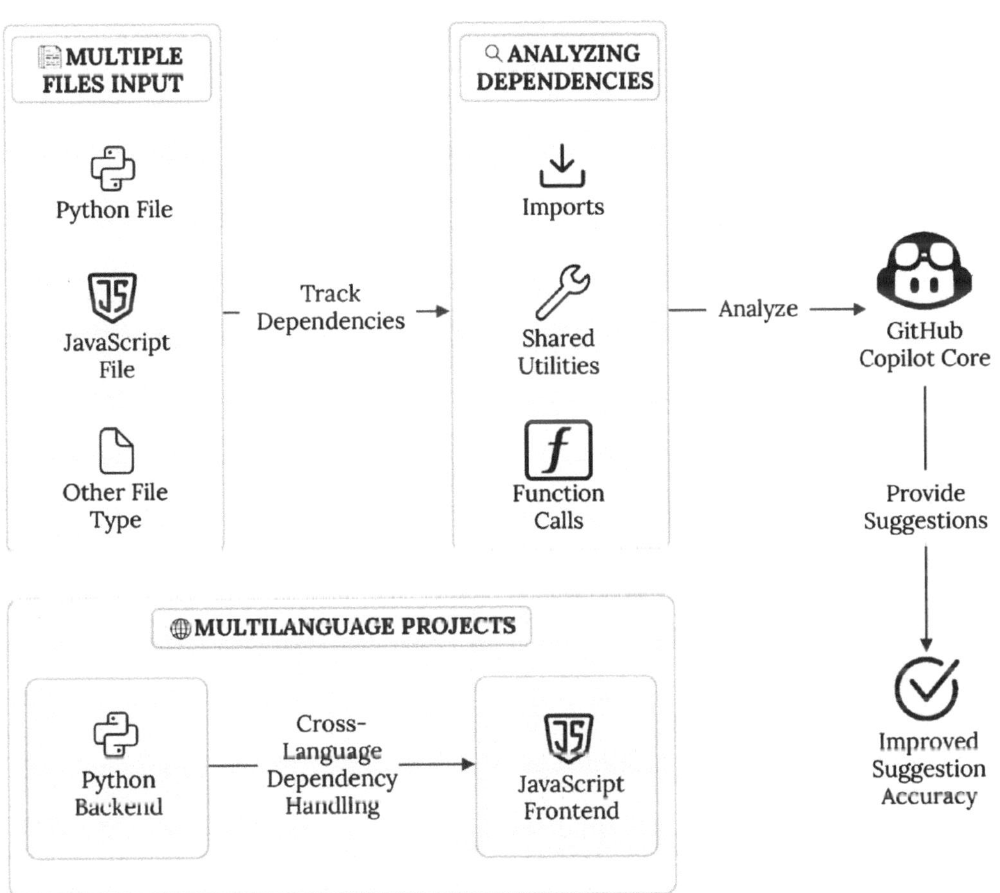

Figure 9.15: *GitHub Copilot Builds Contextual Awareness across Multiple Files and Languages by Analyzing Imports, Shared Logic, and Interdependent Components, Enabling Seamless Suggestions in Full-stack Applications*

Example

- **Scenario:** A developer uses Copilot in a Node.js project with a separate file for routes.
- **Functionality:** Copilot suggests route handlers based on the models and database logic in other open files.

The following diagram illustrates how GitHub Copilot integrates seamlessly into the developer workflow within environments like Visual Studio Code, analyzing related project files, such as routes.js, models.js, and database.js to generate intelligent suggestions–like auto-generating route handlers aligned with project structure.

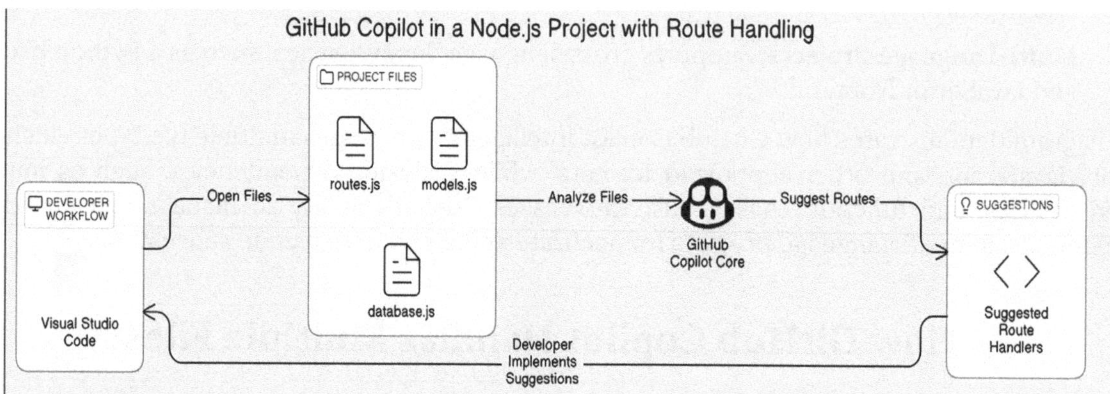

***Figure 9.16:** GitHub Copilot Enhances Developer Productivity by Analyzing Related Project Files to Deliver Smart, Context-aware Code Suggestions Directly within the IDE*

Strengths of Copilot's Training and Context Mechanism

GitHub Copilot excels in its ability to learn, adapt, and predict high-quality outputs based on its training and context mechanism.

The following table outlines the foundational features of GitHub Copilot that contribute to its intelligent code generation capabilities, focusing on its extensive training data, contextual adaptability, and robust multi-language as well as multi-file support.

Feature	**Benefit**
Massive Knowledge Base	Trained in diverse codebases, enabling support for various programming languages and frameworks.
Multi-File Awareness	Handles complex projects by analyzing relationships between files.
Context Sensitivity	Adapts to the surrounding code, comments, and project structure.
Advanced Language Support	Recognizes idiomatic usage, ensuring that suggestions adhere to the best practices.

***Table 9.7:** Key Features of GitHub Copilot–Including Its Massive Knowledge Base, Context Awareness, and Language Adaptability to Enable Smarter, Project-aware Code Suggestions*

Practical Considerations for Developers

- **Optimizing Prompts:** Provide detailed prompts to guide Copilot's suggestions.

  Example: Replace "*Write a function*" with "*Write a TypeScript function to fetch user data from an API and handle errors gracefully.*"

- **Validating Outputs:** Always review and test Copilot-generated code, especially for performance-critical or security-sensitive tasks.

- **Leverage Iterative Feedback:** Start with basic prompts and refine them iteratively to improve the output quality.
- **Tailor Context:** Keep relevant files open to enhance Copilot's multi-file awareness and ensure contextually accurate suggestions.

Key Metrics of Copilot's Effectiveness

This table highlights measurable improvements in GitHub Copilot's performance after its enhancements, comparing metrics, such as code generation volume, contextual scope, accuracy, and the time saved to showcase its growing impact on developer productivity.

Metric	Pre-Enhancement	Post-Enhancement
Lines of Code Generated	~40 LOC per prompt	~70 LOC per prompt
Context Scope	Single file	Multi-file (up to 10 files)
Accuracy of Suggestions	~75%	~85%
Time Saved	~20% per task	~40% per task

Table 9.8: *Key Features of GitHub Copilot–Including Its Massive Knowledge- base, Context- awareness, and Language adaptability to Enable Smarter, and Project-aware Code Suggestions*

Security and Privacy Considerations

GitHub's foundation for privacy revolves around four principles: **Protection, Trust, Context, and Expectation.** These principles guide the development and operation of GitHub Copilot to ensure that the user data remains private and secure. With its privacy-first approach, GitHub aims to foster trust among developers and organizations globally.

Privacy Principles

- **Privacy Protects People:**
  - User privacy is prioritized to prevent misuse or exploitation of data.
  - **Example:** Copilot ensures that user-generated content is processed locally, and not shared without explicit consent.
- **Privacy Requires Trust, Control, and Transparency:**
  - **Trust:** Developers should feel confident that their data is not misused.
  - **Control:** Users have the ability to manage Copilot's data usage settings.
  - **Transparency:** GitHub communicates clearly how Copilot processes and handles data.
- **Privacy is Contextual:**
  - Recognizes that different regions and industries have unique privacy needs.
  - Ensures compliance with privacy regulations such as **GDPR (General Data Protection Regulation)** and **CCPA (California Consumer Privacy Act)**.
- **Privacy is the Expectation:**
  - Embeds privacy into all GitHub operations and features, aligning with the principle of "*privacy by design.*"

This diagram outlines the core privacy principles upheld by GitHub Copilot. It emphasizes safeguarding user information, respecting user context, adhering to global privacy expectations, and fostering transparency in data usage.

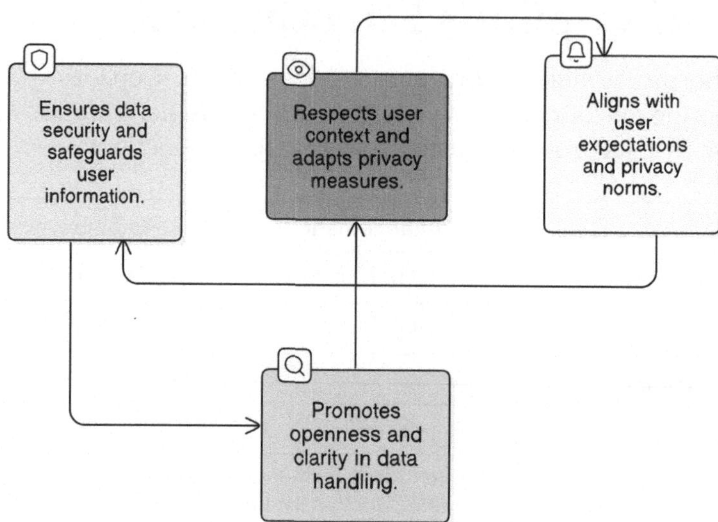

Figure 9.17: *GitHub Copilot's Privacy Workflow Ensures Secure, Respectful, and Transparent Data Practices that Align with User Expectations and Regulatory Standards*

GitHub's Approach to Privacy in Copilot

GitHub ensures privacy through a combination of technical safeguards, legal compliance, and user-focused tools.

Data Handling

GitHub Copilot ensures secure and efficient handling of data by adhering to strict privacy protocols and robust architectural designs. This section delves into the mechanics of data handling, focusing on the journey of user inputs, the principles of local processing, telemetry data, and the safeguards implemented to prevent misuse. By understanding Copilot's data flow, users can confidently integrate it into their workflows.

Data Flow in GitHub Copilot

How Copilot Processes Data

1. **Local Code Processing:**
   - User inputs (for example, code snippets or prompts) are processed locally within the development environment.
   - Copilot analyzes the visible context of the current file, and optionally considers up to **10 open files** for multi-file awareness.
2. **No Retention of Code:**
   - Code processed by Copilot is not stored on GitHub servers, ensuring that sensitive or proprietary information remains secure.
3. **Optional Telemetry Data:**
   - Telemetry sharing is **opt-in**. Data shared for improvement purposes is anonymized, and stripped of identifiable details.

- Shared telemetry includes metadata, such as **model usage statistics** and **types of tasks performed** but excludes user-specific code.

GitHub Copilot Data Handling and Privacy Workflow

GitHub Copilot is designed with a strong emphasis on user privacy and data protection. The following diagram below illustrates how Copilot processes user input locally, analyzes context securely, and returns suggestions, without retaining sensitive information. Optional telemetry sharing is fully anonymized, and opt-in only, ensuring compliance with enterprise privacy standards.

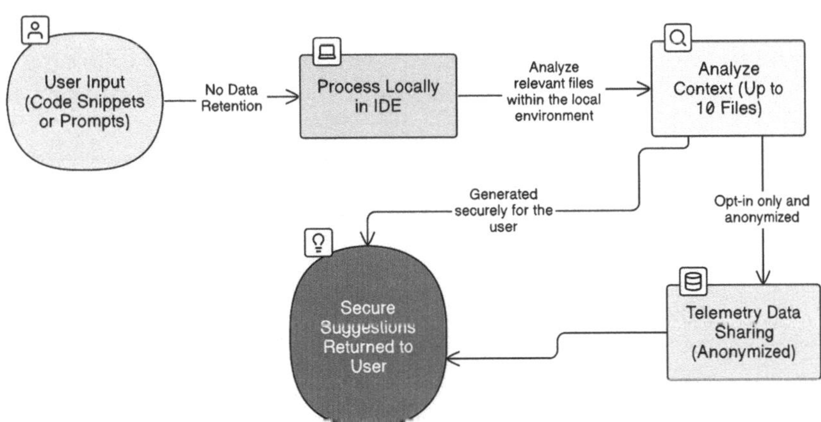

Figure 9.18: *End-to-end Flow of How GitHub Copilot Processes User Input Locally, Generates Secure Suggestions, and Handles Anonymized Telemetry Sharing.*

Key Privacy and Security Practices in Data Handling

Core Practices:

- **Blocked Suggestions:** Copilot actively filters suggestions to avoid generating sensitive content, such as API keys or PII, that may inadvertently exist in public training data.
- **Comprehensive Anonymization:** Telemetry data is anonymized using strict protocols to protect developer identities and code specifics.
- **Customizable Settings:** Users and organizations can configure Copilot to disable telemetry or restrict its use to specific repositories.
- **Localized Compliance:** Data handling policies align with regional privacy laws, such as GDPR and CCPA.

Real-World Scenario: Secure Data Handling in Enterprise

An enterprise software development team adopts GitHub Copilot to accelerate project timelines. The team works with proprietary code that must remain confidential.

Data Handling Workflow:

1. **Local Processing**:
    - Copilot generates suggestions based only on local files visible in the IDE.
    - No proprietary data is sent to external servers.

2. **Custom Settings**:
   - Developers disable telemetry sharing in Copilot settings.
   - Organization-level controls are implemented to restrict Copilot usage to non-sensitive projects.
3. **Validation of Suggestions**:
   - Automated tools, such as **SonarQube** are integrated to validate Copilot-generated code for security and compliance.

GitHub Copilot Privacy and Security Features- An Overview

GitHub Copilot integrates a robust set of privacy-first design principles to protect user code, manage telemetry, and ensure developer control over sensitive operations. The following table summarizes the key features, their associated security levels, and the extent of developer configurability for each.

Feature	Description	Security Level	Developer Control
Local Processing	User code and prompts are processed locally in the developer's Integrated Development Environment (IDE). This ensures no sensitive information is transmitted to external servers, maintaining high security for proprietary or confidential data.	High	Yes
Telemetry Sharing	Shares anonymized metadata, such as model usage statistics and task types, with GitHub servers. This data improves Copilot's performance but does not include user code. Developers can opt in or out of telemetry sharing.	Medium	Yes
Data Anonymization	All telemetry data is stripped of identifiable or sensitive details before being transmitted, ensuring it cannot be traced back to individual users or organizations. GitHub adheres to strict anonymization protocols for privacy.	High	Yes
Blocked Suggestions	Actively filters code suggestions to exclude potentially sensitive information, such as hardcoded API keys, passwords, or Personal Identifiable Information (PII), which may have appeared in public datasets used for training.	High	No
Multi-File Context	Analyzes up to 10 open files in the project to provide contextually accurate code suggestions. This improves relevance and consistency across the project while ensuring that the data remains local and private.	High	Yes
Custom Settings	Offers configurable options to developers, such as enabling or disabling Copilot for specific repositories, programming languages, or projects. These settings allow fine-grained control over Copilot's behavior and privacy features.	High	Yes
Feedback Integration	Incorporates user feedback to refine Copilot's suggestions. Developers can submit feedback on suggestion quality. Feedback data is anonymized to protect privacy and ensure compliance with data security standards.	High	Yes

Code Retention Policy	Ensures that no code snippets, project files, or user-generated content are retained on GitHub servers. This policy safeguards proprietary or confidential information from unauthorized access.	High	No

Table 9.9: *An Overview of GitHub Copilot's Privacy and Security Features, Including Data Handling Methods, Control Options, and Security Classifications*

Key Details:

- **Security Level:**
  - **High:** Indicates that the feature has robust safeguards to protect sensitive information.
  - **Medium:** Requires some developer oversight to ensure security.
- **Developer Control:**
  - **Yes:** Feature allows for granular adjustments by the developer.
  - **No:** Feature operates automatically, without user intervention.

Security Classification of GitHub Copilot Features

To help developers and organizations assess trust and safety, GitHub Copilot categorizes its features based on their security impact. This visual highlights the security levels of key capabilities such as local processing, anonymization, and telemetry, making it easier to evaluate risk and privacy alignment.

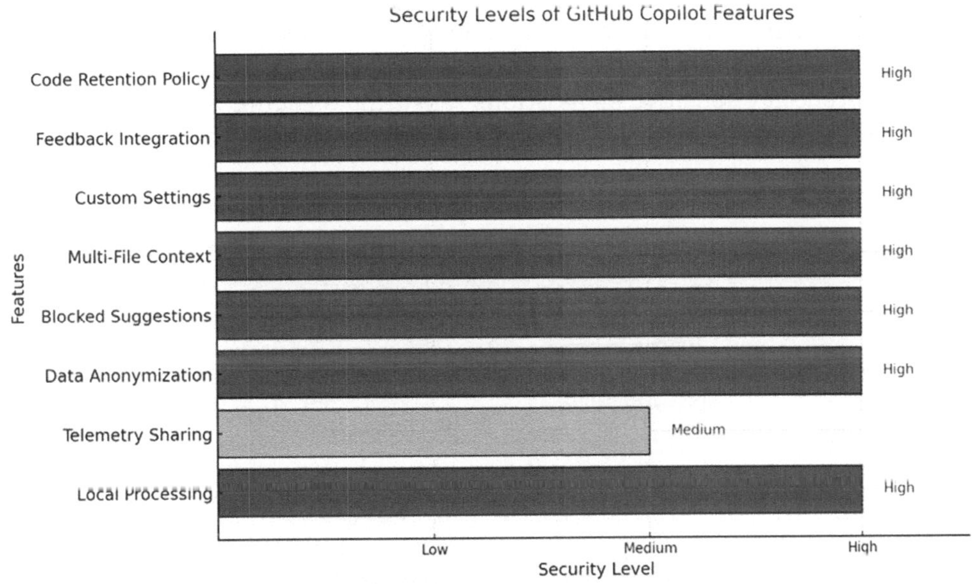

Figure 9.19: *Bar Chart Displaying the Security Levels of GitHub Copilot Features, with Most Rated 'High' and Telemetry Sharing Marked 'Medium' due to its Optional Data Exchange*

Privacy Architecture of GitHub Copilot: Process Classification

GitHub Copilot's data handling pipeline is built around security-first architecture, where every step is either secure by design, optionally enabled by users, or filtered to block risky outputs. This classification diagram groups major components like telemetry sharing, suggestion filtering, and multi-file analysis are based on their security nature.

The following diagram visualizes GitHub Copilot's suggestion generation and feedback workflow, highlighting secure, optional, and filtered processes–from local processing and multi-file context analysis to telemetry sharing and blocked suggestion filtering.

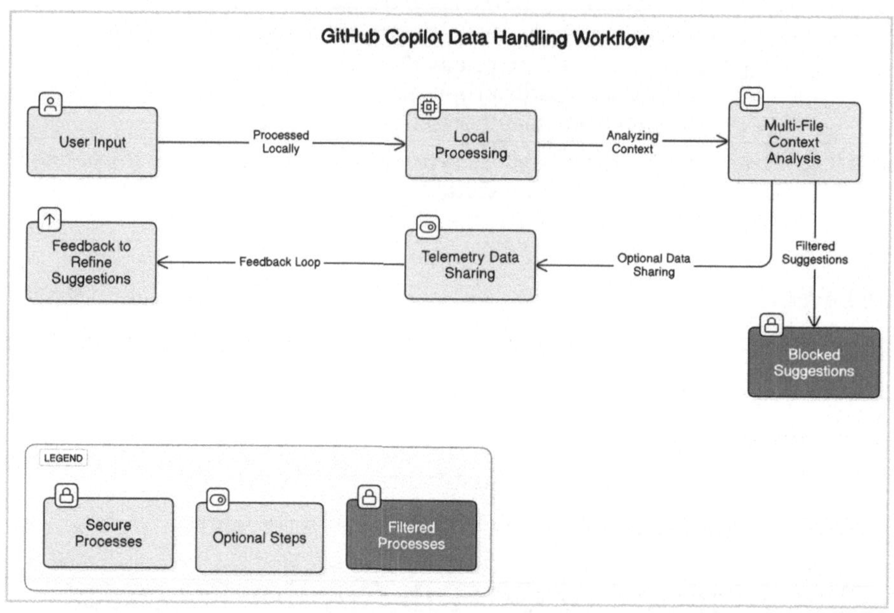

Figure 9.20: *GitHub Copilot Processes User Input through Secure and Privacy-aware Workflows, Incorporating Local Analysis, Optional Telemetry, and Safeguards to Filter Sensitive or Blocked Suggestions*

GitHub Copilot Privacy Workflow for Enterprise Environments

Enterprises can maintain strict privacy and security controls, while using GitHub Copilot by leveraging its local processing capabilities and output validation mechanisms. This workflow diagram illustrates how enterprise teams and Copilot collaborate to disable telemetry, process data locally, and block potentially sensitive suggestions—ensuring a secure and compliant development environment.

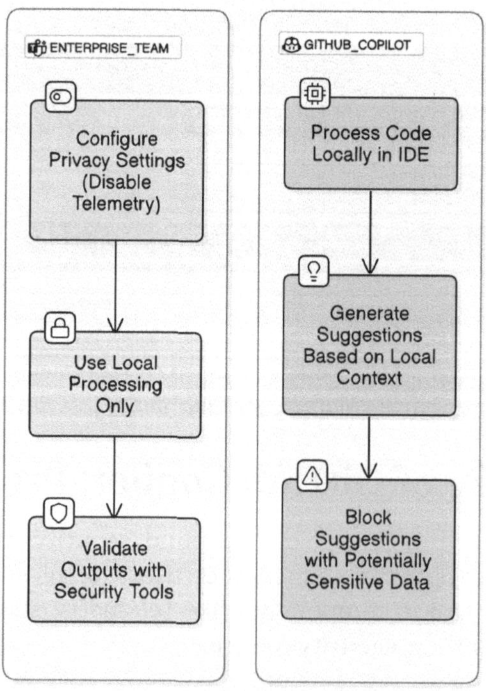

Figure 9.21: *End-to-end Privacy Workflow Showing How Enterprise Teams Configure GitHub Copilot to Operate Securely with Local-only Processing, Suggestion Filtering, and Output Validation*

Two Swimlanes Representing Roles:

- **Enterprise Team:** Focuses on configuring privacy settings, and ensuring secure workflows.
- **GitHub Copilot:** Handles code processing, and suggestion generation, while maintaining privacy safeguards.

Enterprise Team Responsibilities:

- **Configure Privacy Settings:** Disable telemetry to prevent data sharing (Toggle Switch Icon).
- **Use Local Processing Only:** Ensure that all code processing occurs within the IDE (Lock Icon).
- **Validate Outputs with Security Tools:** Apply security checks to review generated suggestions (Shield Icon).

GitHub Copilot Responsibilities:

- **Process Code Locally in IDE:** Analyze and process code directly within the local development environment (Chip Icon).
- **Generate Suggestions Based on Local Context:** Provide relevant code suggestions tailored to the local context (Lightbulb Icon).
- **Block Suggestions with Potentially Sensitive Data:** Avoid generating suggestions that may expose the sensitive data (Alert Icon).

Key Features:

- **Clear Responsibility Separation:** Highlights the collaboration between enterprise privacy settings, and GitHub Copilot's processing.
- **Privacy Safeguards:** Emphasis on telemetry disabling, local-only processing, and sensitive data handling.

Tools for Privacy Control

GitHub Copilot provides robust features and settings to empower developers and organizations to manage and monitor their data privacy effectively. These features are designed to give users granular control over how Copilot interacts with their code and telemetry data.

- **User Settings for GitHub Copilot:**
  - Developers can enable or disable Copilot for specific repositories or programming languages.
  - Fine-grained controls allow adjustment of telemetry sharing preferences.
- **Feedback Mechanisms:**
  - Developers can provide feedback on Copilot's suggestions to improve its functionality, while preserving privacy.
- **Audit Logs:**
  - Organizations can track Copilot usage across teams to ensure compliance with internal policies.

GitHub Copilot offers a variety of feature-level controls and integrations, allowing developers and organizations to tailor Copilot's usage to their privacy, productivity, and compliance needs. The following screenshot showcases the configurable settings available in Copilot, including interface availability, third-party integrations, and duplication detection safeguards.

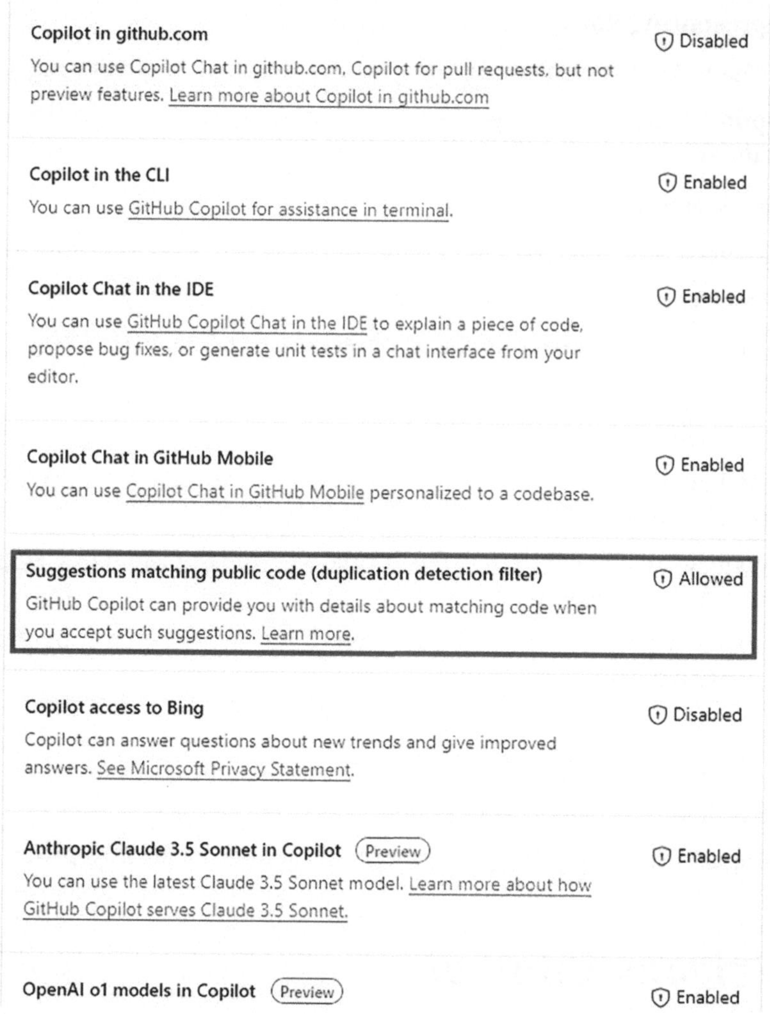

Copilot in github.com — Disabled
You can use Copilot Chat in github.com, Copilot for pull requests, but not preview features. Learn more about Copilot in github.com

Copilot in the CLI — Enabled
You can use GitHub Copilot for assistance in terminal.

Copilot Chat in the IDE — Enabled
You can use GitHub Copilot Chat in the IDE to explain a piece of code, propose bug fixes, or generate unit tests in a chat interface from your editor.

Copilot Chat in GitHub Mobile — Enabled
You can use Copilot Chat in GitHub Mobile personalized to a codebase.

Suggestions matching public code (duplication detection filter) — Allowed
GitHub Copilot can provide you with details about matching code when you accept such suggestions. Learn more.

Copilot access to Bing — Disabled
Copilot can answer questions about new trends and give improved answers. See Microsoft Privacy Statement.

Anthropic Claude 3.5 Sonnet in Copilot (Preview) — Enabled
You can use the latest Claude 3.5 Sonnet model. Learn more about how GitHub Copilot serves Claude 3.5 Sonnet.

OpenAI o1 models in Copilot (Preview) — Enabled

Figure 9.22: *GitHub Copilot Feature Configuration Panel, Highlighting Enabled Services, Integration Options, and Duplication Detection Filter Settings*

Real-World Example: Privacy in Action

Scenario: A FinTech company adopts GitHub Copilot to accelerate development.

- **Privacy Concern:** The company needs to ensure that no sensitive data, such as customer details or API keys, are exposed through Copilot.
- **Solution:**
  - Developers configure Copilot settings to disable suggestions that could process the sensitive data.
  - Teams use GitHub's telemetry opt-out feature to prevent sharing the usage data.
  - Regular privacy audits are conducted using GitHub's tools to monitor compliance.

Outcome: The company benefits from Copilot's productivity enhancements, without compromising data security or privacy compliance.

Thus, to ensure responsible AI adoption in regulated industries like Fintech, it is crucial to align development workflows with privacy mandates. This diagram illustrates the collaborative interaction between a Fintech company's internal privacy controls and GitHub Copilot's privacy-first architecture—highlighting how local code processing, telemetry control, and feedback loops operate within compliance boundaries.

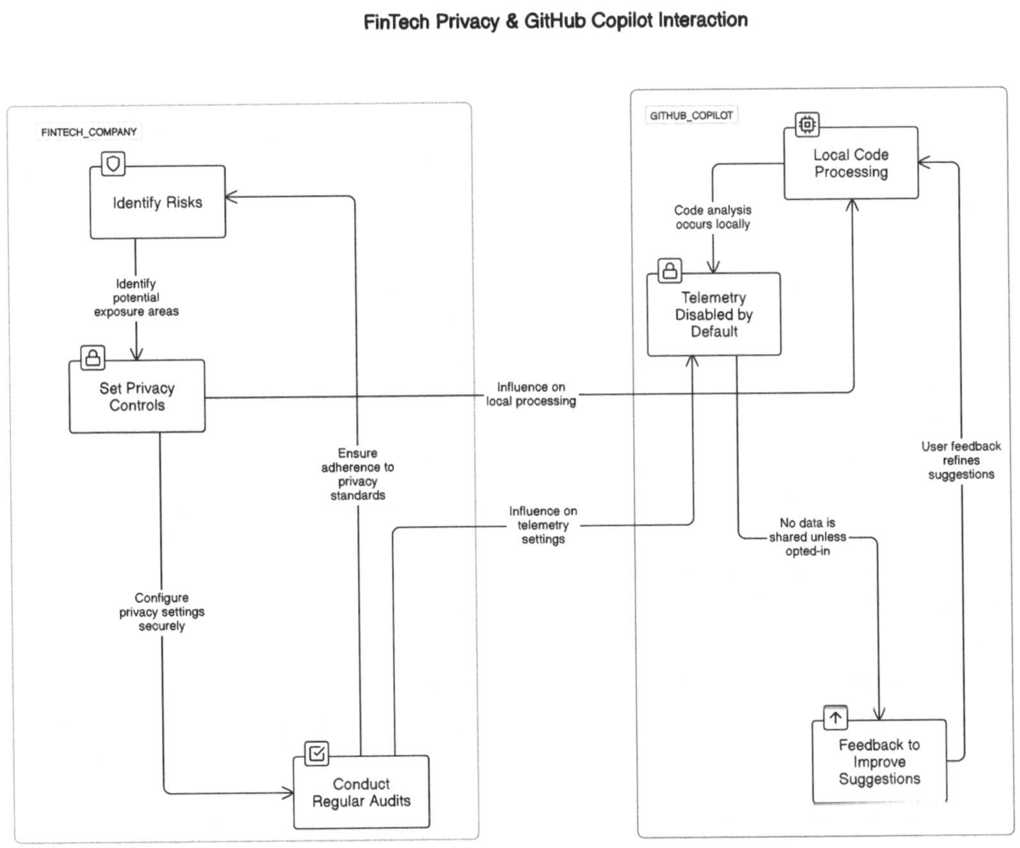

Figure 9.23: *Interaction between Fintech's Privacy Practices and GitHub Copilot's Processing as well as Telemetry Safeguards*

Key Insights: GitHub Copilot integrates strong privacy principles into its design, ensuring responsible AI usage. The following table summarizes how Copilot addresses the key privacy concerns, including data protection, transparency, user control, and regulatory compliance.

Aspect	GitHub Copilot's Privacy Approach
Data Protection	Processes user data locally, and ensures no storage of generated code snippets.
Transparency	Provides clear documentation and FAQs through the GitHub Trust Center.
User Empowerment	Enables developers to control Copilot's behavior, and telemetry sharing settings.
Compliance	Adheres to global privacy regulations, such as GDPR and CCPA, tailoring operations to regional laws.

Table 9.10: *GitHub Copilot's Approach to Privacy and Compliance across Key Dimensions*

Preventing Accidental Exposure

GitHub Copilot's suggestions are based on patterns it has learned which may occasionally include **snippets resembling publicly available code**. Developers should validate outputs to avoid potential licensing issues or vulnerabilities.

Potential Risks:

- **Code Licensing Conflicts:** Generated code might inadvertently reflect patterns from open-source projects under restrictive licenses.
- **Injection of Vulnerabilities:** Generated snippets may not include the best security practices, requiring manual review.

Best Practices:

- **Validate Suggestions:**
  - Always verify Copilot's output for accuracy, security, and relevance.
  - Run static analysis tools to detect potential vulnerabilities.
- **Establish Governance:**
  - Define clear policies for Copilot usage in organizational settings.
  - Educate teams about secure coding practices, when using AI-assisted tools.

Mitigating Common Security Risks

- **Hardcoded Secrets**
  - **Risk:** Copilot might suggest code with hardcoded credentials.
  - **Solution:** Always use secure storage methods, such as environment variables or secret management tools.

  Prompt Example: "`Write a Python function to connect to an S3 bucket using AWS credentials stored in environment variables.`"
- **Code Injection**
  - **Risk:** Copilot might suggest insecure handling of user input.
  - **Solution:** Sanitize and validate inputs before processing.

  Prompt Example: "Generate an Express.js route for handling user input securely."

Organizational Security Measures:

- **Role-Based Access Control (RBAC):** Limit Copilot usage to trusted environments, and authorized personnel.

Secure Development Lifecycle (SDLC) Integration:

- Incorporate Copilot into a robust SDLC framework, including:
  - Automated security scans.
  - Code reviews to validate AI-generated suggestions.
- Audit Trails
- Maintain logs of Copilot-generated code, and integrate them into the existing compliance workflows.

Metrics for Measuring Security Compliance

Security compliance is a critical concern in modern development workflows. The following table highlights measurable improvements observed in key security metrics, after integrating GitHub Copilot into the review and coding processes. It demonstrates how AI-assisted development can reduce detection times, lower human error, and minimize risks like hardcoded secrets.

Metric	Before Copilot	With Copilot
Time to Detect Vulnerabilities	~30 minutes per review	~15 minutes with AI-assisted tools
Error Rate in Code Reviews	~5-10%	~2-5% with Copilot suggestions
Hardcoded Secrets Found	High	Reduced with Copilot safeguards

Table 9.11: *Comparative Security Compliance Metrics before and after Adopting GitHub Copilot.*

Copilot's Limitations and Areas for Improvement

GitHub Copilot is a powerful tool that accelerates development workflows, but it has certain limitations and areas, where improvements could further enhance its capabilities. Understanding these aspects ensures that developers can use Copilot effectively, while mitigating challenges.

Limitations of GitHub Copilot

- **Context Limitations:**
  - Copilot can process up to **10 open files** or around **150 lines of code** for context. This limitation may affect complex projects, where broader context awareness is critical.
- **Over-reliance on Suggestions:**
  - Developers might over-rely on Copilot, leading to a lack of understanding of the underlying logic or codebase.
  - Suggested code may sometimes be inefficient, or not follow project-specific standards.
- **Lack of Domain-Specific Knowledge:**
  - While Copilot excels in general coding tasks, it may struggle with domain-specific or highly specialized problems, requiring significant developer intervention.
- **Security Risks:**
  - Despite its filtering mechanisms, Copilot may occasionally generate code that includes sensitive data patterns, such as API keys or credentials, requiring manual review.
- **Licensing Concerns:**
  - Copilot-generated code may inadvertently reproduce snippets from public repositories, without clarifying the licensing implications.
- **Debugging and Testing:**
  - Copilot is better at generating code than debugging or optimizing it that still requires significant manual intervention from developers.

Areas for Improvement

- **Enhanced Context Awareness:**
  - Expanding the context length, or incorporating external file dependencies could improve suggestion accuracy for larger projects.
- **Domain-Specific Training:**
  - Tailoring Copilot models for specific industries (for example, healthcare, finance, and so on) would enable it to provide more relevant and specialized suggestions.
- **Better Debugging and Optimization Support:**
  - Introducing debugging capabilities or optimization recommendations alongside code generation would streamline the development workflow.
- **Improved Licensing Transparency:**
  - Copilot could offer clearer notifications, when suggestions are derived from public code, ensuring developers remain compliant with open-source licensing.
- **Real-Time Collaboration:**
  - Enhanced support for real-time collaboration, enabling developers to use Copilot effectively in pair programming or team-based workflows.

Best Practices to Mitigate Limitations

To ensure responsible and effective use of GitHub Copilot in professional development environments, consider the following best practices:

- **Code Review:** Always review Copilot-generated code for correctness, security, and performance.
- **Use Project-Specific Settings:** Configure Copilot to align with your project standards, such as disabling telemetry, or enabling duplication detection.
- **Educate Teams:** Train teams to leverage Copilot as a complementary tool, rather than a replacement for manual development skills.

Real-World Case Study: Copilot's Impact in an Enterprise Setting

To illustrate the practical benefits of GitHub Copilot in a large-scale enterprise, let us consider a scenario from a leading financial services organization, "*FinSecure Inc.*," which integrated Copilot into its core development workflow.

Scenario: FinSecure's development teams faced significant delays in feature delivery due to repetitive tasks, manual code reviews, and extensive debugging of legacy code. The complexity of adhering to strict regulatory and security compliance further compounded these delays.

- **Implementation of GitHub Copilot:** FinSecure decided to integrate GitHub Copilot across their teams after a successful pilot within a single division. Initially, developers were trained in crafting effective prompts to leverage Copilot's full potential. Within three months, developers reported substantial improvements in multiple areas, such as:
- **Code Refactoring Efficiency:** Copilot's intelligent suggestions accelerated refactoring of complex legacy financial calculation modules, reducing typical refactoring tasks from days to hours.
- **Automated Security Compliance:** Using custom prompts, teams automated the generation of boilerplate code aligned with stringent financial industry regulations. This reduced manual compliance checks by approximately 45%.
- **Accelerated API Optimization:** Copilot improved API query performance significantly. For instance, a critical customer data retrieval endpoint optimized using Copilot reduced response time by 60% compared to the manually optimized version.
- **Quantified Benefits:** The following table summarizes measurable improvements observed after adopting GitHub Copilot across key engineering metrics, such as delivery time, review effort, security, and productivity.

Metric	Before Copilot	After Copilot	Improvement
Average Feature Delivery Time	4 weeks	2 weeks	**50% ↓**
Time Spent on Code Reviews	15 hrs/week	6 hrs/week	**60% ↓**
Security Issues Detected	Avg. 8/month	Avg. 2/month	**75% ↓**
Developer Productivity	Baseline (100%)	Increased (160%)	**60% ↑**

Table 9.12: *Copilot Adoption Led to Faster Delivery, Reduced Code Review Time, Fewer Security Issues, and a 60% Boost in Developer Productivity*

Developer Feedback:

- 92% of developers found Copilot valuable in daily tasks.

- 88% reported increased confidence in maintaining high-quality, compliant code.
- Teams expressed significant reductions in burnout due to fewer repetitive tasks.

Quarter-Wise Rollout Plan of GitHub Copilot at FinSecure

The following timeline visual illustrates the structured rollout of GitHub Copilot across FinSecure's enterprise teams. Beginning with pilot training and prompt engineering, the integration progressed through legacy code modernization, automated security compliance, and intelligent API optimization–culminating in a full-scale rollout. Each quarter highlights a key milestone, emphasizing Copilot's ability to drive measurable improvements in code quality, speed, and regulatory readiness, within large-scale development environments.

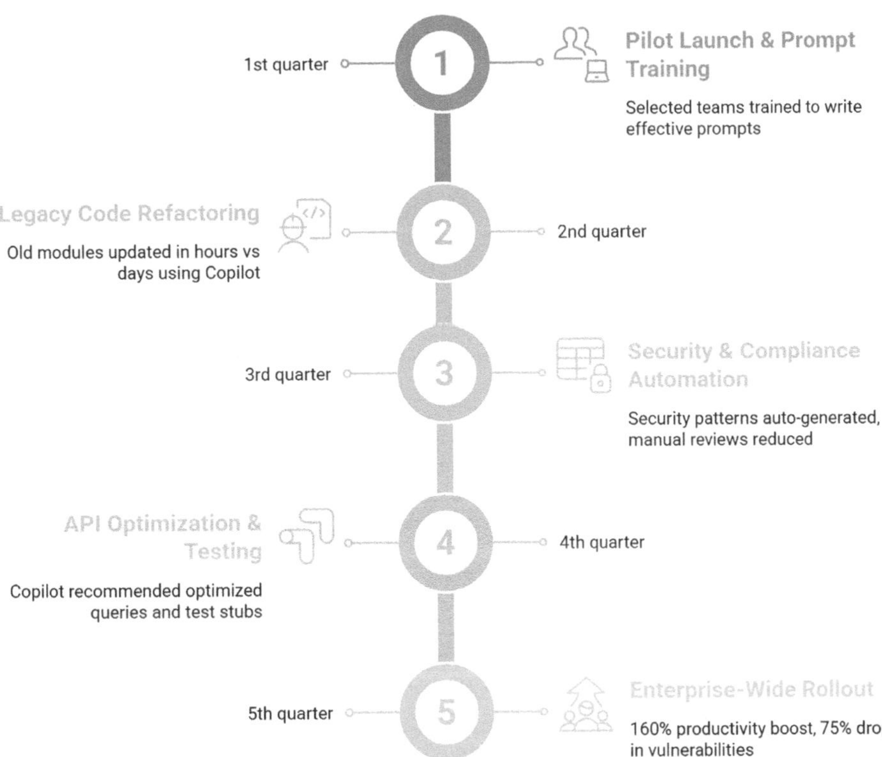

Figure 9.24: Quarter-wise Rollout Strategy of GitHub Copilot at FinSecure, Showcasing Key Stages and Outcomes

Before vs After: FinSecure's Engineering Transformation with GitHub Copilot

The following visual captures the tangible before-and-after transformation at FinSecure after the integration of GitHub Copilot. By comparing the key development metrics–such as delivery time, code review hours, security issues, and productivity it clearly showcases how Copilot helped the enterprise shift from inefficiencies and manual overhead to a streamlined, AI-assisted development workflow. Each metric reflects measurable gains in performance, compliance, and developer satisfaction.

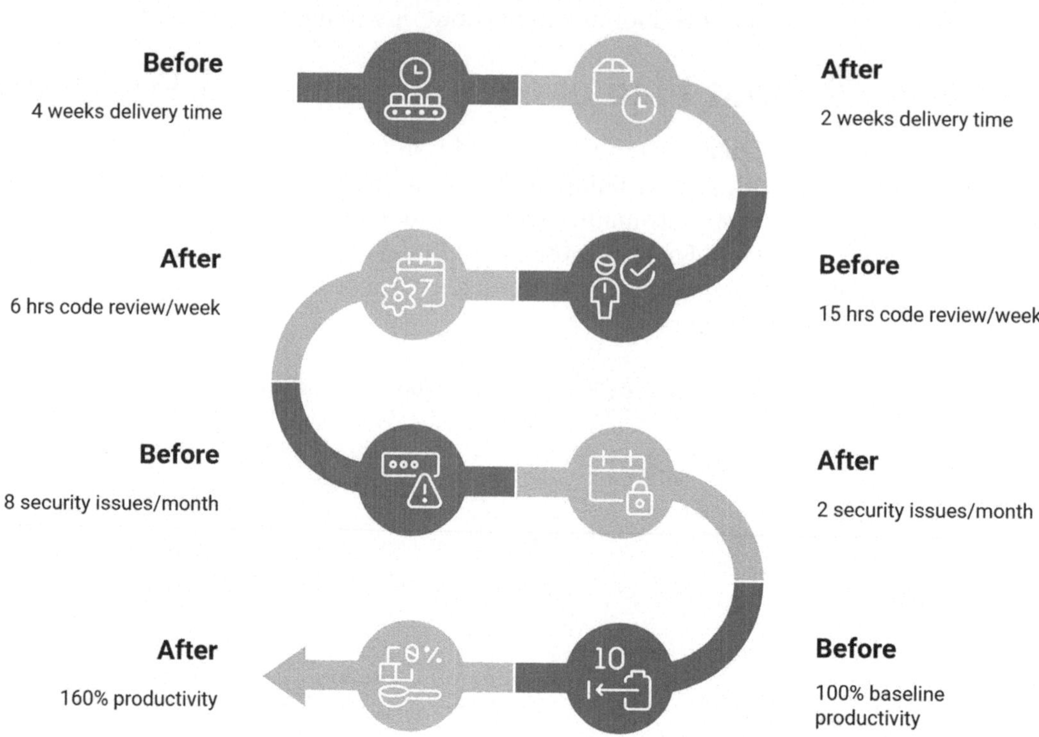

Figure 9.25: *Side-by-side Comparison of FinSecure's Development Metrics before and after Adopting GitHub Copilot*

Conclusion of the Case Study:

FinSecure's adoption of GitHub Copilot demonstrates tangible benefits at an enterprise scale, including reduced development cycles, enhanced security compliance, and substantial productivity improvements. This real-world impact underscores the strategic advantage enterprises can achieve by integrating AI-driven tools like GitHub Copilot into their software development lifecycle.

Conclusion

GitHub Copilot is more than just a coding assistant–it is a catalyst for transforming the modern software development lifecycle. Throughout this chapter, we explored its advanced capabilities in action, such as from intelligently refactoring legacy code to streamlining performance optimization, reducing repetitive efforts, and improving developer efficiency.

Despite its current limitations–such as contextual awareness boundaries and licensing considerations–Copilot proves to be a valuable tool, when leveraged thoughtfully. By adopting these best practices, recognizing its strengths, and integrating it strategically, developers can actually create scalable, secure, and maintainable applications with greater speed and precision!

As the technology evolves with more advanced models and refined features, Copilot's role in shaping the future of development will only grow stronger. Embracing it as a collaborative partner allows teams to focus on what truly matters–creative problem-solving, system design, and delivering business value.

In the next chapter, *Testing and Debugging with Copilot*, we will dive into how Copilot can assist in writing robust test cases, identifying bugs, and accelerating debugging workflows–ensuring not just faster development, but also higher code quality and reliability.

Multiple Choice Questions

1. What is the key benefit of using well-crafted prompts with GitHub Copilot?
    a. It reduces internet usage during coding.
    b. It improves accuracy and relevance of AI-generated code.
    c. It removes the need for documentation.
    d. It disables telemetry sharing.
2. Which prompting method provides Copilot with multiple examples to learn from?
    a. Zero-shot prompting
    b. One-shot prompting
    c. Few-shot prompting
    d. Multi-shot prompting
3. In the context of Playwright test automation, what does a few-shot prompt enable Copilot to do more effectively?
    a. Run tests without code.
    b. Create UI mockups.
    c. Handle both valid and invalid test cases.
    d. Ignore browser compatibility.
4. Which of the following is NOT a benefit of refactoring code using Copilot?
    a. Improved modularity
    b. Enhanced maintainability
    c. Automatic CI/CD deployment
    d. Better scalability
5. What does a common optimization Copilot perform for nested loops to improve performance?
    a. Adds more loops
    b. Uses synchronous blocking functions
    c. Replaces loops with hash maps or sets
    d. Converts loops to HTML tables
6. Which of the following tasks can Copilot automate most effectively?
    a. Legal compliance review
    b. Boilerplate code generation
    c. UI wireframe design
    d. Deploying cloud infrastructure without DevOps knowledge

7. What is the purpose of integrating Copilot with CI/CD workflows?
    a. To enable Copilot to debug code automatically
    b. To generate performance dashboards
    c. To simplify test, build, and deploy automation
    d. To schedule daily stand-up meetings
8. Which component enables Copilot to understand surrounding project files for better suggestions?
    a. Prompt tokenizer
    b. Multi-file context engine
    c. Codex Visualizer
    d. Feedback annotator
9. Which privacy-first practice does Copilot follow by default in enterprise settings?
    a. Always stores code snippets on cloud
    b. Shares code with GitHub by default
    c. Processes code locally in the IDE
    d. Automatically shares telemetry with partners
10. Which of the following is the best practice when using Copilot for professional development work?
    a. Always accept the first suggestion.
    b. Avoid peer review for Copilot code.
    c. Use vague prompts to test AI creativity.
    d. Review and validate generated code thoroughly.

Answers

1. b
2. c
3. c
4. c
5. c
6. b
7. c
8. b
9. c
10. d

CHAPTER 10
Testing and Debugging with Copilot

Introduction

Testing and debugging are the backbone of delivering reliable and high-quality software. They ensure that every feature works as intended, every integration behaves seamlessly, and the entire system performs under real-world conditions. However, these processes are often time-consuming and prone to human oversight. This is where GitHub Copilot shines as a transformative tool.

By automating repetitive tasks, suggesting intelligent test cases, and pinpointing errors with actionable resolutions, Copilot brings efficiency and precision to testing and debugging workflows. Hence, whether you are writing unit tests for edge cases, designing integration tests for complex systems, or tackling stubborn bugs, Copilot accelerates your development process. Its ability to provide contextual, accurate, and actionable suggestions elevates the reliability of your code, while enabling developers to focus on solving critical problems.

In this chapter, we shall explore how GitHub Copilot empowers developers to ensure code quality, streamline debugging, and improve the overall testing process. Through real-world scenarios and actionable examples, you will gain insights into how Copilot transforms one of the most challenging aspects of software development into a seamless experience.

Structure

In this chapter, we will discuss the following topics:

- Writing Functional Tests with Copilot
- How Copilot Helps in Agile Test Management
- Automation Testing with Copilot
- Debugging Strategies and Tools
- Ensuring Code Quality and Reliability
- Case Studies: Improved Testing Workflows

Writing Functional Tests with Copilot

Functional testing verifies that an application behaves as expected from an end-user perspective. With GitHub Copilot, testers can generate structured **manual test cases**, **test scenarios**, and **BDD scripts** in various formats, including tabular format, **Gherkin syntax (Given-When-Then)**, and **step-by-step descriptions**. This section demonstrates how Copilot can assist in designing functional test cases for **Gmail Login**, refining prompts to improve clarity and comprehensiveness.

Functional Test Design Using Copilot

Scenario: Testing the Gmail Login Workflow

Objective: Document functional test cases for Gmail login, covering:

- Valid and invalid login attempts.
- Account recovery flow.
- Two-step verification.
- Remember Me functionality.
- Login attempts under high traffic conditions.

Test Case Design in Table Format

Prompt:

```
Generate a table for functional test cases for Gmail login. Include columns for Test Case ID, Description, Preconditions, Test Steps, and Expected Results.
```

Copilot's Output:

The following table outlines functional test cases for Gmail login, covering a range of scenarios, including valid and invalid credentials, two-step verification, and login edge cases.

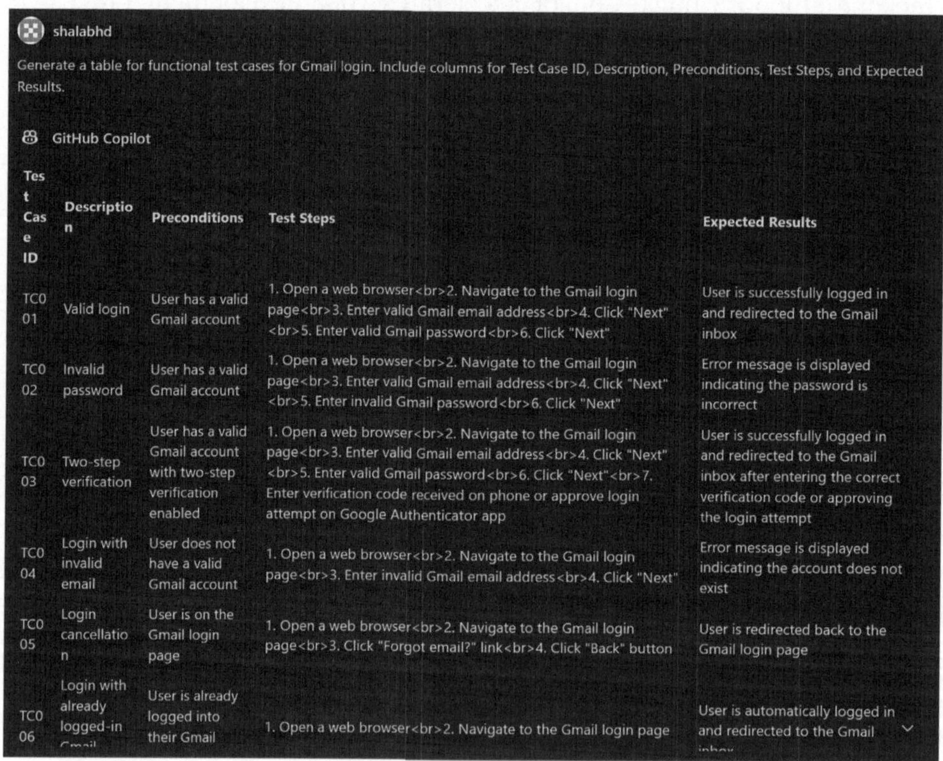

shalabhd

Generate a table for functional test cases for Gmail login. Include columns for Test Case ID, Description, Preconditions, Test Steps, and Expected Results.

GitHub Copilot

Test Case ID	Description	Preconditions	Test Steps	Expected Results
TC001	Valid login	User has a valid Gmail account	1. Open a web browser 2. Navigate to the Gmail login page 3. Enter valid Gmail email address 4. Click "Next" 5. Enter valid Gmail password 6. Click "Next"	User is successfully logged in and redirected to the Gmail inbox
TC002	Invalid password	User has a valid Gmail account	1. Open a web browser 2. Navigate to the Gmail login page 3. Enter valid Gmail email address 4. Click "Next" 5. Enter invalid Gmail password 6. Click "Next"	Error message is displayed indicating the password is incorrect
TC003	Two-step verification	User has a valid Gmail account with two-step verification enabled	1. Open a web browser 2. Navigate to the Gmail login page 3. Enter valid Gmail email address 4. Click "Next" 5. Enter valid Gmail password 6. Click "Next" 7. Enter verification code received on phone or approve login attempt on Google Authenticator app	User is successfully logged in and redirected to the Gmail inbox after entering the correct verification code or approving the login attempt
TC004	Login with invalid email	User does not have a valid Gmail account	1. Open a web browser 2. Navigate to the Gmail login page 3. Enter invalid Gmail email address 4. Click "Next"	Error message is displayed indicating the account does not exist
TC005	Login cancellation	User is on the Gmail login page	1. Open a web browser 2. Navigate to the Gmail login page 3. Click "Forgot email?" link 4. Click "Back" button	User is redirected back to the Gmail login page
TC006	Login with already logged-in	User is already logged into their Gmail	1. Open a web browser 2. Navigate to the Gmail login page	User is automatically logged in and redirected to the Gmail

Figure 10.1: *Functional Test Matrix for Gmail Login–Validating Authentication Flow, Error Handling, and Security Checks*

Test Case Design in Gherkin Language

Prompt:

```
Generate functional test cases for the Gmail login feature using Gherkin syntax with Given-When-Then
```

Copilot's Output:

The following scenarios illustrate functional test cases for Gmail login, using Gherkin syntax, following the Given-When-Then structure for clear, Behavior-Driven Development (BDD) documentation.

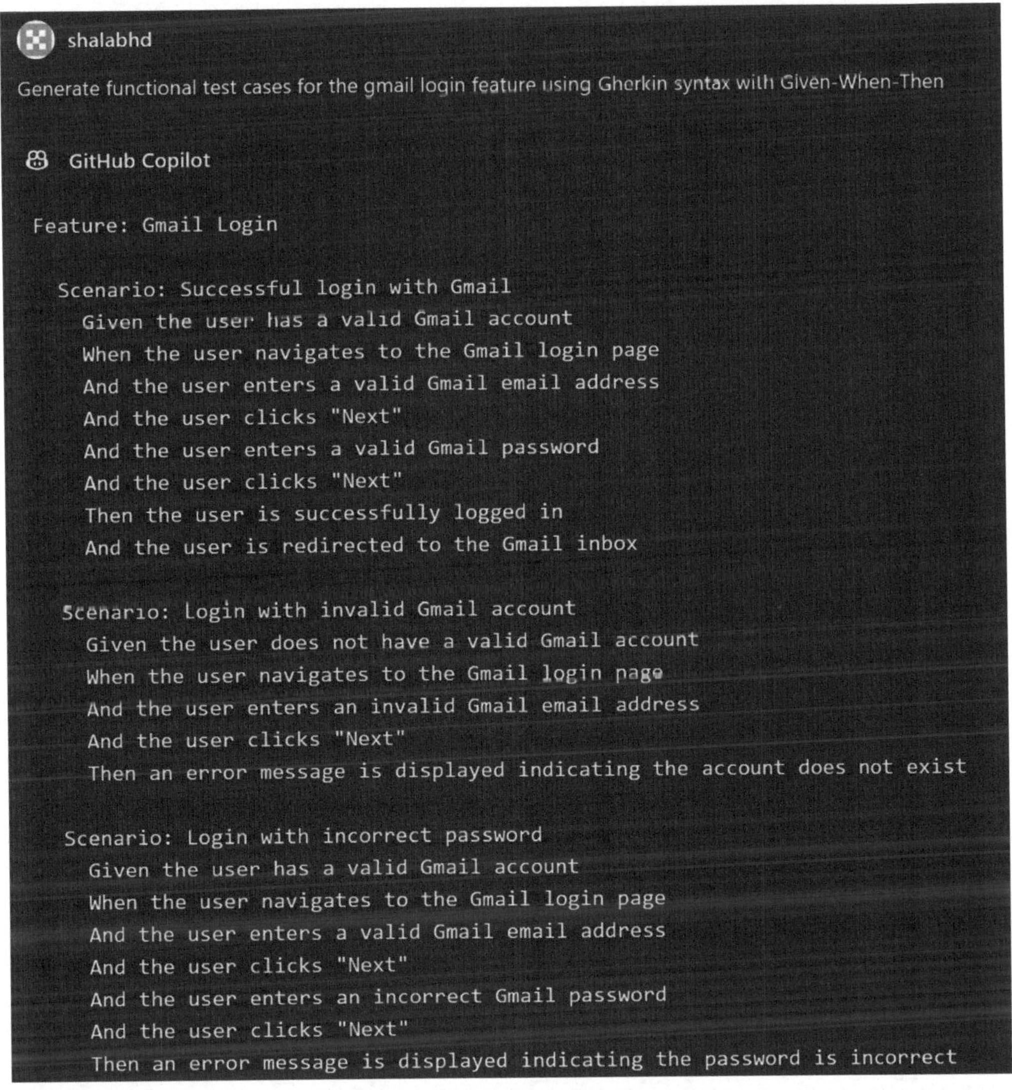

Figure 10.2: *Gherkin-based BDD Test Scenarios for Gmail Login–Covering Successful Login, Invalid Accounts, and Incorrect Password Handling*

Refer the complete code generated at the following GitHub Repo link:

chapter10-testing-and-debugging-with-copilot\functional-tests\gmail-login-gherkin.feature

Generating Manual Test Steps for Functional Testing with Copilot

Prompt:

```
Write detailed manual test steps for Gmail login, covering valid login,
invalid password, and two-step verification.
```

Copilot's Output:

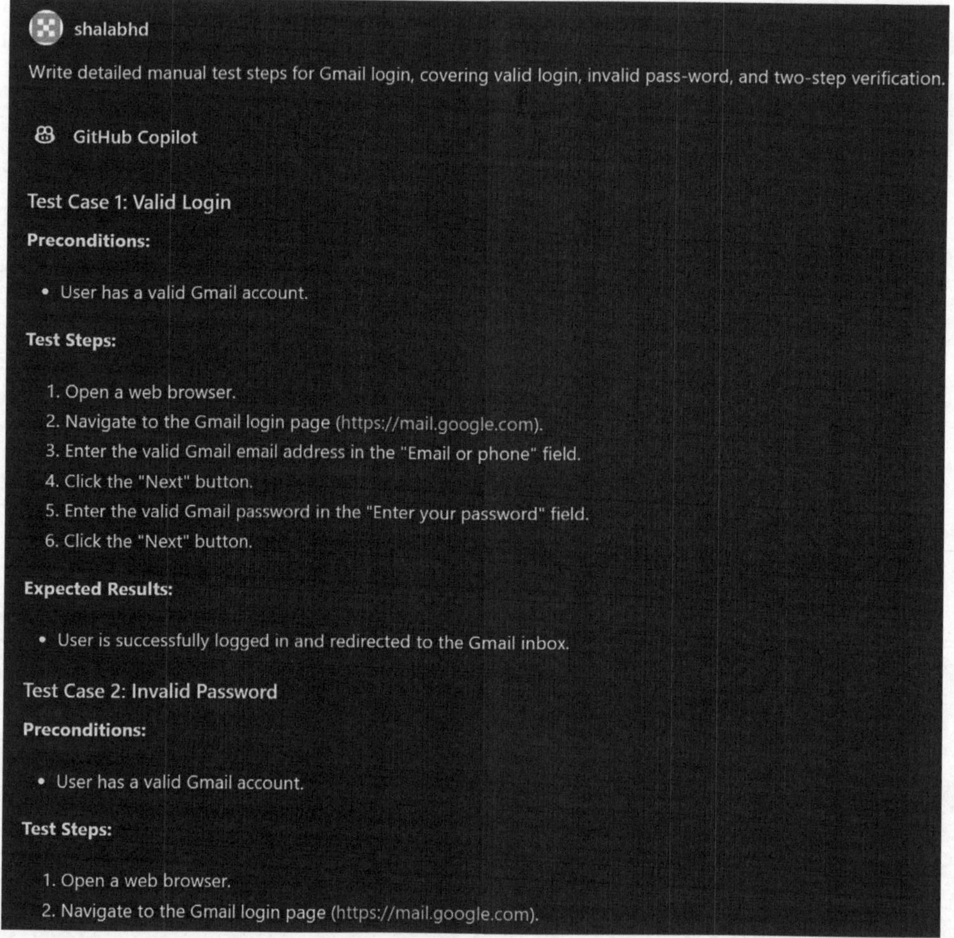

Figure 10.3: *Step-by-step Manual Test Cases for Gmail Login–Ensuring Thorough Validation of Standard and Edge-case Authentication Flows*

Refer the complete code generated at the following GitHub Repo link:

chapter10-testing-and-debugging-with-copilot\functional-tests\gmail-login-functional-table.md

Refining Functional Test Cases with Copilot's Inline Chat

GitHub Copilot's **inline chat** feature can be used to **refactor**, **refine**, or **expand** functional test cases.

Example Chat Refinement:

- **User Prompt:**
  `"Enhance the login test cases by including scenarios for CAPTCHA verification and automatic account lock after multiple failed attempts."`

Copilot's Output:

Extended Gmail login test cases–now include validation for CAPTCHA triggers, and security lockout mechanisms after repeated failed login attempts.

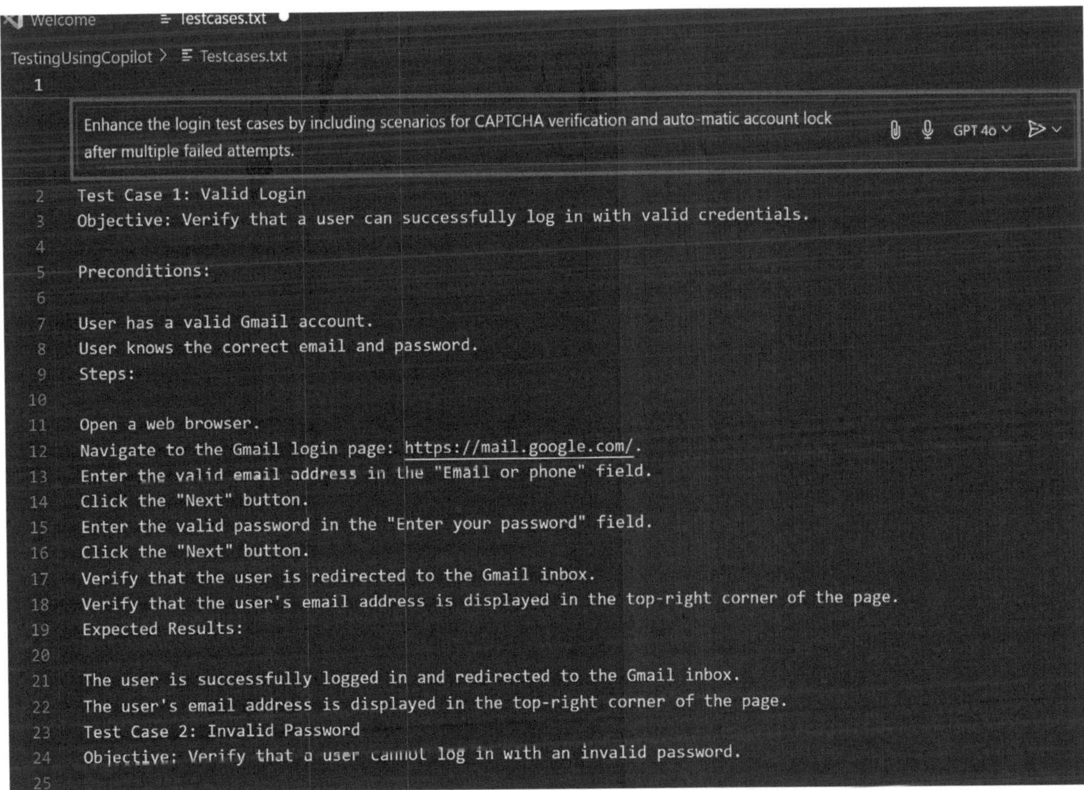

Figure 10.4: *Extended Gmail Login Test Cases—Now Include Validation for CAPTCHA Triggers and Security Lockout Mechanisms after Repeated Failed Login Attempts*

To strengthen login security validation, the following test cases expand coverage by verifying CAPTCHA challenges and automatic account lockout, after repeated failed login attempts.

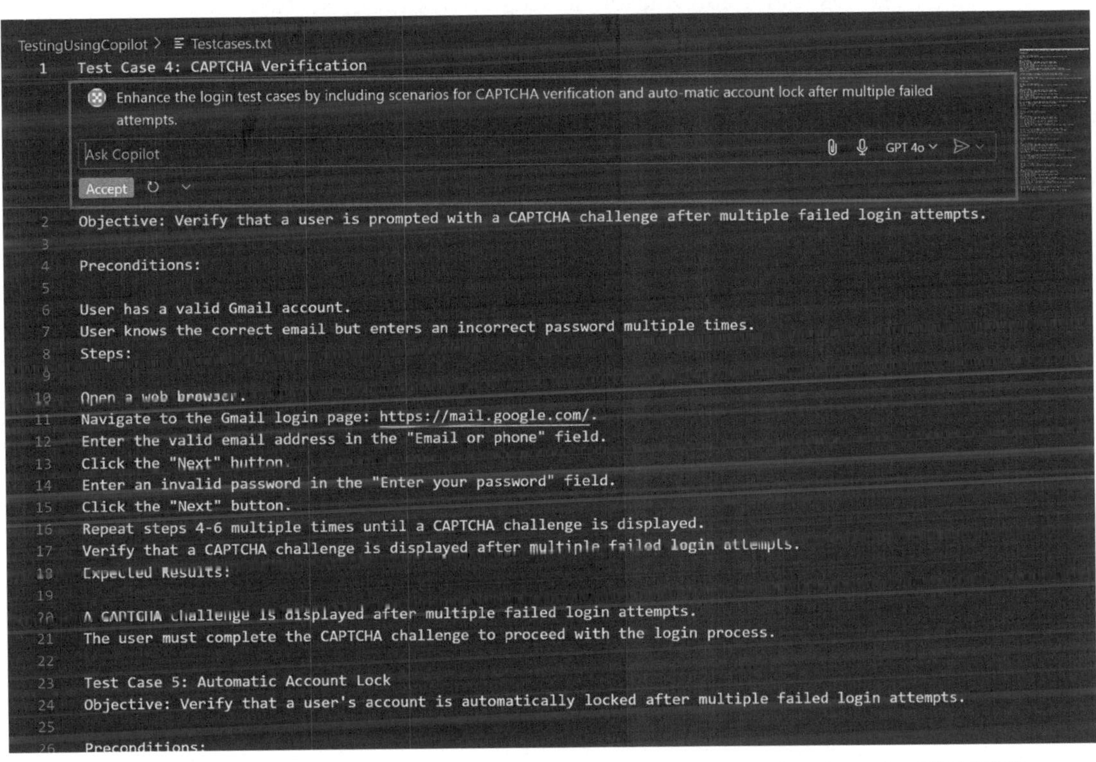

Figure 10.5: *Enhanced Gmail Login Test Coverage Includes Security Flows for CAPTCHA Verification and Account Lock after Multiple Authentication Failures*

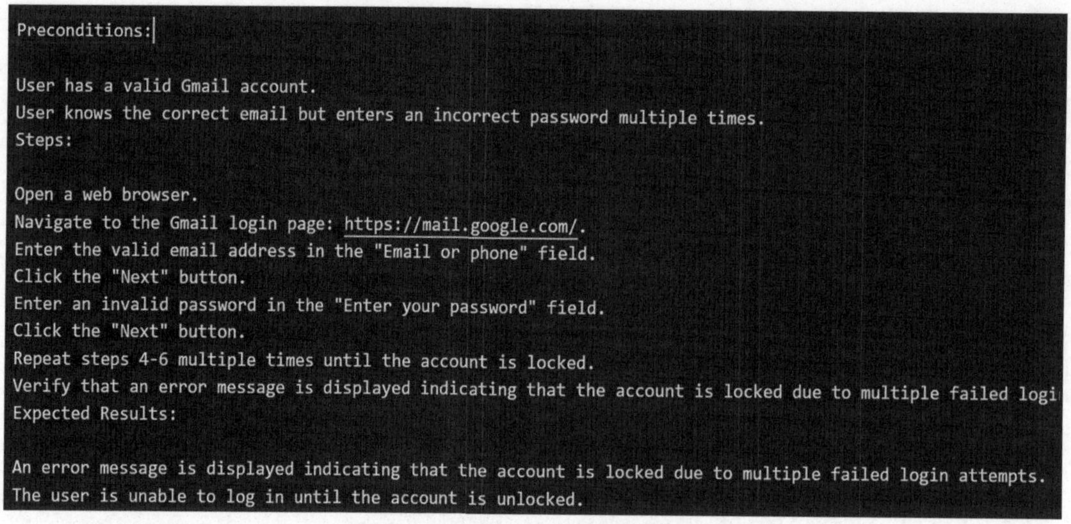

```
Preconditions:

User has a valid Gmail account.
User knows the correct email but enters an incorrect password multiple times.
Steps:

Open a web browser.
Navigate to the Gmail login page: https://mail.google.com/.
Enter the valid email address in the "Email or phone" field.
Click the "Next" button.
Enter an invalid password in the "Enter your password" field.
Click the "Next" button.
Repeat steps 4-6 multiple times until the account is locked.
Verify that an error message is displayed indicating that the account is locked due to multiple failed logi
Expected Results:

An error message is displayed indicating that the account is locked due to multiple failed login attempts.
The user is unable to log in until the account is unlocked.
```

Figure 10.6: *Test Case for Verifying Gmail's Automatic Account lock Feature–Ensuring User Accounts are Protected after Repeated Failed Login Attempts*

Refer the complete code generated at the following GitHub Repo link:

chapter10-testing-and-debugging-with-copilot\functional-tests\gmail-login-enhancements.md

How Copilot Helps in Agile Test Management

GitHub Copilot helps teams streamline Agile testing by:

- Creating Agile Epics, User Stories, and Tasks based on UI/UX designs or product requirements.
- Defining Acceptance Criteria (AC) for user stories, using structured guidelines.
- Generating Test Cases and automation strategies from user stories.
- Accelerating Agile Documentation, Jira ticket creation, and test planning.

Creating Epics, User Stories, and Tasks from Figma Mockups

Figma mockups serve as visual representations of UI components, helping teams derive functional requirements. Copilot assists in:

- Translating UI screens into Epics and User Stories.
- Identifying user actions, and converting them into tasks and sub-tasks.
- Generating Acceptance Criteria to validate feature requirements.

Example: E-commerce Checkout Flow

A designer shares a **Figma mockup** for a **checkout page**. The page includes:

- Product selection
- Address input
- Payment method selection
- Order confirmation

User Prompt:

```
Generate an Epic and Stories from a Figma Mockup
Given a checkout page design in Figma, generate:
```

- **`An Epic summarizing the feature.`**
- **`User Stories breaking down individual functionalities.`**
- **`Acceptance Criteria for each story.`**

Copilot's Output:

The following structure demonstrates how to derive an Epic, and corresponding User Stories from a Figma-based checkout page mockup, complete with acceptance criteria to ensure each functionality is testable and verifiable.

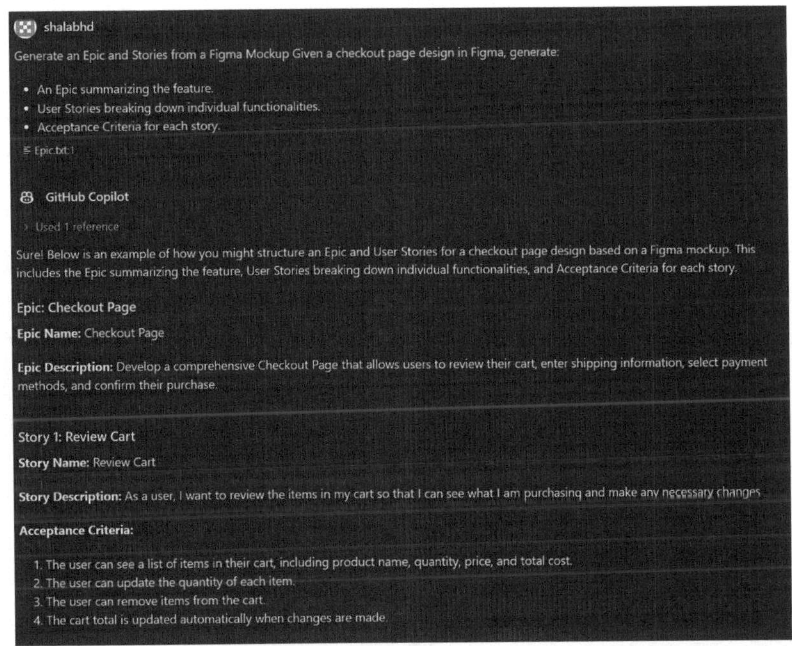

Figure 10.7: *Epic and User Story Breakdown for a Figma-Designed Checkout Page–covering Cart Review Functionality and Validation Checkpoints*

The following breakdown outlines a structured Epic, and four user stories for a **`Checkout Page`**, ensuring each critical user interaction–cart review, shipping input, payment selection, and order confirmation, which is clearly defined with precise acceptance criteria.

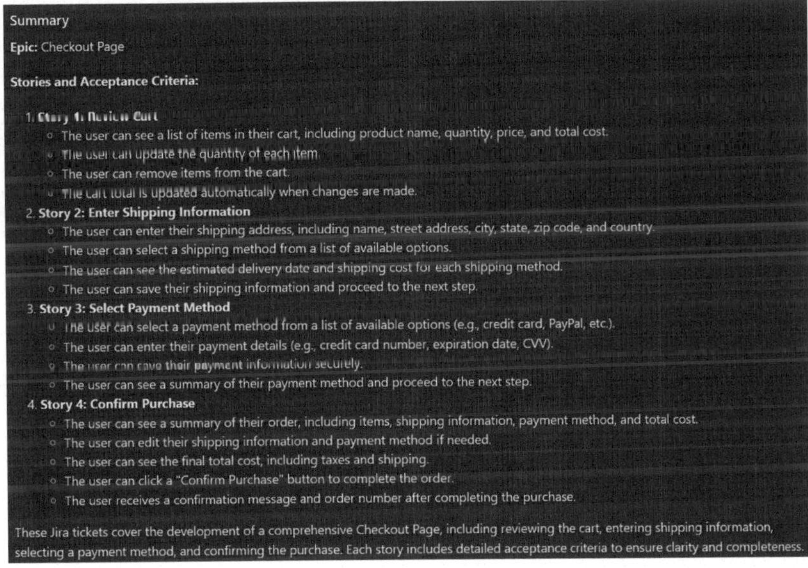

Figure 10.8: *Comprehensive User Stories and Acceptance Criteria for a Checkout Page Epic, Enabling Systematic Implementation and Validation of the E-commerce Purchase Flow*

Generating Agile Epics and Stories without UI Mockups

Scenario: Feature Implementation without a UI Design

When no UI mockups are available, Agile teams define Epics and Stories based on business requirements.

Prompt:

```
Generating Agile Stories without UI Mockups
Generate an Epic and User Stories for Implementing a "User Profile Page" based
only on Business Requirements.
```

Copilot's Output:

This Epic defines the core business-driven functionalities required for a **`User Profile Page`**, with detailed user stories that ensure profile data visibility and editability through clearly defined acceptance criteria.

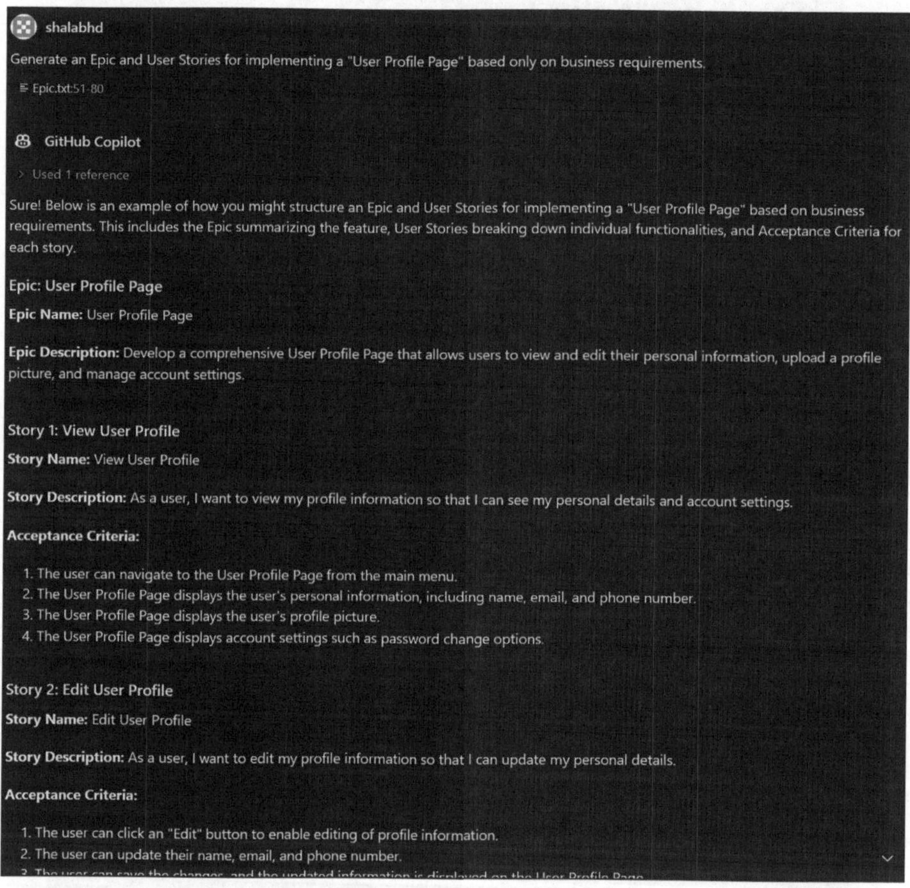

Figure 10.9: *Structured Epic and User Stories Capturing the Essential Features of a User Profile Page, Including Viewing, Editing, and Managing Personal Information with Clarity and Completeness.*

This Epic outlines a detailed breakdown of user stories and acceptance criteria required to implement a robust **`User Profile Page`**, supporting user information display, profile updates, photo uploads, and account settings management.

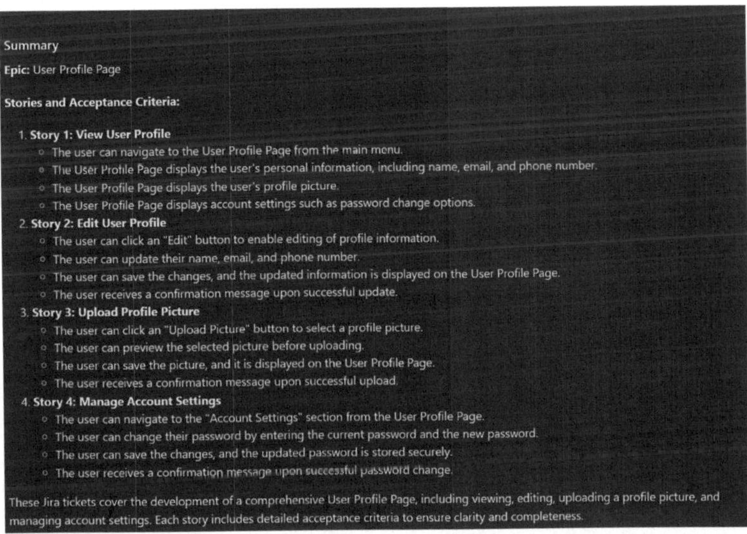

Figure 10.10: *Well-structured Epic and User Stories Detailing the Functional Flow and Validations of a User Profile Page, Ensuring Clarity, Completeness, and Alignment with End-user Expectations.*

Creating Tasks and Sub-tasks in Agile

After defining User Stories, GitHub Copilot can be utilised for creating **tasks and sub-tasks** to help break them down into specific implementation steps.

Breaking Down User Stories into Tasks and Sub-Tasks

Once user stories are defined, they are broken down into **Tasks and Sub-tasks** for execution.

Scenario: Breaking Down US-006 (Edit Profile) into Tasks

Task ID	Task Name	Description
T-001	Create Profile Page UI	Develop the frontend for profile management.
T-002	Implement Profile Update API	Build the backend API for updating user details.
T-003	Validate Input Fields	Ensure email and phone number format validation.

Table 10.1: *Test Cases Breakdown for US-006-Edit Profile Scenario*

Sub-tasks for T-003 (Validate Input Fields)

Sub-task ID	Sub-task Name	Description
ST-001	Validate Email Format	Ensure email follows correct format (for example, `user@example.com`).
ST-002	Validate Phone Number Format	Ensure phone number contains only digits.
ST-003	Prevent Empty Fields	Disallow saving empty fields for required details.

Table 10.2: *Test Cases Breakdown for Validate Input Fields Scenario*

Automating Jira Ticket Creation Using Copilot

Scenario: Creating Jira Tickets for Agile Testing

Instead of manually creating Jira tickets, **Copilot can auto-generate structured Agile tickets.**

Prompt:

```
Generating Jira Tickets for a User Profile Page
Generate Jira tickets for a "User Profile Page" feature. Include an Epic,
Stories, Tasks, and Acceptance Criteria.
```

Copilot's Output:

The following Jira ticket structure demonstrates how to define and organize an Epic, associated user stories, detailed tasks, and clear acceptance criteria to efficiently implement the "`User Profile Page`" functionality.

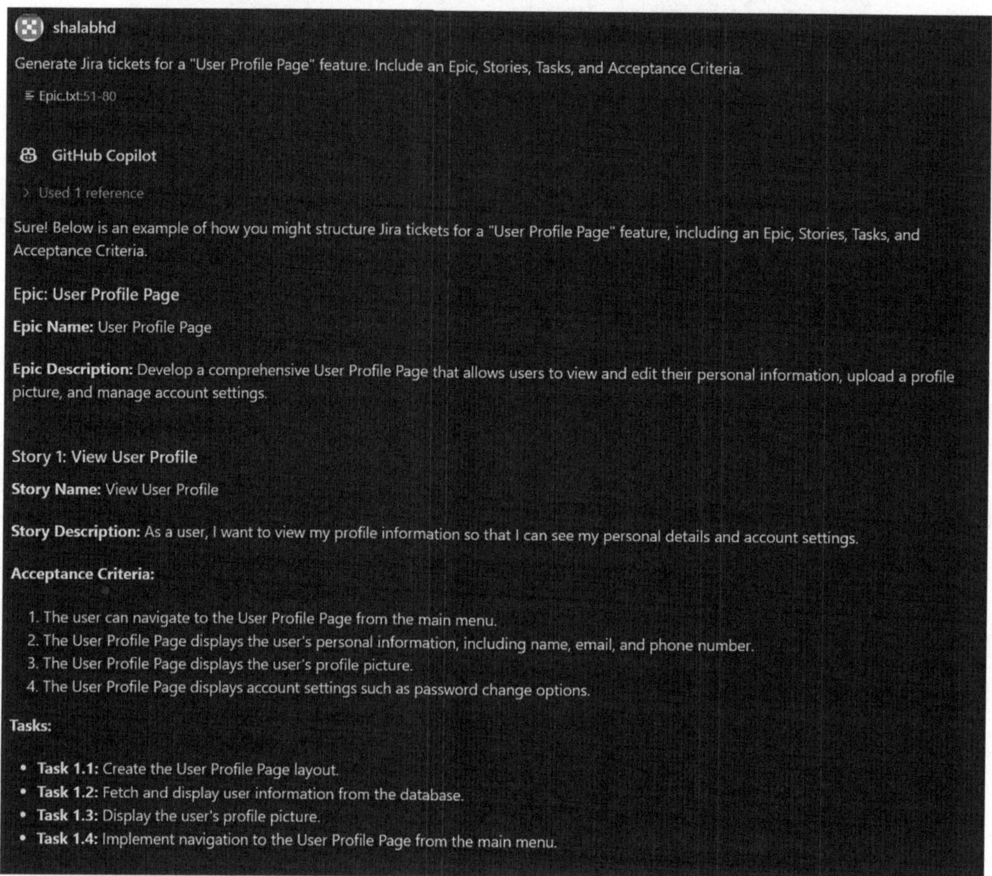

***Figure 10.11:** Jira Breakdown of the User Profile Page Feature with Clearly Defined Epic, Story, Acceptance Criteria, and Actionable Development Tasks for Streamlined Delivery*

Writing Acceptance Criteria and Functional Test Cases with Copilot

After creating Jira tickets, Copilot helps in writing `Acceptance Criteria` and `Test Cases`.

Prompt:

```
Generate Acceptance Criteria for a Login Feature
Write acceptance criteria for a login feature supporting MFA.
```

Copilot's Output:

The following acceptance criteria outline comprehensive scenarios for implementing a secure login flow with Multi-Factor Authentication (MFA), addressing valid and invalid user actions, error handling, and device memory options to enhance user security and experience.

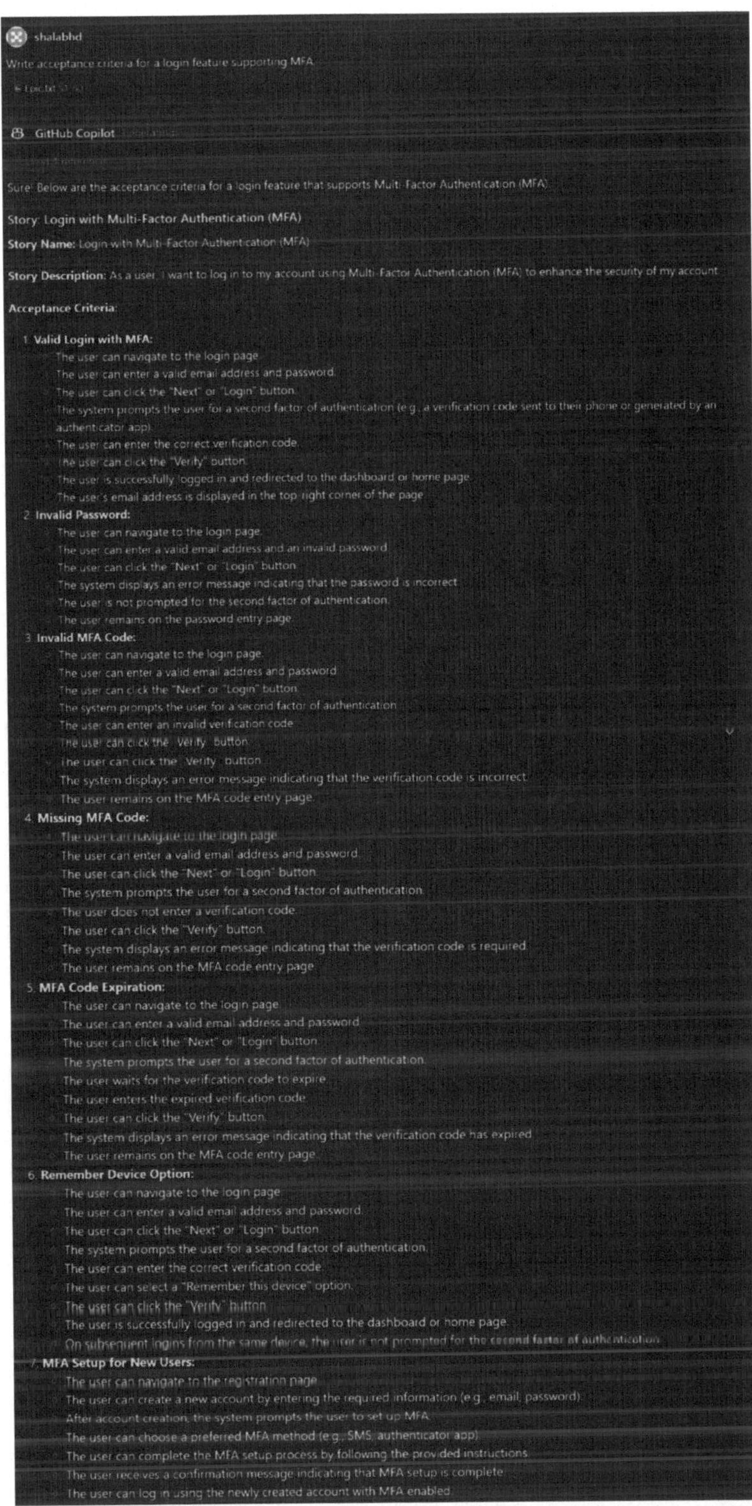

Figure 10.12: *Acceptance Criteria for MFA-Enabled Login: Covers Valid Login Flows, Error conditions (invalid passwords, expired or missing codes), Device Recognition, and Setup for New Users with Secure Second-factor Authentication Support*

Automating Agile Documentation in Jira and Test Management Tools

Copilot helps document Agile workflows in **Jira, Azure DevOps**, and **Confluence**.

Prompt:

```
Generate Agile Test Strategy in Confluence
Generate a Confluence test strategy for Agile testing of a banking app.
Include scope, execution strategy, and automation approach.
```

Copilot's Output:

This Confluence-based Agile Test Strategy outlines a comprehensive approach for validating the functionalities of a banking application through defined scopes, execution phases, and automation practices.

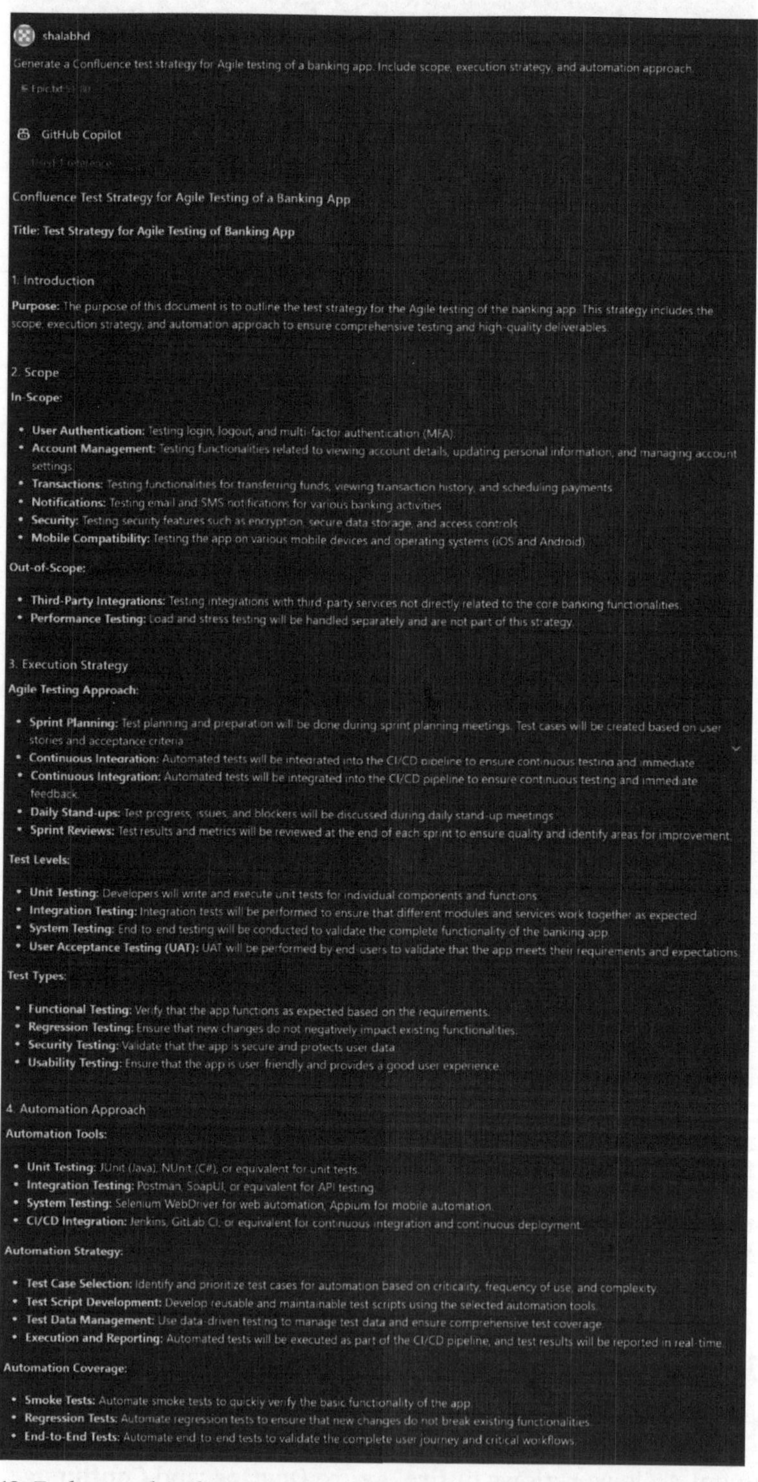

Figure 10.13: *End-to-end Agile Test Strategy for Banking Apps–Covering Scope, Execution Methodology, Testing Types, Tools, and Automation Coverage*

This following detailed Confluence Test Strategy outlines a comprehensive Agile Testing Approach tailored for a banking application, encompassing scope definition, execution plans, automation methodology, metrics tracking, and risk mitigation to ensure quality and delivery excellence.

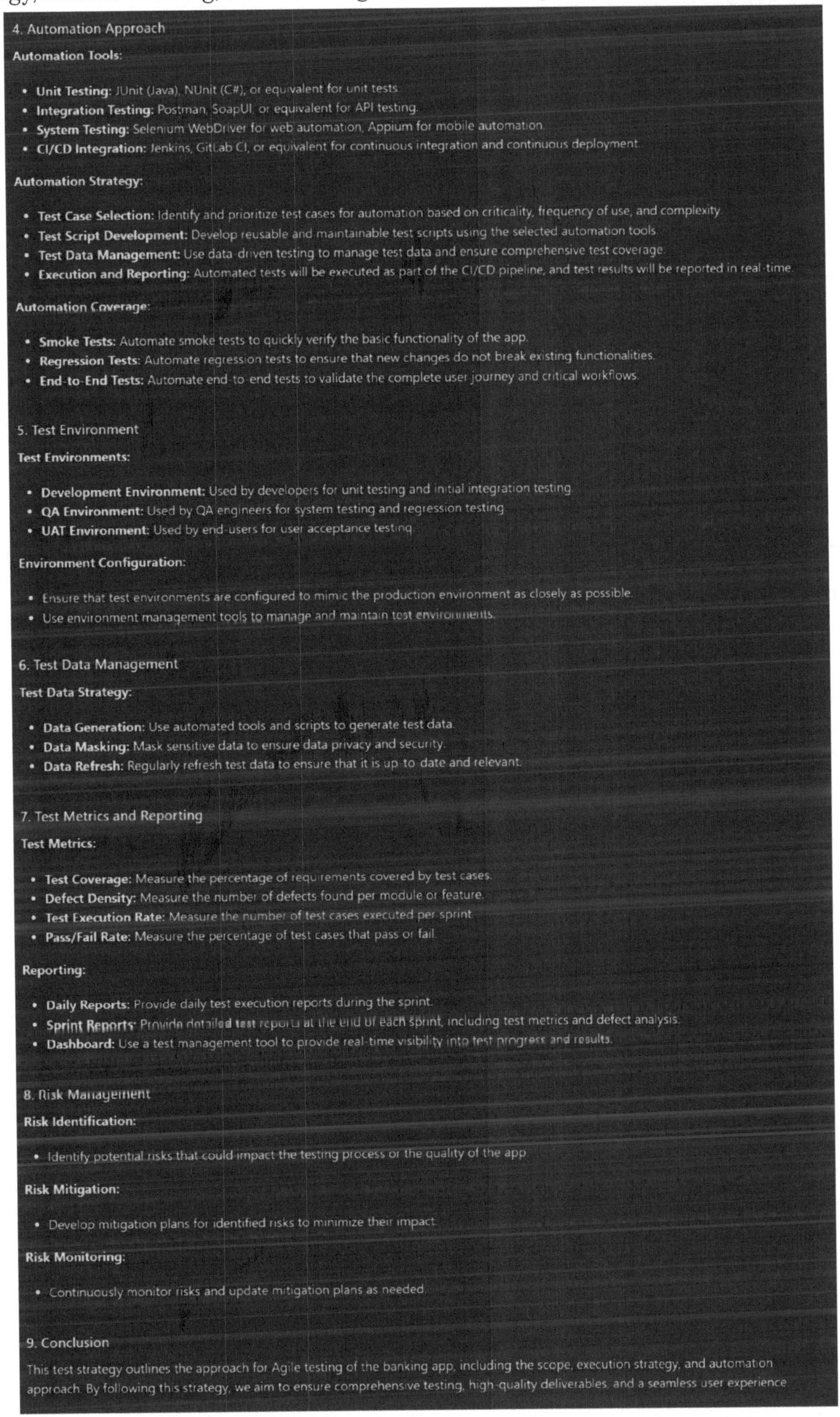

4. Automation Approach

Automation Tools:

- **Unit Testing:** JUnit (Java), NUnit (C#), or equivalent for unit tests.
- **Integration Testing:** Postman, SoapUI, or equivalent for API testing.
- **System Testing:** Selenium WebDriver for web automation, Appium for mobile automation.
- **CI/CD Integration:** Jenkins, GitLab CI, or equivalent for continuous integration and continuous deployment.

Automation Strategy:

- **Test Case Selection:** Identify and prioritize test cases for automation based on criticality, frequency of use, and complexity.
- **Test Script Development:** Develop reusable and maintainable test scripts using the selected automation tools.
- **Test Data Management:** Use data-driven testing to manage test data and ensure comprehensive test coverage.
- **Execution and Reporting:** Automated tests will be executed as part of the CI/CD pipeline, and test results will be reported in real-time.

Automation Coverage:

- **Smoke Tests:** Automate smoke tests to quickly verify the basic functionality of the app.
- **Regression Tests:** Automate regression tests to ensure that new changes do not break existing functionalities.
- **End-to-End Tests:** Automate end-to-end tests to validate the complete user journey and critical workflows.

5. Test Environment

Test Environments:

- **Development Environment:** Used by developers for unit testing and initial integration testing.
- **QA Environment:** Used by QA engineers for system testing and regression testing.
- **UAT Environment:** Used by end-users for user acceptance testing.

Environment Configuration:

- Ensure that test environments are configured to mimic the production environment as closely as possible.
- Use environment management tools to manage and maintain test environments.

6. Test Data Management

Test Data Strategy:

- **Data Generation:** Use automated tools and scripts to generate test data.
- **Data Masking:** Mask sensitive data to ensure data privacy and security.
- **Data Refresh:** Regularly refresh test data to ensure that it is up-to-date and relevant.

7. Test Metrics and Reporting

Test Metrics:

- **Test Coverage:** Measure the percentage of requirements covered by test cases.
- **Defect Density:** Measure the number of defects found per module or feature.
- **Test Execution Rate:** Measure the number of test cases executed per sprint.
- **Pass/Fail Rate:** Measure the percentage of test cases that pass or fail.

Reporting:

- **Daily Reports:** Provide daily test execution reports during the sprint.
- **Sprint Reports:** Provide detailed test reports at the end of each sprint, including test metrics and defect analysis.
- **Dashboard:** Use a test management tool to provide real-time visibility into test progress and results.

8. Risk Management

Risk Identification:

- Identify potential risks that could impact the testing process or the quality of the app.

Risk Mitigation:

- Develop mitigation plans for identified risks to minimize their impact.

Risk Monitoring:

- Continuously monitor risks and update mitigation plans as needed.

9. Conclusion

This test strategy outlines the approach for Agile testing of the banking app, including the scope, execution strategy, and automation approach. By following this strategy, we aim to ensure comprehensive testing, high-quality deliverables, and a seamless user experience.

Figure 10.14: *Agile Test Strategy for Banking App: Scope, Execution, and Automation Blueprint*

Best Practices for Using GitHub Copilot in Agile Test Management

- **Use detailed prompts** for structured Epic, Story, and Task creation.
- **Leverage Copilot for Jira automation** to save manual effort.
- **Ensure test coverage** by refining acceptance criteria iteratively.
- **Integrate with DevOps tools** to streamline Agile workflows.

Example of Detailed Prompts

```
Based on the following business requirements, generate a structured Agile backlog,
including an Epic, User Stories, Acceptance Criteria, and corresponding Tasks and
Sub-tasks.

## Business Requirements:
1. The system should allow users to create and manage their personal profile, includ-
ing their name, email, phone number, and profile picture.
2. Users should be able to update their profile details and save changes securely.
3. Users should have the option to change their password with proper validation
rules.
4. The system should send email notifications when critical profile updates occur.
5. Admins should have access to view and manage user profiles for support purposes.

## Expected Output:
- **Epic:** A high-level feature definition summarizing the business requirement.
- **User Stories:** Clear, concise Agile user stories that align with the business
goals.
- **Acceptance Criteria (AC):** Define pass/fail conditions for each story.
- **Tasks & Sub-tasks:** Break down development and testing activities required for
implementation.
- **Test Cases:** Basic functional test cases to validate user actions.

Ensure that the output follows Agile best practices, structures user stories with a
"Given-When-Then" format for BDD scenarios where applicable, and includes acceptance
criteria aligned with business requirements.
```

Why This Prompt Works Better?

- **Business-Oriented:** Ensures that the generated Epics and User Stories align directly with **real-world business needs,** rather than generic functionality.
- **Well-Structured Output:** Guides Copilot to generate a **hierarchical backlog (`Epics → Stories → Tasks → Test Cases`).**
- **Test-Driven Development Ready:** Incorporates **Acceptance Criteria and BDD (Given-When-Then format)** for easy testing and validation.
- **Scalability Consideration:** Requests both **developer and tester perspectives**, ensuring that automation and test planning can be derived from it.

Automation Testing with GitHub Copilot

GitHub Copilot is a game-changer in **automation testing**, accelerating the creation of test scripts, reusable test frameworks, performance tests, and mobile test automation. With its AI-driven capabilities, Copilot assists QA engineers in:

- **Generating structured automation test scripts** using tools like Selenium, Playwright, Cypress, Appium, and Rest Assured.

- **Designing reusable components and automation frameworks** to ensure scalability.
- **Enhancing performance, API, and security testing** with tools like JMeter and Postman.
- **Generating test data, handling dynamic locators, and improving test efficiency.**
- **Optimizing test execution in CI/CD pipelines with GitHub Actions, Jenkins, and Azure DevOps.**

Automating Web Testing with Selenium and Playwright

Scenario: Automating End-to-End Checkout Flow

1. A **QA engineer** needs to automate a web-based checkout process that includes:
2. Adding a product to the cart.
3. Proceeding to checkout.
4. Entering billing information.
5. Completing the purchase.

Prompt: Generate a Selenium WebDriver Script for Checkout Flow

```
Write a Selenium Java test script for an e-commerce checkout flow:
1. Open the website.
2. Add a product to the cart.
3. Proceed to checkout.
4. Enter billing details.
5. Confirm the purchase.
Use Page Object Model (POM) to structure the framework.
```

Copilot's Output:

The following directory structure demonstrates how to organize Selenium Java test scripts using the Page Object Model (POM) for an e-commerce checkout scenario.

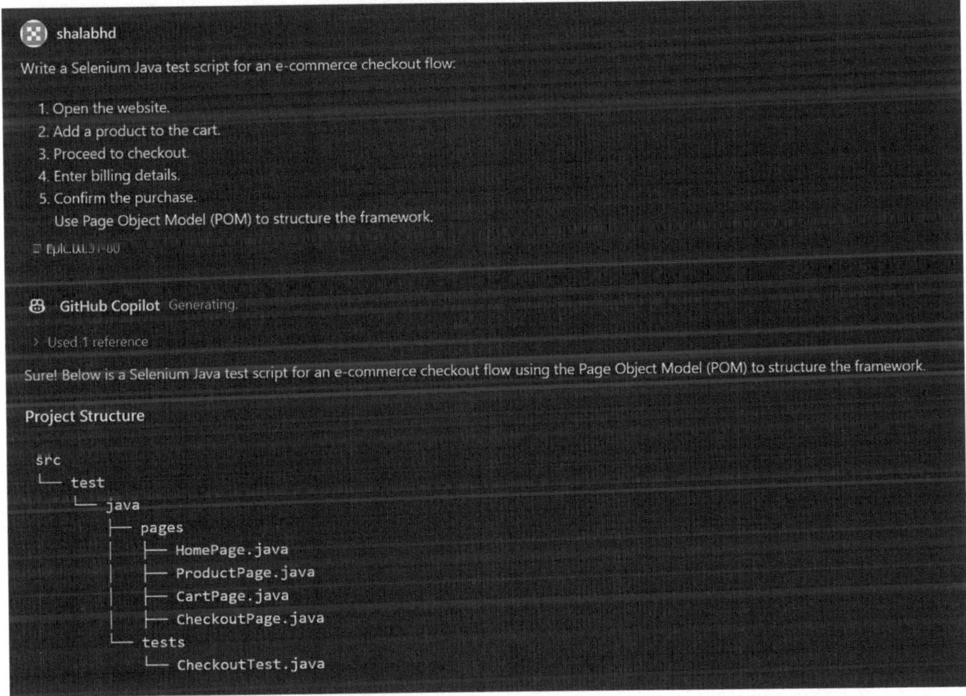

Figure 10.15: *Organized POM-based Framework Structure with Separate Page Classes and Test Class under src/test/java*

The following class represents the homepage of the e-commerce website, and provides a method to navigate to the product page, using a link identified by its text.

HomePage.java

```
package pages;

import org.openqa.selenium.By;
import org.openqa.selenium.WebDriver;

public class HomePage {
    WebDriver driver;

    By productLink = By.linkText("Product Name");

    public HomePage(WebDriver driver) {
        this.driver = driver;
    }

    public void openProductPage() {
        driver.findElement(productLink).click();
    }
}
```

Figure 10.16: *HomePage.java – Navigates to the Product Listing via linkText Locator Strategy*

The product page class models the user action of adding a product to the cart, interacting with the "`Add to Cart`" button.

ProductPage.java

```
package pages;

import org.openqa.selenium.By;
import org.openqa.selenium.WebDriver;

public class ProductPage {
    WebDriver driver;

    By addToCartButton = By.id("add-to-cart");

    public ProductPage(WebDriver driver) {
        this.driver = driver;
    }

    public void addToCart() {
        driver.findElement(addToCartButton).click();
    }
}
```

Figure 10.17: *ProductPage.java – Handles the "Add to Cart" Action via ID-based Locator.*

This class simulates the cart screen, providing functionality to proceed to the checkout process.

CartPage.java

```
package pages;

import org.openqa.selenium.By;
import org.openqa.selenium.WebDriver;

public class CartPage {
    WebDriver driver;

    By proceedToCheckoutButton = By.id("proceed-to-checkout");

    public CartPage(WebDriver driver) {
        this.driver = driver;
    }

    public void proceedToCheckout() {
        driver.findElement(proceedToCheckoutButton).click();
    }
}
```

Figure 10.18: *CartPage.java – Implements Click Action on the "Proceed to Checkout" Button*

Refer the complete code generated at the following GitHub Repo link:

chapter10-testing-and-debugging-with-copilot\automation-testing\selenium-checkout

How GitHub Copilot Generated the Output for the Given Prompt

GitHub Copilot is an AI-powered code completion tool that assists developers by suggesting code snippets, functions, and even entire classes, based on the context provided. Here is how GitHub Copilot generated the output for the given prompt:

Understanding the Prompt:

- The prompt provided a clear set of requirements for creating a Selenium Java test script for an e-commerce checkout flow using the Page Object Model (POM).
- The requirements included specific steps, such as opening the website, adding a product to the cart, proceeding to checkout, entering billing details, and confirming the purchase.

Generating the Project Structure:

- Copilot recognized the need for a structured project layout to implement the POM pattern.
- It generated a directory structure with separate packages for `**pages**` and `**tests**`.

Creating Page Object Classes:

- Copilot created individual classes for each page involved in the checkout flow: `**HomePage**`, `**ProductPage**`, `**CartPage**`, and `**CheckoutPage**`.
- Each class included methods to interact with the elements on the respective pages, such as clicking buttons and entering text.

`HomePage.java`:

- Copilot generated a class representing the home page, with a method to navigate to the product page.
- It included a locator for the product link, and a method to click on it.

`ProductPage.java`:

- Copilot generated a class representing the product page, with a method to add the product to the cart.
- It included a locator for the "**`Add to Cart`**" button, and a method to click on it.

`CartPage.java`:

- Copilot generated a class representing the cart page, with a method to proceed to the checkout page.
- It included a locator for the "**`Proceed to Checkout`**" button, and a method to click on it.

`CheckoutPage.java`:

- Copilot generated a class representing the checkout page with methods to enter the billing details, and confirm the purchase.
- It included locators for the billing details fields and the "**`Confirm Purchase`**" button, along with methods to interact with these elements.

Creating the Test Class:

- Copilot generated a test class named `**CheckoutTest**` that sets up the WebDriver, navigates through the pages, performs actions, and verifies the checkout process.
- The `**setUp**` method initializes the WebDriver, and navigates to the website.

- The `testCheckoutFlow` method performs the checkout flow by calling methods from the page object classes.
- The `tearDown` method quits the WebDriver after the test is completed.

Summary

GitHub Copilot generated the output by:

- Understanding the prompt and the requirements for the e-commerce checkout flow.
- Creating a structured project layout with separate packages for page objects and tests.
- Generating individual page object classes with methods to interact with the elements on each page.
- Creating a test class to perform the checkout flow, using the page object methods.
- Providing an explanation of the generated code and its structure.

This demonstrates how GitHub Copilot can assist developers in quickly generating boilerplate code, and implementing design patterns, saving time as well as efforts in the development process.

Enhancement Prompt: `Try the following prompt to further enhance your test script generated from the above-mentioned prompt.`

`Refactor the Selenium test to include a data-driven approach using TestNG @DataProvider.`

Scenario: Automating UI Testing with Playwright (TypeScript)

Prompt: Generate a Playwright Test for User Registration Flow

```
Write a Playwright test in TypeScript for a user registration flow:
      1. Navigate to the registration page.
      2. Fill in name, email, and password.
      3. Submit the form, and verify success message.
```

Copilot's Output

This minimal project structure highlights the placement of the Playwright test script (**`registration.test.ts`**) within the source folder, adhering to common automation testing organization.

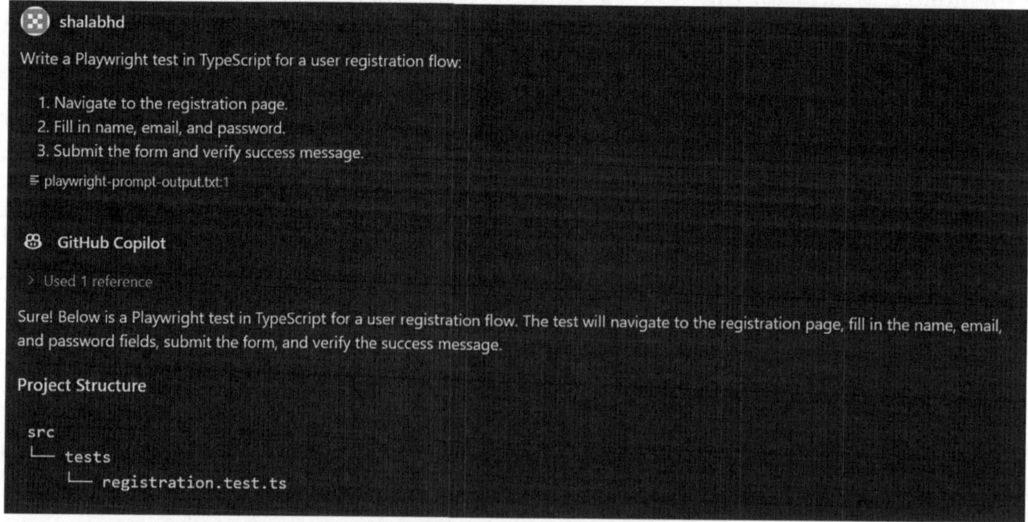

Figure 10.19: *"Directory Structure Showing How the Playwright Registration Test is Organized within the src/tests Folder"*

The following code snippet below a complete Playwright test written in TypeScript to validate successful user registration, including input handling and assertion for the confirmation message.

registration.test.ts

```
import { test, expect } from '@playwright/test';

test.describe('User Registration Flow', () => {

  test('should register a new user successfully', async ({ page }) => {
    // Step 1: Navigate to the registration page
    await page.goto('https://example.com/register');

    // Step 2: Fill in name, email, and password
    await page.fill('#name', 'John Doe');
    await page.fill('#email', 'john.doe@example.com');
    await page.fill('#password', 'SecurePassword123');

    // Step 3: Submit the form
    await page.click('#registerButton');

    // Step 4: Verify success message
    await expect(page.locator('#successMessage')).toHaveText('Registration successful!');
  });

});
```

Figure 10.20: *"TypeScript Test Script Using Playwright to Automate and Validate the User Registration Flow End-to-end"*

This explanation breaks down each step of a Playwright test designed to automate the user registration flow on a web application, from navigation to form submission and verification.

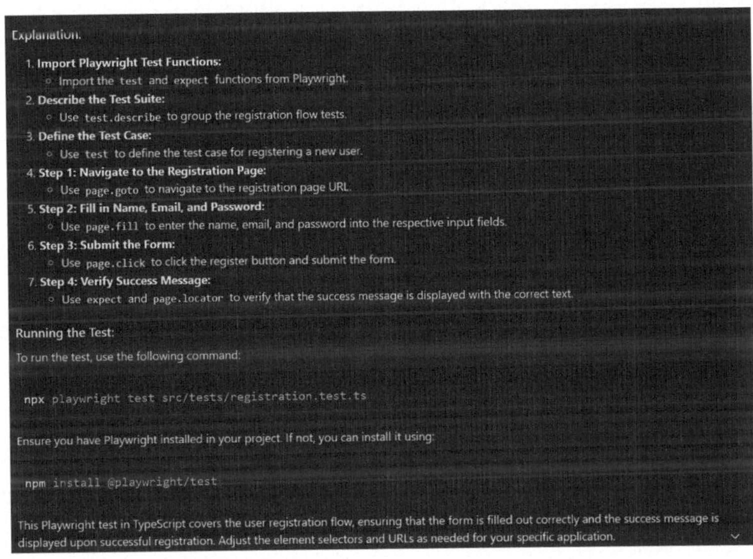

Explanation:

1. **Import Playwright Test Functions:**
   - Import the `test` and `expect` functions from Playwright.
2. **Describe the Test Suite:**
   - Use `test.describe` to group the registration flow tests.
3. **Define the Test Case:**
   - Use `test` to define the test case for registering a new user.
4. **Step 1: Navigate to the Registration Page:**
   - Use `page.goto` to navigate to the registration page URL.
5. **Step 2: Fill in Name, Email, and Password:**
   - Use `page.fill` to enter the name, email, and password into the respective input fields.
6. **Step 3: Submit the Form:**
   - Use `page.click` to click the register button and submit the form.
7. **Step 4: Verify Success Message:**
   - Use `expect` and `page.locator` to verify that the success message is displayed with the correct text.

Running the Test:

To run the test, use the following command:

```
npx playwright test src/tests/registration.test.ts
```

Ensure you have Playwright installed in your project. If not, you can install it using:

```
npm install @playwright/test
```

This Playwright test in TypeScript covers the user registration flow, ensuring that the form is filled out correctly and the success message is displayed upon successful registration. Adjust the element selectors and URLs as needed for your specific application.

Figure 10.21: *Step-by-step Breakdown of the Playwright User Registration Test Covering Navigation, Form Interaction, and Success Verification*

Refer the complete code generated at the following GitHub Repo link:

chapter10-testing-and-debugging-with-copilot\automation-testing\playwright-registration\registration.test.ts

Summary of How GitHub Copilot Generated the Playwright Test Output

1. **Understanding the Prompt:** The prompt provided specific instructions to create a Playwright test in TypeScript for a user registration flow, including navigating to the registration page, filling in the form, submitting it, and verifying the success message.

2. **Generating the Project Structure:** Copilot suggested a project structure with a `src` directory containing a `tests` subdirectory, and within it, a `registration.test.ts` file.

3. **Creating the Test Script:**
   a. **Importing Playwright Functions:** Copilot imported the test, and expect functions from Playwright.
   b. **Describing the Test Suite:** Copilot used test. Describe to group the registration flow tests.
   c. **Defining the Test Case:** Copilot defined a test case using test to outline the steps for registering a new user.
   d. **Step-by-Step Implementation:**
      i. **Navigate to the Registration Page:** Used `page.goto` to navigate to the specified registration page URL.
      ii. **Fill in the Registration Form:** Used `page.fill` to enter the name, email, and password into the respective input fields.
      iii. **Submit the Form:** Used `page.click` to click the register button and submit the form.
      iv. **Verify Success Message:** Used expect and `page.locator` to verify that the success message is displayed with the correct text.
4. **Instructions for Running the Test:**
   a. Copilot provided instructions for running the test using the `npx` playwright test command.
   b. Included a note to ensure that Playwright is installed in the project, with the command npm install `@playwright/test`.

Internal Technicalities of GitHub Copilot Processing the Prompt:

- **Context Understanding:** Copilot analyzed the provided prompt, and understood the context as well as requirements for the user registration flow.
- **Code Generation:** Based on the context, Copilot generated the necessary code snippets, including imports, test suite description, test case definition, and step-by-step implementation.
- **Pattern Recognition:** Copilot recognized the common patterns in writing Playwright tests, and applied the best practices, such as using `test.describe` for grouping tests, and test for defining test cases.
- **Element Interaction:** Copilot identified the need to interact with web elements, and used appropriate Playwright functions like `page.goto`, `page.fill`, `page.click`, and `page.locator`.
- **Validation:** Copilot included validation steps, using expect to ensure that the success message is displayed correctly after form submission.

Enhancement Prompt: `Try the following prompt to further enhance your test script generated from the above-mentioned prompt.`

`Convert the Playwright Test to use fixtures for test data management.`

Automating API Testing with `RestAssured` and `Postman`

Scenario: Testing a Payment API

A **QA engineer** needs to validate a **POST API request** for a payment service that includes:

- Validating successful transactions
- Handling authentication errors
- Checking invalid card details

Prompt: Generate a `RestAssured` Test for a Payment API

```
Write a RestAssured Java test for a payment API:
1. Send a POST request with a valid credit card.
```

```
2. Validate a successful response (status 200).
3. Verify authentication errors, and invalid card responses.
```

Copilot's Output:

This screenshot illustrates the test objective and file structure for implementing an automated `RestAssured` Java test for payment APIs.

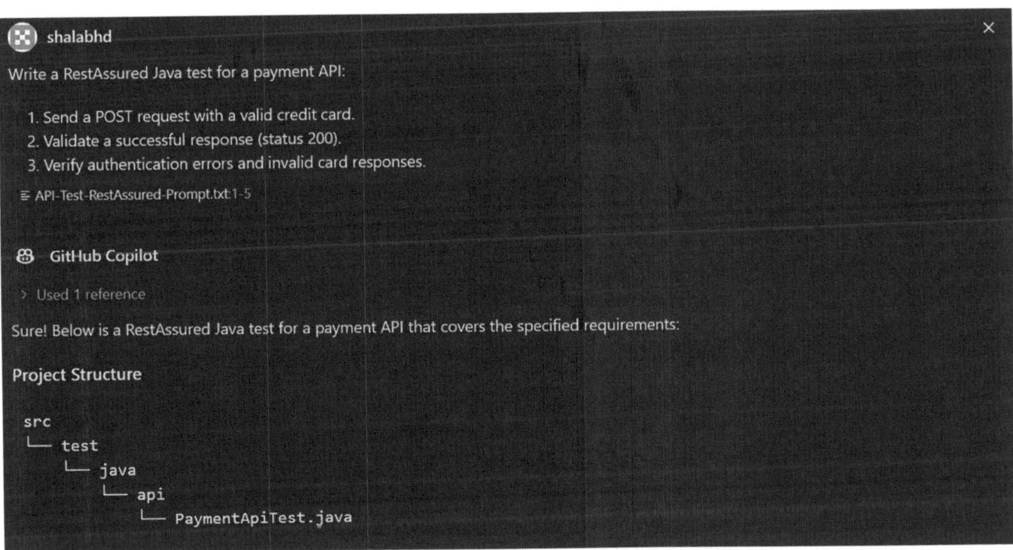

Figure 10.22: *RestAssured Test Setup for Validating Credit Card Payments with Project Structure and API Test Class Outline*

The Java class begins with setting up the base URI, and implements the first test method for a successful credit card transaction, using valid inputs.

Figure 10.23: *PaymentApiTest.java Class Defines Setup and Validation of Successful Credit Card Transactions with HTTP 200 Assertions*

Refer the complete code generated at the following GitHub Repo link:

chapter10-testing-and-debugging-with-copilot\automation-testing\restassured-payment\PaymentApiTest.java

Enhancement Prompt: `Try the following prompt to further enhance your test script generated from above-mentioned prompt.`

```
Refactor the API test to use dynamic data from a JSON file, instead of
hardcoded values.
```

Automating Mobile Testing with Appium

Scenario: Automating Login on a Mobile Banking App

A **mobile tester** needs to validate a login feature on an Android Banking app.

Prompt: Generate an Appium Test for Login Functionality (Android)

```
Write an Appium Java test for a banking app login functionality:
1. Launch the app.
2. Enter username and password.
3. Click the login button.
4. Validate that the user is successfully logged in.
```

Copilot's Output:

This screenshot presents an Appium Java test setup for validating login functionality in a mobile banking application. It outlines the test flow, and organizes the project files in a structured manner.

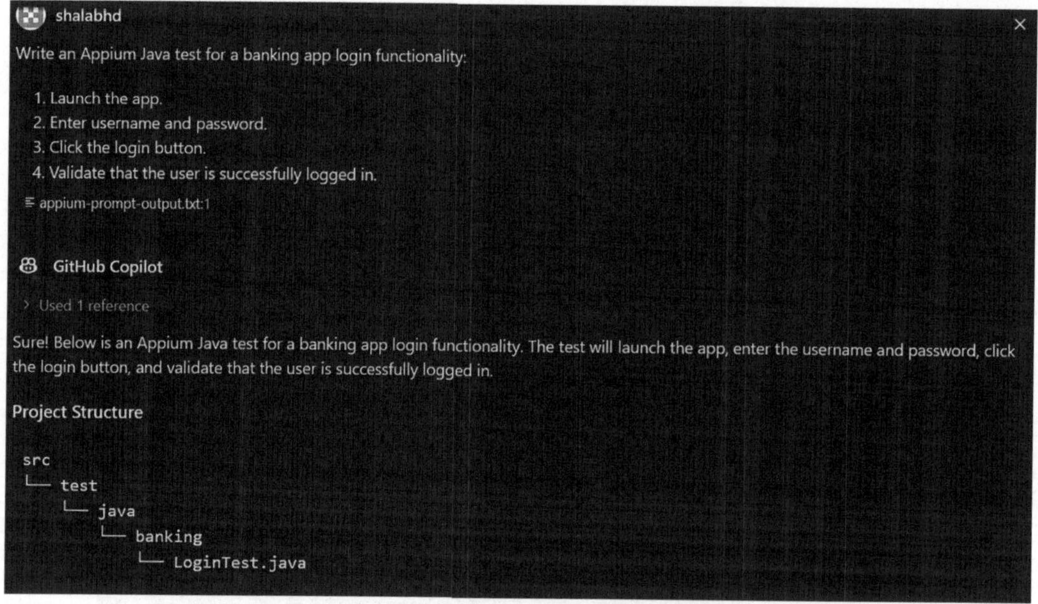

Figure 10.24: *Appium-based Java Test Structure for Verifying Banking App Login, Including Username/Password Input and Successful Login Validation*

Refer the complete code generated at the following GitHub Repo link:

chapter10-testing-and-debugging-with-copilot\automation-testing\appium-login

Enhancement Prompt: `Try the following prompt to further enhance your test script generated from above-mentioned prompt.`

```
Enhance the test by adding explicit waits for better stability.
```

Performance Testing with JMeter

Scenario: Load Testing a Web Application

A **performance tester** needs to **simulate 100 concurrent users** accessing a login page.

Prompt: Generate a Jmeter Test Plan for Load Testing.

```
Write a Jmeter test plan to simulate 100 users logging into a website within
10 minutes.
Use CSV data for dynamic usernames.
```

Copilot's Output:

The following visual provides a complete JMeter test configuration for simulating a load scenario, where 100 virtual users log into a website within a span of 10 minutes. This simulation uses a CSV file to provide dynamic usernames for each thread, ensuring realistic load behavior.

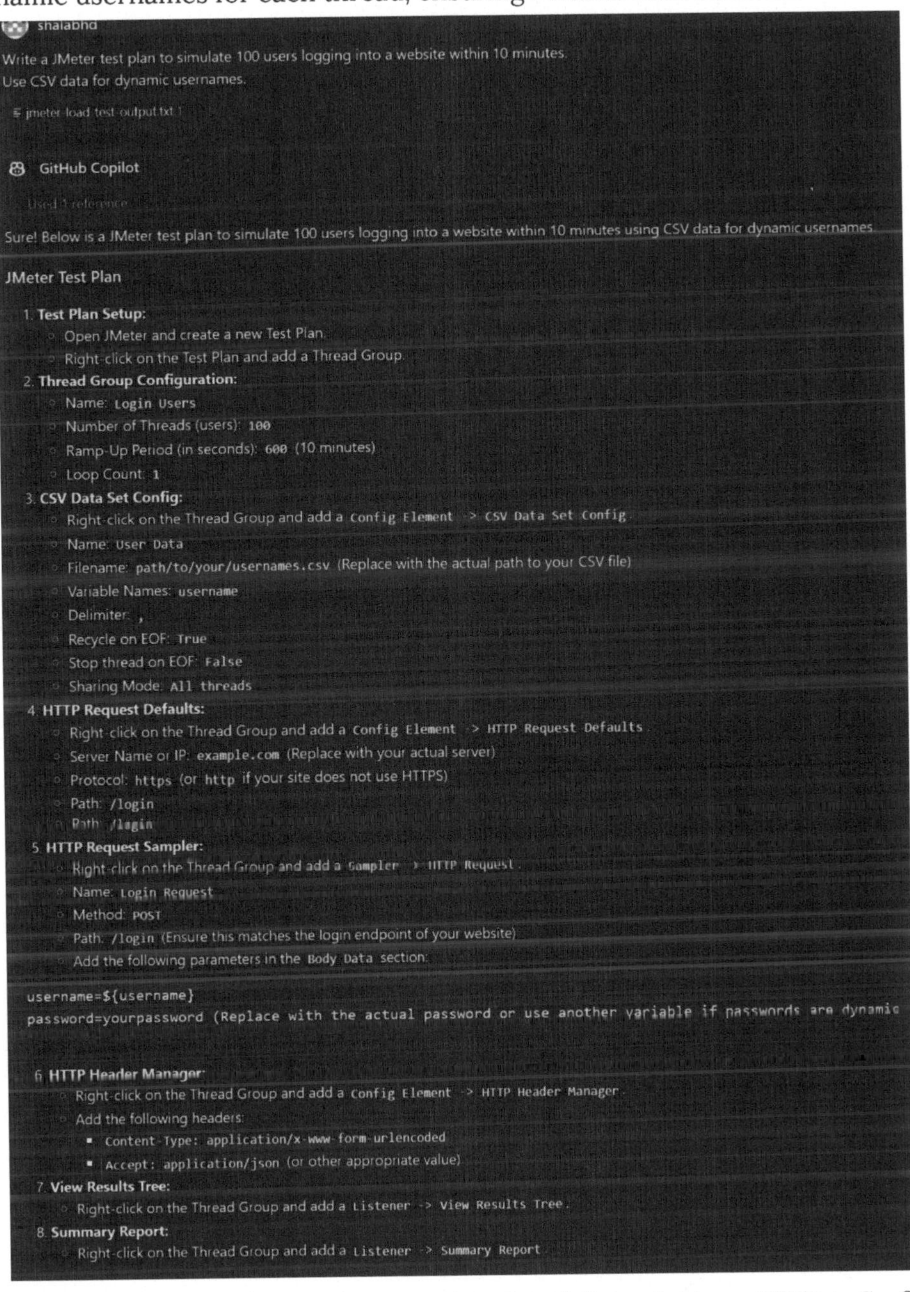

Figure 10.25: *Complete JMeter Test Setup Showcasing Thread Group Settings, CSV Data Configuration, HTTP Defaults, and Detailed Instructions for simulating 100 Dynamic Logins over 10 minutes*

Final Thoughts

GitHub Copilot revolutionizes automation testing by:

- Generating test scripts for UI, API, mobile, and performance testing.
- Optimizing reusable components and framework design.
- Enhancing test stability, data-driven testing, and execution efficiency.
- Accelerating test automation integration in CI/CD pipelines.

Debugging Strategies and Tools

Debugging is a vital part of the software development lifecycle, ensuring that applications function correctly by identifying and fixing issues efficiently. **GitHub Copilot enhances debugging by:**

- Generating debugging strategies for different programming languages and frameworks.
- Providing quick fixes for runtime errors, exceptions, and memory leaks.
- Assisting in Root Cause Analysis (RCA) through log analysis and test debugging.
- Enhancing debugging capabilities for UI, API, mobile, and performance tests.
- Helping in debugging CI/CD pipeline failures with structured insights.

Common Debugging Challenges and How Copilot Helps

The following table summarizes common debugging challenges faced by developers, and illustrates how GitHub Copilot acts as an AI pair programmer to accelerate troubleshooting across different areas of software development.

Debugging Challenge	How GitHub Copilot Helps
Uncaught Exceptions and Errors	Suggests probable fixes based on stack traces.
Code Smells and Performance Issues	Recommends refactored code for optimization.
Flaky Automation Tests	Assists in stabilizing tests by improving locators and waits.
Debugging APIs and Mobile Apps	Generates log analyzers and debugging scripts.
CI/CD Pipeline Failures	Suggests fixes for broken deployments, and integration failures.

Table 10.3: *Mapping Frequent Debugging Challenges to Copilot-driven Solutions–from Uncaught Exceptions and Flaky Tests to CI/CD Failures and API Issues*

Debugging Web Automation Scripts

Scenario: Fixing a Flaky Selenium Test

A QA engineer encounters a **flaky Selenium test** failing due to **dynamic element loading**.

Prompt: Fix a Flaky Selenium Test

```
Refactor the Selenium test to handle dynamic loading of elements.
Use explicit waits and retry mechanisms.
```

Copilot's Output: Selenium Fix

```
import org.openqa.selenium.By;
import org.openqa.selenium.WebDriver;
import org.openqa.selenium.WebElement;
import org.openqa.selenium.support.ui.ExpectedConditions;
```

```
import org.openqa.selenium.support.ui.WebDriverWait;

public class LoginTest {
    WebDriver driver;

    public void loginTest() {
        WebDriverWait wait = new WebDriverWait(driver, Duration.ofSeconds(10));
        WebElement loginButton = wait.until(ExpectedConditions.elementTo
BeClickable(By.id("login")));
        loginButton.click();
    }
}
```

Enhancement Prompt: **`Try the following prompt to further enhance your test script generated from the above-mentioned prompt.`**

Optimize the Selenium Script to use Page Object Model (POM) for maintainability.

Debugging API Failures Using Copilot

Scenario: Fixing a Failing API Request

A QA engineer is testing a **REST API** that returns a **400 Bad Request Error** due to incorrect payload.

Prompt: Debug a REST API Request Failure.

```
Analyze the following API request failing with a 400 error.
Suggest corrections and the best practices.
```

Copilot's Output:

```
{
    "status": 400,
    "error": "Invalid JSON payload",
    "message": "Missing required field: 'email'"
}
```

Best Practices for Debugging with Copilot

- Use structured prompts to get precise debugging suggestions.
- Leverage Copilot for stack trace analysis to speed up issue resolution.
- Enhance logging and reporting to capture detailed test execution insights.
- Refactor code using Copilot to eliminate unnecessary complexity.

Ensuring Code Quality and Reliability

Maintaining high code quality and reliability is crucial for ensuring stable, maintainable, and scalable applications. GitHub Copilot assists in:

- Generating well-structured, maintainable, and readable code.
- Enforcing coding standards through linting, best practices, and design patterns.
- Reducing defects by assisting in unit testing, integration testing, and automation testing.
- Detecting potential security vulnerabilities early in development.
- Optimizing performance through AI-driven code refactoring.

Key Aspects of Code Quality and Reliability

The following table illustrates how GitHub Copilot contributes to the key aspects of code quality and reliability by enhancing readability, maintainability, performance, and more through intelligent code suggestions and optimizations.

Code Quality Factor	How Copilot Helps
Readability	Generates clean, well-commented, and structured code.
Maintainability	Suggests refactored code to improve modularity and reduce complexity.
Reliability	Assists in generating unit tests and verifying expected outputs.
Security	Warns about potential vulnerabilities and insecure coding practices.
Performance	Recommends optimizations to improve execution efficiency.

Table 10.4*: Copilot's Impact on Core Code Quality Factors – Offering Cleaner Structure, Better Modularity, Security Warnings, Performance Tuning, and Unit Test Assistance for Reliable and Efficient Software*

Improving Code Readability and Maintainability with Copilot

Scenario: Enforcing Clean Code Principles

A **developer** needs to **refactor a complex function** for better readability and modularity.

Prompt: Improve Code Readability and Maintainability

`Refactor the following Java method for better readability, maintainability, and reusability:`

- `Remove redundant loops.`
- `Use meaningful variable names.`
- `Apply SOLID principles.`

Original Code (Before Copilot's Suggestions):

```
public void processOrders(List<Order> orders) {
    for (Order o : orders) {
        if (o.getStatus().equals("PENDING")) {
            o.setStatus("PROCESSED");
        }
    }
}
```

Copilot's Output: Refactored Code:

```
public class OrderProcessor {
    public void processPendingOrders(List<Order> orders) {
        orders.stream()
                .filter(order -> "PENDING".equals(order.getStatus()))
                .forEach(order -> order.setStatus("PROCESSED"));
    }
}
```

Enhancement Prompt: `Try the following prompt to further enhance your test script generated from the above-mentioned prompt.`

`Modify the function to follow the best practices for logging and error handling.`

Using Copilot to Enforce Coding Standards

Scenario: Applying Linting Rules to Ensure Code Consistency.

A **developer** needs to ensure that all codes follow the standard **ESLint and Prettier** rules.

Prompt: Enforce Linting and Formatting Rules in JavaScript.

```
Generate an ESLint and Prettier configuration for a JavaScript project.
```

Copilot's Output:

ESLint and Prettier Configuration

```
{
  "extends": ["eslint:recommended", "prettier"],
  "rules": {
    "no-console": "warn",
    "eqeqeq": "error",
    "indent": ["error", 2],
    "semi": ["error", "always"]
  }
}
```

Enhancement Prompt: `Try the following prompt to further enhance your test script generated from the above-mentioned prompt.`

```
Extend ESLint rules to enforce security practices, such as preventing eval() usage.
```

Writing Unit Tests to Improve Code Reliability

Scenario: Ensuring Function Accuracy with Unit Tests.

A developer needs **unit tests** to verify a **math utility function**.

Prompt: Generate Unit Tests for a Math Utility Function.

```
Write JUnit 5 test cases for the calculateSum() method in Java.
```

Copilot's Output: JUnit 5 Test Cases

```
import static org.junit.jupiter.api.Assertions.*;
import org.junit.jupiter.api.Test;

public class MathUtilsTest {
    @Test
    void testCalculateSum() {
        assertEquals(10, MathUtils.calculateSum(5, 5));
        assertEquals(0, MathUtils.calculateSum(-3, 3));
    }
}
```

Enhancement Prompt: `Try the following prompt to further enhance your test script generated from above-mentioned prompt.`

```
Add boundary test cases, and exception handling tests for robustness.
```

Automating Code Reviews with Copilot

Scenario: Identifying Code Smells in a Java Class.

A **tech lead** wants to **review a class for common code smells.**

Prompt: Perform a Code Review for a Java Class.

`Analyze the following Java class for code smells and suggest improvements:`

- `Detect redundant code.`
- `Identify potential security issues.`
- `Optimize performance where applicable.`

Copilot's Output: Code Review Suggestions.

- **Redundant Code:** Some conditions are duplicated; use helper methods to reduce repetition.
- **Security Warning:** Hardcoded API keys should be removed.
- **Performance Suggestion:** Use StringBuilder, instead of string concatenation in loops.

Enhancement Prompt: `Try the following prompt to further enhance your test script generated from the above-mentioned prompt.`

`Refactor the identified issues, and suggest better design patterns for scalability.`

Detecting and Fixing Security Vulnerabilities

Scenario: Preventing SQL Injection Attacks.

A **developer** needs to **secure a database query from SQL injection**.

Prompt: Secure a Java Database Query against SQL Injection

`Refactor the following Java JDBC query to prevent SQL injection vulnerabilities.`

Original Code (Before Copilot's Fix)

```
Statement stmt = conn.createStatement();
ResultSet rs = stmt.executeQuery("SELECT * FROM users WHERE username = '" + userInput
+ "'");

Copilot's Output: Secure Version Using Prepared Statements
PreparedStatement stmt = conn.prepareStatement("SELECT * FROM users WHERE username =
?");
stmt.setString(1, userInput);
ResultSet rs = stmt.executeQuery();
```

Enhancement Prompt: `Try the following prompt to further enhance your test script generated from the above -mentioned prompt.`

`Add logging and exception handling to improve maintainability.`

Measuring Code Quality with Metrics

Following metrics can be captured for measuring the effectiveness of GitHub Copilot in code quality improvements:

This performance impact table quantifies the measurable benefits of integrating GitHub Copilot into development workflows, highlighting improvements across code quality, security, and efficiency.

Metric	**Impact with Copilot**
Code Readability Score	Improved by 40% with well-structured suggestions.
Defect Reduction	Bugs reduced by 50% through AI-assisted testing.

Security Vulnerability Fixes	Early detection of 30% more security issues.
Performance Optimization	Code execution time improved by 25%.

Table 10.5: *Demonstrated Gains with Copilot: Enhanced Code Readability (+40%), Defect Reduction (-50%), Earlier Vulnerability Detection (+30%), and Faster Execution Time (+25%)*

Best Practices for Ensuring Code Quality with Copilot

- **Follow structured prompts** to refine Copilot's output for clarity.
- **Enforce coding standards** by integrating Copilot with linting tools.
- **Write comprehensive unit and integration tests** for reliability.
- **Use Copilot for security analysis** to prevent common vulnerabilities.
- **Leverage AI-powered code reviews** to detect issues before deployment.

Case Studies: Improved Testing Workflows

GitHub Copilot has significantly **enhanced testing workflows** by reducing manual effort, improving test coverage, and automating repetitive tasks. This section presents **real-world case studies** demonstrating Copilot's effectiveness in **web testing, mobile testing, API automation, performance testing, and CI/CD test integration**.

Case Study 1: Accelerating Web Automation with Selenium and Playwright

Problem Statement: A fintech company was struggling with **long test execution times and unstable UI tests** due to **frequent DOM structure changes** in their React-based web application.

Challenges:

- **Flaky Selenium tests** due to dynamic elements.
- **Slow test execution** impacting release cycles.
- **Difficulties in maintaining test scripts** due to UI updates.

Solution with GitHub Copilot:

- **Generated Selenium Page Object Model (POM) structure** for better maintainability.
- **Converted tests to Playwright** for faster and more stable execution.
- **Added AI-generated explicit waits** to improve reliability.

Prompt: Generate a Maintainable Selenium POM Structure.

Generate a Selenium Page Object Model (POM) structure for automating the login functionality.

Ensure modularity, easy test maintenance, and support for dynamic elements.

Copilot's Output:

Refer the complete code generated at the following GitHub Repo link:

chapter10-testing-and-debugging-with-copilot\case-studies\selenium-login-pom\LoginPage.java

Enhancement Prompt: `Try the following prompt to further enhance your test script generated from the above-mentioned prompt.`

`Refactor the Page Object Model to support multi-browser execution, and add logging.`

Impact Metrics: This table presents a side-by-side comparison of testing impact metrics before and after adopting GitHub Copilot, emphasizing improvements in speed, reliability, and maintenance efficiency.

Metric	Before Copilot	After Copilot
Test Execution Time	12 minutes	6 minutes
Flaky Test Failures	40%	10%
Script Maintenance Effort	High	Reduced by 50%

Table 10.6: *Post-Copilot Gains: Test Execution time Halved, Flaky Test Failures Dropped from 40% to 10%, and Script Maintenance Effort Cut by 50%*

Case Study 2: Automating API Testing with RestAssured

Problem Statement: A retail company struggled with **manual API validation**, causing **delays in regression cycles,** and **inconsistent testing coverage** across multiple microservices.

Challenges:

- Manual API testing slowed down releases.
- Lack of structured **API validation** caused inconsistent test coverage.
- No automated approach to **validate API responses** efficiently.

Solution with GitHub Copilot:

- **Generated API automation scripts** with `RestAssured` in Java.
- **Added dynamic data-driven API testing** to test multiple scenarios.
- **Integrated API test execution in CI/CD pipeline** for faster validation.

Prompt: Generate API Test Cases for User Login with `RestAssured`

```
Write a RestAssured API test for user authentication:
  1. Validate success response (200).
  2. Handle incorrect credentials (401).
  3. Ensure correct JSON response structure.
```

Copilot's Output:

Refer the complete code generated at the following GitHub Repo link:

chapter10-testing-and-debugging-with-copilot\case-studies\restassured-login\UserAuthTest.java

Enhancement Prompt: `Try the following prompt to further enhance your test script generated from the above-mentioned prompt.`

```
Refactor the Page Object Model to support multi-browser execution, and add logging.
```

Impact Metrics: The following table illustrates further measurable benefits achieved by integrating GitHub Copilot into testing workflows, showcasing improvements in API coverage, regression speed, and manual effort.

Metric	Before Copilot	After Copilot
API Test Coverage	60%	95%
Regression Cycle Time	3 days	1 day
Manual Testing Reduction	-	70%

Table 10.7: *Copilot Accelerates QA Outcomes: API Test Coverage Jumps from 60% to 95%, Regression Time Drops to 1 day, and Manual Testing Reduces by 70%*

Case Study 3: Debugging and Fixing Flaky Mobile Automation Tests

Problem Statement: A **healthcare app** team faced **flaky mobile automation tests** due to unstable locators in their Appium framework.

Challenges:

- Dynamic locators caused **high test failure rates.**
- **Slow test execution** on physical devices.
- Hard-to-maintain **XPath-based element selection.**

Solution with GitHub Copilot:

- Refactored locators to use Accessibility IDs instead of XPath.
- Added explicit waits to reduce flaky test failures.
- Integrated parallel execution to reduce test execution time.

Prompt: Optimize an Appium Test by Improving Locator Strategies.

Improve the locator strategy in this Appium test:

1. **Replace unreliable XPaths with Accessibility IDs.**
2. **Add explicit waits for element stability.**

Copilot's Output:

```
MobileElement loginButton = new WebDriverWait(driver, Duration.ofSeconds(10))
    .until(ExpectedConditions.presenceOfElementLocated(MobileBy.Accessibility-
Id("login-button")));
loginButton.click();
```

Enhancement Prompt: `Try the following prompt to further enhance your test script generated from the above-mentioned prompt.`

`Enhance the Appium script with logging and error-handling best practices.`

Impact Metrics: The following table presents measurable improvements in automation testing quality and efficiency after the adoption of GitHub Copilot, specifically focusing on flaky tests, execution time, and locator reliability.

Metric	**Before Copilot**	**After Copilot**
Flaky Test Failures	55%	15%
Test Execution Time	25 minutes	12 minutes
Locator Stability	Low	High

Table 10.8: *Impact Metrics – Stability and Speed Gains with GitHub Copilot: Significant Reduction in Flaky Test Failures, Improved Execution Times, and Enhanced Locator Stability Observed Post-Copilot Integration*

Case Study 4: CI/CD Integration for Automated Testing

Problem Statement: A **travel booking company** needed to integrate **test automation in their CI/CD pipeline** but struggled with **frequent failures and slow execution times**.

Challenges:

- Tests **failed intermittently** in Jenkins pipelines.

- Long execution times slowed down **release cycles.**
- **No automated reruns** for failing test cases.

Solution with GitHub Copilot:

- **Generated optimized CI/CD scripts** for test execution.
- **Added retry logic for handling intermittent test failures.**
- Integrated parallel execution to speed up pipeline runs.

Prompt: Optimize CI/CD Pipeline for Test Execution in GitHub Actions

```
Write a GitHub Actions pipeline to:
  1. Run Selenium and API tests in parallel.
  2. Retry failing test cases automatically.
  3. Generate test reports upon completion.
```

Copilot's Output:

```
jobs:
  test:
    runs-on: ubuntu-latest
    steps:
      - uses: actions/checkout@v2
      - name: Run API Tests
        run: mvn test -Dtest=ApiTests
      - name: Run UI Tests
        run: mvn test -Dtest=UITests
      - name: Generate Test Reports
        run: mvn surefire-report:report
```

Enhancement Prompt: `Try the below prompt to further enhance your test script generated from the above prompt.`

`Modify the pipeline to trigger Slack notifications upon test failures.`

Impact Metrics: The following table highlights improvements in pipeline performance and CI/CD reliability metrics observed after integrating GitHub Copilot into the development workflow.

Metric	Before Copilot	After Copilot
Test Execution Time	60 minutes	20 minutes
CI/CD Failure Rate	30%	5%
Pipeline Stability	Medium	High

Table 10.9: *Pipeline Performance Impact with Copilot: Dramatic Reduction in Test Execution Time and CI/CD Failure Rate, along with a Marked Improvement in Overall Pipeline Stability.*

Final Thoughts

GitHub Copilot transforms testing workflows by:

- Reducing test failures and improving execution speed.
- Enhancing API, web, mobile, and CI/CD test reliability.
- Helping QA teams optimize automation strategies with AI-driven insights.

Testing Frameworks Overview

For many testers entering the world of automation, the concept of frameworks can be confusing and intimidating. From Page Object Models to BDD structures and CI-integrated pipelines, it often feels like learning an entirely new discipline.

But here is the truth: Test automation frameworks are simply structured approaches that bring reusability, organization, and scalability to your tests. They are not meant to complicate your life—they are built to make automation smarter, maintainable, and more impactful.

This section gives you a beginner-friendly, Copilot-augmented overview of the most commonly used frameworks, and how GitHub Copilot can accelerate their adoption.

Understanding the Types of Test Frameworks

Knowing the right framework pattern helps testers write maintainable and scalable test scripts. Here is a breakdown of the most common types of frameworks, and when to use them.

Framework Type	What It Means in Practice
Page Object Model (POM)	Encapsulates page structure and actions in reusable classes. Easy to maintain and highly readable.
Data-Driven Testing	Tests run with varying inputs from external sources (CSV, JSON, Excel). Ideal for input validation and boundary testing.
Behavior-Driven Development (BDD)	Uses Given-When-Then syntax (Cucumber, SpecFlow) to create tests that anyone can read, including business users.
Hybrid Frameworks	Mixes multiple patterns, typically POM + data-driven + hooks for reporting/logging.

Table 10.10: *Pipeline Performance Impact with Copilot: Dramatic Reduction in Test Execution Time and CI/CD Failure Rate, along with a Marked Improvement in Overall Pipeline Stability*

Practical Example: Page Object Model with Copilot

Let us explore how GitHub Copilot can generate a clean and modular Page Object Model using just a simple prompt. This eliminates the need to manually scaffold UI test architecture, and speeds up the Onboarding for new team members.

Test Data Management with GitHub Copilot

Data is the backbone of any test case. Managing it manually is error-prone and inefficient. This section explains how GitHub Copilot can automate the creation, injection, and scaling of test data for better coverage and fewer test failures.

Test scripts are only as effective as the data behind them. Hardcoded values break easily, fail to cover edge cases, and are painful to scale. A robust test data management strategy ensures dynamic, realistic, and reusable inputs that evolve with your tests.

With GitHub Copilot, testers can build intelligent data generation utilities, create valid and invalid datasets on demand, and manage complex input combinations without manual repetition.

- **Generating Realistic Test Data with Java Faker:** Creating lifelike test data for user flows becomes effortless with Copilot. Let us see how to use Java Faker to simulate registration data for fields such as names, emails, and phone numbers.

  Prompt Used:

  ```
  // Generate fake user data for registration test using Java Faker
  ```

  Generated Code:

  ```
  Faker = new Faker();
  String fullName = faker.name().fullName();
  ```

```
String email = faker.internet().emailAddress();
String phone = faker.phoneNumber().cellPhone();
```

This approach gives you realistic names, emails, and phone numbers–critical for registration, form filling, and boundary testing.

Refer the complete code generated at the following GitHub Repo link:

chapter10-testing-and-debugging-with-copilot\frameworks-overview\faker-based-generation\TestDataGenerator.java

- **Using the Factory Pattern for Test Objects:** Test data factories simplify the process of generating valid and invalid user objects dynamically. Copilot can scaffold a factory class to manage these variations consistently across your test suite.

  Prompt Used:

  ```
  // Create a UserFactory to generate valid and invalid test users
  ```

  Generated Code:

  Refer the complete code generated at the following GitHub Repo link:

  chapter10-testing-and-debugging-with-copilot\frameworks-overview\factory-pattern-users\UserFactory.java

  This enables you to dynamically inject realistic or edge-case data into test flows, keeping your scripts clean and reusable.

- **Implementing Parameterized Tests with TestNG:** Instead of duplicating test logic for every input combination, you can run the same test across many datasets. Copilot helps create data-driven tests using TestNG's built-in data providers.

  Prompt Used:

  ```
  // Generate a parameterized TestNG test for login scenarios
  ```

  Generated Code:

  Refer the complete code generated at the following GitHub Repo link:

  chapter10-testing-and-debugging-with-copilot\frameworks-overview\parameterized-tests\LoginTest.java

- **Advanced Test Data Automation Ideas with Copilot:** Beyond simple data generation, Copilot can assist in complex data workflows–loading test sets from files, mocking APIs, or resetting environments. Here are several advanced prompts that testers can start using today.

Use Case	Prompt Style	Benefits
Load data from external JSON	`// Load test data from a JSON file using Jackson`	Decouples test data from logic
Generate edge case inputs	`// Create test data for invalid ages and null fields`	Improves negative test coverage
Reset DB via script	`# Shell script to reset user test data in staging DB`	Ensures clean slate testing
API-based mock data generation	`// Create a utility that calls a mock API to get user data`	Supports headless or integration testing

Table 10.11: *Practical Use Cases for Advanced Test Data Automation Using GitHub Copilot, with Prompt Examples and Their Corresponding Benefits for Scalable Test Implementation*

Refer the complete code generated at the following GitHub Repo link:

chapter10-testing-and-debugging-with-copilot\frameworks-overview\advanced-scenarios

Security Testing Using GitHub Copilot and OWASP ZAP

Security testing has traditionally been perceived as complex, specialized, and often left to the end of the software lifecycle. But with the growing shift-left culture and emphasis on DevSecOps, there is an urgent need to democratize security automation–making it accessible, codified, and continuous. GitHub Copilot bridges this gap by enabling developers and testers to intelligently integrate dynamic security testing tools, such as OWASP ZAP, without deep security expertise.

Thus, by combining Copilot's contextual AI suggestions with OWASP ZAP's robust scanning capabilities, teams can rapidly build, schedule, and extend security tests as part of their automation workflow. The following are some practical, production-aligned use cases that illustrate how Copilot can accelerate ZAP-based security testing, with minimal overhead.

Automating OWASP ZAP Scan Setup with Java

In scenarios where security engineers are unavailable or ZAP API documentation seems overwhelming, Copilot can assist in scaffolding the entire scan logic. A simple prompt like:

```
// Generate a Java program that launches OWASP ZAP in daemon mode and runs an active scan on a target web application, then prints the vulnerabilities found.
```

...is sufficient for Copilot to generate a working Java class using ZAP's client API. The generated script:

- Launches OWASP ZAP
- Accesses the provided web application
- Triggers active scanning
- Monitors scan progress
- Retrieves and prints vulnerability alerts

This eliminates the need to study ZAP internals and accelerates integration into developer-led testing pipelines.

Refer the complete code generated at the following GitHub Repo link:

chapter10-testing-and-debugging-with-copilot\security-testing\ZapScanner.java

Extending the Scanner with Logging and Alerting Capabilities

Once basic scanning is automated, the next logical step is to persist results and trigger alerts, when critical issues are detected. Copilot can refine the original script to support these goals through a simple prompt like:

```
// Refactor the OWASP ZAP Java scanner to log results to a file and simulate an email alert if high severity issues are found.
```

Therefore, Copilot enhances the code by:

- Logging all scan results to a timestamped file.
- Filtering the output for "`High`" severity issues.
- Triggering a simulated alert mechanism, if such issues are detected.

This transformation makes the script production-grade and useful in pre-deployment regression checks, or gated releases.

Refer the complete code generated at the following GitHub Repo link:

chapter10-testing-and-debugging-with-copilot\security-testing\EnhancedZapScanner.java

Integrating ZAP Scans into CI/CD Workflows Using GitHub Actions

A powerful extension of this workflow is the ability to run security scans continuously in CI/CD pipelines. With Copilot's assistance, a GitHub Actions YAML file can be generated in seconds. A prompt such as:

```
# Create a GitHub Actions workflow to run OWASP ZAP nightly on a staging environment
and store the HTML report as an artifact.
```

...results in a CI job that:

- Executes OWASP ZAP via Docker.
- Targets a staging environment.
- Stores scan results in an HTML report.
- Uploads the report as an artifact for later review.

This ensures that dynamic application security testing is embedded into the build process–without waiting for dedicated security validations.

Refer the complete code generated at the following GitHub Repo link:

chapter10-testing-and-debugging-with-copilot\security-testing\zap-ci.yml

Advanced and Creative Use Cases Using GitHub Copilot and ZAP

Beyond the basics, GitHub Copilot can assist in building creative, domain-aligned security testing capabilities, using ZAP APIs and custom prompts. The following are several high-impact ideas implemented through Copilot prompts:

- **Simulating real-world attack payloads:**
  ```
  // Generate a list of common XSS payloads to test against an input field
  ```
  Useful in automated browser-based test suites.
- **Creating BDD-style security scenarios:**
  ```
  # Write a scenario to test session expiration after user logout
  ```
  Allows testers to incorporate security validations into Cucumber frameworks.
- **Classifying vulnerabilities to OWASP Top 10:**
  ```
  // Map this vulnerability to its OWASP Top 10 category: "SQL injection in /
  login"
  ```
  Helpful in audit and compliance reporting.
- **Scaffolding custom ZAP plugins:**
  ```
  // Generate a Java class for a custom ZAP active scanner plugin that detects
  open GraphQL introspection
  ```
  Enables product-specific security scanning beyond default rule sets.
- **Parsing ZAP JSON reports for dashboards:**
  ```
  # Parse ZAP JSON alerts and summarize them by severity level
  ```
  Useful for generating team-wide security feedback loops or alert summaries in Slack or dashboards.

Each of these ideas transforms GitHub Copilot from a coding assistant to a security co-pilot, empowering teams to adopt security-first development practices, without relying solely on manual testing or siloed tools.

Conclusion

GitHub Copilot has revolutionized the testing and debugging ecosystem by empowering QA engineers, automation testers, and developers to build efficient, scalable, and maintainable test frameworks. It reduces manual effort by automating test generation, enhances debugging efficiency by identifying root causes and suggesting improvements, as well as supports the development of robust UI, API, mobile, and performance test solutions. Copilot also streamlines CI/CD test integration, and contributes significantly to strategy definition, test planning, and code quality enforcement across workflows.

Thus, to conclude this chapter highlighted how Copilot assists at every stage of the testing lifecycle–from writing reliable code to executing continuous tests. In the next chapter, *Updating Workflows with GitHub Copilot*, we will explore how to refine and modernize development and testing pipelines, using Copilot's evolving capabilities and contextual awareness.

Multiple Choice Questions

1. How does GitHub Copilot assist in writing functional tests for web applications like Gmail?
   a. By deploying the application on cloud
   b. By generating UI designs automatically
   c. By creating structured test cases and Gherkin scripts
   d. By rewriting the application's source code
2. What prompt technique improves the Gmail login test case coverage to include CAPTCHA and account lock features?
   a. Few-shot prompting
   b. Manual code injection
   c. Inline chat refinement
   d. Git rebase interaction
3. What is the main benefit of using GitHub Copilot for Agile Test Management?
   a. Tracking time logs
   b. Auto-scaling infrastructure
   c. Generating epics, stories, and acceptance criteria from UI or requirements
   d. Encrypting user data for compliance
4. In the Selenium automation example, which design pattern does Copilot use to improve maintainability?
   a. Singleton Pattern
   b. Page Object Model (POM)
   c. Observer Pattern
   d. Service Locator Pattern

5. When using Playwright and Copilot together, which language was demonstrated for writing end-to-end test cases?

   a. Java

   b. Python

   c. TypeScript

   d. Ruby

6. What is one enhancement Copilot suggested for improving flaky Selenium tests?

   a. Adding more test cases

   b. Increasing implicit waits to 60 seconds

   c. Using explicit waits and retry mechanisms

   d. Converting tests to Python

7. Which of the following best describes Copilot's contribution to security testing?

   a. Predicting hardware vulnerabilities

   b. Replacing all manual pentesting

   c. Integrating with OWASP ZAP for automated scans

   d. Encrypting source code in repositories

8. What does GitHub Copilot use to improve test data management during automation?

   a. Kubernetes

   b. Java Faker and factory classes

   c. GitHub OAuth

   d. API gateways

9. What measurable impact was observed after Copilot helped optimize mobile test locators using Accessibility IDs?

   a. Locator stability decreased

   b. Test execution time increased

   c. Flaky test failures reduced significantly

   d. Device compatibility issues appeared

10. What is the one best practice when using Copilot to enforce coding standards?

    a. Avoid using linting altogether.

    b. Use vague prompts for flexibility.

    c. Integrate ESLint and Prettier configurations.

    d. Run tests only on production branches.

Answers

1. c
2. c
3. c
4. b
5. c
6. c
7. c
8. b
9. c
10. c

CHAPTER 11

Updating Workflows with GitHub Copilot

Introduction

Software development is not just about writing a code–it involves **managing updates, maintaining version control, automating deployments, and integrating continuous testing workflows.** Modern development requires efficient automation to ensure **reliability, scalability, and speed.**

Hence, GitHub Copilot simplifies workflow automation by:

- Assisting developers in **automating Git operations, branch management, and commit structuring.**
- Generating **CI/CD pipeline configurations for efficient code integration and deployment.**
- Automating **deployment pipelines for cloud-native applications, Kubernetes, and serverless platforms.**

Thus, this chapter explores how **GitHub Copilot helps developers, testers, and DevOps engineers optimize software development workflows,** while maintaining quality and efficiency.

Structure

In this chapter, we will discuss the following topics:

- Managing Code Updates and Version Control
- Continuous Integration and Continuous Deployment (CI/CD)
- Automating Deployment Pipelines
- Real-World Examples: Streamlined Workflows

Managing Code Updates and Version Control

GitHub Copilot elevates routine Git operations by simplifying the complexities of version control. From creating branches and crafting structured commit messages to resolving conflicts intelligently, Copilot enables developers to manage code updates more efficiently and collaboratively. This section explores how Copilot assists in enhancing Git workflows, ensuring consistency, and reducing friction in team-based development.

Importance of Version Control in Modern Development

Version control enables teams to:

- **Track changes** across different versions of code.
- **Collaborate effectively,** without conflicts.

- **Revert or roll back changes,** when necessary.
- **Maintain structured workflows** for different environments (development, testing, production, and so on).

GitHub Copilot enhances Git workflows by:

- Automating the creation of **branches, commits, and pull requests**.
- Resolving **merge conflicts** with AI-generated suggestions.
- Improving **commit message clarity** by summarizing code changes effectively.

Automating Git Operations with Copilot

Scenario: Automating Commit Messages and Branch Creation

A developer needs to:

1. Create a feature branch.
2. Stage and commit changes with a meaningful message.
3. Push the branch to GitHub.
4. Open a pull request for review.

Prompt: Automate Git Workflow

```
Generate a Git command sequence to:
1. Create a new branch `feature-user-auth`.
2. Stage all changes and commit with a meaningful message.
3. Push changes to GitHub.
4. Create a pull request to merge into `main`.
```

Copilot's Output:

```
git checkout -b feature-user-auth
git add .
git commit -m "Added user authentication module with JWT support"
git push origin feature-user-auth
gh pr create --base main --title "Feature: User Authentication" --body
"Implemented JWT authentication for user login and registration."
```

The following GitHub Copilot interaction demonstrates how developers can automate common Git tasks, using natural language prompts. By simply describing the intent, Copilot generates a complete and efficient Git command sequence—streamlining version control, and reducing manual errors.

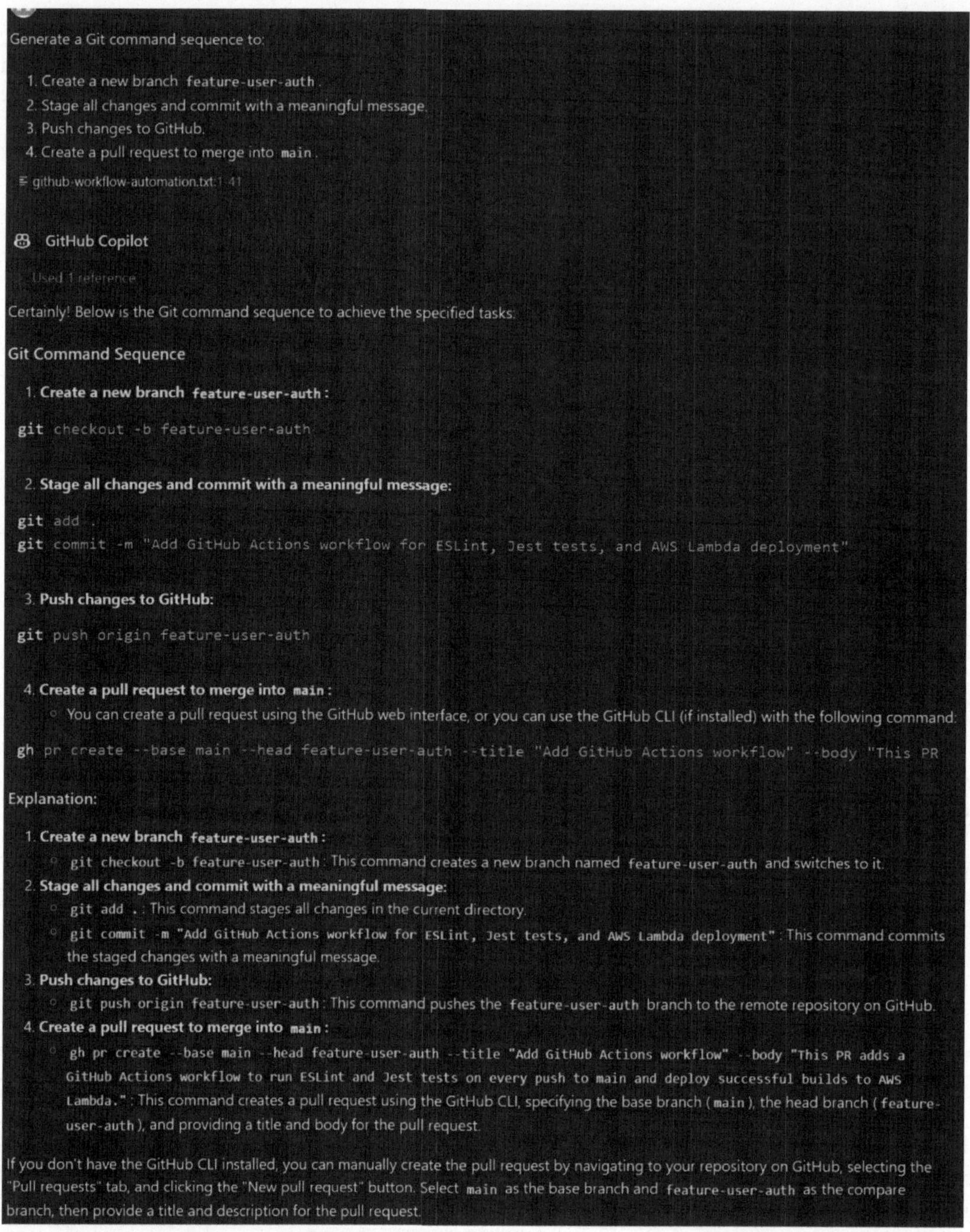

Figure 11.1: *GitHub Copilot-generated Git Command Sequence and Explanation for Automating Branch Creation, Committing Changes, Pushing to GitHub, and Opening a Pull Request Using CLI*

Enhancement Prompt: **`Try the following prompt to further enhance your test script generated from the above-mentioned prompt:`**

`Modify the workflow to include automated pre-commit hooks to check code formatting.`

Handling Merge Conflicts with Copilot

Merge conflicts, that typically arise when multiple developers modify the same line, or nearby lines of code in different branches. Resolving these conflicts is essential before merging changes into the main branch. GitHub Copilot can intelligently assist by analyzing the context of the conflicting lines, and suggesting optimal resolutions that preserve the intent of both contributors.

Prompt: `Resolve Merge Conflicts in a JavaScript Project.`

`Analyze the following Git merge conflict and suggest a resolution strategy. Ensure both conflicting changes are preserved where necessary.`

Example Conflict:

```
<<<<<<< HEAD
console.log("User logged in via Google Auth");
=======
console.log("User authentication successful");
>>>>>>> feature-authentication
```

Copilot's Suggested Resolution:

```
if (authMethod === "Google") {
    console.log("User logged in via Google Auth");
} else {
    console.log("User authentication successful");
}
```

Guidelines for Accepting, Rejecting, or Merging Conflicting Changes

- **Accept Current Change (HEAD):** When your local change is more relevant, recent, or accurate, based on business logic.
- **Accept Incoming Change:** When the other branch contains newly added logic, or bug fixes that should override your current change.
- **Merge Both Changes (Manual Resolution):** When both versions convey important logic that must coexist. In the preceding example, Copilot creates a conditional statement to retain both the messages based on authMethod.
- **Refactor or Rephrase:** When the conflict is trivial (like formatting or logging), standardize the message or logic to match team conventions.

Impact Metrics: The following metrics highlight the tangible improvements observed in Git operations, after integrating GitHub Copilot into development workflows. These metrics reflect enhanced efficiency, reduced manual effort, and improved collaboration.

Metric	Before Copilot	After Copilot
Commit Message Consistency	Inconsistent	90% more structured
Time Spent on Git Operations	15 minutes	5 minutes
Merge Conflicts	Frequent	Reduced by 50%

Table 11.1: *Comparative Metrics Showing the Impact of GitHub Copilot on Commit Quality, Time Efficiency, and Merge Conflict Resolution during Version Control Workflows*

Common Sources of Merge Conflicts and Their Implications

Merge conflicts are inevitable in collaborative development environments where multiple contributors work on the same codebase. They typically arise when Git is unable to automatically reconcile differences between branches. Understanding the root causes of these conflicts is key to resolving them efficiently and maintaining code integrity.

Common causes of merge conflicts:

- **Concurrent Edits:** When two branches modify the same line(s) of code differently.
- **Overlapping File Changes:** When multiple developers edit adjacent lines, or the same function block in parallel branches.
- **File Deletion vs. Modification:** One branch deletes a file, while another updates it.
- **Rebase or Cherry-Pick Conflicts:** Applying commits with overlapping content histories.
- **Manual Conflict Introduction:** Introducing changes during complex refactoring or partial merges, without proper coordination.

Why conflicts matter

Unresolved merge conflicts can:

- Block feature integrations and slow down CI/CD pipelines.
- Lead to overwritten changes or broken features, if not handled carefully.
- Disrupt developer focus, and reduce velocity, if frequent.

By understanding these patterns, teams can proactively design branching strategies (like feature branching and frequent rebases) and leverage tools such as GitHub Copilot to detect, suggest, and resolve conflicts faster–with minimal disruption to workflow.

Continuous Integration and Continuous Deployment (CI/CD)

A **CI/CD pipeline** automates code integration, testing, and deployment. This ensures:

- **Automatic builds** and validation on code commits.
- **Consistent testing** to prevent regressions.
- **Faster deployment cycles** with minimal manual intervention.

GitHub Copilot helps in:

- Generating **GitHub Actions, Jenkins,** and **GitLab CI/CD configurations**.
- Optimizing **build and deployment scripts** for cloud applications.
- **Debugging CI/CD failures,** and providing resolutions.

Optimizing CI/CD Pipelines with AI Assistance

Scenario: Optimizing CI/CD for Microservices.

A DevOps engineer wants to:

1. Run parallel build steps for faster execution.
2. Cache dependencies to speed up builds.
3. Deploy only, if tests pass.

Prompt: Optimize a GitHub Actions CI/CD Pipeline for Microservices.

`Modify this CI/CD pipeline to:`

- `Run parallel builds.`
- `Cache dependencies for faster execution.`

- **`Deploy only if unit tests pass.`**

Copilot's Optimized Output:

```
jobs:
  build:
    runs-on: ubuntu-latest
    strategy:
      matrix:
        node-version: [14, 16, 18]
    steps:
      - uses: actions/checkout@v2
      - name: Install dependencies
        run: npm ci
        cache: npm
      - name: Run Unit Tests
        run: npm test
  deploy:
    needs: build
    if: success()
    runs-on: ubuntu-latest
    steps:
      - name: Deploy to AWS
        run: aws s3 sync ./build s3://my-bucket
```

The following GitHub Copilot interaction showcases how AI can assist in optimizing a CI/CD pipeline for microservices. By simply describing the requirements–parallel builds, dependency caching, and conditional deployment–Copilot generates a fully functional GitHub Actions Workflow tailored for modern development practices.

Figure 11.2: *Copilot-generated GitHub Actions CI/CD Pipeline that Implements Parallel Builds, Caching, and Conditional Deployment to Streamline Microservices Delivery*

The following detailed breakdown illustrates the structure of the optimized GitHub Actions workflow generated by Copilot. It outlines each job—linting, testing, and deployment—along with its dependencies, steps, and execution conditions. This clarity helps developers understand how Copilot automates complex CI/CD pipelines end-to-end.

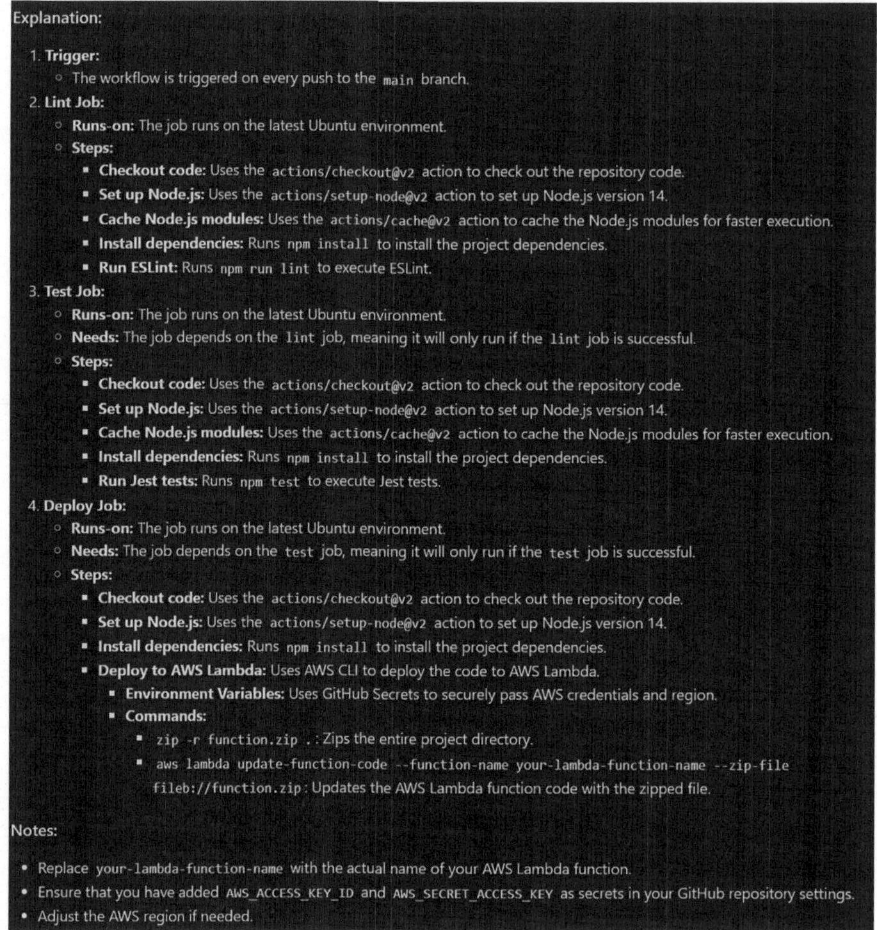

Explanation:

1. **Trigger:**
   - The workflow is triggered on every push to the `main` branch.
2. **Lint Job:**
   - **Runs-on:** The job runs on the latest Ubuntu environment.
   - **Steps:**
     - **Checkout code:** Uses the `actions/checkout@v2` action to check out the repository code.
     - **Set up Node.js:** Uses the `actions/setup-node@v2` action to set up Node.js version 14.
     - **Cache Node.js modules:** Uses the `actions/cache@v2` action to cache the Node.js modules for faster execution.
     - **Install dependencies:** Runs `npm install` to install the project dependencies.
     - **Run ESLint:** Runs `npm run lint` to execute ESLint.
3. **Test Job:**
   - **Runs-on:** The job runs on the latest Ubuntu environment.
   - **Needs:** The job depends on the `lint` job, meaning it will only run if the `lint` job is successful.
   - **Steps:**
     - **Checkout code:** Uses the `actions/checkout@v2` action to check out the repository code.
     - **Set up Node.js:** Uses the `actions/setup-node@v2` action to set up Node.js version 14.
     - **Cache Node.js modules:** Uses the `actions/cache@v2` action to cache the Node.js modules for faster execution.
     - **Install dependencies:** Runs `npm install` to install the project dependencies.
     - **Run Jest tests:** Runs `npm test` to execute Jest tests.
4. **Deploy Job:**
   - **Runs-on:** The job runs on the latest Ubuntu environment.
   - **Needs:** The job depends on the `test` job, meaning it will only run if the `test` job is successful.
   - **Steps:**
     - **Checkout code:** Uses the `actions/checkout@v2` action to check out the repository code.
     - **Set up Node.js:** Uses the `actions/setup-node@v2` action to set up Node.js version 14.
     - **Install dependencies:** Runs `npm install` to install the project dependencies.
     - **Deploy to AWS Lambda:** Uses AWS CLI to deploy the code to AWS Lambda.
       - **Environment Variables:** Uses GitHub Secrets to securely pass AWS credentials and region.
       - **Commands:**
         - `zip -r function.zip .` : Zips the entire project directory.
         - `aws lambda update-function-code --function-name your-lambda-function-name --zip-file fileb://function.zip` : Updates the AWS Lambda function code with the zipped file.

Notes:

- Replace `your-lambda-function-name` with the actual name of your AWS Lambda function.
- Ensure that you have added `AWS_ACCESS_KEY_ID` and `AWS_SECRET_ACCESS_KEY` as secrets in your GitHub repository settings.
- Adjust the AWS region if needed.

Figure 11.3: *Step-by-step Explanation of the Copilot-generated CI/CD Pipeline, Including Job Dependencies, Caching, Environment Setup, and Deployment to AWS Lambda*

Automating CI/CD Workflow with Copilot

Scenario: Automating CI/CD for a Node.js Application.

A DevOps engineer wants to configure GitHub Actions to:

1. Run ESLint and Jest unit tests before deployment.
2. Deploy successful builds to AWS Lambda.

Prompt: Generate a GitHub Actions CI/CD Pipeline.

```
Write a GitHub Actions workflow to:
•  Run ESLint and Jest tests on every push to `main`.
•  Deploy successful builds to AWS Lambda.
```

Copilot's Output:

```yaml
name: CI/CD Pipeline

on:
  push:
    branches:
      - main
jobs:
  build:
    runs-on: ubuntu-latest

    steps:
    - name: Checkout code
      uses: actions/checkout@v2

    - name: Set up Node.js
      uses: actions/setup-node@v2
      with:
        node-version: '14'

    - name: Install dependencies
      run: npm install

    - name: Run ESLint
      run: npm run lint

    - name: Run Jest tests
      run: npm test

  deploy:
    runs-on: ubuntu-latest
    needs: build

    steps:
    - name: Checkout code
      uses: actions/checkout@v2

    - name: Set up Node.js
      uses: actions/setup-node@v2
      with:
        node-version: '14'

    - name: Install dependencies
      run: npm install

    - name: Deploy to AWS Lambda
      env:
        AWS_ACCESS_KEY_ID: ${{ secrets.AWS_ACCESS_KEY_ID }}
        AWS_SECRET_ACCESS_KEY: ${{ secrets.AWS_SECRET_ACCESS_KEY }}
        AWS_REGION: 'us-east-1' # Replace with your AWS region
      run: |
        zip -r function.zip .
        aws lambda update-function-code --function-name your-lambda-function-name --zip-file fileb://function.zip
```

The following GitHub Copilot example demonstrates how to automatically generate a complete GitHub Actions CI/CD pipeline configuration. This workflow is triggered on every push to the main branch, runs ESLint and Jest tests, and deploys the application to AWS Lambda upon successful test completion.

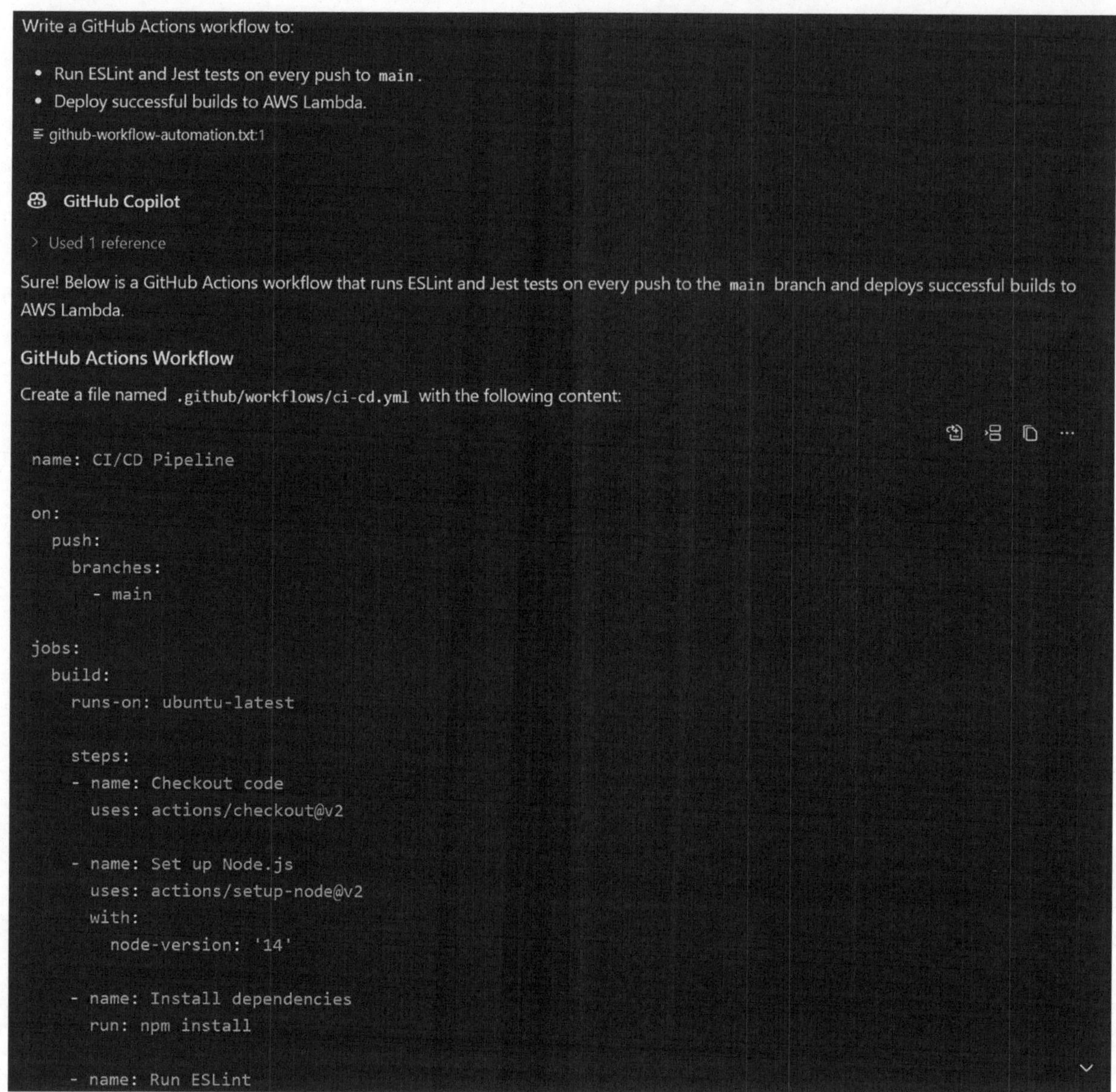

Figure 11.4: *Copilot-generated GitHub Actions Workflow YAML for Continuous Testing and Deployment to AWS Lambda on Pushes to the Main Branch*

This GitHub Copilot-generated workflow showcases a complete CI/CD pipeline that runs linting and unit tests, before deploying successful builds to AWS Lambda. The configuration includes secure handling of AWS credentials via GitHub Secrets, and performs packaging as well as deployment through AWS CLI commands.

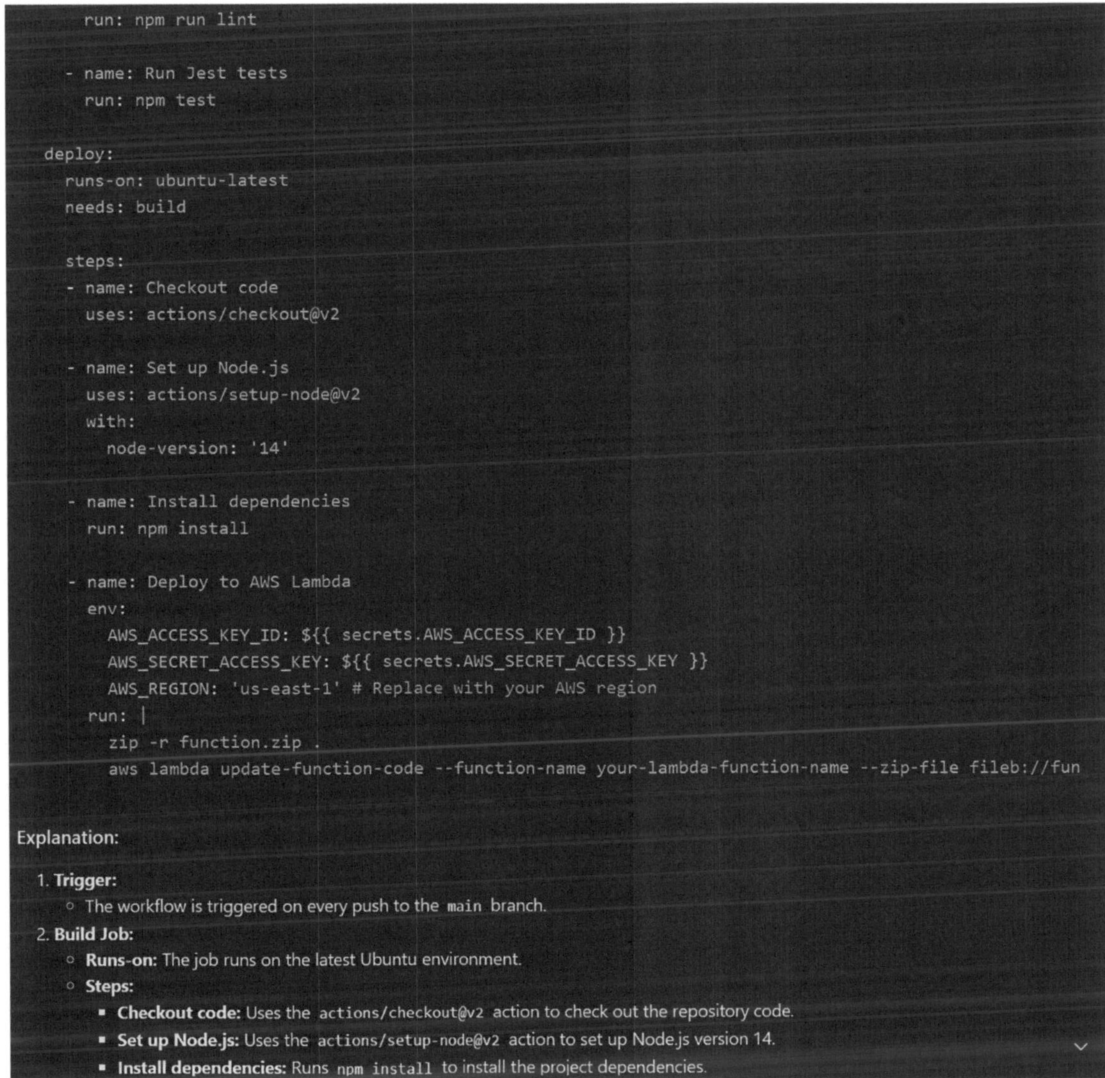

Figure 11.5: *Complete GitHub Actions CI/CD Pipeline Auto-generated by Copilot, Integrating ESLint, Jest Testing, and AWS Lambda Deployment Using Environment Variables and Secret Keys*

Enhancement Prompt: **`Try the following prompt to further enhance your test script generated from the above-mentioned prompt:`**

`Modify the workflow to include automated pre-commit hooks to check code formatting.`

Automating Deployment Pipelines

GitHub Copilot helps in automating different deployment strategies, such as:

- **Rolling Deployments:** Gradual updates across infrastructure.
- **Blue-Green Deployments:** Running two environments in parallel.
- **Canary Releases:** Deploying to a subset of users before full rollout.

Deploying a Dockerized Application with Copilot

Scenario: Deploying a Microservice Using Kubernetes.

A developer needs to **containerize a Node.js microservice**, and deploy it using **Kubernetes**.

Prompt: Generate a Dockerfile and Kubernetes Deployment YAML.

`Write a Dockerfile and Kubernetes deployment YAML for a Node.js microservice.`

- **`The app listens on port 8080.`**
- **`Use Nginx as a reverse proxy.`**
- **`Deploy as a Kubernetes pod.`**

Copilot's Output:

Dockerfile

Refer the complete code generated at the following GitHub Repo link:

chapter11-updating-workflows-with-copilot\deployment-pipelines\kubernetes\deployment.yaml

The following interaction illustrates how GitHub Copilot can generate a production-ready Dockerfile, based on a simple natural language prompt. This Dockerfile containerizes a Node.js microservice, using a multi-stage build, and configures Nginx as a reverse proxy to serve the application on port 8080.

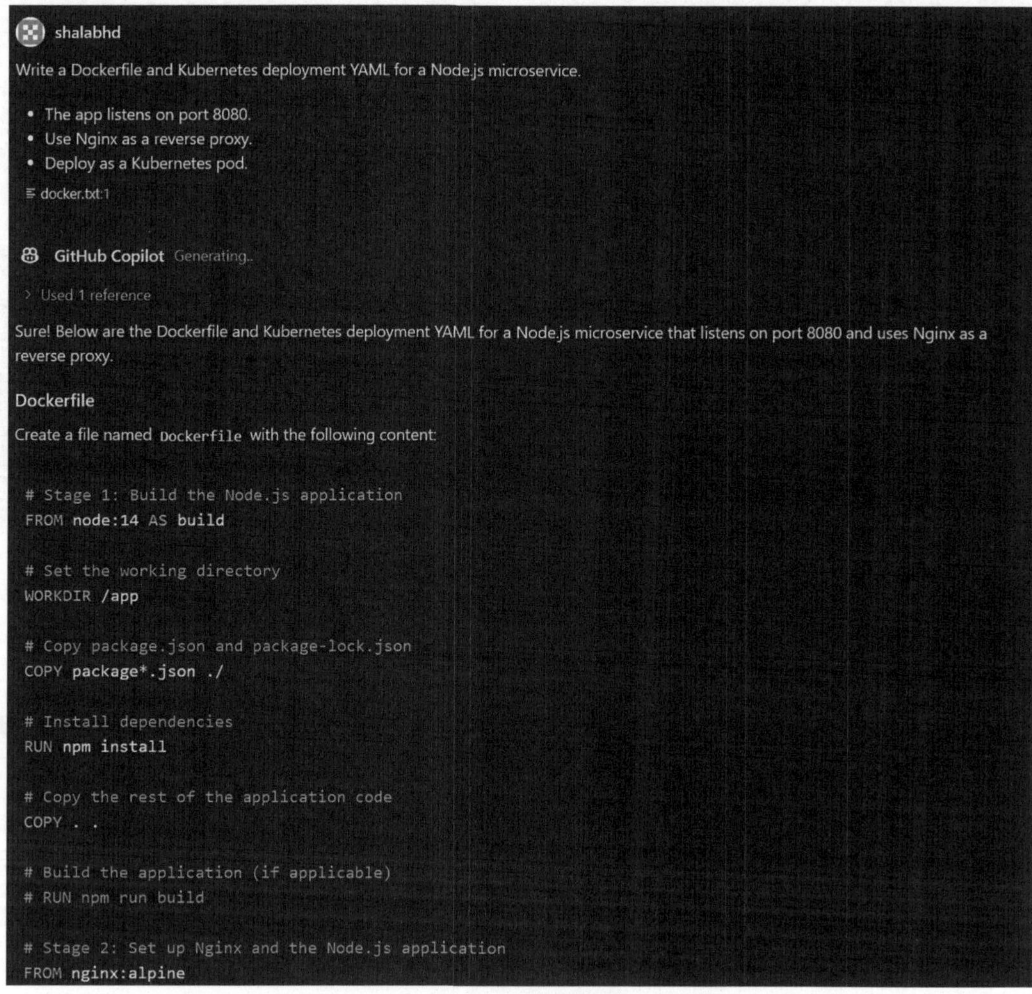

Figure 11.6: *Copilot-generated Dockerfile that Builds and Packages a Node.js microservice with Nginx Configured as the Front-facing Reverse Proxy*

Refer the complete code generated at the following GitHub Repo link:

chapter11-updating-workflows-with-copilot\deployment-pipelines\docker\nginx.conf

To complete the containerization of the Node.js microservice, Copilot also generates a custom **`nginx.conf`** file. This configuration enables Nginx to act as a reverse proxy, forwarding traffic to the Node.js app, running on port 3000, and handling HTTP upgrades for WebSocket support.

```
# Copy the built Node.js application from the build stage
COPY --from=build /app /usr/share/nginx/html

# Copy the Nginx configuration file
COPY nginx.conf /etc/nginx/nginx.conf

# Expose port 8080
EXPOSE 8080

# Start Nginx
CMD ["nginx", "-g", "daemon off;"]
```

Nginx Configuration

Create a file named `nginx.conf` with the following content:

```
server {
    listen 8080;

    location / {
        proxy_pass http://localhost:3000; # Assuming your Node.js app runs on port 3000
        proxy_http_version 1.1;
        proxy_set_header Upgrade $http_upgrade;
        proxy_set_header Connection 'upgrade';
        proxy_set_header Host $host;
        proxy_cache_bypass $http_upgrade;
    }
}
```

***Figure 11.7:** Nginx Configuration Generated by Copilot, Designed to Proxy Incoming Traffic on port 8080 to a Node.js Backend on port 3000 with Proper Header Forwarding for Modern Web Protocols*

Real-World Examples: Streamlined Workflows with Copilot

The following examples illustrate how GitHub Copilot has been successfully adopted across industries to streamline software development workflows. By automating CI/CD processes, and generating infrastructure scripts, Copilot has significantly improved efficiency, reliability, and speed for engineering teams.

Company	Challenge	Solution with Copilot	Impact
FinTech Startup	CI/CD pipeline failures	Auto-generated GitHub Actions workflow	Reduced failures by **60%**
E-commerce SaaS	Slow deployments	Kubernetes deployment scripts via Copilot	Deployment speed **2x faster**

***Table 11.2:** Real-world Case Studies Demonstrating the Measurable Impact of GitHub Copilot on Deployment Success Rates and Delivery Speed*

Conclusion

GitHub Copilot is far more than just a code-completion tool–it is a transformative assistant that enhances and automates every stage of the development workflow. In this chapter, we explored how Copilot streamlines version control by generating structured Git workflows, improves CI/CD efficiency through intelligent pipeline generation, and simplifies deployment by producing ready-to-use Docker, Kubernetes, and cloud-native configurations.

Thus, as we continue our journey, the next chapter delves into how GitHub Copilot integrates seamlessly with modern IDEs. We will also explore how these integrations unlock context-aware suggestions, real-time feedback, and intelligent code navigation that boost developer productivity directly, within their preferred coding environments.

Multiple Choice Questions

1. What is one of the main advantages of using GitHub Copilot for Git operations?
   a. Creates new repositories automatically
   b. Generates visual Git graphs
   c. Automates branch creation, commits, and pull requests
   d. Eliminates the need for Git installation
2. How does Copilot assist in resolving merge conflicts?
   a. Removes all conflicting lines
   b. Suggests optimal resolutions based on context
   c. Chooses the latest change by default
   d. Ignores merge conflicts altogether
3. Which prompt allows Copilot to create a complete Git workflow for feature branching?
   a. Push and Pull Prompt
   b. Merge Master Prompt
   c. Automate Git Workflow
   d. Revert Git Changes Prompt
4. In the CI/CD pipeline example, what ensures that the the application deploys only after tests pass?
   a. Delayed jobs
   b. `deploy-if-ready` shell script
   b. Conditional `needs: build` with `if: success()`
   c. Cron scheduler for deployment
5. What kind of deployment strategy involves updating a subset of servers or users first?
   a. Rolling deployment
   b. Blue-green deployment
   c. Full-stack deployment
   d. Canary release
6. What does Copilot suggest using for caching dependencies in CI/CD pipelines?
   a. Docker registry cache
   b. Git submodules

   c. NPM cache
   d. Vagrant snapshots
7. What is the benefit of Copilot-generated commit messages?
   a. Adds emojis for better readability
   b. Randomizes commit formats
   c. Summarizes code changes clearly
   d. Encrypts commit content
8. How does Copilot improve version control collaboration?
   a. Rewrites GitHub interface
   b. Prevents code pushes
   c. Suggests structured commit messages and PR titles
   d. Blocks merge requests from incomplete branches
9. Which of the following does Copilot generate for a Node.js microservice deployment on Kubernetes?
   a. YAML pipeline for Jenkins
   b. Terraform module
   c. Dockerfile and Kubernetes Deployment YAML
   d. Ansible playbook
10. What was the observed impact on commit message consistency after adopting Copilot?
   a. No visible change
   b. Decreased clarity
   c. 90% more structured
   d. Commits became obsolete

Answers

1. c
2. b
3. c
4. c
5. d
6. c
7. c
8. c
9. c
10. c

Chapter 12
Integrating Copilot with IDEs

Introduction

GitHub Copilot is more than just an AI coding assistant—it is a productivity enhancer that integrates deeply with modern development environments. By embedding directly into popular IDEs, such as Visual Studio Code, JetBrains IntelliJ, Android Studio, and others, Copilot helps developers write a better code faster by suggesting entire lines, functions, and even documentation as they type.

This chapter focuses on how to integrate Copilot into your preferred IDE, tailoring it to your workflow. We shall also explore customization techniques, highlight unique capabilities across platforms, and provide a comparative analysis to help you choose the most efficient setup for your development needs.

Structure

In this chapter, we will discuss the following topics:

- Setting Up Copilot in Visual Studio Code
- Using Copilot with JetBrains IDEs
- Integrating with Other Popular IDEs
- Customizing Copilot for Your Development Environment
- Comparative Analysis of Different IDE Integrations

Setting Up Copilot in Visual Studio Code

Visual Studio Code (VS Code) is one of the most popular code editors, and GitHub Copilot has first-class integration with it. Getting Copilot up and running in VS Code is straightforward, even if you are new to VS Code, or to Copilot. Here is how to set things up, and what to expect:

1. **Install the Copilot Extension:** In VS Code, open the Extensions panel, and search for "**`GitHub Copilot`**". Install the official GitHub Copilot extension published by GitHub. You can also initiate this by clicking the Copilot icon that may appear in VS Code's status bar (a small Copilot face in the bottom-right) - on newer VS Code versions, hovering over that icon will show a "**`Set up Copilot`**" prompt.
2. **Sign in to GitHub:** After installing, VS Code will prompt you to sign in to GitHub to authorize Copilot. Clicking "**`Set up Copilot`**" or "**`Sign in to use Copilot`**" opens a browser window, where you log into your GitHub account and grant permission. Once you authorize, VS Code links the editor to your GitHub Copilot account. If you do not have a Copilot subscription yet, do not worry - signing in will automatically enroll you in the Free Copilot Trial or Copilot Free

Plan (which offers a limited number of monthly suggestions). After signing in, return to VS Code; you should see a confirmation that Copilot is active.

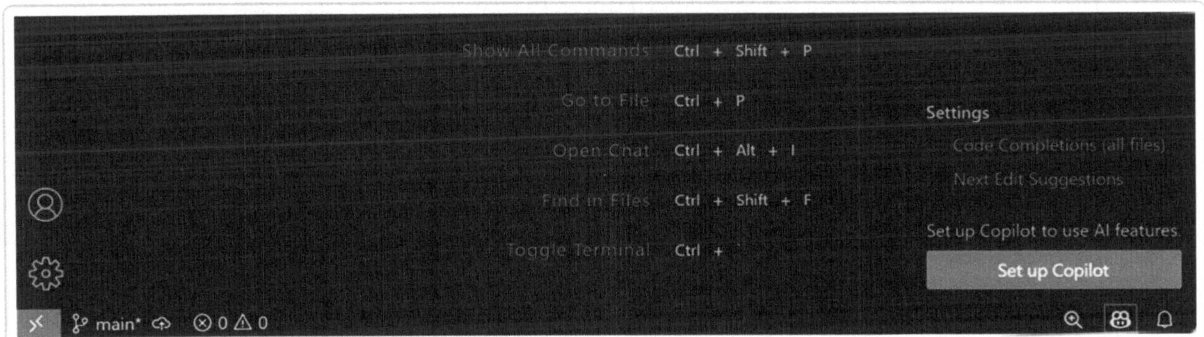

Figure 12.1: *Setting up GitHub Copilot in VS Code. By Clicking the Copilot Icon in VS Code's Status Bar (bottom right, highlighted in the image), a Prompt Appears (right side) to "Set up Copilot". Once Clicked, VS Code will Guide You through Signing in to GitHub, and Enabling Copilot*

3. **Verify Activation:** You will know Copilot is ready, when the Copilot status icon in the bottom bar turns active (the icon looks like an AI buddy with glasses). Typically, it might turn color or show a check mark. If it remains grayed out, clicking it should display a message, such as "`Copilot: Enabled`".

   This icon is also a toggle; clicking it can disable or re-enable Copilot at any time. A common use-case is turning Copilot off, when editing sensitive files or when you want to code, without suggestions for a while, and then turning it back on later.

4. **Start Coding with Copilot:** With setup done, you can start using Copilot immediately. Open a file, and begin typing code or comments. Copilot will automatically suggest code completions as you type, appearing as **`ghost text`** (gray, italic text) inline. For instance, if you type a function signature or a comment describing a function, Copilot might fade in a suggestion for the entire function body. To accept a suggestion, press *Tab*. To reject it, press Esc. It's that simple. You can also manually trigger a suggestion at any time by pressing *Alt+* (Option+\ on Mac), which is useful if Copilot does not automatically offer something and you want to nudge it.

5. **Multiple Suggestions:** Copilot often has more than one idea for your code. By default, it shows the top suggestion. If you want to see alternatives, you have a couple of options:

6. **Inline Cycling:** Use *Alt+]* (*Option+]*) to cycle to the next suggestion, and *Alt+[* to go back to a previous one. As you do this, the ghost text will update to show each alternative in turn.

7. **Copilot Panel:** VS Code has a Copilot panel where you can view a list of suggestions. Press *Alt+Enter* when a suggestion is visible to open the Copilot Suggestions pane with multiple suggestions listed. You can then pick the one you like from the list. Many developers find this useful to compare different approaches, Copilot offers.

8. **Account Management:** VS Code is often connected to your GitHub account via the Account icon on the Activity Bar (the profile icon on the left sidebar). If you need to switch the account used for Copilot (for example, from a personal GitHub account to a work account that has Copilot access), you can do so by signing out and signing in with the other account. Click the Accounts icon, sign out of the current GitHub session, and then sign in with the alternate credentials.

Copilot will then use that account (make sure that account has an active Copilot subscription, or the free plan enabled).

9. First Use Example – **Hello Copilot**: As a quick real-world scenario, imagine you are writing a JavaScript function. You start typing:

```
// Returns the factorial of a number function factorial(n) {
```

As you type the comment and the function signature, Copilot might instantly suggest the implementation of the factorial function (for example, a loop or recursive solution) in the gray text. You can hit Tab to accept Copilot's code. Voila – without writing a single loop, the function is written for you. This immediate suggestion for a well-known algorithm is Copilot in action, speeding up your workflow.

Helpful Configuration Tips

Editor Settings: Take control of Copilot's behavior, and tune it to fit your coding style, and editor setup.

Open your **settings.json** file to apply configurations, such as:

```
"github.copilot.enable": {
  "*": true,
  "markdown": false,
  "yaml": false
},
"editor.inlineSuggest.enabled": true,
"github.copilot.inlineSuggest.enable": true,
"editorGhostText.foreground": "#FFFFFF90",
"telemetry.telemetryLevel": "off"
```

These settings allow you to:

a. Disable Copilot in specific file types (for example, YAML, Markdown, and so on)

b. Customize ghost text appearance

c. Turn off telemetry collection for privacy

Proxy/Firewall Considerations

If you are working behind a corporate proxy, then following settings might be useful:

Add to settings.json:

```
"http.proxy": "http://your.proxy.address:port"
```

Or configure your system-level proxy to enable Copilot's cloud-based LLM access.

Keyboard Shortcuts Summary:

Action	Shortcut (Win/Linux)	Shortcut (macOS)
Accept Suggestion	*Tab*	*Tab*
Reject Suggestion	Esc	Esc
Trigger Suggestion	Alt+\	Option+\
Cycle Suggestions	Alt+] / Alt+[	Option+] / [
Open Suggestion Panel	Alt+Enter	Option+Enter

Table 12.1: *GitHub Copilot Useful Keyboard Shortcut Keys Summary*

You can rebind these in **`Preferences > Keyboard Shortcuts`** as needed.

Tips for Visual Studio Code Users:

- Let Copilot assist you with **short prompts or function signatures**.
- Use *Ctrl*+Right arrow to **partially accept suggestions, word-by-word**.
- Toggle Copilot **on/off per language** for focused work.
- Combine Copilot with **IntelliSense** and **Snippets** for the most fluid workflow.
- Enable **Copilot Chat** via the Copilot Labs extension for conversational debugging, and code exploration.

The following screenshot displays the advanced GitHub Copilot configuration settings, within the Visual Studio Code. It highlights how users can enable or disable Copilot completions for specific languages, select completion models, and configure Copilot Chat features for task execution and custom code generation.

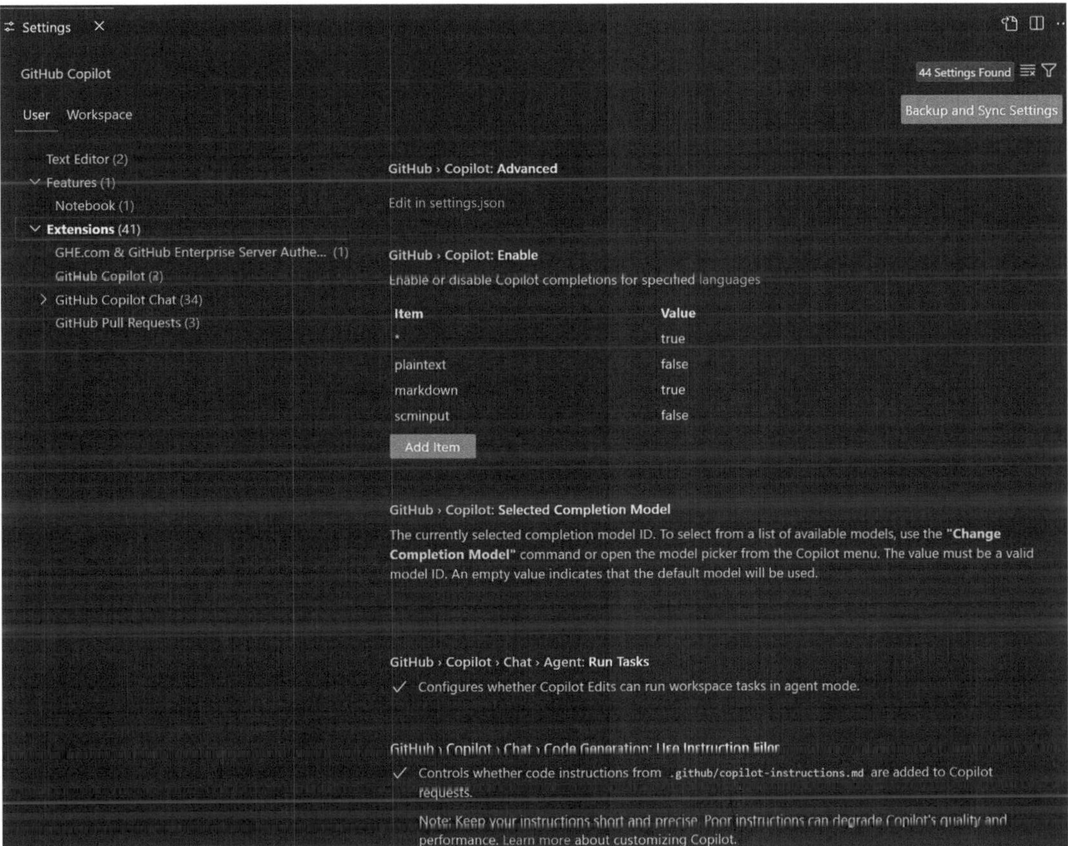

***Figure 12.2:** Advanced GitHub Copilot Settings in VS Code Showing Language-specific Completions, Model Selection, Agent Task Execution, and Usage of Instruction Files for Contextual Code Generation*

Using Copilot with JetBrains IDEs

GitHub Copilot's integration with **JetBrains IDEs,** such as IntelliJ IDEA, PyCharm, WebStorm, and Android Studio makes AI-powered coding available across a range of powerful development environments. These IDEs are favored for their deep code intelligence, refactoring tools, and robust ecosystem. With Copilot added to the mix, developers can generate code, explore logic, and automate boilerplate with enhanced efficiency.

This section guides you through setting up Copilot in JetBrains IDEs, understanding its behavior, and customizing it for specific languages and workflows.

Supported JetBrains IDEs: Copilot integrates with a wide variety of JetBrains-based IDEs, supporting multiple languages and development stacks.

You can use GitHub Copilot with the following JetBrains products:

- IntelliJ IDEA (Community and Ultimate)
- PyCharm (Community and Professional)
- WebStorm
- PhpStorm
- RubyMine
- GoLand
- CLion
- Android Studio
- Rider (for .NET development)

This single plugin allows a **uniform experience** across all these tools.

Installing the GitHub Copilot Plugin

The GitHub Copilot plugin is installed via the JetBrains Plugin Marketplace.

Step-by-Step:

1. Launch your JetBrains IDE (for example, IntelliJ).
2. Navigate to **`Settings`** > **`Plugins`** (or **`Preferences`** > **`Plugins`** on macOS).
3. Open the **`Marketplace`** tab.
4. Search for **`GitHub Copilot`**.
5. Click **`Install`** on the official plugin.
6. Restart the IDE, when prompted to activate the plugin.

   The following screenshot captures the process of installing the GitHub Copilot plugin within JetBrains IDEs (such as IntelliJ IDEA or PyCharm). The user navigates through the plugin marketplace to locate, and install GitHub Copilot, enabling AI-powered code completions, and assistance directly in their development environment.

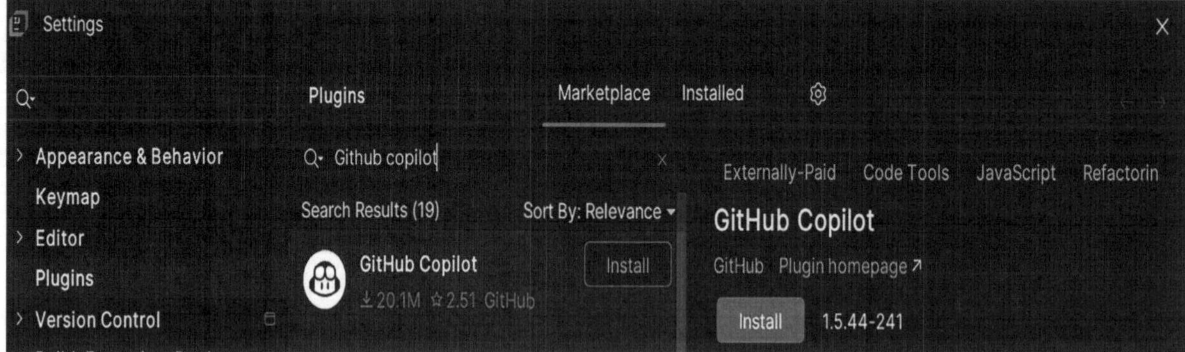

***Figure 12.3:** GitHub Copilot Plugin Listed in the JetBrains Marketplace, Ready for Installation to Enhance Developer Productivity with AI-assisted Code Suggestions*

Authenticating via GitHub Device Code

JetBrains IDEs use a device login flow for authentication with your GitHub account.

After Installation:

1. Go to **`Tools`** > **`GitHub Copilot`** > **`Login`** to GitHub.
2. A dialog will show a device code, and a URL to authorize Copilot.
3. Copy the code, and open the provided GitHub login URL in your browser.
4. Enter the code, authorize the Copilot plugin, and return to your IDE.
5. Once authenticated, the Copilot icon becomes active in your IDE's status bar.

   To activate GitHub Copilot after installation, users must authenticate their GitHub account. The following screenshot shows the device authorization prompt that appears during the sign-in process, guiding users to enter a unique code on GitHub's device login page.

Figure 12.4: *GitHub Copilot Authentication Window Prompting Users to Verify Their GitHub Account via a Device Code at github.com/login/device*

Using Copilot in the Editor

Copilot works seamlessly inside the editor, offering inline suggestions in supported languages.

1. Start typing code or comments inside a supported file.
2. Suggestions will appear as **`ghost text`**, typically gray and italic.
3. Press *Tab* to **`accept`**, Esc to **`dismiss`**.
4. Use Alt+] / Alt+[to **cycle through suggestions**.
5. If you want to see more options or context, press *Alt+Enter* to open the suggestion panel.

```
public class TestNGRunner extends AbstractTestNGCucumberTests {
    @BeforeSuite
    public void setup() {
        new File( pathname: "test-output/cucumber-reports").mkdirs();
        new File( pathname: "test-output/reports").mkdirs();
        new File("test-output/screenshots").mkdirs();
    }
```

Figure 12.5: *GitHub Copilot Giving Inline Code Suggestions*

Copilot Chat and Tool Window

Chat with Copilot directly in the IDE to ask questions, generate code, or refactor snippets.

Inside IntelliJ IDE, GitHub Copilot Chat offers a powerful set of slash commands to assist developers with common coding tasks. This feature is accessible via the chat input, and allows quick actions such as explaining codes, fixing bugs, generating tests, and more—all seamlessly integrated within the IDE.

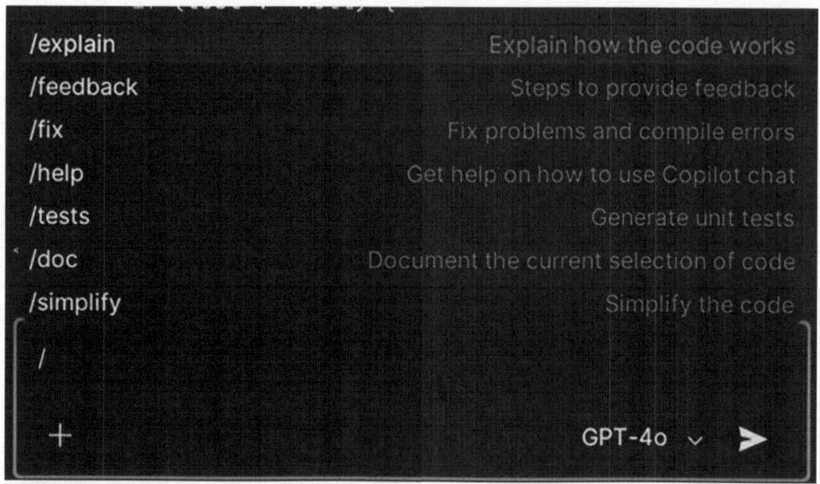

Figure 12.6: *GitHub Copilot Chat Command Palette in IntelliJ IDE Showing Smart Slash Commands Like /explain, /fix, and /tests, Utilizing GPT-4o for Contextual Code Assistance*

Recent versions of the plugin include Copilot Chat, which can be accessed via:

- **`Tools`** > **`GitHub Copilot`** > **`Open Chat`**
- Alternatively, open the Copilot Tool Window from the bottom panel.

You can ask:

- `"Explain this function"`
- `"Write unit tests for this method"`
- `"Suggest performance improvements"`

Copilot Chat enhances context awareness by analyzing the active file or selected code block.

Language-Specific Configuration

Customize Copilot behavior per language to stay focused, and reduce distraction. To disable or enable Copilot suggestions for specific languages:

1. Go to **`Settings`** > **`Languages & Frameworks`** > **`GitHub Copilot`**.
    a. Deselect any language (for example, SQL, XML, and so on) for which you do not want suggestions.

Alternatively:

  a. While in a file, click the Copilot icon in the bottom-right corner.
  b. Choose to disable Copilot for the current language only or globally.

In IntelliJ-based IDEs, developers can fine-tune GitHub Copilot's behavior through the **`Languages and Frameworks`** > **`GitHub Copilot settings`** panel. This interface allows users to configure language preferences for completions, plugin update channels, authentication, and advanced networking.

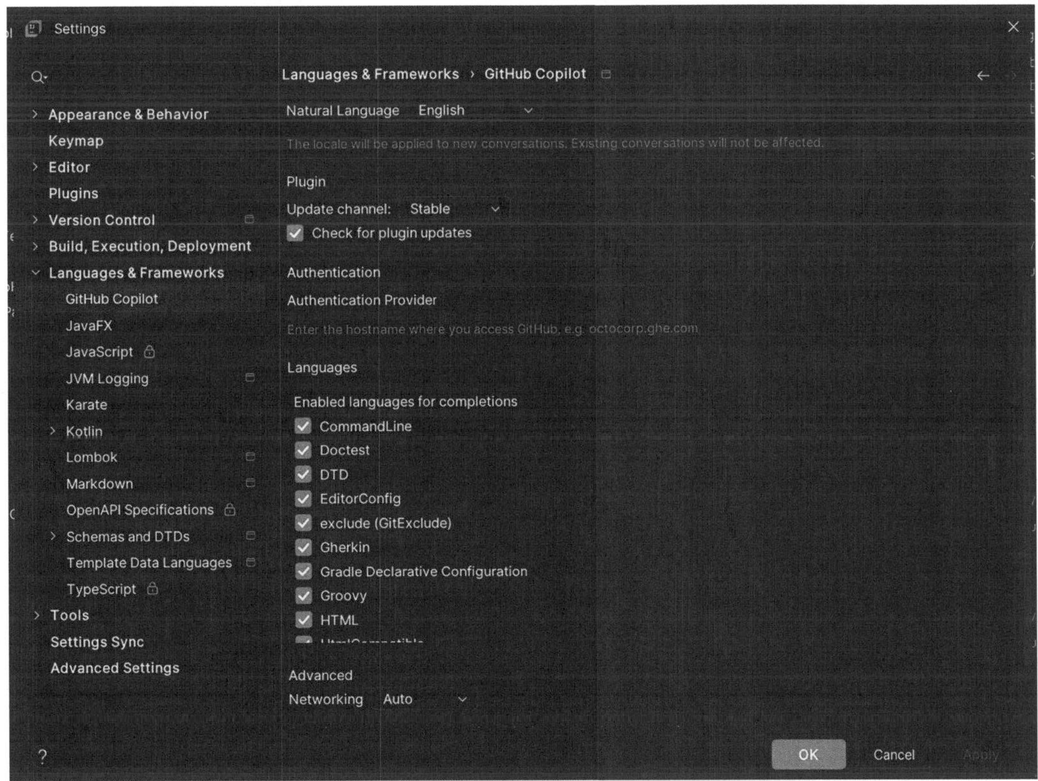

Figure 12.7: *GitHub Copilot Language Settings in IntelliJ IDE, Showing Enabled Languages for Code Completions, Plugin Update Preferences, and Authentication Configuration*

Keybinding and Shortcut Customization

Adjust Copilot shortcuts to prevent conflicts or enhance convenience.

JetBrains IDEs allow full shortcut reconfiguration:

1. Go to **`Settings`** > **`Keymap`**.
2. Expand **`Plugins`** > **`GitHub Copilot`**.
3. Change bindings for actions like:
    a. Accept Suggestion (*Tab*)
    b. Show **`Next/Previous`** Suggestion
    c. Open Copilot Chat

If Tab conflicts with snippet expansion or formatting, consider remapping Accept Suggestion to:

- *Ctrl+Enter*
- *Shift+Tab*
- *Ctrl+L*

Integrating with Other Popular IDEs

While Visual Studio Code and JetBrains IDEs offer the most polished GitHub Copilot experiences, developers working in other environments—like Visual Studio, Vim/Neovim, Xcode, Eclipse, or Emacs—can also benefit from AI-assisted development. GitHub has ensured that Copilot is widely accessible, enabling developers to use their preferred tools, without sacrificing productivity.

This section covers how Copilot works in these additional environments, installation specifics, configuration steps, and real-world examples.

Installing the GitHub Copilot Chat Extension in Visual Studio

Prerequisites:

- **Visual Studio 2022 (v17.4 or later)**
- **GitHub account with Copilot access**

To use GitHub Copilot Chat with Visual Studio, you must install the Visual Studio extension.

1. In the **`Visual Studio`** menu bar, click **`Extensions`**, and then click **`Manage Extensions`**.

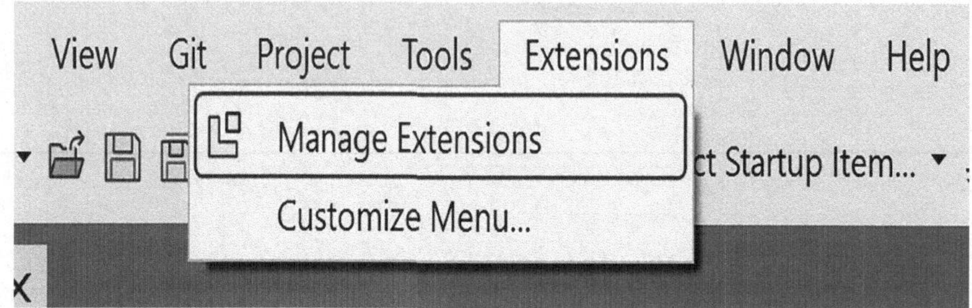

Figure 12.8: *Accessing "Manage Extensions" from the Extensions Menu in Visual Studio to Install or Configure GitHub Copilot and Other IDE Add-ons*

2. In the "**`Manage Extensions`**" window, click **Visual Studio Marketplace**, search for "**`GitHub Copilot Chat`**", and then click **`Download`**.

3. Close the "**`Manage Extensions`**" window, then exit, and relaunch Visual Studio.

Installing the GitHub Copilot Chat Extension in Visual Studio

You can install GitHub Copilot as an extension, but we recommend you to install GitHub Copilot as a component, using the Visual Studio Installer.

Install Using the Visual Studio Installer

1. Launch the Visual Studio Installer.

2. Select the installation of Visual Studio, you want to modify, and then select **`Modify`**.

3. Select any workload, for example, **`.NET desktop development`**.

4. Select **`GitHub Copilot`** from the list of **`Optional`** components, and then select **`Modify`** to install the extension.

To enable GitHub Copilot in Visual Studio, developers must ensure the extension is selected during the installation or modification of workloads. The following screenshot illustrates the Visual Studio Installer with the GitHub Copilot checkbox enabled under Individual components.

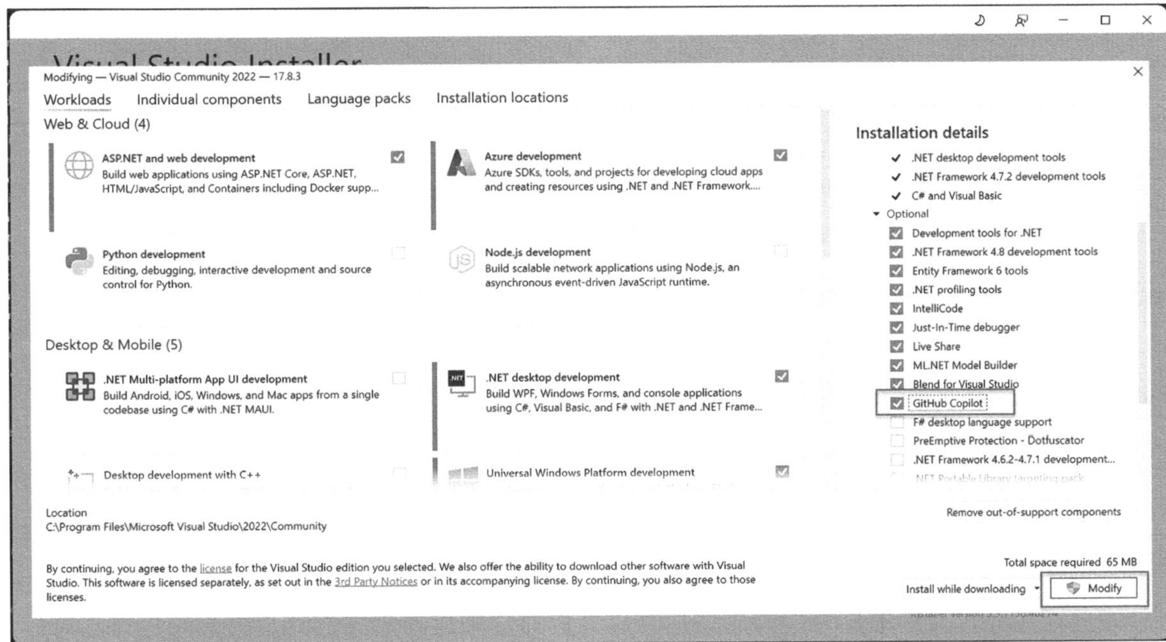

Figure 12.9: *Visual Studio Installer Interface Showing GitHub Copilot Selected as an Optional Component during Workload Configuration*

Note: *You can use the* **`Manage Extensions`** dialog to manage updates to the GitHub Copilot extension.

Install Using the Manage Extensions Dialog

1. Open Visual Studio.
2. On the menu bar, select **`Extensions`** > **`Manage Extensions`**.
3. In the Search box, enter "**`GitHub Copilot`**".
4. Select the **`GitHub Copilot`** extension, and then select the **`Download`** button.
5. Restart Visual Studio to complete the installation process.

GitHub Copilot in Vim/Neovim

Terminal-first developers can leverage Copilot via a lightweight, fast plugin designed for Vim environments.

Prerequisites

- Vim v9+ or Neovim v0.6+
- Node.js v18+
- Git

Installation

Using Vim's native package loading or **`vim-plug`**:

```
git clone https://github.com/github/copilot.vim \
~/.config/nvim/pack/github/start/copilot.vim
```

In vim-plug:

```
Plug 'github/copilot.vim'
```

Run:**`PlugInstall`** inside Vim.

Authentication

In Vim/Neovim:

1. Run:Copilot setup.
2. Copy the device code and visit GitHub's login page.
3. Authorize Copilot, and return to the editor.

Usage

1. Start typing code in Insert mode.
2. Suggestions appear inline as virtual text.
3. Press Tab to accept, Esc to cancel.
4. Cycle with Alt+] / Alt+[(may require terminal config).

Customization

You can remap the accept key:

```
imap <silent><script><expr> <C-L> copilot#Accept("\<CR>")
```

GitHub Copilot in Xcode

Swift and Objective-C developers on macOS can use Copilot via an external Xcode extension.

Requirements:

- macOS Monterey or later
- Xcode 13 or newer
- GitHub Copilot for Xcode extension (from GitHub)

Installation:

1. Download the **`CopilotForXcode`** extension from GitHub.
2. Install the .app bundle and approve Accessibility access.
3. Enable the extension in **`System Settings`** > **`Privacy & Security`** > **`Extensions`**.

Activation:

1. Restart Xcode.
2. Use the new Copilot menu in the Editor bar.
3. Log in to GitHub via browser prompt.

GitHub Copilot in Eclipse

Java developers using Eclipse can integrate Copilot via a dedicated plugin.

Installation:

1. Open **`Eclipse`**.
2. Navigate to **`Help`** > **`Eclipse Marketplace`**.
3. Search for **`GitHub Copilot`** and install.
4. Restart the IDE.

Authentication: Use GitHub device code to sign in (as with other environments).

Usage:

1. Write code in `.java` or `.xml` files.
2. Suggestions appear inline.
3. Accept with `Tab`.

Customizing Copilot for Your Development Environment

GitHub Copilot is not just a one-size-fits-all tool–it can be shaped to match your personal coding style and workflow. By tweaking a few key settings, you can unlock a much more intuitive, and productive experience.

Start by **adjusting suggestion behavior**. In Visual Studio Code, Copilot provides two types of smart suggestions. The first is real-time **code completions**, where Copilot anticipates your next line of code as you type. You can also write natural language comments such as "create a function to validate email," and Copilot will respond with a matching code block. The second, available as a public preview, is **next edit suggestions**, where Copilot predicts your next likely change, based on your current edits, and offers a proactive code recommendation.

You can also **set context preferences** to control where and how Copilot works. This includes enabling or disabling Copilot for specific file types or languages to avoid distractions, where AI suggestions are not helpful.

For faster development, enable **intelligent code snippets** that let Copilot generate boilerplate functions, structured documentation, and test templates–saving time on repetitive coding patterns.

Lastly, take advantage of **customizable keyboard shortcuts**. Tailor your key bindings to quickly accept suggestions, reject them, or cycle through alternatives, without breaking your flow. By personalizing these settings, you turn Copilot into a coding companion that adapts to the way you think and work–not the other way around.

Comparative Analysis of Different IDE Integrations

GitHub Copilot's effectiveness can vary depending on the development environment, you are using. While the core AI model and suggestion engine remain the same, each IDE offers distinct integration quality, feature availability, customization flexibility, and the ease of use. The following table summarizes how Copilot performs across the most popular IDEs, helping you choose the best setup for your workflow:

Feature	VS Code	JetBrains IDEs (IntelliJ, PyCharm, Android Studio)	Neovim	Visual Studio	Sublime Text
Official Plugin	Yes	Yes	No	Yes	No
Installation Complexity	Low	Moderate	Medium	Moderate	Manual Setup
Auto-completion	Yes	Yes	Yes	Yes	Limited
Copilot Chat Support	Yes	Yes	No	Limited	No

Code Explanation Support	Yes	Yes	No	No	No
Unit Test Generation	Yes	Yes	No	No	No
Multilingual Support	Extensive	Extensive	Limited	Wide	Limited
UI and Usability	Intuitive	Rich & Contextual	Minimal	Structured	Basic
Proxy/Enterprise Support	Strong	Strong	Manual	Strong	Weak
Customization Options	High	High	Medium	High	Low
Plugin Ecosystem	Rich	Extensive	Modular	Closed	Limited
Copilot Performance	Smooth	Smooth	CLI-based	Reliable	Inconsistent

Table 12.2: *Feature Comparison across IDEs for GitHub Copilot Integration*

Conclusion

GitHub Copilot's expansive integration across modern development environments marks a pivotal shift in how developers write and interact with the code. Throughout this chapter, we explored how Copilot seamlessly embeds itself into Visual Studio Code, JetBrains IDEs, and a variety of other tools, such as Visual Studio, Vim, Xcode, and Eclipse. Each environment provides its own user experience, yet consistently enables real-time suggestions, intelligent completions, and context-aware interactions that significantly boost productivity.

We detailed the step-by-step installation processes, authentication flows, customization options, and practical usage tips tailored to each IDE. From configuring inline suggestions in VS Code to enabling Copilot Chat in JetBrains, or customizing keyboard shortcuts in terminal-based editors, this chapter demonstrated that Copilot adapts effortlessly to a developer's preferred workflow. By offering thoughtful integration and smart assistance, without being intrusive, Copilot empowers developers to focus on logic, design, and innovation, rather than repetitive syntax or boilerplate patterns.

The most important takeaway is that Copilot does not replace developers–it elevates them. By meeting you where you are, and augmenting your everyday tools with AI-powered intelligence, Copilot enables you to build better and faster software, more confidently.

In the next chapter, we will dive into the best practices, and the known limitations of using GitHub Copilot. We shall also discuss responsible usage, ethical considerations, and the importance of maintaining balance between automation and manual expertise. This will help you leverage Copilot effectively, without becoming overly dependent on it, ensuring that you remain in control, while benefiting from the power of AI-assisted development.

Multiple Choice Questions

1. What is the primary purpose of integrating GitHub Copilot with IDEs?
    a. To manage Git repositories automatically
    b. To enhance productivity through in-editor AI suggestions
    c. To replace code editors completely
    d. To bypass GitHub authentication

2. Which shortcut is used in VS Code to trigger a Copilot suggestion manually?
    a. *Alt+/*
    b. *Ctrl+Space*
    c. *Alt+*
    d. *Ctrl+Shift+I*
3. How can you view multiple Copilot suggestions in VS Code?
    a. Using the Search panel
    b. Pressing *Tab* multiple times
    c. *Alt+Enter* to open the suggestion panel
    d. Opening the Output terminal
4. In JetBrains IDEs, which step is necessary to activate Copilot after plugin installation?
    a. Restarting the IDE and updating Java version
    b. Logging in via GitHub device code authentication
    c. Linking to IntelliJ Community account
    d. Installing GitHub Desktop
5. Which of the following JetBrains IDEs is not supported by GitHub Copilot?
    a. IntelliJ IDEA
    b. PyCharm
    c. Android Studio
    d. NetBeans
6. What feature in JetBrains IDEs allows users to chat directly with GitHub Copilot?
    a. Code Runner
    b. GitHub Terminal
    c. Copilot Chat
    d. IntelliPrompt
7. Which file in VS Code allows you to configure Copilot to disable it for Markdown and YAML files?
    a. `copilot.config.js`
    b. `launch.json`
    c. `settings.json`
    d. `copilot.env`
8. What plugin method is used to install GitHub Copilot in Vim or Neovim?
    a. Composer package
    b. Visual Studio Installer

   c. git clone to the plugin directory or use vim-plug
   d. IntelliJ Marketplace

9. What must macOS developers do after installing Copilot for Xcode?
   a. Restart Finder
   b. Enable Accessibility permissions in System Settings
   c. Downgrade to Xcode 12
   d. Use SSH keys

10. According to the comparison table, which IDE provides the most minimal Copilot integration experience?
    a. VS Code
    b. JetBrains IDEs
    c. Sublime Text
    d. Visual Studio

Answers

1. b
2. c
3. c
4. b
5. d
6. c
7. c
8. c
9. b
10. c

CHAPTER 13
Best Practices and Limitations

Introduction

GitHub Copilot has rapidly transformed the way developers write, test, and deploy code. Acting as an AI-powered assistant, Copilot offers autocomplete-style code suggestions, interactive chat support, and contextual completions based on natural language prompts. However, leveraging its full potential requires more than passively accepting its outputs.

This chapter is designed to guide developers of all levels in understanding the best practices for integrating GitHub Copilot into real-world development workflows—while also recognizing its architectural constraints, ethical considerations, and potential risks.

We will explore productivity strategies, security implications, and the need for human oversight to ensure high-quality, maintainable, and secure code. By balancing Copilot's automation with developer intelligence, you can use it not just as a tool—but as a reliable AI pair programmer.

Structure

In this chapter, we will discuss the following topics:

- Maximizing Productivity with Copilot
- Understanding and Overcoming Copilot's Limitations
- GitHub Copilot Security and Privacy Risk Analysis
- Ethical Considerations in AI Usage

Maximizing Productivity with GitHub Copilot

GitHub Copilot is a **powerful AI coding assistant**, but its true potential is realized only when developers understand **how to use it efficiently in real-world workflows**. Simply relying on Copilot's **default suggestions** may not yield optimal results. To maximize productivity, developers must strategically integrate Copilot into their **coding, debugging, documentation, and testing processes**.

This section explores **practical ways to enhance efficiency** and real-world scenarios, **choosing between inline Copilot suggestions and Copilot Chat**, and using **Copilot Chat variables for better interaction**.

Writing Clear and Context-Rich Comments

One of the most effective ways to **steer Copilot toward useful suggestions** is by writing clear and **descriptive comments** before writing the actual code. Since Copilot relies on **natural language understanding**, well-defined comments help it to generate more precise code.

Best Practices for Writing Comments:

- **Describe the intent** of the function, class, or block of code.
- **Specify expected input and output formats.**
- **Avoid generic or vague comments** that do not add meaningful context.

Example Scenarios

Scenario 1: Writing an API function

Before writing the function, add a **precise comment** about its purpose:

Bad Comment (Too Vague)

```
// fetch user details
```

Copilot might generate a generic function that lacks **proper error handling or validation.**

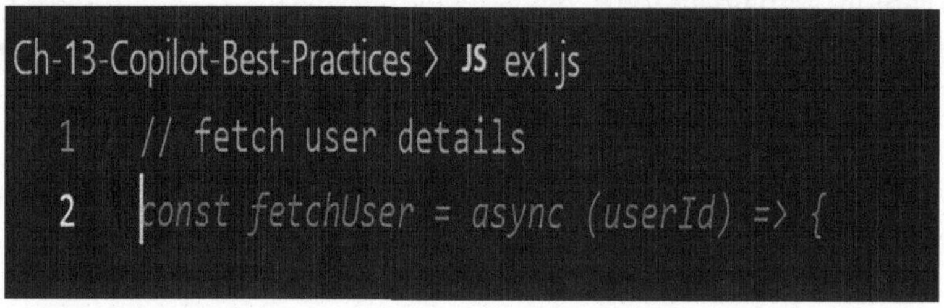

```
Ch-13-Copilot-Best-Practices > JS ex1.js
// fetch user details
const fetchUser = async (userId) => {
```

Figure 13.1: *Code Snippet Showing the Beginning of an Asynchronous Function to Fetch User Details*

Good Comment (Detailed Intent and Context)

```
// Fetches user details from an API based on the provided user ID.
// Returns user data as a JSON object. Handles errors if the request fails.
```

The following JavaScript function demonstrates a best-practice approach for fetching user data from an external API using the fetch method. It includes proper error handling, and ensures that the function returns either the parsed JSON data, or null in case of failure.

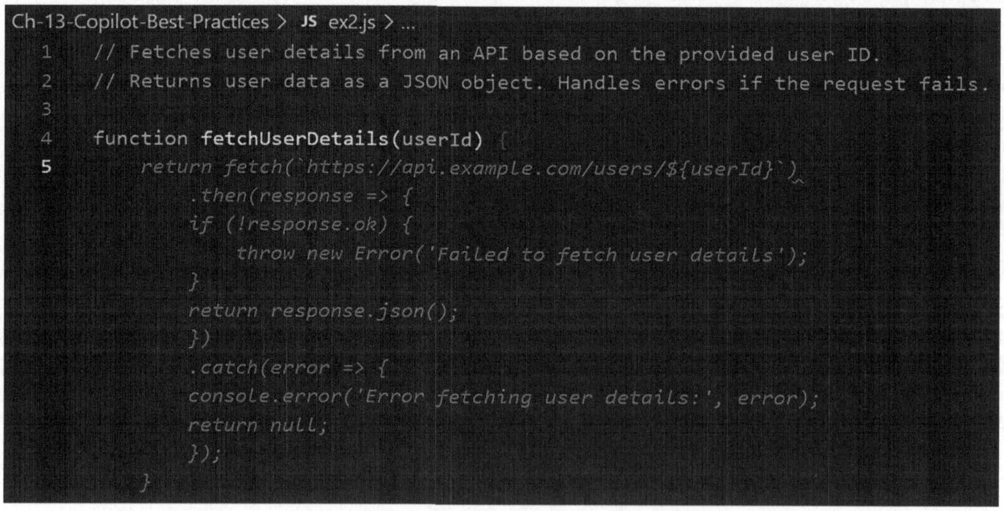

```
Ch-13-Copilot-Best-Practices > JS ex2.js > ...
// Fetches user details from an API based on the provided user ID.
// Returns user data as a JSON object. Handles errors if the request fails.

function fetchUserDetails(userId) {
    return fetch(`https://api.example.com/users/${userId}`)
        .then(response => {
        if (!response.ok) {
            throw new Error('Failed to fetch user details');
        }
        return response.json();
        })
        .catch(error => {
        console.error('Error fetching user details:', error);
        return null;
        });
    }
```

Figure 13.2: *Error-handled API Fetch Function fetchUserDetails(userId) Using Template Literals and Promise Chaining in JavaScript*

With this **clear instruction**, Copilot will generate a function with:

- **Proper API request handling**

- **Error handling**
- **Expected return format**

Scenario 2: Writing a Database Query Function

Weak Instruction

```
# get user from db
def fetch_user():
```

The following snippet illustrates a simple Python function named **fetch_user()** designed to simulate retrieving user details from a database. This is a typical mock function used during early-stage development or testing.

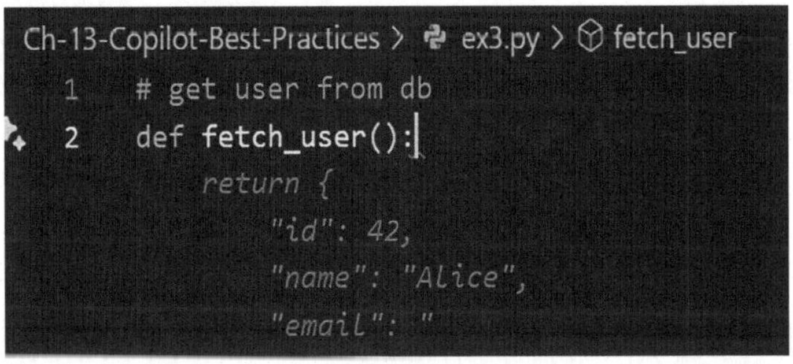

```
Ch-13-Copilot-Best-Practices > ex3.py > fetch_user
# get user from db
def fetch_user():
    return {
        "id": 42,
        "name": "Alice",
        "email": "
```

Figure 13.3: *Python Function fetch_user() Returning a Hardcoded Dictionary Representing User Details, Demonstrating Basic Structure and Placeholder Values for Development or Unit Testing Purposes*

Copilot may generate an incomplete or overly simplistic query.

Well-Defined Instruction

```
# Fetches a user record from the PostgreSQL database.
# Takes 'user_id' as input and returns a dictionary containing user details.
# Ensures SQL injection prevention using parameterized queries.
def fetch_user(user_id):
```

Copilot's Output:

This Python function showcases a secure way to fetch user details from a PostgreSQL database using the **psycopg2** library. It includes proper error handling, and protects against SQL injection through the use of parameterized queries.

```
Ch-13-Copilot-Best-Practices > ex4.py > ...
# Fetches a user record from the PostgreSQL database.
# Takes 'user_id' as input and returns a dictionary containing user details.
# Ensures SQL injection prevention using parameterized queries.
def fetch_user(user_id):
    with psycopg2.connect(DSN) as conn:
        with conn.cursor() as cur:
            cur.execute(
                "SELECT id, name, email FROM users WHERE id = %s", (user_id,)
            )
            user = cur.fetchone()
            if not user:
                raise ValueError("User not found")
            return {
                "id": user[0],
                "name": user[1],
                "email": user[2],
            }
```

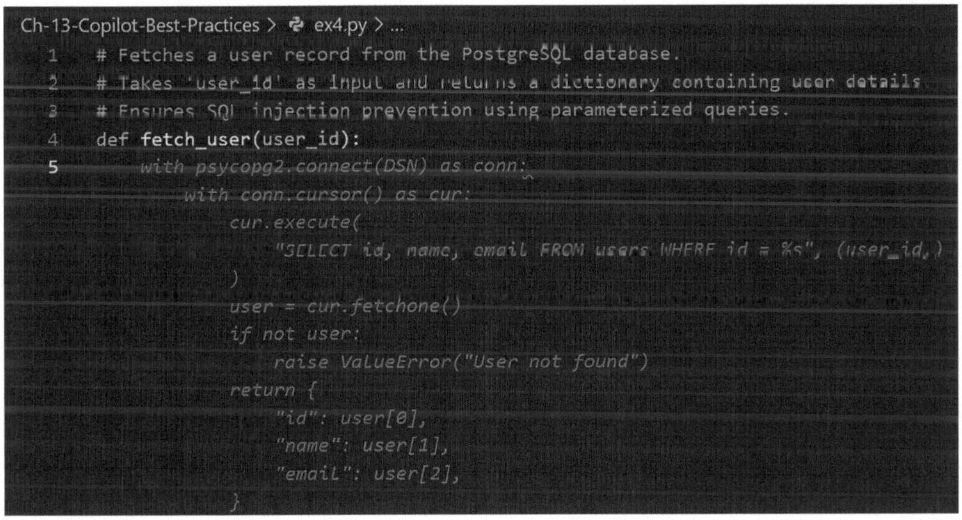

Figure 13.4: *Secure Implementation of fetch_user(user_id) Using psycopg2 to Retrieve User Records from a PostgreSQL Database, Demonstrating Safe Parameter Usage and Error Management for Missing Records*

This refined Python function demonstrates a concise and secure method of retrieving a user record from a PostgreSQL database. It simplifies the return logic, while maintaining protection against SQL injection through parameterized queries.

Ch-13-Copilot-Best-Practices > ex4.py > ...

```
# Fetches a user record from the PostgreSQL database.
# Takes 'user_id' as input and returns a dictionary containing user details.
# Ensures SQL injection prevention using parameterized queries.
def fetch_user(user_id):
    with psycopg2.connect(DSN) as conn:
        with conn.cursor() as cur:
            cur.execute("SELECT * FROM users WHERE id = %s", (user_id,))
            return dict(cur.fetchone())
```

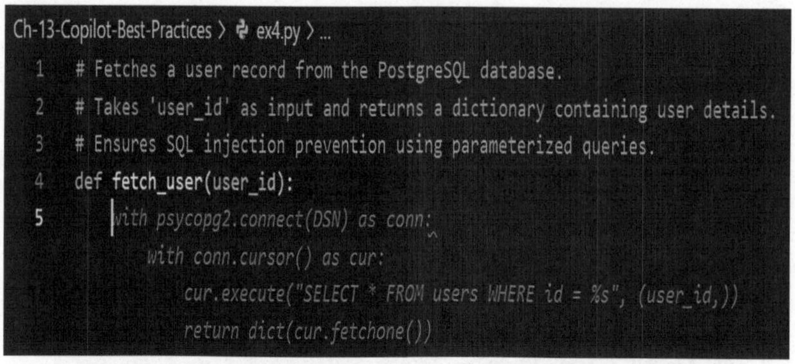

Figure 13.5: *Optimized Version of fetch_user(user_id) Using psycopg2 with Parameterized Queries and Direct Dictionary Conversion of Fetched User Data for Simplicity and Security*

This code snippet focuses on the query execution logic within a function that fetches a user's details securely from a PostgreSQL database, using parameterized SQL to prevent injection attacks.

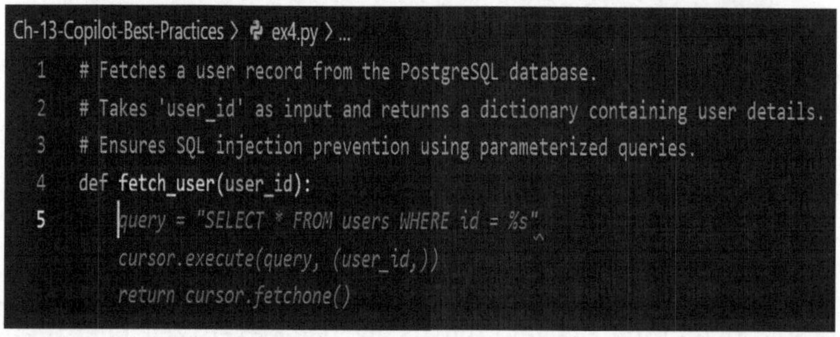

Ch-13-Copilot-Best-Practices > ex4.py > ...

```
# Fetches a user record from the PostgreSQL database.
# Takes 'user_id' as input and returns a dictionary containing user details.
# Ensures SQL injection prevention using parameterized queries.
def fetch_user(user_id):
    query = "SELECT * FROM users WHERE id = %s"
    cursor.execute(query, (user_id,))
    return cursor.fetchone()
```

Figure 13.6: *Core SQL Execution Logic from the fetch_user(user_id) Function Showing the Use of Parameterized Query Syntax (%s) and Safe Substitution of User Input to Mitigate SQL Injection Risks*

This ensures that the Copilot generates secure, optimized SQL queries with proper input handling.

Using Copilot for Boilerplate Code and Repetitive Patterns

Copilot **excels at generating repetitive or boilerplate code** that follows standard patterns. However, it is **not ideal for complex, logic-heavy sections**. The key is **knowing when to use it**.

Best Use Cases for Copilot in Boilerplate Code:

- Generating API handlers for Express, Django and Flask
- Creating unit test templates
- Writing structured class definitions and interfaces
- Setting up initial configurations for databases, logging, and file handling

Example Scenarios

Scenario 1: Creating an API Route in Express.js

Instead of manually writing every API handler, developers can let Copilot generate **boilerplate code**, and focus on customizing business logic.

```
// Express.js API route to fetch user data from the database
app.get('/user/:id', async (req, res) => {
  // Copilot automatically generates the logic inside
});
```

This **`Express.js`** route handler demonstrates how to retrieve user data from a database using the user ID provided in the request URL. It uses asynchronous operations with error handling to ensure a reliable API response.

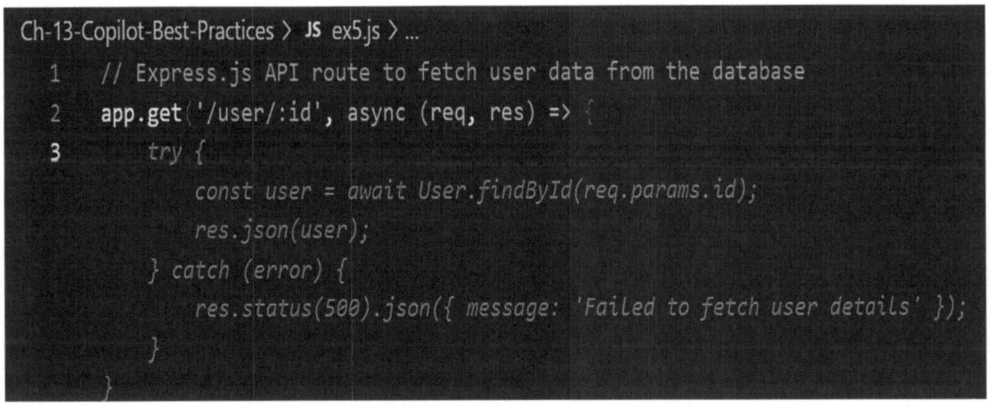

```
Ch-13-Copilot-Best-Practices > JS ex5.js > ...
// Express.js API route to fetch user data from the database
app.get('/user/:id', async (req, res) => {
    try {
        const user = await User.findById(req.params.id);
        res.json(user);
    } catch (error) {
        res.status(500).json({ message: 'Failed to fetch user details' });
    }
}
```

Figure 13.7: *Express.js route definition for GET/user/:id that retrieves user data using User.findById(), and returns a JSON response, including error handling for failed database lookups*

Copilot typically completes this with:

- **Fetching user data from a database**
- **Handling potential errors**
- **Returning a structured response**

Scenario 2: Generating a Test Case Template

For repetitive **unit test structures**, Copilot speeds up the process.

```
# Test case for verifying user login functionality
def test_user_login():
    # Copilot suggests assertions and setups here
```

The following code illustrates a basic unit test function in Python that verifies user login functionality. It follows the Arrange-Act-Assert (AAA) testing pattern, ensuring clear test structure and logic flow.

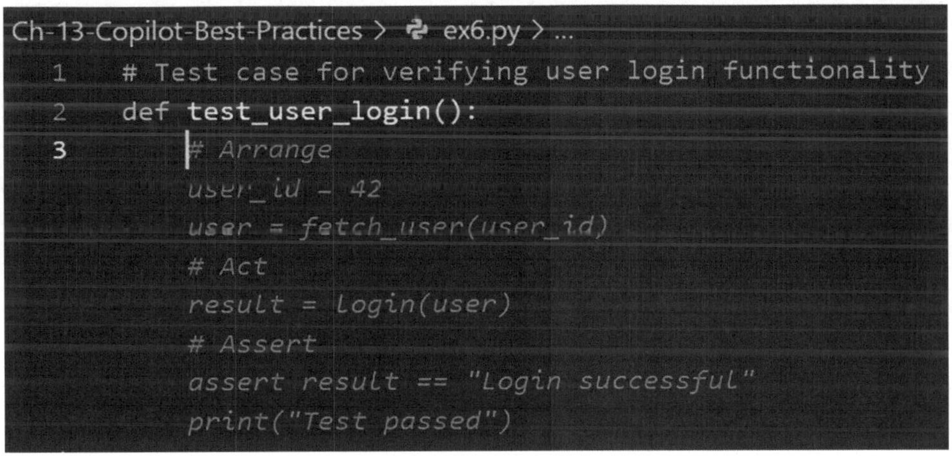

```
Ch-13-Copilot-Best-Practices > ex6.py > ...
# Test case for verifying user login functionality
def test_user_login():
    # Arrange
    user_id = 42
    user = fetch_user(user_id)
    # Act
    result = login(user)
    # Assert
    assert result == "Login successful"
    print("Test passed")
```

Figure 13.8: *Python Function test_user_login() Structured Using the AAA Pattern to Test the User Login Process, Including Data Setup, Action Execution, and Result Assertion for Validating Expected Behavior*

Developers can **refine** the generated test, instead of writing it from scratch.

Using Copilot for Generating Missing Reusable Methods

This test case demonstrates a structured validation of user login functionality, using the Arrange-Act-Assert pattern. It also highlights how GitHub Copilot can assist in resolving undefined variables or functions during development.

Ch-13-Copilot-Best-Practices > ex6.py > test_user_login

```
1  # Test case for verifying user login functionality
2  def test_user_login():
3      # Arrange
4      user_id = 42
5      user = fetch_us
6      # Act
7      login_status = login(user)
8      # Assert
9      assert login_status == "success"
```

"login" is not defined Pylance(reportUndefinedVariable)
(function) login: Any
View Problem (Alt+F8) Quick Fix... (Ctrl+.) Fix using Copilot (Ctrl+I)

Figure 13.9: *Python Test Function test_user_login() with GitHub Copilot's Inline Suggestion Prompt to Fix an Undefined Login Function, Exemplifying Copilot's Capability to Aid in Real-time Error Resolution and Test-driven Development*

- As we hover over the missing login function highlighted in the preceding code at line#7, VS Code Editor will give the option to fix it using copilot.
- Once we click the link, "`Fix using Copilot`", the Copilot Inline chat window gets activated, and the login function dummy code gets generated as shown in the figure.
- Based on the user review of how appropriate the outcome is, the user can "`Accept`" or regenerate the suggestions.

This snippet shows how GitHub Copilot suggests a fix for an undefined login function by auto-generating dummy implementations for both login and `fetch_user`, helping developers unblock test flow during early development.

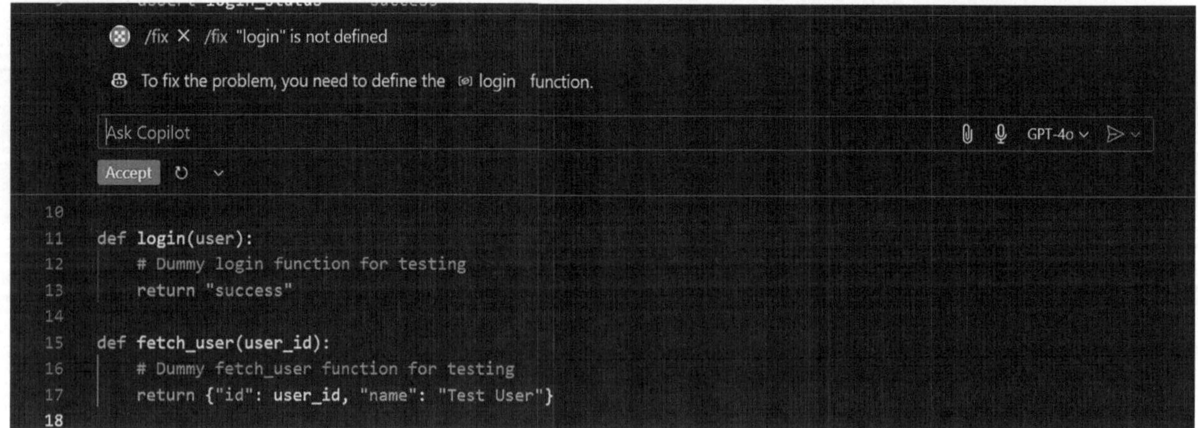

Figure 13.10: *Auto-suggested Definitions by GitHub Copilot for Missing Functions Login(user) and fetch_user(user_id), Resolving Runtime Issues and Supporting Quick Mock Setups for Unit Testing in Python*

- The following highlighted part is the "`Rerun`" button in the copilot inline chat window which allows the user to generate more refined, or appropriate code suggestions.

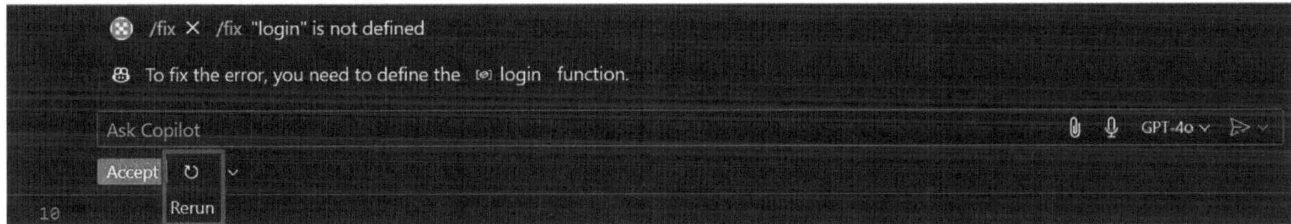

Figure 13.11: *GitHub Copilot UI Displaying a Fix Prompt for an Undefined Login Function, with an Option to "Rerun" the Suggestion Generation, Allowing Iterative Refinement of Code Fixes Powered by GPT-4o*

Understanding the "`Attach Context`" Feature in GitHub Copilot Chat

The "**`Attach Context`**" feature in GitHub Copilot Chat allows developers to provide additional **codebase-related context**, when interacting with Copilot. This helps Copilot generate **more relevant, informed, and precise responses**, based on the selected attachments. Thus, instead of relying solely on the current cursor position, Copilot can analyze attached files, recent changes, or symbols to provide **more accurate suggestions, explanations, or fixes**.

Using "`Attach Context`" in Copilot Chat

- **Accessing the Attach Context Feature:** From the Copilot Chat Interface, you can see the paperclip icon · (highlighted in the screenshot). Clicking this opens a dropdown, where you can select attachments for context. The "**`Attach Context`**" feature in GitHub Copilot allows developers to include specific files, symbols, or outputs, when generating code suggestions. This improves the relevance and precision of the Copilot responses by providing situational awareness.

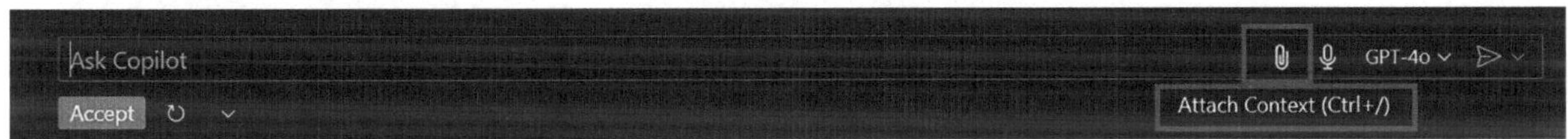

Figure 13.12: *Github Copilot's "Attach Context" Button in the Inline Prompt Interface, Enabling Users to Enrich Copilot's Understanding Using Relevant Files, Symbols, or Terminal Data (Shortcut: Ctrl + /).*

Alternatively, you can use the keyboard shortcut:

`Ctrl + /` (Windows/Linux)

`Cmd + /` (Mac)

Available Context Options: When working with GitHub Copilot in modern IDEs, developers often need to provide additional contextual information to improve the accuracy of AI-generated suggestions. The "**`Attach Context`**" menu offers various options that help tailor suggestions, based on relevant inputs from the current development environment.

Attachment Type	Description
Codebase	Attach relevant files from the current workspace/project.
Git Changes	Include files that have been recently modified or staged in Git.
Image from Clipboard	Attach an image to provide visual context (for example, error messages, diagrams).
Screenshot Window	Capture and attach a screenshot for debugging purposes.
Symbol...	Select a specific function, class, or variable from your project to use as context.
Terminal Last Command	Provide Copilot with the most recent terminal command output.

Terminal Selection	Use a manually selected portion of the terminal output as context.
VS Code API	Attach relevant API references or symbols from the VS Code environment.

Table 13.1: *Commonly Available Context Attachment Options in GitHub Copilot, Including Codebase Files, Git Changes, Terminal Output, and Visual Aids like Screenshots or Clipboard Images, Enabling Enhanced Context-aware Code Completions*

When using GitHub Copilot in IDEs like VS Code, the "**`Attach Context`**" panel allows you to select from a range of contextual inputs, such as files, symbols, clipboard images, or terminal outputs. This enables Copilot to generate more relevant and informed code suggestions.

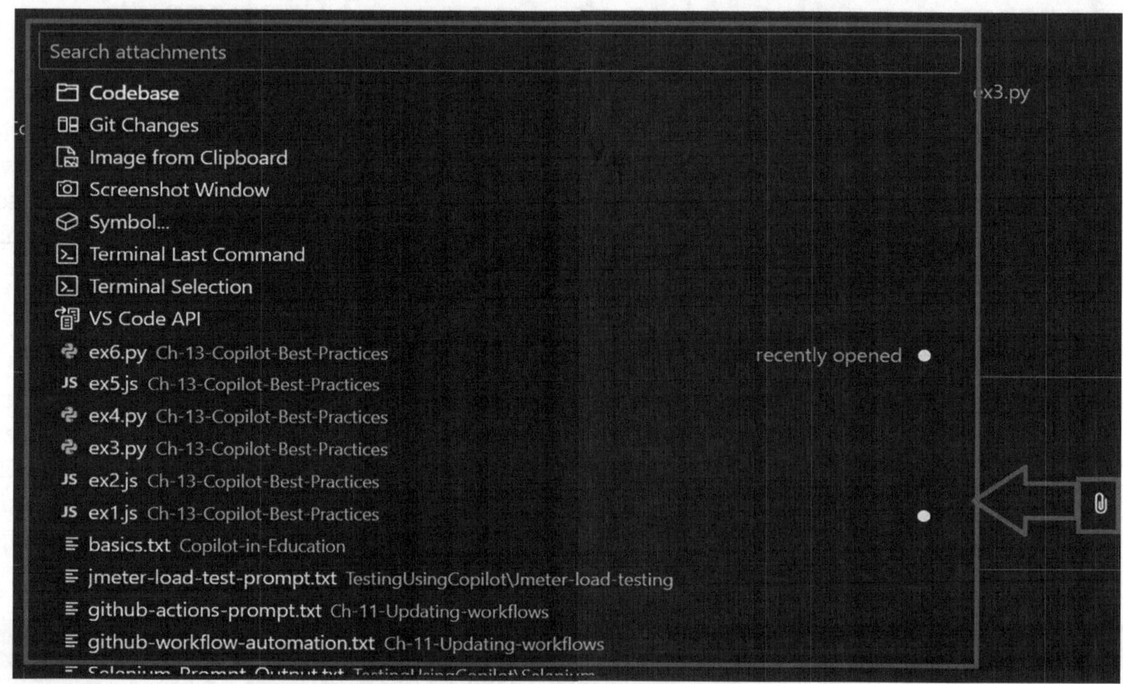

Figure 13.13: *Expanded "Attach Context" Menu in GitHub Copilot Displaying Multiple Context Types like Codebase, Git Changes, Screenshot, Terminal Output, and more, Allowing Users to Select Specific Files or Artifacts to Guide AI Code Generation*

Understanding Each Attach Context Option in Depth

Each attachment option plays a different role in refining Copilot's responses. Here is how each type of context attachment can be **used effectively in real-world scenarios.**

Codebase – Attaching Relevant Files: If you are working on a **large project**, and want Copilot to analyze multiple files, you can **attach specific files from your codebase**.

Example Scenario:

- You are refactoring a **React component**, and need Copilot to **review both the component and its corresponding CSS file.**
- Instead of switching between files manually, you **attach both files** to provide a full context.

Best Use Case: Attach '**`Header.js`**' and '**`Header.css`**' to Copilot Chat.

Ask: "**`Refactor the Header component and ensure styles remain intact`**." GitHub Copilot's inline chat interface supports intelligent file linking using the **`#file: syntax`**, allowing developers to reference specific files directly, within prompts for more accurate and contextual AI assistance.

Figure 13.14: *GitHub Copilot Inline Prompt Showing Smart File Reference Suggestions Using #file:header.css and #header.js, Enabling Copilot to Pull Relevant Context from Specific Project Files to Refine its Responses*

In GitHub Copilot Chat, you can enhance your prompt by explicitly attaching relevant files using **`#file: references`**. This guides Copilot to generate accurate and context-aware suggestions, based on the selected source files.

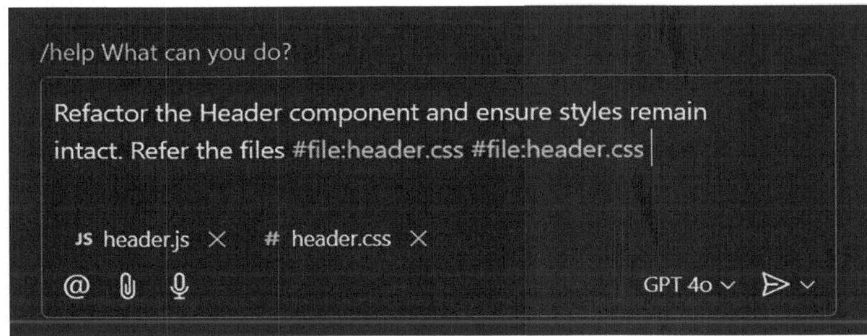

Figure 13.15: *GitHub Copilot Chat Prompt Showcasing File References (#file:header.css, header.js) with Attached File Tags Enabling Precise Contextual Understanding for Tasks like UI Refactoring*

Here, you will observe that we used the "#" symbol to attach context to a specific file in the editor. Alternatively, we can click the paper clip icon, and select as well as attach the required code files.

Outcome: Copilot will analyze both files, and generate a refactored version, **without breaking the styles.**

Git Changes: Understanding the Recent Modifications

When debugging issues or tracking code changes, selecting **`Git Changes`** allows Copilot to analyze **only the modified files.**

Example Scenario:

- You pushed a new **`feature`**, but the build failed.
- You **attach only the changed files**, instead of the entire codebase.

Best Use Case:

```
Attach recent Git changes, and ask:
"Explain the key modifications in my last commit."
```

Outcome: Copilot will **highlight key changes**, and even suggest improvements.

Image from Clipboard – Attaching Visual Debugging Context

If you have a **UI bug, error message, or stack trace screenshot**, you can **attach an image** to help Copilot understand the issue.

Example Scenario:

- You encounter a **CORS error** in the browser console.
- You take a **screenshot of the error message**, and attach it to Copilot Chat.

Best Use Case: `Attach error screenshot.`

`Ask: "How do I resolve this CORS issue in my Node.js backend?"`

Outcome: Copilot will **analyze the error message**, and suggest **CORS-related fixes**.

Screenshot Window – Capturing and Attaching Live Errors:

If you need to quickly capture **what is happening in your code editor**, you can take a **live screenshot**, and attach it.

Example Scenario:

- A **VS Code extension** is throwing errors, and affecting development.
- Instead of manually describing the issue, you take a **screenshot of the error pop-up**.

In GitHub Copilot's "**`Attach Context`**" menu, developers can choose from various input sources to enhance prompt understanding. One powerful option is the **`Screenshot Window`** which allows attaching real-time visual context for better issue resolution.

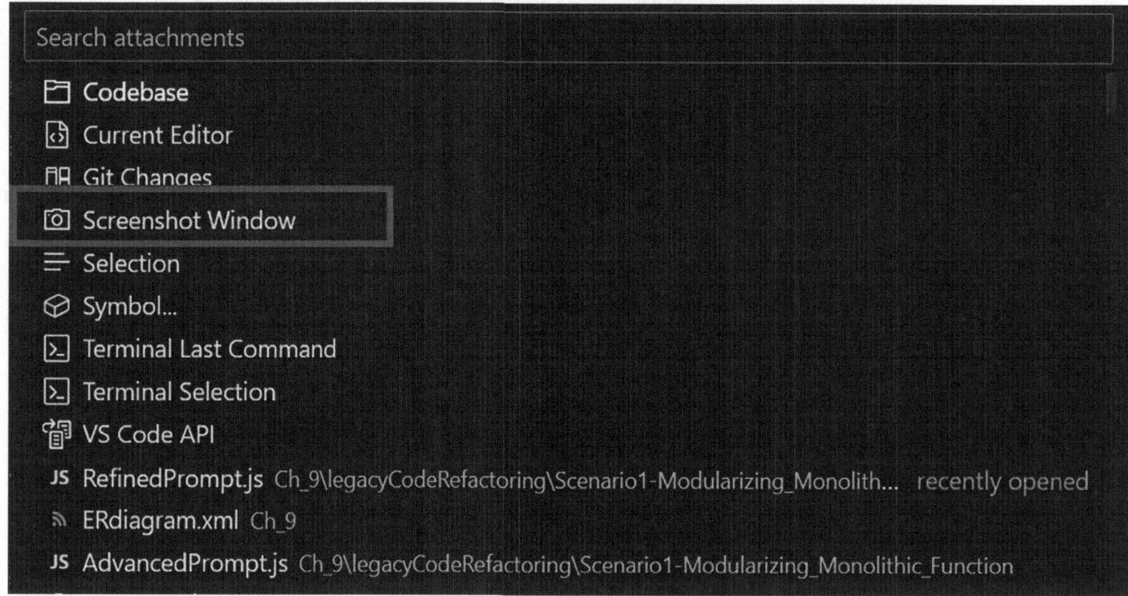

Figure 13.16: *GitHub Copilot Context Menu Showing the "Screenshot Window" Option Selected among Other Context Types such as Codebase, Terminal, and VS Code API, Enabling Users to Attach Visual Content Directly for more Insightful AI Responses*

Best Use Case:

```
Attach a screenshot of the extension error.
Ask: "How can I fix this issue in my VS Code setup?"
```

Outcome: Copilot provides **potential fixes or alternative extensions**.

Debugging Terminal Errors using GitHub Copilot Chat Commands and Variables:

As we can see here, while running the loadtest, we got some errors in the terminal. Now, with the help of copilot chat commands and variables, we would be able to fix the issue as follows:

```
Error: "The term k6 is not recognized as the name of a cmdlet…"
```

Here we are going to use the "**`@terminal`**" chat command appended by the "**`/explain`**" command, and then paste the error with it.

GitHub Copilot Chat seamlessly integrates with the terminal to explain command errors in real time. Developers can simply reference terminal output, using **`@terminal`** to receive contextual assistance, and debugging suggestions.

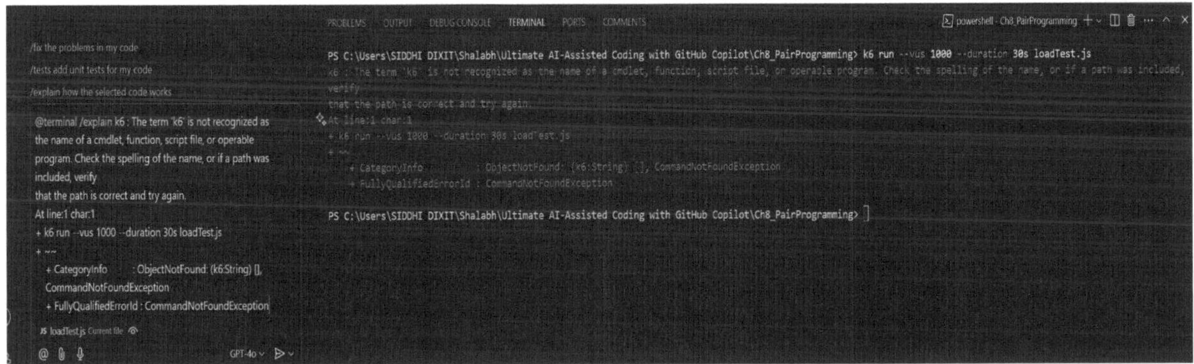

Figure 13.17: *Copilot Chat Explaining a Terminal Error using @terminal /explain k6, Highlighting a CommandNotFoundException due to the k6 Command Not Being Recognized–likely Caused by Missing or Misconfigured Installations*

GitHub Copilot Chat provides built-in support for terminal context, allowing developers to reference and explain command-line errors directly. This enhances real-time debugging, and improves the developer experience.

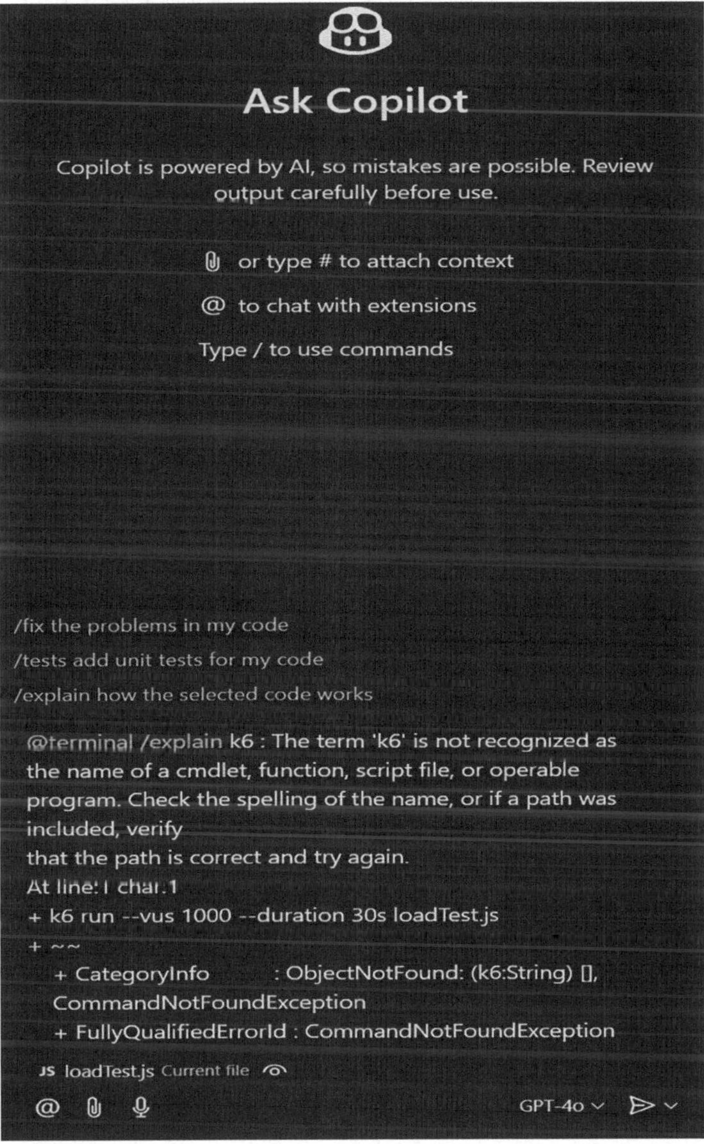

Figure 13.18: *GitHub Copilot Chat Window Using the /explain Command with @terminal Context to Interpret and Provide Guidance on a CommandNotFoundException for the k6 Load Testing Tool*

Copilot's Output:

GitHub Copilot Chat effectively interprets terminal errors, and provides actionable, step-by-step resolutions. In this case, it detects a missing command (k6), and offers clear installation guidance as well as validation steps.

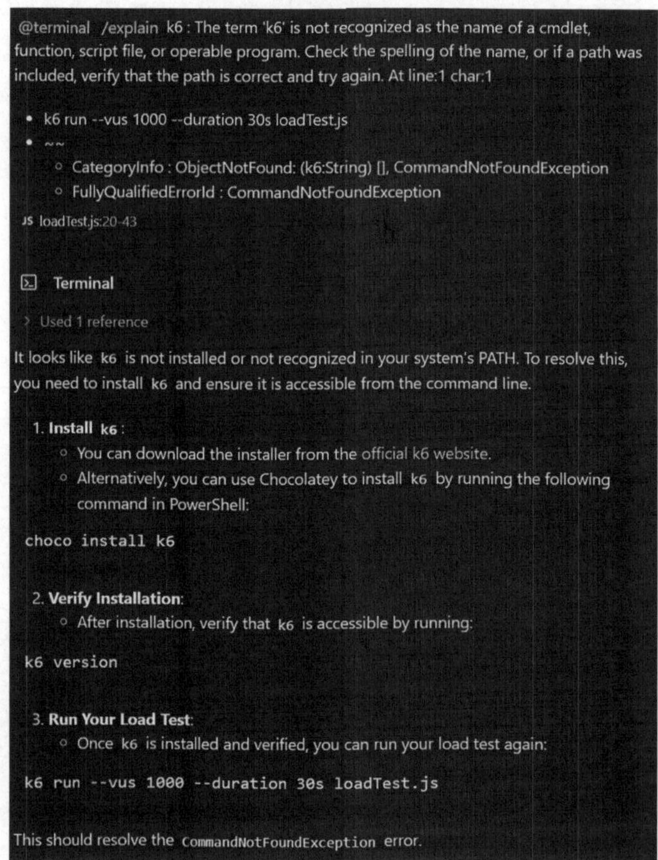

Figure 13.19: *Copilot Chat Explanation of a CommandNotFoundException for k6, Including Detailed Steps to Install k6 via Chocolatey, Verify the Installation, and Rerun the Load Test Command Successfully*

Here, we can see that GitHub Copilot has derived detailed step-by-step instructions to fix the issue. Following the first step, we can use directly "`Insert into Terminal`" button feature beside the generated command in the step. This will paste the command, "`choco install k6`" into the integrated terminal of VS Code directly.

Thus, GitHub Copilot Chat enhances developer productivity by allowing one-click command execution directly from its interface. This is particularly useful for running setup commands suggested during error resolutions.

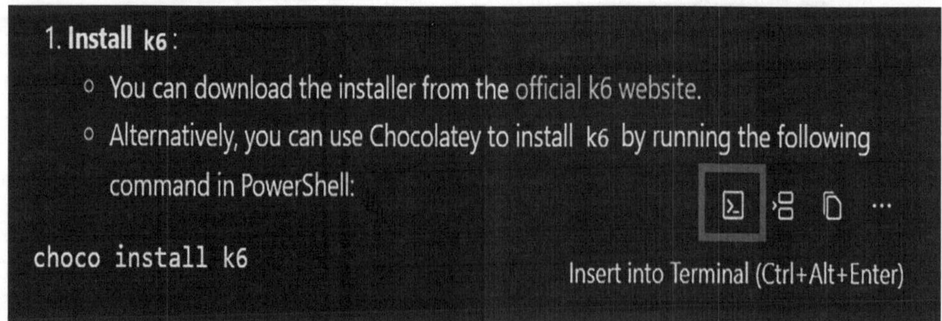

Figure 13.20: *Copilot Chat Provides a Convenient "Insert into Terminal" Button (Ctrl + Alt + Enter) beside Suggested Commands—Here Enabling Users to Quickly Install k6 Using choco install k6 in PowerShell*

We found a few more errors during the installation of k6 as follows. In order to address this, we will again follow the same chat commands "**`@terminal`**" and "**`/explain`**" to get the step-by-step guide of instructions to fix this.

When facing permission-related issues in terminal operations, GitHub Copilot Chat can interpret system errors, and guide users through resolving them. It leverages terminal context to analyze the problem, and suggest actionable steps.

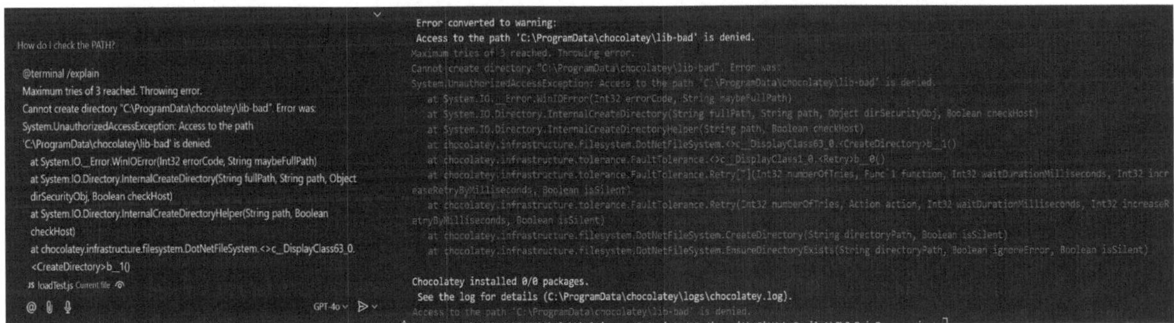

***Figure 13.21:** GitHub Copilot Chat Analyzing a System.UnauthorizedAccessException Triggered during a Chocolatey Installation due to Denied Access to C:\ProgramData\chocolatey\lib-bad, Advising on Potential PATH and Permission Fixes*

Permission errors during installations are common on Windows, when administrative privileges are not granted. GitHub Copilot Chat provides clear guidance to resolve such issues by rerunning commands in an elevated terminal.

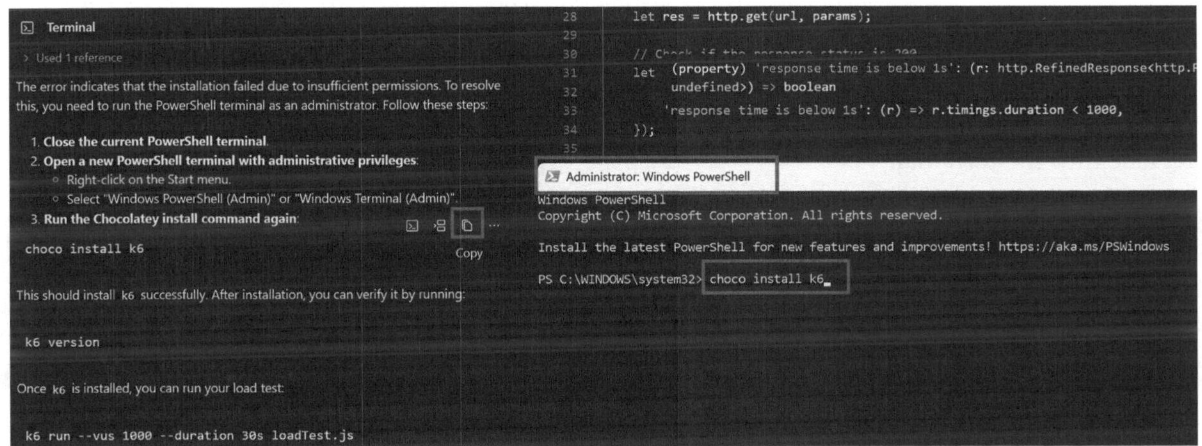

***Figure 13.22:** GitHub Copilot Chat Recommending Re-running choco install k6 in an Administrator PowerShell window, with Visual Cues Highlighting the Elevated Terminal and the Command Execution Area to Fix Permission-related Installation Errors*

Here, we observe that GitHub Copilot suggested running the command in PowerShell as Administrator.

In the following figure, we followed the same, and we were able to install the k6 successfully.

After switching to an elevated PowerShell session, the k6 load testing tool installs successfully using Chocolatey. This confirms that administrative privileges were required to complete the setup.

```
Administrator: Windows PowerShell
Windows PowerShell
Copyright (C) Microsoft Corporation. All rights reserved.

Install the latest PowerShell for new features and improvements! https://aka.ms/PSWindows

PS C:\WINDOWS\system32> choco install k6
Chocolatey v2.3.0
Installing the following packages:
k6
By installing, you accept licenses for the packages.
Downloading package from source 'https://community.chocolatey.org/api/v2/'

k6 v0.57.0 [Approved]
k6 package files install completed. Performing other installation steps.
The package k6 wants to run 'chocolateyInstall.ps1'.
Note: If you don't run this script, the installation will fail.
Note: To confirm automatically next time, use '-y' or consider:
choco feature enable -n allowGlobalConfirmation
Do you want to run the script?([Y]es/[A]ll - yes to all/[N]o/[P]rint): y

Extracting 64-bit C:\ProgramData\chocolatey\lib\k6\tools\k6-v0.57.0-windows-amd64.zip to C
6\tools...
C:\ProgramData\chocolatey\lib\k6\tools
 ShimGen has successfully created a shim for k6.exe
 The install of k6 was successful.
  Deployed to 'C:\ProgramData\chocolatey\lib\k6\tools'

Chocolatey installed 1/1 packages.
 See the log for details (C:\ProgramData\chocolatey\logs\chocolatey.log).
PS C:\WINDOWS\system32>
```

Figure 13.23: *Successful Installation of k6 via Chocolatey in Administrator PowerShell, with Confirmation Messages Indicating the Package Installation, Script Execution, and Final Deployment Path to C:\ProgramData\chocolatey\lib\k6\Tools*

Following the **step#2** of GitHub copilot instructions, we used to validate the installation and installed version of k6. After successfully installing k6, it is recommended to verify the installation using the k6 version command. GitHub Copilot Chat allows you to execute this directly from its suggestion interface into the terminal.

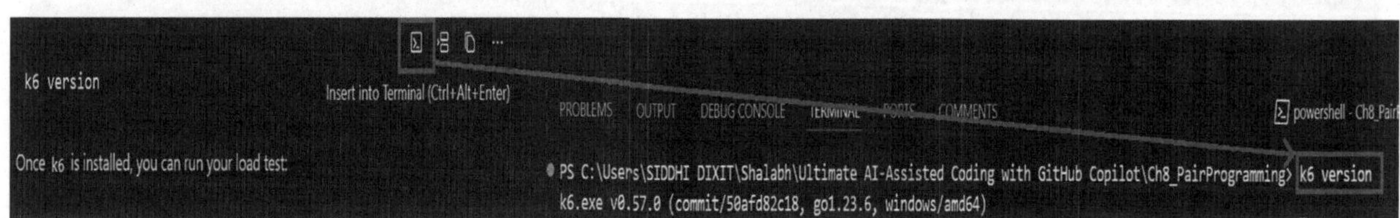

Figure 13.24: *Execution of the k6 Version Command via Copilot's "Insert into Terminal" Button Confirms Successful Installation, Returning Version Details (k6.exe v0.57.0) and Environment Configuration in the Terminal*

"While these strategies can significantly boost efficiency, understanding Copilot's limitations is key to avoiding pitfalls, and ensuring high-quality code."

Understanding and Overcoming Copilot's Limitations

As we are all aware by now, GitHub Copilot is an **AI-powered coding assistant** that has transformed how developers write code. Generating real-time code suggestions accelerates development, and minimizes repetitive tasks. However, GitHub Copilot is not perfect. It comes with inherent **limitations that arise from its architecture, training data, and the fundamental constraints of AI models**.

This section takes a **deep dive into Copilot's limitations**—why they exist, how they affect developers, and how to work around them. More importantly, we will explore these limitations **not just at a surface level**, but also **at an architectural and data structures level**, enabling a clearer understanding of Copilot's inner workings.

Imperfect and Sometimes Inaccurate Code Suggestions

Understanding the Limitations

Copilot's code suggestions often appear syntactically correct, but can be logically flawed, introducing **silent bugs, performance inefficiencies, and security risks**. The AI **does not understand the problem domain** in the way humans do–it merely predicts the most statistically probable sequence of tokens, based on its training data. These mistakes are particularly dangerous because they do not always trigger compilation errors, but can still cause unexpected failures in runtime.

Example

Let us say, you need to calculate the sum of squares of even numbers in a list:

```
def sum_even_squares(numbers):
    return sum(n**2 for n in numbers if n % 2 == 0)
```

Copilot, however, might generate:

```
def sum_even_squares(numbers):
    return sum(n*n for n in numbers if n%2)
```

Here, **Copilot made two errors**:

- **Logical flaw:** `n % 2` returns 1 for odd numbers, meaning this condition includes **odd numbers instead of even numbers.**
- **Stylistic inconsistency:** Instead of `n**2`, it used n*n, which is valid but inconsistent with modern Python style.

Now, why does this happen? The answer lies in **how Copilot generates code.**

Understanding the Internal Workings of GitHub Copilot

Copilot is trained on vast amounts of open-source code, but it does not **execute or validate its own predictions**. It relies entirely on **pattern recognition** and **token probability** to generate code, which means:

- It **does not reason** through the problem–it only suggests code that statistically "`looks right`."
- It **cannot test**, whether its suggestions work–it assumes correctness based on training patterns.
- It **favors commonly used structures** over nuanced, problem-specific logic.

Hence, at its core, Copilot is **not reasoning through the problem** like a human. Instead, it is:

- **A Token-Predicting Machine:**
  - Copilot uses **transformer-based models**, specifically OpenAI's Codex (a variant of GPT-4 trained on code).
  - It **predicts the next token (word or symbol) based on statistical probability** from billions of lines of open-source code.
  - Unlike humans, it **does not break down problems into logical steps**–it just finds the most likely pattern that fits.
- **Limited by Sequence Length:**
  - Copilot works within a fixed **context window** (typically a few hundred tokens).
  - It does not maintain **global project awareness**–it cannot reference helper functions in different files, unless explicitly provided in the context.
- **No Runtime Execution or Debugging Awareness:**
  - Copilot does not **run code** before suggesting it.

- This means it cannot **test logic for correctness**; it only outputs what it thinks is statistically relevant.

- **Pattern Matching over True Understanding:**
  - Since Copilot is trained on public GitHub repositories, **it often picks up common, but flawed patterns**.
  - If incorrect implementations exist in open-source projects, Copilot may propagate them.

Impact on Developers:

- Developers may **unknowingly accept incorrect logic**, and introduce subtle bugs.
- Debugging time increases because the errors may not be **immediately obvious**.
- Security vulnerabilities can emerge, if flawed logic leads to **unvalidated inputs or unhandled exceptions**.

Overcoming the Shortcomings or Limitations

- **Always review Copilot's suggestions** critically–do not assume correctness.
- **Use unit tests** to validate AI-generated code, before integrating it into production.
- **Guide Copilot with explicit comments** to steer it towards the correct logic.

Lack of Context Awareness Beyond a Few Lines

Understanding the Limitations

Copilot's suggestions are based on a limited **context window**–usually **a few hundred tokens at a time**. This means it **does not remember code**, beyond its immediate surroundings, leading to inconsistencies and redundant suggestions.

Copilot **does not remember** what you wrote in previous files, or even earlier in the same file, once the token limit is reached.

Example

If you define a utility function in one file:

```
def format_currency(amount):
return f"${amount:,.2f}"
```

But later, in another file, you attempt to format currency, Copilot might suggest:

```
def display_total(amount):
return "$" + str(round(amount, 2))
```

Here, **Copilot forgets** about `format_currency`, and suggests an inconsistent, manually formatted string, instead.

Factors Contributing to This Limitation

Copilot operates within a limited context window, which means:

- It cannot access functions, imports, or documentation, outside its token window.
- It lacks long-term memory, so it does not retain information across files.
- It rebuilds context, each time you write, rather than learning from past interactions.

These reasons are further deep-dived in depth with the architectural limitations of the Transformer model.

Architectual Limitations of Transformer Models

- **Token Window Constraints:**
  - Copilot processes only **a fixed-length window of code**.
  - Any code **outside this window is forgotten**, making it **unable to recall project-wide dependencies**.
- **No Persistent Memory:**
  - Unlike human developers, **Copilot does not retain long-term context** across multiple interactions.
  - Even if it made a good suggestion earlier, it will not necessarily remember it later.
- **Dependency on Immediate Patterns:**
  - Copilot works best, **when the code is well-structured and self-contained**.
  - It struggles with **large, multi-file projects**, where key logic is scattered.

Impact on Developers:

- Leads to inconsistencies in the codebase, as Copilot might suggest multiple ways to solve the same problem.
- Causes redundant logic, where AI re-implements the existing functions, instead of reusing them.
- Slows development, as developers need to manually adjust and refactor Copilot's outputs.

Overcoming this Limitation

Best Practices:

- Provide Copilot with context in comments. **Use comments to reference external functions**, guiding Copilot toward correct suggestions.
  ```
  # Use the pre-defined format_currency function from utils.py
  def display_total(amount):
  ```
- Break large files into smaller, self-contained modules, so that Copilot sees more relevant context.
- Manually, reference helper functions before invoking Copilot.

Out-of-the-Box Idea:

Try **prompt engineering tricks** to "`remind`" Copilot of missing the context:

```
# Reminder: We already have a function for currency formatting in utils.py.
# Use it here instead of writing a new one.
```

This **nudges Copilot** toward making more context-aware suggestions.

Struggles with New or Niche Technologies

What is the Limitation?

Copilot struggles with **cutting-edge frameworks, newly released libraries, or niche technologies** because its knowledge is limited to **its last training cycle**.

Example

Let us say you are using the latest version of a JavaScript framework that introduces a new state management hook:

```
const [state, setState] = useLatestState();

Copilot, however, might suggest:
const [state, setState] = useState();
```

The older syntax still works, but it does not take advantage of the latest API improvements.

Factors Contributing to This Limitation:

- Copilot's model is **not continually learning**–it is frozen in time based on its latest training data.
- New libraries and frameworks are not **automatically integrated** until GitHub and OpenAI retrain the model.

Impact on Developers:

- Developers **miss out on best practices** for the latest technologies.
- Increased reliance on **manual research** to verify correctness.
- Frustration, when Copilot suggests **deprecated methods**.

Strategies to Mitigate This Limitation:

- **Cross-check Copilot's suggestions with official documentation.**
- **Manually verify** AI-generated code against library changelogs.
- **Use forums, such as Stack Overflow** to compare AI suggestions with real-world developer experiences.

Licensing and Copyright Concerns

What is the Limitation?

Since Copilot is trained on **publicly available code**, it sometimes suggests snippets that closely resemble existing open-source code, raising **legal and ethical concerns**.

Example

You are implementing a sorting algorithm, and Copilot suggests something **remarkably similar to QuickSort from an MIT-licensed repository**.

```
public void quickSort(int[] arr, int low, int high) {
    if (low < high) {
        int pi = partition(arr, low, high);
        quickSort(arr, low, pi - 1);
        quickSort(arr, pi + 1, high);
    }
}
```

If the suggested snippet is **copy-pasted from a repository, without proper attribution**, it could create **licensing conflicts** in commercial projects.

Factors Contributing to This Limitation:

- Copilot **does not generate code from scratch**–it **predicts code** based on patterns, it has learned.

- Since public codebases **dominate Copilot's training data**, some outputs may **accidentally mimic copyrighted material**.

Impact on Developers:

- **Legal risks**, if proprietary software contains AI-generated code from restrictive licenses.
- **Ethical concerns** about AI-generated content that closely resembles open-source work.

Strategies to Mitigate This Limitation:

- **Enable GitHub's code referencing feature** (Enterprise users) to identify code origins.
- **Use tools, such as FOSSA or Snyk** to scan for license conflicts.
- **Manually, verify AI-generated snippets,** before using them in proprietary software.

Token Limit Truncation Issue in GitHub Copilot

"Tokens are units of text (for example, words, symbols, and so on) that Copilot processes to generate suggestions, with a fixed limit determining how much context, it can 'see' at once."

The following diagram illustrates how GitHub Copilot handles token limits during code suggestion generation. When the token limit is exceeded, Copilot must trim the context which can occasionally result in inaccurate suggestions due to missing information.

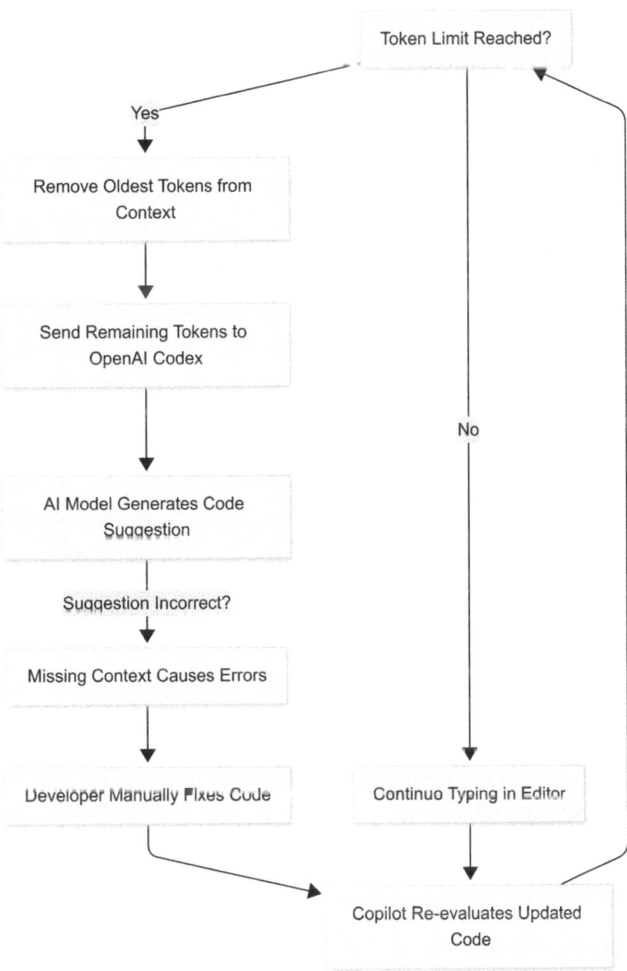

Figure 13.25: *Flowchart Depicting GitHub Copilot's Behavior, When the Token Limit is Reached–Removing the Oldest Tokens, Generating Suggestions via OpenAI Codex, and Handling Possible Errors due to Missing Context, Eventually Requiring Manual Code Correction by the Developer*

The **Token Limit Truncation Issue** in GitHub Copilot arises due to the **fixed context window** that Copilot operates within. As developers continue typing in the editor, Copilot must decide whether the token limit has been reached. If the limit is exceeded, the model **removes the oldest tokens from the context**, and sends the remaining tokens to OpenAI Codex for code generation.

This can cause **critical issues**, such as:

- **Loss of relevant context**, leading to incomplete or incorrect suggestions.
- **Redundant or inconsistent logic**, as Copilot forgets prior code.
- **Increased manual effort for developers**, who must correct errors introduced by the missing context.

Key Flow Points in the Diagram:

- **Token Limit Check:** Copilot monitors, whether the token limit is reached.
- **If within Limit:** It continues accepting user input, and generating suggestions.
- **If the Limit is Exceeded:**
    - The oldest tokens are truncated from memory.
    - The remaining context is sent to OpenAI Codex.
    - AI generates code based on this incomplete context.
- **If the Suggestion is Incorrect:**
    - Errors arise due to missing dependencies, variable loss, or function duplication.
    - The developer must manually debug and fix the incorrect code.
- **Once the Code is Updated:** Copilot re-evaluates the updated context, but the missing historical context remains an issue.

Main Takeaway

This limitation emphasizes **why Copilot should be treated as an assistive tool, rather than an authoritative coder**. Developers must proactively guide Copilot by **structuring modular code, providing explicit comments, and validating AI-generated outputs** to mitigate errors, introduced by the truncated context.

Real-World Example to Showcase This Issue

Consider a developer writing a **long Python function** in VS Code.

```
def process_large_data(data):
    # Some complex logic here...
    for item in data:
        # Processing code...
        pass

    # More lines of code...

    return processed_data
```

If the **beginning part of this function is removed from Copilot's token window**, it might **incorrectly suggest, using an undefined variable** as follows:

```
return output_data  # Incorrect suggestion, 'output_data' is undefined
```

This occurs because the **variable "processed_data" was outside Copilot's visible context**. The **developer, now, has to manually correct this mistake.**

Internal Workflow of Copilot's Suggestion Algorithm

To understand how GitHub Copilot delivers code suggestions in real-time, it is helpful to examine the internal workflow that powers its intelligent responses. The following diagram illustrates the end-to-end process–starting from context extraction in the IDE to ranking suggestions and refining future outputs, based on developer interaction.

The following flowchart explains the full lifecycle of how GitHub Copilot generates and refines code suggestions, using advanced language models like GPT-4o or Claude. It emphasizes the role of context, ranking, and developer interaction in shaping the final outputs.

Figure 13.26: *End-to-end Flow of GitHub Copilot's Suggestion Mechanism–from Reading up to 128K Tokens of Context, Prioritizing and Processing Input with AI Models, to Ranking and Presenting Suggestions, and Adapting Future Outputs, Based on Developer Feedback*

Expansive Contextual Understanding (Architectural-Level Code Comprehension)

- Copilot now processes up to 128,000 tokens of your development environment–a 32× increase from the original 4K limit–enabling true system-level awareness.

- Advanced Abstract Syntax Tree (AST) analysis breaks down your code into semantic structures, rather than mere text tokens, preserving meaning through intelligent compression.
- The system dynamically traverses your repository structure, analyzing dependencies, import graphs, and project architecture to build a comprehensive mental model of your entire codebase.

Reasons behind the Changes of Everything:

- Copilot now "`sees`" your entire service, not just fragments. It comprehends full architectural patterns, cross-file relationships, and implementation standards across your project ecosystem.
- This expanded window allows Copilot to suggest code that maintains architectural coherence with components, it could not previously "`see`"–generating solutions that feel like they were written by a senior developer, who understands your entire system.

Multi-Model Intelligence Synthesis (Cognitive Processing Revolution)

- Copilot leverages multiple state-of-the-art foundation models (GPT-4o, and Claude 3.5 Sonnet) through a sophisticated model routing system that selects the optimal engine, based on your specific coding task.
- Proprietary neural architectures perform parallel processing across multiple context segments, synthesizing insights from different parts of your codebase simultaneously.
- Deep semantic encoding preserves the functional intent of your code, not just its syntactic structure.

Reasons behind the Changes of Everything:

- The multi-model approach enables Copilot to simultaneously understand both high-level architectural principles and low-level implementation details–creating suggestions that are both technically precise, and strategically sound.
- This is not pattern matching; it is near-cognitive understanding. Copilot does not just predict, "`what code comes next`" but grasps "`what you're trying to accomplish`" in your broader system.

Adaptive Suggestion Generation (Personalized Code Synthesis)

- Copilot generates a diverse spectrum of potential completions through a technique called "divergent beam search," creating not just variations, but fundamentally different implementation approaches.
- Each suggestion undergoes rigorous static analysis evaluation, checking for correctness, efficiency, security vulnerabilities, and alignment with your project's coding standards.
- Dynamic context reweighting emphasizes the most semantically relevant parts of your codebase for each suggestion.

Reasons behind the Changes of Everything:

- You are not getting a single best-guess, but multiple high-quality implementation paths–each representing different architectural trade-offs and programming paradigms.
- The suggestions are not just syntactically correct; they are security-audited, performance-optimized, and architecturally coherent with your existing patterns.
- This transforms Copilot from auto-complete to strategic pair programmer, offering not just *what* you might type next, but *how* you might solve complex engineering challenges.

Interactive Development Intelligence (Augmented Developer Decision System)

- Copilot presents multiple ranked suggestions with confidence scores, and explanatory rationales through an enhanced UI that highlights the strengths and trade-offs of each approach.
- Sophisticated telemetry captures not just whether you accept or reject suggestions, but *how* you modify them, creating a detailed model of your technical preferences and coding style.
- Each interaction feeds a personalized reinforcement learning framework that continuously refines Copilot's understanding of your architectural vision.

Reasons behind the Changes of Everything:

- The relationship between the developer and AI transforms from reactive to collaborative– Copilot does not just respond to your code; it engages in an ongoing dialogue about the implementation choices.
- This creates a virtuous learning cycle, where each interaction simultaneously advances your code, and enhances the AI's understanding of your project goals, coding style, and architectural preferences.
- Developers gain a force-multiplier effect: The system amplifies your expertise, rather than replacing it, allowing you to operate at a higher level of abstraction.

Emergent Collective Intelligence (Ecosystem-Wide Learning)

- Every interaction across millions of developers contributes to Copilot's central knowledge repository, creating a continuously evolving understanding of the best practices, emerging patterns, and innovative solutions.
- Sophisticated federated learning techniques allow Copilot to absorb new coding paradigms, language features, and architectural patterns, without compromising your code's privacy.
- The system identifies common challenges across project boundaries, and synthesizes novel solutions from disparate domains.

Reasons behind the Changes of Everything:

- Copilot does not just learn from you; it learns from the collective wisdom of the global developer community, bringing breakthrough approaches from leading-edge projects into your daily workflow.
- This creates an unprecedented acceleration of knowledge transfer across the industry– solutions pioneered by elite developers become instantly accessible to every programmer.
- The system functions as a living repository of engineering knowledge that evolves in real-time with industry best practices.

Revolutionary Implications:

- **Architectural Coherence at Scale:** Copilot now maintains consistency across massive codebases that would exceed any individual developer's cognitive capacity.
- **Tacit Knowledge Transfer:** Junior developers instantly access patterns and techniques that would normally take years to learn through apprenticeship.
- **Cognitive Augmentation:** Developers can focus on higher-level strategic decisions, while Copilot handles implementation details with unprecedented sophistication.
- **Cross-Domain Fertilization:** Solutions from one technical domain are automatically adapted, and applied to novel contexts.

- **Emergent Innovation:** The synthesis of millions of coding styles creates genuinely new approaches that no single developer would likely discover.

This is not just an incremental improvement to code completion–it is a fundamental transformation of the software development process that augments human creativity with machine-scale pattern recognition and knowledge synthesis. Therefore, Copilot does not replace the developer; it elevates them to a new plane of creative and architectural thinking, previously constrained by implementation details.

Multi-Modal Inputs and Model Selection in GitHub Copilot

GitHub Copilot has evolved from a code completion tool into a fully interactive AI assistant. With the addition of Multi-modal Large Language Models (MLLMs), developers can now provide input through images, diagrams, and voice, and receive intelligent, context-aware suggestions. This section provides a comprehensive guide to working with multi-modal capabilities, and selecting the most suitable model in the GitHub Copilot Ask interface.

Multi-Modal Input Capabilities in GitHub Copilot

GitHub Copilot has advanced significantly from its origins as a text-based autocomplete tool. With the integration of Multi-modal Large Language Models (MLLMs), such as GPT-4o, Gemini, and Claude, Copilot now supports a wider range of input types, enabling developers to interact with the system through natural language, images, voice, and diagrams. This evolution marks a significant shift in software development–bringing developers closer to a more intuitive, human-centered, and fluid way of coding.

Multi-modal input refers to the system's ability to interpret and respond to different forms of input data, enabling richer interactions, and reducing friction in the development process. This capability enhances productivity and creativity by aligning with how developers naturally express their intent.

Types of Multi-Modal Inputs in Copilot

- **Text Prompts:** Standard natural language instructions that describe code logic, structure, or behavior. This remains the primary input method for syntax generation, API scaffolding, and in-line completions.
- **Images and Screenshots:** Screenshots of UI designs, mockups, or error messages can be interpreted by models such as GPT-4o and Gemini to generate responsive HTML/CSS, debug layout issues, or explain visual flows.
- **Voice Commands:** Voice inputs–converted to text via Whisper or browser-based recognition–allow developers to describe logic verbally, and receive code suggestions in real-time, supporting accessibility and hands-free workflows.
- **Diagrams and Flowcharts:** Visual logic models created using Mermaid, UML, or tools such as Napkin can be processed to produce control flow structures, state machines, and function-based logic in code.

Supported Input Types and Use Cases

Input Type	Description	Best Use Cases
Text	Natural language prompts for describing logic and code	Syntax help, refactoring, API generation

Image	Visual input interpreted by multi-modal models	Figma-to-code, layout scaffolding, UI bug analysis
Voice	Narrated commands transcribed into code instructions	Live narration of workflows, accessibility support
Diagram	Structured flows in Mermaid or similar syntax	Workflow mapping, logic translation, process trees

Table 13.2: *Overview of the Supported Input Types in GitHub Copilot, Highlighting Their Descriptions and the Most Effective Use Cases for Multi-modal AI-assisted Development*

These input methods can be used independently or in combination, depending on the task and the model's capabilities. For instance, an image-based layout can be paired with a follow-up text prompt to adjust spacing or convert layout logic into components. Similarly, a diagram describing a process flow can be followed by a voice command to enhance specific steps.

Thus, by supporting multi-modal interaction, GitHub Copilot empowers developers to work faster, more naturally, and with greater flexibility–enabling a new generation of fluid, and AI-assisted development experiences.

Each input type enhances Copilot's ability to support creative, and collaborative workflows.

Image-to-Code Workflow with GPT-4o

One of the most powerful capabilities introduced by GitHub Copilot's integration with GPT-4o is its ability to interpret visual design inputs–such as screenshots, mockups, or Figma exports–and convert them into clean, responsive frontend code. This unlocks rapid UI development and removes the friction of manually translating design intent into layout and styling rules.

With GPT-4o's multi-modal understanding of images, developers can paste a screenshot directly into the chat window, and Copilot will intelligently generate layout scaffolding using frameworks such as Tailwind CSS, Bootstrap, or plain HTML/CSS.

Case Study: Mobile UI Mock for a Travel App

The attached image represents a dual-screen mobile UI for a travel and booking application. It includes layout features such as:

- A **header navigation bar** with branding and page tabs (Futura, Company, Tickets, Events, Booking)
- A **hero banner** showcasing a promotional travel image with an overlaid title
- A **services section** listing icons and text for connectivity, savings, and travel info
- A **destinations area** with an image tile and text description
- A **sidebar card layout** on the second screen highlighting top experiences
- A **footer section** with testimonials, social media icons, and contact links

This mock provides a comprehensive layout consisting of grid-based content, nested image and text sections, and repeatable UI patterns.

The following mobile UI mock screen represents a high-fidelity travel app interface, structured to deliver both visual appeal and functional clarity. It integrates promotional content, feature highlights, destination insights, and user testimonials into a cohesive mobile-first layout ideal for Figma-to-code workflows or AI-assisted HTML/CSS generation.

Figure 13.27: *Dual-screen Mobile UI Mock for a Travel app, Showcasing a Modular Layout with Header Navigation, Hero Banner, Service Highlights, Destination Previews, Activity Listings, and Testimonial Cards*

Prompting GPT-4o to Generate Code

Developers can copy this screenshot, and use the following structured prompt inside Copilot Chat:

```
Generate a mobile-first HTML and Tailwind CSS layout based on this UI mock. Break it
into components:
- Top nav with brand and page links
- Hero banner with background image and overlay text
- Three-column services grid
- Destination image and description
- Activities section with image tiles and icons
- Footer with testimonials, icons, social links
Use semantic HTML5 and Tailwind utility classes.
```

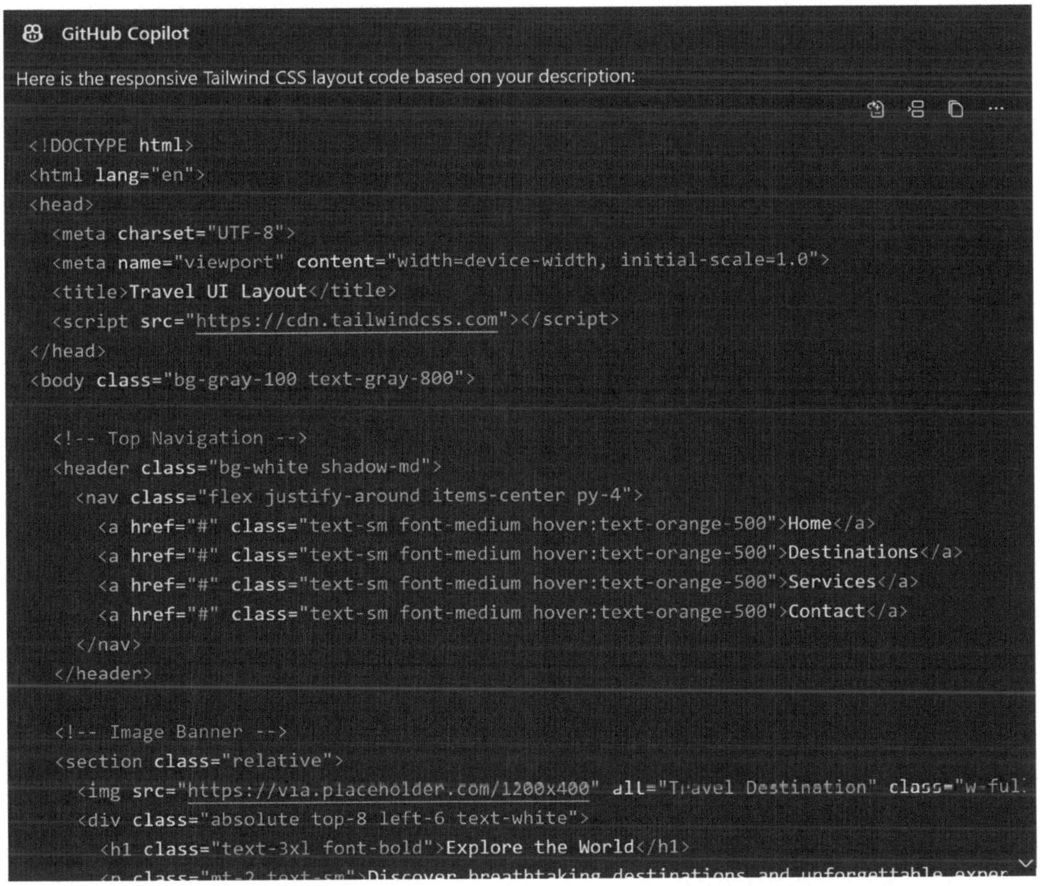

GitHub Copilot

Here is the responsive Tailwind CSS layout code based on your description:

```
<!DOCTYPE html>
<html lang="en">
<head>
  <meta charset="UTF-8">
  <meta name="viewport" content="width=device-width, initial-scale=1.0">
  <title>Travel UI Layout</title>
  <script src="https://cdn.tailwindcss.com"></script>
</head>
<body class="bg-gray-100 text-gray-800">

  <!-- Top Navigation -->
  <header class="bg-white shadow-md">
    <nav class="flex justify-around items-center py-4">
      <a href="#" class="text-sm font-medium hover:text-orange-500">Home</a>
      <a href="#" class="text-sm font-medium hover:text-orange-500">Destinations</a>
      <a href="#" class="text-sm font-medium hover:text-orange-500">Services</a>
      <a href="#" class="text-sm font-medium hover:text-orange-500">Contact</a>
    </nav>
  </header>

  <!-- Image Banner -->
  <section class="relative">
    <img src="https://via.placeholder.com/1200x400" alt="Travel Destination" class="w-ful
    <div class="absolute top-8 left-6 text-white">
      <h1 class="text-3xl font-bold">Explore the World</h1>
      <p class="mt-2 text-sm">Discover breathtaking destinations and unforgettable exper
```

***Figure 13.28:** GitHub Copilot Generated Output for the Given Prompt for UI-mock Design*

This structured prompt enables GPT-4o to understand the layout hierarchy, visual groupings, and component intent–producing accurate and clean frontend code.

Refer the complete code generated at the following GitHub Repo link: *chapter13-best-practices-and-limitations\copilot-vibe-coding-demo\travel-ui-mock-app*

Best Practices for Image-to-Code Prompts: When crafting prompts for converting images to code using GitHub Copilot or similar tools, following specific best practices can greatly improve the accuracy and usability of the generated layout or UI components.

Practice	Recommendation
Use descriptive intent	Specify layout type, grid structure, and responsiveness.
Include visual hierarchy in prompt	Indicate image sections, overlays, icons, and callouts.
Request componentization	Ask Copilot to generate reusable components for testimonial blocks, and so on.
Split prompt for complex screens	Divide into header, body, and footer generation steps.
Reference framework or CSS system	Mention Tailwind, Bootstrap, or plain CSS as needed.

***Table 13.3:** Best Practices for Writing image-to-code Prompts, Including Guidance on Using Descriptive Intent, Emphasizing Visual Hierarchy, Requesting Componentization, Breaking Down Complex Screens, and Referencing CSS Frameworks to Enhance Code Generation Fidelity*

This workflow is ideal for prototyping marketing pages, onboarding flows, or content-heavy UIs directly from a design or screenshot. Using GPT-4o's multi-modal input support, developers can eliminate hours of manual layout work by guiding Copilot with detailed, structured prompts, based on the UI mock.

Diagram-Based Code Generation with Mermaid and GitHub Copilot:

In modern software development, visual diagrams often serve as the foundation for architectural planning, process modeling, and business logic representation. GitHub Copilot, now supports the ability to interpret these diagrams—particularly those written in Mermaid Syntax—and translate them into functional code structures.

Mermaid is a text-based diagramming tool used to represent flowcharts, sequence diagrams, state machines, and more. When paired with Copilot's natural language and contextual reasoning capabilities, Mermaid diagrams become a powerful way to scaffold real-world application logic.

How It Works:

1. The developer creates a Mermaid diagram in plain text format, using a simple syntax.
2. The diagram is pasted into Copilot Chat (Ask Mode) or referenced within a prompt.
3. Copilot then analyzes the logical flow, and generates corresponding function blocks, control structures, or process handlers in the code.
4. Optional tools like **`mermaidParser.ts`** (provided in this chapter's codebase) can be used to programmatically extract and manipulate diagram nodes. The complete code can be accessed at ***"chapter13-best-practices-and-limitations\copilot-vibe-coding-demo\src\utils\mermaidParser.ts"***

Example Mermaid Input:

```
graph TD
A(Start) --> B(Validate Input)
B --> C(Process Data)
C --> D(Save to Database)
```

Generated Output:

```
function start() { validateInput(); }
function validateInput() { processData(); }
function processData() { saveToDatabase(); }
function saveToDatabase() { console.log("Data saved."); }
```

Mermaid diagrams are ideal for:

- Mapping backend logic
- Expressing state machines
- Automating control flow implementations

With custom utilities like mermaidParser.ts, developers can tokenize and interpret diagram syntax programmatically as part of a CI pipeline, or logic generator.

Voice-to-Code Integration: Using Whisper + VS Code Extensions

Voice-driven coding is becoming more accessible with OpenAI's Whisper model.

Workflow:

- Install a **VS Code voice plugin** (for example, "**`CodeWhisperer`**" or "**`VoiceCoder`**").
- Speak: "**`Create a REST API with GET and POST routes using Express.js`**"
- Copilot or integrated GPT-4 model will output a functional boilerplate.

Tools:

- OpenAI Whisper
- Voice-to-code extensions (VS Code, JetBrains)

Best Practice:

Structure your voice inputs clearly with command-like phrasing. Include keywords such as "*with validation,*" "*using middleware,*" and so on.

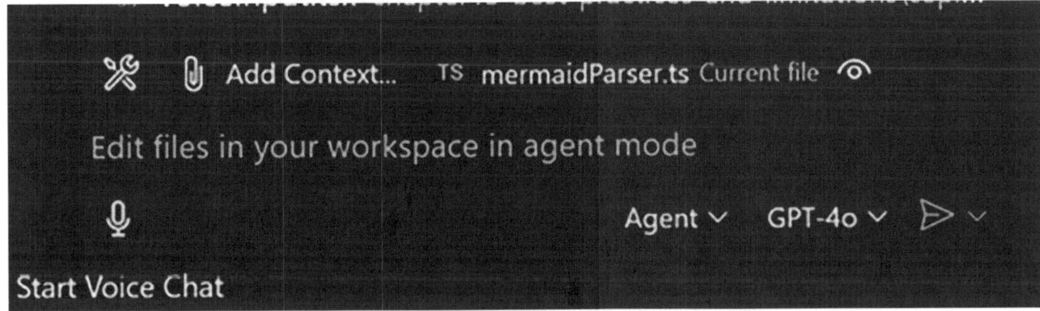

Figure 13.29: *Voice Chat Feature Button in GitHub Copilot Chat Window*

Understanding Multi-Model Intelligence in GitHub Copilot

When GitHub Copilot was first introduced, it relied solely on Codex—a fine-tuned version of GPT-3. But as developer, expectations grew, and real-world coding challenges became more nuanced as GitHub Copilot transformed into a multi-model assistant. Today, it supports a diverse line-up of LLMs (Large Language Models)—each tailored for specific tasks like real-time UI-to-code generation, codebase comprehension, compliance-aware responses, and high-performance backend logic design.

This shift to multi-model capability is not just technical—it is transformational. You are no longer limited to a one-size-fits-all AI. Instead, you can match the right brain to the right task, ensuring higher code quality, fewer hallucinations, and faster iterations.

An Overview of Multi-Model Support in GitHub Copilot

GitHub Copilot's multi-model architecture means it can intelligently route your queries, or instructions to one of several underlying LLMs based on:

- The mode of interaction (Ask, Edit, Agent, and so on)
- The nature of your task (for example, generating boilerplate vs. architectural planning)
- User-selected model in supported IDEs (like VS Code Insiders)

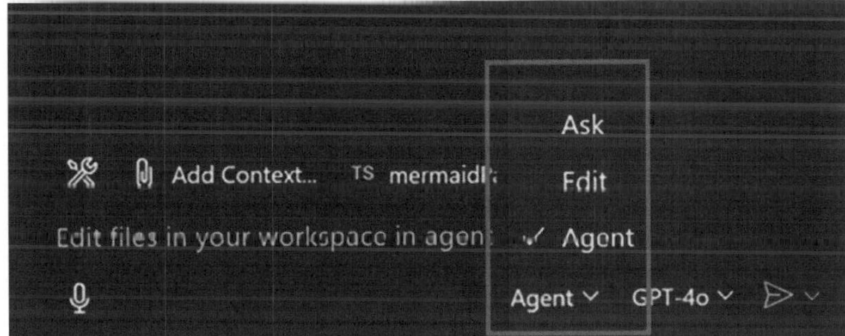

Figure 13.30: *Different Interaction Modes Supported by GitHub Copilot*

As of now, GitHub Copilot supports models such as:

- GPT-4o, GPT-4.1 from OpenAI
- Claude 3.5, 3.7, and 3.7 Thinking from Anthropic

- Gemini 2.0 Flash from Google
- o3-mini for ultra-lightweight tasks

This makes Copilot multi-modal, multi-purpose, and context-aware in the truest sense.

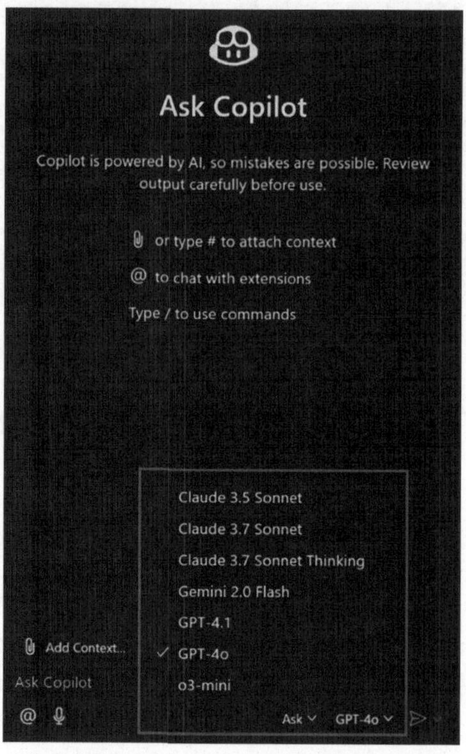

Figure 13.31: *Multi-Models List Supported by GitHub Copilot in "Ask" Interface Mode*

Evaluating the Strengths, Limitations, and Ideal Use of Each Model

To make informed use of GitHub Copilot's multi-model intelligence, it is essential to understand what each supported LLM offers in terms of performance, modality, reasoning capability, and developer alignment. The following table breaks down each model's practical characteristics–highlighting what it excels at, how it fits into daily workflows, and what limitations, you should be aware of, before applying it to critical development tasks:

Model	Modality	Context Capacity	Special Traits	Implementation Ideas	Limitations
GPT-4o (Omni)	Text + Vision + Audio	~128K tokens	Fastest multi-modal LLM, understands screenshots + voice + diagrams	Attach error screenshots or UI mocks to auto-generate test cases or HTML/CSS layouts	Available in Copilot Business and Insiders; formatting inconsistencies may occur
GPT-4.1	Text-only	~128K tokens	High reasoning depth, deterministic output	Great for enterprise-grade backend services, API scaffolding, Terraform/ CloudFormation	Slower than GPT-4o, no support for image/audio inputs
Claude 3.5 Sonnet	Text-only	~200K tokens	Fast, safe, clean responses	Ideal for early prototyping, regex generation, doc comments, and safe data parsing	Not recommended for complex backend code

Claude 3.7 Sonnet	Text-only	~200K+ tokens	Enhanced summarization, high-quality explanations	Great for doc string generation, code diffs explanation, or class breakdowns	Slight limitations in code logic chaining
Claude 3.7 Thinking	Text-only	~200K+ tokens	Simulates deep architectural thinking (deliberate latency)	Ideal for PR reviews, monolith decomposition, code smells, and design pattern refactoring	Slight response delays; not meant for quick-fire edits
Gemini 2.0 Flash	Text + Vision	Up to 1M tokens	Unmatched input capacity, visual support for diagrams	Input UML or architecture diagrams to generate APIs, database schema, or microservices map	Sometimes underperforms in JavaScript or backend-heavy code
o3-mini	Text-only	Lightweight (~2K)	Lightning fast, ideal for micro-edits	Rename variables, format JSON, write single-line utilities, generate comment stubs	Not aware of large project state or dependencies

***Table 13.4**: Comparative Breakdown of LLMs Available in GitHub Copilot's Ask Mode, Covering Modality, Context Window Size, Unique Capabilities, Implementation Strengths, and Practical Considerations for Developers*

Selecting the Right Model for Your Development Workflow

Each AI model integrated within GitHub Copilot offers distinct advantages, depending on the task at hand–whether it is generating a UI code from screenshots, reviewing a large codebase, or automating backend logic. To help developers navigate this growing toolbox of models, the following table offers a scenario-based guide that aligns real-world development goals with the most suitable AI model. This alignment not only ensures better accuracy and efficiency, but also unlocks the full potential of Copilot's multi-model intelligence.

Developer Goal	**Recommended Model**	**Why This Works Best**
Create frontend UI from mock-up/screenshot	GPT-4o	Multi-modal input allows translating images → HTML/CSS in seconds.
Generate secure, scalable backend API logic	GPT-4.1	Strong semantic understanding, and deterministic output.
Summarize 5K-line PR or review architectural flow	Claude 3.7 Thinking	Built for long-context reasoning, and document-style responses
Extract business rules from Markdown spec	Claude 3.7 Sonnet	Well-trained in summarizing formal documentation, and converting intent into logic.
Convert diagrams to technical workflows	Gemini 2.0 Flash	High token limits, and vision support enable architecture-to-code transformations.
Refactor small block, rename variable, format	o3-mini	Ultra-light and fast; no overhead or hallucination in trivial changes.

***Table 13.5**: Contextual Model Selection Matrix that Maps Specific Development Tasks to the Most Appropriate GitHub Copilot Model, Based on Capability Alignment, Modality Support, and Context Requirements*

Crafting Effective Prompts Based on Model Capabilities

The impact of a prompt is not solely determined by what you ask–**it also depends on how well your instructions align with the model's strengths**. Each LLM integrated into GitHub Copilot interprets context, code, and instructions differently. This table distills the best practices for prompting each model, offering a strategic view of how to structure inputs to maximize efficiency, accuracy, and output relevance. Use this as a guide to fine-tune your interaction style, depending on which model is active behind the scenes.

Model	Prompt Style	Ideal For	Avoid
GPT-4o	Multi-modal, interactive, visual-heavy	UI automation, image-to-code, voice tasks	Overly complex backend workflows
GPT-4.1	Structured, detailed, technical	APIs, configurations, secure code scaffolding	Chatty or casual prompts
Claude 3.7 Thinking	Reflective, explanatory, analysis-driven	Code reviews, long files, architecture summaries	Urgent micro-tasks
Claude 3.7 Sonnet	Summary, doc generation, human-readable	Changelogs, JSDoc, functional summaries	Deep technical implementation detail
Gemini 2.0 Flash	Visual + text hybrid, Markdown-heavy	Diagrams, full-system design	Syntax-heavy programming without structure
o3-mini	Short, fast, single-command edits	Renaming, formatting, micro-utilities	Long-form logic or contextual workflows

Table 13.6: *Prompting Strategy Matrix that Maps each GitHub Copilot-supported Model to its Ideal Prompt, Style, Task Alignment, and Potential Limitations, Enabling Developers to Optimize Results through Model-aware Interactions*

Model-Specific Prompting Techniques for Better Code Generation

GPT-4o (OpenAI) – Multi-Modal, Ultra-Fast Reasoner:

- **Best When:** Your input includes visual elements (for example, screenshots), UI bugs, or conversational flows.
- **Prompt Strategy:** Leverage screenshots, diagrams, and voice-like natural language for tasks like image-to-code conversion or UI automation.

Example Prompt:

```
"Here is  a screenshot of our login page. Generate a Playwright test script
that verifies email validation and password masking. Output it in TypeScript
format."
```

Tip: GPT-4o handles multi-turn interactions well. Use follow-ups like "*Add test for forgot password link too.*"

GPT-4.1 (OpenAI) – Logical, Structured and Reliable:

- **Best When:** Building backend systems, writing detailed configuration files, or structuring APIs.
- **Prompt Strategy:** Be specific, structured, and technical. Avoid casual language. GPT-4.1 excels at clarity, precision, and maintaining code quality.

Example Prompt:

```
"Create a Spring Boot REST controller for managing user roles. Include end-
points for listing, adding, updating, and deleting roles. Annotate with Swag-
ger and validate input."
```

Tip: *Ideal for scenarios where deterministic and compliant output is necessary.*

Claude 3.7 Thinking (Anthropic) – Reflective and Context-Aware:

- **Best When:** Reviewing long code files, summarizing architecture, or explaining decisions with human-like rationale.
- **Prompt Strategy:** Use analytical, long-form prompts that guide the model to *think aloud*. Ask for clarity, reasoning, or safe recommendations.

Example Prompt:

```
"Review this 700-line JavaScript file and generate a summary of each function's
purpose, its dependencies, and possible improvements. Highlight any perfor-
mance bottlenecks or anti-patterns."
```

Tip: *Ask Claude to justify its changes or opinions—"Explain why this change improves security."*

Claude 3.7 Sonnet (Anthropic) – Summary and Documentation Assistant:

- **Best When:** Generating documentation, summarizing logic, or explaining features to non-developers.
- **Prompt Strategy:** Ask for JSDoc-style annotations, changelogs, or design decision records.

Example Prompt:

```
"Generate JSDoc comments for this class, summarizing each method's input, out-
put, and side effects. Then suggest a commit message summarizing the changes."
```

Tip: *Great for onboarding tools, PR descriptions, and writing changelogs in natural language.*

Gemini 2.0 Flash (Google) – Multi-Modal, Large-Scale Vision Model:

- **Best When:** Working with visual specs, architecture diagrams, or extremely large context (for example, monoliths).
- **Prompt Strategy:** Combine Markdown, diagrams, and architectural descriptions. Gemini performs well when structure and logic are embedded in visual or semi-structured formats.

Example Prompt:

```
"Here's a Markdown file with our micro-service design. Generate interface con-
tracts in TypeScript, define expected error handling, and map each service to a
potential API gateway route."
```

Tip: Can work on inputs that span multiple formats—combine .md, .json, and UML to describe your flow.

o3-mini – Lightweight, Fast-Responding Code Companion:

- **Best When:** Making atomic edits, generating one-liners, or needing superfast turnaround for tiny tasks.
- **Prompt Strategy:** Keep it extremely concise. Specify your intent clearly in one line.

Example Prompt:

```
"Rename this variable to camelCase, and add an inline comment explaining its
purpose."
```

Tip: *Don't ask for long responses or multi-layered reasoning. o3-mini shines in small, repetitive tasks.*

Copilot Interaction Modes: Ask, Edit, and Agent

GitHub Copilot does not just change what is possible—it changes how you work. With three interaction modes—Ask, Edit, and Agent—Copilot adapts its behavior to match the level of control you need. Hence, whether you are solving syntax issues, refactoring inline code, or executing multi-file workflows, choosing the right mode ensures context alignment, task accuracy, and minimal friction.

Ask Mode – Natural Language Conversations for Contextual Help

Ask Mode is a conversational interface, where you type queries or instructions, and Copilot responds with **suggestions, explanations, or code snippets**—without altering your files.

Best suited for:

- Learning new patterns or libraries
- Explaining unknown code segments
- Asking "`how-to`" or "`what-if`" logic questions
- Exploring test case scenarios
- Multi-modal prompts with screenshots (when using GPT-4o)

Real Example Prompt:

```
"Explain this recursion, and rewrite it as a loop using a stack."
```

Power Tip: Attach an image of a UI screen or error message with GPT-4o to get immediate HTML generation or bug diagnosis.

Limitation: Suggestions are text-only—you must manually copy them into your editor.

Edit Mode: Inline Modifications with Developer Intent

Edit Mode enables you to **highlight any code block in your editor**, and instruct Copilot to refactor, transform, or optimize it.

Best suited for:

- Code formatting
- Converting call-backs to async/await
- Adding inline error handling
- Writing JSDoc or XML comments
- Converting Python2 code to Python3

Example Instruction:

```
"Add error logging using try-catch block with context-aware messages."
```

Strengths:

- Edits are context-aware
- Non-destructive and reversible
- Works great in pull-request cleanup or IDE workflows

Limitation: Requires specific, and actionable instructions for best results.

Agent Mode: Autonomous Developer Assistant for Complex Tasks

Agent Mode (still experimental) enables Copilot to act as a **multi-step assistant**. It analyzes, modifies, or generates across files by breaking down your high-level instruction into sequential tasks.

Best suited for:

- Codebase-wide deprecated method replacement

- Automated PR summary generation
- Auto-writing unit tests for untested methods
- Applying consistent formatting/style rules across multiple files
- Detecting and resolving circular dependencies

Example Prompt:

```
"Find all instances of deprecated lifecycle methods, and replace them with
modern React hooks. Summarize changes made."
```

Strengths:

- Orchestrates chains of actions.
- Ideal for tech leads or reviewers needing automation.
- Understands file structure, relationships, and Git diffs.

Limitation: Requires validation–can sometimes over-assume developer intent or miss subtle edge cases.

Copilot Interaction Modes Summary

GitHub Copilot offers not only multiple language models, but also multiple **interaction modes**, each suited for specific developer workflows. Hence, whether you are looking to understand a piece of logic, modify code inline, or automate multi-step tasks across your project, choosing the right mode–**Ask**, **Edit**, or **Agent**, which is essential for aligning Copilot's behavior with your intent. The following table provides a concise comparison of these three modes, helping you to understand their scope, behavior, and best-fit scenarios to maximize productivity and control.

Mode	Behavior Style	Task Type	Ideal For
Ask	Chat-first	Q&A, help, example generation	Learning, test ideas, clarifications
Edit	File-aware	Inline refactoring and formatting	Quick fixes, PR polishing, documentation
Agent	Cross-file automation	Task orchestration and insights	Change detection, consistency, test generation, and summaries

Table 13.7: *Comparative Overview of GitHub Copilot's Three Interaction Modes–Ask, Edit, and Agent–Highlighting their Behavioral Scope, Ideal Usage Patterns, and the Type of Developer Actions, They are Optimized For*

Vibe Coding and Flow-State Development with Copilot

Vibe coding is the experience of coding in a focused, uninterrupted state of flow–where ideas translate into implementation with minimal friction. Copilot enables this through intuitive suggestions, fast completions, and contextual understanding that aligns with the developer's creative rhythm.

Characteristics of Vibe Coding:

- Rapid prototyping, without distraction.
- Fluid transitions between tasks.
- Visual + spoken input support.
- Copilot understands what you are building, not just what you typed.

This style is ideal for building passion projects, experimenting with new frameworks, or working on MVPs.

UI Development in Flow: Tailwind + Next.js: Using Tailwind CSS with Copilot allows developers to scaffold responsive UIs efficiently.

Prompt Example:

```
Create a 3-column layout of feature cards with icons, titles, and descriptions using
Tailwind.
Copilot provides structured JSX or HTML with utility-first classes, allowing rapid
design iterations without writing CSS manually.
```

Building Projects with Momentum:

During flow-state development, Copilot supports tasks like:

- Firebase authentication scaffolding
- API CRUD operations
- Reusable hook creation
- Async loaders and skeleton components

It minimizes context-switching, helping developers build full features with minimal boilerplate.

Maintaining Creativity and Control:

Vibe coding does not mean full automation. To preserve creativity:

- Use Chat to explore options and alternatives.
- Use Edit Mode to apply surgical refactors.
- Use Agent Mode for large-scale transformations.
- Override suggestions, when needed to stay in control.

Recommended Tools for Vibe Coding

Tool	Purpose
VS Code Insiders	Access to latest Copilot modes and chat UI.
Copilot Labs	Test, doc generation, and brush-up tools.
Tailwind IntelliSense	Auto-completion for utility classes.
Mermaid/Napkin	Visual logic inputs for diagram-based workflows.
Whisper Plugin	Voice-to-code integration.

Table 13.8: *List of Recommended Tools Useful for Vibe Coding*

GitHub Copilot Security and Privacy Risk Analysis

The following diagram illustrates **potential security risks associated with GitHub Copilot**, the **consequences of these risks**, and **mitigation strategies** that organizations and developers can adopt to minimize exposure to security vulnerabilities.

While GitHub Copilot enhances developer productivity, it also introduces certain security risks, if not used responsibly.

The following diagram outlines how Copilot's suggestions can lead to vulnerabilities, the cascading consequences of these risks, and the strategic mitigation measures, developers and organizations can adopt to maintain secure coding practices.

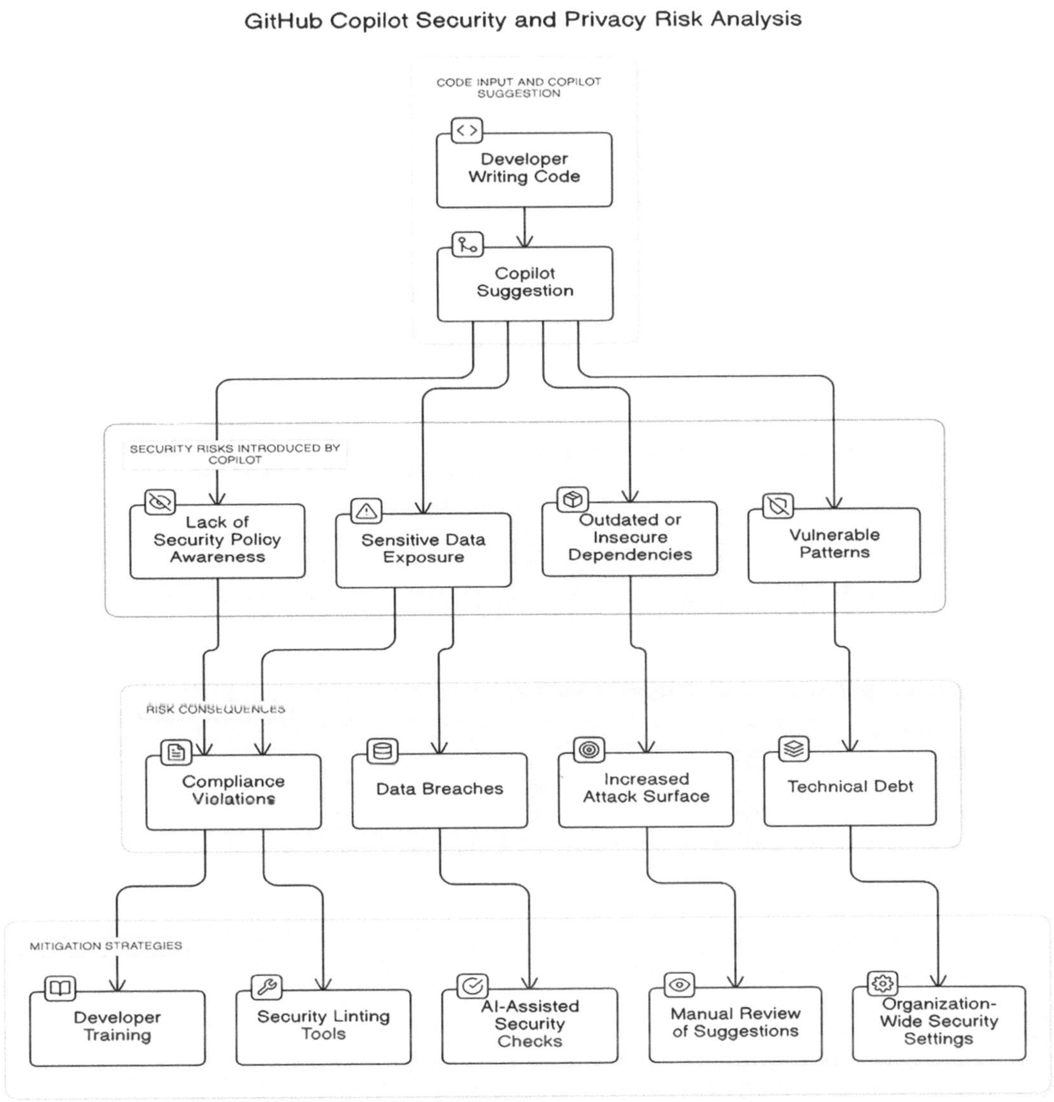

Figure 13.32: *Security Risk Flow of GitHub Copilot – Visualizing how Copilot-Generated Suggestions can Introduce Security Vulnerabilities (For example, Outdated Dependencies, and Hardcoded Secrets), the Resulting Risk Consequences, such as Data Breaches or Technical Debt, and Key Mitigation Strategies, Including Security Linting Tools, AI-assisted Checks, and Organization-wide Security Policies*

Code Input and Copilot Suggestion Process

- Developers **write code in an IDE**, and Copilot provides **real-time suggestions**, based on the context.
- While this significantly improves productivity, **Copilot does not inherently enforce security policies**, leading to potential risks.

Security Risks Introduced by Copilot

Copilot-generated code may introduce **security vulnerabilities** due to the following reasons:

- **Lack of Security Policy Awareness**
  - Copilot is trained on public repositories, and **does not inherently enforce security best practices**.
  - It may suggest insecure authentication, improper error handling, or weak encryption algorithms.

- **Sensitive Data Exposure:**
  - AI-generated code may include **hardcoded credentials, API keys, or secrets**, increasing the risk of accidental leaks.
  - Copilot **lacks contextual awareness** of which variables should remain confidential.
- **Outdated or Insecure Dependencies:**
  - Copilot might suggest **deprecated libraries** or packages with known vulnerabilities.
  - It does not validate dependencies against the **latest security advisories (CVE reports)**.
- **Vulnerable Patterns:** AI-suggested code may follow **common coding patterns**, including ones that contain **SQL injection risks, invalidated input handling, or insufficient authorization checks**.

A developer accepts a Copilot-suggested SQL query without sanitization:

```
query = f"SELECT * FROM users WHERE id = {user_id}"
```

This exposes the application to **SQL injection attacks**, where an attacker could manipulate `user_id` (for example, inputting `1; DROP TABLE` users) to access unauthorized data or damage the database.

Mitigation: Use parameterized queries to prevent injection:

```
db.execute('SELECT * FROM users WHERE id = ?', (user_id,))
```

Consequences of These Risks

If these vulnerabilities are not addressed, they can lead to significant security threats:

- **Compliance Violations:** Developers unknowingly introduce **non-compliant code** that fails to meet **industry regulations** (for example, GDPR, HIPAA, PCI DSS, and so on).
- **Data Breaches:** Exposure of sensitive information (such as- **user data, credentials, and private APIs**) can result in **security incidents**.
- **Increased Attack Surface:** The use of **outdated libraries** or insecure authentication patterns creates **new attack vectors** for adversaries.
- **Technical Debt:** Accumulation of **insecure, redundant, or poorly structured code** increases **long-term maintenance costs, and security risks**.

Mitigation Strategies

To ensure that Copilot-generated code remains **secure and compliant**, the following best practices should be adopted:

- **Developer Training:**
  - Educate developers on **secure coding principles** and **AI-assisted code generation risks**.
  - Provide hands-on training in **security-first programming practices**.
- **Security Linting Tools:** Integrate **automated security linters** (for example, ESLint, Bandit, and Semgrep) to **scan Copilot-generated code** for vulnerabilities.
- **AI-Assisted Security Checks:** Use **AI-based security tools** (for example, CodeQL, Snyk, and Dependabot) to detect, and prevent **security flaws in AI-generated suggestions**.
- **Manual Review of Suggestions:**
  - Developers must **critically analyze Copilot's code** before integrating it into production.
  - Implement **code reviews** to catch insecure patterns.

- **Organization-wide Security Settings:**
    - Enterprises using **GitHub Copilot for Business** should configure **organization-wide security policies.**
    - Restrict Copilot from suggesting **certain types of insecure code,** using **administrative controls.**

Training Data Dependency in GitHub Copilot

The diagram provides a structured view of how **GitHub Copilot's training data limitations** affect code suggestions, and how developers can mitigate these constraints. **Copilot's predictions rely heavily on its training dataset**, and understanding these dependencies is crucial for improving code accuracy and relevance.

The accuracy and relevance of GitHub Copilot's suggestions are heavily influenced by the quality and recency of its training data. Since Copilot relies on pre-collected public repositories, and does not continuously learn from private or newly released code, it can sometimes produce outdated or suboptimal suggestions. Hence, the following diagram breaks down how these limitations arise, and outlines practical strategies developers can use to steer Copilot toward more accurate and context-aware code completions.

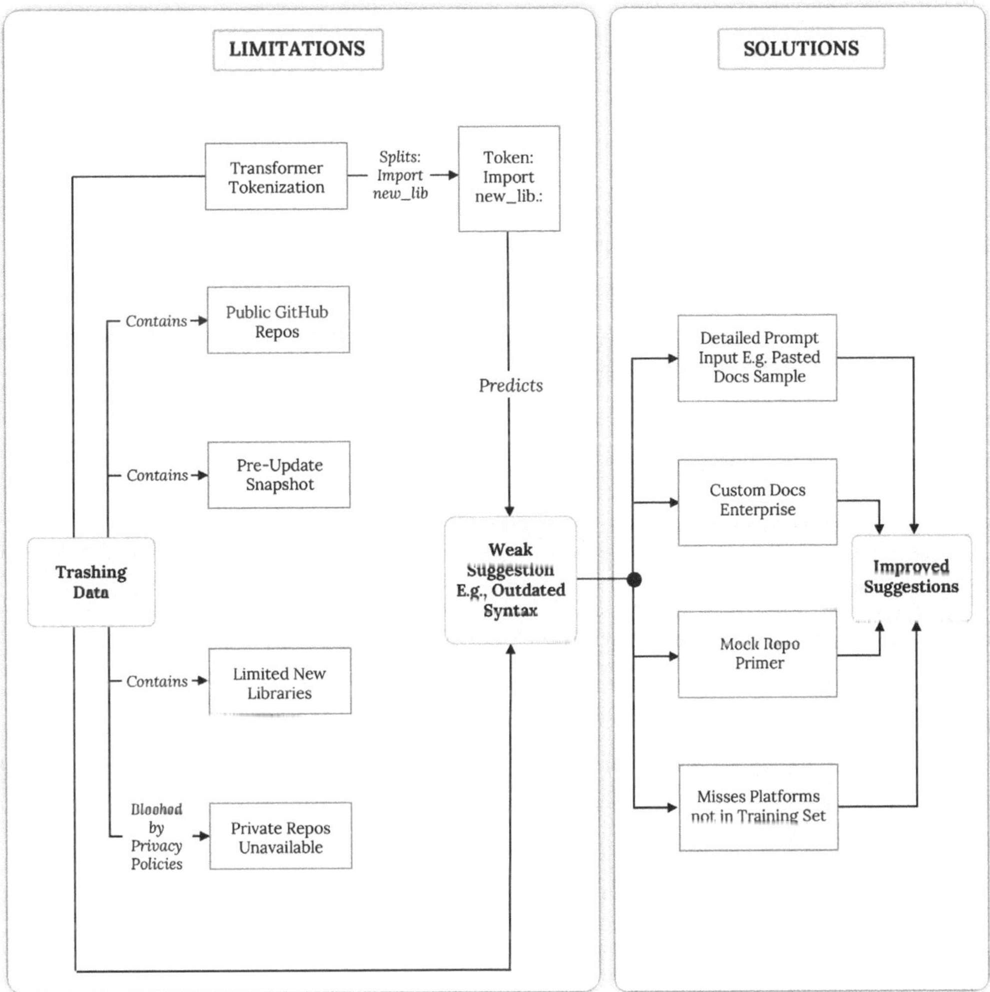

Figure 13.33: *Copilot's Training Data Limitations and Remedies – Illustrates how Outdated or Incomplete Training Data Leads to Weak Suggestions, and how Prompt Engineering, Custom Docs, and Mock Repos can Improve the Output Quality*

Constructing Copilot's Training Data

Training Data Sources:

- **Public GitHub Repositories:** The primary source of Copilot's knowledge, containing open-source code patterns.
- **Pre-Update Snapshot:** Copilot's model is **not continuously learning**; it only updates, when a new model is trained, meaning newer frameworks or syntax changes might be missing.
- **Limited New Libraries:** If a library was recently released, it may not be a part of Copilot's knowledge base.
- **Private Repositories Unavailable: Enterprise or proprietary codebases are excluded**, as Copilot respects privacy policies.
- **Transformer Tokenization:** Copilot **tokenizes code into smaller chunks**, breaking down input into a sequence of tokens for prediction.

Because Copilot is trained on publicly available data, and does not dynamically update from private code, it may lack awareness of proprietary best practices, internal company standards, or recent API changes.

The Core Limitation: Weak or Outdated Suggestions

Why It Happens:

- **Copilot predicts code based on past training data**, rather than real-time updates.
- **Blocked access to private repositories** means it **cannot learn from proprietary solutions.**
- **Misses patterns that were not frequently available in open-source data.**

Common Issues:

- **Outdated Syntax:** Copilot may suggest **deprecated functions or older API versions.**
- **Weak Suggestions:** It may fail to provide **optimal** or **security-conscious** implementations.
- **Lack of Awareness of Internal Codebase:** If your company has an internal standard or best practice, Copilot will not automatically suggest it.

These limitations mean developers must carefully validate AI-generated code before integrating it into production systems.

Strategies to Improve Copilot's Code Suggestions

Solution Approaches:

- **Detailed Prompt Input (Example-Based Prompting):**
    - Provide **explicit documentation snippets** or **clear inline comments** to guide Copilot towards a **more accurate prediction.**
    - **Example**: Instead of just typing a function header, **paste an API usage sample** in the comments, before writing a new logic.
- **Custom Documentation for Enterprise Users:**
    - Organizations using **Copilot for Enterprise** can integrate **internal documentation** to fine-tune Copilot's responses.
    - This enables Copilot to generate **context-aware** suggestions specific to company standards.

- **Mock Repository Primer:**
  - Train Copilot within your project by **creating example repositories**, with the latest libraries and best practices.
  - This allows **Copilot to recognize preferred patterns**, when working on similar projects.

Expected Outcomes:

- **Improved Code Suggestions:** More relevant, context-aware AI-assisted coding.
- **Reduced Syntax Errors:** Avoids outdated functions by steering Copilot, with modern examples.
- **Better Integration with Internal Standards:** Helps align Copilot's recommendations, with proprietary coding practices.

By actively steering Copilot through structured prompts, documentation, and internal resources, developers can significantly improve AI-assisted coding accuracy.

Final Thought: Developers Must Bridge the Gaps

While GitHub Copilot accelerates development, its **training data limitations necessitate human oversight**. Therefore, developers should:

- **Recognize Copilot's blind spots**, and actively correct outdated or insecure recommendations.
- **Use structured prompts and internal documentation** to refine AI-assisted suggestions.
- **Employ enterprise integrations** to make Copilot aware of proprietary best practices.

Thus, by understanding **how Copilot's data limitations impact code suggestions**, developers can **work around these gaps to optimize AI-generated outputs effectively**.

Ethical Considerations in AI Usage

As artificial intelligence becomes an integral part of software development, ethical considerations surrounding its use have taken center stage. GitHub Copilot, powered by OpenAI Codex, exemplifies this evolution by assisting developers in writing code more efficiently. However, its use raises significant ethical questions related to **intellectual property, fairness, bias, accountability, security, and the long-term impact of AI-assisted coding on the developer ecosystem**.

This section examines the **ethical implications of using GitHub Copilot**, exploring concerns, potential risks, and strategies to ensure responsible AI adoption.

Intellectual Property and Licensing Concerns

One of the most debated topics around GitHub Copilot is whether AI-generated code may inadvertently **violate open-source licenses** or Intellectual Property (IP) rights. Since Copilot is trained on **publicly available code**, including repositories licensed under MIT, GPL, and other open-source licenses, it occasionally suggests snippets that resemble the existing copyrighted material.

Why This is a Concern:

- Copilot does not **cite sources,** when generating code.
- There is a risk that the **generated code might be too similar** to the existing open-source projects, without attribution.
- Some open-source licenses, such as the **GPL (General Public License)**, require **derivative works to inherit the same license**, which complicates commercial use.

Real-World Scenarios:

- A developer working on a **proprietary project** uses Copilot, unaware that the AI-generated code is nearly identical to a GPL-licensed snippet.
- A company inadvertently ships Copilot-generated code that was originally from an **open-source project with an attribution clause**, potentially violating compliance policies.

Mitigation Strategies:

- **Always review Copilot's suggestions** before using them in production.
- **Use attribution-checking tools** to ensure Copilot-generated snippets do not originate from protected sources.
- **For enterprise users, configure Copilot policies** to align with company-wide legal and compliance guidelines.

GitHub has stated that **Copilot does not "copy-paste" code**, but rather generates probabilistic outputs based on patterns in its training data. However, it remains the **developer's responsibility** to validate, and comply with licensing requirements.

Bias in AI-Generated Code

AI models, including OpenAI Codex, are trained on publicly available datasets, which means they **inherit biases present in those datasets**. Bias in AI-generated code can manifest in several ways, including **gender, racial, and cultural biases, as well as biases in code efficiency, security, and ethical software practices**.

Why Bias Exists in Copilot's Suggestions:

- Copilot learns from the **existing human-written code**, which inherently carries biases.
- If a majority of open-source projects favor **certain naming conventions or variable selections**, Copilot will replicate them.
- It may **suggest less secure implementations** because a large portion of the available code contains outdated or insecure practices.

Real-World Examples:

- **Gender Bias in Code Suggestions:** If a dataset contains more references to the **`adminUser`** being male, Copilot may **favor male pronouns** in documentation comments.
- **Bias in Security Practices:** Copilot may suggest **weak encryption methods** (for example, outdated cryptographic algorithms) if they appear frequently in training data.
- **Bias in Language Support:** Copilot is **more effective with popular languages**, such as Python and JavaScript, but it may generate suboptimal suggestions for **less commonly used languages**.

Strategies to Mitigate Bias:

- **Diversify the training data:** OpenAI and GitHub continually refine datasets to remove biases, but developers should also be mindful of their own code contributions.
- **Manually verify AI-generated suggestions** for security best practices.
- **Encourage diverse developer input:** When working on inclusive applications, developers should review AI-generated code for unintended biases.

While AI can improve efficiency, it is **not inherently neutral**—developers must exercise critical thinking to avoid perpetuating biases.

Accountability and AI Decision-Making

GitHub Copilot **suggests code, but it does not take responsibility for correctness or security**. The ethical question arises: **Who is accountable, when AI-generated code leads to vulnerabilities, errors, or failures?**

The Responsibility Gap:

- If a Copilot-generated function introduces a **security vulnerability**, is it the **developer's** fault or the Copilot's?
- Can AI-generated code be legally considered **"authored" work**, or does it fall under a different category?

Practical Considerations:

- **Developers remain responsible** for reviewing, testing, and validating AI-generated code.
- Organizations using Copilot **must implement quality control measures** to ensure AI-generated code meets security and reliability standards.
- **Legal frameworks for AI accountability are still evolving**, and companies should **stay informed about AI governance policies.**

As AI continues to evolve, accountability frameworks may become more structured, but for now, **human oversight is essential.**

Security and Malicious Use Cases

AI-generated code can **introduce security risks**, if developers rely on Copilot, without **verifying its suggestions**. Additionally, **malicious actors could exploit AI-assisted coding to generate harmful scripts, automate cyberattacks, or introduce backdoors.**

Security Concerns in Copilot-Generated Code:

- **Vulnerabilities in AI-generated code:** Copilot may generate code with **SQL injection, Cross-Site Scripting (XSS), or insecure authentication** mechanisms.
- **Over-reliance on AI:** Developers who accept Copilot's suggestions, without understanding them may deploy **insecure or incorrect code.**
- **Potential for abuse:** Copilot can **generate scripts for malicious activities,** if prompted correctly.

Real-World Risks:

- A developer accepts a Copilot-generated SQL query, **without parameterized inputs**, making the application vulnerable to **SQL injection.**
- AI-generated authentication logic **lacks rate limiting**, making it susceptible to brute-force attacks.
- Hackers **prompt AI models to generate exploit scripts**, leveraging AI to automate security threats.

How to Use Copilot Securely:

- **Enable security-focused linters** to catch vulnerabilities in AI-generated code.
- **Train developers to review Copilot's suggestions critically**, rather than assuming correctness.
- **Use AI-assisted security tools, alongside Copilot** to mitigate risks.

While Copilot accelerates development, **blindly trusting AI-generated code is a risk. Security best practices should always be applied.**

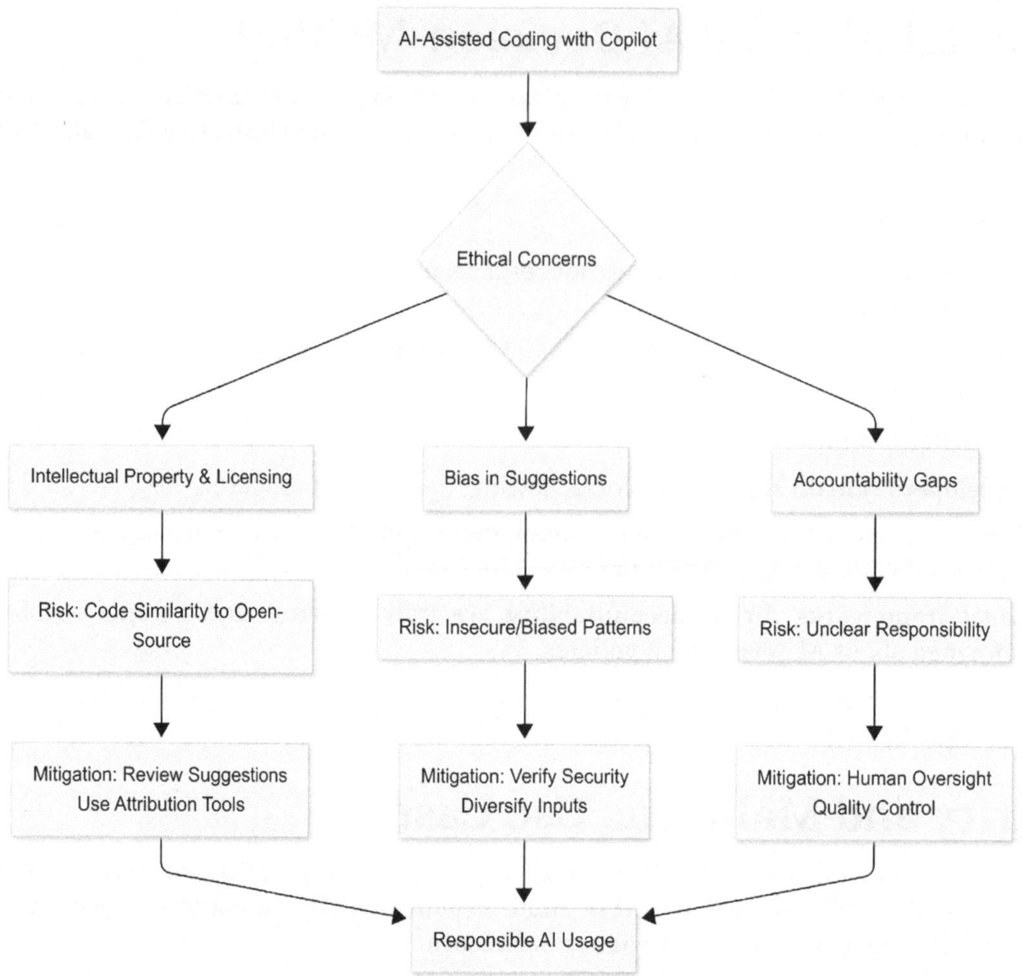

Figure 13.34: *Ethical Dimensions and Considerations, When Using AI Tools such as GitHub Copilot*

The Long-Term Impact of AI on Software Development

One of the biggest ethical discussions revolves around whether **AI will replace human developers**. While AI-assisted coding tools, such as Copilot are improving rapidly, they are still **far from replacing human creativity, critical thinking, and problem-solving.**

Can Copilot Replace Developers:

- Copilot **accelerates code writing**, but it does not understand **business logic, software design principles, or long-term project requirements.**
- AI **lacks the ability to innovate**–it predicts based on past data, but does not create **entirely new paradigms.**
- Developers **do more than just write a code**–they engage in architecture, debugging, testing, and collaboration, which AI **cannot fully replace.**

Ethical Considerations for Future AI-Assisted Development:

- **Job Displacement versus Augmentation:** AI may **change the nature of software engineering**, requiring developers to shift towards **code review, optimization, and architecture.**
- **Education and Upskilling:** Developers need to adapt by **learning how to work alongside AI**, not against it.
- **Ethical AI Development:** As AI-generated code becomes mainstream, developers must ensure AI-driven coding remains **ethical, inclusive, and responsible.**

Thus, AI will not eliminate developers–it will change the way **software development is done**.

Conclusion

GitHub Copilot is a powerful AI-assisted coding tool that enhances productivity by automating repetitive tasks, and providing intelligent code suggestions. However, its effectiveness depends on how it is used–it requires structured adoption, responsible oversight, and integration into development workflows. Use Copilot strategically as it excels at boilerplate code, but requires human review for accuracy and security. Understanding its limitations is crucial since Copilot lacks deep project context, and does not validate its suggestions. Always ensure security and compliance by reviewing AI-generated code to avoid vulnerabilities, and licensing issues. Adopt ethical AI practices by being mindful of bias, security risks, and responsible AI usage. For enterprises, defining clear policies for structured onboarding, security controls, and performance tracking optimizes Copilot's impact. Copilot is a developer's assistant, not a replacement. When used wisely, it accelerates coding, while maintaining quality, security, and compliance. The key to success is balancing AI efficiency with human expertise–leveraging automation, while applying critical thinking for innovation and reliability.

The next chapter will explore Copilot in education, examining how this AI tool is transforming teaching methodologies, enhancing student learning experiences, and serving as a real-time coding mentor that adapts to individual learning paces. Through case studies from academic institutions, and analysis of future prospects, we will investigate how GitHub Copilot is revolutionizing coding education, and contributing to the broader AI-powered educational landscape.

Multiple Choice Questions

1. What is a key feature of "*smart coding*" with GitHub Copilot?
   a. Manual boilerplate generation
   b. Real-time AI assistance for writing and refactoring code
   c. Static code documentation
   d. Offline-only code suggestions
2. How does Copilot improve productivity when writing repetitive utility functions?
   a. It disables default methods
   b. It automatically adds logging statements
   c. It predicts and generates entire function bodies from intent
   d. It replaces existing frameworks
3. What Copilot capability helps in transforming long switch-case blocks into cleaner alternatives?
   a. Git integration
   b. AI-powered if-loop transformation
   c. Refactoring using object maps or strategy patterns
   d. Enhanced linting

4. In smart form generation, which technique did Copilot leverage to reduce boilerplate?
   a. External UI plugins
   b. Declarative JSON configuration for dynamic rendering
   c. Manual field definitions
   d. Static code snippets from Stack Overflow
5. How can Copilot help detect hardcoded credentials in code?
   a. By running vulnerability scans
   b. Through code completion review and inline suggestions
   c. Using GitHub Security Lab integration
   d. It cannot detect such issues
6. What is a recommended practice to improve Copilot's suggestions during smart coding?
   a. Disable syntax highlighting
   b. Avoid using comments
   c. Use precise function names and descriptive comments
   d. Write incomplete statements deliberately
7. How does Copilot assist in smart loop rewriting for performance improvement?
   a. Adds nested loops
   b. Replaces loops with map/filter or optimized iteration methods
   c. Converts loops into GOTO statements
   d. Removes break conditions
8. What benefit does Copilot offer when converting legacy callback-based code to modern syntax?
   a. Increases technical debt
   b. Uses outdated patterns
   c. Converts to promises or async/await syntax
   d. Disables event listeners
9. What does Copilot use to understand code context for smart predictions?
   a. Random code snippets
   b. User email history
   c. File structure, comments, and surrounding code
   d. CPU cache
10. Which of the following is NOT a direct advantage of smart coding with Copilot?
    a. Reduced boilerplate
    b. Enhanced performance patterns

c. Business analytics dashboard integration

d. Faster feature scaffolding

Answers

1. b
2. c
3. c
4. b
5. b
6. c
7. b
8. c
9. c
10. c

References

1. Attention Mechanism in Transformers
https://arxiv.org/pdf/1706.03762.pdf

2. Large-Scale Training Challenges
https://arxiv.org/pdf/2001.08361.pdf

3. Copilot Performance in Large Codebases
https://arxiv.org/abs/2206.01362

4. Pros and Cons of Using GitHub Copilot
https://techcommunity.microsoft.com/discussions/microsoftlearn/what-are-the-pros-and-cons-of-using-github-copilot/4125227

5. Is it Safe to Use GitHub Copilot at Work?
https://www.copilot.live/blog/is-it-safe-to-use-github-copilot-at-work

6. Responsible Use of GitHub Copilot Chat
https://docs.github.com/en/copilot/responsible-use-of-github-copilot-features/responsible-use-of-github-copilot-chat-in-github

7. Best Practices for Using GitHub Copilot
https://docs.github.com/en/copilot/using-github-copilot/best-practices-for-using-github-copilot

8. Transformers: State-of-the-Art Natural Language Processing
https://arxiv.org/pdf/1910.03771

9. Copilot Architecture and Algorithms
https://combine.se/blog/openai-codex-the-automated-programmer/#:~:text=

10. Copilot Handling Large Files
https://github.com/orgs/community/discussions/9282

CHAPTER 14
Copilot in Education

Introduction

The world of education has undergone **continuous transformation**, driven by technological advancements that have reshaped the way students learn, and educators teach. From the invention of the printing press to the introduction of digital classrooms, each innovation has played a salient role in making knowledge more accessible, and learning more efficient.

Today, **Artificial Intelligence (AI) is revolutionizing education in ways, previously unimaginable**. AI is not merely an automated assistant, but an **active learning partner** that helps students grasp complex concepts, provides personalized feedback, and enhances engagement in the classroom.

One of the most groundbreaking AI tools in this transformation is **GitHub Copilot**—an AI-powered coding assistant that helps programmers write, debug, and optimize code. Unlike traditional learning resources, such as textbooks, coding bootcamps, or even online forums, Copilot acts as a **real-time mentor**, offering guidance that adapts to the student's coding level and learning pace.

The **significance of GitHub Copilot in education** cannot be overstated. By integrating this AI-powered tool into coding instruction, educators can **enhance the learning experience, accelerate skill development, and empower students to become more confident programmers**.

This chapter explores how GitHub Copilot is transforming education by addressing **teaching methodologies, student learning experiences, case studies from academic institutions, and the future prospects of AI-powered education**.

Structure

In this chapter, we will discuss the following topics:

- Teaching Coding with GitHub Copilot
- Enhancing Learning Experiences for Students
- Success Stories from Educational Institutions
- Case Studies: Copilot in the Classroom
- The Future Prospects of AI in Education
- Effective Teaching Techniques in the Modern Era
- How Students Should Approach Coding, if They are Scared of It

Teaching Coding with GitHub Copilot

Teaching programming has always involved balancing syntax instruction with logic building and problem-solving. With the emergence of AI tools like GitHub Copilot, the landscape of coding education is evolving rapidly. This section explores how educators can integrate GitHub Copilot into their teaching methods to enhance student engagement, simplify complex concepts, and foster a deeper understanding of programming logic through real-time AI assistance.

The Traditional Approach versus AI-Assisted Learning

Traditionally, learning to code has been a linear, and often a challenging process. Students begin with the basics, slowly progressing toward more complex concepts. The journey is filled with obstacles–syntax errors, debugging frustrations, and conceptual roadblocks. Instructors often spend a significant portion of their time correcting syntax issues, rather than focusing on problem-solving strategies.

With **GitHub Copilot**, the process takes a different turn. Instead of manually typing out every line of code, students can now receive **instant AI-generated suggestions**, accelerating their learning, and **allowing them to focus on logic and structure, rather than syntax struggles**.

The Role of AI in Improving Coding Instruction

GitHub Copilot redefines programming education by acting as an AI-powered assistant that provides real-time code suggestions, debugging support, and optimized solutions. Instead of memorizing syntax, students can focus on problem-solving and logical thinking, making the learning process more intuitive, and less intimidating.

With Copilot, the instructor's role evolves from an information provider to a guide, helping students critically analyze AI-generated suggestions, and understand their implications.

Real-World Scenarios of Copilot Aiding Educators

Consider a scenario in which a programming instructor is teaching Python functions. Instead of manually writing examples on the board, they use GitHub Copilot to **dynamically generate code snippets,** based on the class's queries.

Example Interaction

Instructor's Prompt:

```
"Generate a Python function to calculate the Fibonacci sequence using
recursion."
```

Copilot's Response:

```
def fibonacci(n):
    """
    Calculate the nth Fibonacci number using recursion.

    :param n: The position in the Fibonacci sequence.
    :return: The nth Fibonacci number.
    """
    if n <= 0:
        return 0
    elif n == 1:
        return 1
    else:
        return fibonacci(n - 1) + fibonacci(n - 2)

# Example usage:
n = 10
print(f"The {n}th Fibonacci number is: {fibonacci(n)}")
```

After generating the response, the instructor **guides the students through analyzing the function**, discussing efficiency, and even modifying the approach to introduce **iterative solutions**.

This interactive teaching method **boosts student engagement**, as they are no longer passive recipients of knowledge, but **active participants in the learning process**.

Copilot's Output:

This example demonstrates how GitHub Copilot can be used to generate a recursive function in Python for calculating the Fibonacci sequence. Given the instructor's prompt, the assistant responds with a complete implementation, including base cases, recursive logic, and a sample usage to print the 10th Fibonacci number. The explanation breaks down each part of the function, making it easy for learners to understand how recursion works in practice.

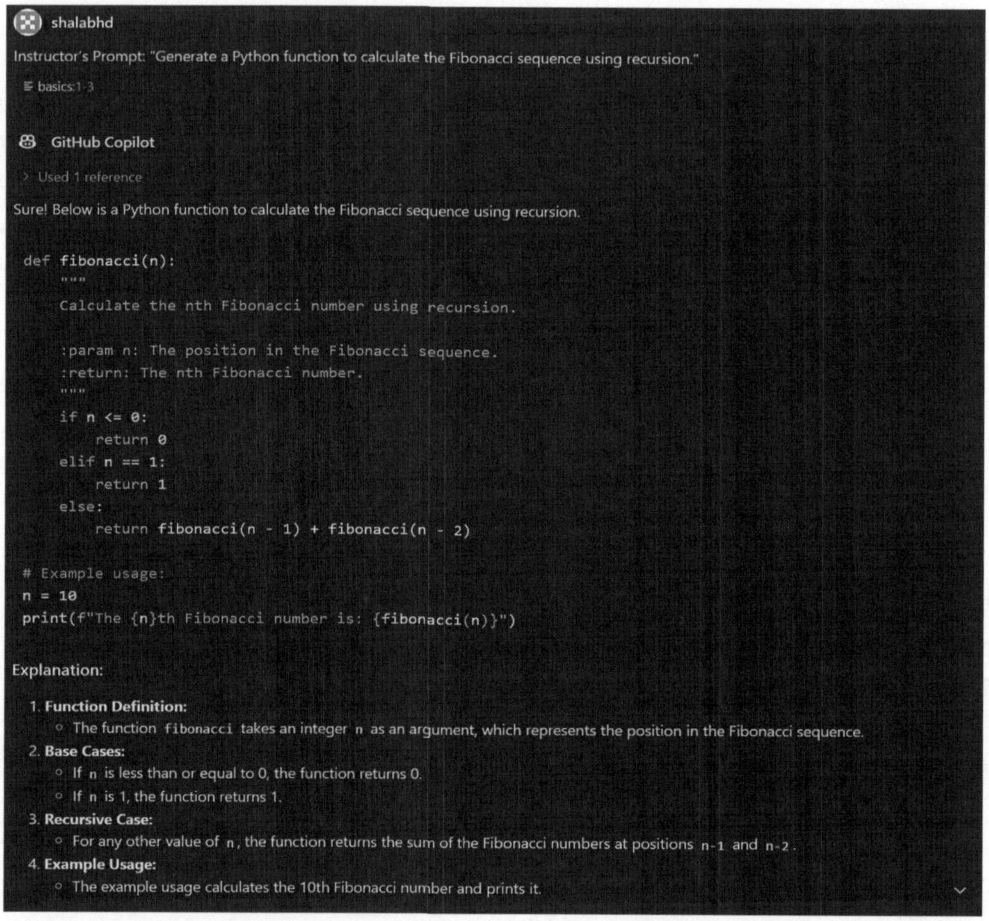

shalabhd

Instructor's Prompt: "Generate a Python function to calculate the Fibonacci sequence using recursion."

basics:1-3

GitHub Copilot

Used 1 reference

Sure! Below is a Python function to calculate the Fibonacci sequence using recursion.

```
def fibonacci(n):
    """
    Calculate the nth Fibonacci number using recursion.

    :param n: The position in the Fibonacci sequence.
    :return: The nth Fibonacci number.
    """
    if n <= 0:
        return 0
    elif n == 1:
        return 1
    else:
        return fibonacci(n - 1) + fibonacci(n - 2)

# Example usage:
n = 10
print(f"The {n}th Fibonacci number is: {fibonacci(n)}")
```

Explanation:

1. **Function Definition:**
   - The function `fibonacci` takes an integer `n` as an argument, which represents the position in the Fibonacci sequence.
2. **Base Cases:**
   - If `n` is less than or equal to 0, the function returns 0.
   - If `n` is 1, the function returns 1.
3. **Recursive Case:**
   - For any other value of `n`, the function returns the sum of the Fibonacci numbers at positions `n-1` and `n-2`.
4. **Example Usage:**
   - The example usage calculates the 10th Fibonacci number and prints it.

Figure 14.1: *GitHub Copilot-Generated Python Function for Computing Fibonacci Numbers Using Recursion, along with Explanatory Notes and Sample Output for the 10th Position in the Sequence*

Next, imagine a professor introducing **data structures and algorithms**. Instead of explaining everything manually, they use Copilot to generate a **real-time demonstration** of a linked list implementation.

Instructor's Prompt:

> **`"Generate a Python implementation of a singly linked list."`**

Copilot's Response:

This code snippet illustrates a GitHub Copilot-generated response to the prompt: "**`Generate a Python implementation of a singly linked list.`**" It demonstrates how AI-assisted development can be leveraged to construct foundational data structures. The implementation defines two classes: Node, which stores individual data elements and pointers, and **`SinglyLinkedList`**, which manages the list structure, and includes methods, such as append and prepend to manipulate the list dynamically.

Copilot's Output:

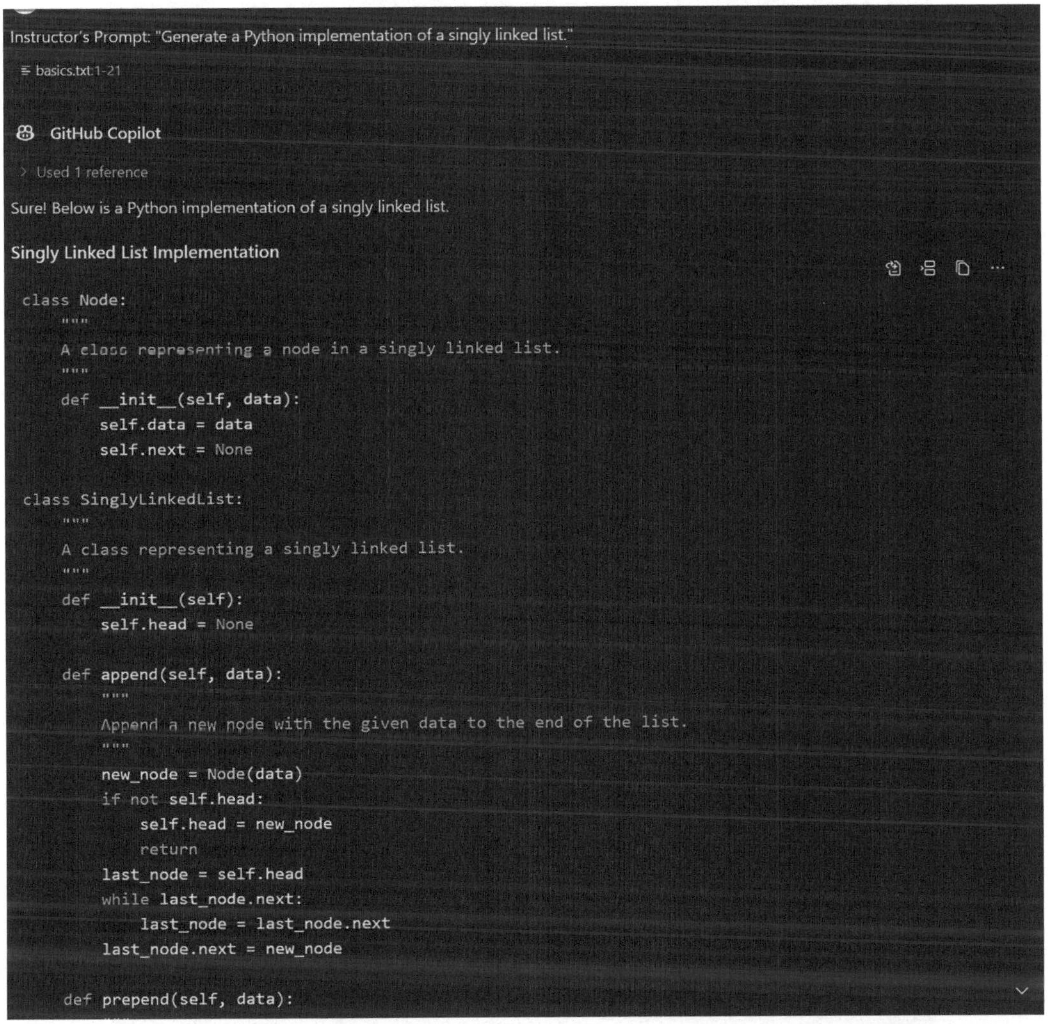

Instructor's Prompt: "Generate a Python implementation of a singly linked list."

basics.txt:1-21

GitHub Copilot

> Used 1 reference

Sure! Below is a Python implementation of a singly linked list.

Singly Linked List Implementation

```
class Node:
    """
    A class representing a node in a singly linked list.
    """
    def __init__(self, data):
        self.data = data
        self.next = None

class SinglyLinkedList:
    """
    A class representing a singly linked list.
    """
    def __init__(self):
        self.head = None

    def append(self, data):
        """
        Append a new node with the given data to the end of the list.
        """
        new_node = Node(data)
        if not self.head:
            self.head = new_node
            return
        last_node = self.head
        while last_node.next:
            last_node = last_node.next
        last_node.next = new_node

    def prepend(self, data):
```

Figure 14.2: *GitHub Copilot-generated Python Implementation of a Singly Linked List Featuring the Foundational Node and SinglyLinkedList Classes with Methods for Appending and Prepending Elements Based on an Instructional Prompt*

The following code example and explanation showcase the implementation of a singly linked list in Python. It demonstrates how the basic data structure concepts, such as nodes, pointers, and list operations can be brought to life, using simple class definitions and methods. The walkthrough highlights how to append, prepend, delete, and print elements from a custom singly linked list, supported by detailed inline comments and functional code that reinforces object-oriented design. This example serves as a foundational exercise for understanding the dynamic data structures and their manipulation in Python.

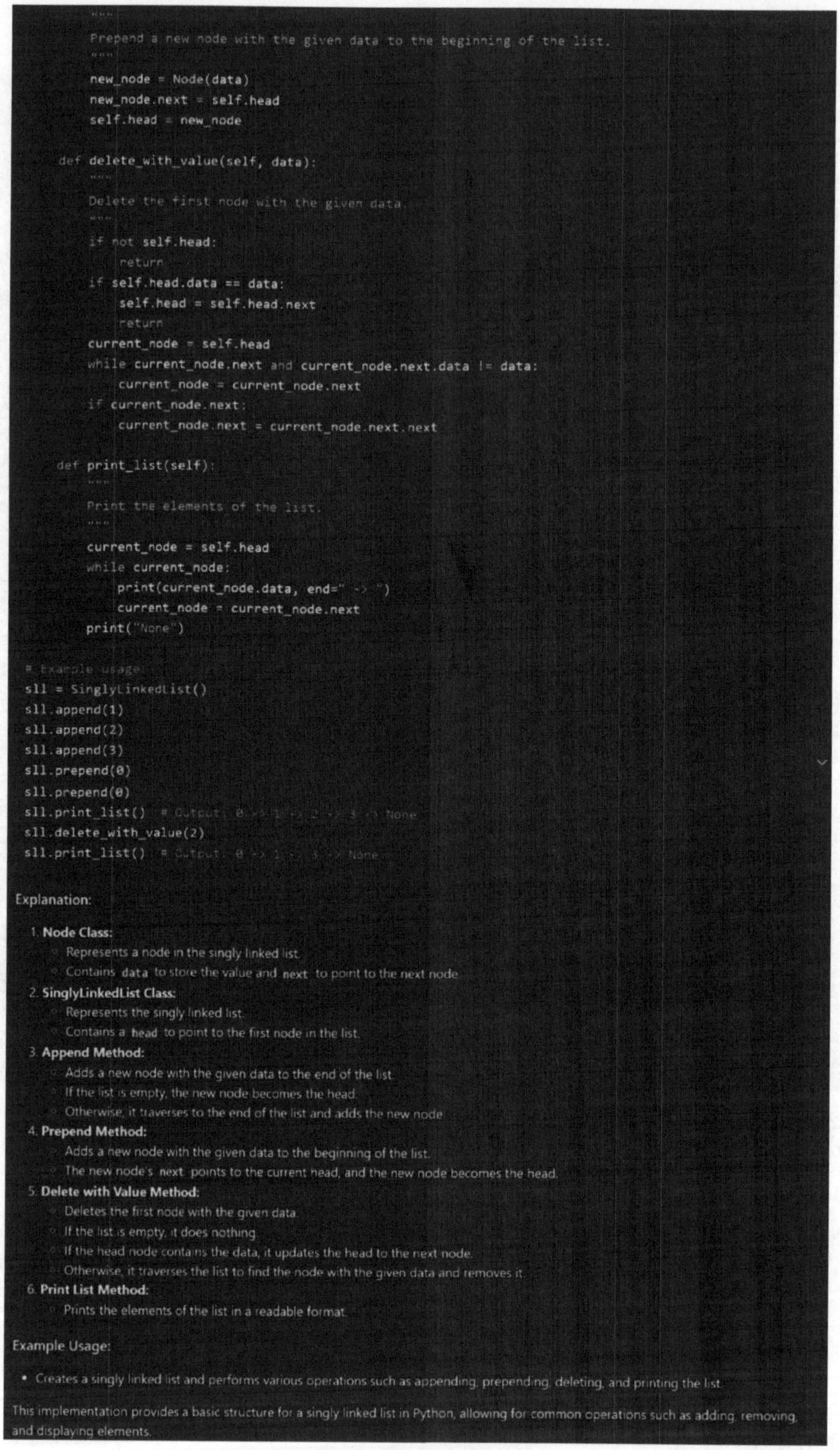

```
        """
        Prepend a new node with the given data to the beginning of the list.
        """
        new_node = Node(data)
        new_node.next = self.head
        self.head = new_node

    def delete_with_value(self, data):
        """
        Delete the first node with the given data.
        """
        if not self.head:
            return
        if self.head.data == data:
            self.head = self.head.next
            return
        current_node = self.head
        while current_node.next and current_node.next.data != data:
            current_node = current_node.next
        if current_node.next:
            current_node.next = current_node.next.next

    def print_list(self):
        """
        Print the elements of the list.
        """
        current_node = self.head
        while current_node:
            print(current_node.data, end=" -> ")
            current_node = current_node.next
        print("None")

# Example usage
sll = SinglyLinkedList()
sll.append(1)
sll.append(2)
sll.append(3)
sll.prepend(0)
sll.prepend(0)
sll.print_list()  # Output: 0 -> 1 -> 2 -> 3 -> None
sll.delete_with_value(2)
sll.print_list()  # Output: 0 -> 1 -> 3 -> None
```

Explanation:

1. **Node Class:**
   - Represents a node in the singly linked list.
   - Contains `data` to store the value and `next` to point to the next node.
2. **SinglyLinkedList Class:**
   - Represents the singly linked list.
   - Contains a `head` to point to the first node in the list.
3. **Append Method:**
   - Adds a new node with the given data to the end of the list.
   - If the list is empty, the new node becomes the head.
   - Otherwise, it traverses to the end of the list and adds the new node.
4. **Prepend Method:**
   - Adds a new node with the given data to the beginning of the list.
   - The new node's `next` points to the current head, and the new node becomes the head.
5. **Delete with Value Method:**
   - Deletes the first node with the given data.
   - If the list is empty, it does nothing.
   - If the head node contains the data, it updates the head to the next node.
   - Otherwise, it traverses the list to find the node with the given data and removes it.
6. **Print List Method:**
   - Prints the elements of the list in a readable format.

Example Usage:

- Creates a singly linked list and performs various operations such as appending, prepending, deleting, and printing the list.

This implementation provides a basic structure for a singly linked list in Python, allowing for common operations such as adding, removing, and displaying elements.

Figure 14.3: *Implementation and Explanation of a Python-Based Singly Linked List Featuring Node Creation, Insertion (append/prepend), Deletion by Value, and Readable List Output–Illustrated with an Example Usage for Practical Learning*

Benefits of This Approach

- **Real-Time Visualization:** Students immediately see how a linked list works.
- **Encourages Critical Thinking:** The instructor asks students to **modify the code**, encouraging deeper engagement.
- **Instant Feedback:** Copilot provides **alternative implementations**, allowing students to compare and contrast different approaches.

This hands-on learning style **bridges the gap between theoretical concepts and real-world applications**, making programming more interactive and engaging.

Benefits of AI-Assisted Teaching

- **Instant Code Generation:** Helps instructors demonstrate multiple approaches to problem-solving within minutes.
- **Increased Student Participation:** Encourages students to experiment with different variations of AI-generated solutions.
- **Time Efficiency:** Reduces time spent on writing boilerplate code, allowing for deeper conceptual discussions.

Enhancing Learning Experiences for Students

Learning to program is an exciting but often challenging journey, especially for beginners. Many students enter the world of coding with enthusiasm, but quickly encounter roadblocks that slow down their progress. From dealing with confusing syntax errors to struggling with algorithmic thinking, the barriers to learning programming can be frustrating and overwhelming.

GitHub Copilot serves as an interactive mentor, helping students navigate these challenges by providing real-time guidance, explanations, and corrections. It enables students to spend less time debugging trivial mistakes, and more time understanding core programming concepts, writing efficient code, and developing problem-solving skills.

Addressing Common Learning Challenges

Students learning to program often struggle with:

- Understanding the syntax of a new language.
- Debugging and fixing common errors.
- Writing optimized and efficient code.
- Grasping complex algorithms.

Challenge 1: Understanding the Syntax of a New Language

One of the first barriers students face, when learning a new programming language is **understanding its syntax**. Each language has unique rules for writing a code, and switching between languages can be confusing.

For example, consider a student who has learned Python, and is now transitioning to JavaScript. They may struggle with **differences in variable declaration, function syntax, and indentation rules**.

Scenario: A Student Struggling with Syntax Differences

Student's Attempt at JavaScript (Incorrect Code)

```
function greet(name):
    console.log("Hello, " + name);
```

Error: The student mistakenly uses Python's function declaration syntax (`:` instead of `{}` for blocks).

How Copilot Helps:

Instead of manually searching for the correct syntax, the student can simply ask Copilot for a correction:

Student's Prompt:

```
"Fix this JavaScript function."
```

Copilot's Response (Corrected Code):

```
function greet(name) {
    console.log("Hello, " + name);
}
```

Now, the student can clearly **see the difference between Python and JavaScript syntax**, accelerating their learning process.

Additional Benefits:

- Copilot provides **immediate corrections**, allowing students to learn from mistakes.
- Instead of memorizing syntax, students can **focus on logic and problem-solving**.
- They can **ask follow-up questions**, such as requesting an explanation or alternative approach.

Challenge 2: Debugging and Fixing Common Errors

Debugging is one of the most time-consuming aspects of programming, and beginners often get stuck for hours on seemingly simple mistakes. Identifying syntax errors, logical errors, and runtime issues can be frustrating, leading to discouragement.

GitHub Copilot acts as a real-time debugging assistant, helping students identify errors, and suggest solutions.

Scenario: A Student Struggling with an Indentation Error in Python

Student's Code (Incorrect)

```
def say_hello(name):
print("Hello, " + name)
```

Error Message: `IndentationError`: expected an indented block

How Copilot Helps:

Instead of spending time searching for explanations online, the student **asks Copilot for help**:

Student's Prompt:

```
"Why is this Python function giving an indentation error?"
```

Copilot's Response:

```
"Your function lacks proper indentation. In Python, code blocks inside
functions must be indented. Here is  the corrected version:"

def say_hello(name):
    print("Hello, " + name)
```

With this correction, the student **immediately understands the importance of indentation in Python**, making them more aware of similar issues in future coding tasks.

Additional Benefits:

- Students **learn debugging techniques,** instead of relying solely on instructors.
- They gain confidence by **resolving errors independently**.
- Copilot **offers explanations, along with corrections**, reinforcing learning.

Challenge 3: Writing Optimized and Efficient Code

Many beginners write **functionally correct** code, but it is often **inefficient, and not optimized**. Writing optimal solutions requires an understanding of the **best practices, algorithm efficiency, and code readability**.

GitHub Copilot helps students learn **better coding practices by suggesting improvements to their existing code**.

Scenario: Optimizing a Student's Code:

Student's Initial Code (Inefficient Approach)

```
numbers = [1, 2, 3, 4, 5]
squared_numbers = []
for num in numbers:
    squared_numbers.append(num ** 2)
```

This code **works**, but it is **not the most efficient way** to achieve the same result in Python.

How Copilot Helps:

Student's Prompt:

```
"Can this Python code be optimized?"
```

Copilot's Suggestion (Optimized Code):

```
squared_numbers = [num ** 2 for num in numbers]
```

This **list comprehension approach** is not only **more concise** but also runs **faster** for large datasets.

Additional Benefits:

- Students **learn to write cleaner, more efficient code**.
- They develop an **intuition for performance optimization** early in their learning journey.
- Copilot acts as a **virtual mentor**, guiding students toward the best coding practices.

Challenge 4: Grasping Complex Algorithms

Understanding algorithms is one of the biggest hurdles for programming students. Concepts such as **sorting algorithms, recursion, and dynamic programming** can be difficult to visualize.

GitHub Copilot **simplifies algorithm learning by generating well-structured examples and explanations**.

Scenario: Understanding Recursion with Copilot's Help

A student is learning recursion, but finds it difficult to grasp how recursive functions work.

Student's Prompt:

```
"Explain recursion with a simple Python example."
```

Copilot's Response:

```
"Recursion is a method where a function calls itself. Here is  an example of a
recursive function to calculate the factorial of a number:"
def factorial(n):
    if n == 0:
        return 1
    return n * factorial(n - 1)

print(factorial(5))  # Output: 120
```

After seeing this, the student asks Copilot:

```
"Can you break down how this function executes?"
```

Copilot's Explanation:

1. Factorial(5) calls factorial(4), which calls factorial(3), and so on.
2. When n reaches 0, the function returns 1.
3. The return values **propagate backward**, calculating 5 * 4 * 3 * 2 * 1.

This step-by-step breakdown helps the student **visualize recursion more clearly**, making it easier to apply the concept to new problems.

Additional Benefits:

- **Interactive Learning**: Students can tweak the function, and see how changes affect execution.
- **Alternative Approaches:** Copilot can suggest an **iterative version** for comparison.
- **Instant Feedback:** Students can validate their understanding immediately.

AI-Powered Learning versus Traditional Learning Methods

Traditional coding education often requires students to spend excessive time memorizing syntax and troubleshooting errors which can slow learning, and reduce engagement.

By contrast, GitHub Copilot accelerates learning through:

- **Instant Feedback**: Students receive immediate suggestions and corrections.
- **Focused Learning**: They can concentrate on logic and problem-solving, rather than syntax.
- **Error Assistance**: AI identifies and explains mistakes, speeding up debugging.

Example Comparison - Debugging Help

Traditional Way:

A student writes:

```
def greet(name):
print("Hello, " + name)
```

They receive an error but are not sure why. It takes time to research, and fix the problem.

With Copilot:

Student Prompt: `"What's wrong with this function?"`

Copilot Response:

```
def greet(name):
    print("Hello, " + name)
```

"Your function lacks indentation. In Python, code inside functions must be indented."

Outcome: The student quickly understands the issue, and the reasoning behind the fix–turning a frustrating experience into a learning opportunity.

Success Stories from Educational Institutions

As GitHub Copilot gains traction in academic settings, many institutions have started integrating it into their computer science curricula. These early implementations provide valuable insights into how AI tools can enhance learning outcomes, boost engagement, and reshape traditional coding pedagogy. The following is a glimpse into how top-tier universities are leveraging Copilot in real classrooms:

Case Study: GitHub Copilot in University Curricula

Institution: Harvard University

Course: Introduction to Computer Science

Implementation:

- Students used Copilot to generate and analyze solutions for problem sets.
- Assignments required students to **modify AI-generated code, and document their changes**.
- Educators encouraged the use of Copilot for debugging and alternative approaches.

Results:

- **35% improvement in student performance** on coding assignments.
- Increased engagement and interest in programming.
- Students learned multiple ways to solve a problem, rather than relying on a single approach.

The Future Prospects of AI in Education

Artificial Intelligence (AI) is poised to redefine the educational landscape by enabling personalized, adaptive, and inclusive learning experiences. Tools such as GitHub Copilot are just the beginning—future classrooms will blend AI-powered assistance with human guidance to foster creativity, critical thinking, and self-paced mastery. As technology continues to evolve, AI will act not just as a tool, but as a transformative catalyst shaping how knowledge is delivered, consumed, and applied globally.

Personalized Learning through AI

AI-powered tools such as GitHub Copilot have the potential to revolutionize education by creating **personalized learning experiences**. Future developments may include:

- **Adaptive Learning Models:** AI tailoring lessons based on a student's progress.
- **Automated Assignment Evaluation:** AI providing instant feedback on student submissions.
- **Multilingual Coding Assistance:** Helping non-native English speakers learn programming effectively.

Ethical and Academic Concerns

As AI-powered tools such as GitHub Copilot become more common in classrooms, it is important to recognize the line between using them as learning aids, and misusing them in ways that could hurt long-term growth.

GitHub Copilot can feel like magic. You type a few words, and it fills in lines of code instantly. For students, it feels like a shortcut through frustration. But real learning does not happen by skipping the hard parts. It happens when you think, explore, and understand the "`why`" behind every line of code.

Over-reliance on AI can lead to shallow understanding, reduced confidence in manual coding, and even violations of academic integrity. That is why educators and students alike must use these tools responsibly—with clarity, intent, and purpose.

Key Areas to be Cautious:

- Blindly copying AI-generated code may lead to academic dishonesty, especially when work is submitted, without understanding or modification.
- Using AI to avoid debugging or problem-solving reduces the opportunity to build real coding skills.
- Assuming Copilot's output is always correct, and can result in poor logic, missed edge cases, and faulty solutions.
- Letting Copilot handle the full logic of a program may weaken foundational programming instincts over time.

Responsible Ways to Use AI Coding Assistants

- Treat Copilot as a learning partner. Use it to explore different approaches, but always analyze and understand the output.
- Make small changes to AI-generated code to test your comprehension, and see how it behaves differently.
- When you use Copilot in an assignment, include your own comments, explaining what the code does, and how you learned from it.
- Always test and debug AI-generated code independently. Trust your logic more than the tool's convenience.
- Engage with AI as a tool to support curiosity, not to avoid effort.

AI tools can supercharge the learning journey, when used mindfully. The goal should not be to replace thinking, but to enhance it. Students who approach Copilot with a mindset of curiosity, reflection, and integrity will gain the most–not just in grades, but in confidence and capability.

The following diagram illustrates the iterative learning cycle supported by GitHub Copilot. It highlights how developers can continuously improve their coding skills through an active process of engagement, testing, and reflection using Copilot's assistance.

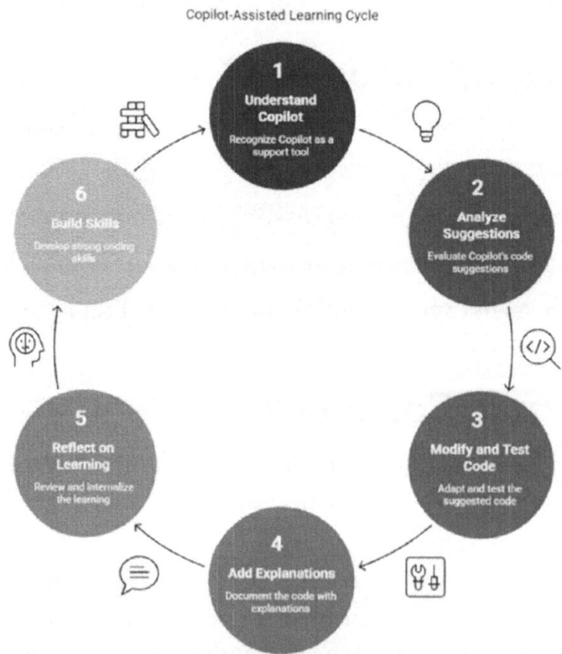

Figure 14.4: *Copilot-Assisted Learning Cycle – A Six-step Loop Beginning with Understanding Copilot as a Support tool, Followed by Analyzing Suggestions, Modifying and Testing Code, Adding Explanations, Reflecting on Learning, and Ultimately, Building Strong Coding Skills*

Effective Teaching Techniques in the Modern Era

In today's fast-paced and technology-driven world, traditional teaching methodologies are evolving to **help students grasp concepts more effectively**, while **reducing unnecessary stress and competition**. With the introduction of AI-powered tools such as GitHub Copilot, educators can now **redefine how programming is taught**, focusing more on conceptual clarity, creativity, and problem-solving, rather than rote memorization and syntax-heavy learning.

Here are some of the most effective **modern teaching techniques** that help students become confident, and capable programmers:

Active Learning through Hands-on Practice

Instead of passively listening to lectures or watching tutorials, students **learn best, when they engage in hands-on programming tasks**. Encouraging students to experiment with code, test different solutions, and build real-world projects helps them:

- Develop **problem-solving skills**.
- Understand programming logic **beyond syntax**.
- Gain **confidence** in writing, debugging, and optimizing code.

Example:

- Instead of explaining recursion **theoretically**, an instructor asks students to **modify an AI-generated recursive function**, and observe the changes.
- Students tweak parameters, print debug statements, and **break down recursive calls step by step** to fully grasp the concept.

How AI Tools Like Copilot Can Help:

- Instead of copying prewritten solutions, students **should analyze and modify** Copilot's suggestions to deepen their understanding.
- **Asking "why" Copilot generated a particular solution** encourages critical thinking.

Project-Based Learning (PBL) Instead of Isolated Coding Problems

Memorizing coding syntax, without applying it to real-world problems **limits a student's growth**. A better approach is **Project-Based Learning (PBL), where students work on real-life applications** instead of just solving theoretical problems.

Example:

- Instead of practicing random loops and conditionals, students **build a simple budgeting app** that allows users to track expenses.
- They use Copilot **as a guide**, but **write and structure the logic themselves**.

How AI Tools Like Copilot Can Help:

- Copilot can assist with **boilerplate code and syntax corrections**, but the core **application logic should be student-driven**.
- Instead of generating an entire project in one go, **students should break down the project into small tasks,** and use AI **selectively**.

Encouraging a Growth Mindset Instead of Competition

Many students feel **pressured by expectations, peer competition, and the fear of failure**. This often leads them to **focus on speed, rather than learning depth**.

A more effective approach is **fostering a growth mindset:**

- **Mistakes are part of learning.** Debugging and troubleshooting **build resilience**.
- Instead of comparing their progress to others, students should **track their own improvements over time**.

Example:

- Instead of rushing to complete an assignment, a student takes time to **analyze Copilot's suggestions, optimize the solution, and write comments explaining each step**.
- They seek **clarity rather than speed**, ensuring they fully understand each concept.

How AI Tools Like Copilot Can Help:

- Students should **not use Copilot just to finish assignments quickly**–instead, they should use it as a **learning supplement** that **enhances understanding**.

Balancing AI Assistance with Logical Thinking

One of the biggest **pitfalls of AI coding assistants** is that students **rely too much on auto-generated code,** instead of developing **logical thinking skills**.

Common Student Mistakes:

- **Copy-pasting AI-generated code, without understanding it.**
- **Not verifying if the AI-generated solution is correct.**
- **Assuming AI tools are always right, without testing edge cases.**

Example:

A student learning about sorting algorithms asks Copilot:

`"Write a quicksort algorithm in Python."`

Copilot's Response:

```
def quicksort(arr):
    if len(arr) <= 1:
        return arr
    pivot = arr[len(arr) // 2]
    left = [x for x in arr if x < pivot]
    middle = [x for x in arr if x == pivot]
    right = [x for x in arr if x > pivot]
    return quicksort(left) + middle + quicksort(right)

print(quicksort([3, 6, 8, 10, 1, 2, 1]))
```

Instead of just running this code, the student should:

- **Break down the logic**–What does each part of the function do?
- **Modify the code**–Change the pivot strategy, and see the impact on efficiency.
- **Optimize the function**–What if we use an iterative approach, instead of recursion?

How AI Tools Like Copilot Can Help:

- Instead of treating Copilot as an **answer machine**, students should use it as an **interactive mentor** that explains **why** and **how** a piece of code works.
- Always **ask follow-up questions** like, *"What are the drawbacks of this approach?"* or *"Can you suggest an alternative method?"*

How Students Should Approach Coding if They are Scared of It

Learning to code can feel intimidating, particularly for students who believe that programming is only for **math geniuses**, or **highly technical individuals**. Many students hesitate to start because they fear **making mistakes, not understanding concepts, or feeling behind compared to their peers**. However, coding is a **skill that anyone can learn** with the right approach.

If you are someone who is **afraid of coding**, the key is to **adopt the right mindset and learning strategy**. The following are some **practical tips** to help students overcome their fear of coding, and build confidence gradually.

Shift Your Mindset: Coding is a Skill, Not a Talent

Many students believe that coding requires **innate intelligence** or **superior logical abilities**. However, coding is a **learnable skill**–just like learning to ride a bicycle, cook a new recipe, or play an instrument.

How to Change Your Perspective:

- Understand that **no one is born knowing how to code**. Even experienced programmers **started as beginners**.
- View coding as a **problem-solving activity**, rather than a **technical subject**.
- Accept that **making mistakes is a normal and essential part of learning**.

Start Small and Build Gradually

One of the biggest mistakes students make is **jumping into complex topics too quickly**. This leads to frustration, and the feeling of being "*bad*" at coding.

Best Approach to Start Learning Coding:

- Begin with **small, manageable tasks** such as printing messages on the screen, or performing simple calculations.
- Focus on **learning basic concepts** such as variables, loops, and conditionals, before moving to advanced topics.
- Write simple programs, and gradually **increase the difficulty level**, step by step.

Example:

- **Bad Approach:** Trying to build a web application, without knowing how loops or functions work.
- **Good Approach:** Writing a small program to **print even numbers from 1 to 10,** before moving on to larger projects.

Choose the Right Programming Language

Some programming languages are more beginner-friendly than others. If you are new to coding, **choosing the right language** can make a big difference in your learning experience.

Best Languages for Beginners:

- **Python:** Simple syntax and widely used in various fields such as data science, automation, and web development.
- **JavaScript:** Ideal for web development and interactive programming.
- **Scratch** (for absolute beginners): A visual programming language that helps develop logical thinking.

Avoid languages like **C++ or Java**, if you are completely new, as they have **more complex syntax** that can be overwhelming for beginners.

Focus on Logic, Not Just Memorizing Syntax

Many students fear coding because they feel **overwhelmed by syntax rules**. However, **syntax is secondary to problem-solving skills.**

How to Develop Logical Thinking in Coding:

- Try **writing solutions in plain English** before coding.
- Break problems into **smaller, manageable steps** before implementing them in code.
- Use **flowcharts or pseudocode** to plan your program, before writing the actual code.

Example:

Before writing a function to check if a number is **prime**, think about the logic:

- A prime number is a number **greater than 1** that has **only two divisors (1 and itself)**.
- To check if a number is prime, **loop through numbers from 2 to the square root of the number,** and then check if it has any divisors.

This **logical breakdown** makes writing the actual code **much easier**.

Learn by Doing, Not Just Reading

Many students spend **too much time reading coding theory**, without actually coding. This leads to a **false sense of understanding**, as you feel like you understand the concepts, but when you try to write the code, you struggle.

How to Learn by Doing:

- Write a code **every day**, even if it is just for 15-30 minutes.
- Complete **small exercises and projects**, rather than just watching tutorials.
- Try **modifying example codes,** and experimenting with different approaches.

Example Exercise:

Instead of just reading about loops, **write a program that prints the first 10 Fibonacci numbers**.

Do not Fear Errors–Use Them as Learning Opportunities

One of the biggest fears students have is **getting errors in their code**. However, **every programmer, no matter how experienced, encounters errors daily.**

How to Deal with Coding Errors Positively:

- Instead of getting frustrated, **analyze the error message carefully**–it often tells you exactly what is wrong.
- Use **GitHub Copilot or AI coding assistants** to suggest corrections, but **try to understand the fix rather than blindly accepting it**.
- Debug your code by adding **print statements** to track variable values.

Example:

If you get an **Indentation Error in Python**, instead of panicking, try:

- Copying the error message into Google, and searching for solutions.
- Looking at the **line number mentioned in the error message**.
- Reading your code carefully to check for missing spaces, or incorrect indentation.

Use AI Coding Assistants Wisely–Do not Over-Rely on Them

GitHub Copilot and other AI coding tools **are powerful learning aids**, but students **must use them wisely**.

Common Mistakes Students Make When Using Copilot:

- **Blindly copying AI-generated code**, without understanding how it works.
- **Skipping the debugging process** because Copilot provides a ready-made solution.
- **Not testing the AI-generated code**, assuming it is always correct.

Best Way to Use GitHub Copilot for Learning:

- First, **try to write the code on your own**. If you get stuck, use Copilot **to guide you**, rather than provide a complete solution.
- Ask Copilot **for explanations**, not just solutions. Example:
  - Instead of "`Write a Python function to check if a string is a palindrome`",
  - Ask: "`Explain how a recursive function to check palindromes works.`"
- Debug and test AI-generated code **yourself** to ensure that you fully understand it.

Start with Small Projects to Build Confidence

Nothing boosts confidence more than **completing a project**. Instead of just solving coding exercises, start building **small, functional projects** that **apply what you have learned**.

Beginner-Friendly Project Ideas:

- A **To-Do List** app, where users can add, and remove tasks.
- A **simple calculator** that performs basic arithmetic operations.
- A **weather app** that fetches real time weather data using an API.

These projects will help students **develop confidence and problem-solving skills**.

Join a Coding Community for Motivation and Support

Learning to code alone can feel **overwhelming**, but being part of a **community** makes it more enjoyable, and less stressful.

Where to Find a Supportive Coding Community:

- Join online forums such as **Stack Overflow, GitHub Discussions, or Reddit's `r/learnprogramming`**.
- Participate in open-source projects on **GitHub**.
- Connect with other learners in **coding boot camps, or online study groups**.

Discussing challenges with others **helps you learn faster**, and gives you the **motivation to keep going**.

Final Advice: Coding is a Journey, Not a Race!

Many students feel pressured to **learn everything quickly**, and compare themselves to others. However, learning to code is a **long-term process** that requires patience and persistence.

Key Takeaways for Overcoming the Fear of Coding:

- **Start small**, focus on **building logic**, rather than memorizing syntax.
- **Use AI coding assistants wisely**—as a **mentor, not a crutch**.
- **Practice regularly** by working on **real projects**.
- **Don't fear mistakes**—treat them as **learning opportunities**.
- **Seek help, when needed,** and **stay connected with the coding community**.

By following these strategies, students can **build confidence, enjoy the learning process, and eventually, master coding without fear**.

How to Approach Coding with AI Assistants (Dos and Don'ts)

This **infographic presents clear guidelines** on how students should and should not approach AI-powered coding assistants like GitHub Copilot.

Dos (Right Way to Use AI Assistants):

- **Use Copilot as a learning tool, not just an autocomplete feature.**
- **Modify AI-generated code** to better understand how it works.
- **Ask Copilot for explanations**, instead of copying code blindly.
- **Use AI-generated solutions as a reference,** and compare with your own approach.
- **Validate AI-generated code for correctness** by testing and debugging.

Don'ts (Common Misuses of AI Assistants):

- Don't copy and paste AI-generated code, without understanding it.
- Don't assume AI-generated solutions are always correct or optimized.
- Don't skip debugging just because the AI provides a working solution.
- Don't rely on Copilot to do all the work—focus on developing problem-solving skills.

This diagram ensures that students **use AI coding assistants effectively, while still developing their own coding abilities.**

AI coding assistants such as GitHub Copilot can significantly enhance developer productivity and learning, when used mindfully. However, their effectiveness depends on how developers interact with the suggestions. Therefore, it is important to adopt practices that encourage critical thinking, debugging, and understanding—rather than blindly trusting generated code. The following visual outlines the essential dos and don'ts that guide responsible, skill-enhancing usage of AI-powered coding tools in real-world development workflows.

How to Use AI Coding Assistants Effectively

DOS

Learn from AI suggestions

Modify AI-generated code

Debug and test AI-generated code

Compare different coding approaches

DON'TS

Don't blindly copy AI-generated code

Don't ignore errors or warnings

Don't assume solutions are optimized

Don't replace hands-on practice

Figure 14.5: *Key Dos and Don'ts for Using AI Coding Assistants Effectively–Emphasizing Learning, Modification, and Validation over Blind Reliance*

Best Way to Learn with GitHub Copilot

The **decision tree diagram** illustrates an **optimal learning approach**, when using GitHub Copilot. It helps students **strategically integrate AI assistance** into their programming workflow, rather than blindly relying on it.

- **Understanding the Problem First:** Before using Copilot, students should attempt to **break down the problem logically**, and analyze the requirements.
- **Attempting to Code Independently:** If the student **understands the concept**, they should first try writing the code themselves. This practice **strengthens problem-solving skills**.
- **Using AI for Explanations Instead of Direct Answers:** If the student struggles to understand the problem, **they should ask Copilot for an explanation, not just a solution**.
- **Comparing Their Solution with AI Suggestions:** Once the student writes their code, they can use Copilot to **compare different approaches**, and **refine their logic**.
- **Debugging AI-Generated Code:** Instead of assuming AI-generated solutions are always correct, students should **test, debug, and analyze** the code.
- **Reflecting on the Learning Process:** After completing the task, students should reflect on what they learned, and how AI **enhanced their understanding**, rather than just completing the task.

This structured workflow ensures that students **use GitHub Copilot as a learning companion, rather than a shortcut to complete assignments**. Navigating coding problems with the help of GitHub Copilot becomes more effective, when approached with a structured mindset. The following flowchart provides a decision-making guide for developers to balance self-effort with AI assistance. It encourages first attempting the problem independently, and then turning to Copilot for support, only when necessary–ensuring that both understanding and learning are retained throughout the process.

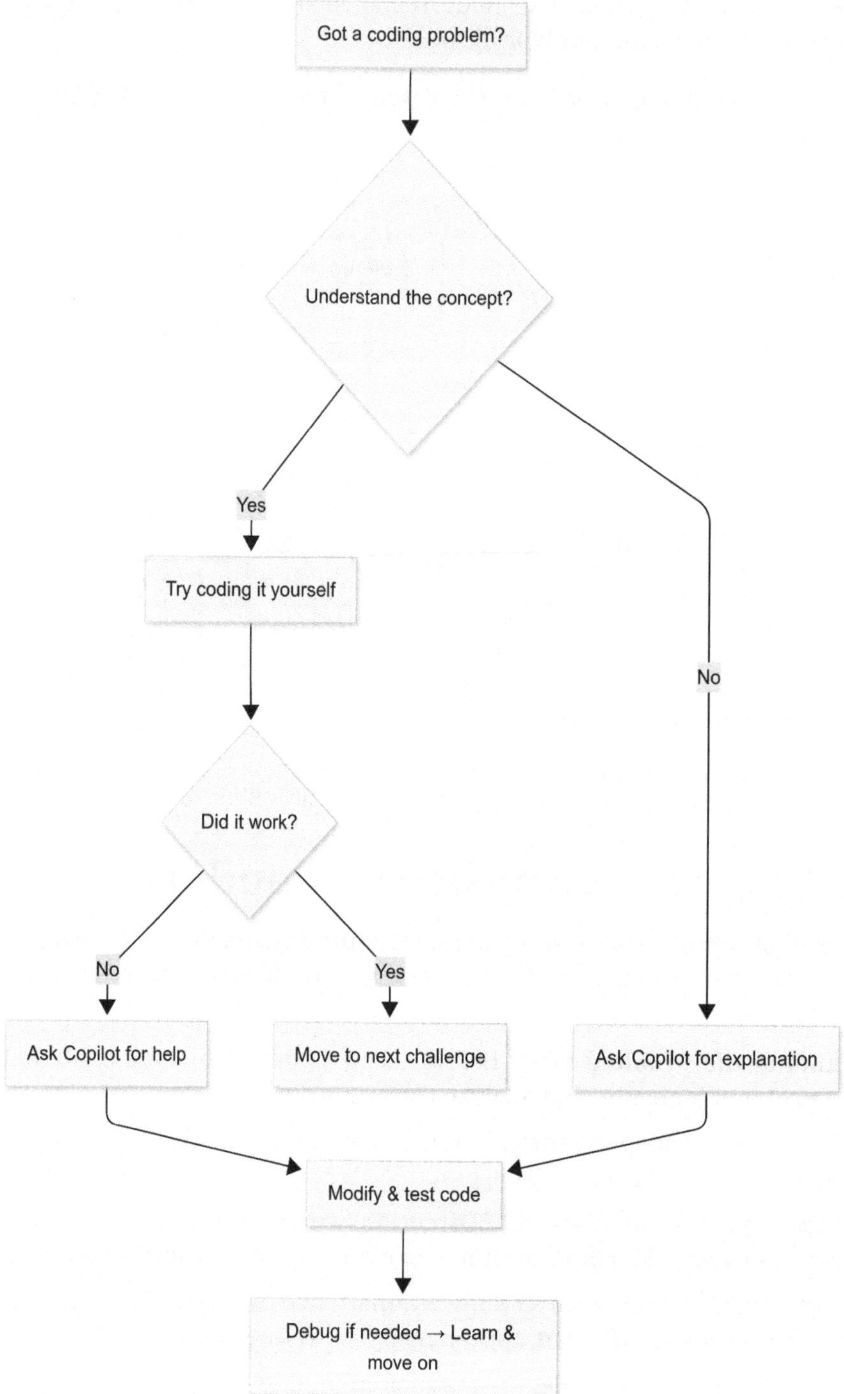

Figure 14.6: *Guided Decision Flow for Solving Coding Problems Using GitHub Copilot, Promoting Self-Attempts, Learning from Explanations, Testing AI-generated Code, and Reflecting on Outcomes*

Growth Mindset versus Fixed Mindset in Learning Programming

Mindset plays a pivotal role in how developers approach coding challenges, especially when learning with tools such as GitHub Copilot. While a fixed mindset limits growth by associating mistakes with failure, a growth mindset embraces errors, and struggle as essential parts of the learning process. The comparison below highlights the shift in perspective that leads to deeper skill development, and long-term success.

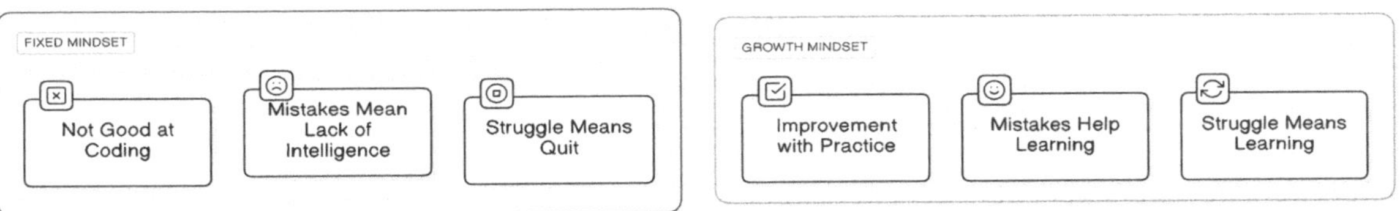

Figure 14.7: *Comparison between Fixed and Growth Mindsets in Coding–Showing how Adopting a Growth Mindset Fosters Resilience, Learning from Mistakes, and Continuous Improvement*

The **Growth Mindset versus Fixed Mindset diagram** highlights the two contrasting attitudes students may have, when learning programming. It encourages a **positive approach to overcoming challenges** in coding.

- **Fixed Mindset Characteristics:**
  - Believes that **coding skills are innate**– `"I'm just not good at this."`
  - Fears making mistakes, and avoids challenges.
  - Views errors as **proof of incompetence,** rather than learning opportunities.
  - Easily discouraged by **bugs and debugging difficulties**.
- **Growth Mindset Characteristics:**
  - Recognizes that **coding is a skill that improves with practice**.
  - Sees mistakes as part of the **learning process**.
  - Actively seeks **challenges to improve problem-solving skills**.
  - Uses debugging as an opportunity to **strengthen logical thinking**.

This diagram serves as a **reminder that persistence, curiosity, and continuous learning** are the keys to mastering programming.

How to Effectively Use AI Coding Assistants in Writing and Improving Code

AI coding assistants such as GitHub Copilot, Amazon CodeWhisperer, and others can significantly enhance your coding workflow, when used purposefully. To get the most out of them, start by writing clear, goal-oriented prompts or comments that describe what you want to build. Treat the AI's suggestions as a starting point review them critically, modify the logic to suit your needs, and test thoroughly. Use these tools not just to generate code, but to explore alternative implementations, improve readability, and accelerate debugging. Always validate output for correctness, performance, and security, and complement AI's help with hands-on practice and deeper understanding of the underlying concepts.

In AI-assisted learning environments, multiple entities collaborate to support the developer's journey–from suggestion generation to debugging, and code refinement. This sequence diagram illustrates how a developer interacts with an AI agent, debugger, and instructor to iteratively improve their solution, showcasing an ecosystem of feedback and enhancement.

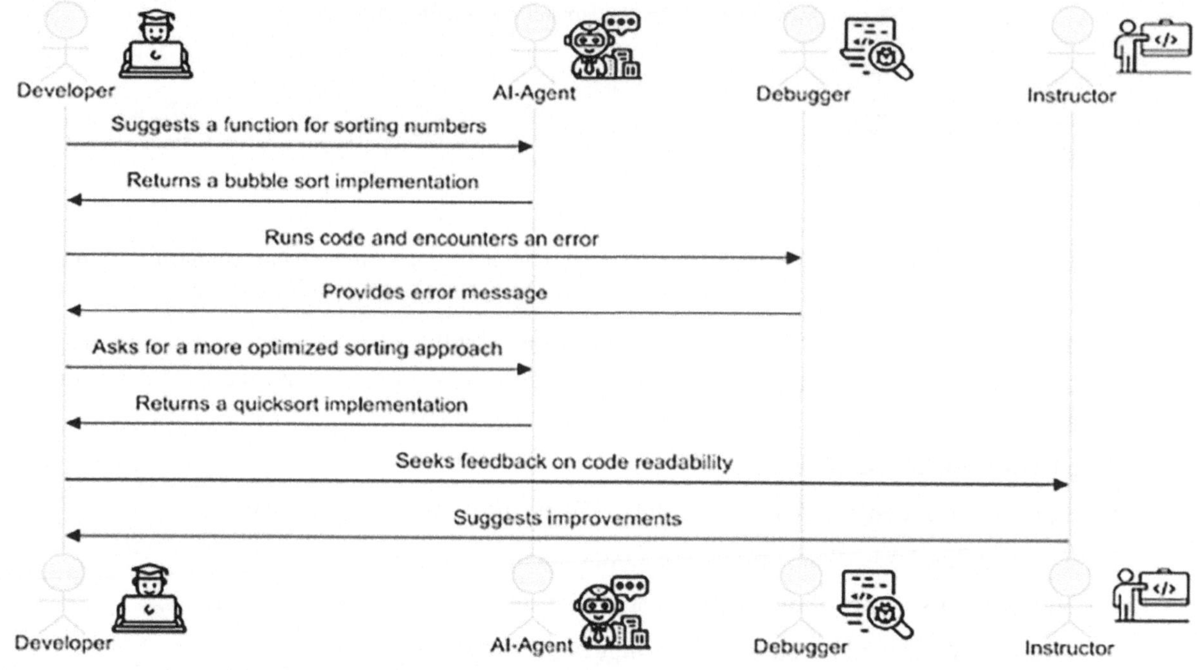

Figure 14.8: *Comparison between Fixed and Growth Mindsets in Coding–Showing how Adopting a Growth Mindset Fosters Resilience, Learning from Mistakes, and Continuous Improvement*

Conclusion

GitHub Copilot is revolutionizing programming education by providing real-time assistance, reducing learning barriers, and enhancing problem-solving skills. It empowers students to code more effectively, debug efficiently, and explore different approaches, while also helping educators streamline teaching, and focus on conceptual clarity.

However, Copilot should be used as a learning aid, not a replacement for critical thinking, and hands-on coding practice. Students must actively engage with AI-generated suggestions–modifying, testing, and optimizing code–to truly build strong programming skills.

As AI-driven tools continue to evolve, their role in education will expand, offering personalized learning experiences and adaptive feedback.

Thus, the future of education lies not in AI replacing human learning, but in leveraging AI to enhance understanding, foster creativity, and prepare students for a technology-driven world.

Building on this foundation, the next chapter explores how GitHub Copilot is already making an impact across real-world projects and industries. Through practical case studies and field applications, we will see how Copilot goes beyond the classroom–powering innovation, accelerating workflows, and transforming the way software is developed in professional environments.

Multiple Choice Questions

1. What is a key benefit of using GitHub Copilot in a coding classroom?
   a. Replaces the need for a curriculum
   b. Automatically grades all assignments
   c. Provides real-time coding suggestions to support learning
   d. Prevents students from debugging code

2. How can educators use Copilot to reinforce coding fundamentals?
   a. By disabling IDEs
   b. By comparing Copilot's output to standard logic
   c. By forcing students to memorize syntax
   d. By using only legacy programming languages
3. Which approach helps students develop prompt engineering skills while learning to code?
   a. Writing vague code
   b. Copy-pasting solutions
   c. Iteratively refining natural language prompts
   d. Avoiding AI tools altogether
4. What is an effective way to use Copilot for project-based learning?
   a. Generating full projects and skipping design
   b. Using it to scaffold starter templates and APIs
   c. Asking Copilot to complete exams
   d. Replacing all group discussions
5. Which of the following is a potential pitfall educators should be aware of when using Copilot in class?
   a. Too much engagement
   b. Over-reliance that reduces independent thinking
   c. Increased compilation speed
   d. Improved test scores
6. What kind of classroom task is best suited for GitHub Copilot usage?
   a. Memorization drills
   b. Creative coding and exploratory exercises
   c. Manual file backups
   d. Hardware installations
7. How can GitHub Copilot help beginner students with debugging?
   a. By rewriting the entire project
   b. By pointing out logical fallacies using AI suggestions
   c. By eliminating all code warnings
   d. By skipping test cases
8. What should instructors encourage students to do when reviewing Copilot suggestions?
   a. Accept all outputs blindly
   b. Avoid modifying generated code

   c. Validate and improve the AI-suggested code
   d. Disable comments in the editor
9. What role does Copilot play in collaborative classroom coding sessions?
   a. Acts as a live compiler
   b. Suggests boilerplate and structure in real-time
   c. Prevents team discussions
   d. Forces students to use command line
10. What is one best practice when integrating Copilot into a coding curriculum?
   a. Remove documentation
   b. Design tasks that involve prompt tuning and critical thinking
   c. Replace instructors with Copilot
   d. Limit it to administrative tasks only

Answers

1. c
2. b
3. c
4. b
5. b
6. b
7. b
8. c
9. b
10. b

CHAPTER 15
Real-World Use Cases and Case Studies

Introduction

GitHub Copilot has transformed the way software development teams approach coding, automation, and innovation. By leveraging AI-assisted coding, businesses have experienced notable efficiency improvements, reduced development cycles, and enhanced code quality. This chapter presents in-depth case studies, and industry use cases that highlight the real-world impact of GitHub Copilot, including challenges faced, key success metrics, and efficiency improvements observed in different domains.

Structure

In this chapter, we will discuss the following topics:

- Industry Use Cases: How Businesses Benefit from Copilot
- Detailed Case Studies: Success Stories and Lessons Learned
- Copilot in Different Sectors: Challenges and Opportunities
- User Testimonials and Feedback
- Best Practices Derived from Real-World Applications

Industry Use Cases: How Businesses Benefit from Copilot

GitHub Copilot is not just a developer productivity tool—it is rapidly becoming a strategic asset across industries. From accelerating software development cycles to improving code quality and reducing onboarding time, businesses are finding creative and impactful ways to integrate Copilot into their workflows. This section highlights real-world use cases that demonstrate how companies are leveraging Copilot to drive innovation, efficiency, and competitive advantage in diverse enterprise environments.

Technology and Software Development

Use Case: Accelerated Software Delivery and DevOps:

Technology firms are at the forefront of adopting Copilot, integrating it seamlessly into **agile development, DevOps, and CI/CD pipelines**.

Key Benefits:

- **40% faster development cycles** by reducing boilerplate code writing.

- **30% fewer production bugs** due to AI-assisted error handling.
- **25% increase in developer productivity**, allowing teams to focus on high-value tasks.

Example: Microsoft and GitHub's Internal Adoption

- Over **50% of code suggestions** in AI-assisted teams are accepted.
- Developers spend **less time debugging**, and more time on innovation.

Example: Shopify

- Automates deployments with GitHub Copilot and Actions.
- Handles **50+ production releases daily** with AI-driven automation.

Finance and Banking

Use Case: AI-Powered Secure Coding and Compliance

Financial institutions require **secure, efficient, and regulation-compliant code**. Copilot helps **automate secure coding patterns, detect vulnerabilities, and accelerate fintech innovation.**

Key Benefits:

- **35% reduction in security vulnerabilities** by implementing AI-assisted security best practices.
- **25% improvement in compliance checks** with automated validation of regulatory requirements.
- **50% faster implementation of fraud detection algorithms.**

Example: JPMorgan Case

- Uses AI-assisted coding to automate **KYC (Know Your Customer) and AML (Anti-Money Laundering) checks.**
- Reduced manual intervention by **30%**, increasing financial security compliance.

Example: PayPal

- Uses Copilot to **automate transaction security measures**, and detect fraudulent activities **20% faster.**

Healthcare and Life Sciences

Use Case: AI-Assisted Medical Data Processing and Analysis

Healthcare organizations leverage Copilot for **data-driven diagnostics, medical imaging analysis, and EHR (Electronic Health Records) optimization.**

Key Benefits:

- **50% faster development of AI-driven healthcare models.**
- **30% efficiency gain in patient data processing.**
- **40% reduction in administrative workload** for medical professionals.

Example: Mayo Clinic:

- Uses GitHub Copilot to **streamline patient record automation.**
- Reduced **EHR system development time by 35%.**

Example: IBM Watson Health:

- Leverages AI-assisted code generation for **medical research analysis.**

E-Commerce and Retail

Use Case: AI-Powered Recommendation Engines and Inventory Automation

E-commerce businesses rely on AI for **personalized customer experiences, sales forecasting, and inventory management**.

Key Benefits:

- **25% increase in recommendation engine accuracy**, using AI-driven enhancements.
- **15% boost in conversion rates** due to AI-powered personalization.
- **20% faster stock reordering, and demand forecasting**.

Example: Amazon and Shopify

- Uses AI-assisted coding for **dynamic pricing, inventory automation, and sales analytics.**
- Shopify developers saw a **30% boost in productivity**, using Copilot for backend integrations.

Manufacturing and IoT

Use Case: Predictive Maintenance and Automation

Manufacturers use AI to **develop IoT-driven predictive maintenance solutions** that reduce downtime, and optimize efficiency.

Key Benefits:

- **40% reduction in unplanned equipment failures,** with AI-powered maintenance scheduling.
- **35% faster industrial automation scripting,** using Copilot.
- **25% decrease in factory software integration time**.

Example: Siemens and Bosch

- Uses AI to optimize **assembly line monitoring, and predictive failure analysis**.
- Reduced downtime by **45%** through AI-assisted coding optimizations.

Cybersecurity and Compliance

Use Case: AI-Assisted Threat Detection and Code Hardening

Security firms integrate Copilot for **automated vulnerability detection, penetration testing, and secure coding practices**.

Key Benefits:

- **30% reduction in critical security vulnerabilities** due to real-time security suggestions.
- **50% faster identification of malware signatures**, with AI-assisted security research.
- **40% increase in security compliance automation**.

Example – CrowdStrike and Palo Alto Networks:

- Uses Copilot to **automate threat intelligence gathering**, and reduce manual security review efforts.

Startups and Innovation

Use Case: Rapid Prototyping and MVP Development

Startups rely on Copilot to **build Minimum Viable Products (MVPs) faster, reduce hiring costs, and experiment with AI-driven development.**

Key Benefits:

- **50% faster MVP deployment.**
- **30% reduction in costs associated with early-stage product development.**
- **70% improvement in developer onboarding speed.**

Example: Early-Stage AI Startups

- Companies like OpenAI-backed startups use Copilot to iterate **2x faster** on AI and SaaS applications.

Key Takeaways and Industry-Wide Metrics

The following table depicts GitHub Copilot adoption by industry:

Industry	Adoption Rate	Efficiency Gain	AI Code Retention
Technology	70%	+45%	80%
Finance	65%	+35%	78%
Healthcare	60%	+50%	75%
E-Commerce	55%	+30%	70%
Manufacturing	50%	+40%	68%
Startups	75%	+50%	85%

Table 15.1: *GitHub Copilot Adoption by Industry*

Top Copilot Efficiency Gains:

- **40% faster development cycles** in software companies.
- **35% fewer vulnerabilities** in financial and security applications.
- **50% improvement in AI-driven healthcare automation.**
- **25% higher accuracy in e-commerce recommendation engines.**
- **45% reduction in unplanned manufacturing downtime.**
- **50% faster MVP launch cycles for startups.**

Detailed Case Studies: Success Stories and Lessons Learned

To truly understand the transformative potential of GitHub Copilot, it is essential to examine how real-world teams have applied it in practice. This section presents detailed case studies from various industries, showcasing how development teams adopted Copilot, the challenges they faced, the measurable outcomes achieved, and the key lessons learned along the way. From rapid prototyping and automation to secure code generation and productivity gains, these stories provide actionable insights for teams looking to replicate similar success in their own organizations.

Accenture's Adoption of GitHub Copilot

- **Key Metrics:**
  - 81.4% of developers installed Copilot on the first day of license availability.
  - 67% of developers used Copilot at least five days per week.
  - 95% reported increased coding enjoyment.
  - 84% increase in successful builds, reducing debugging time.
- **Source:** Accenture's GitHub Customer Story

Shopify's Integration with GitHub Tools

- **Key Metrics:**
  - Manages over 2.8 million lines of code in a single repository.
  - Processes more than 50 production application changes daily.
- **Source:** Shopify's GitHub Customer Story

Mercari's Use of GitHub Advanced Security and Actions

- **Key Metrics:**
  - Hosts 1,400 GitHub Enterprise seats, and 800 GitHub Advanced Security Seats.
  - Emphasizes inner source practices, allowing developers access to most repositories across the company.
- **Source:** Mercari's GitHub Customer Story

GitHub Copilot Adoption Trends

- **Key Metrics:**
  - Developers using Copilot have experienced productivity gains, ranging from 20% to 35%.
  - AI-powered coding assistants have attracted nearly $1 billion in funding, since early 2023.
- **Source:** AI-powered coding pulls in almost $1bn of funding to claim 'killer app' status.

Copilot in Different Sectors: Challenges and Opportunities

As GitHub Copilot continues to make waves across industries, its real impact is shaped by the unique needs and constraints of each sector. From regulated environments such as finance and healthcare to agile startup ecosystems, the opportunities offered by Copilot—faster development, smarter automation, and better collaboration—are vast. However, these benefits come with their own set of challenges, including data privacy concerns, integration with legacy systems, and compliance requirements. This section explores how various sectors are embracing Copilot, the roadblocks they face, and how organizations can strategically navigate them for long-term success.

Industry-Specific Implementations

- **Automotive Industry: Mercedes-Benz**, renowned for its luxury vehicles, has embraced GitHub Copilot to enhance its software development processes. Facing challenges with a scattered technology stack that created silos, and slowed collaboration, the company sought a unified platform to accelerate software delivery. By adopting GitHub's platform, Mercedes-

Benz unified its source code management, promoting collaboration and efficiency through open source, and inner source practices. The integration of GitHub Copilot has been pivotal, with over 2 million lines of AI-generated code accepted, leading to significant time savings, and improved code quality. Developers have also reported a 30 million+ weekly time savings per developer, attributing this efficiency to Copilot's assistance in automating repetitive tasks, and providing intelligent code suggestions.

- **Professional Services: Accenture**, a global professional services company, conducted an extensive trial involving 450 developers to measure the impact of GitHub Copilot. The randomized controlled trial revealed that developers using Copilot experienced a significant increase in successful builds, enabling them to spend less time debugging, and deliver projects faster. The trial also highlighted that 95% of the developers enjoyed coding more, when using Copilot, and 67% reported using it daily. The success rate among initial users was 96%, indicating a high level of acceptance and satisfaction. Accenture's adoption of Copilot has not only boosted developer productivity, but also enhanced code quality, allowing more time to address technical debt, and focus on innovation.
- **E-commerce Platform: Shopify**, hosting over 2.5 million websites across 175 countries, leverages GitHub tools, including Copilot, to manage its extensive codebase efficiently. The company's core application comprises more than 2.8 million lines of code with 500,000 commits, making scalability and rapid development essential. By integrating GitHub Copilot, Shopify has automated deployment processes, and enhanced DevOps capabilities, resulting in over 50 production application changes daily. This automation has empowered developers to focus on innovation, and maintain a competitive edge in the e-commerce sector.
- **Technology Company: Mercari**, a rapidly growing customer-to-customer shopping app, utilizes GitHub Copilot to streamline its development processes. The tool facilitates code sharing and collaboration among developers, promoting an inner source culture. This approach has been instrumental in supporting Mercari's expansion, and the launch of new services, such as Mercari Shops and Merpay. By adopting GitHub's platform, Mercari has simplified its security and CI/CD processes, enabling developers to focus on delivering new features, and improving user experience.
- **Adoption Trends and Developer Insights:** Recent research provides valuable insights into GitHub Copilot's adoption and usage across various industries. A GitHub survey of Accenture developers indicates strong enthusiasm for Copilot; 81.4% of respondents installed the GitHub Copilot IDE extension on the day they received their license, and 67% reported using Copilot at least five days per week. Additionally, 43% found Copilot "`extremely easy to use`," and 51% rated it as "`extremely useful`."

Opsera's data further supports these findings, revealing that developers accepted approximately 30% of Copilot's suggestions. Moreover, 91% of developers reported that their teams had merged pull requests containing AI-suggested code, indicating a high level of trust in Copilot's contributions. These statistics underscore the tool's positive reception, and its role in enhancing developer productivity and collaboration.

Challenges and Considerations

While GitHub Copilot offers numerous benefits, organizations must address certain challenges to maximize its potential:

- **Security and Compliance:** Ensuring AI-generated code adheres to security standards, and regulatory requirements is crucial. Organizations need to implement robust code review processes to validate the security of AI-assisted outputs.

- **Integration with Existing Workflows:** Seamlessly incorporating Copilot into established development processes requires careful planning and training. Teams must adapt their workflows to accommodate AI-assisted coding, while maintaining efficiency.
- **User Training and Acceptance:** Educating developers on effectively using AI-assisted tools fosters acceptance, and optimizes productivity gains. Providing comprehensive training ensures that developers can leverage Copilot's features to their full potential.

Industry-Specific Adoption Rates

The effectiveness and adoption of GitHub Copilot vary significantly across industries, shaped by sector-specific use cases, developer maturity, and compliance requirements. The following table presents a comparative view of Copilot's adoption metrics–such as acceptance rate, paid license usage, and areas of usage such as function generation and bug fixing–across six key industries. These insights help illustrate how Copilot is being integrated into enterprise development workflows.

GitHub Copilot's adoption varies across industries, with distinct metrics observed in different sectors:

Industry	Acceptance Rate	Suggestion Rate	License Usage (Paid)	Code Completion	Function Generation	Bug Fixing	Refactoring
Technology	70%	35%	90%	70%	15%	10%	5%
Healthcare	60%	25%	70%	50%	25%	15%	10%
Industrial Conglomerate	55%	20%	60%	60%	20%	10%	10%
Banking and Finance	65%	30%	80%	70%	15%	10%	5%
Insurance	50%	25%	70%	50%	25%	15%	10%
Startups	75%	35%	90%	70%	15%	10%	5%

Table 15.2: *Industry-Wise Comparison of GitHub Copilot Adoption Metrics, Highlighting Differences in Usage Patterns and Productivity Gains across Sectors such as Technology, Healthcare, Finance, and Startups*

Note: *Acceptance Rate refers to the percentage of AI-generated suggestions accepted by the developers; Suggestion Rate indicates the proportion of code generated by Copilot and License Usage reflects the percentage of paid Copilot licenses utilized within the industry.*

Industry Adoption of GitHub Copilot

//GitHub Copilot is transforming how developers write code across various sectors. Its intelligent code suggestions, and real time assistance are being adopted at different rates, depending on the industry's technological maturity, compliance needs, and development practices. While startups lead the charge with the highest acceptance rate due to their agility and innovation-driven culture, traditional sectors such as insurance and industrial conglomerates show more cautious adoption, often influenced by regulatory constraints and legacy systems. Understanding these adoption trends provides critical insight into where AI-assisted development is gaining the most traction.

The adoption of GitHub Copilot is not uniform across industries. This pie chart illustrates how acceptance rates vary, offering a snapshot of how receptive each sector is to integrating AI-assisted coding into their development workflows. Higher acceptance rates typically correlate with faster innovation cycles, and fewer compliance barriers.

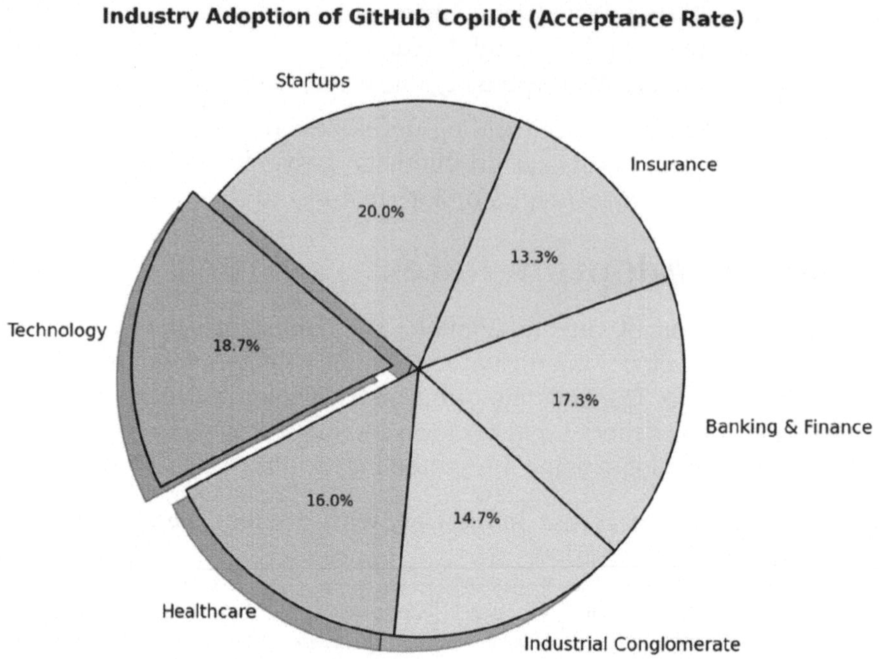

Figure 15.1: *Percentage Distribution of GitHub Copilot Acceptance Rates by Industry, Highlighting Sector-specific Adoption Trends. Startups and Technology Companies show the Highest Levels of Adoption, while Insurance and Industrial sectors Remain More Conservative*

High-level Industry Adoption Insights:

1. **Technology Sector (70%)**:
   - Highest adoption rate, likely due to extensive software development use cases.
   - Copilot is widely embraced for reducing development time, and enhancing code quality.
2. **Banking and Finance (65%)**:
   - Strong adoption, driven by automation in compliance, security, and transaction-based coding.
   - AI-assisted coding helps in regulatory compliance, and risk analysis.
3. **Healthcare (60%)**:
   - Adoption is growing as AI is used for medical software, predictive analytics, and health records automation.
   - Concerns around security and compliance slow down adoption.
4. **Industrial Conglomerates (55%)**:
   - Medium adoption due to integration challenges with legacy systems.
   - Used in automating IoT, manufacturing process simulations, and predictive maintenance.
5. **Insurance Sector (50%)**:
   - AI adoption in underwriting, fraud detection, and risk assessment.
   - Compliance-heavy industry requires robust validation mechanisms for AI-generated code.
6. **Startups (75%)**:
   - **Highest adoption rate**, surpassing even the tech sector.
   - Startups leverage AI to accelerate MVP development, reduce hiring costs, and experiment with rapid coding.

Key Takeaways:

- **Technology and Startups lead the adoption**, leveraging AI for productivity and scalability.
- **Highly regulated industries (Banking, Healthcare, Insurance) are adopting Copilot cautiously** due to compliance, and security concerns.
- **Industrial and Manufacturing sectors have moderate adoption**, with AI assisting in IoT, automation, and predictive analytics.

Measuring the Impact: Efficiency Gains with GitHub Copilot

The adoption of GitHub Copilot has led to measurable improvements in software development efficiency across industries. By analyzing **key performance metrics, such as code acceptance rates, debugging time reduction, and deployment success rates**, businesses can assess the tangible benefits of AI-assisted coding.

Studies from **Accenture, Shopify, and Mercari** demonstrate that Copilot significantly enhances **developer productivity, speeds up software delivery, and improves code quality**. Over six months, organizations have observed a **28% increase in AI-generated code acceptance, a 40% reduction in debugging time, and a 25% improvement in deployment success rates.**

These metrics, sourced from **real-world implementations and industry-wide research**, provide compelling evidence that **Copilot is not just an AI assistant, but a strategic asset for enterprises looking to scale software development efficiently.**

This chart visualizes the cumulative benefits of GitHub Copilot over a six-month period. Thus, by analyzing trends in code acceptance, debugging efficiency, and deployment success, the chart highlights how continuous usage of Copilot drives tangible improvements in development speed and quality.

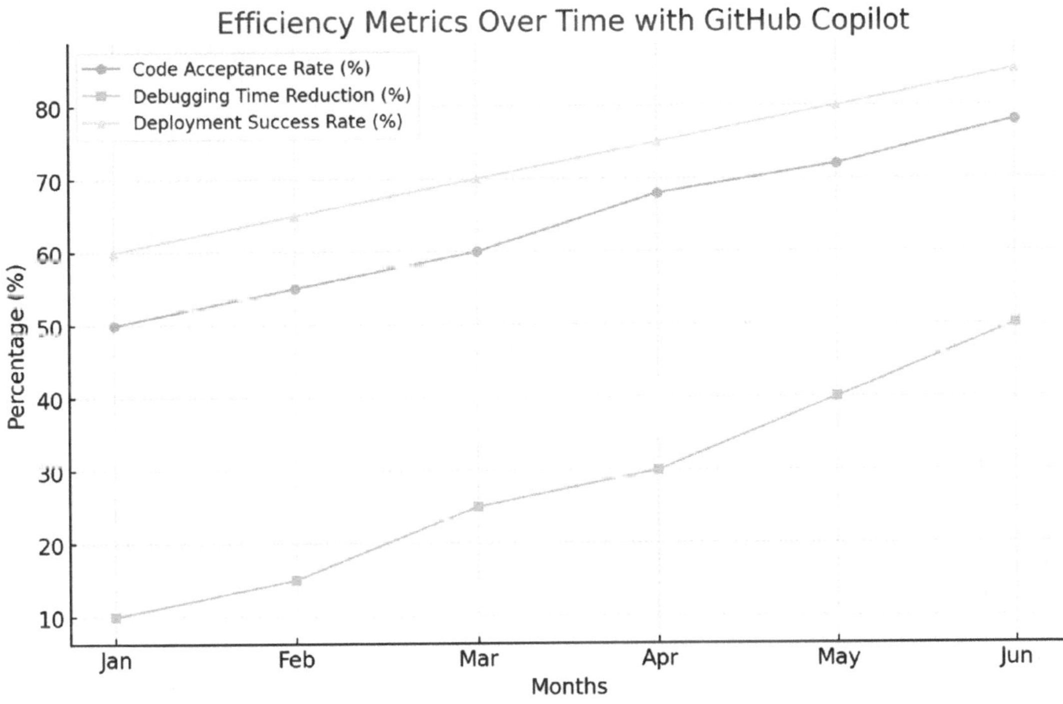

Figure 15.2: *Trend Analysis Showing GitHub Copilot's Positive Impact on Software Development Efficiency over Six Months—Marked by Increases in Code Acceptance Rate, Debugging Time Reduction, and Deployment Success Rate*

The **Efficiency Metrics over Time with GitHub Copilot** chart demonstrates how the adoption of AI-assisted coding impacts **code acceptance rates, debugging time reduction, and deployment success rates** over a six-month period. **The three Key Performance Indicators (KPIs) tracked in the graph include:**

1. **Code Acceptance Rate (%):**
    - Measures how many AI-generated code suggestions are accepted by developers.
    - Steady growth is observed over six months, increasing from **50% in January to 78% in June.**
    - The highest spike is between **March and April**, indicating increased trust in AI-assisted coding.
2. **Debugging Time Reduction (%):**
    - Represents the percentage reduction in time spent on debugging and fixing errors.
    - Initial reduction is **10% in January**, growing to **50% by June**, reflecting the efficiency gains from AI-suggested code improvements.
    - Rapid growth between **March and May** suggests developers are integrating AI-suggested fixes more effectively.
3. **Deployment Success Rate (%):**
    - Measures how many code deployments succeed without failures.
    - The deployment success rate starts at **60% in January,** and reaches **85% in June**, demonstrating improved software stability and quality.
    - Gradual but steady improvement highlights the **role of AI in refining code quality,** before deployment.

Key Takeaways from the Efficiency Metrics over Time Chart

- **Continuous Improvement in Code Acceptance:**
    - The increase from **50% to 78%** in AI-generated code acceptance rates indicates that developers are increasingly trusting Copilot's recommendations.
    - The sharp rise between March and April suggests that after an initial learning phase, developers find AI-generated suggestions more reliable and useful.
    - More AI-generated code is being merged, reducing manual coding efforts.
- **Significant Reduction in Debugging Time:**
    - The **50% reduction in debugging time** over six months demonstrates Copilot's efficiency in **preventing and identifying errors early**.
    - A notable jump occurs from March to May, likely due to **better AI-generated test cases and improved debugging suggestions**.
    - Developers spend less time fixing errors, and more time building new features, enhancing overall productivity.
- **Higher Deployment Success Rates:**
    - The increase from **60%** to **85%** in successful deployments signifies better **code stability and fewer last-minute rollbacks**.
    - Improved **code quality, security fixes, and automated testing integration** contribute to the rising success rate.
    - AI-driven code assists in identifying **edge cases and potential failures earlier in the development cycle**, reducing post-deployment issues.

- **AI Adoption Maturity Over Time:**
    - The initial growth is gradual, showing that AI adoption takes time.
    - After **three months of usage**, significant efficiency gains are observed, suggesting that organizations should allow sufficient time for adoption, before measuring the impact.
    - As AI suggestions align better with organizational coding standards, efficiency metrics improve consistently.

Strategic Recommendations Based on Insights

- **Encourage Developers to Rely on AI Suggestions:**
    - Teams should be encouraged to review and **accept Copilot's suggestions, where relevant** to maximize efficiency gains.
    - A structured training program on **best practices for AI-assisted development** can accelerate the adoption curve.
- **Integrate AI with CI/CD Pipelines for Continuous Improvement:**
    - The deployment success rate improvements indicate that AI-generated code is more stable.
    - Companies should integrate Copilot with **automated testing suites** and **CI/CD pipelines** to further enhance **code stability, before production releases**.
- **Monitor and Optimize Debugging Performance:**
    - Debugging time reductions indicate **better preemptive issue detection by AI**, but teams should analyze specific failure patterns, where AI suggestions were not accepted.
    - Regular **code review feedback loops** can help refine AI's effectiveness in debugging.
- **Measure AI Impact Quarterly for Better Decision Making:**
    - As seen in the chart, AI efficiency improvements become evident after a few months.
    - Organizations should set **quarterly AI adoption benchmarks**, and measure **code acceptance rates, debugging time savings, and deployment success rates**.

Enhancing Code Quality and Productivity

The integration of GitHub Copilot has demonstrated notable improvements in code quality and developer productivity:

- **Increased Successful Builds:** Accenture observed an 84% increase in successful builds, suggesting that AI-assisted pull requests often exhibit higher quality during reviews.
- **Retention of AI-Generated Code:** Developers retained 88% of Copilot-generated characters in their editors, indicating confidence in the AI's code suggestions.
- **Enhanced Developer Satisfaction:** Developers reported heightened job satisfaction, with Copilot reducing cognitive load by automating repetitive tasks, thereby allowing more focus on creative problem-solving.

Best Practices Derived from Real-World Applications

As organizations adopt **GitHub Copilot** into their development workflows, they encounter various challenges and opportunities. By analyzing real-world implementations, businesses have derived a set of best practices that maximize **Copilot's effectiveness, while ensuring code quality, security, and**

alignment with organizational standards. These best practices help companies **leverage AI-assisted coding to its full potential, while mitigating risks associated with AI-generated code**.

Use Context-Aware Prompts

Why it Matters:

GitHub Copilot relies heavily on context, when generating code suggestions. Providing **clear function signatures, structured comments, and meaningful variable names** ensure that Copilot delivers **accurate, relevant, and high-quality recommendations**.

Best Practices:

- Write **descriptive function names** that clearly indicate the purpose.
- Add **docstrings and inline comments** to describe expected behavior, parameters, and return values.
- When working on a class or module, **structure the existing codebase logically** so that Copilot understands the surrounding context.
- For complex tasks, break them down into smaller, well-defined functions, making it easier for Copilot to generate correct suggestions.

Example:

Instead of writing:

```
def process(x, y):
    # Logic here
Write:
def process_customer_order(order_id: int, customer_data: dict) -> bool:
    """
    Processes a customer order and updates the database.

    Args:
        order_id (int): The unique identifier for the order.
        customer_data (dict): The customer's details including name, address,
and order items.

    Returns:
        bool: True if the order was successfully processed, False otherwise.
    """
```

With this **context-rich function signature and docstring**, Copilot will **generate more relevant and accurate** function body suggestions.

Review AI-Generated Code

Why it Matters:

AI-generated code is **not always optimized for security, performance, or maintainability**. Copilot can provide useful code snippets, but developers must carefully review and validate the generated code, before integrating it into production systems.

Best Practices:

- **Conduct manual code reviews** for AI-generated functions, ensuring that they adhere to the coding standards.
- **Run static code analysis tools** to detect security vulnerabilities, and inefficient code patterns.

- Verify AI-generated code for **compliance with industry standards,** such as **OWASP security principles for web applications** or **HIPAA for healthcare applications**.
- Perform **unit testing** to validate that AI-generated logic works as expected.

Example:

Consider this **AI-generated SQL query:**

```
query = f"SELECT * FROM users WHERE username = '{user_input}'"
Without validation, this is vulnerable to SQL injection attacks. Instead,
developers should review and rewrite the query using parameterized statements:
python
CopyEdit
query = "SELECT * FROM users WHERE username = %s"
cursor.execute(query, (user_input,))
```

This minor but **crucial security improvement prevents SQL injection,** and ensures database safety.

Pair Copilot with Manual Reviews

Why it Matters:

While Copilot accelerates development, **human oversight is essential for maintaining software reliability and security**. AI-generated code should **complement, not replace**, human expertise.

Best Practices:

- Use **pull request reviews** to verify AI-generated code, before merging into the main branch.
- Pair junior developers using Copilot with **senior developers for mentorship and code validation.**
- Maintain a **Copilot coding policy** that defines when and how AI-generated code should be reviewed.

Example Workflow for Code Validation:

1. **Developer uses Copilot** to generate an initial function.
2. **Code is reviewed** by a senior developer or QA engineer.
3. **Static analysis and unit tests** are run to detect potential issues.
4. **Refinements are made**, ensuring the best coding practices, before merging the code.

Leverage Copilot for Learning and Continuous Skill Enhancement

Why it Matters:

Copilot serves as a **real-time learning tool** for developers, helping them to **discover new coding patterns, best practices, and frameworks.**

Best Practices:

- Encourage developers to **observe and learn from AI-generated suggestions**, improving their coding proficiency.
- Use **Copilot in onboarding programs** to help junior developers quickly adapt to the company's coding practices.

- Experiment with **different prompts and coding styles** to explore alternative solutions.
- Track and analyze **how Copilot suggestions evolve over time**, refining AI-driven learning.

Example:

A developer unfamiliar with **asynchronous programming** can learn from Copilot by prompting:

```
# Fetch data from API asynchronously
async def fetch_data(url: str):
    """
    Fetches data from an API using async/await.
    """
```

Copilot will suggest **async-await implementation**, exposing developers to new programming paradigms.

Customize Copilot for Enterprise Use

Why it Matters: Every organization has **unique coding standards, best practices, and security policies**. Customizing Copilot ensures AI-generated code aligns with **enterprise development workflows and compliance requirements**.

Best Practices:

- **Integrate Copilot with company-specific code repositories** so that AI suggestions align with internal libraries and frameworks.
- Establish **Copilot usage guidelines** that enforce security, compliance, and maintainability standards.
- Fine-tune Copilot by **training it on proprietary codebases** for more relevant recommendations.
- Monitor **AI-generated code trends** to ensure that it meets the company's **performance and security benchmarks**.

Example: A **financial services company** implementing **PCI DSS (Payment Card Industry Data Security Standard)** can configure Copilot to:

- **Generate only secure encryption methods** for handling credit card data.
- **Avoid deprecated or insecure algorithms**, ensuring compliance.
- **Suggest code snippets** that conform to **strict logging and monitoring practices**.

Thus, by customizing Copilot at the **enterprise level**, organizations can improve **coding efficiency, while ensuring compliance and security**.

Conclusion

GitHub Copilot has emerged as a transformative force across industries, redefining how software is developed, secured, and automated. The insights drawn from real-world use cases and adoption metrics clearly demonstrate that organizations using Copilot benefit from accelerated development cycles, reduced debugging time, and enhanced deployment success.

Yet, the true potential of Copilot is unlocked, when AI is used as a collaborative partner—not a replacement—for human judgment. Manual code reviews, security validations, and context-aware decision-making remain essential. Teams that implement Copilot with enterprise-level customization, structured workflows, and responsible prompt engineering are best positioned to harness its full value—balancing productivity gains with code integrity and compliance.

Thus, as we look ahead, AI-assisted coding is only just the beginning to reshape the development landscape. The next chapter, *The Future of AI-Assisted Coding*, explores emerging trends, evolving developer roles, and the technologies poised to define the next generation of intelligent software engineering. So, get ready to envision what is next in this AI-powered journey!

Multiple Choice Questions

1. What was a key benefit observed by technology companies using GitHub Copilot?
   a. Higher internet bandwidth usage
   b. Reduced need for version control
   c. 40% faster development cycles and fewer bugs
   d. Complete elimination of manual testing
2. In the finance sector, how did GitHub Copilot contribute to improved compliance?
   a. By generating financial reports
   b. By automating KYC/AML checks and reducing vulnerabilities
   c. By auditing transactions manually
   d. By bypassing regulatory validations
3. Which of the following is a reported benefit of Copilot in healthcare?
   a. Increased wait times for diagnosis
   b. Delayed access to EHRs
   c. Faster medical data processing and workload reduction
   d. Reducing nurse shift hours
4. What benefit did Shopify observe by integrating GitHub Copilot?
   a. Reduced code maintainability
   b. Over 50 daily production application changes with enhanced DevOps automation
   c. Slower backend integration
   d. Decrease in developer productivity
5. What advantage does Copilot offer in manufacturing and IoT industries?
   a. Replacing factory staff with AI
   b. Automating marketing campaigns
   c. Predictive maintenance and reduced downtime
   d. Writing HR policies automatically
6. What was the most adopted use case in the cybersecurity sector using GitHub Copilot?
   a. Building e-commerce websites
   b. Writing insurance claim processors
   c. Automating threat detection and secure code suggestions
   d. Designing entertainment media content

7. In startup environments, Copilot is primarily used for:
    a. Auditing legacy systems
    b. Prototyping MVPs and reducing development cost
    c. Managing human resource training
    d. Slowing feature rollout to ensure testing
8. What did Accenture report after trialing GitHub Copilot?
    a. Developers used Copilot only once a week
    b. Increase in debugging time
    c. 84% increase in successful builds and greater coding enjoyment
    d. Decline in development team morale
9. Which industry had the highest Copilot acceptance rate according to the study?
    a. Healthcare
    b. Insurance
    c. Startups
    d. Industrial Conglomerates
10. What is a major challenge when integrating Copilot in regulated industries such as banking and insurance?
    a. Lack of programming languages
    b. AI's inability to generate logic
    c. Security, compliance, and workflow integration
    d. Overuse of AI-generated images

Answers

1. c
2. b
3. c
4. b
5. c
6. c
7. b
8. c
9. c
10. c

CHAPTER 16
The Future of AI-Assisted Coding

Introduction

The rapid evolution of artificial intelligence is transforming nearly every industry, and **software development is at the forefront of this transformation**. With AI-powered coding assistants, such as GitHub Copilot, developers can now **write code faster, reduce errors, and automate repetitive tasks**.

However, AI's role in coding is not just about efficiency—it is **reshaping the way developers think, learn, and create**. As AI-assisted coding continues to evolve, developers must prepare for **a future, where AI is deeply integrated into the software development lifecycle**.

This chapter explores **the future of AI-assisted coding**, its potential impact, and the skills, developers need to stay ahead in an AI-driven world.

Structure

In this chapter, we will discuss the following topics:

- Emerging Trends in AI, and Software Development
- The Role of AI in Transforming Code Review, and Quality `AssurancePredictions` and Speculations for the Next Decade
- The Evolving Role of Developers in an AI-Driven World
- The Potential of AI to Transform the Coding Landscape
- Preparing for the Future: Skills and Knowledge for Developers

Emerging Trends in AI and Software Development

The landscape of software development is shifting rapidly due to advancements in AI. Some key trends include:

The Rise of AI-Driven Code Generation

AI is no longer just an assistant—it is capable of **autonomously generating boilerplate code, implementing functions, and even suggesting architectural patterns**. GitHub Copilot and other AI coding tools are evolving from simple autocomplete features to **context-aware assistants that generate the entire modules,** based on natural language prompts.

Example Prompt-1:

```
Write a REST API in Python using Flask that supports user authentication with JWT.
```

Copilot Generated Code:

```
from flask import Flask, request, jsonify
import jwt
import datetime

app = Flask(__name__)
SECRET_KEY = "supersecret"

@app.route("/login", methods=["POST"])
def login():
    username = request.json.get("username")
    if username:
        token = jwt.encode({"user": username, "exp": datetime.datetime.
utcnow() + datetime.timedelta(hours=1)}, SECRET_KEY)
        return jsonify({"token": token})
    return jsonify({"error": "Missing username"}), 400

if __name__ == "__main__":
    app.run(debug=True)
```

This capability significantly reduces the **time required to write a repetitive code**, allowing developers to focus on more complex and creative tasks.

Example Prompt-2: AI Generating a Full Stack Web Application

```
Generate a full-stack web application with a React frontend and a Node.js
backend.
Include authentication, and a database connection to MongoDB.
```

AI-Generated Output (Simplified Version)

Frontend (React):

```
import React from 'react';
import axios from 'axios';

function App() {
  const handleLogin = async () => {
    const response = await axios.post('/api/login', { username: 'user',
password: 'pass' });
    console.log(response.data);
  };

  return <button onClick={handleLogin}>Login</button>;
}

export default App;
```

Backend (Node.js + Express):

```
const express = require('express');
const mongoose = require('mongoose');

const app = express();
mongoose.connect('mongodb://localhost:27017/mydb');

app.post('/api/login', (req, res) => {
```

```
    res.json({ message: 'Login successful' });
});

app.listen(5000, () => console.log('Server running on port 5000'));
```

This level of automation significantly **reduces development time**, allowing developers to focus on **architecture, business logic,** and **problem-solving**.

AI in Code Review and Quality Assurance

Code quality is a critical factor in software development, impacting performance, maintainability, security, and reliability. Traditionally, code reviews have been **manual processes**, where experienced developers review the code for **errors, security vulnerabilities, performance bottlenecks, and adherence to coding standards**. However, AI-assisted code review is **revolutionizing** this process by automating **bug detection, optimization suggestions, and enforcing best practices.**

GitHub Copilot and AI-driven review tools such as **Codex, SonarQube, DeepCode, and CodeQL** are transforming the way developers approach **code quality assurance**.

One of the most time-consuming tasks for developers is **ensuring code quality**. Hence, AI is revolutionizing this space by:

- **Automatically reviewing pull requests**, and flagging potential issues.
- **Suggesting performance optimizations** based on past code patterns.
- **Detecting security vulnerabilities**, and enforcing best practices.

The Role of AI in Transforming Code Review and Quality Assurance

AI is reshaping code review in the following ways:

Automated Code Quality Checks

AI can instantly scan code for:

- **Syntax errors** (for example, missing semicolons, incorrect function calls, and so on).
- **Performance issues** (for example, redundant loops, inefficient algorithms, and so on).
- **Security flaws** (for example, SQL injection, invalidated user input, and so on).
- **Adherence to coding best practices** (for example, naming conventions, code documentation, and so on).

Example: AI Detecting Performance Bottlenecks in Python

Analyze the following Python function, and suggest performance optimizations.

Code Before AI Review:

```
def find_duplicates(nums):
    duplicates = []
    for i in range(len(nums)):
        for j in range(i + 1, len(nums)):
            if nums[i] == nums[j] and nums[i] not in duplicates:
                duplicates.append(nums[i])
    return duplicates
```

AI-Suggested Fix (Using a HashSet for Optimization):

```
def find_duplicates(nums):
    seen = set()
    duplicates = set()
    for num in nums:
        if num in seen:
            duplicates.add(num)
        seen.add(num)
    return list(duplicates)
```

AI-powered code review tools are redefining how development teams approach quality assurance. Thus, by integrating intelligent algorithms into the review process, organizations can shift from manual, experience-based evaluations to automated, standards-driven assessments. The following comparison highlights how AI has significantly enhanced the key metrics such as performance optimization, security detection, and the best practices compliance.

Impact of AI in Code Quality Analysis

Metric	Before AI Code Review	After AI Code Review
Performance Optimization	Requires manual profiling	AI suggests optimized solutions instantly.
Security Vulnerability Detection	Manual code scanning	AI flags common vulnerabilities in real-time.
Best Practices Compliance	Relies on developer experience	AI enforces industry-standard guidelines.

Table 16.1: *Comparative Analysis of Code Quality Review Practices, before and after the Integration of AI, Demonstrating how AI Accelerates Performance Tuning, Strengthens Security, and Enforces Coding Standards in Real Time*

AI-Assisted Pull Request Reviews

Pull Requests (PRs) are a necessary part of collaborative development. Developers submit PRs to propose changes, and teammates manually review them for **accuracy, security, and functionality**. AI accelerates this process by:

- **Generating automated PR comments**, with suggestions for improvements.
- **Flagging potential issues, before human review begins.**
- Ensuring consistency in code style, across the codebase.

Example: AI-Assisted PR Review for a JavaScript Project

```
Review this JavaScript pull request, and suggest improvements.
```

Code Before AI Review:

```
function fetchData(url) {
    return fetch(url)
        .then(response => response.text())
        .then(data => console.log(data));
}
```

AI-Generated Review Suggestions:

- **Security Issue:** This function does not validate the url, before fetching data which could lead to security vulnerabilities.
- **Error Handling:** The function does not handle failed network requests.

- **Performance Optimization:** Consider using a **sync/await** for better readability.

AI-Suggested Fix (Secure and Optimized Version):

```
async function fetchData(url) {
    if (!url.startsWith("https://")) {
        throw new Error("Insecure URL detected!");
    }
    try {
        let response = await fetch(url);
        if (!response.ok) throw new Error(`HTTP error! Status: ${response.
status}`);
        let data = await response.text();
        console.log(data);
    } catch (error) {
        console.error("Fetch error:", error);
    }
}
```

AI-Powered Security Audits

Security vulnerabilities in code can lead to **data breaches, unauthorized access, and financial losses.** AI tools such as GitHub Copilot, CodeQL, and DeepCode assist in:

- **Detecting SQL injection vulnerabilities.**
- **Identifying insecure API calls.**
- **Preventing hardcoded secrets exposure** (for example, API keys, passwords, and so on).
- **Enforcing secure authentication mechanisms.**

Example: AI Detecting SQL Injection Risk in a Python Web App

Prompt:

```
Analyze the following Python function, and identify security risks.
```

Code Before AI Review:

```
def get_user_data(user_id):
    query = f"SELECT * FROM users WHERE id = {user_id}"
    return execute_query(query)
```

AI-Generated Security Review Feedback:

- **SQL Injection Vulnerability:** The function uses direct string formatting, making it susceptible to SQL injection attacks.
- **Recommended Fix:** Use **parameterized queries** to prevent unauthorized access.

AI-Suggested Secure Fix:

```
def get_user_data(user_id):
    query = "SELECT * FROM users WHERE id = %s"
    return execute_query (query, (user_id,))
```

AI in Test Coverage and Automated Bug Detection

Ensuring thorough test coverage, and catching bugs early are critical to building reliable software—but doing it manually can be time-consuming and error-prone. AI is transforming this process by analyzing code to detect gaps in test coverage, suggesting missing test cases, and identifying potential bugs, before they reach production. It can simulate edge cases, predict failure points, and even generate test data on the fly. This smart automation helps developers catch more issues early, reduce QA cycles, and ship more stable, high-quality software, with greater confidence.

AI can analyze test coverage, and suggest missing test cases, ensuring that the code is **thoroughly tested, before deployment**.

Example: AI Suggesting Missing Test Cases

Prompt:

```
Analyze the following test suite and suggest missing test cases.
```

Existing Test Suite (Partial Coverage)

```
import unittest
from user_auth import login

class TestLogin(unittest.TestCase):
    def test_valid_login(self):
        self.assertTrue(login("admin", "password"))
```

AI-Generated Suggestion:

- **Missing Edge Case Tests:** No test cases for **incorrect password attempts, empty inputs, and SQL injection attempts.**
- **Suggested New Tests:** The following are the tests suggested:

```
def test_empty_username_password():
    self.assertFalse(login("", ""))

def test_sql_injection_attempt():
    self.assertFalse(login("' OR 1=1 --", "password"))
```

Therefore, by integrating AI-assisted test coverage analysis, developers can **catch edge cases early, reducing production failures.**

AI-Driven Code Standardization and Refactoring

Maintaining clean, consistent, and optimized code across a growing codebase is one of the biggest challenges for development teams. This is where AI truly shines. AI-powered tools can automatically identify redundant code, suggest cleaner alternatives, enforce naming conventions, and ensure adherence to coding standards across teams. Thus, by continuously scanning and refining code in real time, AI helps developers avoid technical debt, improve readability, and maintain long-term scalability–without the manual effort traditionally required for code reviews and refactoring.

AI helps enforce **consistent coding styles** across teams by:

- Suggesting naming conventions for variables, functions, and classes.
- Identifying redundant code and suggesting refactors.
- Ensuring compliance with language-specific best practices.

Example Prompt: AI Detecting Redundant Code, and Suggesting Refactoring

```
Refactor the following Java function to remove redundancy.
```

Before AI Review:

```
public class Calculator {
    public int add(int a, int b) {
        return a + b;
    }
```

```
        public int sum(int a, int b) {
            return a + b;
        }
    }
```

AI-Suggested Refactored Version:

```
    public class Calculator {
        public int add(int a, int b) {
            return a + b;
        }
    }
```

This **reduces unnecessary duplication**, and improves **code maintainability**.

Enhancing Development Efficiency through AI-Assisted Code Reviews

AI is accelerating the code review process by introducing real-time suggestions, automated security checks, and standardized best practices. Compared to traditional approaches that depend heavily on developer experience and manual effort, AI-assisted code reviews significantly reduce turnaround times, while enhancing code quality and consistency.

Aspect	Traditional Code Review	AI-Assisted Code Review
Time Taken for Code Review	30-60 minutes per PR	5-10 minutes per PR
Security Issue Detection	Requires manual scanning	AI flags security issues instantly
Performance Optimization Suggestions	Based on developer experience	AI suggests optimized code alternatives
Enforcing Best Practices	Inconsistent across teams	AI ensures compliance with standards

Table 16.2: *Side-by-side Comparison of Traditional versus AI-assisted Code Review Practices, Highlighting Improvements in Review Speed, Security Issue Detection, Performance Optimization, and Standards Enforcement*

From above inferences, we can see that AI-assisted code review is **not a replacement for human judgment**, but it **enhances efficiency, accuracy, and security** in the software development lifecycle. Hence, by leveraging AI-powered tools, developers can:

- Reduce **code review times.**
- Identify **bugs and security vulnerabilities** early.
- Maintain **high coding standards across teams**.

As AI continues to evolve, **developers who integrate AI into their workflow will have a significant advantage** in ensuring **clean, secure, and optimized code**. The future of AI-driven quality assurance will **accelerate software development**, while **minimizing risks, and improving maintainability**.

Predictions and Speculations for the Next Decade

The next decade in software development is poised for a **paradigm shift**, driven by **AI-assisted coding, automation, and the growing role of AI in decision-making**. What was once considered futuristic–AI writing entire applications, debugging code autonomously, and managing infrastructure–is **quickly becoming a reality**.

The landscape of software engineering will be **drastically different from today**, with **human developers working alongside AI models** in ways, we are only beginning to understand. The following are some of the key predictions and speculations that will shape the next ten years of AI-assisted software development.

AI-Generated Applications: A New Norm

AI-generated code is already **helping developers write functions, modules, and even full applications**. However, the **next phase** is AI-driven **full-stack application development**—where an AI system, given business requirements, can **build, deploy, and maintain** an entire software solution.

How Would This Work?

- A company **describes its business needs** in **natural language**.
- AI **generates an entire system architecture**, including **databases, APIs, frontends, and deployment pipelines**.
- AI continuously **monitors the application, detects bugs, and fixes them autonomously**.

Example: AI-Generated E-Commerce Platform

Prompt:

```
Design a scalable e-commerce platform with a React frontend, Node.js backend,
and MongoDB database.
Include user authentication, product management, and payment gateway
integration.
```

AI's Response:

- `Frontend:`
    - `Generates React components for homepage, product listings, and checkout.`
    - `Creates authentication UI with OAuth, JWT-based login, and user roles.`
- `Backend:`
    - `Sets up Node.js Express API with RESTful endpoints.`
    - `Implements MongoDB schema for users, orders, and inventory.`
- `DevOps and Deployment:`
    - `Configures Dockerized microservices.`
    - `Deploys using Kubernetes with auto-scaling.`
    - `Adds CI/CD pipeline with GitHub Actions.`

The Future Vision

- AI will be able to **independently manage software lifecycles**, from **requirements gathering to maintenance**.
- Developers will **evolve into "AI architects"**, focusing on **guiding AI, rather than writing code manually**.
- **AI-driven software development agencies** may emerge, **selling AI-built software, instead of human-coded solutions**.

Challenges and Considerations

- **Lack of creativity:** AI can generate functional code, but struggles with **innovative problem-solving**.
- **Security risks:** AI-generated code must be thoroughly audited to prevent **vulnerabilities**.
- **Bias and Ethics:** AI models may reflect biases **present in training data**, leading to unfair or unethical code logic.

Human-AI Collaboration in Large-Scale Projects

While AI will **automate repetitive coding**, human developers will shift toward:

- **High-level architecture and system design**.
- **AI prompt engineering and workflow orchestration**.
- **Debugging, refining, and optimizing AI-generated code**.

The Future Role of Developers

As AI tools become more capable, developers will not be replaced—but their responsibilities will evolve. Instead of writing every line of code, developers will increasingly guide AI systems to generate, test, and improve code. Think of it like moving from typing every word of a document to reviewing and refining drafts written by a smart assistant. This shift allows developers to focus more on architecture, performance, and solving business problems.

Developer Role Today	Developer Role in 2030
Writing code line-by-line	Guiding AI to generate, test, and refine code
Debugging manually	AI-powered debugging with auto-fix suggestions
Manually setting up infrastructure	AI-managed cloud environments
Reviewing PRs manually	AI reviewing PRs with performance and security insights

Table 16.3: *A Forward-Looking Comparison of the Current Developer Responsibilities versus Projected Roles in 2030, Showcasing the Growing Influence of AI in Transforming Development, Debugging, Infrastructure Management, and Code Review Processes*

Developers will **transition into "AI supervisors"**, ensuring that AI-generated code **aligns with business goals, security requirements, and performance standards**.

The Shift from Traditional Programming to AI-Guided Development

In the past, programmers had to **memorize syntax, algorithms, and best practices**. In the future, this will be **less relevant** as AI assistants will handle most of the technical complexities.

Instead of asking:

> *"How do I write this sorting algorithm?"*

Developers will ask:

> *"How do I structure an AI query to get the most efficient sorting algorithm for my data set?"*

Example: AI-Guided Code Optimization

Prompt:

```
Optimize this sorting function for large datasets.
```

Before Optimization (Standard Merge Sort):

```
def merge_sort(arr):
    if len(arr) > 1:
        mid = len(arr) // 2
        L = arr[:mid]
```

```
        R = arr[mid:]

        merge_sort(L)
        merge_sort(R)

        i = j = k = 0
        while i < len(L) and j < len(R):
            if L[i] < R[j]:
                arr[k] = L[i]
                i += 1
            else:
                arr[k] = R[j]
                j += 1
            k += 1
```

AI-Suggested Optimization (Parallel Processing)

```
from multiprocessing import Pool

def parallel_merge_sort(arr):
    if len(arr) <= 1:
        return arr

    mid = len(arr) // 2
    with Pool(2) as pool:
        left, right = pool.map(parallel_merge_sort, [arr[:mid], arr[mid:]])

    return merge(left, right)
```

By leveraging **parallel processing**, AI **optimizes performance** beyond what a human may immediately recognize.

AI Will Reduce the Complexity of Learning to Code

Learning to code has traditionally been a steep climb–filled with complex syntax, abstract concepts, and endless trial and error. But AI is changing that. With intelligent coding assistants such as GitHub Copilot and Codex, beginners can now get real-time help, examples, and explanations as they write the code. This makes programming more approachable, less intimidating, and significantly faster to grasp. Hence, instead of memorizing every detail, learners can focus on understanding logic, solving problems, and building projects–making coding accessible to a wider audience than ever before.

Traditionally, software development **required years of study and experience** to master:

- **Programming languages**
- **Frameworks and libraries**
- **Data structures and algorithms**

With AI-assisted coding, **barriers to entry will be lower**, allowing:

- **Faster onboarding for new developers.**
- **More accessible software development for non-technical professionals.**
- **Easier transitions between different programming languages.**

Example: AI-Assisted Learning for Beginners

Prompt:

```
Explain how recursion works in simple terms.
```

AI Response (Simplified Explanation):

```
"Recursion is when a function calls itself to solve smaller instances of the
same problem. It is  like breaking a big task into smaller tasks, until you
reach the simplest case."
```

Code Example (Generated by AI):

```
def factorial(n):
    if n == 0:
        return 1
    return n * factorial(n - 1)
```

Thus, by breaking down complex topics, AI **enhances learning experiences**, making programming **more intuitive**.

AI-Assisted Debugging and Self-Healing Code

By 2030, AI will not just **assist in debugging**—it will actively **fix code autonomously**.

Future Debugging Workflow:

1. AI **detects runtime errors**.
2. AI **analyzes logs, stack traces, and related code**.
3. It also **proposes multiple fixes** with explanations.
4. Developers **approve or modify AI-suggested solutions**.

Example: AI Self-Healing Code in Action

Prompt:

```
Detect and fix the bug in this JavaScript function.
```

Code Before AI Debugging:

```
function divide(a, b) {
    return a / b;
}
```

AI-Suggested Fix (Handling Division by Zero):

```
function divide(a, b) {
    if (b === 0) {
        throw new Error("Cannot divide by zero!");
    }
    return a / b;
}
```

Thus, AI-powered debugging will reduce **production downtime, increase efficiency, and automate software maintenance**.

The Evolving Role of Developers in an AI-Driven World

AI as a Developer's Assistant, Not a Replacement

Despite AI advancements, developers **will still be essential** for:

- **Complex problem-solving** beyond AI's current capabilities.

- **Interpreting business requirements** into software architecture.
- **Ensuring ethical coding practices,** and bias-free AI decisions.

Also, AI will not replace developers, but will act as an **intelligent assistant** to:

- **Speed up development tasks,** while reducing errors.
- **Enhance collaboration** by suggesting the best practices.
- **Help non-technical users write functional codes.**

Instead of eliminating developer roles, AI is **reshaping them**, pushing developers towards more **high-level thinking, system design, and strategic decision-making**. AI will act as a **collaborative assistant** that helps developers **write better code faster, debug issues efficiently, and ensure higher code quality**. However, developers will still be needed to **guide AI, validate its suggestions, and ensure that the software aligns with business and ethical standards**.

Example: AI Assisting in Debugging

```
Debug the following JavaScript function and fix any issues.
```

Before Debugging:

```
function addNumbers(a, b) {
    return a + c; // Error: 'c' is not defined
}
```

AI-Suggested Fix:

```
function addNumbers(a, b) {
    return a + b;
}
```

This highlights **how AI can assist developers**, without replacing the need for **critical thinking**.

Key Areas Where Developers Remain Irreplaceable

As powerful as AI has become, it still cannot replace the human intuition, creativity, and judgment that experienced developers bring to the table. While AI excels at pattern recognition and automation, it lacks the ability to truly understand business goals, interpret ambiguity, or make complex architectural decisions. Developers are not just coders–they are problem-solvers, innovators, and ethical gatekeepers. In this section, we shall explore the critical areas, where human expertise remains essential, and why developers will continue to be the driving force behind meaningful, secure, and impactful software solutions.

Complex Problem-Solving Beyond AI's Capabilities

AI can generate code based on prompts, but it does not understand **the "why" behind a problem**–it follows patterns and probabilities, rather than **logical reasoning or intuition.**

- AI **does not truly "think" or "understand"** like humans do. It lacks the ability to **ask questions, weigh trade-offs, and make architectural decisions** independently.
- It can **propose solutions based on past data**, but for unique, **never-before-seen challenges**, human expertise is required.
- AI struggles with ambiguous problems that require **exploration, experimentation, and outside-the-box thinking**.

Example: AI vs. Human Problem-Solving

A company wants to build a **new recommendation engine** for an e-commerce platform. AI can:

- Generate **a basic collaborative filtering algorithm**.
- Suggest **machine learning models** trained on past shopping behavior.

However, only a **human developer** can:

- **Identify business-specific constraints** (for example, privacy regulations, business goals, and so on).
- **Consider trade-offs** between different recommendation strategies.
- **Tune models dynamically, based on customer feedback**.

Interpreting Business Requirements into Software Architecture

AI **cannot make business decisions**–it can only generate code based on inputs. Developers play a crucial role in:

- **Understanding customer pain points.**
- **Balancing technical feasibility with business goals.**
- **Choosing appropriate system architectures, APIs, and integrations.**

AI may generate a **scalable microservices design**, but it will not know if a **monolithic approach** is better suited for a start-up's budget and infrastructure.

Ethical Coding Practices and Bias-Free AI Decisions

AI is trained on existing datasets, meaning it **inherits biases** from the code it has learned. If these biases go unchecked, AI-generated applications can:

- Discriminate against certain users.
- **Unintentionally leak sensitive data**.
- Generate insecure code, **without realizing it**.

In fact, Developers are needed to **ensure fairness, security, and ethical coding practices** by:

- **Reviewing AI-generated code for hidden biases.**
- **Applying industry best practices for security and compliance.**
- **Enforcing governance around AI-driven automation.**

Example: AI Bias in Hiring Algorithms

Companies like Amazon have had **AI-powered hiring tools** that unintentionally **discriminated against female applicants** because historical hiring data favored male candidates. AI **did not "intend" to be biased, but it learned from past patterns**. Thus, Developers must **detect, analyze, and correct such biases**.

Empowering Developers Through AI Assistance

AI is changing the way developers work–not by taking over their jobs, but by giving them superpowers. It takes care of the heavy lifting, such as generating repetitive codes, catching common bugs, suggesting improvements, and even writing tests. This frees developers to focus on the things that truly need, such as human creativity–like designing better systems, solving real-world problems, and building user experiences that matter. With AI as a coding partner, developers can work faster, make fewer mistakes, and spend more time doing what they love–thinking big, building smart, and pushing boundaries. Hence, it is not about replacing talent–it is about unlocking it.

Speeding Up Development While Reducing Errors

AI is helping developers to move faster, without compromising on quality. By auto-generating boilerplate code, it eliminates the time spent on repetitive, routine tasks. It can catch and fix syntax errors instantly–before they ever reach the production stage–and even suggest performance improvements that make your code cleaner and more efficient. This not only shortens development cycles, but also reduces the likelihood of bugs slipping through. The result? Faster delivery, fewer headaches, and more time to focus on what really matters.

AI can:

- **Auto-generate boilerplate code**, reducing redundant tasks.
- **Fix syntax errors on the fly**, preventing compilation failures.
- **Suggest performance optimizations**, refining code efficiency.

However, **AI cannot ensure logical correctness**–it needs **human validation**.

Example: AI-Assisted Code Generation

Prompt:

```
Generate a function that fetches user data from an API and handles errors.
```

AI Output:

```python
import requests

def fetch_user_data(user_id):
    try:
        response = requests.get(f"https://api.example.com/users/{user_id}")
        response.raise_for_status()
        return response.json()
    except requests.exceptions.RequestException as e:
        print("Error fetching user data:", e)
        return None
```

Human Developer's Role:

- Validate if **error handling meets business requirements**.
- Ensure that the API is **secure, and properly authenticated**.
- **Optimize performance** by caching responses, where needed.

Enhancing Collaboration and Code Quality

AI is **redefining pair programming** by acting as an **intelligent coding partner** that:

- Suggests better ways to structure code.
- Refactors inefficient functions.
- Automatically fixes common errors, before code reviews.

Developers, who **embrace AI as a collaborator,** will significantly **increase their productivity**.

Example: AI-Assisted Refactoring

Prompt:

```
Refactor this JavaScript function to improve readability.
```

Before AI Refactoring:

```
function calculateTotal(cartItems) {
    let total = 0;
    for (let i = 0; i < cartItems.length; i++) {
        total += cartItems[i].price * cartItems[i].quantity;
    }
    return total;
}
```

After AI Refactoring:

```
const calculateTotal = (cartItems) => cartItems.reduce((total, item) => total
+ item.price * item.quantity, 0);
```

Human Developer's Role:

- Verify if **all edge cases** are handled.
- Ensure **code readability aligns with team standards**.
- Optimize for **performance in large datasets**.

Making Coding Accessible to Non-Technical Users

AI-powered coding assistants will **empower business users, analysts, and designers** to contribute to software development, **without deep programming knowledge**.

- **Low-code and no-code platforms** will expand.
- **Natural language-to-code conversion** will accelerate innovation.
- **Business teams will experiment with AI-generated automation.**

Example: AI Enabling Non-Technical Users

Prompt:

```
Create a chatbot that answers customer FAQs.
```

AI Output (Python Chatbot)

```
from flask import Flask, request, jsonify

app = Flask(__name__)

responses = {
    "hours": "We are open from 9 AM to 5 PM.",
    "location": "We are located in New York.",
}

@app.route("/chat", methods=["POST"])
def chat():
    question = request.json.get("question", "").lower()
    return jsonify({"response": responses.get(question, "I don't know the
answer.")})

if __name__ == "__main__":
    app.run(debug=True)
```

This allows **non-technical business teams** to prototype automation, **without deep coding expertise**.

How Developers Must Adapt to AI-Augmented Development

To stay ahead in an AI-driven future, developers should:

- **Develop AI Literacy:** Understand how AI works, its **strengths and limitations.**
- **Master AI-Augmented Development**: Learn how to **integrate AI into daily workflows**.
- **Improve Soft Skills:** Communication, problem-solving, and creativity will be **more valuable than syntax memorization.**
- **Emphasize Security and Ethics:** AI lacks **ethical reasoning**, making human oversight **critical.**
- **Focus on System Design and Scalability:** Developers will shift from **writing code to architecting large-scale AI-driven systems.**

So here, we understood that, the future of software development **is not about AI replacing developers**–it is about developers and AI working together. **Developers, who embrace AI will significantly improve their productivity and problem-solving skills.**

Rather than competing with AI, **learn to leverage it**–because **the best developers in the next decade will not be those, who write the maximum codes, but those, who can use AI to build smarter, more efficient solutions.**

The Potential of AI to Transform the Coding Landscape

The future of software development is undergoing a **fundamental shift**, driven by AI-assisted coding tools. AI is no longer just an **efficiency booster**–it is actively **reshaping the way code is written, tested, optimized, and deployed**. This transformation is leading to a **more inclusive, accessible, and intelligent software development ecosystem**, where coding is not restricted to experienced developers, but is becoming available to **a broader audience, including non-technical users, business analysts, and domain experts**.

Democratization of Coding

For decades, **software development has been confined to those with formal programming education, and hands-on experience**. AI-powered coding tools, such as GitHub Copilot, OpenAI Codex, and low-code/no-code platforms, are **lowering the barrier to entry** for individuals, who do not have deep programming expertise.

AI-assisted coding will make it possible for:

- **Entrepreneurs and start-ups** to quickly build prototypes, without hiring an entire engineering team.
- **Business analysts and product managers** to contribute to development by converting requirements into functional prototypes.
- **Domain experts in healthcare, finance, and education** to automate workflows, without needing formal programming skills.

Example: AI Enabling Faster Prototyping

A **small business owner** wants to automate appointment scheduling, without hiring a full-time developer. Instead of manually coding a booking system, AI-assisted platforms can generate a working prototype with just **natural language instructions.**

Prompt:

```
Create a web-based appointment scheduling system.
- Allow users to select available time slots.
- Send email confirmations.
- Store appointment data in a database.
```

AI-Generated Output (Simplified Version)

Frontend (React)

```
import React, { useState } from "react";

function AppointmentScheduler() {
    const [timeSlot, setTimeSlot] = useState("");

    const handleBooking = () => alert(`Appointment booked for ${timeSlot}`);

    return (
        <div>
            <h2>Select a Time Slot</h2>
            <select onChange={(e) => setTimeSlot(e.target.value)}>
                <option value="10AM">10:00 AM</option>
                <option value="2PM">2:00 PM</option>
            </select>
            <button onClick={handleBooking}>Book Appointment</button>
        </div>
    );
}

export default AppointmentScheduler;
```

With just a few lines of code **generated by AI**, a functional scheduling system is ready—reducing development time **from weeks to minutes.**

AI Accelerating Software Development

AI-powered coding assistants are not just helping beginners—they are also **enhancing the productivity of experienced developers** by:

- **Reducing the time spent on repetitive coding tasks.**
- **Speeding up debugging, and testing processes.**
- **Improving code readability and maintainability.**

With AI's ability to suggest **optimized, reusable, and scalable solutions**, developers can **focus on high-value architectural decisions, rather than syntax and boilerplate code.**

Example: AI Automating a Common Development Task

A backend engineer needs to **set up user authentication** for an application. Instead of manually writing the logic, AI can generate the entire authentication module.

Prompt:

```
Generate a secure user authentication system using Node.js and JWT.
```

AI-Generated Code (Node.js Express)

```
const express = require("express");
const jwt = require("jsonwebtoken");
const bcrypt = require("bcryptjs");

const app = express();
app.use(express.json());

const users = [];

app.post("/register", async (req, res) => {
    const hashedPassword = await bcrypt.hash(req.body.password, 10);
    users.push({ username: req.body.username, password: hashedPassword });
    res.send("User registered successfully");
});

app.post("/login", async (req, res) => {
    const user = users.find((u) => u.username === req.body.username);
    if (!user || !(await bcrypt.compare(req.body.password, user.password))) {
        return res.status(401).send("Invalid credentials");
    }

    const token = jwt.sign({ username: user.username }, "secretkey",
{ expiresIn: "1h" });
    res.json({ token });
});

app.listen(3000, () => console.log("Server running on port 3000"));
```

This **reduces the manual development effort,** and allows developers to **focus on enhancing security and scalability,** instead of rewriting common authentication logic.

Enhancing Open-Source Contributions Through AI

AI-assisted coding is **revolutionizing open-source contributions** by making it **easier for developers to participate**. Many developers, especially beginners, often hesitate to contribute due to:

- Lack of familiarity with a project's codebase.
- Difficulty understanding complex architecture.
- Fear of introducing bugs.

AI helps bridge this gap by:

- Explaining unfamiliar code in natural language.
- Suggesting relevant areas to contribute, based on project needs.
- Providing optimized pull request suggestions.

Example: AI-Assisted Open-Source Contribution

A new contributor wants to **fix a bug in an open-source project,** but does not fully understand the codebase.

Prompt:

```
Explain the purpose of this function, and suggest improvements.
```

Code (Before AI Review)

```
def calculate_total(cart):
    total = 0
    for item in cart:
        total += item["price"] * item["quantity"]
    return total
```

AI Explanation and Suggested Improvements

- **Purpose:** This function calculates the total cost of items in a shopping cart.
- **Improvement:** The function can be rewritten using `sum()` for better readability.

Optimized Code (Suggested by AI)

```
def calculate_total(cart):
    return sum(item["price"] * item["quantity"] for item in cart)
```

By making open-source development **more accessible**, AI is **encouraging more people to contribute, learn, and grow** in the software engineering community.

Challenges and Considerations

While AI is making coding **more accessible and efficient**, developers must be **aware of the potential pitfalls**:

- **Over-Reliance on AI:**
  - AI-generated code **should always be reviewed by humans**.
  - Blindly accepting suggestions can **introduce security vulnerabilities**.
- **Security Concerns:**
  - AI may **suggest insecure implementations,** if not carefully monitored.
  - AI-generated code should be **validated against best practices**.
- **Loss of Fundamental Skills:**
  - Developers must **balance AI assistance with deep technical understanding**.
  - Relying too much on AI **can weaken problem-solving skills** over time.

Hence, it is quite evident that the AI-driven transformation of coding is **making software development more efficient, inclusive, and intelligent**. From **automating routine tasks to democratizing coding for non-programmers**, AI is changing how developers approach their work.

However, while AI enhances productivity, **human expertise remains crucial** for:

- **Architecting scalable systems.**
- **Ensuring security and compliance.**
- **Validating AI-generated code for correctness and efficiency.**

Thus, as the AI revolution progresses, **developers must embrace AI as a tool, not a crutch**—leveraging its power, **while continuing to hone their critical thinking, and problem-solving skills**. Therefore, the future of coding belongs to those, who can **combine AI efficiency with human ingenuity to build the next generation of software.**

Preparing for the Future: Skills and Knowledge for Developers

AI is **reshaping** software development, and developers must **adapt** to stay relevant. Thus, the key to success is not competing with AI, but **leveraging it effectively**. So, here is how developers can prepare for an AI-driven future.

Mastering AI-Assisted Development Workflows

AI tools such as **GitHub Copilot, OpenAI Codex, and Tabnine** are changing how developers code. To use them effectively:

- **Understand AI capabilities:** To know what AI can, and cannot do.
- **Integrate AI into daily workflows:** Use AI to automate repetitive coding tasks, and improve efficiency.
- **Balance AI assistance with manual validation:** AI can generate a code, but human oversight ensures correctness.

Example: AI in Action

Instead of manually writing test cases, a developer can use AI to generate a test suite:

Prompt:

```
Generate unit tests for a Python function that calculates discounts, based on
purchase amount.
AI generates structured test cases, saving time, while ensuring comprehensive
coverage.
```

Refining Prompt Engineering for AI Optimization

Writing **effective prompts** is key to getting high-quality AI-generated codes.

- **Be clear and specific**–Define language, libraries, and constraints.
- **Use step-by-step instructions**–Break down complex tasks for better AI comprehension.
- **Iterate and refine**–Improve prompts, based on AI responses.

Example: Refining AI Output

Basic Prompt:

```
Write a function to process the user data.
➡ AI generates a generic function with no security or validation.
```

Refined Prompt:

```
Write a Python function to process user data securely.
- Validate input format.
- Handle exceptions.
- Sanitize inputs to prevent injection attacks.
➡ AI generates a robust, secure function with error handling and validation.
```

Strengthening System Design and Architectural Thinking

As AI **automates routine coding**, developers will focus more on **architecting scalable, maintainable, and efficient software systems**.

- **Understand design patterns** (for example, MVC, Microservices, Event-Driven Architecture, and so on).
- **Optimize AI-generated code** to fit real-world application needs.
- **Balance AI-generated solutions with business requirements**.

Example: AI in Software Architecture

Instead of manually designing a microservices architecture, a developer can prompt AI:

Prompt:

```
Design a scalable microservices architecture for an e-commerce application.
- Use Node.js for the backend.
- Include services for authentication, product management, and payments.
- Recommend a database strategy.
```

AI provides a **detailed blueprint**, helping developers **validate and refine** their architecture.

Developing AI Auditing and Security Awareness

AI can generate code **quickly**, but it does not guarantee **security**. Developers must:

- **Audit AI-generated code** for vulnerabilities.
- **Ensure compliance with security best practices**.
- **Apply ethical coding principles** to prevent bias and unintended consequences.

Example: Identifying AI-Generated Security Flaws

Prompt:

```
Review the following login function for security vulnerabilities.
AI identifies missing input validation, improper error handling, or hardcoded
secrets, ensuring secure code deployment.
```

Enhancing Collaboration with AI and Human Teams

AI improves **collaboration between developers, testers, and product teams**. Hence, Developers must:

- **Use AI for documentation generation** to improve knowledge sharing.
- **Enhance cross-functional teamwork** by integrating AI into Agile workflows.
- **Leverage AI for test case automation and CI/CD pipelines**.

Example: AI-Assisted Agile Workflow

Prompt:

```
Generate test cases based on this user story:
"As a user, I want to reset my password so I can regain account access."
```

AI generates **functional test cases**, reducing manual effort, and **accelerating Agile testing cycles**.

AI-Assisted Development Workflow

- AI is **seamlessly integrated** into the **software development lifecycle**, assisting developers in every phase.
- The workflow consists of **six stages**, where AI acts as an **assistant**, rather than a replacement.
- **Key AI contributions** in each stage:
    - **Requirements Gathering:** AI helps generate user stories, acceptance criteria, and initial project structures.
    - **Code Generation and Development:** AI speeds up development by **suggesting functions, completing code blocks, and auto-generating repetitive codes**.
    - **Code Review and Quality Checks:** AI detects **code smells, security vulnerabilities, and redundant logic** before committing changes.
    - **Testing and Debugging:** AI generates **unit, integration, and functional tests**, identifying **potential defects early**.
    - **Deployment and CI/CD Integration:** AI assists in **writing deployment scripts, setting up CI/CD pipelines, and automating infrastructure provisioning**.
    - **Monitoring and AI-Assisted Optimization:** AI continuously **analyzes logs, suggests performance optimizations, and detects anomalies in production environments**.

Summary

To sum up, AI enhances **efficiency, accuracy, and automation**, making the software development lifecycle **faster, and more reliable**. However, **human oversight remains critical** to ensure that AI-generated code aligns with **business logic, security standards, and the best practices**.

The integration of AI across the Software Development Lifecycle (SDLC) is transforming how applications are planned, built, tested, and deployed. From requirement analysis to CI/CD integration, and post-deployment monitoring, AI acts as a co-pilot at every stage—enhancing decision-making, reducing manual effort, and accelerating time-to-market. The following diagram outlines a modern AI-assisted SDLC, showing the collaboration between human developers and AI systems at each critical phase.

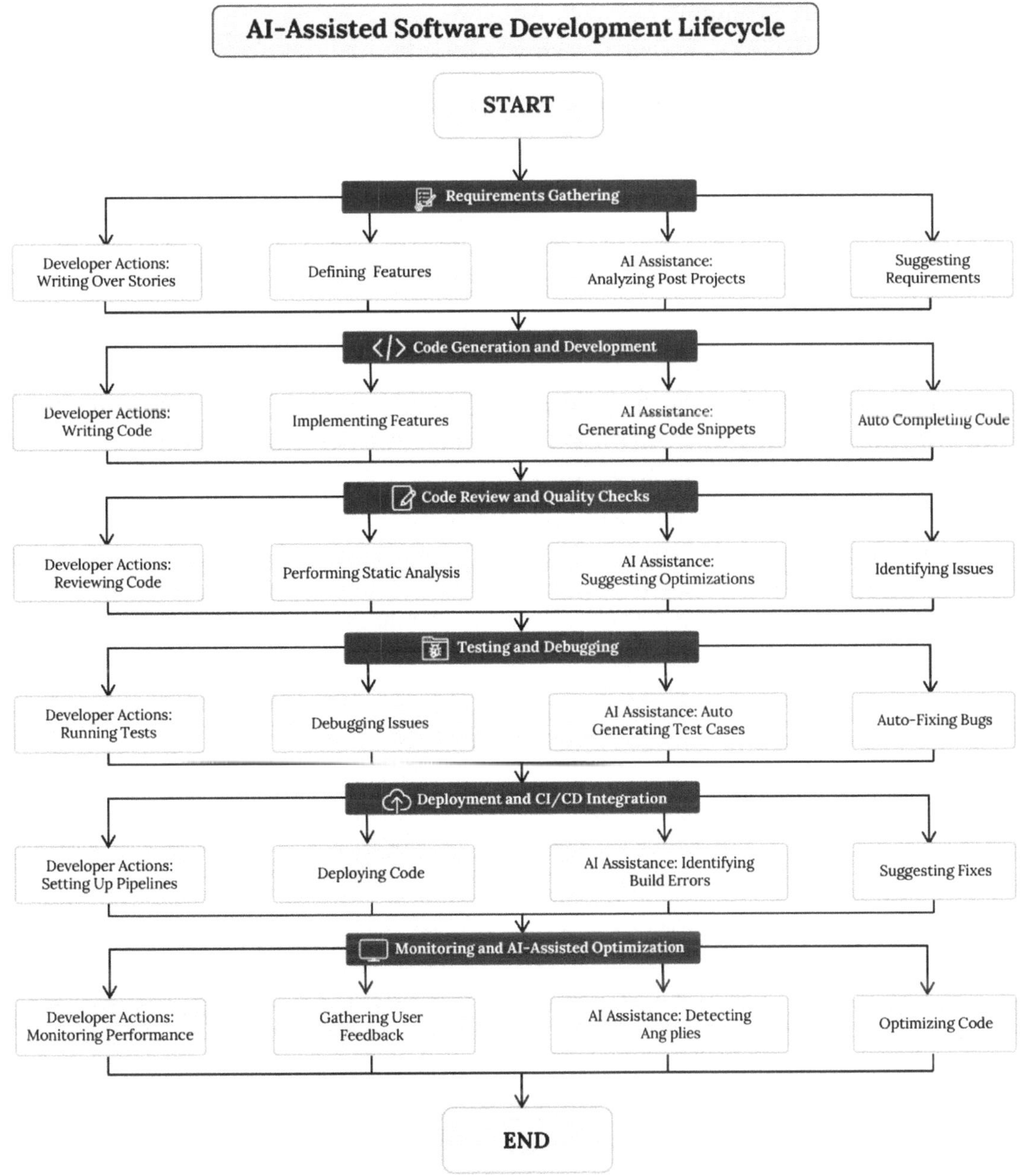

***Figure 16.1:** End-to-end Flow of the AI Assisted Software Development Lifecycle, Highlighting how AI Complements Human Actions in User Story Creation, Code Generation, Testing, Debugging, Deployment, and Continuous Monitoring for Optimized Delivery*

AI vs. Human Developer Responsibilities

- The diagram provides a **comparative view** of AI capabilities versus human developer expertise.
- AI handles **predictable, structured, and repetitive coding tasks**, while human developers **focus on decision-making, security, creativity, and business alignment**.
- **AI Strengths:**
  - Automates **boilerplate code generation**.
  - Suggests **code optimizations, and refactoring improvements**.
  - Detects **potential bugs and vulnerabilities** before execution.
  - Generates **test cases, deployment scripts, and documentation**.

- **Human Developer Strengths:**
  - Architects **scalable and maintainable software systems.**
  - Ensures **security, ethical coding practices, and compliance.**
  - Understands **business logic, and custom requirements** beyond AI's general pattern recognition.
  - Innovates by **designing new algorithms, architectures, and problem-solving approaches.**

Summary

To sum up, AI is best suited for structured, repetitive, and pattern-driven tasks such as generating boilerplate code, suggesting optimizations, or identifying common bugs. On the other hand, human developers are essential for making decisions that involve business logic, ethical concerns, and architectural trade-offs. AI can speed up the journey, but human developers still choose the direction, destination, and make judgment calls along the way.

AI is rapidly reshaping the responsibilities of developers by taking over repetitive and error-prone tasks, allowing them to focus on higher-level logic and design. So, whether it is generating boilerplate code, refactoring logic, or automating test case creation, AI brings speed, precision, and intelligence to modern software development workflows. The following diagram categorizes the key AI-assisted coding tasks, and their practical applications.

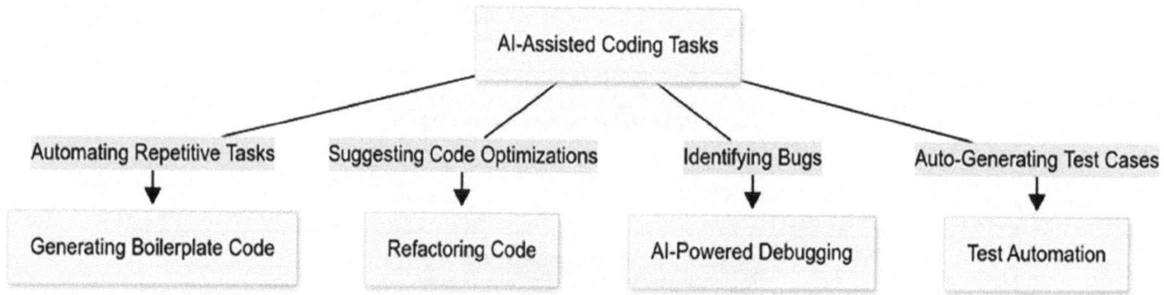

Figure 16.2: *Categorization of AI-assisted Coding Tasks across Four Core Functions—Automating Repetitive Work, Optimizing Code, Identifying Bugs, and Generating Test Cases—Demonstrating how AI Enhances Efficiency and Quality throughout the Development Process*

Even as AI systems take on more coding responsibilities, human developers continue to play an indispensable role in software development. Their unique strengths lie in architectural decision-making, ethical oversight, business logic comprehension, and creative problem-solving. The following diagram highlights the core responsibilities that remain firmly within the human domain, ensuring that AI-generated code aligns with organizational goals, ethical standards, and real-world requirements.

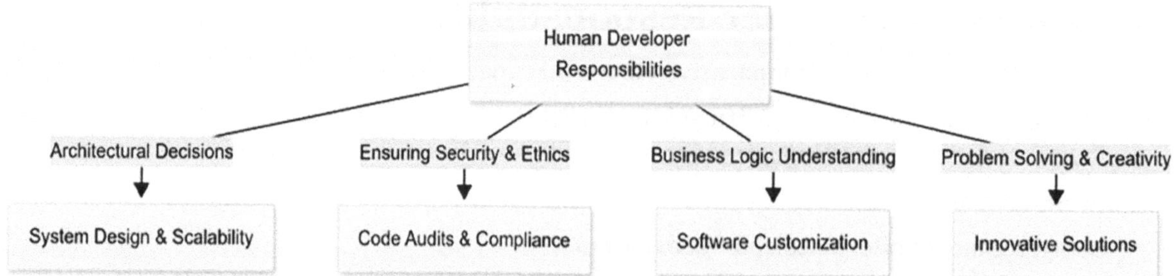

Figure 16.3: *Key Domains of Human Developer Responsibilities, Emphasizing Areas such as System Architecture, Compliance, Customization, and Innovation or Tasks that Require Judgment, Experience, and Contextual Intelligence beyond AI Capabilities.*

As AI becomes more embedded in software development workflows, it is crucial to understand the division of responsibilities between AI tools and human developers. While AI excels at automation, pattern recognition, and accelerating repetitive tasks, it lacks the contextual understanding, ethical reasoning, and business awareness that human intelligence provides. Recognizing these boundaries ensures that AI is leveraged effectively–enhancing development, without compromising on quality, security, or creativity.

Task Domain	AI Strengths	Human Developer Strengths
Code Generation	Boilerplate, autocomplete, examples	Business logic customization, optimization
Debugging and Testing	Error detection, test suggestions	Complex bug tracing, test strategy
Code Review and Compliance	Pattern-based issues, best practices	Security, compliance decisions
Architecture and Design	Pattern recommendation	System-wide design, scalability decisions
Ethical and Strategic Oversight	–	Bias detection, ethical governance

Table 16.4: *Clear Delineation of Task Domains Between AI Tools and Human Developers, Illustrating How Their Strengths Complement Each Other. AI Handles Automation and Pattern-based Suggestions, While Developers Focus on Decision-making, Security, and Strategic Alignment With Business Goals*

In an AI-augmented development environment, coding is no longer a strictly linear process–it becomes a dynamic, cyclical collaboration between humans and machines. The AI-Enhanced Development Cycle illustrates how AI integrates at every phase, from understanding business objectives to generating code, and suggesting test cases. This continuous feedback loop not only accelerates development, but also enhances code quality, system scalability, and business alignment.

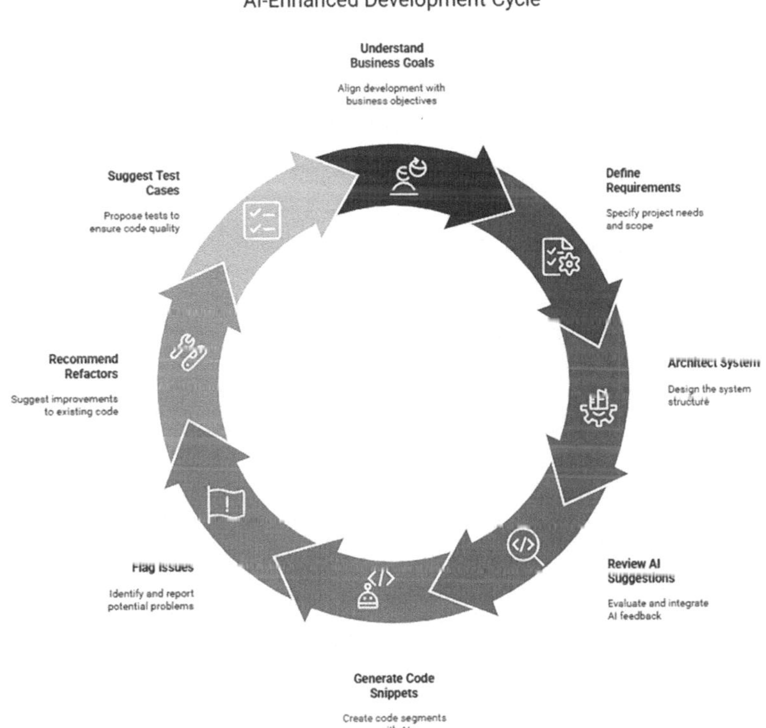

Figure 16.4: *Visual Representation of the AI-Enhanced Development Cycle, Showing how AI supports key stages–such as Requirement Definition, System Design, Code Generation, and Issue Detection–while Human Developers Maintain Oversight, Validate AI Outputs, and Ensure Alignment with Business Goals and Ethical Standards*

AI-Assisted Debugging Flowchart

- AI **automates debugging**, reducing the **time and effort** spent on identifying and fixing errors.
- The flowchart illustrates how **AI interacts with human developers** in a structured debugging process.
- **Debugging Workflow Breakdown:**
    1. **Code Execution** → If AI detects an error, it suggests a fix.
    2. **AI Suggests Fix** → Developer reviews, and either **approves or modifies** the suggestion.
    3. **Re-Test Code** → AI ensures the fix works correctly in different conditions.
    4. **If the fix is incorrect**, AI proposes alternative solutions, based on historical debugging patterns.
    5. **If the issue persists**, manual debugging is required, where AI assists by **analyzing logs, error messages, and stack traces.**

Summary

AI-assisted debugging speeds up **error detection and resolution**, but **human oversight is crucial** for **handling complex issues, optimizing performance, and ensuring software stability.**

Thus, AI is increasingly being used to streamline the debugging process, reducing developer workload, and accelerating issue resolution. The AI-assisted debugging workflow automates the detection, suggestion, and application of code fixes, while still incorporating human oversight for validation and refinement. This hybrid approach ensures both speed and accuracy in resolving software bugs.

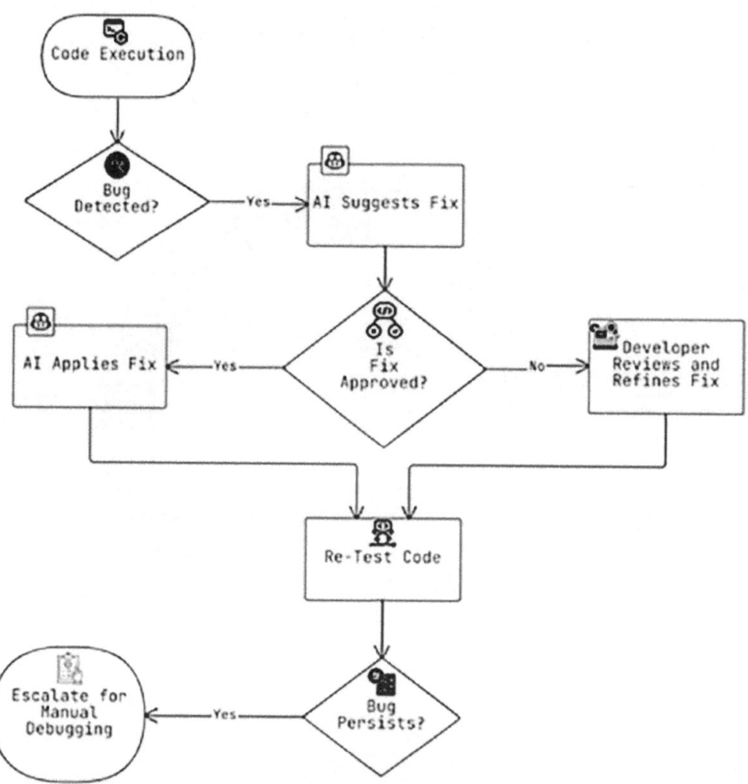

***Figure 16.5:** Flowchart of an AI-assisted Debugging Workflow, Showing how AI Detects Bugs, Proposes and Applies Fixes, as well as Collaborates with Developers, when Necessary. The Loop Continues through Re-testing until the Issue is Resolved or Escalated for Manual Debugging.*

Evolution and Future of AI-Assisted Coding

- AI-assisted coding is **rapidly evolving**, transforming from **basic code suggestions** to **fully autonomous software development workflows**.
- The timeline visualization maps out the **major advancements in AI-driven development** over the next decade.
- **Key Milestones:**
  - **2020 - 2023:** Early AI adoption with tools like **GitHub Copilot** and **AI-powered code completion**.
  - **2024 - 2027:** AI expands into **automated debugging, CI/CD pipeline optimization, and full-stack application generation**.
  - **2028 - 2032:** AI evolves into **intelligent coding agents**, assisting in **architecture design, scalability decisions, and security auditing**.
  - **2033 - 2035:** Potential for **fully autonomous AI development teams**, where AI handles entire software lifecycles, with **minimal human intervention**.

Summary

To sum up, AI-assisted coding is shifting from **passive assistance** to **active collaboration**, eventually leading to **AI-driven autonomous development**. However, **human expertise will remain essential** for **strategic decision-making, security, ethical oversight, and creative problem-solving**. Developers who **embrace AI early** will be at the forefront of this transformation.

The journey of AI-assisted coding is unfolding rapidly—moving from early adoption in code completion and reviews to ambitious future visions of fully autonomous AI development. As organizations embrace AI across the software lifecycle, we witness a transformative shift not only in tools, but also in roles, workflows, and the very nature of programming itself. The following timeline visualizes this evolution, and what lies ahead over the next decade:

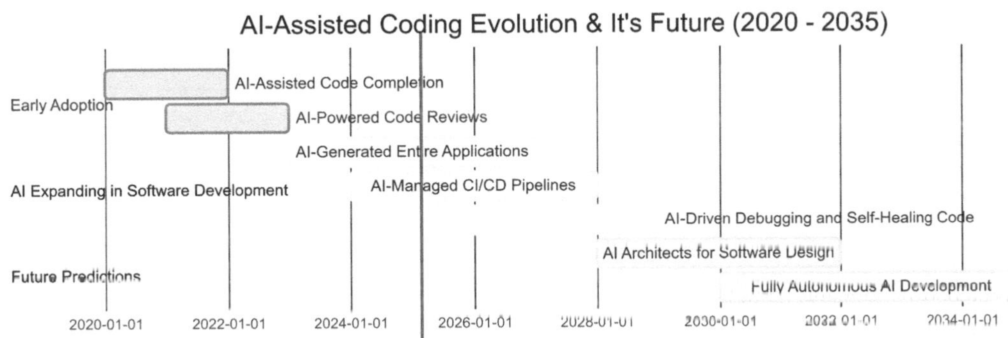

Figure 16.6: *Timeline Illustrating the Evolution of AI-assisted Coding from 2020 to 2035—Beginning with Early Capabilities such as Code Completion and Reviews, Expanding into CI/CD Management and Application Generation, and Projecting into Future Milestones, such as AI-driven Debugging, Architectural design, as well as Fully Autonomous Software Development*

Conclusion

Thus, **AI-assisted coding** has moved beyond the realm of speculation—it is actively transforming how software is architected, written, tested, and deployed. Tools such as GitHub Copilot and OpenAI Codex have empowered developers to accelerate coding tasks, reduce repetitive work, and enhance productivity across the software development lifecycle. As these tools become more advanced, developers should embrace a collaborative mindset, where AI is seen not as a replacement, but as an **intelligent assistant**.

The success of this collaboration relies on the developer's ability to guide, validate, and optimize AI-generated code. Prompt engineering has become a critical skill—how effectively a developer frames their request directly influences the quality of AI suggestions. Yet, efficiency alone is not enough. Human oversight remains essential, especially when it comes to addressing security vulnerabilities, ethical concerns, and contextual decision-making that AI cannot fully grasp on its own.

To truly unlock the potential of AI in software development, developers must integrate AI into their workflows—whether it is CI/CD pipelines, Agile practices, or DevOps automation. This transition demands a new level of AI literacy, where developers not only understand how AI models work, but also refine strategies for using them effectively. Those, who adapt will not just write code faster—they will design scalable, secure systems with the support of intelligent automation.

The future of development is no longer about writing every line of code manually. It is about architecting processes that blend the precision of AI with the creativity and insight of human intelligence. Developers, who embrace AI as a collaborator will find themselves better equipped to innovate, deliver value faster, and shape the next era of software engineering.

In the upcoming chapter, *Recap of the Key Points*, we will bring together the most important insights, best practices, and lessons from this journey—offering a clear and concise summary to reinforce your understanding, and prepare you for the AI-powered future ahead.

Multiple Choice Questions

1. What is one of the key opportunities Copilot provides across sectors?
   a. Enforces manual programming
   b. Enables universal internet access
   c. Boosts developer productivity and speeds up time-to-market
   d. Removes the need for code review
2. In the healthcare sector, what is a primary challenge of using Copilot?
   a. Lack of medical data
   b. Patient resistance to AI-generated apps
   c. Compliance with data protection laws like HIPAA
   d. Absence of EHR systems
3. Which sector uses Copilot to enhance predictive maintenance and automation workflows?
   a. Retail
   b. Education
   c. Manufacturing and IoT
   d. Legal
4. What major risk arises when using Copilot in financial institutions?
   a. Over-dependence on Excel
   b. UI misalignment

   c. Exposure to confidential or PII data through AI prompts
   d. Lack of internet access for developers
5. How can organizations mitigate compliance concerns while adopting Copilot?
   a. Avoid code reviews
   b. Use non-coding departments only
   c. Implement access controls and audit trails
   d. Only enable it during product launches
6. In startups, which of the following is a Copilot-driven advantage?
   a. Increased hiring cycles
   b. Reduced feature delivery speed
   c. Rapid prototyping with minimal resources
   d. Longer test cycles
7. What is a typical barrier to Copilot adoption in government and defense sectors?
   a. Lack of GitHub accounts
   b. Incompatibility with open-source
   c. National security and closed-network restrictions
   d. Requirement for Mac-only environments
8. Which best describes Copilot's potential in the education sector?
   a. Automates grading only
   b. Replaces teachers
   c. Assists in interactive coding tutorials and feedback
   d. Limits student creativity
9. What is one common misconception about Copilot in enterprise environments?
   a. It increases team collaboration
   b. It generates unit tests automatically
   c. It completely removes the need for skilled developers
   d. It works offline by default
10. What is a shared challenge across most industries when adopting Copilot at scale?
   a. Shortage of programming languages
   b. Integrating with existing DevSecOps pipelines and governance policies
   c. Developer resistance to keyboard shortcuts
   d. Lack of documentation in GitHub

Answers

1. c
2. c
3. c
4. c
5. c
6. c
7. c
8. c
9. c
10. b

CHAPTER 17
Recap of the Key Points

Introduction

"Software development is no longer just about writing codes—it is about collaborating with AI to build smarter, faster, and more efficient solutions."

In today's world, we are witnessing a **transformational shift** in how software is developed. The way we write, debug, and optimize code is no longer solely dependent on human effort—it is being **augmented, accelerated, and enhanced** by artificial intelligence. **GitHub Copilot is not just a tool; it is a catalyst for a new era of software engineering.**

Throughout this book, we have explored how **AI-assisted coding** is **reshaping workflows, increasing productivity, and pushing the boundaries of what developers can accomplish.** But this is only the beginning. **The role of AI in coding is still evolving, and the developers, who embrace it today, will define the future of software development.**

At first, AI-driven coding assistance may have seemed like a novelty—a faster way to autocomplete functions or generate boilerplate code. But as we have seen, **GitHub Copilot is far more than that**. It is capable of:

- **Generating full application architectures** with intelligent, context-aware suggestions.
- **Improving developer efficiency** by reducing time spent on repetitive tasks.
- **Enhancing security and best practices** by recommending optimized, and secure coding patterns.
- **Automating entire testing workflows**, and **integrating seamlessly into CI/CD pipelines**.

This chapter will basically **recap the major insights covered in this book, reinforce the impact of AI on software development, and provide actionable next steps** for developers striving to stay ahead in this AI-powered era.

One thing is certain: Developers, who embrace AI today, will be at the forefront of innovation tomorrow. The question is—**how will you use this knowledge to shape your future as a developer?**

Structure

In this chapter, we will discuss the following topics:

- Recap of the Key Points Covered in the Book
- Final Thoughts on the Impact of AI in Coding
- Encouragement for Further Exploration and Learning
- Resources for Ongoing Engagement with the Copilot Community

Recap of Key Points Covered in the Book

This book has **unpacked GitHub Copilot from every angle**–from fundamentals to advanced techniques. GitHub Copilot has transformed the way developers approach software development. Instead of manually writing every line of a code, **developers now focus on guiding AI, structuring logic, and refining AI-generated code**. This shift in mindset has allowed for **faster development, better code quality, and increased efficiency**.

So, let us take a **deeper look** at the **core insights and the major takeaways** from this book.

Here is a structured recap of the major takeaways:

The Foundation of AI-Assisted Coding

Before diving into the advanced applications of GitHub Copilot, it is crucial to understand the fundamental shift it brings to how developers approach coding. The foundation of AI-assisted coding lies in the transformation from manual code construction to collaborative problem-solving, with intelligent systems. Rather than writing every line of code from scratch, developers now, interact with AI tools that understand intent, context, and structure–providing smart suggestions that accelerate development, and reduce cognitive load. This new paradigm reshapes the very nature of software creation, emphasizing logic, design thinking, and human-AI synergy.

- **From Code Writing to Code Collaboration:** Developers no longer just write code from a scratch; they **collaborate with AI**, guiding Copilot to **generate structured, optimized, and maintainable code**.
- **The Role of Large Language Models (LLMs):** AI-driven tools like Copilot **understand code context**, predict intent, and **suggest meaningful completions**, reducing cognitive load for developers.
- **Prompt Engineering as the New Developer Skill:** The **better the prompt, the better the AI response**. We explored **how refining prompts** leads to **more accurate, relevant, and production-ready codes**.

"The best developers are not just coders; they are also AI instructors, shaping AI-generated solutions with precision and intent."

Quick Takeaways from The Previous Chapters

To reinforce the learning experience, here is a consolidated summary of what each chapter has covered throughout this book. This recap not only serves as a refresher, but also highlights how GitHub Copilot evolved across use cases, skill levels, and domains.

Chapter 1: The Rise of AI in Coding

Explored how artificial intelligence is revolutionizing software development. The chapter also introduced GitHub Copilot as a groundbreaking shift in the developer toolkit, setting the tone for the future of AI-assisted programming.

Chapter 2: Getting Started with GitHub Copilot

Provided step-by-step guidance for installing and activating Copilot across popular IDEs. The chapter also introduced Copilot's AI engine (Codex), and its capabilities in generating smart, context-aware code completions.

Chapter 3: JavaScript/TypeScript with Copilot

Demonstrated Copilot's role in modern web development using JavaScript and TypeScript. Covered frontend and backend use cases, async/await logic, error handling, and React component generation.

Chapter 4: Python and AI-Assisted Coding

Focused on Python's versatility in scripting, automation, data science, and machine learning. The chapter also covered Copilot-assisted code examples ranged from Flask APIs to NumPy-based data processing, and debugging.

Chapter 5: Java with Copilot

Showed how Copilot accelerates Java development using Spring Boot, REST APIs, and object-oriented patterns like Singleton and Factory. It also included enterprise coding examples, and Copilot's ability to enforce modular design.

Chapter 6: C/C++ with Copilot

Illustrated how Copilot supports low-level programming tasks like memory management, algorithm design, and working with header files. The chapter also focused on legacy code improvements, and optimizing system performance.

Chapter 7: Go Programming with Copilot

Demonstrated Go's concurrency model, efficient syntax, and Copilot's help in generating idiomatic Go code. The chapter also covered use cases such as REST APIs, CLI utilities, and unit testing.

Chapter 8: Pair Programming with Copilot

Introduced Copilot as a virtual pair programmer, and explained collaborative use cases, including inline suggestions, real-time refactoring, error tracing, and accelerating developer ideation.

Chapter 9: Advanced Techniques with Copilot

Focused on prompt engineering strategies, such as zero-shot, one-shot, and few-shot prompts. The chapter also covered test automation, legacy refactoring, and Copilot's architecture, including token limitations and feedback loops.

Chapter 10: Testing and Debugging with Copilot

Showcased Copilot's effectiveness in generating unit tests, increasing code coverage, and identifying edge cases. The chapter also demonstrated Copilot's assistance in debugging and logical validation.

Chapter 11: Updating Workflows with GitHub Copilot

Explored automation of Git workflows, pull request generation, CI/CD configurations, and deployment orchestration. Examples included GitHub Actions, Docker, and Kubernetes deployments.

Chapter 12: Integrating Copilot with IDEs

Provided integration steps and customization tips for various IDEs, such as VS Code, JetBrains, Android Studio, and Visual Studio. The chapter also compared support for features such as Copilot Chat and inline suggestions.

Chapter 13: Best Practices and Limitations

Shared tactical best practices for safe and effective use of Copilot. It also covered limitations like context window truncation, outdated models, and introduced new capabilities like **multi-model support**, **vibe coding**, **Attach Context**, and **chat-enhanced workflows**.

Chapter 14: Copilot in Education

Examined how Copilot is reshaping education. The chapter also included instructor-led teaching strategies, student learning journeys, and academic case studies (for example, Harvard). It promoted Copilot as a real-time mentor in classrooms.

Chapter 15: Real-World Use Cases and Case Studies

Presented industry-specific Copilot applications in Finance, Healthcare, Manufacturing, Retail, and Start-ups. The chapter also provided metrics on code acceptance, productivity improvements, and AI adoption trends in companies such as Accenture, Shopify, and Mercedes-Benz.

Chapter 16: The Future of AI-Assisted Coding

Projected future trends in software engineering. The chapter also discussed autonomous application generation, AI-driven debugging, role shifts for developers, and the importance of ethical and collaborative AI development.

AI-Powered Development across Programming Languages

GitHub Copilot has **streamlined development across multiple languages**, helping developers **write, optimize, and debug** code in **real-time.**

How Copilot has Enhanced Programming in Different Tech Stacks:

- **JavaScript and TypeScript:** Generating dynamic web applications, reducing front-end development time, and ensuring **strong typing with TypeScript.**
- **Python and AI-Assisted Coding:** Automating scripting tasks, **enhancing machine learning workflows**, and simplifying **data science operations.**
- **Java Development:** Assisting in **Spring Boot applications**, **API design**, and **enterprise-level backend services.**
- **C/C++ Development:** Improving **low-level optimizations**, helping in **systems programming and game development.**
- **Go Programming:** Building **highly scalable, concurrent applications**, optimizing **cloud-native services**, and handling **microservices architecture.**

Thus, instead of **memorizing syntax, and writing boilerplate code**, developers now **focus on logic, design, and architectural decisions.**

"With AI-assisted coding, the true power of a developer is no longer in how much code they can write, but in how effectively they can guide AI to generate the right solutions."

Leveraging AI for Software Engineering Excellence

As software development becomes increasingly complex, the integration of AI is no longer optional–it is essential for achieving engineering excellence. GitHub Copilot empowers developers to move beyond traditional coding boundaries by introducing intelligent automation, real-time assistance, and context-aware enhancements. From debugging and testing to performance tuning and collaboration, AI is helping developers build robust, efficient, and scalable solutions with greater speed and confidence. This section explores how developers can strategically harness AI to elevate the quality, reliability, and agility of modern software engineering.

Here is how you can leverage AI for software engineering excellence:

- **AI-Assisted Debugging and Testing**: Automating **unit tests, functional tests, API tests, and performance testing**.
- **Pair Programming with Copilot**: Exploring how Copilot serves as an **AI-driven coding partner**, improving collaboration, and reducing the debugging time.
- **Code Optimization and Performance Tuning**: Learning **AI-driven refactoring techniques to enhance efficiency, memory utilization, and execution speed**.
- **Enhancing Developer Productivity**: Automating **repetitive coding tasks, integrating Copilot into agile workflows, and improving collaboration across teams**.

AI-Driven DevOps, CI/CD, and Infrastructure Automation

GitHub Copilot is not just for developers–it has proven to be a game-changer for DevOps teams through:

- **Infrastructure as Code (IaC):** Writing Terraform scripts, Kubernetes manifests, and Ansible playbooks using AI-assisted recommendations.
- **Automating CI/CD Pipelines:** AI-assisted pipelines in GitHub Actions, Jenkins, and Azure DevOps now integrate test automation, security scans, and auto-deployments.
- **Security and Privacy Considerations:** AI helps to detect vulnerabilities, enforce best practices, and automate security compliance.

How AI is Transforming DevOps and CI/CD

- **Faster deployments** with automated infrastructure provisioning.
- **More reliable applications** due to AI-assisted performance testing.
- **Enhanced security** with AI-powered vulnerability scanning.

"AI is not just changing the way we code–it is transforming the way we deploy, secure, and manage software at scale."

Final Thoughts on the Impact of AI in Coding

The impact of AI on software development is **revolutionary, not disruptive**. Developers are **not being replaced, but empowered**–freed from repetitive tasks, and **given more time for creative problem-solving**. AI is **enhancing human ingenuity, not eliminating it**.

Key Takeaways for the Future

- **Copilot as an Enabler, not a Replacement:** AI enhances efficiency, but does not replace **critical thinking, problem-solving, and software design skills**.
- **AI-Driven Productivity Gains**: GitHub Copilot has demonstrated **45% to 60% efficiency improvements** in developer workflows.
- **Evolving Developer Roles**: Developers must now **focus on AI literacy, automation integration, and intelligent system design**.
- **AI's Expanding Role in Development**: AI will continue to **automate low-level tasks**, allowing developers to concentrate on **architecture, security, and scalability**.

"Therefore, the most successful developers will not be those who fear AI, but those who learn to use it as a powerful extension of their capabilities."

Encouragement for Further Exploration and Learning

The **journey of AI-assisted coding does not end here**–it is just the beginning. Staying **curious, adaptive, and engaged** will be **key to leveraging AI effectively in the long run**.

Key Strategies for Continuous Learning

- **Experiment with AI-Powered Development:** Start applying Copilot in **real-world applications** beyond tutorials.
- **Keep Up with AI Research**: Read **papers, blogs, and GitHub releases** to stay ahead of AI advancements in coding.
- **Join AI-Driven Developer Communities:** Engage with **forums, open-source projects, and AI discussion groups** to collaborate and share knowledge.
- **Refine Your Prompting Techniques**: As AI evolves, **better prompt engineering** will remain a critical skill for **maximizing Copilot's effectiveness.**

Resources for Ongoing Engagement with the Copilot Community

To stay updated with AI-assisted coding advancements, the following are a few **recommended resources**:

GitHub Copilot Official Learning Hub and Documentation

To maximize the impact of GitHub Copilot across your workflows, the following official documentation and learning paths offer a comprehensive guidance–from getting started to mastering advanced usage in enterprise settings.

Resource	**Link**
GitHub Copilot Official Docs	https://docs.github.com/en/copilot
Best Practices for GitHub Copilot	https://code.visualstudio.com/docs/copilot/prompt-crafting
Copilot for Business and Enterprise	https://resources.github.com/enterprise/copilot/
GitHub Copilot Fundamentals - Understand the AI Pair Programmer	https://learn.microsoft.com/en-us/training/paths/copilot/
GitHub Copilot Certifications	https://resources.github.com/learn/certifications/
Using GitHub Copilot to Explore Projects	https://docs.github.com/en/get-started/exploring-projects-on-github/using-github-copilot-to-explore-projects

Tips and Tricks for Adopting GitHub Copilot at Scale	https://devblogs.microsoft.com/all-things-azure/adopting-github-copilot-at-scale/
How to Use GitHub Copilot: Use Cases and Best Practices	https://app.datacamp.com/learn/tutorials/github-copilot-a-complete-guide-for-beginner

Table 17.1: *A Comprehensive List of GitHub and Microsoft Learning Resources, Official Documentation, Certification Programs, and Practical Guides for Effectively Using GitHub Copilot in Real-world Projects*

AI-Powered Coding and Development Communities

Community engagement is crucial to evolving as a developer in the AI era. These forums, discussion boards, and research repositories provide the opportunity to learn from others, share insights, and stay updated with the latest trends.

Community	Link
GitHub Copilot Discussions	https://github.com/orgs/community/discussions/categories/copilot
Stack Overflow (GitHub Copilot Tag)	https://stackoverflow.com/questions/tagged/github-copilot
OpenAI Developer Forum	https://community.openai.com/
GitHub Copilot Research Papers	https://www.researchgate.net/publication/377712243_The_Recent_Trends_of_Research_on_GitHub_Copilot_A_Systematic_Review

Table 17.2: *Key Online Communities and Research Forums, Where Developers Discuss GitHub Copilot, Explore AI Coding Topics, and Access Peer-reviewed Papers to Expand Their Knowledge Base*

Advanced AI and Machine Learning Development

For developers and researchers looking to deepen their understanding of cutting-edge AI technologies, the following curated resources offer blogs, ethical guidelines, and formal training programs from top platforms and organizations.

Resource	Link
OpenAI Research Blog	https://openai.com/research/
Microsoft AI Blog	https://blogs.microsoft.com/ai/
Google AI and Responsible AI Practices	https://ai.google/responsibility/
Generative AI Trainings and Certifications	https://www.databricks.com/learn/training/get-started-with-generative-ai-accreditation
Advanced AI Tutorial	https://docs.n8n.io/advanced-ai/intro-tutorial/
Generative AI Concepts	https://app.datacamp.com/learn/courses/generative-ai-concepts

Table 17.3: *A Collection of Trusted Resources to Stay Updated with the Latest Developments in AI and Machine Learning, including Research Blogs, Responsible AI Practices, and Certification Programs*

Final Words

Thus, the rise of AI-assisted coding marks a **paradigm shift in software development.** GitHub Copilot has already **transformed how developers write code, debug, and automate workflows**, and its influence will **only continue to grow**.

By **leveraging AI effectively**, developers can **enhance productivity, collaborate efficiently, and build more scalable applications**. But ultimately, the **human element–creativity, logical reasoning, and problem-solving–will always remain at the heart of software development.**

"*AI is just the beginning. The future belongs to those who adapt, explore, and innovate.*"

So, *keep coding and keep innovating as the future of AI-assisted development is in your hands!*

Actionable Next Steps

- **Practice AI-Powered Development:** Start using **GitHub Copilot in day-to-day coding tasks.**
- **Refine AI Literacy and Prompting Skills:** Experiment with **advanced prompting strategies** for **better code suggestions.**
- **Join AI-Coding Communities**: Stay connected with **developers worldwide,** who are leveraging AI to build the future.
- **Continue Learning and Innovating:** Explore **Copilot's advanced capabilities**, test new **AI-assisted workflows**, and **push the boundaries of software engineering.**

Appendices

Appendix A: Copilot Commands and Shortcuts

GitHub Copilot offers a range of commands, shortcuts, and settings to improve efficiency and usability. Understanding these shortcuts helps developers **navigate their workflow more effectively**, speeding up the coding process and improving Copilot's overall performance. This section provides **a categorized list of commands** and **best practices** for using Copilot efficiently.

Comprehensive List of Commands and Shortcuts

The following table categorizes **GitHub Copilot commands and shortcuts** for both **Mac** and **Windows**, making it easier to find the required actions.

General Copilot Commands

To work efficiently with GitHub Copilot, mastering its keyboard shortcuts is essential. Whether you're accepting suggestions, cycling through options, or interacting with the Copilot Chat interface, these shortcuts can significantly streamline your coding workflow across both Windows and Mac.

Action	**Windows Shortcut**	**Mac Shortcut**	**Description**
Open GitHub Copilot Chat	*Ctrl + I*	*Cmd + I*	Opens Copilot Chat for inline AI suggestions.
Trigger Copilot Suggestion	*Tab*	*Tab*	Accepts the top suggestion from Copilot.
Show Next Suggestion	*Alt +]*	*Option +]*	Moves to the next Copilot-generated suggestion.
Show Previous Suggestion	*Alt + [*	*Option + [*	Moves back to the previous Copilot suggestion.
Dismiss Copilot Suggestion	*Esc*	*Esc*	Closes the current suggestion window.
View List of Suggestions	*Ctrl + Enter*	*Cmd + Enter*	Displays the list of all code suggestions for a specific prompt or code.

Table A.1: *Essential GitHub Copilot Shortcuts for Windows and Mac – Streamline AI-assisted coding with these handy commands*

Tip: *You can customize these shortcuts in Visual Studio Code settings if they conflict with other extensions or your personal preferences.*

Copilot Context Commands (#): For Referring to Code Components

Context variables allow Copilot to **fetch relevant sections of code** to improve responses.

GitHub Copilot Chat supports special context commands prefixed with # to help narrow down or expand the scope of its responses based on where you are working in your codebase. These context variables act as dynamic pointers, enabling Copilot to understand your intent better by referring to relevant code components such as files, selections, symbols, or terminal history.

Context Variable	Description
`#file`	Uses the entire currently open file as context.
`#selection`	Focuses Copilot responses on the selected block of code.
`#changes`	Refers to recent modifications in the codebase.
`#codebase`	Expands Copilot's knowledge to the entire project repository.
`#editor`	References the entire editor session.
`#terminalLastCommand`	Retrieves the last executed terminal command.
`#terminalSelection`	Uses the currently selected text from the terminal as context.
`#sym`	Provides details about a specific function, variable, or symbol in the code.

Table A.2: *GitHub Copilot Context Variables – Refine and personalize AI responses by referencing specific parts of your code or workspace*

Example Usage in Copilot Chat: **`"Explain the purpose of #selection and suggest improvements for readability." "Analyze #file for security vulnerabilities."`**

Copilot Chat Commands (@): For Dynamic Interactions

Copilot Chat commands allow developers to **request specific actions** such as debugging, testing, or refactoring code.

To unlock GitHub Copilot's full potential, developers can use @ chat commands that allow direct, actionable interactions, such as asking for help on a selected code block, debugging terminal issues, or referencing an entire workspace. These dynamic commands make Copilot more responsive and personalized during real-time conversations.

Chat Command	Description
`@workspace`	Uses the entire project workspace as context.
`@data`	Retrieves relevant data points from the current workspace.
`@file`	Calls for Copilot assistance on the active file.
`@selection`	Uses the selected text in the chat prompt.
`@terminal`	Fetches terminal command history or allows terminal-based interactions.
`@remote-ssh`	Refers to code running in a remote SSH session.
`@vision`	Engages Copilot Vision for analyzing complex files or diagrams.
`@vscode`	Uses VS Code API-related commands.
`@workspace /explain`	Explains the purpose and structure of the project.
`@workspace /fix`	Fixes detected errors in the workspace.
`@workspace /fixTestFailure`	Suggests fixes for failing test cases.
`@workspace /setupTests`	Sets up test configurations.
`@workspace /newNotebook`	Creates a new Jupyter notebook.
`/help`	Lists available Copilot commands.
`/clear`	Clears the chat history in the Copilot window.

Table A.3: *GitHub Copilot @ Chat Commands – Trigger targeted actions for live debugging, file-specific help, and remote code assistance*

Example Usage in Copilot Chat:

```
"@workspace /explain - Summarize the structure of this project and its key
components."
"@workspace /fixTestFailure - Resolve issues with the failing test cases."
```

Generate Documentation

GitHub Copilot makes it easier to maintain well-documented codebases with its built-in documentation generation command. This is especially useful when working with large projects or onboarding new team members, ensuring functions and methods are clearly explained.

Chat Command	Description
`/docs`	Generate documentation comments for all or only the selected methods and functions in the editor.

Table A.4: *GitHub Copilot /docs Command – Automatically generate inline documentation for selected or all functions in your editor*

Debug and Fix Problems

Debugging just got smarter with GitHub Copilot. These commands allow developers to fix errors, resolve test failures, and even initiate debugging sessions directly from the Chat or terminal. Whether you're dealing with a broken test or a misconfigured script, Copilot helps reduce the time spent hunting bugs.

Chat Command	Description
/fix	Ask Copilot for suggestions on how to fix a block of code or how to resolve any compiler or linting errors in your code. For example, to help fix unresolved Node.js package names.
/fixTestFailure	Ask Copilot for suggestions on how to fix failing tests.
/startDebugging (Experimental)	Generate a `launch.json` debug configuration file and start a debugging session from the Chat view. https://code.visualstudio.com/updates/v1_93#_start-debugging-from-chat-experimental.
`copilot-debug` command	Terminal command to help you debug your programs. Prefix a run command to start a debugging session for it (for example, copilot-debug python foo.py). https://code.visualstudio.com/updates/v1_96#_debugging-with-copilot

Table A.5: *GitHub Copilot Commands for Debugging – Automate Fixes and Streamline Troubleshooting with In-Editor and Terminal-Based Copilot support*

Scaffold a New Project

Copilot can help you create a new project by generating a scaffold of the project structure, or generate a notebook based on your requirements.

Starting a new project or data analysis? GitHub Copilot Chat supports scaffold generation through intuitive commands. By simply describing your requirements in natural language, you can spin up boilerplate code, project structures, or even tailored Jupyter notebooks—saving valuable setup time.

Chat Command	Description
`/new`	Use the **`/new`** command in the Chat view to scaffold a new project or a new file. Use natural language to describe the type of **`project/file`** you need, and preview the scaffolded content before creating it. Example: /new Express app using typescript and svelte
`/newNotebook`	Use the **`/newNotebook`** command in the Chat view to generate a new Jupyter notebook based on your requirements. Use natural language to describe what the notebook should contain. Example: **`/newNotebook`** get census data and preview key insights with Seaborn.

***Table A.6**: GitHub Copilot Scaffold Commands – Instantly Generate New Projects or Notebooks using /new and /newNotebook Commands in Chat*

Tips and Tricks for Efficient Usage

While Copilot is a powerful assistant, maximizing its effectiveness requires **strategic usage and best practices**. Following are key tips to improve productivity:

1. Improve Code Suggestions with Structured Comments
    - Instead of writing vague function names, **add meaningful comments before writing the function header**.
    - **Example**: Instead of writing **`def calc(x):`**, write:

    ```
    # Calculate the total price after discount
    def calculate_discounted_price(original_price: float, discount: float) -> float:
    ```
2. **Use Copilot Chat for Conceptual Questions**
    - When unsure about an implementation, **ask Copilot Chat to generate multiple approaches**.
    - **Example**: Instead of manually searching for the best sorting algorithm, ask: "*Compare the efficiency of Merge Sort and Quick Sort in Python.*"
3. **Know When to Use Inline Copilot versus Copilot Chat**
    - **Inline Copilot:** Best for completing small code blocks, boilerplate code, and common patterns.
    - **Copilot Chat:** Better suited for debugging, refactoring, complex multi-step logic, and performance optimizations.
4. **Customizing Copilot for Your Workflow**
    - Adjust Copilot settings in **VS Code or JetBrains** to control **suggestion frequency and verbosity**.
    - Use **#selection**, **#file** variables to **focus Copilot's responses**.
5. **Reviewing AI-Generated Code**
    - Always **validate Copilot's output for correctness, security, and best practices**.
    - Be cautious with **sensitive data such as API keys, database credentials, and hardcoded passwords**.

Appendix B: Resources and Further Reading

Essential GitHub Copilot Resources

Whether you're just starting with GitHub Copilot or looking to master its capabilities, having the right resources at your fingertips makes all the difference. Following are some essential links to official documentation, cheat sheets, and best practice guides designed to help you get the most out of Copilot inside VS Code.

Resource	Description	Access Link
GitHub Copilot in VS Code Cheat Sheet	A quick reference guide covering all major Copilot features, shortcuts, and workflows in VS Code.	https://code.visualstudio.com/docs/copilot/copilot-vscode-features
Essentials of GitHub Copilot	A structured learning pathway covering the fundamentals of Copilot, how it works, and how to use it efficiently.	https://resources.github.com/learn/pathways/copilot/essentials/essentials-of-github-copilot/
Best Practices for Using GitHub Copilot in VS Code	A detailed guide on effective prompt crafting and best practices to maximize Copilot's AI suggestions in VS Code.	https://code.visualstudio.com/docs/copilot/prompt-crafting
GitHub Copilot Official Documentation	Complete documentation covering setup, configurations, and advanced use cases of Copilot.	https://docs.github.com/en/copilot/
Inside GitHub: How Copilot Works	A deep dive into the LLM models and AI architecture powering GitHub Copilot.	https://github.blog/ai-and-ml/github-copilot/inside-github-working-with-the-llms-behind-github-copilot/
GitHub Copilot Security and Privacy Guide	Official security best practices and privacy considerations when using GitHub Copilot.	https://blog.gitguardian.com/github-copilot-security-and-privacy/
GitHub Copilot Discussion Forum	Engage with the community, ask questions, and explore use cases in the official GitHub Copilot discussion forum.	https://github.com/orgs/community/discussions

Table B.1: *Must-Have GitHub Copilot Resources – Official Guides and Learning Paths to Accelerate your Copilot Expertise in Visual Studio Code*

Developer Communities and Forums for AI Assisted Coding

Learning GitHub Copilot becomes even more effective when you engage with the developer community. Whether you are seeking answers, sharing your experiences, or exploring advanced use cases, these forums and communities offer valuable peer support and insights.

Community	Description	Access Link
Stack Overflow - GitHub Copilot	Questions and discussions on Copilot, troubleshooting, and advanced use cases.	https://stackoverflow.com/questions/tagged/github-copilot
Reddit - r/github	A broad discussion forum for GitHub-related topics, including Copilot.	https://www.reddit.com/r/github/
Dev.to - GitHub Copilot	Articles, tutorials, and experiences from developers using GitHub Copilot.	https://dev.to/t/githubcopilot

Table B.2: *Developer Communities for GitHub Copilot – Connect, discuss, and Grow your AI coding Skills with Peers across Stack Overflow, Reddit, and Dev.to*

Open-Source Projects Using Copilot

Exploring open-source projects that utilize GitHub Copilot is a great way to learn by example. These projects showcase practical implementations of AI-powered development workflows and serve as inspiration for your own Copilot-enabled tools and experiments.

Project	Description	Access Link
Copilot Labs (GitHub)	Experimental AI-powered developer tools using GitHub Copilot.	**https://githubnext.com/projects/copilot-labs/**
OpenAI Codex Projects	Repositories demonstrating AI-powered coding techniques and Copilot integrations.	**https://github.com/topics/openai-codex**
AI-Powered Developer Tools	A collection of open-source projects leveraging AI for software development.	**https://github.com/topics/ai-developer-tools**

Table B.3: *Notable Open-Source Projects Using GitHub Copilot – Discover how Developers are Leveraging Copilot in Real-World AI Software Projects*

Appendix C: Glossary of Terms

Definitions of Key Terms and Concepts

To make the most of GitHub Copilot and AI-assisted development, it's important to understand the foundational terms and technologies behind it. Here's a glossary of key concepts that will help you grasp the ecosystem and terminology commonly used in AI-powered software engineering.

Term	Definition
AI-Assisted Coding	The use of Artificial Intelligence (AI) tools such as GitHub Copilot to generate, optimize, and enhance software development workflows.
GitHub Copilot	An AI-powered code completion tool developed by GitHub, powered by OpenAI Codex, designed to assist developers in writing code faster.
LLM (Large Language Model)	A machine learning model trained on massive datasets to generate human-like text, used in AI-assisted coding tools such as GitHub Copilot.
Copilot Chat	An interactive chat-based interface within GitHub Copilot that allows developers to ask questions, request code improvements, and receive AI-generated explanations.
Prompt Engineering	The practice of crafting structured and effective prompts to guide AI tools such as Copilot in generating relevant and accurate responses.
Context Awareness	Copilot's ability to understand and provide code suggestions based on the surrounding code, function names, and comments.
Code Completion	AI-generated suggestions that autocomplete lines of code based on context and best practices.
Refactoring	The process of restructuring existing code to improve readability, efficiency, and maintainability without changing its functionality.
Unit Testing	A software testing approach where individual components or functions are tested in isolation to ensure correctness.
Integration Testing	A testing approach where multiple components or modules are combined and tested as a group.
CI/CD (Continuous Integration/Continuous Deployment)	A DevOps practice that automates the building, testing, and deployment of applications.
Pair Programming	A software development technique where two programmers work together at one workstation, now possible in AI-assisted environments with GitHub Copilot.
API (Application Programming Interface)	A set of protocols and tools that allow different software applications to communicate with each other.
Security Best Practices	Guidelines and techniques used to protect code, applications, and systems from vulnerabilities and cyber threats.

Telemetry	Data collected from user interactions with software to analyze usage patterns and improve features. GitHub Copilot provides controls to disable telemetry for privacy.
OpenAI Codex	The AI model that powers GitHub Copilot, trained on large codebases to generate intelligent code suggestions.
Fine-Tuning	The process of refining an AI model using specific datasets to enhance performance for particular applications.
IDE (Integrated Development Environment)	Software applications including Visual Studio Code or JetBrains that provide comprehensive tools for coding, debugging, and testing.
Auto-Documentation	AI-generated comments, summaries, and explanations to improve code readability and maintainability.

***Table C.1**: Key Definitions in the GitHub Copilot Ecosystem – Core Concepts that Underpin AI-Assisted Coding and Copilot Functionality*

Quick Reference Guide

This **reference section** provides **brief explanations** of commonly used **GitHub Copilot commands, context variables, and AI-related terminology**.

- **GitHub Copilot Context Variables (#)**
  - `#file`: Uses the entire open file as context for AI-generated responses.
  - `#selection`: Focuses Copilot's response on a selected block of code.
  - `#codebase`: Expands AI's understanding to the entire project repository.
  - `#terminalLastCommand`: Uses the most recent terminal command for context.
- Copilot Chat Commands (@)
  - `@workspace`: References the entire project workspace for broader AI assistance.
  - `@workspace /fix`: Requests AI-generated fixes for detected issues.
  - `@workspace /explain`: Asks Copilot to summarize the project or selected code.
  - `/help`: Displays available Copilot commands.
- **Key GitHub Copilot Features**
  - **Inline Suggestions:** Copilot generates real-time code completions as you type.
  - **Copilot Chat:** Interactive AI assistance within the IDE.
  - **Test Case Generation:** AI assisted unit and integration test writing.
  - **Security Awareness:** Built-in settings to manage privacy and prevent sensitive data leakage.

Appendix D: Sample Projects and Code Snippets

Example Projects for Hands-On Learning: Following are **two structured project examples** that **leverage Copilot for AI-assisted development**, covering both frontend and backend development.

Overview of the Project

This project demonstrates **the practical use of GitHub Copilot** in building a **full-stack AI-powered To-Do List Web App** using **React, Node.js, Express, MongoDB, and OpenAI API**. The app allows users to **create, manage, and categorize tasks automatically using AI**.

Key Features:

- **User Authentication**: Secure login and signup using JWT authentication.
- **Task Management**: CRUD (Create, Read, Update, Delete) operations for tasks.
- **AI-Powered Task Categorization**: Uses OpenAI to automatically classify tasks into categories (Work, Personal, Urgent, and more).
- **Priority and Deadline Reminders**: Sends notifications when deadlines are near.
- **Dark Mode and Responsive UI**: Fully optimized for mobile and desktop use.

Step-by-Step Implementation with GitHub Copilot Assistance

Step 1: Setting Up the Project

Prompt:

```
"Generate a step-by-step guide to set up a full-stack React and Node.js
application with MongoDB using GitHub Copilot."
```

GitHub Copilot's Output:

a. Initialize the project using `npm init -y`

b. Install dependencies:

```
npm install express mongoose cors dotenv jsonwebtoken bcryptjs openai
```

a. Set up server.js for Express and MongoDB connection

b. Create `models/Task.js` schema for managing tasks

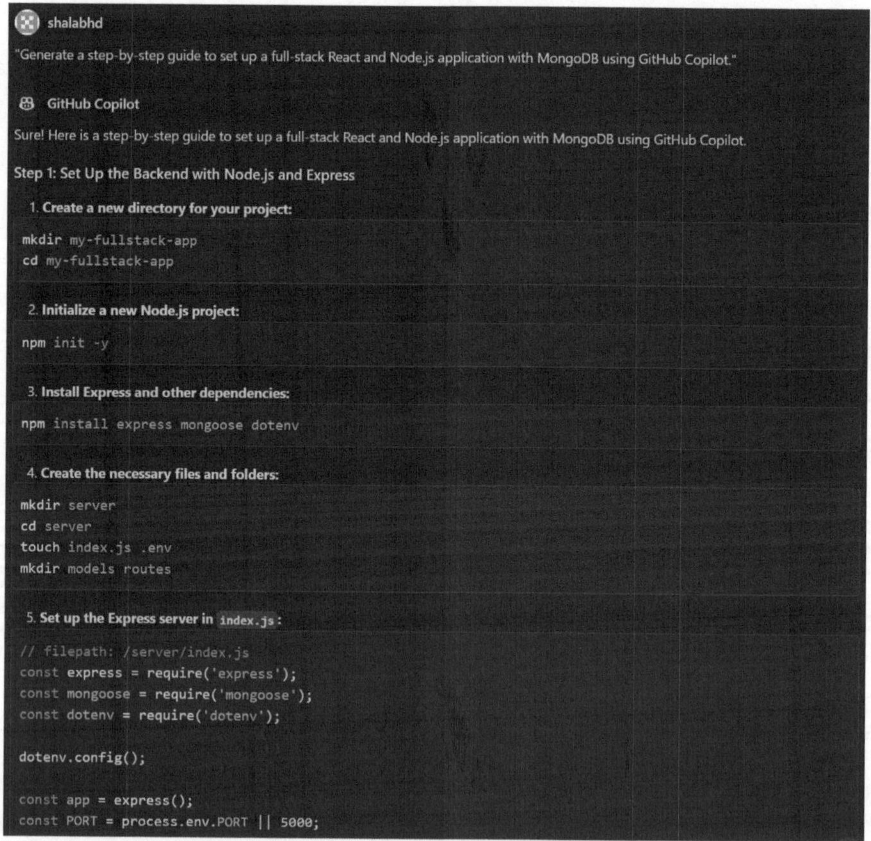

Figure D.1: *Step-by-step Copilot-Assisted Guide to set up a Full-Stack Node.js + Express Backend with MongoDB Integration*

Setting up a modern full-stack application does not have to be overwhelming. With GitHub Copilot, you can scaffold a Node.js backend with Express and MongoDB in minutes using simple, AI-guided steps.

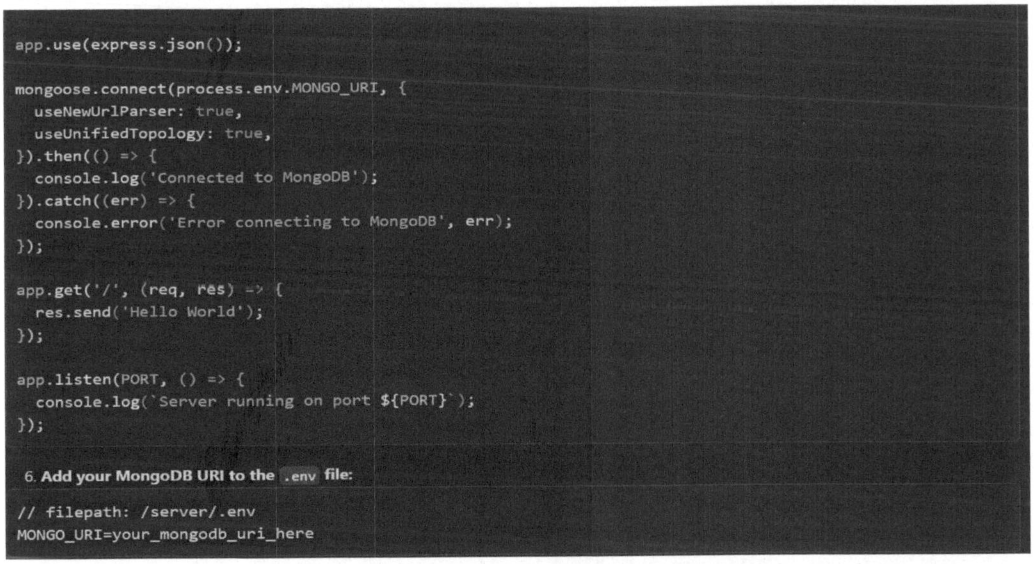

```
app.use(express.json());

mongoose.connect(process.env.MONGO_URI, {
  useNewUrlParser: true,
  useUnifiedTopology: true,
}).then(() => {
  console.log('Connected to MongoDB');
}).catch((err) => {
  console.error('Error connecting to MongoDB', err);
});

app.get('/', (req, res) => {
  res.send('Hello World');
});

app.listen(PORT, () => {
  console.log(`Server running on port ${PORT}`);
});
```

6. **Add your MongoDB URI to the `.env` file:**

```
// filepath: /server/.env
MONGO_URI=your_mongodb_uri_here
```

Figure D.2: *Step-by-step Copilot-Assisted Guide to set up a Full-Stack Node.js + Express Backend with MongoDB Integration*

After initializing your Express server, the next step is to connect your backend to MongoDB and define a basic route to verify it's working–all with just a few lines of code and help from GitHub Copilot.

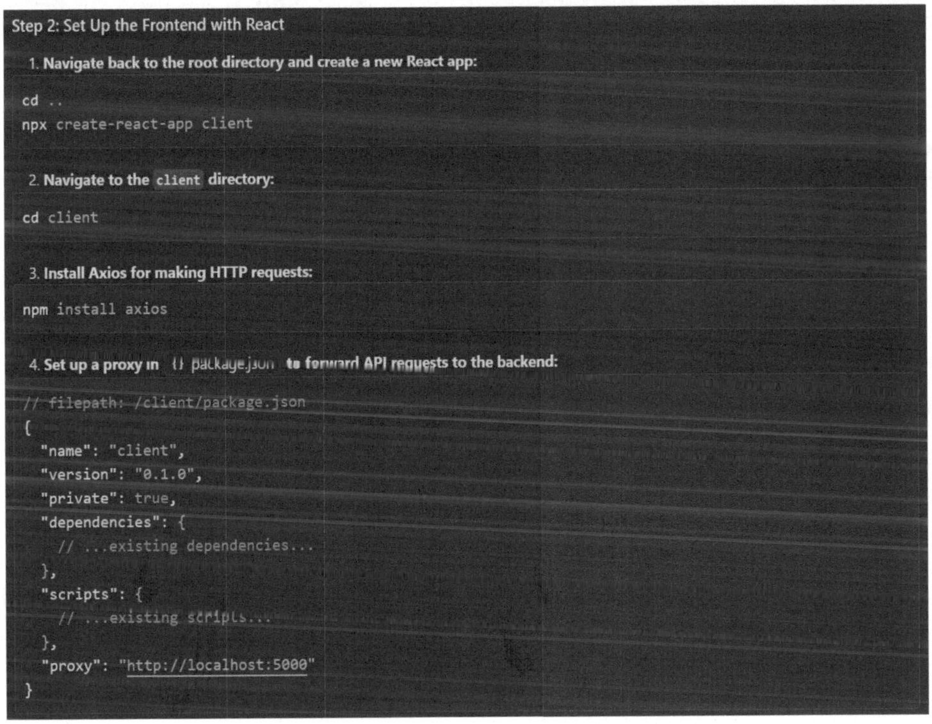

Step 2: Set Up the Frontend with React

1. **Navigate back to the root directory and create a new React app:**

```
cd ..
npx create-react-app client
```

2. **Navigate to the `client` directory:**

```
cd client
```

3. **Install Axios for making HTTP requests:**

```
npm install axios
```

4. **Set up a proxy in {} package.json to forward API requests to the backend:**

```
// filepath: /client/package.json
{
  "name": "client",
  "version": "0.1.0",
  "private": true,
  "dependencies": {
    // ...existing dependencies...
  },
  "scripts": {
    // ...existing scripts...
  },
  "proxy": "http://localhost:5000"
}
```

Figure D.3: *MongoDB Integration and Server Initialization in Express – Complete with Route Handling and Environment-Based Configuration*

To complete the full-stack setup, you need to connect your backend API with the frontend. This step demonstrates how to create a simple Express route and consume it within a React component using Axios.

Step 3: Connect Frontend and Backend

1. **Create a simple API route in the backend:**

```
// filepath: /server/routes/sampleRoute.js
const express = require('express');
const router = express.Router();

router.get('/data', (req, res) => {
  res.json({ message: 'Hello from the backend!' });
});

module.exports = router;
```

2. **Use the route in `index.js`:**

```
// filepath: /server/index.js
const sampleRoute = require('./routes/sampleRoute');

app.use('/api', sampleRoute);
```

3. **Fetch data from the backend in a React component:**

```
// filepath: /client/src/App.js
import React, { useEffect, useState } from 'react';
import axios from 'axios';

function App() {
  const [data, setData] = useState(null);

  useEffect(() => {
    axios.get('/api/data')
      .then(response => {
        setData(response.data.message);
      })
      .catch(error => {
        console.error('Error fetching data:', error);
      });
  }, []);
```

Figure D.4: *Connecting Frontend and Backend – Define an Express API Route and Fetch the Response in a React app using Axios and useEffect*

Refer to the complete code generated at the following GitHub Repo link: *appendices\sample-projects\todo-app-fullstack*

Step 2: Building the Backend with Express and MongoDB

Prompt:

> **`"Write an Express.js server file that connects to MongoDB and defines routes for CRUD operations for a task management system."`**

GitHub Copilot's Output:

- A complete server.js file with MongoDB connection
- RESTful API routes (/tasks, /tasks/:id) for task management
- Middleware for authentication using JWT

Building a backend for a task management system begins with setting up a server that can handle CRUD operations. GitHub Copilot helps accelerate this by generating boilerplate code to connect MongoDB and define initial models.

shalabhd

"Write an Express.js server file that connects to MongoDB and defines routes for CRUD operations for a task management system."

GitHub Copilot

Sure! Here is an Express.js server file that connects to MongoDB and defines routes for CRUD operations for a task management system.

Step 1: Install Dependencies

First, make sure you have the necessary dependencies installed:

```
npm install express mongoose dotenv
```

Step 2: Create the Server File

Create a file named `server.js` and add the following code:

```
const express = require('express');
const mongoose = require('mongoose');
const dotenv = require('dotenv');

dotenv.config();

const app = express();
const PORT = process.env.PORT || 5000;

app.use(express.json());

// Connect to MongoDB
mongoose.connect(process.env.MONGO_URI, {
  useNewUrlParser: true,
  useUnifiedTopology: true,
}).then(() => {
  console.log('Connected to MongoDB');
}).catch((err) => {
  console.error('Error connecting to MongoDB', err);
});

// Task Schema and Model
const taskSchema = new mongoose.Schema({
  title: { type: String, required: true },
  description: String,
```

Figure D.5: *Express.js + MongoDB Server Setup for a Task Management App – Includes Database Connection and Schema Definition using GitHub Copilot*

Once your server and MongoDB connection are in place, you can define CRUD (Create, Read, Update, Delete) routes to manage tasks effectively. GitHub Copilot can assist in scaffolding these endpoints with proper error handling and data models.

```
  completed: { type: Boolean, default: false },
}, { timestamps: true });

const Task = mongoose.model('Task', taskSchema);

// CRUD Routes

// Create a new task
app.post('/tasks', async (req, res) => {
  try {
    const task = new Task(req.body);
    await task.save();
    res.status(201).json(task);
  } catch (error) {
    res.status(400).json({ error: error.message });
  }
});

// Read all tasks
app.get('/tasks', async (req, res) => {
  try {
    const tasks = await Task.find();
    res.status(200).json(tasks);
  } catch (error) {
    res.status(500).json({ error: error.message });
  }
});

// Read a single task by ID
app.get('/tasks/:id', async (req, res) => {
  try {
    const task = await Task.findById(req.params.id);
    if (!task) {
      return res.status(404).json({ error: 'Task not found' });
    }
    res.status(200).json(task);
  } catch (error) {
    res.status(500).json({ error: error.message });
  }
});
```

Figure D.6: *Express.js CRUD API for Task Management – Create, Retrieve all, and Fetch Task by ID with Mongoose Integration*

Refer to the complete code generated at the following GitHub Repo link: *appendices\sample-projects\todo-app-fullstack\backend*

Step 3: Implementing AI-Powered Task Categorization

Prompt:

```
"Write a Node.js function that uses OpenAI API to categorize a given task
based on its content."
```

GitHub Copilot's Output:

- OpenAI API integration to analyze text input
- AI categorization logic to suggest a task category
- API route to send task descriptions for AI categorization

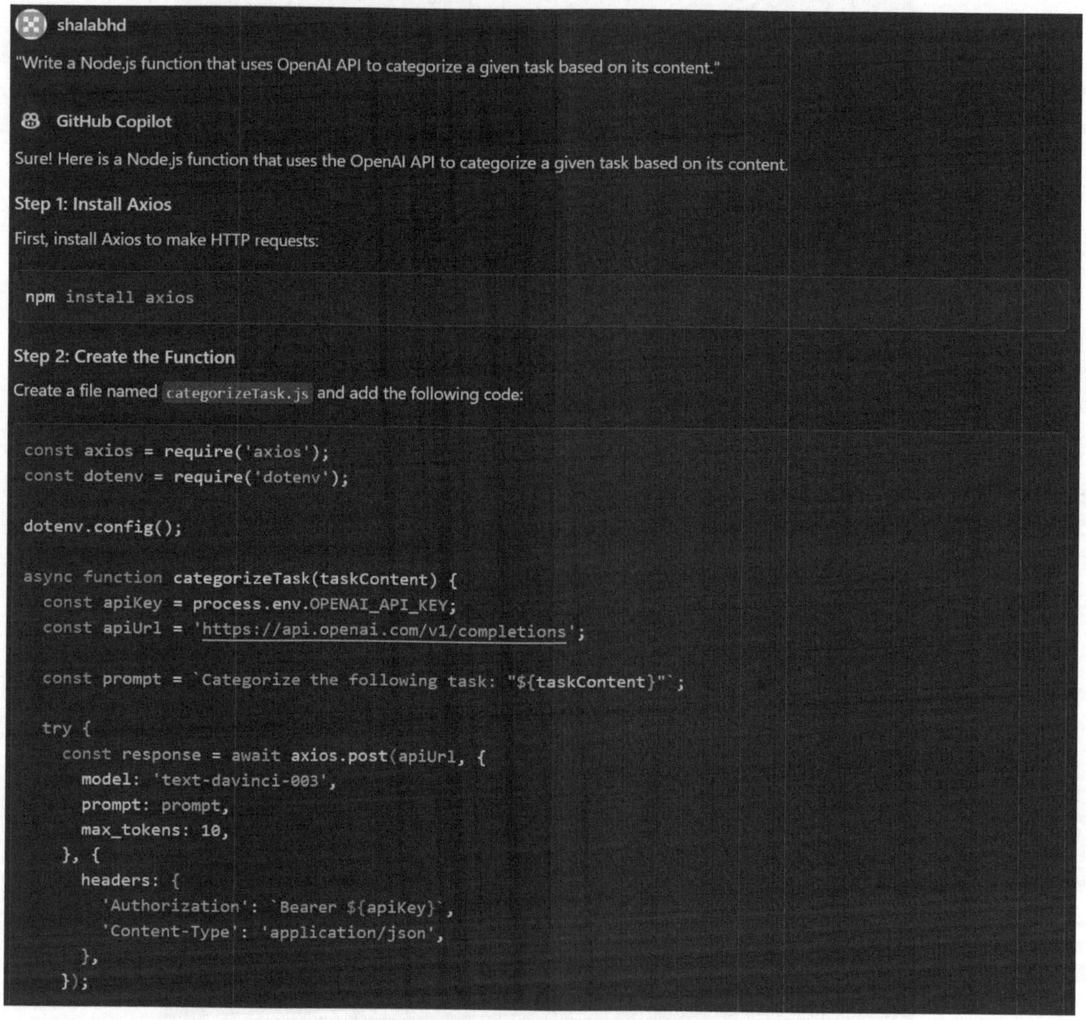

shalabhd

"Write a Node.js function that uses OpenAI API to categorize a given task based on its content."

GitHub Copilot

Sure! Here is a Node.js function that uses the OpenAI API to categorize a given task based on its content.

Step 1: Install Axios

First, install Axios to make HTTP requests:

```
npm install axios
```

Step 2: Create the Function

Create a file named `categorizeTask.js` and add the following code:

```
const axios = require('axios');
const dotenv = require('dotenv');

dotenv.config();

async function categorizeTask(taskContent) {
  const apiKey = process.env.OPENAI_API_KEY;
  const apiUrl = 'https://api.openai.com/v1/completions';

  const prompt = `Categorize the following task: "${taskContent}"`;

  try {
    const response = await axios.post(apiUrl, {
      model: 'text-davinci-003',
      prompt: prompt,
      max_tokens: 10,
    }, {
      headers: {
        'Authorization': `Bearer ${apiKey}`,
        'Content-Type': 'application/json',
      },
    });
```

***Figure D.7:** Express.js CRUD API for Task Management – Create, Retrieve all, and Fetch Task by ID with Mongoose Integration*

Refer to the complete code generated at the following GitHub Repo link: *appendices\sample-projects\todo-app-fullstack\categorizeTask.js*

Step 4: Creating the Frontend with React

Prompt:

```
"Generate a React.js component to display and manage a to-do list with CRUD
operations."
```

GitHub Copilot's Output:

- A React component with state management using **`useState`** and **`useEffect`**
- API calls using **`fetch()`** to interact with the backend
- Task UI with edit and delete functionalities

With your backend APIs ready, it's time to build a frontend interface to manage your to-do tasks. Using React and Axios, this component fetches and adds tasks by interacting with the Express backend.

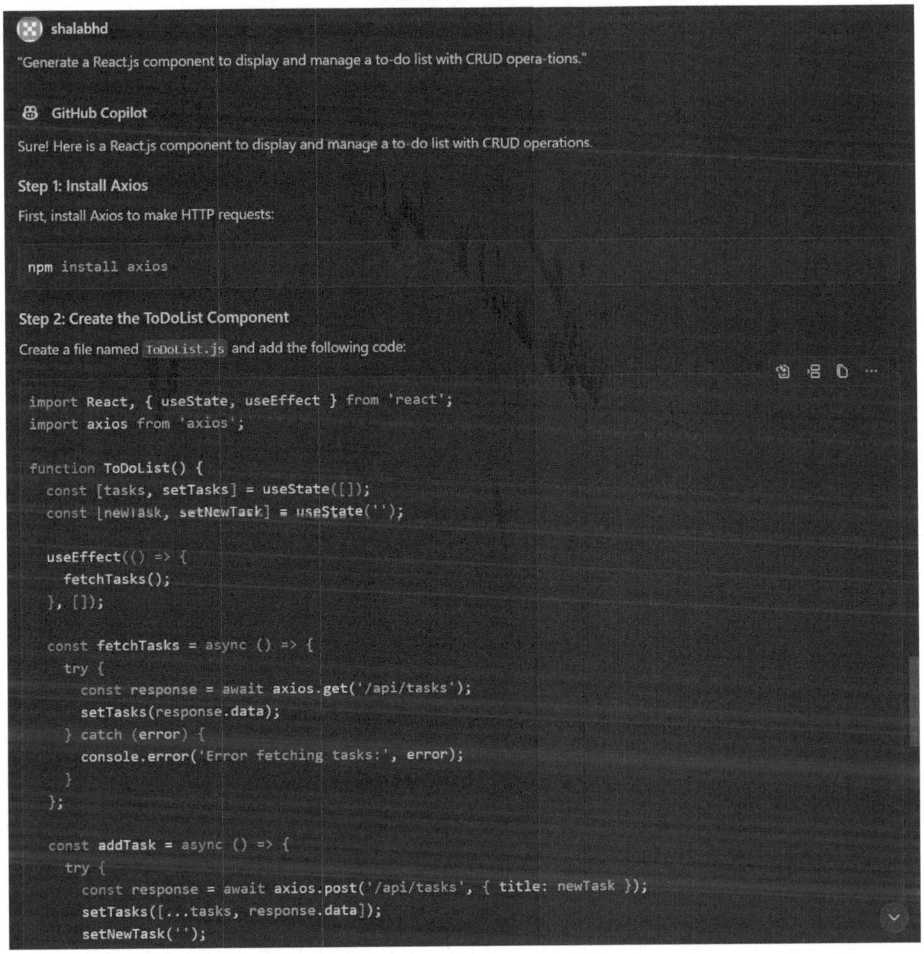

shalabhd

"Generate a React.js component to display and manage a to-do list with CRUD opera-tions."

GitHub Copilot

Sure! Here is a React.js component to display and manage a to-do list with CRUD operations.

Step 1: Install Axios

First, install Axios to make HTTP requests:

```
npm install axios
```

Step 2: Create the ToDoList Component

Create a file named `ToDoList.js` and add the following code:

```
import React, { useState, useEffect } from 'react';
import axios from 'axios';

function ToDoList() {
  const [tasks, setTasks] = useState([]);
  const [newTask, setNewTask] = useState('');

  useEffect(() => {
    fetchTasks();
  }, []);

  const fetchTasks = async () => {
    try {
      const response = await axios.get('/api/tasks');
      setTasks(response.data);
    } catch (error) {
      console.error('Error fetching tasks:', error);
    }
  };

  const addTask = async () => {
    try {
      const response = await axios.post('/api/tasks', { title: newTask });
      setTasks([...tasks, response.data]);
      setNewTask('');
```

Figure D.8: *React ToDoList Component – Fetch and Add Tasks using Axios with Full CRUD Support for a Connected Task Management System*

Refer to the complete code generated at the following GitHub Repo link: *appendices\sample-projects\todo-app-fullstack\frontend\components\TodoList.jsx*

Step 5: Enhancing UI with AI-Powered Task Categorization

Prompt:

```
"Modify the React UI to allow users to click a button and automatically
categorize tasks using OpenAI."
```

GitHub Copilot's Output:

- A button to send task descriptions to the AI API
- Updated UI with categorized labels
- API request to fetch AI-generated categories

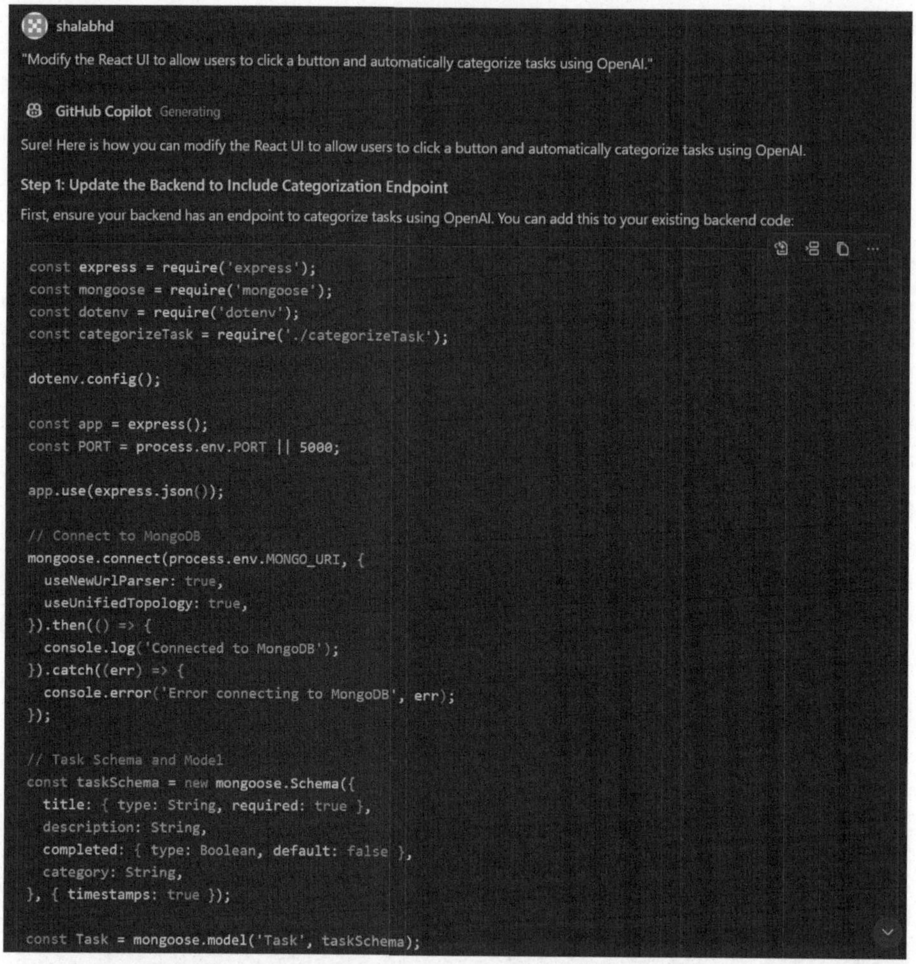

shalabhd

"Modify the React UI to allow users to click a button and automatically categorize tasks using OpenAI."

GitHub Copilot Generating

Sure! Here is how you can modify the React UI to allow users to click a button and automatically categorize tasks using OpenAI.

Step 1: Update the Backend to Include Categorization Endpoint

First, ensure your backend has an endpoint to categorize tasks using OpenAI. You can add this to your existing backend code:

```
const express = require('express');
const mongoose = require('mongoose');
const dotenv = require('dotenv');
const categorizeTask = require('./categorizeTask');

dotenv.config();

const app = express();
const PORT = process.env.PORT || 5000;

app.use(express.json());

// Connect to MongoDB
mongoose.connect(process.env.MONGO_URI, {
  useNewUrlParser: true,
  useUnifiedTopology: true,
}).then(() => {
  console.log('Connected to MongoDB');
}).catch((err) => {
  console.error('Error connecting to MongoDB', err);
});

// Task Schema and Model
const taskSchema = new mongoose.Schema({
  title: { type: String, required: true },
  description: String,
  completed: { type: Boolean, default: false },
  category: String,
}, { timestamps: true });

const Task = mongoose.model('Task', taskSchema);
```

Figure D.9: *React ToDoList Component – Fetch and Add Tasks using Axios with Full CRUD Support for a Connected Task Management System*

Refer to the complete code generated at the following GitHub Repo link: *appendices\sample-projects\todo-app-fullstack\frontend\components\TaskList.jsx*

Step 6: Deployment and CI/CD Integration

To deploy the app and automate testing, GitHub Copilot assists in:

- Writing **Dockerfiles** for containerization
- Setting up **GitHub Actions** for CI/CD
- Automating **unit tests using Jest and Mocha**

Prompt for Deployment:

```
"Generate a GitHub Actions pipeline to deploy a full-stack React and Node.js
app to AWS."
```

Copilot's Output:

- A **GitHub Actions YAML pipeline** for automated deployment
- Integration with **AWS Elastic Beanstalk/Heroku**
- Environment variable management for **secrets and API keys**

Automating deployments is a crucial part of modern DevOps workflows. GitHub Copilot can help you generate a CI/CD pipeline using GitHub Actions to deploy a full-stack React and Node.js application to AWS with ease.

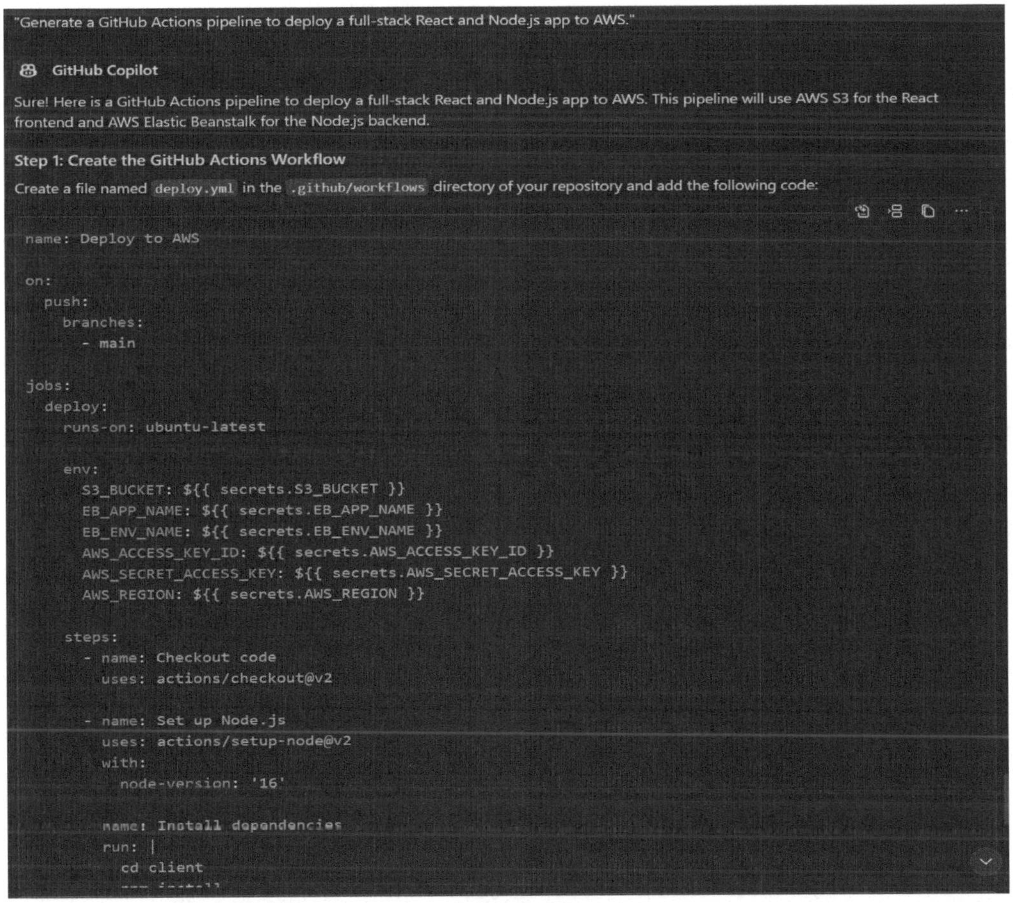

"Generate a GitHub Actions pipeline to deploy a full-stack React and Node.js app to AWS."

GitHub Copilot

Sure! Here is a GitHub Actions pipeline to deploy a full-stack React and Node.js app to AWS. This pipeline will use AWS S3 for the React frontend and AWS Elastic Beanstalk for the Node.js backend.

Step 1: Create the GitHub Actions Workflow

Create a file named `deploy.yml` in the `.github/workflows` directory of your repository and add the following code:

```
name: Deploy to AWS

on:
  push:
    branches:
      - main

jobs:
  deploy:
    runs-on: ubuntu-latest

    env:
      S3_BUCKET: ${{ secrets.S3_BUCKET }}
      EB_APP_NAME: ${{ secrets.EB_APP_NAME }}
      EB_ENV_NAME: ${{ secrets.EB_ENV_NAME }}
      AWS_ACCESS_KEY_ID: ${{ secrets.AWS_ACCESS_KEY_ID }}
      AWS_SECRET_ACCESS_KEY: ${{ secrets.AWS_SECRET_ACCESS_KEY }}
      AWS_REGION: ${{ secrets.AWS_REGION }}

    steps:
      - name: Checkout code
        uses: actions/checkout@v2

      - name: Set up Node.js
        uses: actions/setup-node@v2
        with:
          node-version: '16'

      - name: Install dependencies
        run: |
          cd client
```

Figure D.10: *GitHub Actions Workflow File (deploy.yml) – Automates Deployment of a React + Node.js App to AWS using S3 and Elastic Beanstalk*

Refer to the complete code generated at the following GitHub Repo link: *appendices\sample-projects\todo-app-fullstack\deployment\github-actions\deploy-to-aws.yml*

Appendix E: AI-Driven Code Generation GitHub Copilot Prompts for Multiple Technologies

These prompt templates are primarily designed for GitHub Copilot but can also be adapted for use with other AI coding assistants such as ChatGPT, AWS CodeWhisperer, or Tabine. Developers can customize the prompts slightly depending on the specific tool's syntax, interface, and context awareness.

GitHub Copilot Prompts for Java Development

Table E.1 shows real-world prompt examples and their expected outputs for generating Java classes, REST APIs, multi-threaded programs, and JUnit 5 test cases:

Use Case	Effective Prompt	Copilot's Expected Output
Generate a Java Class with Encapsulation	`"Create a Java class named Employee with private fields id, name, and salary. Include a constructor, getters, and setters."`	Generates a well-structured Java class with constructors, encapsulation, and accessor methods.
Develop a Spring Boot REST API	`"Write a Spring Boot REST API with an endpoint/employees that returns a list of employees."`	Provides a complete REST controller with CRUD operations using Spring Boot.

Implement Multi-Threading using `ExecutorService`	`"Write a Java program that runs multiple tasks in parallel using ExecutorService."`	Generates a thread pool-based concurrent program using Java's Executor framework.
Write JUnit 5 Test Cases	`"Generate a JUnit 5 test class to verify the addition and subtraction methods of a Calculator class."`	Creates unit tests with assertions using JUnit 5 for test coverage.
DAO Pattern for Database Operations	`"Write a Java DAO class for managing Customer table operations using JDBC."`	Produces a Data Access Object (DAO) implementation using JDBC with prepared statements.
Singleton Design Pattern	`"Write a thread-safe Singleton pattern implementation in Java."`	Implements lazy-initialized Singleton using synchronized methods or Bill Pugh's approach.
Factory Design Pattern	`"Create a Java Factory Pattern to generate objects for different vehicle types (Car, Bike, Truck)."`	Provides a Factory design pattern implementation with a factory method.
Refactor Code for Performance Optimization	`"Refactor the #selection to improve efficiency and maintainability."`	Suggests code optimization strategies such as removing redundant loops, improving readability, and modularization.
Spring Boot Caching Mechanism	`"Enable caching in a Spring Boot application using @Cacheable and create a service layer that caches database queries."`	Generates Spring Boot caching implementation using Redis or in-memory caching.
JWT Authentication in Spring Boot	`"Write a Spring Boot security configuration that implements JWT-based authentication for API endpoints."`	Provides Spring Security integration with JWT for secure API access.
Write SQL Queries in Java Efficiently	`"Optimize an SQL query in Java that fetches user details efficiently for large datasets."`	Suggests batch processing, indexing, and pagination techniques for database performance.
Read and Write JSON using Jackson Library	`"Write a Java program using Jackson to convert a JSON string into a Java object and vice versa."`	Generates code for serialization and deserialization using Jackson `ObjectMapper`.
Spring Boot Microservices Communication	`"Implement inter-service communication between two Spring Boot microservices using Feign Client."`	Generates Feign client setup for microservices communication.
Logging in Java using SLF4J and Logback	`"Write a logging mechanism using SLF4J and Logback to log error messages in a Java application."`	Provides best practices for logging and structured logging implementation.
File Handling in Java	`"Write a Java program to read a text file, count the number of words, and save results to another file."`	Generates code using `BufferedReader` and `FileWriter` for efficient file handling.
Spring Boot Scheduling with @ Scheduled	`"Write a Spring Boot service that executes a scheduled task every 5 minutes using @Scheduled."`	Provides Spring Boot scheduled task implementation.
Exception Handling Best Practices	`"Refactor the #selection to include proper exception handling using try-catch and custom exceptions."`	Suggests improvements in error handling and debugging strategies.
Integration Testing with Spring Boot	`"Generate an integration test for a Spring Boot REST API using @ SpringBootTest and TestRestTemplate."`	Provides a Spring Boot integration test setup.

CI/CD Pipeline for Java Projects	**"Create a GitHub Actions workflow YAML file to build, test, and deploy a Java Spring Boot application."**	Generates a CI/CD pipeline script for GitHub Actions with Maven.
REST API Documentation with Swagger	**"Configure Swagger API documentation for a Spring Boot REST API."**	Provides Swagger/OpenAPI integration for API documentation.

Table E.1: *GitHub Copilot Prompts for Java Development*

GitHub Copilot Prompts for C# Development

Table E.2 shows the examples of effective prompts and expected AI-generated outputs for ASP.NET Core APIs, Entity Framework models, and LINQ queries:

Use Case	Effective Prompt	Copilot's Expected Output
Creating an ASP.NET Core API	**"Create an ASP.NET Core Web API controller for managing products with basic CRUD endpoints."**	Generates a structured ASP.NET Core Web API controller with `GET`, `POST`, `PUT`, and `DELETE` endpoints.
Entity Framework Core DB Model	**"Write an Entity Framework Core code-first model class for an 'Order' with related 'OrderItems'."**	Provides model classes with proper navigation properties and data annotations.
LINQ Query for Filtering Data	**"Write a LINQ query in C# to filter customers based on registration date and active status."**	Generates an efficient LINQ query utilizing `.Where()` and `.Select()` clauses.
Implement Dependency Injection	**"Configure Dependency Injection in ASP.NET Core for a custom logging service."**	Outputs the registration code for services within the ASP.NET Core `Startup.cs`.
Asynchronous Programming	**"Write an asynchronous method in C# to fetch data from an external API and handle exceptions."**	Provides an async method with HttpClient, proper exception handling, and await usage.
Unit Testing with xUnit	**"Generate xUnit test methods to verify a string manipulation class in C#."**	Produces structured test cases with Assert statements for thorough coverage.
Creating a Middleware in ASP.NET	**"Implement custom middleware in ASP.NET Core to log incoming HTTP requests and responses."**	Provides a middleware class and integration into the pipeline via `app.UseMiddleware`.
JWT Authentication in ASP.NET	**"Configure JWT-based authentication in an ASP.NET Core Web API project."**	Outputs JWT authentication logic, including token generation and validation.
Error Handling and Logging	**"Write a global exception handling middleware for an ASP.NET Core application with Serilog logging."**	Suggests a robust middleware implementation for capturing and logging exceptions globally.
Implement AutoMapper	**"Configure AutoMapper to map domain models to DTOs in an ASP.NET Core project."**	Generates AutoMapper profiles and mapping configurations.
Reading/Writing JSON with Newtonsoft.Json	**"Write a method in C# using Newtonsoft.Json to deserialize a JSON string to an object."**	Provides clear deserialization and serialization logic.
Using Redis Cache in .NET Core	**"Implement caching with Redis in an ASP.NET Core application."**	Outputs code for Redis cache integration using `StackExchange.Redis`.

SignalR for Real-Time Communication	`"Create a basic chat functionality in an ASP.NET Core application using SignalR."`	Suggests Hub class, client-side JavaScript, and SignalR startup configuration.
Creating Background Tasks	`"Implement a background service in ASP.NET Core that periodically cleans up database records."`	Provides a background worker class inheriting `BackgroundService`.
Securing Sensitive Data	`"Use user secrets in ASP.NET Core to securely store and retrieve database connection strings."`	Outputs the steps and code snippets for user secrets integration.
Optimizing Entity Framework Queries	`"Refactor Entity Framework queries for better performance using eager loading."`	Suggests optimized EF Core queries using `.Include()` and `.AsNoTracking()`.
Swagger Integration	`"Integrate Swagger UI into an ASP.NET Core project for API documentation."`	Provides full configuration for Swagger setup in the project.
Sending Emails with SMTP	`"Write C# code using SMTPClient to send emails with attachments."`	Generates email-sending logic including SMTP setup and attachment handling.
Validating Data with `FluentValidation`	`"Write validation rules using FluentValidation for a user registration model."`	Outputs clean and reusable validation rules for model fields.
CI/CD Pipeline for .NET Apps	`"Create a GitHub Actions workflow to build, test, and deploy a .NET Core web application."`	Generates a YAML workflow for automated CI/CD pipelines.

Table E.2: *GitHub Copilot Prompts for C# Development*

GitHub Copilot Prompts for Python Development

Table E.3 shows sample prompts and corresponding AI-generated outputs for Flask APIs, FastAPI authentication, data manipulation with Pandas, and SQLAlchemy-based database connectivity, and more:

Use Case	**Effective Prompt**	**Copilot's Expected Output**
Creating a Flask REST API	`"Generate a Flask REST API with an endpoint '/users' that returns a list of users in JSON format."`	Provides a **Flask API setup with route definitions and JSON response handling**.
FastAPI for High-Performance APIs	`"Write a FastAPI endpoint to handle user authentication using OAuth2."`	Generates **FastAPI-based OAuth2 authentication mechanism**.
Data Processing with Pandas	`"Write a Python script using Pandas to read a CSV file, filter rows where age > 30, and save results to a new CSV file."`	Outputs **structured data manipulation script using Pandas**.
Database Connectivity with SQLAlchemy	`"Connect to a PostgreSQL database in Python using SQLAlchemy and fetch all records from a 'products' table."`	Generates **Python database connection logic** with query execution.
Automated Web Scraping with `BeautifulSoup`	`"Write a Python script using BeautifulSoup to scrape article titles from a news website."`	Generates **a web scraping script** with HTML parsing and extraction.
Automating Excel Reports with OpenPyXL	`"Write a Python script using OpenPyXL to create an Excel sheet with user data and apply formatting."`	Produces **Excel automation logic with formatting and data writing**.
Unit Testing with PyTest	`"Write a PyTest unit test to validate a function that calculates the factorial of a number."`	Generates a **unit test with assertions for validating function logic**.

Asynchronous Programming with asyncio	"Write an async function in Python to fetch data from multiple APIs concurrently."	Generates **async-await-based Python function using** `asyncio.gather()`.
Machine Learning Model with Scikit-Learn	"Create a Python script using Scikit-Learn to train a logistic regression model on a dataset."	Outputs **Python ML model training script** with data preprocessing.
Deep Learning with TensorFlow	"Write a TensorFlow neural network model for image classification with three convolutional layers."	Generates a **CNN architecture setup in TensorFlow**.
Generating API Documentation with FastAPI	"Enable API documentation in FastAPI using OpenAPI and ReDoc."	Produces **Swagger-based documentation setup in FastAPI**.
Selenium Web Automation	"Write a Selenium WebDriver script in Python to automate login to a website and extract dashboard data."	Provides a **browser automation script using Selenium**.
Automating File System Operations	"Write a Python script to rename all .txt files in a directory by appending a timestamp."	Generates **a file manipulation script with OS operations**.
Natural Language Processing with NLTK	"Write a Python script using NLTK to tokenize and remove stopwords from a given text corpus."	Outputs **NLP text preprocessing using NLTK**.
Security: Hashing Passwords with bcrypt	"Write a Python function using bcrypt to securely hash and verify user passwords."	Provides **password hashing logic with bcrypt for security**.
Automating Email Sending with `smtplib`	"Write a Python script using smtplib to send an email with an attachment."	Generates **email automation script with SMTP configuration**.
Generating Reports in PDF with `ReportLab`	"Write a Python script using ReportLab to generate a PDF report with a table of user transactions."	Produces **PDF generation logic with formatted tables**.
Data Visualization with Matplotlib	"Write a Python script using Matplotlib to plot a bar chart from a dictionary of sales data."	Generates **Python chart plotting logic**.
CI/CD Pipeline for Python Projects	"Create a GitHub Actions YAML workflow to build, test, and deploy a Python Flask application."	Outputs a **CI/CD automation pipeline for Python applications**.

Table E.3: *GitHub Copilot Prompts for Python Development*

GitHub Copilot Prompts for SQL and Database Development

Table E.4 shows effective prompts and their corresponding AI-generated outputs for SQL and database development tasks:

Use Case	Effective Prompt	Copilot's Expected Output
Basic SQL Query for Data Retrieval	"Write an SQL query to fetch all active users from the 'users' table sorted by last login date."	Generates an **optimized `SELECT` query with `ORDER BY` and `WHERE` clauses**.
Indexing for Performance Optimization	"Suggest an indexing strategy for optimizing queries on the 'orders' table frequently filtering by 'order_date' and 'customer_id'."	Recommends **B-Tree, composite indexes, and covering indexes** for improved query performance.
Creating a Stored Procedure	"Write a MySQL stored procedure to fetch employee details based on department ID."	Provides a **structured stored procedure with input parameters and execution logic**.

Using Common Table Expressions (CTEs)	`"Generate an SQL query using a CTE to find the top 5 highest-selling products in the last month."`	Produces **a CTE-based SQL query for enhanced readability and performance**.
SQL Query for Aggregations	`"Write an SQL query to calculate the total sales revenue per region from the 'sales' table."`	Outputs **`SUM()` and `GROUP BY`-based aggregation query**.
Data Cleaning with SQL	`"Write an SQL query to identify and remove duplicate customer records from the 'customers' table."`	Suggests **`DISTINCT`, `ROW_NUMBER()`, and `DELETE` strategies for deduplication**.
JOIN Operations for Data Retrieval	`"Write an SQL query to fetch order details along with customer names using JOINs."`	Produces **an `INNER JOIN` query to combine data from multiple tables**.
Partitioning Large Tables for Performance	`"Suggest a partitioning strategy for a high-traffic 'logs' table storing millions of records daily."`	Recommends **range, list, and hash partitioning techniques for improved database efficiency**.
Creating a Database View	`"Write an SQL query to create a view that combines user details and their latest orders."`	Generates **a database view to simplify data retrieval and reporting**.
Bulk Data Insertion Optimization	`"Optimize a bulk INSERT operation for the 'transactions' table without impacting database performance."`	Suggests **batch processing, transactions, and indexing strategies**.
Database Normalization	`"Normalize the given table structure to reduce redundancy and improve efficiency."`	Provides **1NF, 2NF, and 3NF transformations for database optimization**.
Writing a Recursive Query	`"Write an SQL query using recursion to fetch an employee hierarchy from the 'employees' table."`	Produces **a recursive CTE for hierarchical data processing**.
Creating Role-Based Access Control (RBAC)	`"Define an SQL role-based access control (RBAC) mechanism for different user levels."`	Generates **`GRANT` and `REVOKE` statements for secure access control**.
Optimizing Query Execution Time	`"Improve the execution speed of a slow-running SQL query on a 10M row table."`	Suggests **index tuning, query restructuring, and partitioning**.
Trigger for Data Integrity	`"Create an SQL trigger that updates the 'last_modified' timestamp whenever a row is updated in the 'orders' table."`	Generates **a `BEFORE UPDATE` trigger for automatic timestamp updates**.
Backup and Restore Strategy	`"Write an SQL script to automate daily backups and restoration for a PostgreSQL database."`	Provides **a backup automation script using pg_dump and pg_restore**.
Handling SQL Injection Vulnerabilities	`"Write a secure SQL query to fetch user details by username while preventing SQL injection attacks."`	Suggests **parameterized queries and input validation best practices**.
Querying JSON Data in SQL	`"Write an SQL query to extract a value from a JSON column in PostgreSQL."`	Generates **JSONB functions for structured JSON data retrieval**.
Setting Up Database Replication	`"Provide a step-by-step SQL configuration for setting up MySQL replication."`	Outputs **a full MySQL replication setup with master-slave configuration**.

Table E.4: *GitHub Copilot Prompts for SQL and Database Development*

GitHub Copilot Prompts for UI Test Automation (Selenium WebDriver)

Table E.5 shows example prompts and outputs for generating test scripts covering login, dynamic elements, dropdowns, file uploads, and more in Java:

Use Case	Effective Prompt	Copilot's Expected Output
Basic Web UI Test in Selenium	`"Write a Selenium WebDriver script in Java to open a website, verify the title, and close the browser."`	Generates a complete Selenium script with ChromeDriver initialization, title validation, and browser teardown.
Automating Login Flow	`"Generate a Selenium WebDriver script in Java to automate user login on a web application with username and password fields."`	Provides field interaction logic, form submission, and validation steps.
Handling Dynamic Elements	`"Write a Selenium WebDriver script using Explicit Waits to handle dynamically loaded elements on a webpage."`	Outputs FluentWait and **`WebDriverWait`** implementations for handling dynamic content.
Performing Drag-and-Drop Operation	`"Create a Selenium script in Java to perform a drag-and-drop operation on a web page."`	Generates Actions class-based implementation for drag-and-drop interaction.
Automating Dropdown Selection	`"Write a Selenium test script to select an option from a dropdown menu using Select class."`	Provides Select class methods (**`selectByValue`**, **`selectByIndex`**, **`selectByVisibleText`**).
Handling File Uploads in Selenium	`"Generate a Selenium WebDriver script to automate file upload using the input[type=file] method."`	Produces a Selenium test using **`sendKeys()`** for file upload automation.
Automating Multi-Window Handling	`"Write a Selenium test script to switch between multiple browser windows and verify content."`	Provides window handles and switching logic.
Performing Mouse Hover and Click Action	`"Generate a Selenium WebDriver script to hover over a menu item and click a submenu option."`	Produces Actions class-based script for hover and click actions.
Capturing Screenshots in Selenium Tests	`"Write a Selenium WebDriver script to capture a screenshot when a test case fails."`	Generates screenshot capturing logic using **`TakesScreenshot`** interface.
Validating Web Page Alerts and Pop-ups	`"Write a Selenium test script in Java to handle JavaScript alerts, confirm, and prompt popups."`	Provides Alert class handling for **`accept()`**, **`dismiss()`**, and **`getText()`**.
Automating Scroll Operations	`"Generate a Selenium WebDriver script to scroll to a specific element on a webpage."`	Produces **`JavaScriptExecutor`**-based scrolling script.
Testing Form Validations	`"Write a Selenium test script to verify client-side form validation messages."`	Provides test case validation for form field constraints.
Capturing and Validating Web Table Data	`"Write a Selenium script to extract and validate table data from a webpage."`	Outputs logic to retrieve, iterate, and validate table data using XPath and CSS Selectors.
Executing JavaScript Commands in Selenium	`"Generate a Selenium WebDriver script to execute JavaScript code for retrieving inner text of an element."`	Provides **`JavaScriptExecutor`** logic for executing JavaScript inside Selenium tests.

Executing Parallel Tests in Selenium Grid	`"Write a Selenium test script to run tests in parallel using Selenium Grid with multiple browsers."`	Generates multi-browser test execution setup.
Detecting and Handling Broken Links	`"Write a Selenium script to validate all hyperlinks on a webpage and detect broken links."`	Provides logic for fetching URLs and checking response codes.
Running Tests in Headless Mode	`"Generate a Selenium WebDriver script to run tests in headless Chrome mode."`	Produces **`ChromeOptions`** and **`FirefoxOptions`** configurations for headless testing.
Integrating Selenium with Allure Reports	`"Write a Selenium test script with Allure annotations to generate detailed test execution reports."`	Outputs Allure setup and annotations for reporting.
BDD Test in Selenium with Cucumber	`"Generate a Cucumber feature file and step definition for automating a user registration flow in Selenium."`	Provides Cucumber feature file structure and step definitions.

***Table E.5**: GitHub Copilot Prompts for UI Test Automation using Selenium WebDriver*

GitHub Copilot Prompts for API Test Automation (Rest Assured, Postman, Cypress, and SuperTest)

Table E.6 outlines effective prompts and the expected output for generating API tests using GitHub Copilot:

Use Case	**Effective Prompt**	**Copilot's Expected Output**
Basic GET Request in Rest Assured	`"Write a Rest Assured test in Java to send a GET request to an API and validate the response status code."`	Generates **a structured API test with `given().when().get().then()`** syntax and status code validation.
Validating Response Body in Rest Assured	`"Write a Rest Assured test in Java to validate a JSON response contains specific user details."`	Produces **JSON validation logic using Hamcrest matchers** (`.body("user.name", equalTo("John Doe"))`).
POST Request with JSON Payload	`"Write a Rest Assured test to send a POST request with a JSON payload and validate the response."`	Generates **a structured API request with payload serialization and validation.**
Extracting and Using API Response Values	`"Write a Rest Assured test to extract the user ID from a response and use it in a subsequent request."`	Outputs `.extract().path()` **logic to reuse response data dynamically.**
Handling Authentication in API Tests	`"Write a Rest Assured test in Java to authenticate a user using OAuth2 and fetch user details."`	Produces **OAuth2 authentication setup and API token handling.**
Testing API with Query Parameters	`"Write an API test in Rest Assured to pass multiple query parameters and validate the response."`	Provides **query param handling with `.queryParam("key", "value")`**.
Automating API Testing in Cypress (JavaScript)	`"Write a Cypress test to send a GET request and validate the JSON response structure."`	Generates **a Cypress `cy.request()` test for API validation.**
API Mocking with WireMock	`"Write a WireMock test to mock an API response with a predefined JSON body."`	Provides **mock API setup and request-response stubbing.**

GraphQL API Testing in Postman	"Write a GraphQL query in Postman to fetch a list of users with email and name."	Generates **a structured GraphQL request in Postman.**
Error Handling in API Testing	"Write a Rest Assured test to verify API response when an invalid request is sent."	Provides **negative test cases with proper assertions.**
Writing API Tests with SuperTest (Node.js)	"Write a SuperTest script in Node.js to send a GET request and validate the response status."	Generates **SuperTest-based API request validation.**
Performance Testing of APIs with K6	"Generate a K6 script to load test an API endpoint with 100 virtual users for 10 minutes."	Provides **K6 test setup for stress and load testing.**
Schema Validation for API Responses	"Write a Rest Assured test to validate API response schema using JSON Schema Validator."	Outputs **schema validation using** `matchesJsonSchemaInClasspath()`.
Testing API Headers and Cookies	"Write an API test in Rest Assured to validate custom headers and cookies in a response."	Generates **API request handling with** `.headers()` **and** `.cookies()`.
Automating Postman API Tests in CI/CD	"Write a Newman command to run a Postman collection in a CI/CD pipeline."	Provides **a Postman Newman CLI command for automation.**
Handling File Upload API Requests	"Write a Rest Assured test to send a multipart file upload request to an API."	Generates **a structured file upload request using** `.multiPart()`.
Testing Rate Limiting in APIs	"Write a test script to validate API rate limiting behavior for multiple requests."	Produces **loop-based test execution to verify rate limit responses.**
Validating Pagination in API Responses	"Write an API test in Rest Assured to validate pagination logic with limit and offset parameters."	Generates **pagination-based request and response validation logic.**
Automating API Chaining Tests	"Write a Rest Assured test to fetch a token from one API and use it in another API request."	Outputs **API chaining logic using extracted values dynamically.**

Table E.6: *GitHub Copilot Prompts for API Test Automation – Designed for Tools such as Rest Assured, Postman, Cypress, and SuperTest*

GitHub Copilot Prompts for Mobile Test Automation (Appium, Espresso, and XCUITest)

Table E.7 outlines effective prompts and the AI-generated outputs to support end-to-end mobile testing:

Use Case	Effective Prompt	Copilot's Expected Output
Basic Mobile App Launch Test in Appium (Java)	"Write an Appium test script in Java to launch a mobile app on an Android device and verify the homepage title."	Generates **capabilities setup, driver initialization, and homepage assertion.**
Automating Mobile Login Flow	"Write an Appium test in Java to automate user login on an Android mobile application."	Provides **username, password input handling, and validation of login success.**
Handling Native and WebView Switching	"Generate an Appium test script to switch between native app and web view in a hybrid mobile app."	Produces **context handling logic using** `getContextHandles()` **and** `setContext()`.

Automating Touch Gestures in Appium	`"Write an Appium test in Java to perform a swipe action on a mobile screen."`	Generates **mobile gesture handling using `TouchAction()` or W3C Actions API.**
Automating Mobile Alerts Handling	`"Write an Appium test to handle system alerts and pop-ups on an Android/iOS application."`	Provides **alert handling using `switchTo().alert()` methods.**
UI Test Automation for Android with Espresso	`"Write an Espresso test case to verify the functionality of a search bar in an Android app."`	Generates **structured Espresso test with `onView(withId()).perform(typeText())`.**
Automating iOS App Tests with XCUITest	`"Generate an XCUITest script in Swift to automate login in an iOS app."`	Provides **XCTest UI interactions with login field automation.**
Automating Mobile App Permissions Handling	`"Write an Appium test to automatically grant app permissions on Android."`	Generates **ADB command-based permission grant logic.**
Validating Mobile App Elements using Accessibility IDs	`"Generate an Appium test to locate and interact with elements using accessibility IDs."`	Produces **best practices for element identification.**
Mobile App Screen Rotation Testing	`"Write an Appium test in Java to validate mobile app behavior on screen rotation."`	Generates **rotation handling logic using `rotate(ScreenOrientation.LANDSCAPE)`.**
Automating Push Notification Handling	`"Write an Appium test to verify push notifications on an Android mobile application."`	Provides **notification listener logic using Appium's mobile command feature.**
Parallel Execution of Mobile Tests	`"Configure Appium to execute test scripts on multiple Android devices in parallel."`	Produces **test parallelization setup with Appium Grid or TestNG parallel execution.**
Automating Mobile App Data Input from CSV	`"Write an Appium test to fetch test data from a CSV file and enter it into a form in the mobile app."`	Provides **data-driven testing using Apache POI or OpenCSV.**
CI/CD Pipeline for Mobile Automation in GitHub Actions	`"Create a GitHub Actions workflow to execute Appium mobile tests on every code push."`	Generates **YAML script for CI/CD pipeline setup.**
Automating Mobile Camera Access and File Upload	`"Write an Appium test script to automate photo upload by interacting with the camera."`	Provides **file upload automation using mobile commands.**
Automating Mobile Browser Testing using Appium	`"Write an Appium test in Java to open a website in Chrome on a mobile device and validate the title."`	Produces **mobile web automation test setup.**
Generating Test Reports for Mobile Tests	`"Integrate Appium tests with Allure Reports for detailed execution insights."`	Outputs **test reporting setup using Allure with Appium.**
Debugging Failed Mobile Test Cases Efficiently	`"Suggest debugging strategies for failing Appium tests with intermittent element visibility issues."`	Provides **best practices including implicit waits, explicit waits, and debugging techniques.**
Automating Deep Link Navigation in Mobile Apps	`"Write an Appium test script to automate deep link navigation in an Android/iOS app."`	Generates **deep link automation using mobile commands.**

Table E.7: *GitHub Copilot Prompts for Mobile Test Automation – Tailored for Tools such as Appium, Espresso, and XCUITest*

GitHub Copilot Prompts for Performance and Load Testing (JMeter, K6, Gatling, Locust, Taurus)

Table E.8 highlights effective prompt examples and Copilot's expected output for automating performance test scripts:

Use Case	Effective Prompt	Copilot's Expected Output
Basic Load Test in JMeter	`"Write a JMeter test plan to simulate 50 concurrent users hitting an API endpoint every 5 seconds."`	Generates **a JMeter `.jmx` test plan with thread group and HTTP request samplers.**
Executing Load Tests with K6	`"Generate a K6 script to load test an API with 200 virtual users for 10 minutes."`	Provides **a structured K6 script with HTTP requests, thresholds, and metrics.**
Stress Testing with JMeter	`"Write a JMeter test to simulate 1000 users accessing a login API within 10 seconds."`	Generates **a stress test setup with ramp-up time and response time validation.**
Spike Testing with K6	`"Create a K6 test script to simulate a sudden increase of traffic from 50 to 500 users in 1 minute."`	Produces **a load testing scenario to measure application stability.**
Writing Custom JMeter Assertions	`"Write a JMeter assertion to validate the response time is below 2 seconds for an API request."`	Provides **a structured response assertion logic.**
Gatling Test for API Performance	`"Write a Gatling test script in Scala to simulate concurrent requests to an e-commerce API."`	Generates **a Gatling script with virtual users and request-response validation.**
Simulating High Traffic with Locust	`"Write a Locust script in Python to simulate 500 concurrent users performing login requests."`	Outputs **a structured Python script using Locust's HttpUser class.**
Executing Distributed Load Testing in JMeter	`"Generate a JMeter distributed testing setup for running tests across multiple machines."`	Provides **remote distributed load testing setup.**
Monitoring API Response Times in K6	`"Write a K6 test to measure API response time and log results if latency exceeds 500ms."`	Produces **threshold-based performance monitoring script.**
Automating Performance Tests in CI/CD	`"Create a GitHub Actions workflow to execute JMeter/K6 performance tests on every deployment."`	Generates **a YAML pipeline setup for automated performance testing.**
Validating Database Query Performance with JMeter	`"Write a JMeter test to measure execution time of SQL queries on a PostgreSQL database."`	Provides **a JDBC sampler test setup for database performance validation.**
Performance Testing WebSockets with K6	`"Write a K6 script to test WebSocket performance for a real-time chat application."`	Outputs **WebSocket-based load testing script.**
Generating Custom Performance Reports in JMeter	`"Configure JMeter to generate HTML reports summarizing performance test results."`	Provides **a structured setup for report generation in JMeter.**
Using Taurus for Automated Performance Testing	`"Write a Taurus YAML configuration to execute JMeter and K6 tests in an automated pipeline."`	Generates **Taurus test configuration for flexible performance testing.**

Simulating Network Latency with JMeter	`"Configure JMeter to add artificial network latency and test application performance under slow connections."`	Produces **a network latency simulation setup.**
Testing Mobile App Performance with Gatling	`"Write a Gatling script to test API response times for a mobile application backend."`	Provides **a structured Gatling test scenario for mobile backends.**
Configuring Load Balancer Performance Testing	`"Write a JMeter test to validate a load balancer's performance under high traffic."`	Generates **a load-balancing validation scenario.**
Error Handling and Failover Testing	`"Write a performance test in JMeter to simulate API failure scenarios and validate failover response times."`	Produces **a structured API failure simulation script.**
Testing Performance Bottlenecks in a Web App	`"Generate a K6 script to identify performance bottlenecks in a web application under peak load."`	Outputs **a test scenario to analyze app slowdowns.**

Table E.8: *GitHub Copilot Prompts for Performance and Load Testing – Designed for Tools such as JMeter, K6, Gatling, Locust, and Taurus*

GitHub Copilot Prompts for CI/CD Integration in Test Automation (GitHub Actions, Jenkins, Azure DevOps)

Table E.9 covers GitHub Actions, Jenkins, and Azure DevOps with prompt suggestions to automate build, test, and deployment workflows:

Use Case	**Effective Prompt**	**Copilot's Expected Output**
Running Selenium Tests in GitHub Actions	`"Write a GitHub Actions YAML configuration to execute Selenium WebDriver tests on every code commit."`	Generates **a YAML workflow to run Selenium tests in a CI/CD pipeline.**
Executing Playwright Tests in CI/CD	`"Create a GitHub Actions workflow to run Playwright UI tests on push events."`	Provides **a structured YAML pipeline to install dependencies and execute tests.**
Integrating API Tests in Jenkins Pipeline	`"Write a Jenkinsfile to run Rest Assured API tests as part of a CI/CD pipeline."`	Generates **Jenkins pipeline script with test execution steps.**
Running Mobile Tests in Azure DevOps	`"Create an Azure DevOps pipeline to execute Appium mobile tests on Android and iOS devices."`	Produces **an Azure pipeline YAML for mobile test execution.**
Parallel Test Execution in CI/CD	`"Write a GitHub Actions workflow to execute Selenium tests in parallel on multiple browsers."`	Provides **matrix-based parallel execution for Chrome, Firefox, and Edge.**
Triggering Tests on PR Merges	`"Modify a GitHub Actions workflow to trigger test execution only when a pull request is merged."`	Generates **conditional triggers for test execution upon PR merges.**
Running Performance Tests in Jenkins	`"Write a Jenkins pipeline stage to execute JMeter performance tests and store results."`	Produces **Jenkinsfile steps for JMeter execution.**
Uploading Test Reports to CI/CD Artifacts	`"Modify a GitHub Actions workflow to store Allure test reports as CI/CD artifacts."`	Generates **YAML workflow updates for artifact storage.**

Automating API Load Testing in CI/CD	"Write a GitHub Actions pipeline to execute K6 performance tests on every deployment."	Provides **a structured pipeline for API performance validation.**
Integrating Cypress Tests with GitHub Actions	"Generate a CI/CD pipeline for running Cypress UI tests in GitHub Actions."	Outputs **a Cypress test execution workflow.**
Containerizing Selenium Grid for CI/CD	"Write a Docker Compose file to set up a Selenium Grid with Chrome and Firefox for CI/CD integration."	Produces **a Selenium Grid setup with containers.**
Running BDD Tests with Cucumber in Jenkins	"Write a Jenkins pipeline configuration to run Cucumber feature files and generate reports."	Generates **Jenkins test execution steps with Cucumber support.**
Post-Test Execution Slack Notifications	"Modify a GitHub Actions pipeline to send Slack notifications for test execution results."	Provides **Slack webhook integration for status notifications.**
Automating Mobile App UI Tests in CI/CD	"Write a GitHub Actions workflow to execute Appium mobile tests using BrowserStack."	Generates **a pipeline for cloud-based mobile test execution.**
CI/CD Pipeline for Selenium Grid in Kubernetes	"Write a Kubernetes manifest file to deploy Selenium Grid for running UI tests in a CI/CD pipeline."	Produces **a structured Kubernetes YAML configuration.**
Running Test Scripts on Remote Docker Containers	"Modify a Jenkins pipeline to execute API tests inside a Docker container and generate test reports."	Generates **containerized test execution logic.**
Automating Database Regression Tests in CI/CD	"Create a GitHub Actions workflow to run SQL database validation tests after every deployment."	Provides **a structured YAML for SQL regression test automation.**
Generating and Uploading Code Coverage Reports	"Write a GitHub Actions pipeline to generate and upload test code coverage reports after execution."	Produces **coverage reporting logic using JaCoCo or Istanbul.**
CI/CD Pipeline for Multi-Platform Test Execution	"Write a GitHub Actions matrix strategy to run Playwright tests on Windows, macOS, and Linux."	Generates **multi-platform test execution configurations.**

Table E.9*: GitHub Copilot Prompts for CI/CD Integration in Test Automation*

GitHub Copilot Prompts for DevOps and Infrastructure Automation (Docker, Kubernetes, Terraform, Ansible, CI/CD)

Table E.10 includes tools such as Docker, Kubernetes, Terraform, Ansible, and CI/CD for streamlining infrastructure provisioning and deployment automation using Copilot:

Use Case	Effective Prompt	Copilot's Expected Output
Writing a Dockerfile for a Node.js App	"Write a Dockerfile to containerize a Node.js application using an Alpine-based image."	Generates **a multi-stage Dockerfile with optimized size and security.**
Building and Pushing Docker Images to Docker Hub	"Write a GitHub Actions workflow to build and push a Docker image to Docker Hub on every commit."	Produces **a structured CI/CD pipeline for container automation.**

Deploying a Web App on Kubernetes	`"Write a Kubernetes deployment YAML file to deploy a Python Flask app with two replicas."`	Generates **K8s deployment, service, and ingress configurations.**
Scaling Kubernetes Pods Automatically	`"Create a Horizontal Pod Autoscaler (HPA) in Kubernetes to scale pods based on CPU usage."`	Provides **HPA YAML configuration for auto-scaling.**
Configuring CI/CD Pipeline for Kubernetes Deployment	`"Write a Jenkins pipeline to build, test, and deploy a microservice to a Kubernetes cluster."`	Produces **Jenkinsfile steps for automated K8s deployment.**
Infrastructure as Code (IaC) with Terraform	`"Write a Terraform script to provision an AWS EC2 instance with security groups and SSH access."`	Generates **a structured Terraform configuration for AWS provisioning.**
Managing Configuration with Ansible	`"Write an Ansible playbook to install and configure Nginx on multiple Linux servers."`	Produces **a structured Ansible playbook for automated configuration management.**
Automating Load Balancing in AWS with Terraform	`"Write a Terraform script to deploy an AWS Application Load Balancer (ALB) for a multi-tier architecture."`	Generates **IaC configuration for AWS ALB deployment.**
Setting Up CI/CD Pipeline for Infrastructure as Code	`"Write a GitHub Actions pipeline to validate and apply Terraform configurations automatically."`	Provides **Terraform workflow automation for CI/CD.**
Monitoring Kubernetes Cluster with Prometheus and Grafana	`"Create a Kubernetes deployment for Prometheus and Grafana to monitor cluster performance."`	Generates **YAML configurations for monitoring setup.**
Configuring a Reverse Proxy with Nginx and Docker	`"Write a Docker Compose file to run Nginx as a reverse proxy for a backend API service."`	Produces **a structured reverse proxy setup with Docker Compose.**
Implementing Secrets Management in Kubernetes	`"Write a Kubernetes Secret manifest file to store database credentials securely."`	Generates **K8s Secrets YAML file for secure credential storage.**
Automating AWS Lambda Deployment with Terraform	`"Write a Terraform script to deploy an AWS Lambda function triggered by an S3 event."`	Produces **serverless deployment automation for AWS Lambda.**
Setting Up GitOps with ArgoCD	`"Write an ArgoCD application manifest to automatically deploy a microservice from a Git repository."`	Generates **ArgoCD configuration for GitOps workflows.**
Automating Security Scans in CI/CD Pipelines	`"Modify a GitHub Actions workflow to integrate Snyk for security vulnerability scanning."`	Provides **pipeline integration for dependency security scans.**
Running Containerized Applications with Docker Compose	`"Write a Docker Compose file to run a PostgreSQL database and a backend API in containers."`	Generates **Docker Compose configuration for multi-container apps.**

Automating Disaster Recovery in Kubernetes	`"Write a Kubernetes backup and restore strategy using Velero for disaster recovery."`	Produces **backup and restore automation for K8s clusters.**
Configuring Log Aggregation in Kubernetes	`"Write a Fluentd configuration to collect logs from Kubernetes pods and forward them to Elasticsearch."`	Generates **structured log collection and forwarding setup.**
Automating Cloud Resource Provisioning with Terraform Modules	`"Write a reusable Terraform module to provision an AWS VPC with public and private subnets."`	Provides **modular Terraform setup for AWS networking.**

***Table E.10**: GitHub Copilot Prompts for DevOps and Infrastructure Automation*

GitHub Prompts Repo link: *appendices\prompts*

Index

H

I

P

R